Out of Darkness

Out of Darkness

essays on corporate power and civic resistance

RALPH NADER

introduction by
LEWIS LAPHAM

Seven Stories Press
New York • Oakland • London

Seven Stories Press
140 Watts Street
New York, NY 10013
www.sevenstories.com

College professors and high school and middle school teachers may order free examination copies
of Seven Stories Press titles. Visit https://www.sevenstories.com/pg/resources-academics or email
academic@sevenstories.com.

Library of Congress Cataloging-in-Publication Data

Names: Nader, Ralph, author.
Title: Out of darkness : essays on corporate power and civic resistance,
    2012-2022 / Ralph Nader ; introduction by Lewis Lapham.
Description: New York : Seven Stories Press, 2024. | Includes index.
Identifiers: LCCN 2023043348 | ISBN 9781644213735 (trade paperback) | ISBN
    9781644213742 (ebook)
Subjects: LCSH: Business and politics--United States. | Corporate
    power--United States. | Political culture--United States.
Classification: LCC JK467 .N339 2024 | DDC 322/.30973--dc23/eng/20231229
LC record available at https://lccn.loc.gov/2023043348

Printed in the USA.

9 8 7 6 5 4 3 2 1

Contents

1. PHILOSOPHICAL RUMINATIONS

2. ON DONALD TRUMP

3. ON THE COVID-19 PANDEMIC AND HEALTH CARE

4. ON ENVIRONMENT, HEALTH, AND SAFETY

5. ON CORPORATE CRIME AND CORPORATE WELFARE

6. ON VOTING AND THE 2012, 2016, AND 2020 ELECTIONS

7. ON THE MEDIA

8. ON IMPERIAL POWER AND THE MILITARY

9. ON MONEY, BANKING, AND CLASS

10. HEROES

11. ON THE LAW AND CORPORATE POWER

12. ON CONGRESS AND CIVIC ENGAGEMENT

SELECTED LETTERS

INTRODUCTION

A Citizen in Full

LEWIS LAPHAM

The judges on the bench of prime-time opinion say that Ralph Nader lacks charisma, but the word admits of different interpretations, and if it can be referred to a lively intelligence as well as a bright smile, Nader seems to me a good deal more charismatic than David Letterman or Brad Pitt. I know of few spectacles more entertaining than the play of a mind being put to constructive or imaginative use, and I like to listen to Nader talk. I never fail to learn something new, and in Nader's idealism I find an antidote for the cynicism that constitutes an occupational hazard on the shop floors of the image-making industries in New York.

Accepting the Green Party nomination in Denver on June 27, 2000, Nader presented his campaign as a question—"How badly do we want a just and decent society, a society that raises our expectations of ourselves?"—and in Washington three days later he supplemented it with further commentary and explanation.

"Unlike Gush and Bore," he said, "I don't promote myself as a solution to the nation's problems. The idea is to encourage a lot of other people to use the tools of democratic government to take control of the assets they hold in common—the public lands, the public broadcast frequencies, the public money. Whatever your issue is, whether it's racism, homophobia, taxes, health care, urban decay, you're not going to go anywhere with it unless you focus on the concentration of power. We have an overdeveloped plutocracy and an underdeveloped democracy, too many private interests commandeering the public interest for their own profit. Most Americans don't realize how badly they're being harmed by the unchecked commercialization of what belongs to the commonwealth. If enough people knew what questions to ask, we have both the ways and means to achieve better schools, a healthier environment, a more general distribution of decent health care."

Nader has been asking the questions for sixty-five years. He established his credibility as a consumer advocate in 1965 when he published *Unsafe at Any Speed*, a fierce indictment of the carelessness with which General Motors manufactured its cars. The book resulted in legislation that forced G.M. to improve its automotive designs, and Nader went on to search out further proofs of malfeasance almost everywhere else in corporate America, filing investigative briefs against oil companies, banks, hospitals; publishing another twenty books (about corporate accountability, the judiciary and banking committees in both the Senate and the House, etc.); organizing numerous civic-minded committees (among them the Center for the Study of Responsive Law and the Public Interest Research Group); and bringing about, or at least setting in train, changes for the better in the management of the country's pension funds, classified information, and toxic wastes.

"The oligarchy," he said, "never wants anyone to know what, or how much, ordinary citizens can accomplish if they learn to use the power of their own laws. Apathy is good for business-as-usual; so is cynicism. The lie that all the worthy causes are dead is like the lie that art is dead. Both lies serve the interests of entrenched mediocrity. Convince the kids that all the wars are over, that history is at an end, that nothing important remains to be discovered, done, or said, and maybe they won't ask why a corporate CEO receives a salary four hundred times greater than that of the lowest paid worker in his own company.

"I hear young people saying that they're not turned on to politics, and I tell them that if you do not turn on to politics, politics will turn on you."

"One of the ways to define freedom," Ralph Nader has said, "is as a taking part, even a very small part, in the dispositions of political power. If every year in this country one million people gave one hundred hours of their time to some sort of public purpose, one hundred hours and one hundred dollars, I think we'd be surprised by the number of changes we could make."

"Critics tell me that I ought to work 'within the system,' but people 'within the system' don't welcome new ideas. They like to talk about social change, but when it comes to actually doing something, they remember that social change is outrageous, un-American, and wrong. Look at the history of the country. I don't care whether you're talking about the Revolution of 1776, or abolitionists forcing the issue of slavery in the 1850s, about women's suffrage, the late nineteenth-century populist revolt against the eastern banks and railroads, the trade-union movement, Social Security, meat inspection, civil rights. The change invariably begins with people whom the defenders of the status quo denounce as agitators, communists, hippies, weirdos. And then, ten or twenty years later, after the changes have taken place, the chamber of commerce discovers that everybody's profits have improved. The captains of industry never seem to understand that a free democracy is the precondition for a free market; try to turn the equation the other way around, and you end up with an economy like the one in Indonesia."

Ralph Nader reminds us that a democratic republic knows no higher rank or title than that of citizen. The media prefer celebrities, who come and go like soup cans or summer moths, unthreatening and ephemeral. Cheaply produced and easily replaced, made to the measure of our own everyday weakness, celebrities ask nothing of us except a round of applause. Like President Clinton, they let us off the hook. Nader sets the hook on the sharp points of obligation to a higher regard for our own intelligence and self-worth.

—LEWIS LAPHAM
NYC, November 2023
(Adapted from "A Citizen in Full,"
Harper's Magazine, September 2000.)

Out of Darkness

1.

PHILOSOPHICAL RUMINATIONS

Indicators for Measuring Injustice and Societal Decay

AUGUST 14, 2020

Economic indicators—data points, trends, and microcategories—are the widgets of the Big Information industry. By contrast, indicators for our society's democratic health are not similarly compiled, aggregated, and reported. Its up-and-down trends are presented piecemeal and lack quantitative precision.

We can get the process started and lay the basis for qualitative and quantitative refinement. Years ago, when we started "redefining progress" and questioning the very superficial gross domestic product and its empirical limitations, professional economists took notice. Unfortunately, with few exceptions, economists cling to the yardsticks that benefit and suit the plutocrats and CEOs of large corporations.

Here are my offerings in the expectation that readers will add their own measures:

1. A society is decaying when liars receive mass-media attention while truth-tellers are largely ignored. Those who are chronically wrong, with outrageous and baseless predictions, are featured on news broadcasts and op-ed pages and as convention and conference speakers. On the other hand, those who forewarn and are proven to be accurate are not regaled, but instead excluded from the media spotlight and significant gatherings. Consider the treatment of George W. Bush, Dick Cheney, Donald Rumsfeld, and Paul Wolfowitz post–Iraq invasion, compared to people like Congressman Dennis Kucinich, Noam Chomsky, and Howard Zinn, all of who factually warned Washington not to attack illegally a country that didn't threaten us.

2. A society is decaying when rampant corruption is tolerated and its perpetrators are rewarded with money, votes, and praise. When Pres-

ident Eisenhower's chief of staff, former New Hampshire governor Sherman Adams, accepted a vicuña coat from a textile manufacturer, he was forced to resign. The daily corruption of Trump and the Trumpsters towers beyond measure over Adams's indiscretion. Yet calls for Trump and his cronies to resign are rare and anemic. Tragically, the law and the norms of decency have done little to curb the corrupt, criminogenic, and criminal excesses of Trump and company. Even government prosecutors and inspectors general have been fired, chilled, and sidelined by Trump and his toady, Attorney General Bill Barr.

3. A society is decaying when a growing number of people believe in fantasies instead of realities. Social media makes this an ever more serious estrangement from what is actually happening in the country and in the world. Believing in myths and falsehoods leads to political servitude, economic disruption, and social dysfunction. The corrupt concentration of power ensues.

4. An expanding economy focusing increasingly on "wants and whims" while ignoring the meeting of basic "needs and necessities" shatters societal cohesiveness and deepens miseries of many people. Adequate housing, health care, food, public services, education, mass transit, health and safety standards, and environmental protections are the prerequisites for a humane democracy. The economy is in shambles for tens of millions of Americans, including hungry children. Minimal economic security is beyond the reach of tens of millions of people in our country.

5. With few exceptions, the richer the wealthy become, the more selfishly they behave, from severely diminished contributions to charities to the failure to exert leadership to reverse the breakdown of society. Moreover, those in power do little to address all the failures of the election machinery, from obstructing voters to simply counting the votes honestly with paper records. The US Senate won't vote to give the states the $4 billion needed for administering the coming elections despite the COVID-driven need for expanded voting by mail. The undertaxed megabillionaires of Silicon Valley could make a $4 billion

patriotic donation to safeguard the voting process in November and not even feel it.

6. Rampant commercialism knowing no boundaries or restraints—even to protect young children—is running roughshod over civic values. Every major religion has warned about giving too much power to the merchant class going back more than two thousand years. In our country, justice arrived after commercial greed was subordinated to humane priorities such as abolishing child labor and requiring crashworthy cars, cleaner air and water, and safer workplaces. Mercantile values produce predictable results, from excluding civic groups from congressional hearings and the mass media to letting corporations *control* what the people *own* such as the vast public lands and public airwaves.

7. Then there is the American empire astride the globe, enabled by an AWOL Congress and propelled by the avaricious military-industrial complex. In his 1961 farewell address, President Dwight Eisenhower presciently forewarned that, "[W]e must guard against the acquisition of unwarranted influence, whether sought or unsought, by the military-industrial complex. The potential for the disastrous rise of misplaced power exists and will persist." All empires devour themselves until they collapse on the countries of their origins. Over 55 percent of the federal government's operating spending goes to the Pentagon and its associated budgets. The military-industrial complex increasingly leads to quagmires and creates adversaries abroad as it starves the social-safety-net budgets in our country. Our country's military spending with all its waste is surging and un-audited. The US spent more than $732 billion on direct defense spending in 2019; this is more than the next ten countries with the largest military expenditures.

8. A society that requires its people to incur crushing debt to survive, while relying on casinos and other forms of gambling to produce jobs, is going backward into the future.

9. Public officials who repeatedly obstruct voters from having their votes

received and counted accurately and in a timely fashion continue with impunity to try to steal elections. Then-Georgia secretary of state Brian Kemp (now governor of Georgia) "stole" the election in 2018 from gubernatorial candidate Stacey Abrams. Abrams said Kemp was an "architect of voter suppression," and that because Kemp was the Georgia secretary of state during the race, he was "the referee, the contestant, and the scorekeeper" for the 2018 gubernatorial election. He escaped accountability. Democracy decays.

10. Access to justice is diminishing. Tort law—the law of wrongful injuries—has been weakened in many states with arbitrary caps on damages for the most serious injuries. It is also harder than ever for citizens to get through to real people in government agencies.

Shame of a Nation: The 1 Percent Rules, the 99 Percent Lets Them!

OCTOBER 3, 2019

1. There has never been more access to food—domestic and imported—yet hunger is an ongoing problem everywhere. In the US alone, 16.5 million children go to bed hungry, and 20 percent of community college students are experiencing food insecurity.

2. Never have there been more communications technologies, yet it is harder to get through to people personally than it was fifty years ago.

3. Never have people been able to use their right to free speech so unencumbered, yet a torrent of lies now spreads freely, and often goes unchallenged.

4. Never have there been higher corporate profits, yet staggering amounts of poverty and near-poverty remain, along with stagnant wages.

5. Never have there been more medications to alleviate pain, yet far too many of these painkillers have caused widespread fatalities and addiction.

6. Never has there been more liquid corporate capital piled up, yet corporate investment is proportionately lower than before. Instead, CEOs have burned over $7 trillion in unproductive stock buybacks in the past decade.

7. Never have there been more exercise outlets, exercise machines, and apps, yet obesity is still rampant.

8. Never have there been more tax breaks for big businesses, yet big busi-

nesses use so little of the windfalls for productive investments, good jobs, and shoring up pensions.

9. Never has there been more free access to information, yet so little retained knowledge.

10. Never have there been more impressive muckraking film documentaries and books that expose corporate and government crimes, yet this media attention produces less impact and reform.

11. Never have there been more ongoing impeachable offenses and statutory violations by a president, yet the opposing party in Congress has been reluctant to move on the many articles of impeachment. Remember how fast the unified House of Republicans moved to impeach Bill Clinton in 1998 for perjury and obstruction of justice?

12. Never have there been more trainers, sports physicians, protective equipment, and guards for professional athletes, yet there are far more injuries and days lost by players than was the case sixty years ago. Now there are helmets, gloves, pads, cushioned walls, better shoes, etc. Why?

13. Never has there been more to read, yet there are so few readers reading. Historically, we have gone from illiteracy to literacy to aliteracy!

14. Never before has technology made it so easy for heads of government to meet, yet fewer international treaties (e.g., cyber, water, environmental, consumer, labor) are made.

15. Never has there been such an outrageous corporate crime wave, yet law enforcement budgets have decreased! The more that big CEOs are paid, the worse their management is (e.g., the big banks twelve years ago, General Electric for years).

16. Never before have there been so many wrongful injuries, yet the court budgets are becoming tighter and the law of torts is being restricted. Without the defense of and use of our civil justice system, wrongful injury cases cannot go to court with a trial by jury.

17. Never before has there been more corporate fraud, yet agencies tasked with bringing this fraud to justice have smaller budgets and more limitations. The budget of the Federal Trade Commission is a third of one day's worth of health care billing fraud, which is estimated this year to be $350 billion, according to Harvard's national expert on the subject, professor Malcolm Sparrow. The Consumer Financial Protection Bureau has been straitjacketed by the evil corporate crime abettor Mick Mulvaney, the acting White House chief of staff for corrupt Donald.

18. Never has the drug industry accumulated more profits and government subsidies, yet so many patients cannot begin to afford lifesaving medicines.

19. Never have the undertaxed super-rich been so rich, yet on average give a smaller proportion of their money to "good works." Actually, middle- and lower-income people give more proportionally than do the ultrawealthy.

I could go on and on. Pick up the pace, readers. Senator Elizabeth Warren has correctly called for "big structural changes."

Professional Societies: Corporate Service, or Public Services for You?

MAY 30, 2018

They call themselves nonprofit "professional societies," but they often act as enabling trade associations for the companies and businesspeople who fund them. At their worst, they serve their paymasters and remain in the shadows, avoiding publicity and visibility. When guided by their better angels, professional societies can be authoritative tribunes for a more healthy and safe society.

I am referring to the organizations that stand for their respective professions—automotive, electrical, chemical, and mechanical engineers; physicians; architects; scientists; and accountants. The people working in these occupations all want to be members of a "professional" association, not a "trade" association.

So, let's start by distinguishing how a "profession" is supposed to differ from a "trade." First, profit is not to be the end-all of a profession and its practitioners. Moral and public-interest codes of ethics are supposed to be paramount when they conflict with maximizing sales and income.

The National Society of Professional Engineers's code of ethics stipulates that an engineer has a professional duty to go to the appropriate authorities should the engineer be rebuffed by an employer or client who was notified of a dangerous situation or product.

Physicians have a duty to prevent the trauma or disease that they are trained to treat. A half dozen physicians in the 1960s aggressively pressed the auto industry to build more crash-protective vehicles to prevent trauma casualties they had to treat regularly.

A profession has three basic characteristics. First is a learned tradition—otherwise known as going deep and keeping up with a profession's literature and practices. Second is to continue a tradition of public service. Third is to maintain the independence of the profession.

How do professional societies measure up? Not that well. They are too monetized to fulfill their public-service obligations and retain their independence. The Society of Automotive Engineers (SAE) has a notorious history of following the technological stagnation of the auto companies. Their standards almost never diverge from what is permitted by GM, Ford, and others. Indeed, the SAE's standards committees are mostly composed of company engineers whose employers provide funding and facilities for any testing.

The Institute of Electrical and Electronics Engineers is waist-deep in the automation and artificial intelligence drive. You'll not hear from that society about the downsides, collateral risks, or undisclosed data by the companies in this portentous area.

The American Society of Mechanical Engineers has not distinguished itself regarding the safety of gas and oil pipelines, allowing industry lobbyists to take over the federal regulators without as much as a warning whistle. This history was exposed years ago by retired DuPont engineer Fred Lang.

The American Institute of Chemical Engineers knows about the scores of vulnerable plants resisting regulatory efforts to safeguard their premises from sabotage that could destroy a nearby town or city. Ask Rick Hind, former legislative director for Greenpeace, about this evasion (see: "Chemical Security Testimony by Greenpeace's Rick Hind").

The American Medical Association (AMA) received peer-reviewed studies by the medical schools of Harvard and Johns Hopkins pointing to at least five thousand patient deaths per week from preventable problems in hospitals—from malpractice to hospital-induced infections. Despite this clear medical emergency, the AMA refuses to move into high drive against this epidemic. Mum's the word. When the AMA does act, it's against tort law and the civil justice system, which every once in a rare while hold negligent or criminally behaved physicians accountable to their victims.

Possibly the most complicit profession facilitating, covering for, and explaining away corporate greed and deception is the American Institute of Certified Public Accountants. Too many corporate accountants specialize in complex cooking of the books for their corporate clients. The 2008–2009 Wall Street crash is a major case in point. Donald Trump knows about such accountants from his business career of obfuscation.

The American Institute of Architects, after a long period of submissiveness, woke up to the energy waste and pollution crisis of modern buildings and developed standards with labels to give builders incentives toward more responsible construction. But by and large, it remains a profession, apart from modern technologies, that has left its best days back in the eighteenth and nineteenth centuries (e.g., the classic cities of Europe).

Now what about the scientific societies? The Federation of American Scientists has led the way for nuclear arms control and other weaponized discoveries of the warfare state. On the other hand, the American Association for the Advancement of Science—by far the largest membership organization, and the publisher of *Science* magazine—has been utterly timid in putting muscle behind its fine pronouncements.

The large street protests by scientists in Washington after the Electoral College selected Donald Trump were started by young social and physical scientists. They stood up for scientific integrity and conscience and opposed Trump's defunding of such governmental organizations as the National Science Foundation and the Centers for Disease Control and Prevention. These scientists' efforts have been met with some success.

What most Americans do not know is that many of the state and federal safety and health standards are taken in considerable measure from the weak "consensus" standards advanced by professional societies. These societies, so heavily marinated in their respective industries, see their important role of feeding their industry standards into state, national, and international standards, which are enforceable under domestic law or treaty.

Maybe these societies continue a learned tradition at their annual meetings and workshops and in their publications. But they far too often fail to maintain their professions' standards of independence (from commercial supremacy) and commitment to public service.

These professional societies, and other associations not mentioned here, need to be brought out of their convenient shadows into the spotlight of public scrutiny, higher expectations, and broader participation.

Can the World Defend Itself
from Omnicide?

JULY 26, 2017

Notice how more frequently we hear scientists tell us that we're "wholly unprepared" for this peril or for that rising fatality toll? Turning away from such warnings may reduce immediate tension or anxiety, but it only weakens public awareness and distracts us from addressing the great challenges of our time, such as calamitous climate change, pandemics, and the rise of a host of other self-inflicted disasters.

Here are some warnings about rising and looming risks.

1. The opioid epidemic is here now and poised to become further exacerbated. It is the US's deadliest drug overdose crisis ever, taking more than a thousand lives a week. Even that figure is underestimated, according to a report by the Centers for Disease Control (CDC). These fatalities, many of them affecting people in the prime of their lives, stem from legally prescribed drugs taken to relieve chronic pain. Tragically ironic!

2. Congress is figuring out how to budget for many billions of dollars to combat this toll—much greater than the deaths by motor vehicle crashes or AIDS. Republican and Democratic state officials are suing the drug companies for excessive, misleading promotion for profit. Still, the awful toll keeps rising.

3. Cyberattacks and cyber warfare are increasingly becoming a facet of daily life. Although IBM and other firms are trying to develop more effective defenses, the current scale of cyberattacks is "crazy," according to specialist Christopher Ahlberg. As he said in a recent interview with the *Wall Street Journal*, "If you told anybody ten years ago about what's going on now, they wouldn't believe it."

4. Negotiations are not even underway for a cyberwarfare treaty among nations. The sheer scale and horrific implications of this weaponry seems to induce societies to bury their heads in the sand. Former host of ABC's *Nightline* Ted Koppel discusses this emerging threat in his acclaimed recent book, *Lights Out: A Cyberattack, A Nation Unprepared, Surviving the Aftermath*. Koppel's book describes how "a well-designed attack on just one of the nation's three electric power grids could cripple much of our infrastructure . . . And a cybersecurity advisor to President Obama believes that independent actors—from "hacktivists" to terrorists—have the capability as well." Koppel makes it clear "that the federal government has no plan for the aftermath of an attack on the power grid."

5. Former secretary of defense and CIA director Leon Panetta says Koppel's book is "an important wake-up call for America." Yet neither he nor the enormous military-industrial complex, of which he remains a supportive part, are doing much of anything about this doomsday threat to national security. The big manufacturers are too busy demanding ever more taxpayer money for additional nukes, aircraft carriers, submarines, fighter planes, missiles, and other weaponry of an increasingly bygone age.

6. "The World Is Not Ready for the Next Pandemic" read the headline of a recent *Time* magazine article. The authors note that the "US Centers for Disease Control and Prevention . . . ranks H7N9 as the flu strain with the greatest potential to cause a pandemic—an infectious disease outbreak that goes global." They predict the disease could claim "tens of millions" of lives.

7. In between his Twitter tantrums, President Trump approved an insanely myopic $1 billion proposed budget cut to the CDC's programs used to predict and combat rising pandemics from China, African countries, and elsewhere. Fortunately, cooler heads may prevail in Congress, backed by some private foundations.

8. The number of new diseases per decade, *Time* reports, has increased nearly fourfold over the past sixty years. Antibiotics are being over-

ridden by adaptive mutations of bacteria. Dr. Trevor Mundel of the Gates Foundation asserts, "There's just no incentive for any company to make pandemic vaccines to store on shelves." That profit-driven rejection is exactly why government must act to produce the drugs, as the Department of Defense did successfully with new antimalarial drugs in the seventies and eighties.

9. University of Minnesota professor Michael Osterholm, one of the nation's leading experts on infectious diseases, warns that for all our world-class scientists and high-tech isolation units, the US health care system is not ready for the stresses of a major pandemic. Not even close.

10. It isn't just Elon Musk, CEO of the Tesla company, who is warning that the advent of artificial intelligence (AI) is "the greatest risk we face as a civilization." In 2015, hundreds of other scientists, such as renowned physicist Stephen Hawking, and technologists, such as Steve Wozniak, signed a public letter that was a one-day story, instead of an alarmed world turning it into a galvanizing event. In a 2014 piece in the *Independent*, Professor Hawking warns us: "Success in creating AI would be the biggest event in human history. Unfortunately, it might also be the last, unless we learn how to avoid the risks. In the near term, world militaries are considering autonomous-weapon systems that can choose and eliminate targets." We humans, Hawking adds in the *Washington Post*, "are limited by slow biological evolution, couldn't compete and would be superseded by AI." In short, the robots race out of control, become self-actuating, and are not held back by any moral boundaries.

From Lincoln to Einstein, we have been counseled that new situations require new thinking. A massive reversal of our world's priorities toward reverence for life and posterity, toward diplomacy and waging peace, toward legal and ethical frameworks for exploding science and technology (including biotechnology and nanotechnology) must receive our focus, from families nurturing their children to the philosophers, ethical specialists, engineers, and scientists pausing their exponential discoveries to ponder the serious adverse consequences of their creations.

Our present educational systems—from Harvard Law School to MIT to K–12—are not rising to these occasions for survival. Our mass media, wallowing in trivia, entertainment, advertisements, and political insults, is not holding the politicians accountable to serious levels of public trust and societal safety. Time for new movements awakening our best angels to foresee and forestall. Do any potential leaders at all levels want to be first responders?

A Clarion Call for Our Country's Pillars to Demand Justice

JULY 12, 2017

It is time for an urgent clarion call.

Given the retrograde pits inhabited by our ruling politicians and the avaricious overreach of myopic big-business bosses, the self-described pillars of our society must step up to reverse the decline of our country. Here is my advice to each pillar:

1. Step up, lawyers and judges of America. You have no less to lose than our constitutional observances and equal justice under law. A few years ago, brave Pakistani lawyers marched in the streets in open protest against dictatorial strictures. As you witness affronts to justice such as entrenched secrecy, legal procedures used to obstruct judicial justice, repeal of health and safety protections, and the curtailment of civil liberties and access to legal aid, you must become vigorous first responders and exclaim: *Stop!* A just society must be defended by the courts and the officers of the court—the attorneys.

2. Step up, religious leaders, who see yourselves as custodians of spiritual and compassionate values. Recall your heroic forebears who led non-violent civil disobedience during the repression of civil rights in the 1960s—as with the leadership of the late greats Martin Luther King Jr. and William Sloane Coffin. Champion the Golden Rule for those who don't believe that "he who has the gold makes the rules."

3. Step up, businesspeople—businesses both large and small. Some of you are enlightened and motivated enough to stand tall against the cruel, monetized minds that are harming low-paid workers, cheating consumers, denying insurance to patients, avoiding or evading taxes, swindling investors, and undermining communities across the country.

4. You have good examples from history, including those business leaders who recently quit the US Chamber of Commerce over the necessity to confront climate change or the 150 business leaders who issued strong support for the successful Legal Services Corporation for low-income Americans that Trump's budget would eliminate entirely.

5. Step up, professors and teachers, and protect your students from politicians intent on undermining the public school system and turning its budgets into cash cows for commercial vendors. You can help the cause by demanding that practical civic skills and experience become part of the curriculum. You can demand that Trump's increasingly bloated war budget not be funded at the expense of our children's education and deteriorating physical facilities. You can point out waste and administrative bureaucracy to strengthen this already-compelling call. University professors can establish active brain trusts to educate the public and rebut the avalanche of fake news and political insults.

6. Step up, doctors and nurses, in whose trust are placed the lives of millions of people. Polls show over half of you want full "Medicare for all" with free choice of physician and hospital. This should come as no surprise since it is much more efficient, eliminating much of the bookkeeping and lengthy billings that drain your time away from practicing healthcare. Above all, Medicare for all saves lives and prevents trauma and disease when people can afford early diagnoses and treatment.

7. Already, prominent economists, business magnates like Warren Buffett, and over 60 percent of Americans want single-payer. Your strong voices together can sober up those politicians in Congress hell-bent on coarse pullbacks that will make the present situation even worse and more perilous. Imagine our well-insured elected representatives pushing a huge tax cut for the rich, at the expense of hospitals and clinics and big-time reductions in Medicaid.

8. Step up, PR professionals, who can take an active role in facilitating a public conversation on the need for important social services and reforms that improve their implementation.

9. Step up, veterans, including high-ranking military, national security, and diplomatic retirees, who can advocate for waging peace instead of reckless wars of aggression and other violations of US and international law by the armed forces. Some people incorrectly think that veterans monolithically support all military interventions. But no one knows the horror of war better than those soldiers who have fought them. (According to a January 2005 poll, a large majority of soldiers in Iraq wanted us to get out of that disastrous quagmire.)

10. Over three hundred retired generals, admirals, and national security officials openly opposed Bush/Cheney's criminal invasion of Iraq in 2003. Veterans For Peace makes eloquent arguments for waging peace. Now is the time to learn from their experience, stand for smart diplomacy, and avoid succumbing to provocations and the boomeranging impacts of empire.

11. Step up, members of the media, both corporate and public. Give voice to the vast civil society and citizen groups that are vital to our democracy. They have long been practicing and strengthening democratic practices. Allow their voice of reason, sanity, and evidence-based proposals to reach millions of Americans.

12. Step up, scientists and technologists. You must strongly organize against the corrosive effect of medieval myths about the natural world and habitat-destroying toxins pouring from unaccountable industry. Champion the necessity of science for the people, not for militarism and a global arms race.

13. Urge the restoration of the acclaimed, nonpartisan Office of Technology Assessment in Congress that Newt Gingrich and his Republicans terminated in 1995, plunging Congress into ignorant darkness and costly, wrongful budgeting.

14. Step up, students. Show the country your earnest idealism, supported by knowledge and your hope for a brighter future. Fight for tuition-free education, reform of student debt gouging, and an ecologically benign economy that will work for you and the planet. Really get out the vote for next year!

15. Step up, leaders of the vast number of charity and service clubs. Without a sense of justice, there will be fewer charitable resources for ever-increasing needs.

Many of you have the moral authority to speak truth to the power of the 1 percent and resist attempts to diminish support to those vulnerable members of our society who most need it.

In times of crisis, routines must be replaced with urgent awakenings, bringing out the better angels and wisdom from these underachieving pillars of the American community. A few leaders can take the first steps, and many more will follow your example. Stand tall in support of justice in these trying times.

Schooling for Myths and Powerlessness

MAY 16, 2017

All over America, school children are completing another academic year before their summer vacation. This invites the questions, what did they *learn* and what did they *do* with what they learned?

I'm not talking about their test scores, nor the latest fads in rebranding education, like the STEM (Science, Technology, Engineering, and Mathematics) curriculum that de-emphasizes the first two-thirds of the old mantra—reading, writing, and arithmetic. Rather, I am questioning what they learned about their real-world surroundings, about preparing themselves for life as citizens, workers, consumers, taxpayers, voters, and members of various communities.

Not very much, sad to say. The same is true of my generation. Instead of receiving an enriching and well-rounded education, we were fed myths. All societies perpetuate lavish myths that enable the few to rule over the many, repress critical thinking, and camouflage the grim realities. Our country was, and remains, no exception.

In school we learned that our country was number one, the greatest in the world. We sang "Onward Christian Soldiers" in music class. Being the "greatest" was neither defined nor questioned. We simply had a vague sense that "great" meant militarily and economically "big."

In practice, however, "great" was associated with knee-jerk patriotism and served as a barrier to thinking critically about what we were told to take for granted. For were we to have parsed the deeper meaning of the word "great," we might have had to make specific comparisons of the United States, in concrete ways, to other countries such as Canada and those in Europe. And we might have discovered that we weren't first in many areas of human and environmental well-being.

Early in elementary school we were told that Christopher Columbus "discovered" America and what followed was the arrival of the pioneers of "civilization." This myth served to justify the white man's domination

23

over "inferior races," whether native or brought in as slaves from Africa. In truth, as my father taught me, Columbus invaded America in search of gold and, with his soldiers, slaughtered Caribbean tribes that long preceded Columbus's arrival in their lands.

Along the way in school, we were told that, unlike other "evil" countries, American soldiers did not intentionally kill civilians, as did our cruel enemies. Somehow General Sherman's march to the sea during the Civil War escaped our attention, as did later mass slaughter of human beings in the Philippines and the deliberate targeting and incineration of entire civilian residential areas in World War I and World War II—to, in the language of the official strategies, "terrorize the populations."

The myth of an America without imperial intentions camouflaged the purposes of several wars and many imperial assaults and overthrows. Who were we to question? Other countries were empires; America was guided by "manifest destiny."

Then there was the fictional character, Paul Bunyan, the giant lumberjack from American folklore who was hijacked and commercialized by the timber industry to propagandize the minds of millions of children. With his huge blue ox, Babe, Bunyan conquered and cut down forests. One of the Paul Bunyan stories ended with our hero leaving Montana for Alaska's vast wilderness. Bunyan and Babe, we were assured, would persevere "until the last tree was down." Progress, the myth instructed, was the exploitation of the natural world, not the preservation of nature in sustainable ways.

The most pervasive myth, which persists to this day, is that the free market provides the supreme pathway to economic prosperity. Never mind monopolies, business crimes and deceptions, government subsidies, bailouts and taxpayer giveaways, patent monopolies, fine-print contract servitude, and the abuse of our air, water, and soil as toxic corporate sewers. The free-market myth teaches that government regulation is inherently bad, that suing businesses in court harms the economy, and that unions and consumer cooperatives are un-American, even communistic. This dogma has no room for the honest assertion that the market can "make a good servant, but a bad master," in the words of Amory Lovins of the Rocky Mountain Institute.

With the exception of some marvelous teachers, our many hours in class teach us to believe—not to think, obey, or challenge. For too many of our school years, the process was, and is, memorization and regurgitation. At the most, we are given some cursory training, but not *educated* in any deep or productive sense.

It is unsurprising that such mythical conditioning does not give us the training to fight back, decade after decade, against forces that impoverish, gouge, fire, harm, exclude, disrespect, and perpetuate the three afflictions of corporatism, militarism, and racism.

Just look at today's headlines and ponder the joint partnership of plutocracy and oligarchy—often called the corporate state. No wonder "we the people" are not working to resist and overcome these destructive forces of greed and power.

A meaningful answer starts with replacing our years of schooling, punctuated by years of being commercially entertained and distracted. It starts with acquiring the civic motivations and skills necessary to build a society that can move us toward "liberty and justice for all." As Thomas Jefferson observed at our nation's conception, "An educated citizenry is a vital requisite for our survival as a free people."

Animals to Humans:
"Listen, Learn and Respect!"

NOVEMBER 23, 2016

I have long wondered what the animal kingdom—mammals, reptiles, birds, fish, and insects—would want to tell us humans if we and the animals had a common language.

Well, in my new fable—*Animal Envy* (Seven Stories Press)—a "Human Genius" invents a digital translation application whereby animals can speak with each other across species and also speak one way to humans so they learn to listen. The response by "subhumans" is so overwhelming that the Human Genius reserves one hundred hours of global TV time for the denizens of the natural world to tell their stories before billions of mesmerized humans all over the Earth.

An Elephant, Owl, and Dolphin—sensing the need for some sort of production order and fair play—call themselves "*The Triad*" and convene the "*Great Talkout.*" Driven by the complexity of raising their young and surviving generation after generation, the animals, led by the wisdom of *The Triad*, develop a strategy born out of their keen sense of observing the human animal, whom they internally call "*The King of Beasts.*"

To make their core messages palatable, they have to frame their approach during those early television hours to be seen as ingratiating and flattering to humans' self-interest. They know that humans have their doubts and their dissenters, but overall, their long-touted "conquest of nature" as a measure of their "progress" reflected a level of ongoing aggressive behavior, marked by arrogance and violence that had no equal on Earth.

The Triad suggests that all species commence with flattery of humans to get them to open their minds. Animals could better show how useful the animal kingdom is to humans once humans accept and understand them.

The animals are not going to rely on appeals to justice and fairness. They want to speak directly from their experience and conditions of their existence.

It turns out that different species make different demands on *The Triad*'s program management. There are the dire urgencies of species facing severe habitat loss and extinction. *The Triad* gives them special emergency access to the television stage. There are species who disagree on using flattery and go right into their priorities. Other species say to heck with mutual self-interest—look what humans can learn from our far superior physical capabilities, such as our senses of sound, smell, and sight—from dogs to owls to octopi—and our unique relation to our biological environments. Think of beavers, bees, spiders, beetles, and the critical earthworm.

Many species want to convey to humans that they are far more than genetically determined organisms—they have what humans call instinct. "Multiple intelligences" come into play soon after birth. They are forms of feedback—fear, hunger, heat, cold, weather eruptions, and intricate mating and social rituals. In short, animals learn and adapt.

To the massive human audience, the Great Talkout is beyond fascinating. All ages are glued to the screen. The sheer variety and recounting of different species are startlingly new to all but animal scientists, ecologists, and other specialists. After all, animals have been stereotyped simplistically over the centuries.

Humans have known, for example, that elephants have extraordinary memory, but we did not know that they also have compassion, empathy, courage, sorrow, even grief. And so do other species beyond just mammals.

The book describes a revolt of the insects, who feel their massive numbers, variety, beauty, and impact on humans (e.g., that of mosquitoes) deserve more airtime. They organize a challenging parade to impress upon *The Triad* their importance to the environment and their ability to command the attention of humans, who fear them. They get their time on stage.

Some animals speak directly to *The Triad* to convey warnings to humans. Particularly vociferous are the Asian beetles, known as emerald ash borers, who have destroyed tens of millions of urban and rural ash trees. Foresters estimate losses so far of about $25 billion and much more to come.

One ash borer, speaking for all of them, declares, "We want you, oh mighty Triad, to broadcast this message: 'Humans, know that we came from China, hitchhiking in packing materials. We're a half-inch long with green wings and a reddish stomach. You can't stop us from our meal. Neither Chinese wasps nor birds, like those hated woodpeckers, can stop us.

They can eat a whole lot of us but we still multiply. You might be asking why I'm telling you all this. It's because you need to be more humble, but humility can become a great asset to your survival and health.'"

Because the various species know that humans are much "smarter" than they are, they caution the humans to beware of their past habit of out-smarting themselves and succumbing to the intensifying hubris that could cause ever bigger disasters and extinction on our small planet.

There are many consequential facts about the animal kingdom, including domesticated animals for food and pets, which should fascinate readers of all ages. This may be partially why *Animal Envy* has been praised by leaders of how humans must and should deal with other sentient beings, such as Princeton professor Peter Singer, environmental attorney Eric Glitzenstein, and scholar-author Marc Bekoff.

A special comment came from singer and poet Patti Smith, who described the fable as "a tale of two kingdoms, mirroring that reflective insight of animals and closing eyes of human kind. *Animal Envy* is a clarion call!"

Authors, naturally, want their books to be read. Such reactions are indeed welcome.

The Downsides of Cheap Abundance

OCTOBER 22, 2015

In college, Economics 101 is often described as the social science discipline that deals with the production, distribution, and consumption of goods and services. MIT economist Paul Samuelson liked to focus on scarcity, or, more specifically, the allocation of scarce resources.

"Abundance" was always a pretty word with an idyllic connotation for Professor Samuelson. I often wonder why there weren't a few classes about the real-life consequences of abundance, along with scarcity and people's material welfare.

The present generation of internet technology is a proper subject of study within an economic framework. It might help us understand what is happening to our society.

Let's start with today's highly touted information age. At our fingertips is the greatest free trove of information in human history. We can get it quickly and efficiently. Are we more informed? Are we hungry for more information? Do we read more books in an era of record production of books? Do we know more about what our congressional and state legislators are about? Are we more knowledgeable about history and its lessons?

My sense is that the present generation of students knows about popular art and music and has a nascent awareness of current events. But an unfortunate consequence of information abundance is that too many students have left themselves less informed than their predecessors about serious information regarding our overall society and the world. This includes geography; politics; economics; literature; history; the side effects of technology; the interactions between consumers, workers, taxpayers, and corporations; the doings of city hall; or even how to cultivate gardens. Alas, the virtual reality of the culture of addictive distractions and stupefying daily routines still reigns.

Just about everyone now has a smartphone with which they can enter an endless world of spectator entertainment, video games, and checking of messages by the minute, to name a few of the engagements. Granted, serious news, feature stories, lectures, rallies, programs, and other materials are also available. Judging by the Twitter followers of Hollywood celebrities and even famous cats, dogs, and horses, for some internet users there is a crowding out of information that matters most for a functioning democracy. And unless you're in one's inner circle, try having a two-way communication with someone without long waits using any of the new technologies. The age of dial phones and letters had more than charm.

Energy presents another example of abundance. Historically, the United States had abundant, cheap energy, and, with Canada, set the world record for wasting it. Meanwhile Japan had limited domestic energy resources and became much more efficient in using what it produced, favoring efficient cars, homes, and appliances. Energy efficiently used means less pollution and fewer greenhouse gases.

Abundant cheap water has led to much waste of water. When water rates go up there is more efficient usage. California is experiencing water shortages, and, as a result of scarcity in combination with regulatory restrictions, people in California are wasting less water.

Making our abundant "commons"—owned by the American people—available for corporations to exploit freely (or nearly so) has led to vast wastelands. The public lands—one-third of the US landmass plus huge offshore areas—are open to oil mining and timber companies for ridiculously low-price leases. For hard-rock minerals like gold and silver, the General Mining Act of 1872 only requires as little as five dollars an acre to extract billions of dollars of minerals a year. No royalties are required. Such unlimited use takes away the people's resources with nothing but cleanup costs for the mining wastes left behind for taxpayers. (See bollier. org.)

When FCC chairman Newton Minow called television a "vast wasteland" in 1961, he wasn't just speaking metaphorically. The radio and television broadcast stations control our public airways twenty-four hours a day. Because "We the People," who are the landlords, do not reserve time daily for audience networks and also do not charge the stations for their use of public airwaves, broadcasters can waste their round-the-clock abundance (see Claire Riley's "Oh Say Can You See: A Broadcast Network for the Audience," *Virginia Law Review* [Fall, 1988]).

A relatively new entry in the world of abundance is corporate capital.

The cries from business about a capital shortage in the 1970s, so as to get more tax breaks, have long been muted by the trillions of dollars the US's big businesses have lying inert here and abroad. Such abundance has led to hundreds of billions of dollars in unproductive stock buybacks since 2000.

A leading analyst of big-business behavior, Robert A. G. Monks, has called such buybacks a clear sign of incompetent or unimaginative management. By this he means that such profits should be used for productive investment, better wages, or more dividends to shareholders, mutual funds, and pension trusts, which should be exercising more of their ownership leverage.

Instead, the corporate bosses prefer to apply such profits, derived from the sweat of their workers and from government-provided corporate welfare, to reduce the earnings-per-share ratio, which enhances the criteria for increasing their already sky-high executive compensation. Stock buybacks rarely sustain a higher share price.

What to do with this expanding phenomenon of "abundance" in a world wracked by public and private poverty and its damaging fallouts? We must impose wisely used charges or taxes on the abundant commons. For example, charging royalties for hard-rock mining and raising leases to market-based prices for other publicly owned resources can be used for needed land reclamation. Charging rent for the use of public airways can pay for better interactive programming and establishing audience networks. Imagine how an audience network could facilitate the potential for the people to summon campaigning politicians to real debates on their own radio and TV stations.

Requiring telecommunications companies to donate some of the profits they make from customers who pay exorbitant fees to use smartphones could provide revenues for the development of civic applications and would help to offset the trivialization that has arrived with the technology.

As for the capital glut, an excess accumulated profits tax will provide an incentive to put such capital to productive work or return it to shareholders—the owners of the corporations.

We'd better think more about "abundance" and its negative consequences.

Fast, Faster, Fastest: Why the Rush?

SEPTEMBER 11, 2015

Socrates and Plato were not in a hurry. Neither was Aristotle nor Heraclitus. They took time to think deeply. As far back as twenty-five centuries ago, they offered insights and observations about the human condition, character, and personality that are as true today as they were then.

Fast-forward to our fast-paced society. Many people think if they talk faster, people will think they're smarter. Talking fast is not talking smart. Evening TV news interviews of individuals may average five or fewer seconds—what are called sound bites—while they averaged about eighteen seconds in the 1970s. Standardized tests put a premium on how fast you can answer the questions, putting an emphasis on speed and memory rather than understanding. With standardized testing, deeper learning never really had a chance. Marketers aim for your instant gratification when selling you junk food and other impulse buys. "One-click" ordering has taken this system to a completely new level. Smart traders surrender to computerized trading, speculating in split seconds on the stock exchanges. I could give you ten reasons why this is a bad idea.

You can now hear the evening news on National Public Radio in just three or so minutes—an absurdity. There are radio shows called *The Academic Minute* and the *Corporate Crime Reporter Morning Minute*, dedicated to shrinking attention spans.

To state the obvious, there are fast-food outlets everywhere—so many that a modest slow-food movement is underway. Many hospitals have been known to admit women in labor and discharge these new mothers less than twenty-four hours after they have given birth—exhibiting a corporate form of attention-deficit disorder. Advertisements for drugs and other consumables end with warnings of adverse effects that are described so swiftly that they are simply incomprehensible. A top sushi restaurant in Tokyo charges by the minute, not the amount ordered—running you about $300 for a thirty-minute meal.

Ever count how many images flit by in an ordinary TV news show while it is being narrated? Play it again—does the viewer even have a chance to absorb and mentally react? TV advertisements are, of course, more emotionally charged this way.

Then there is Twitter with its limited 140-character tweets, the ping-pong exchanges of text messaging scores of times throughout the day, and the constant immersion in video games. Back in 1999, Barbara Ehrenreich, in her review of James Gleick's book *Faster: The Acceleration of Just About Everything*, pauses to ponder: "What we lose, as 'just about everything' accelerates, is the chance to reflect, to analyze and, ultimately, to come up with moral judgments."

Not quite everything in our society, however, is speeding up. Rush-hour speeds have slowed to ten or fifteen miles per hour in many cities. Banks, in a computer age, deliberately take days to clear checks, maybe hoping to penalize you with a thirty-five-dollar bounced-check fee. Try getting through to a business or another institution on an automated phone line. You may have to work through ten levels of "press one, press two." After choosing, you may only have the opportunity to leave a voicemail.

As a society, it has taken far too long to implement proven policies that could address and abolish poverty, including raising the minimum wage that has long been gutted by inflation. As a society, we are too slowly expanding mass transit, confronting climate change, converting to renewable energy, and improving the miles per gallon of our automobiles.

Except for Medicare reimbursements, physicians know how long it takes for insurance companies to pay up. Our companies and governments take a long time to clean up their own pollution or respond to complaints from consumers and citizens. These days, it's looking like a contest of who can care less.

On the other hand, a bizarre, frantic emphasis has emerged to get the packages you order delivered faster and faster. Amazon is following through on their wildest dreams and even thinking about using drones to make deliveries. Likewise, Walmart is gearing up to deliver to your homes and businesses as fast as they can. Pretty soon people won't have to go to stores; they'll just order everything online and never see any other shoppers or have chance meetings with friends and neighbors. Let's hear the applause from those people who haven't thought through these "improvements" and the resulting destruction of communities.

Entertainment is a bubble waiting to burst. People do not have more than two eyes, two ears, or twenty-four hours in a day. In the 1950s, there were three national television networks. Now, there are hundreds of cable channels and over-the-air TV stations, not to mention the avalanche of internet-based programs and diversions. The pressure for ratings is starting to implode on its vendors. In an article published on August 31, 2015, in the *New York Times* titled "Soul-Searching in TV Land Over the Challenges of a New Golden Age," reporter John Koblin sums up the "malaise in TV these days," namely that "there is simply too much on television." "Too much" is colliding with "too fast," and our technological wonderland is fraying.

Hewlett Packard (HP) has just started an advertising campaign with the slogan: "The future belongs to the fast." The text includes this message: "HP believes that when people, technology, and ideas all come together, business can move further, faster."

By contrast, fifteen years ago, Bill Joy, the famous technology inventor and innovator, wrote an article titled "Why the Future Doesn't Need Us," citing the oncoming converging technologies of artificial intelligence, biotechnology, and nanotechnology.

So, which is it? Got a minute to think about it? Hurry! Oops, you've just lost sixty-three nanoseconds already trying to decide.

Coming Soon: No More Coming in Second and Winning the Presidency

JUNE 12, 2015

In the history of the United States, four presidential candidates who came in second in the popular vote were "elected" president (John Quincy Adams in 1824, Rutherford B. Hayes in 1876, Benjamin Harrison in 1888, and George W. Bush in 2000). This inversion of democratic elections was due to the fifty states' winner-take-all laws and the absurdity of the Electoral College. To political observers in other democratic countries, the US is a laughingstock for its failure to change this system that rejects the popular will.

Change is in the wind. A remarkable civic movement is taking on this overlooked issue. The nonprofit group National Popular Vote is successfully pressing for an interstate compact, whereby states pass laws declaring that they will give all their electoral votes to the winner of the national popular vote for president. Presto! Therefore, there is no need for a constitutional amendment to repeal the Electoral College. What the compact does is align the electoral vote with the popular vote, since the Constitution exclusively accords the states the authority to select the manner of choosing their presidential electors.

Remember from your history book, voters do not vote for presidential candidates directly; they vote for a slate of presidential electors who then vote for the real candidates.

So far, led by philanthropist Steve Silberstein and his colleagues, ten states (and the District of Columbia), possessing 165 electoral votes together—or 61 percent of the 270 electoral votes necessary to prevail—have enacted laws for this interstate compact. In order of when the law was enacted, they are Maryland, New Jersey, Illinois, Hawaii, Washington, Massachusetts, District of Columbia, Vermont, California, Rhode Island, and New York. (Visit nationalpopularvote.com for state-by-state details and a list of their bipartisan advisory board with both retired Republican and Democratic members of Congress.)

There are numerous other benefits of this long-overdue reform that has been backed by public opinion polls in the past few decades. With such a reform, presidential candidates will become more likely to campaign in more states, regardless of whether they are blue states, red states, or closely divided states. Presidential elections will no longer be focused on a tiny number of so-called battleground states, such as Florida, Ohio, Virginia, and Iowa.

In 2012, a majority of the general-election presidential campaign events were just in those four states. That means most Americans never see these candidates in their states to meet, question, support, or oppose them. Mitt Romney did not campaign in California or New York; Barack Obama did not campaign in South Dakota or Texas.

As a presidential candidate, I always thought ignoring states, by so pragmatically reflecting the winner-take-all Electoral College, was disrespectful to the American people of the states who were visited less frequently or not at all. Each time I ran for president, I campaigned in all fifty states, though there was no need for me to be concerned about the winner-take-all rule.

This interstate compact, once it reflects a majority of the electoral votes—enough to elect a president (270 of 538)—assures that, in Mr. Silberstein's words, "*every* vote, in *every* state, will matter in *every* presidential election." When people know that their vote matters, they are going to be more motivated to turn out to vote.

Beyond the aforementioned four instances in which the second-place candidate in the popular vote became president, there were more close calls. Mr. Silberstein explains that "a shift of 59,393 votes in Ohio in 2004 would have elected John Kerry despite President Bush's nationwide lead of over three million votes. A shift of 214,393 votes in 2012 would have elected Mitt Romney despite President Obama's nationwide lead of almost five million votes."

With importance placed on the popular vote over the electoral vote, voter suppression or messing with the counting of the votes in specific swing states (e.g., Florida in 2000 or Ohio in 2004) will not be as likely.

The present skewed system gives more importance to a tiny number of battleground states, which tip the election. Politicians favor these states with more visits and more tangible benefits once the candidate is in office. Perhaps it is a coincidence, but, as pointed out by National Popular Vote, battleground states receive 7 percent more federal grants than spectator states, twice as many presidential disaster declarations, and more exemptions for Superfund enforcement and No Child Left Behind.

Applying my theory that it takes 1 percent or less of the citizenry to make major changes in American government (so long as they reflect majoritarian opinion), this tiny group, the National Popular Vote, could be nearing a historic triumph with their educational and advocacy efforts at the state legislative level.

There is a lot of talk these days about growing inequality in the country. That inequality is exacerbated by the lack of direct influence in elections that a popular vote would give those currently underrepresented groups. This nationwide citizen drive working to reduce inequality among voters could be an important step toward closing the inequality gap.

To join the effort for the national popular election of the president, go to nationalpopularvote.com for clear and crisp guides toward becoming a participant in your state.

Why the Future Doesn't Need Us—Revisited

AUGUST 17, 2015

When the stunning article "Why the Future Doesn't Need Us," by Bill Joy, chief scientist for Sun Microsystems, made the cover of *WIRED* magazine in April 2000, it created quite a rumble in high-tech circles. Its argument was that "our most powerful 21st-century technologies—robotics, genetic engineering, and nanotech—are threatening to make humans an endangered species."

Bill Joy was writing about out-of-control, self-replicating technologies that, though once the stuff of science fiction, were now on the way in decades if not years. Tens of thousands of scientists, engineers, mathematicians, and systems analysts are working in countries all over the world churning out theories and specialized applications without much consideration of their overall impacts.

The funding has been coming from various governments' military budgets, which are heavily contracted out to industrial corporations, and, now increasingly, it comes from the commercial pursuits of global corporations. The rate of knowledge production has been exponential as computers become faster and are programmed to become more self-reliant.

Around 70 percent of the volume of stock trading in the US is now driven by computers and their algorithms—a mere glimmer of the future pictured by Mr. Joy.

Sensitive futurists worry about both the intended and unintended consequences. Autonomous weaponry, for example, may be intended for typical purposes by government militaries, but then cause more dreaded unintended consequences when, for instance, these weapons decide for themselves when and whom to strike.

Last month, astrophysicist Stephen Hawking, Apple cofounder Steve Wozniak, and Elon Musk of Tesla were some of many specialists who signed an open letter that called for a ban on autonomous weapons. The letter says, "If any major military power pushes ahead with AI weapon development, a global arms race is virtually inevitable," adding that "unlike nuclear weapons, they require no costly or hard-to-obtain raw materials, so they will become ubiquitous and cheap for all significant military powers to mass-produce."

Artificial intelligence (AI), or "thinking machines," are worrying far more of the serious scientists and technologists than those few who speak out publicly.

Last December, in an interview with the BBC, Stephen Hawking, through his computer-generated voice, warned that "the development of full artificial intelligence could spell the end of the human race. . . . It would take off on its own and redesign itself at an ever-increasing rate." Hawking, a big thinker, noted that "humans, who are limited by slow biological evolution, couldn't compete, and would be superseded."

Self-restraint is not a characteristic of the companies developing robotics for businesses that want to replace tens of millions of both white-collar and blue-collar jobs. Look at the latest factories, refineries, and warehouses to illustrate what is coming fast. Even the work of lawyers is being automated.

But wider audiences need to hear the warnings coming from people like Nassim Nicholas Taleb, author of the runaway bestseller *The Black Swan*, and Stuart Russell, a computer scientist at the University of California, Berkeley, and coauthor of the textbook on AI, who writes about "risks that could lead to human extinction."

Complex systems can be very fragile in ways not foreseen until they happen! That is why Bill Joy saw all three of these technologies—nanotechnology, genetic engineering, and AI—as interwoven systems expanding over the globe beyond human control.

In a recent interview (July 17, 2015) by *Science* magazine, Professor Russell was asked, "What do you see as a likely path from AI to disaster?" He replied: "The routes could be varied and complex—corporations seeking a super-technological advantage, countries trying to build [AI systems] before their enemies, or a slow-boiled frog kind of evolution leading to dependence and enfeeblement not unlike E. M. Forster's *The Machine Stops*."

He told *Science* that he is "not aware of any large movement calling for regulation either inside or outside AI, because we don't know how to write such regulation." Such, he noted, is the "bewildering variety of software that we cannot yet describe."

In the meantime, Congress is oblivious to these grim scenarios. The Republicans in charge have no interest in holding educational public hearings because the corporations who own them have no such interest. Meanwhile, the myopic Democrats are too busy dialing for commercial campaign dollars to grease their campaigns so as to retake Congress in 2016.

Some of these Democrats know better. They championed the Office of Technology Assessment (OTA), an arm of Congress established to research and advise members of Congress about such matters. When Congressman Newt Gingrich toppled the Democrats in 1994, one of his first acts was to defund and shut down OTA.

Congress has played ostrich ever since. The American people will surely pay the price unless a tiny few, including leaders of the scientific community, organize and demand that Congress reinstate the technical warning system that OTA provided. With a tiny annual budget of $22 million, OTA saved far more in prevented boondoggles that were circulating on Capitol Hill.

None of this domestic inaction should preclude international efforts to expand the Geneva Conventions against chemical and biological warfare to cover these latest mass-destruction weapons against humanity. This initiative would constitute an updated declaration of profound human rights.

Enduring Security: Volunteer
Fire Departments

MARCH 28, 2014

"What do you know about Winsted's firemen?" my mother asked me one day when I was eleven years old. "They jump into fire trucks and go put out fires fast," I replied. "Well, you should also know," she added, "that they're volunteers and they risk their lives for the townspeople."

Recently, I had the opportunity to update and expand my knowledge of the Winsted Fire Department (WFD) and the Winchester Volunteer Fire Department (WVFD) that work the higher elevations of this picturesque Connecticut town nestled in the Litchfield Hills. I met with several volunteer firefighters, as they are now called, as well as their paid chief Robert J. Shopey II and their volunteer chief Peter Marchand. I learned an astonishing historical fact: the WFD was organized with four fire companies in 1862.

Now, 152 years later, these companies—the Union Hose Company One, the Deluge Engine Company Two, the Niagara Engine Company Three, and the Cascade Engine Company Four are still operating with volunteers on call and ready to move twenty-four hours a day, seven days a week! Benjamin Franklin, who started the first volunteer fire department in Philadelphia, Pennsylvania, in 1736, would be proud.

Nationwide, volunteer firefighters still make up over two-thirds of all firefighters—the rest being paid public servants.

In Winsted and Winchester, volunteers have to be physically qualified with a certification of "Firefighter I" given by the state of Connecticut, after many hours of training and passing a test. Further training qualifies them to handle forest fires, vehicle extraction, chemical and environmental spills, confined space rescues, cold-water rescues, and other hazardous situations such as downed power lines and search and rescue operations.

They practice regularly each month, learn to use the latest equipment, and keep the doors open for new volunteers, which is more difficult than earlier decades due to changing economic conditions, longer commutes to

41

jobs, and more intensive training requirements. Chief Shopey explained that the WFD used to have 150 volunteers, but now has 80 such stalwarts.

They are managing quite well with a response time of only seven minutes before first firefighter contact is made in this community of about eleven thousand residents. That is under the twelve-minute standard set by the National Fire Protection Association's codes, the chief noted. They get about nine hundred calls a year. There are around ninety "structure" fires, including kitchen fires.

Like other fire departments around the country, Winsted and Winchester receive grants from time to time from various federal departments for equipment, training, and retention. They also receive the local support of the volunteer "fire police," who control traffic around fire locations, and the Winsted Area Ambulance Association and its dedicated volunteer emergency medical technicians.

Of course, not everything that they do is about emergency and preparation. The two departments are alert to prevention, detection, and suppression requirements in residences and other building structures, and protection of the safety of firefighters and apparatuses.

Little-noticed in the national mass media is that fires and fire fatalities have been declining since 1979. Amazing progress in reduction of fire-related deaths has been made in the United States. Nationally in 2012 there were 2,855 civilian deaths and 16,500 civilian injuries, which is well under half the toll in 1979, when the population was tens of millions fewer in number. What is remarkable is that a national policy of improved fire safety has surpassed even the record in Japan—a country that forty years ago had one of the lowest fatality rates per capita in the industrialized world.

There is still progress to be made, however, on preventing the hidden hazards of synthetic chemicals that make up more and more combustible materials and can be deadly threats to the longer-term health of all firefighters.

The very perils that volunteer (and paid) firefighters choose to face at any time (recall the catastrophic loss of hundreds of New York City firefighters during 9/11) produce the solidarity, mutual aid, and camaraderie for which they are properly famous.

Around the country, difficulties and exclusionary practices remain to be overcome. Also, incentives like workers' compensation and some later pension benefits remain to be improved. But the volunteer tradition is an exceptional reminder of how many of our enduring and important volunteer and civic traditions originated in the eighteenth and nineteenth centuries. It's important that we catch up with the new needs of modern society, given the decline of volunteerism seen everywhere.

In Winsted/Winchester every August there is the historic firefighters' parade with engine companies and bands from communities across Connecticut and Western Massachusetts. This tradition started in 1912 and was called by the local paper—the *Winsted Evening Citizen*—"The Most Magnificent Spectacle Ever Witnessed on Winsted Streets."

Next week (April 6–12) is the National Volunteer Fire Council's Volunteer Firefighters Appreciation Week.

If there is an open house at your nearby fire station, do consider attending. You'll meet some self-reliant and valiant volunteers who will welcome your recognition and support in the community. Visit nvfc.org for more information.

Newtown's Moral Authority for Action

DECEMBER 20, 2012

Po Murray, a mother of four children in Newtown, Connecticut, the location of the shooting rampage that took the lives of twenty youngsters and six adults, met with about forty of her townspeople in the local public library to take their grieving to a new level of resolve that they call Newtown United.

PBS *NewsHour* carried the conversation. "This catastrophe happened in our town," Murray said. "This is an opportunity for us to do something really good from a very tragic event that happened. This is a watershed for meaningful change. And I think that we could do something big. And I want to be defining our town by that, not by the tragic event that happened."

Others agreed. James Belden, who runs an environmental nonprofit, said that Newtown, finding itself in "an unfortunate place right now," has "a little more of a voice than we did on Thursday." Tom Bittman, a technology consultant, added: "And if nothing else, if we can get a good national discussion going, and keep it going and get to a resolution, then we win."

From such horrible tragedies emerge the beginnings of a national movement that moves sanctimonious politicians from talking to acting. Newtown has a moral authority to be heard and respected in Washington, DC, and around the country. It is an authority born of a determination that these children and brave adults shall not have perished in vain. Imagine twelve thousand human beings in the US who, in columnist Richard Cohen's words, annually succumb "to the routine mayhem caused by guns," not counting thousands of suicides.

In other countries where such rampages have occurred—Australia and Norway—legislative reforms followed quickly and worked not to eliminate but to reduce risks and harms. Drawing on his experience as chief domestic adviser to President Lyndon B. Johnson, Joseph A. Califano Jr.

provided President Obama with important advice in the *Washington Post*, "Demand action on comprehensive gun control immediately from this Congress or lose the opportunity during your presidency."

In Japan, which has a third of the US's population, eleven people lost their lives to guns in 2008, a tiny fraction of 1 percent of the gun casualties in the United States that year. New York City mayor Michael Bloomberg, who has organized hundreds of mayors in a group called Mayors Against Illegal Guns, said: "We are the only industrialized country that has this problem. In the whole world, the only one."

The problems are numerous, some more tractable than others. The greatest consensus starts with requiring stricter criminal background checks on gun sellers and gun buyers. This receives majority support among National Rifle Association (NRA) members. Next in public support would be the renewal and strengthening of the ban on assault weapons and other military hardware, followed by limits on high-capacity magazines and certain kinds of ammunition.

There are, of course, more controversial measures, including two proposed by President Johnson—licensing all gun owners, suitably trained, as we do with those wanting to drive, and registering firearms, as we do with motor vehicles. Also, as noted by Dr. E. Fuller Torrey and Doris A. Fuller in the *Wall Street Journal*, there would be fewer mass shootings "if individuals with severe mental illnesses received proper treatment."

Officially, the NRA continues to urge stronger enforcement of existing laws. Yet its congressional lobbyists and those of the gun industry have worked hard to keep the budget of the enforcement agency in the Justice Department inadequate to the task. And they're succeeding; there are fewer enforcers now than there were forty years ago. In the Senate, these advocates are even blocking President Obama's nominee for director of the ATF (Bureau of Alcohol, Tobacco, Firearms and Explosives).

Now, back to Newtown United. Tom Bittman, sensing that the current public shock and outrage may soon atrophy, declared, "But now is the time where we can do the most. So we have to do it now."

Who is we? "We the People," that is who, led by the abiding mourning of Newtowners, in sympathy with the daily fatalities on the streets and the same tragedies in Tucson, Aurora, Columbine, and other places of slaughter—for the president and members of Congress are susceptible to "bogging down" and being otherwise predisposed. It's happened many times before.

Joe Nocera, columnist for the *New York Times*, found an apt precedent with Mothers Against Drunk Driving (MADD), started by Candy Lightner, who lost her thirteen-year-old daughter to a drunk driver. She and other grieving mothers raised funds, hired staff and lobbyists, and toughened many of the drunk driving laws and penalties around the country with a salutary though obviously not perfect effect. "Minimize risk and reduce harm" are the pathways to addressing the gun problem, sourced in multiple causations and conditions.

The *Wall Street Journal* devoted an entire page in color to pictures of the Newtown children. That page or its likeness should be sent to the White House and your representatives in Congress again and again, to remind them of those innocent little ones and of the nearly three thousand children every year who are killed by guns in this country.

People across the nation and especially from the surrounding, affluent towns—such as Greenwich, Darien, and Wilton—should help provide the resources to Newtown United so that its sorrowful determination is solidly supported with enough resources to catapult its effort into an America United.

Having "Skin in the Game"

DECEMBER 6, 2012

Nassim Nicholas Taleb's new tour-de-force book *Antifragile: Things That Gain from Disorder* is a frame-of-reference-altering work that a *Wall Street Journal* reviewer confessed he would have to read "again and again," presumably to figure out its "somersaults of the mind," to borrow a phrase from Yoko Ono.

Antifragile, following Taleb's *The Black Swan* that sold three million copies and was a worldwide bestseller, is actually six books in one, as Taleb says. Most reviewers did not comment on "book six," titled "Skin in the Game." In Washington, DC, and on Wall Street, the absence of skin in the game is the presence of power without responsibility or vulnerability.

Taleb writes: "The worst problem of modernity lies in the malignant transfer of fragility and antifragility from one party to the other, with one getting the benefits, the other one (unwittingly) getting the harm, with such transfer facilitated by the growing wedge between the ethical and the legal."

Recognizing the use of self-serving law by the powerful as an instrument of oppression to engage in blatantly unethical conduct, Taleb offers former Secretary of the Treasury Robert Rubin as an example. With Bill Clinton, Rubin pressed Congress in 1999 to repeal the Glass-Steagall Act. Just before the repeal's passage, he resigned and quickly joined Citigroup, the giant financial conglomerate where he was making $40 million within a few months.

It was not a coincidence that Citigroup was the major lobbyist for repealing Glass-Steagall, an FDR-era success that separated commercial banking from investment banking to assure stability and minimize conflicts of interest that were very risky to trusting investors. But it wasn't Rubin who took any risks. After disastrously codirecting Citibank's strategy to the edge of bankruptcy, he proceeded to rack up millions of dollars in bonuses while pushing to make sure that Washington directly bailed out his bank and other financial giants.

Because of Rubin's avaricious and wrongheaded behavior, pension funds, mutual funds, individual investors, taxpayers, and workers all paid the price for the 2008 Wall Street collapse. Despite this wreckage, Rubin popped up after Obama's election as one of the president-elect's leading advisers.

This is what Taleb means when he says executives possess this type of "heads I win, tails you lose" privilege. He adds that "this system is called 'incentive-based' and supposed to correspond to capitalism. Supposedly managers' interests are aligned with those of the shareholders. What incentive? There is upside and no downside, no disincentive at all." In short, "no skin in the game."

Likewise, when Congress abdicated their constitutional war-declaring authority to President George W. Bush in 2003, members of Congress and their families had no skin in the game. These politicians who gave Bush the power to unlawfully invade Iraq paid no price. Indeed, they retained their upwardly mobile status. The White House with its mass propaganda machine and the cowardly Congress paid no penalties for violating the Constitution.

Had there been a law requiring the drafting of able-bodied, age-qualified members of legislators' families whenever the government plunged the country into war, they would have had a personal downside. There would have been deliberative public hearings, where some of the hundreds of high-ranking retired military officers and national security and diplomatic officials who were vocally antiwar would have exposed the Bush/Cheney lies, deceptions, and cover-ups that led to catastrophe for the people of Iraq, the US economy, and military families who especially suffered the downsides.

Taleb gives examples from history in which high performance came from being forced to have "skin in the game," as in Roman times when engineers had "to spend some time under the bridge they built—something," he says, "that should be required of financial engineers today."

To those who impose political and economic power over the people, we should ask them at every opportunity, "Do you have skin in the game?"

The virtue of *Antifragile* is that it is hard to summarize because, in the words of Random House executive editor Will Murphy, it attempts nothing less than to build a guide to thriving—as societies and individuals—in a world too complex to understand: a world governed by the unforeseen events that Taleb, in his previous book, dubbed "black swans."

Daniel Kahneman, Nobel laureate and author of the book *Thinking, Fast and Slow*—no slouch himself—says of Taleb's writings that they "changed my view of how the world works."

Antifragile, a book drawing on the wisdom of many ancient cultures, is an explanation for all ages and all tunnel visions—a boisterous and witty antidote to bureaucratic and individual anomie.

Time for Full-Time Town Jesters

OCTOBER 17, 2012

There's an old saying: "In humor there is truth." Until the eighteenth century, British monarchs, surrounded by sycophantic entourages, retained court jesters who would tell them the truth in the garb of satire and motley costumes with donkey ears, red-flannel coxcomb, and bells.

Of course, the jester also played the fool, made famous in Shakespeare's plays, laughing and joking with his mock scepter. Jesters often played music, clowned around, spoke in riddles, and generally reduced the tensions and pomposity of the royal court.

Queen Elizabeth (who reigned from 1558 to 1603) reportedly "rebuked one of her fools for being insufficiently severe with her." In Shakespeare's *Twelfth Night*, Feste the jester is described as "wise enough to play the fool."

Some jesters became historical figures, such as Jeffrey Hudson, Muckle John, and Archibald Armstrong. James VI of Scotland signed documents lazily without reading them until his jester, George Buchanan, got him to sign his abdication. The king got the message. No one else could have survived such a sobering trick other than the lowly jester.

In *King Lear*, Shakespeare used the jester as a symbol "of common sense and honesty . . . for insight and advice on the part of the monarch, taking advantage of his license to mock and speak freely to dispense frank observations and highlight the folly of his monarch," according to Wikipedia.

In various towns and guises across cultures, the court jester performed in ancient, medieval, and renaissance times at many royal courts, going back to ancient Egypt and across the Atlantic to the Aztec people of Middle America until Cortés's invasion.

Why am I writing about jesters, given all the problems, injustices, greed, deprivation, and perils facing our country? Because even though we do not have emperors or kings, we do have "kingly" presidents, imperial CEOs, and a need to have town jesters from the peaks of power down to our village squares and town meetings.

Concurring pragmatists can call it a jobs program. For you civic advocates, full-time jesters can counter the censorship, self-censorship, and knee-jerk polarization of both civic and political life in America. They can also counter the smugness, arrogance, ignorance, and phoniness of our "deciders."

Face it, how many times a year do you notice political, military, labor, and corporate leaders with marbles in their mouth or, alternatively, speaking with forked tongues? Thinking twice about telling the truth or saying what's really on their mind is an occupational prerequisite to keep their position and entertain promotions. "Mum's the word" behavior in so-called high places is what keeps Jon Stewart and Stephen Colbert getting high television ratings.

Consider a jester in New England towns with populations of up to 75,000. It would be a field day of humor and satire for the jester—getting truth and facts and throwing light on needed reforms. Up and down Main Street; during town meetings and referenda, parades, sports contests; at schools, playgrounds with the children, city hall—the colorful, costumed, bell-ringing jester would lessen the stresses with laughter and open the minds of their immediate audiences. Comedic authenticity is quite different than the canned guffaws emitting from our television screens.

Although a strong case can be made that taxpayer-funded town jesters would more than pay for themselves through the waste, chicanery, and misdeeds they harpoon, why not try to promote fundraising? Foundations? Wealthy people? One spring week in May of personal door-to-door canvassing by the jester and their biggest fans, special performance fees, an annual jester dinner. The possibilities are numerous.

A column by the town manager of Winsted, Connecticut (population about eleven thousand), Dale Martin, literally begging citizens to experience their right to directly vote on a budget referendum for themselves, sparked my imagination. Most Americans don't get to vote directly on their governmental budget. Winsted has a last-resort direct democracy, and over half the voters do not vote either to approve or disapprove of their municipal budgets. And never mind doing a little homework in addition to saying yes or no.

Time for a town jester. Who in, near, or far outside of Winsted, Connecticut, wants to help find perhaps the first career town jester in America? Résumés describing the useful skills, knowledge, personality, artistry, and stamina are invited. Send them and any relevant imaginative essays to Town Jester, PO Box 500, Winsted, Connecticut 06098.

2.

ON DONALD TRUMP

Against the Trumpian GOP Onslaught—the Dems Are Like Deer in the Headlights

APRIL 29, 2022

There is something about entrenched bureaucracies that transcends nations and cultures. When bureaucracies are confronted with unanticipated or new challenges, they freeze—like a deer facing headlights.

Sears, Roebuck and Company saw Walmart coming out of Arkansas and spreading all over the country for years, but the Sears bosses could not adjust to deal with this swarming business model. Sears, once the premium retail and mail-order company in the nation, is now almost gone.

The lumbering General Motors (GM) had years to confront the electric-car challenge of Tesla. Tiny Tesla took on giant GM, which built electric cars as prototypes long before Elon Musk was born. GM launched the much-troubled Chevrolet Volt and other converted model brands, but Musk isn't losing any sleep over competition from GM or the other giant auto manufacturers. He just reported last-quarter sales of more than three hundred thousand electric vehicles, which means expected sales of well over one million vehicles in 2022 or 50 percent more than the previous year. Tesla's profits are skyrocketing as well, as more Tesla manufacturing plants open. The GM bureaucracy, under CEO-engineer Mary Barra, just can't put it together no matter its bold promises to convert to all electric vehicles.

Similarly, the national Democratic Party bureaucrats are inept or bewildered. With its record-setting campaign fundraising, the party can't seem to figure out how to go on the offensive against the overtly lying, cruel, corrupt, law-breaking, Wall Street–over–Main Street, Trumpian Republican Party. GOP fictions are fabricated and reinforced with wild falsifications—e.g., critical race theory being taught in elementary schools, Democratic politicians wanting to defund the police, Democrats being "socialists," and, the latest, Democrats supporting teaching gay rights and gay lifestyles to early elementary school children. These accusations have left the Democratic apparatchiks tongue-tied. They can neither come up with easily pummeling rebuttals, exciting slogans, nor even authentic boasting about delivered and proposed social-safety-net and infrastructure programs that provide necessary assistance. How hard is it to boast about the $300 per month to over sixty million children cut off by GOP congressional callousness? Or a fifteen-dollar minimum wage? Or good-paying jobs repairing and expanding public services for all workers also opposed by the GOP?

Article after article in the mainstream media depicts the Democratic Party as depressed, discouraged, and predicting their own defeat in the November election. They are searching for effective "messaging" by looking over each other's shoulders.

Bear in mind that many of their Republican opponents are political crooks, law violators, and voter suppressors. Senator Rick Scott (R-FL), who is in charge of the Senate November campaigns, wants to tax one hundred million low-income Americans and sunset Social Security and Medicare (see Senator Scott's "An 11 Point Plan to Rescue America").

Democratic political operatives are frantic and down in the dumps. Yet they cling to their corporate-conflicted consultancies that are making it worse for them. Facing their self-fulfilling prophecies of November doom in the Senate and the House, they are still not welcoming the advice and know-how of the civic community, which fifty years ago worked with the Democratic Party to enact fundamental consumer, environmental, and worker-safety legislation.

GOP strategists mock the Democrats regularly as not having a clue what ordinary Americans want. Unfortunately, whether it is arrogance, stupidity, or historical ignorance, the Dems rarely return calls of civic leaders who know how to connect with Americans where they live, work, and raise their families.

Of course, it doesn't help that the mainstream media has excluded the activities and reports by these national and state organizations. They gave coverage to the work of these groups in the past.

Can, at the very least, the Democratic National Committee and its network of related federal and state committees, pollsters, fundraisers, and consultants learn from Harry S. Truman in his underdog 1948 presidential campaign against the former prosecutor and New York governor Thomas Dewey? Pollsters and pundits described Truman as a sure loser and a has-been. Southern segregationists, or Dixiecrats, walked out of the Democratic nominating convention and formed their States' Rights Party.

These setbacks just got "Give 'Em Hell, Harry!" underway. He called Congress back into session so he could show the public the differences between his policies and those of the retrograde Republicans. As related in Robert Kuttner's new book, *Going Big*, Truman pushed "legislation on housing, aid to education, a higher minimum wage, development and reclamation programs for the South and West, increased Social Security, and expanded public power." With these popular hammers, Truman provoked the fierce opposition of what he repeatedly called the "Do-nothing Eightieth Congress," controlled by Republicans, and set the stage for highlighting the sharp differences of the GOP in his presidential campaign.

Come September 1948, Truman spent thirty-three days covering 21,928 miles on the railroad campaign trail, attacking the Republicans and their "big-money boys." In Dexter, Iowa, Kuttner reports, "He told a crowd of some ninety thousand people:"

> I wonder how many times you have to be hit on the head before you find out who's hitting you? . . . These Republican gluttons of privilege are cold men. They are cunning men. . . . They want a return of the Wall Street economic dictatorship. . . . I'm not asking you to vote for me. Vote for yourselves!

This was the language of class warfare that still resonates as well in 2022 as it did in 1948 or in 1933. The Democrats can even quote megabillionaire Warren Buffett, who candidly said there is class warfare in America, "but it's my class, the rich class, that's making war, and we're winning."

The Democrats have memories of many inept races for the White House and Congress that they should have won handily over the last twenty-five years. What they should remind themselves of now is how the FDR, Truman, and LBJ Democrats won their elections against much more tame Republicans than the now vicious, snarling, anything-goes GOP candidates that have turned themselves into Trumpian lackeys.

Democrats Must Demolish Trump's Delusional Law-Breaking Dystopia

AUGUST 28, 2020

Donald Trump continually breaks multiple laws. Yet the serial law-breaking, lying Trump is playing the "law and order" card against street protesters reacting to fatal cases of police brutality. Armed pro-Trump provocateurs are attending civic protests and generating casualties and property damage, as was the case recently in Kenosha, Wisconsin. Trump uses such mayhem to attack Joe Biden and his hyped "radical leftists." This is grotesque, but then that is how corrupt, dangerous, devious Donald operates when cornered by falling polls and growing opposition from top retired military leaders and national intelligence officials. Trump's attack on the US Postal Service is also producing a nationwide backlash, and even red-state conservatives are troubled by delays in deliveries of medicine and Social Security checks.

Devious Donald has a practice of doing exactly what he mostly falsely accuses his opponents of doing. It is puzzling, though not surprising, that the Democrats have not repeatedly restated the highlights from corrupt Donald's rap sheet. Shining a spotlight on Trump, with specific indictments, would demonstrate that his actions suspend law and order in favor of dictates.

Every day, Trump is committing crimes and civil violations of federal law. Every day, Trump is violating the Constitution with serious impeachable offenses (December 18, 2019, *Congressional Record* H12197). Do the Democrats think that the American people do not care about the rule of law and observing the Constitution, those bulwarks against destructive dictatorial power by an ego-obsessed, delusional wannabe monarch?

Yesterday's acceptance speech to the Republican Party by Trump turned the White House into a federal crime scene. The Hatch Act states that having federal employees enable, with federal property, the political campaigns of the president is a criminal violation with serious jail time. Why? Because Congress did not want the power of the federal government to be used to further an incumbent's political objectives against challengers. When Trump ordered Treasury Department staff to place his signature on the memo line of millions of relief checks, that was also a criminal violation of the Hatch Act. Attorney General William Barr, a Trump toady, is not about to prosecute. Barr refuses to respond to demands that he investigate this and other legal violations by the Trump administration.

But lawless Donald has gotten away with more serious violations, such as seizing, unconstitutionally and illegally, the congressional power of the purse and the power to tax. Trump moves money, for purposes not approved by Congress, from one agency to another, as he did for building the wall, thereby violating the Antideficiency Act, which carries a criminal penalty.

Trump has defied more than one hundred congressional subpoenas and more formal demands for his subordinates to testify. These are first-class impeachable offenses. The Founding Fathers provided Congress with the power to compel the disclosure of information that is critical to all other congressional authorities.

President Richard Nixon was on the way, in 1974, to being impeached and convicted in the Senate, during the Watergate scandal, for defying just one subpoena and one count of obstruction of justice. Trump obstructs justice, the processes of law enforcement, all the time, as documented in part by the Mueller Report.

Trump talks about supporting law enforcement on the streets while inciting his supporters to violence, yet he fires and intimidates prosecutors and inspectors general who investigate or expose violations of law by Trump and his Trumpsters. Both his current government and personal businesses, as well as his previous ongoing personal business and taxation entanglements, are under investigation by federal and state prosecutors.

The list goes on. Trump unlawfully nullifies statutory mandates by executive orders. His failure to enforce environmental, health, worker safety, and consumer protection laws is a direct violation of federal law and the Constitution. He is dismantling these protections, driving out civil servants and scientists, and abandoning law and order for corporate crooks by defunding the corporate crime police.

Trump's outlaw regime brags about destroying controls on pesticides (especially harmful to children), coal ash, and other sickening emissions that will attack the health of all Americans. Trump and his henchmen also recently shredded controls on the release of methane, a global warming gas many times worse than carbon dioxide.

Why don't the Democrats use what even the *Wall Street Journal* has regularly exposed about Trump's riddance of law and order to allow runaway big businesses to cheat, pollute, and overcharge people, as well as to defraud the federal government big-time with procurement rackets? Trump is pushing for twenty million Americans to lose their health insurance, with no substitute proposal, and weakening nursing-home safety regulations—in the middle of a giant pandemic!

One answer may be that the Democrats have done some similar things when in power, especially in the area of unauthorized wars and mass surveillance of the people. However, Trump sinks to utterly unprecedented levels of outlawry and openly embraces the monarchical boast that "I have an Article II, where I have the right to do whatever I want as president."

The daily tweeting, lying king, the man who boasted about abusing women and behaving as a sexual predator, is a ruler who brings out the worst from this country. Trump deliberately divides America and stokes conflict and disruption. Trump is a reality denier and chaotic bungler who is aiding and abetting the climate crisis and preventing scientists and public health managers from controlling COVID-19, the cause of the worst global pandemic in our lifetimes. He is also blocking relief for a crashing economy and still escapes accountability.

The Democrats are not matching Trump's or his party's propaganda. In 2004, author and former prominent Republican political analyst Kevin Phillips argued that the Democrats go for the capillaries while the GOP goes for the jugular. By not going full force against dictator Trump, the Democrats are failing to overwhelmingly counter the most criminally, unconstitutionally culpable, vulnerable, and dislikable president in US history. With just over two months until the November 3 election, a strong, independent, civic drive to oppose and vote out Trump and Pence is required. Standing on the sidelines hoping that the Democrats will retire the failed gambling czar didn't work in 2016 and it won't work in 2020 either.

Trump: Letting Big Corporations Get Away with Whatever They Want

MAY 15, 2020

Throughout his presidency, Donald Trump has allowed large corporations to run rampant, exploit people, and get away with it. Trump considers himself above the law, boldly claiming, "I have an Article II, where I have the right to do whatever I want as president." For more information about Trump's misdeeds, please see the Articles of Impeachment proposed by me and constitutional law experts Bruce Fein and Louis Fisher in the December 18, 2019, *Congressional Record*, page H12197.

In 2017, Trump betrayed his own voters by giving the corporate rich a nearly $2 trillion tax cut instead of fulfilling his promise to invest in repairing infrastructure and expanding well-paid job opportunities.

These tax cuts for the rich and big corporations, which benefited the Trump family, ran up the deficit for our children and were largely used to give executives bonuses and let CEOs waste money on stock buybacks. In short, the corporate bosses lied to Congress, saying they wanted these tax cuts to invest and create jobs, but actually used them to enrich themselves.

After his Trumpian giveaway, Trump crushed health and safety law enforcement, unleashing more disease-producing corporate polluters and corporate thieves. The result: harm to workers, consumers, and defenseless communities.

The *New York Times* reported that ninety-eight lifesaving regulations were revoked, suspended, or simply replaced with weaker versions. What remains on the books is not enforced.

Similar wreckage of corporate law and order has exacerbated the crisis of working people. Trump has worked to further punish student borrowers, diminish workplace and auto safety, and remove safeguards against banking, credit, and payday-loan rackets.

Trump, during his failed business career and bankruptcies, saw the law as a nuisance and breaking and escaping justice as a competitive advantage.

While raising huge sums for his reelection campaign from business lobbyists, Trump keeps giving them no-law government, more loopholes for tax escapes ($170 billion more buried in the $2.2 trillion relief and bailout legislation), more corporatist judges to shut you down in the courtroom, and more of your taxes for their endless corporate welfare greed.

Big companies such as banks, insurance companies, real-estate behemoths, and Silicon Valley giants have so many tax escapes and cuts that they're moving toward tax-exempt status.

Howard Stern, a longtime friend of Trump who promoted Trump's notoriety early on, has recently called on Trump to resign. Stern said that, in reality, Donald Trump was "disgusted" by his own voters. Why won't more Trump voters realize that Trump has nothing but contempt for them? Trump will betray his followers at every turn.

During the COVID-19 pandemic—which Trump dismissed and scoffed at for eight critical weeks, leaving the country defenseless—Trump has had no qualms about aiding and abetting a corporate crime epidemic.

Trump, with congressional Republicans, wants more legislation that gives big companies immunity from lawsuits brought by victims who take them to task for their negligently harmful products and services. Another rigging of the system.

Trump's agencies actually announced that they're putting their law enforcers on the shelf. The Food and Drug Administration astonishingly told foreign importers of food and medicine that inspections overseas are suspended. The Environmental Protection Agency signaled similar retreats, as have other enforcement agencies. Why would the Trumpsters signal green lights for corporate crooks? Especially since corporate scams and other corporate crimes—some crude, others sophisticated—are exploding as trillions pour out of Washington.

A year ago, Public Citizen reported a steep decline in corporate prosecutions and fines under Trump. Now, compared to the size of the previous corporate crime wave, they've fallen off a cliff. You can ignore the stern warnings by Attorney General William Barr. He is a phony. He has neither allocated nor asked Congress for a budget that will provide the Department of Justice the capacity to crack down.

In fact, Trump has fired inspectors general and not filled vacant inspector-general positions. Trump's boasts bear repeating: Congress can't watchdog him because "[he has] an Article II, where [he has] the right to do whatever [he wants] as president."

With vicious madness, Trump pushes for federal deregulation of nursing homes where residents are dying from COVID-19. He pursues court cases in attempts to end Obamacare, the result of which would be throwing twenty million Americans off their insurance during a lethal pandemic. He is cravenly freeing corporations that emit life-destroying mercury and coal ash into our air and condemned pesticides and toxins into our drinking water, and whatever else is on the deadly wish list given to him by his corporate paymasters.

Trump's actions that dismantled protections for all American families have been expertly documented. Yet few critics are calling for his resignation or removal from office, despite the clear and present danger he poses to the American people and the republic.

Trump is doing whatever he wants. He is getting away with abandoning the rule of law and the dismantling of crucial government institutions as he embraces American-style fascism and nepotism.

Perhaps people will learn how to effectively fight back against Trump, a delusional, flailing, ego-obsessed, foul-mouthed, self-enriching bully. The people must stand up to this corrupt politician who lies every hour and turns our government over to Wall Street. He sacrifices the people on Main Street to enrich fat cats and oligarchs.

One person, Eugene Jarecki, offers a rebuttal to Trump. In a *Washington Post* op-ed, Jarecki's sources found that "had the guidelines been implemented earlier, a crucial period in the exponential spread of the virus would have been mitigated and American lives saved." According to conservative estimates from epidemiologists, "had the Trump administration simply implemented mitigation guidelines by March 9, approximately 60 percent of American COVID-19 deaths could have been avoided." On his website, TrumpDeathClock.com, Jarecki "displays both the number of people who have died in the country from COVID-19 and an estimate of that portion whose lives would have been saved had the president and his administration acted just one week earlier." Jarecki has also erected a fifty-four-foot-high Trump death clock in New York City's historic Times Square.

See the numbers yourself on TrumpDeathClock.com. Email david@theeisenhowerproject.org to see how Eugene Jarecki's team can help you set up such an accountability clock in your community.

Full Impeachment for Trump Will Shake Senate Republicans from Kangaroo Court

JANUARY 9, 2020

Many Americans have forecasted that the outlaw Donald Trump will commit even more illegal acts to increase his support in the 2020 presidential year. Remember *Wag the Dog*, a film about using a fabricated war to draw attention away from presidential misdeeds? Those Americans have been proven right by Donald Trump's attempt to provoke an unlawful war with Iran. Likewise, Trump has illegally ordered his staff or ex-staff to ignore congressional subpoenas to testify and provide documents.

As the most impeachable president in American history, Trump continues to shred our Constitution and its critical separation of powers. Trump has repeatedly, brazenly seized congressional authority in an attempt to turn the presidency into a monarchy. Trump once went so far as to say, "I am the chosen one."

Unlike Nixon, who slinked away because of the Watergate scandal, every day Trump is providing more evidence to Congress about his impeachability. He never stops. He never expresses remorse or apologizes for violating the Constitution or federal criminal statutes, such as the Antideficiency Act. Likewise, Trump has shown no respect for international treaties to which the US is a solemn signatory.

Trump's mantra of usurpation is clear. He declared that because of Article II of the Constitution, "I have the right to do whatever I want as president." Trump seems to have neglected Article I, which gives Congress the exclusive authority to declare war, to appropriate funds, and to conduct investigations of the executive branch with the plenary authority, i.e., issue and enforce subpoenas. Congress is the primary branch of government, not a coequal branch.

Trump has refused to turn over his tax returns, unlike previous presidents who released them every year. Trump has much to hide in terms of entanglements with foreign entities. He is a walking violation of the emoluments clause (Article I, Section 9, Clause 8), which prohibits any president from profiting from foreign interests. Trump profits when foreign dignitaries patronize his hotels and other properties.

The Constitution requires Trump to faithfully execute the law. Instead, he is destroying health, safety, workplace, and environmental laws through his corrupt henchmen. The Trump regime is dismantling congressionally mandated federal agency law enforcement programs and, in so doing, is removing lifesaving protections. At the same time, Trump is corruptly raising money from the corporate interests that want to dismantle these agencies, from Wall Street to Houston's oil barons.

The most morally distinguishing impeachable offenses come under the heading of what Alexander Hamilton called "abuse of the public trust."

Consider these abuses of the public trust:

1. Trump's chronic, obsessive, pathological lying and falsifications (according to the *Washington Post*, he has made over fifteen thousand false or misleading claims since January 21, 2017);

2. Trump's history of being a serial sexual predator working to delay numerous court cases and escape demands for depositions under oath by many victims;

3. Trump's endless racism and bigotry in words and deeds. Since becoming president, Trump has backed voter suppression aimed at minorities; and

4. Trump's incitement of violence on more than one occasion.

Trump should be impeached and convicted. If the supine Republican-controlled Senate fails to convict Trump, the voters should landslide him in November.

It is almost as if Trump looks to set a record for how many parts of the constitution he can violate. He interceded with the prime minister of Israel, Benjamin Netanyahu, to prevent two members of Congress from getting visas to Israel. Trump's actions prevented these members of Congress from exercising their oversight responsibilities under the speech and debate clause (Article I, Section 6, Clause 1). No president has ever dared such an intervention.

For the elaboration of twelve impeachable counts under one major article, see the letter by me and constitutional law experts Bruce Fein and Louis Fisher in the *Congressional Record* (December 18, 2019, page H12197).

Speaker Pelosi must add some of these impeachable offenses, backed by constitutional law specialists, or Trump will trumpet that though she had the votes to do so, she didn't because they are "fake, lies." Exonerating him will prove to be a devastating precedent for future presidents behaving similarly, as the standards for presidential behavior keep dropping lower and lower into lawless immunity and impunity.

Conservative Fox News commentator, constitutional law scholar, and former judge Andrew Napolitano has said if he were the Democrats, he would reopen the impeachment case "on the basis of newly acquired evidence. . . . That would justify holding onto the articles of impeachment the articles of impeachmentbecause there's new evidence, perhaps new articles."

Pelosi can strengthen her hand constitutionally by enlarging the impeachment case against Trump. This move would give millions of Americans a stake in impeachment because it would directly relate to protections and services they lost because of lawless Trump. In addition, more articles of impeachment would make the Senate Republicans, led by "Moscow Mitch" McConnell, far less able to hold a hasty kangaroo-court trial without witnesses.

Fein, Fisher, and I have written Speaker Pelosi and Senator McConnell urging that the trial's procedures should be established by Chief Justice John Roberts, subject to Senate majority repeal, to assure not only fairness but the perception of fairness. Right now in the Senate there is too much bias, prejudgment, and conflict to avoid a farce.

Moreover, when will the American Bar Association, with over 194,000 lawyer-members, insist on constitutional observance and the rule of law? When will all those original members of Trump's cabinet, whom he fired in favor of yes-men, stand up patriotically for America? When will Colin Powell, George Shultz, and other leading figures from past administrations stand tall and speak out? When will former president Barack Obama stand up to Donald Trump? All of these people are privately worried sick over what Trump is doing and will do to our country.

These are very dangerous times for our republic, its democratic processes, and our freedoms. Trump is going to "wave the flag" and try to intimidate and bully his opponents and the citizenry. *Don't fall for it, America!*

Trump: Importing Dangerous Medicines and Food and Keeping Consumers in the Dark

MAY 15, 2019

Conservatives favor consumer choice. Consumer information is vital to make that choice meaningful. Corporatists, masquerading as conservatives, do not care about informed consumer choice. Donald Trump is a corporatist, as are the vast majority of Republicans in his cabinet and in Congress. Corporatists do not even want you to know where products are made. Today, producers and retail sellers do not have to tell you the country of origin for beef and pork products. Before 2015, when Congress bowed to the dictates of the World Trade Organization (WTO), Congress had enacted a law that required country of origin labels on meat products.

People wanted to know whether the beef and pork sold in their local stores was from the US, or Canada, Brazil, China, Mexico, or South Africa, among other importers. But after the WTO judges in Geneva, Switzerland, decided, bizarrely, that country of origin labeling was an impermissible non-tariff trade barrier, Congress meekly passed a bill that repealed the labeling law, and President Obama signed this legislation into law.

While Donald Trump claims to reject free-trade treaties, he has been silent on country of origin regulations. State Cattlemen's Associations want laws mandating country of origin labels, believing that consumers are more trusting of the US meat industry than the meat industries in most other countries. These associations know that the USDA Food Safety and Inspection Service has a much less rigorous inspection process for imported meats. Unfortunately, the rest of the meat industry likes to import meat, without labeling, and mix it up with the US products. Trump—a prodigious meat eater—has yet to tweet in favor of the American cattle industry, even though many people in this part of the US meat industry voted for him in 2016.

Even worse, we cannot tell where our drugs are being manufactured. Rosemary Gibson, author of *China Rx: Exposing the Risks of America's Dependence on China for Medicine*, thinks American patients are endangered by imported medicines. Gibson is about to testify before Congress on her very disturbing findings regarding importation of medicines from China. I've been trying to get the attention of Donald Trump; his secretary of health and human services, Alex Azar; and the secretary of agriculture, Sonny Perdue, regarding the risks of importing food and drugs. Letters, emails, and calls have been met with silence. By not responding, they're telling us who they primarily support—corporate profiteering interests. That is one reason why Trump has broken his promise to the American people to bring down staggeringly high drug prices.

It will be harder for the Trump administration to ignore journalist Katherine Eban. Eban provides us with a terrifying glimpse of her new book, *Bottle of Lies: The Inside Story of the Generic Drug Boom,* in a *New York Times* article published on Sunday, May 11, 2019. The article, "Americans Need Generic Drugs. But Can They Trust Them?" exposes the widespread unsafe conditions in many Indian and Chinese labs and plants that manufacture generic drugs for the US market (generics amount to 90 percent of the US supply of drugs). One of her sources was an intrepid Food and Drug Administration (FDA) inspector, Peter Baker (he has since left the agency).

Baker was a bold and honest auditor. He refused to announce lab inspections in advance, as is FDA's lackadaisical practice. From 2012 to 2018, Baker discovered "fraud or deceptive practices in almost four-fifths of the drug plants he inspected" in India and China. Indian and Chinese manufacturers engaged in data manipulation that could prove deadly.

At one firm, the Wockhardt plant in India, Baker caught the company knowingly releasing insulin vials containing metallic fragments from a defective sterilizing machine into Indian and foreign markets. Eban reports that "[Baker] learned that the company had been using the same defective equipment to make a sterile injectable cardiac drug for the American market." Two months later, the FDA banned imports from that plant.

Eban continues, shockingly: "In some instances, deceptions and other practices have contributed to generic drugs with toxic impurities, unapproved ingredients, and dangerous particulates reaching American patients." This is nothing new. In 2008, at least eighty-one American patients died in hospitals after being given heparin, a blood thinner that contained a contaminated ingredient from China.

You'd think that the FDA would demand from Trump more inspectors abroad, and the US Department of Agriculture would ask the White House for more USDA Food and Safety inspectors, along with tougher laws and penalties on unsafe imports to transmit to Congress. After all, the sheer scope of US drug companies going to China and India to produce drugs cheaply, so as to swell their already swollen profits, is simply stunning.

Another chilling statistic from Eban is that "nearly forty percent of all our generic drugs are made in India. Eighty percent of active ingredients for both our brand and generic drugs come from abroad, the majority from India and China. *America makes almost none of its own antibiotics anymore*" (my emphasis). The outsourcing of drug production to foreign countries presents vast challenges for health and safety regulators.

One would think this surrender to imports, whose sole purpose is to fatten US drug companies' profits, would be considered both a consumer safety threat and a national security matter. Why isn't Trump doing anything to keep Americans safe from dangerous foreign products as he crows about tariffs?

Of course, the FDA responds with their usual phony assurances about its reliable inspections, putting out a statement that reads: "The FDA inspects all brand-name and generic manufacturing facilities around the world which manufacture product for the US market."

Is that why the FDA, which has largely conducted unannounced inspections of US plants, still allows preannouncement of the vast majority of its foreign inspections? Eban reports that the FDA investigators are treated as "the company's guests and agree on an inspection date in advance. Plant officials have served as hosts and helped to arrange local travel."

Messrs. Trump, Azar, and Perdue better wake up before innocent Americans lose their lives due to corporate-indentured government officials failing to properly do their jobs. Do they want a major disaster to land on their derelict desks?

They are on full public notice.

Trump versus Congress and Our Constitution

MAY 2, 2019

Donald Trump is the most impeachable president in American history. Many Democrats, however, are running away from the word "impeachment" for tactical political reasons. Some Democrats say they have a sworn duty under the Constitution to present articles of impeachment for a vote in the House of Representatives, regardless of the refusal by the Republican-controlled Senate to hold a trial.

Interestingly, when Republicans in the House impeached President Bill Clinton in 1998, he was more popular in polls than Donald Trump is now. The Republican-controlled Senate, however, failed to get the two-thirds vote needed to remove President Clinton from office. Clinton's offenses—lying under oath and obstruction of justice—pale in comparison to the many mega-offenses of Trump.

The six major House committees are investigating issues ranging from his tax returns and business dealings to the serial obstructions of justice documented in the Mueller report. As these investigations move well beyond what is already on the public record and more Americans learn their contents, there will be more than enough to substantiate numerous articles of impeachment. Plus a new one of Trump's own creation: the wholesale, broadside obstruction of all these congressional investigations, defying subpoenas for sworn testimony and documents, amounting to a gigantic contempt of Congress—itself an impeachable offense.

Trump is trying to bar key witnesses from testifying. He is suing his own accounting firm and Deutsche Bank to shield his sordid business relationships and potential tax violations.

I'll bet he's never even read our Constitution—he says out loud that whatever Congress does on impeachment, the Supreme Court will rescue him. Donald, when it comes to congressional impeachment and conviction, the decision by Congress is final.

The House Democrats can strengthen their case with the American people by connecting impeachable offenses with actions that endanger the lives, health, and economic well-being of adults and children.

For starters, Trump and his henchmen have brazenly, openly, and defiantly refused to faithfully execute the laws of the land as required in Article II, Section 3, of the Constitution. By not enforcing the law, he has opened the floodgates for deadly emissions from various industries to get into the lungs of millions of Americans. By allowing more pollution of the water, air, food, and workplaces of the American people, by immobilizing, if not firing, the federal cops on the corporate crime beat; pulling back on existing enforcement; eliminating critical safeguards on the books; and cutting enforcement budgets, he has jeopardized the health of millions of Americans. This is a gift to the lethal coal industry; the reckless drug industry; the chemical pesticide companies; the oil, gas, and nuclear industries; and all those extractive companies licking their chops to plunder more of our beautiful public lands such as the Arctic National Wildlife Refuge and our national forests.

Physicians have pleaded with the Trumpsters to protect the vulnerable infants and children from toxins and microparticulates in the air and water. "Hell no," cry his craven gangsters who were chosen to run our health and safety agencies *precisely* because they want to run them into the ground.

For the first time ever, life expectancy in the United States is declining. This lawlessness is way beyond what should be excused by "prosecutorial discretion." Trump's defiant, wholesale repeal of the rule of law begs for impeachment.

Trump's impeachable brew is deep, hot, and deadly. He violates the Constitution, federal statutes, and international treaties with his war crimes anywhere he wants to conduct them around the world. John Bolton, the unconfirmed national security adviser, and Mike Pompeo, Trump's secretary of state, are looking for new wars—whether in Iran or Venezuela. Bolton and Pompeo are prime examples of unindicted war criminals.

These men violently threaten regimes, except those run by Trump's favorite dictators (he says he's "fallen in love" with North Korea's Kim), as if there are no laws whatsoever to restrain their dangerous missions. The fact that previous presidents, such as Clinton, the two Bushes, and Obama, committed war crimes does not exonerate Trump. Congress is also culpable. It has to stop the lawless foreign and military policies of empire that eventually will boomerang and undermine our nation's national security. It has already produced devastating costs in casualties and dollars.

Impeachable offenses include violating Article I, Section 8, by conducting wars of choice without a congressional declaration, as well as other provisions of the Constitution (Article 1, Section 9, Clause 7) and statutes banning spending tax monies without congressional appropriation. Consider the support of the war on Yemen and bombing of Syria with immense civilian destruction as illustrations.

This is the road to tyranny and the de facto overthrow of our "constitutional order."

Then there are Trump's campaign finance violations, his tax frauds, and his threats to use blanket pardons of Trump associates who are now convicted criminals. Not to mention Trump's "indifference to wrongdoing," in the words of the late, eminent constitutional scholar Charles Black. Such "indifference," Black declared, "may be in effect equivalent to ratification of wrongdoing."

Another standard for impeachment is the widely quoted criterion by Alexander Hamilton—behavior that constitutes "abuse or violation of some public trust." How about Trump's more than ten thousand recorded lies or misleading fabrications? How about his bigotry, misogyny, and lying about his sexual misconducts and payoffs? How about Trump allowing the enrichment of his businesses (which he refused to sell or put into a blind trust) by foreign governments spending lavishly at his hotels and other properties, in violation of our Constitution's emoluments clause?

Our founders condemned behavior, shorn of minimal honor and integrity, that brings the office of the presidency into disrepute and undercuts the legitimacy of the US government or the ability of the government to function.

Recall the five-week shutdown of the US government by our pouting juvenile president over not getting his porous border wall funded. Trump's actions shut down critical, lifesaving governmental services. That tantrum alone should be an impeachable offense.

Congress was handed a mass of evidence by the Mueller report, and congressional hearings are likely to find this evidence provides a solid basis for impeachment. Bear in mind, Mueller decided he couldn't recommend any criminal enforcement due to his hands being tied by a Justice Department "opinion," not a law, that sitting presidents could not be criminally indicted. Instead, he punted his damning report to Congress with such statements as, "Our investigation found multiple acts by the president that were capable of exerting undue influence over law enforcement investigations, including the Russian-interference and obstruction investigations." Over a dozen listed acts, to be specific.

As the laws start catching up with Trump, he will resort to raucous mass rallies where he will warn of violence in the streets, as he did during his campaign in 2016 when discussing his potential loss. He will start military actions, which explains why he had to pressure former generals Mattis and Kelly to resign from the Department of Defense and White House. Trump doesn't like generals who advocate restraint.

Trump himself has said that he will be secure so long as the police and military are with him. Get ready for a fast-approaching major constitutional crisis between Trump and members of Congress who are adherents of the rule of law.

Our lying, lawless president is about to face the laws of the land, backed by our Constitution. It is time for Republicans to start looking at themselves in the mirror of history. And it is time for all Americans to challenge their elected officials to stand tall and uphold the rule of law.

Look How the Real Trump Is Endangering America

MARCH 27, 2019

Special counsel Robert Mueller spent almost two years to produce a $25 million report that is a flat tire. Still unreleased in full to the American people, Trump's acolyte Attorney General William Barr, a longtime friend of Republican Mueller, gave us what Trump long craved by stating that "the investigation did not establish that members of the Trump campaign conspired or coordinated with the Russian government in its election interference activities" during the 2016 election. As for obstruction of justice by Trump, Attorney General Barr cryptically burped, "The special counsel states that 'while this report does not conclude that the president committed a crime, it also does not exonerate him"—whatever that means. Give people the whole report now, as the House of Representatives voted 420–0 to do.

What a farce and distraction this whole exercise turned out to be! Mueller's assigned subject was Trump. So, does this prosecutor demand to interview Trump, to subpoena Trump? No. Does this special investigator conclude with any legal recommendations at all? No. He just wants to be forgotten as he slinks away into deliberate silence (unless he is made to testify before the House Judiciary Committee).

Really, what should we have expected from someone who, as FBI director, testified before Congress as part of the Bush/Cheney regime, pushing for the criminal invasion of Iraq in 2003?

The assignment to Mueller was doomed from the start. Its charge was far too narrow, and proof in such matters is very difficult to find. Intent to collude requires direct examination of the president himself. But why would Trump have to collude at all? The Russians interfered in his favor in various ways to the detriment of Hillary Clinton, and all he had to do was accept such foreign largess.

An inquiry into Trump and all his business deals and business proposals with various governments points to Trump's disregard for the law. By the way, whatever happened to the IRS audit that Tricky Donald kept using as an excuse in 2016 for not releasing these voluminous tax records depicting suspicious relations that Pulitzer Prize–winner David Cay Johnston has written about for years (see his book *The Making of Donald Trump*)?

The endless speculation and successful prosecutions of Trump's associates largely focused on ancillary lies and thefts not leading directly to the White House.

Trump couldn't have distracted the mass dittohead media any better from his true crimes. Those include unlawful war-making, corruption, wasting public funds, and unlawfully handcuffing or firing the federal "cops" whose job is to save the lives, health, safety, and economic assets of all the American people from big corporate predators across the land.

Consider all the print, TV, and radio time the mass media used on the Mueller Russian probe compared to Trump's cruelty and viciousness from his brazen "deregulation" or open flouting of statutorily mandated government missions.

These policies have directly harmed innocent children, the elderly, patients, consumers, and workers and have wreaked environmental ruin, polluting the air, water, and soil with lethal toxins. He proudly took away protections, leaving defenseless humans to suffer more deadly coal dust, coal ash, and coal pollution.

He has blocked our government's responses to the climate crisis, which is looming everywhere.

He has gotten away with massive federal deficits caused by his tax holidays for corporations and the rich, including the Trump family. Take that, next generation of Americans!

He backs for-profit colleges that have committed serial crimes against their impoverished students while heavily subsidizing these corporations with your tax dollars.

He is pushing to weaken or eliminate modest controls over imperial Wall Street, upsetting even Wall Streeters like Timothy Geithner, setting the stage for another Wall Street collapse on the economy, causing workers to lose their pensions and savings before they, as taxpayers, are required to again bail out the Wall Street speculators and crooks.

He lies repeatedly about current realities, falsely brags about conditions he is actually worsening. He opposes any increase in the frozen federal minimum wage of $7.25 an hour and does not adequately enforce fair labor standards. He has hired and personally profited from many undocumented workers while attacking their presence in the US.

He pays more attention to one golf ball than he does to the estimated $60 billion in annual wage theft or $350 billion a year in the health industry's computerized billing fraud, or the gouged drug prices he falsely promised the people he would reduce.

Never mind impeachment—millions of Trump's victims, regardless of how they voted in 2016, should demand his resignation. A million-person march should surround the White House and peacefully make this demand repeatedly.

Enough of lying Trump's slimy bigotry and his snarling, hateful, bullying speech always directed at the powerless. Enough of his destructive impact on millions of children imitating his coarseness toward siblings and parents who, when admonished, blurt out that the president says *this* and does *that*. That daily acidic intrusion into family life—a cultural time bomb—has yet to properly interest the media.

Cheating Donald J. Trump has gotten away with everything in his failed businesses and his Electoral College–caused presidency. In so doing, he has taught us much about ourselves; how much we tolerate with chronic indifference the flaying of the rule of law; and the principles of decency, helpfulness, peace, and justice.

He has taught us about the costs of not doing our political homework, of staying home civically and electorally. He has taught us that if we do not look ourselves in the mirror, the three horsemen of fascism, lawless plutocracy, and oligarchy will run our beloved country into the ground, if not over the fiscal cliff.

Mugger Mick Mulvaney—
Trump's Sadist-in-Chief

JUNE 27, 2018

Mr. Mulvaney's title seems uninterestingly bureaucratic—director of the Office of Management and Budget (OMB). But as Trump's chief hatchet man extraordinaire, Mugger Mick Mulvaney is easily one of the cruelest, most vicious presidential henchmen in modern American history. From his powerful perch next door to the White House, he is carving a bloody trail against tens of millions of Americans who are poor, disabled, frail, or elderly. He has gone after defenseless children and injured or sick patients with little or no access to health care.

It is difficult to exaggerate the relentless, savage delight that this former congressman from South Carolina—handpicked for Trump by the brutish, oil-funded Heritage Foundation—takes in attacking the most vulnerable members of our society.

A human wrecking ball, Mugger Mick has pushed to eliminate the Meals on Wheels assistance for isolated elderly, to increase rents for poor tenants, to severely gut SNAP (food stamps) and nutritious food standards, and to diminish Medicaid. In addition, the Trump administration wants to impose work requirements as a condition of eligibility for Medicaid. Many adult Medicaid recipients are already working. Where will the new jobs come from? Those who want to work but can't find jobs are not Mr. Mulvaney's concern.

His hellish agenda, undertaken on behalf of his plutocratic rulers, is comprehensive. He wants to smash consumer, environmental, and workplace health and safety standards. To Mugger Mick, killing and disabling Americans doesn't even qualify as collateral damage. To Mulvaney's fevered, psychopathic mind, eliminating Americans' health and safety protections is worth it if it means "efficiency" and less spending of tax dollars (more on that lie later).

He even would plunge a dagger into Social Security and Medicare. President Trump has the political sense to restrain Mugger Mick from this attack on the elderly. However, biding his time, Mulvaney has led the campaign for the enacted corporate and wealthy tax cuts that are already swelling the forthcoming massive deficits. Mulvaney wants to use the deficit to persuade Trump to eventually butcher these two pillars of our society's foresight and compassion for seniors.

The *New York Times* reports that Mulvaney is at the core of the Trump regime's "rollback in the enforcement of fair housing, educational equity, payday lending, and civil rights cases pursued aggressively under the Obama administration intended to protect vulnerable populations from discrimination and abusive business practices."

Nowhere has Mugger Mick been more blatant about his ugly mission than in his efforts to freeze and dismantle the Consumer Financial Protection Bureau (CFPB). The CFPB was created after the Wall Street collapse of the economy, which displaced millions of workers and drained trillions of dollars from pension and mutual funds. Remember Wall Street then had to be bailed out by America's taxpayers.

Mulvaney has jettisoned ongoing enforcement actions, driven or reassigned personnel, zeroed out the CFPB's first-quarter budget, and prioritized the protection of Wall Street in the CFPB mission statement. How grotesque a response to the corporate crime wave in this country that has been stealing trillions of dollars from defenseless consumers, workers, and investors!

There is, of course, more to this colossal bully. Mulvaney is also a colossal coward and a greasy hypocrite at that. He shuts his foul mouth when it comes to the bloated defense budget and the corporate contractors profiting from endless Pentagon golden handshakes. He shuts his mouth when confronted with thousands of corporate subsidies, handouts, giveaways, and bailouts. In these crony-capitalistic binge arenas, he demands no corporate self-reliance or worries about taxpayer losses. Why would he argue with his future paymasters and the corporate donors who funded his prior congressional campaigns?

Mugger Mick is a walking candidate for impeachment, a poster boy for high crimes and misdemeanors, as well as a lawsuit by members of Congress for the deliberate dereliction of duties that aids and abets corporate criminality. Every day he has been systematically defying and violating existing congressional mandates, called federal statutes.

So where are the Democrats? Aside from a few members, such as Senators Elizabeth Warren and Sherrod Brown, pummeling Mugger Mick at congressional hearings that go nowhere, action by the Democratic Party on Capitol Hill is largely AWOL. Mulvaney just laughs at the Democrats' verbal darts.

Forget about their own pride—these lawmakers have little fortitude in preserving the best work of their forbears in Congress and in the White House. They're too busy having fun ridiculing Trump's foibles, fibs, and fantasies. Such distractions emanating from the Trumpsters and their media dittoheads may well cause Democrats not to urgently focus on what is happening to the American peoples' freedom, urgent necessities, and livelihoods.

November is coming fast.

What Does Trump Mean by "Make America Great Again"?

DECEMBER 13, 2017

Donald Trump's now ubiquitous slogan, "Make America Great Again," is often chanted at rallies but rarely scrutinized in public discourse. What era in America's past is Mr. Trump referring to when he says "again"?

Would Mr. Trump prefer America return to the days of slavery, Jim Crow, and labor exploitation in unsafe factories, mines, foundries, and plantations? How about the late nineteenth century when robber barons monopolized one industry after another? Is he longing for the days when women were second-class citizens and couldn't vote, until securing this right less than one hundred years ago, only to still be paid lower wages than their male colleagues for performing the same jobs and to face consumer and educational discrimination?

Or is Trump referring to a time when the US was less of a giant empire than it is today?

Or, more optimistically, in the 1960s and early 1970s when America had its highest real wages and a large trade surplus? Has anyone heard him say he wanted to return America to that prominence that peaked in the 1960s?

He surely doesn't want to raise wages for workers. On the campaign trail last year he said wages were too high and has not championed raising the frozen federal minimum wage ($7.25 an hour) since.

He has spoken often about revising trade agreements to reduce our trade deficit, but he's not going to take on the opposition of the emigrating giant global corporations to reduce our trade deficit.

Maybe he wants to go back to the America before there was Medicare or Medicaid, before dangerous cars had to be recalled, before food had to be labeled, before unions existed to collectively bargain with large companies in the auto, steel, and oil industries?

Does he miss the days when there were segregated restaurants, hotels, trains, and buses? What about when people could smoke in your space in airplanes, college lecture halls, hospital waiting rooms, cafes, offices, and just about all public spaces, no matter the presence of children and asthmatics? Or when people with disabilities faced greater physical exclusion and career discrimination?

More benignly, perhaps Mr. Trump is longing for the days when there was less soil erosion, fewer toxic chemicals in the environment, and more family farms. Or when there was far less obesity and diabetes and less aggressive marketing to children of fast food full of fat, sugar, and salt. If so, he sure is not going to Make America Great with the corporatists he's appointed to run the Food and Drug Administration, the Environmental Protection Agency, or the Department of Agriculture.

Does he want to Make America Great Again by returning to the days when there were fewer people in prisons per capita; fewer nonviolent drug offenders serving long sentences, including juveniles; fewer, if any, private corporate prisons? If so, he is going to have problems with his attorney general, Jeff Sessions. What about when casino gambling was highly restricted and only legal in Nevada? It's unlikely Mr. Trump would have wanted to prohibit gambling in his Atlantic City Casinos before they failed or went bankrupt. With his flurry of statements and tweets endorsing sexual harasser, accused pedophile, and defeated Senate candidate Roy Moore, Trump, given his boastful aggression toward women, certainly does not want to return to an America when such widely publicized misbehavior would have kept men from even running for office.

Maybe, Mr. Trump has a limited meaning to "again." Maybe he means going back to a time when America was respected and feared in the world. Going back to the days when a smaller Japan and Germany made war on the US or when Britain played Woodrow Wilson and the US for suckers and got us into World War I, which led to World War II. Oh, such glorious nostalgia for Donald J. Trump.

What a speech Trump could give were he to explain what Making America Great Again means to him. He could explain his desire to go back to the prosperous sixties when big corporations and the rich paid much higher taxes, didn't dare pay their CEOs more than thirty times the average wage in their companies, and had to comply with a higher real minimum wage. He could wax nostalgic over the larger relative infrastructure budgets of the federal government, or the days when student debt was small or nonexistent compared to the huge student debt load now imposed on this younger generation of Americans.

If all this sounds a little confusing, it is. Voters should have rejected such an unrebutted slogan repeated to applauding crowds again and again by Donald Trump in his get-away-with-anything presidential campaign of 2016.

Trump's Hundred Days of Rage and Rapacity

APRIL 26, 2017

The lawless-loving corporatists have worked overtime to besmirch the word "regulation" (or law and order for corporations) and edify the word "deregulation" to help bring about their dream state of dismantled or weakened regulation.

Here is one little-mentioned ongoing disaster of nonregulation costing our country. The patsy Federal Aviation Administration (FAA), for decades after the hijacking of planes to Castro's Cuba, refused to require the airlines to install toughened cockpit doors and stronger locks to prevent entry by terrorists bent on making the aircraft a destructive weapon. Why? Because the airlines objected to the mere $3,000 cost per aircraft and, by its very nature, the FAA acquiesced.

Then came 9/11, followed by "mad dog" George W. Bush (and Dick Cheney, his handler) launching an all-out attack on Afghanistan rather than leading a multilateral force to apprehend the backers of the attackers. Later, Bush's criminal war devastated the country and people of Iraq. Iraq is still convulsing violently today.

This was all because the FAA didn't regulate the airlines to protect their cockpits and pilots. Sure, the hijackers could still have hijacked the planes, but they could not have piloted them into the World Trade Center and the Pentagon.

Government regulations have led to lifesaving motor vehicle standards. They have required safer pharmaceuticals; improved the safety of mines, factories, and other workplaces; and diminished the poisonous contaminants of air, water, food, and soil. According to the Center for Auto Safety, the federal programs for highway and vehicle safety have averted 3.5 million deaths in the US between 1966 and 2015.

In an industrialized economy with corporations, hospitals, and other commercial activities producing old and new hazards, regulations are needed to foresee and forestall many human casualties and damage to the natural world.

The role of sensible regulations has been all but ignored by Donald J. Trump in his regime's first hundred days of rage and rapacity. The Trump administration continues to take away basic protections that save both money and lives. With his cruel and monetized Republicans controlling Congress, he has eliminated thirteen safeguards issued by the Obama administration.

Proudly, he and House Speaker Paul Ryan and Senate Majority Leader Mitch McConnell have turned their backs on ensuring cleaner waterways, making coal-polluted air less toxic, enforcing workplace protections, and preserving our public lands. Disastrously for our country, Trump has joined forces with the Republicans in Congress to immobilize our government's research and action regarding accelerating climate change. He is even scaring big business, including the insurance industry.

The worst of Trump's egregious attacks on regulatory protections are coming out of his mindless executive orders to federal agencies. While many are of dubious legality—they would require congressional legislation—his intent is clear: roll back major protections of Americans wherever they eat, breathe, drink, work, drive, and receive health care.

One executive order requires agencies to repeal two regulations for every one they issue. Such an empty but dangerous gesture is mindless but emblematic of the prevaricating, boasting, failed gambling czar. The Trump administration's rejection of essential roles for government is stunning.

Trump would weaken the laws protecting your savings, investments, and retirement security from what shredded them during the 2008–2009 Wall Street crash. No Wall Street bosses were ever jailed, so they're prone to keep speculating with your money and pocketing huge fees from your accounts in the process.

Trump is even putting off a Department of Labor rule requiring your investment advisers to put your interests ahead of their conflicting interests—the so-called fiduciary rule. Trump—who betrayed creditors, employees, investors, and consumers alike during his business career—readily knows what that accountability mechanism is all about.

When Trump's formal budget is announced next May, it will starve the already strained enforcement budgets of the health and safety regulatory agencies such as the Federal Drug Administration, Environmental Protection Agency, and Occupational Safety and Health Administration. Trump even wants a sharp cut of the Centers for Disease Control's program to head off deadly global epidemics.

In addition, Trump has broken his campaign promises, surrounding himself with Wall Street insiders and intensifying Obama's belligerent and militaristic foreign policy around the globe. He is also demanding that Congress add $52 billion more to the already bloated Pentagon budget, decried by many liberals and conservatives. Fifty-two billion dollars is far greater than all the combined federal regulatory budgets for the agencies that provide the health, safety, and economic protections for Americans from costly corporate crimes, abuses, and frauds.

The fallout of these ominous hundred days is not escaping millions of lawyers, accountants, physicians, engineers, scientists, and teachers at all levels. And it isn't escaping those blue-collar workers who rolled the dice and voted for Trump, despite his opposition to raising the minimum wage and fair labor standards.

Yes, there are signs of stirrings among these citizens. But will there be action against the Trumpsters and Trumpism in the coming weeks and at the polls next year? Will the people continue to turn out in ever greater numbers at marches, rallies, and congressional town meetings (see indivisibleguide.com), whether arranged by their senators and representatives or, if not, by the citizenry summoning its 535 members of Congress to peoples' town meetings?

Only you, the American people, one by one and by joining together, can answer these questions.

How Unpatriotic Is Donald Trump?

JULY 1, 2016

Samuel Johnson famously considered patriotism "the last refuge of a scoundrel." His biographer, James Boswell, who passed along that judgment, clarified that Johnson "did not mean a real and generous love for our country, but that pretended patriotism which so many, in all ages and countries, have made a cloak for self-interest."

This could be describing Donald Trump. And yet the *Wall Street Journal*'s Peggy Noonan theorized in an April 2016 column that Trump's major appeal to Republican voters came not from his adherence to any political ideology, but rather from his radiant patriotism that has, in her view, been absent from the political status quo. "What Trump supporters believe, what they perceive as they watch him," she wrote, "is that he is on America's side."

There is little in Trump's rambling, off-the-cuff speeches and media interviews, or in his reactionary stream-of-consciousness tweets, that demonstrates his understanding of patriotism. Trump is a snake-oil salesman, and he is arguably in the midst of his greatest pitch to date. Smart consumers should do their research to find out the truth about the "product" they are being sold by Mr. Trump.

Here are some examples of where the real estate plutocrat comes up short on patriotism.

- Peeved by the *Washington Post*'s coverage of his presidential campaign and its investigation of the details surrounding his grand claims, Trump has revoked the paper's press credentials for attending his rallies and political events. He has also banned reporters from *Politico*, *Univision*, *Mother Jones*, the *Daily Beast*, *Huffington Post*, and others. What's patriotic about muffling the free press when you are running for the highest office in the land?

- Despite lofty rhetoric about "bringing jobs home," Trump has used cheap foreign production in China and Bangladesh for his signature clothing brands. "They don't even make this stuff here," the ever-defensive Trump told ABC News's George Stephanopoulos when questioned about it. Stephanopoulos informed Trump that Brooks Brothers clothing does, in fact, "make this stuff" here. What's patriotic about making profits on the backs of poorly paid foreign workers who are often suffering under dictatorial rule?

- Big talker Trump has claimed to have given millions of dollars to many different charities over the years. According to a recent *Washington Post* investigation, he's given far, far less than he's boasted—and far less than other billionaires of his (allegedly) comparable wealth. Most of his donations have come through the Trump Foundation, to which he has donated little of his own fortune. All in all, over the past seven years, the *Post* reports that Trump has personally given less than $10,000 to charities. What's patriotic about lying about your own philanthropy?

- One of Trump's more preposterous statements has been calling for a "total and complete shutdown of Muslims entering the United States." Drawing much justified criticism, Trump has been pressured into clarifying and restating his position. He now claims that only immigration from "terrorist countries" would fall under his proposed ban. He also stated last fall that he was "open" to the idea of creating an Orwellian database of all Muslims living in the United States. Is accusatory language of ethnic stereotyping reflective of our patriotic traditions? The inscription on the Statue of Liberty is: "Give me your tired, your poor, your huddled masses yearning to breathe free." Is repudiating Lady Liberty patriotic?

- Donald Trump's bid for the presidency has been based on the supposed strength of his talent and judgment as a businessman and dealmaker. These skills, however, are not totally verifiable, since Trump refuses to release his tax returns. Trump has managed to avoid any severe blows to his personal wealth by strategically insulating himself from failed corporate business endeavors. He has bragged that he "used, brilliantly," corporate bankruptcy as a competitive advantage. When Trump fails, only the little guys suffer. Not exactly reflecting the last words of the pledge of allegiance—"with liberty and justice for all."

- Last year, Donald Trump shamefully criticized Senator John McCain, who spent over five years as a prisoner of war in North Vietnam. The ever-brash Trump dismissed McCain's extraordinary ordeal, claiming: "He's not a war hero." Trump continued, "He was a war hero because he was captured. I like people who weren't captured." Is degrading the suffering of an American veteran patriotic? Unlike McCain, Trump did not serve in the Vietnam War. He has gone on the record, however, for making a different kind of sacrifice. Trump described his romantic escapades in the 1980s as his "personal Vietnam" due to how he put himself at risk of sexually transmitted diseases. He told Howard Stern that this made him feel "like a great and very brave soldier."

- "I believe that Trump University was a fraudulent scheme," Ronald Schnackenberg, a former employee of the unaccredited Trump University, stated in testimony, "and that it preyed upon the elderly and uneducated to separate them from their money." Indeed, much of the information that has come to light about Donald Trump's "university" reveals that it was little more than a scam meant to drain people of their money while promising them success. Cornered by the allegations, Trump resorted to accusing Judge Gonzalo P. Curiel, who is scheduled to hear the class action suit in November, of being "a hater" of his due to Curiel's Mexican ethnicity. Are these the words of man who loves America or those of a con man caught with his hand in the cookie jar?

  Since starting his bid for the presidency, Donald Trump has produced a veritable Trump Tower of outrageously false statements. According to the nonpartisan Politifact, nearly 80 percent of the statements made by Donald Trump fall under the categories of Mostly False, False, or "Pants on Fire." His campaign won the distinction of 2015 Politifact Lie of the Year for its entire spider web of deceptions. What's patriotic about chronically lying when you're running for the presidency of the United States?

So what does it truly mean to be patriotic? My parents defined it quite simply. They taught my siblings and me that loving one's country meant working hard to make it more lovable. This means working to end poverty, discrimination, corruption, greed, cheating, and other injustices that weaken the promise and potential of America.

Trump for President? Giving the GOP Nightmares

Donald Trump, the bombastic builder of Trump towers and Trump casinos is moving from his reality TV show to the theater of presidential elections. If he survives the first three months of mass media drubbing him and his notorious affliction of "leaving no impulsive opinion behind," he's going to be trouble for the other fifteen or so Republican presidential candidates.

Already the commentators have derided his massive egotism—he said "I" 195 times in his announcement speech, not counting the twenty-eight times he said "my" or "mine" or the twenty-two mentions of "me." But Trump revels in self-promotion and, as one commentator wrote, "plays the media like a harp."

If he is still campaigning by Labor Day, watch out Republicans! He will be a big nightmare for Republican contenders—from Jeb Bush to Ted Cruz, from John Kasich to Scott Walker. Here are some reasons why:

1. Many American voters love to vote for very rich candidates, whether they are Republicans or Democrats. They believe they can't be bought. They love business success stories. And being very rich, the media CEOs keep the very rich candidates in the limelight, as do the national polls.

2. He can pay for his own media. Remember billionaire Ross Perot and his purchase of national television to show his charts on deficits? People laughed. But Mr. Perot got nearly 20 million votes in 1992, even after dropping out of the campaign in the summer and being labeled a conspiracy theorist before again becoming a candidate in the fall!

3. Trump consistently and personally attacks the other candidates, which makes for regular news. The other candidates do not like to engage in personal attacks unless under political duress.

4. Trump turns liabilities into assets, including his vaunted forthcoming disclosures of his net worth—he focused on assets while ignoring many complex liabilities. While Jeb Bush and Mitt Romney before him tried to play down their wealth, Trump insisted he's worth over $10 billion. He even ridiculed Bush, who announced his candidacy without wearing a suit and tie. To accusations that he has taken public subsidies and eminent-domain protections for his giant projects, Trump replies that capital and tax money create jobs and more businesses.

5. Trump will crowd other candidates out from valuable TV, radio (Rush Limbaugh thinks highly of him), and print space. To adjust, they may have to become more flamboyant, further expanding the circus-like atmosphere of the Republican primaries while the Democratic Party leaders chortle.

6. Some of Trump's positions have sizable support among Republican voters. He believes in public-works programs on a big scale. He talks jobs, jobs, jobs and says he's the only one among the candidates who has been creating jobs. He objects strongly to the trade agreements, including the proposed Trans-Pacific Partnership deal now in the news, on the grounds that other countries, such as Japan and China, are superior negotiators and are taking us to the cleaners. He wants to build a tall wall on the Mexican border. He is against Common Core and federalizing education. He warned against invading Iraq in some detail, predicting it would expand Iran's influence. He is for a strong military and talks about the mistreatment of veterans. He exudes self-confidence and attaches it to American national interests.

7. Having survived tough, acidic New York journalism for years, he is almost scandal-proof. Attacks from his business and political enemies have helped to immunize the big-time scrapper from serious reporting. He feeds off public cynicism about politics.

8. If the Republican bigwigs try to exclude or humiliate him, Trump has the means to run as an independent candidate for president—as Mr. Perot essentially did under the banner of his Reform Party. Just

the prospect of that added nightmare might induce caution at the top levels of the GOP.

9. He is not going to run out of money and, unlike his competitors, doesn't have to spend any precious campaign time dialing for dollars or making campaign promises. He can hire the smart strategists, speechwriters, election lawyers, and primary delegate–seekers.

One hurdle Trump may not be able to surmount is Lorne Michaels's Saturday Night Live (SNL). Michaels, SNL's forever producer, uses exaggeration and satire to lampoon politicians. How can he satirize buffoonish satire itself? How can he exaggerate Trump, who brags that the master bathroom on his private jet has a 24-karat-gold-plated sink?

3.

ON THE COVID-19 PANDEMIC
AND HEALTH CARE

~~~~~~~~~~~~~~~~

Trump and Pence—Step Aside for Professional Pandemic Scientists and Managers

JULY 2, 2020

Major changes in society can be accomplished by a fast-emerging, broad-based *civic jolt* so obvious and persuasive that it overwhelms the entrenched powers. The most urgent job is for people to organize to get Trump and Pence to *step aside* from their bungling, making-matters-worse mismanagement of the COVID-19 pandemic. The White House should let a professional pandemic control specialist with public health experience and an appreciation of science replace the current and ongoing Trump horror show.

Many Republican operatives watching the daily *Trump virus* spectacle are terrified by how the president fabricates and fantasizes, confusing and endangering the country. As Trump lowers his and their poll numbers, Republicans would welcome a replacement.

"We the People" are seeing the failing Donald Trump overriding his own scientists and paralyzing any federal leadership and coordination of state efforts, as he measures all moves by his delusional ego. The citizenry must quickly mount irresistible pressure for Trump and Pence to step aside. Let Trump focus on the November election, which is all he cares about anyway, apart from watching Fox News for hours each day, lying to the public, and endlessly tweeting slanders and insults.

Trump is so cruel and out of touch that he is letting his henchmen cut nursing-home safety regulations; end health and safety protections for workers, consumers, and communities, and pursue the end of Obamacare by stripping now twenty-three million Americans of their health insurance. Doing this in the middle of a worsening killer pandemic is sheer madness. We have a president at the helm of the careening ship of state acting worse than Captain Queeg.

Would any community tolerate, in Maureen Dowd's words, such "chaos, cruelty, deception, and incompetence" in their local public-safety officials?

To be sure, there have been thousands of articles, columns, editorials, and TV/radio reports of the grotesque delays, perverse actions, quackery, and glossing over the grim realities by Trump and Pence. All this takes place against the backdrop of his blundering son-in-law who is overseeing and furthering corrupt corporate bailouts. But inexplicably, reporters and columnists avoid the conclusions that should stem from their own convictions and writings. One exception is the *Washington Post* editorial, in May 2020, calling for Trump and Pence to step aside and let people who know what they're doing take the reins.

The country simply cannot wait until Inauguration Day, January 20, 2021. Every day the Trump virus spreads further, while its presidential enabler is making sure sick Americans are left unprotected and workers are left unemployed. More and more innocents are paying the ultimate price for this public health and economic disaster.

The failed gambling czar, selected to be our fake president by the unelected Electoral College, crazily gives himself a "ten" rating, admits no mistakes, and refuses to learn from other nations' comparative successes against the virus.

Putting health professionals in charge of the "war" against the COVID-19 pandemic has worked in Taiwan, New Zealand, Thailand, Uruguay, Canada's British Columbia, and other countries with sane leadership. These countries are showing far, far superior lifesaving results and fewer economic convulsions.

Mr. Trump, if you're not going to resign for America's sake, at the least, step aside for your own political campaign's sake. A coordinated civic jolt and a laser-beam demand from the people can make you and the alarmed GOP realize you are not capable of doing the job that needs to be done. Of course, if Congress wasn't a rubber stamp, our first branch of government could stop this lethal incompetence by mandating professional pandemic management.

For those who doubt this could happen, remember the ringing statement by the demanding abolitionist Frederick Douglass: "Power concedes nothing without a demand. It never did and it never will." Trump is a papier-mâché figure who hides behind bluffs and snarls. A civic jolt can displace him much like the statutes of slavers.

Start your "step aside" demand by calling the White House opinion phone number 202-456-1111. Urge your friends to do the same. There is no time to delay.

Beware of the Medicare "Disadvantage" Corporate Trap—Wake Up, AARP

NOVEMBER 21, 2019

While the Democratic presidential candidates are debating full Medicare for All, giant insurance companies like UnitedHealthcare are advertising to the elderly in an attempt to lure them from Original Medicare (OM) to the so-called Medicare Advantage (MA)—a corporate plan that United-Healthcare promotes to turn a profit at the expense of enrollees.

Almost one-third of all elderly people over sixty-five are enrolled in these numerous, complex MA policies the government pays so much for monthly. The health insurance industry wants more enrollees as they continue to press Congress for more advantages.

Medicare *Dis*advantage would be a more accurate name for the programs, as insurance companies push to corporatize all of Medicare, yet keep the name for the purposes of marketing, deception, and confusion.

Elderly people enrolled in MA will experience its often merciless denials when they get sick. As hospital expert, attorney, and physician Dr. Fred Hyde put it: "It's not just what you pay, it's what you get."

Start with the cross-subsidization of MA from OM. In 2009, the Congressional Budget Office estimated these overpayments would cost the federal government $157 billion over the coming decade. Obama's Affordable Care Act started to reduce these subsidies to the giant insurers, but they still amount to many billions of dollars per year.

Add that with Medicare *Dis*advantage, you are restricted to networks of vendors. That restricts your choice for competence and skills and sometimes requires you to travel longer distances for treatment. This could mean fewer enrollees will utilize their health care, and insurance companies will gain more profits.

Under Medicare *Dis*advantage, you are subject to all kinds of differing plans, maddening trapdoor fine print, and unclear meaning when the insurers argue no "medical necessity" to deny you care.

The advertisements for Medicare *Dis*advantage stress that you can sometimes get perks—gym memberships, hearing aids, and eyeglasses—as enticements, but they avoid telling you they are not so ready to cover serious needs like skilled nursing care for critically ill patients.

Under Medicare *Dis*advantage, there is no Medigap coverage as there is for OM. Copays and deductibles can be large. Under a recent Humana Medicare Advantage plan in Florida, your copay for an ambulance could be up to $300, lab services up to $100, and outpatient X-rays another $100.

A few years ago, UnitedHealthcare corporations dismissed thousands of physicians from their MA networks, sometimes immediately, sometimes telling their patients before telling their physicians.

Dr. Arthur Vogelman, a gastroenterologist, said he received a termination letter in 2013 from UnitedHealthcare. He appealed, documenting his successful treatment of many patients. The company denied his appeal, with no reason, as it had for thousands of network physicians.

Dr. Vogelman called it "an outrage. I have patients in their eighties and nineties who have been with me twenty years, and I'm having to tell them that their insurer won't pay for them to see me anymore. The worst thing is I can't even tell them why." Except that the company wanted more profits.

After a lengthy protest by national and state medical societies in 2013, UnitedHealthcare began to be less aggressively dismissive.

Studies show the main reason MA enrollees return to OM is how badly the corporate insurers treated them when they became sick.

Medicare itself is getting overly complex. But nothing like the ever-changing corporate rules, offerings, and restrictions of Medicare *Dis*advantage. How strange it is that AARP, with its Medigap insurance business run by UnitedHealthcare, doesn't advise its members to go with the obviously superior Original Medicare. AARP reportedly receives a commission of 4.95 percent for new enrollees on top of the premiums the elderly pay for the Medigap policy from UnitedHealthcare. This money—about $700 million a year—is a significant portion of AARP's overall budget.

AARP responded to my inquiries into its MA policy saying that it does not recommend one plan over another, leaving it to the uninformed or misinformed consumer. That's one of AARP's biggest cop-outs—they know the difference.

There is no space here to cover all the bewildering ins and outs of what corporations have done to so-called managed Medicare and managed Medicaid. That task is for full-time reporters. The government does estimate a staggering $60 billion in billing fraud annually just on Medicare—manipulating codes, phantom billing, etc. You need the equivalent of a college-level course just to start figuring out all the supposed offerings and gaps.

Suffice it to say that, in the words of Eleanor Laise, senior editor of *Kiplinger's Retirement Report*, "the evidence on health care access and quality decidedly favors original Medicare over Medicare Advantage, according to a Kaiser Family Foundation review of 40 studies published between 2000 and 2014."

All this anxiety, dread, and fear; all these arbitrary denials of care—prompted by a pay-or-die commercial profit motive; all these restrictions of what doctors or hospitals you can go to do not exist in Canada. All Canadians have a Medicare card from birth; they have free choice of health care vendors. There are few American-style horror stories there; patients have better outcomes and almost never even see a bill. The whole universal system costs half *per capita* of that in the US, where over eighty million people are uninsured or underinsured—still! (See singlepayeraction.org for civic action to rid Americans of this perverse chaos.)

25 Ways the Canadian Health Care System is Better than Obamacare for the 2020 Elections

SEPTEMBER 18, 2019

Dear America:

Costly complexity is baked into Obamacare, and although it has improved access to health care for some, tens of millions of Americans still cannot afford basic medical care for their families. No health care system is without problems, but Canadian-style single-payer—full "Medicare for all"—is simple, affordable, comprehensive, and universal for all basic and emergency medical and hospital services.

In the mid-1960s, President Lyndon Johnson enrolled nearly twenty million elderly Americans into Medicare in six months. There were no websites. They did it with index cards!

Below please find twenty-five ways the Canadian health care system— and the resulting quality of life in Canada—is better than the chaotic, wasteful, and often cruel US system.

Replace it with the much more efficient Medicare for all: everybody in, nobody out, free choice of doctor and hospital. It will produce far less anxiety, dread, and fear. Hear that, Congress and the White House!

NUMBER 25:

In Canada, everyone is covered automatically at birth—everybody in, nobody out. A human right.

In the United States, under Obamacare, over twenty-eight million Americans (9 percent) are still uninsured, and eighty-five million Americans (26 percent) are either uninsured or underinsured. Obamacare is made even worse by Trumpcare restrictions. (See *Struggling and Dying Under Trumpcare*, by John Geyman, MD [2019].)

NUMBER 24:

In Canada, the health system is designed to put people, not profits, first.

In the United States, Obamacare has done little to curb the insurance industry's massive profits and in fact has caused them to increase.

NUMBER 23:

In Canada, coverage is not tied to a job or dependent on your income—rich and poor are in the same system, the best guaranty of quality.

In the United States, under Obamacare, much still depends on your job or income. Lose your job or lose your income and you might lose your existing health insurance or have to settle for lesser coverage.

NUMBER 22:

In Canada, health care coverage stays with you for your entire life.

In the United States, under Obamacare, for tens of millions of Americans, health care coverage stays with you only for as long as you can afford your insurance.

NUMBER 21:

In Canada, you can freely choose your doctors and hospitals and keep them.

In the United States, under Obamacare, the in-network list of places where you can get treated is shrinking—thus restricting freedom of choice—and if you want to go out of network, you pay dearly for it.

NUMBER 20:

In Canada, the health care system is funded by income taxes, sales taxes, and corporate taxes that, combined, are much lower than what Americans pay in insurance premiums directly and indirectly per employer.

In the United States, under Obamacare, for thousands of Americans, it's "pay or die"—if you can't pay, you die. That's why many thousands will still die every year under Obamacare from lack of health insurance to get diagnosed and treated in time. The survivors are confronted with very high, often unregulated drug prices.

NUMBER 19:

In Canada, there are no complex hospital or doctor bills. In fact, usually you don't even see a bill.

In the United States, under Obamacare, hospital and doctor bills are terribly complex and replete with massive billing fraud estimated to be at least $350 billion a year by Harvard professor Malcolm Sparrow.

NUMBER 18:

In Canada, costs are controlled. Canada pays 10 percent of its gross domestic product (GDP) for its health care system, covering everyone.

In the United States, under Obamacare, costs continue to skyrocket. The US currently pays 17.9 percent of its GDP and still doesn't cover tens of millions of people.

NUMBER 17:

In Canada, it is unheard of for anyone to go bankrupt due to health care costs.

In the United States, health-care-driven bankruptcy will continue to plague Americans.

NUMBER 16:

In Canada, simplicity leads to major savings in administrative costs and overhead.

In the United States, under Obamacare, often staggering complexity ratchets up huge administrative costs and overhead.

NUMBER 15:

In Canada, when you go to a doctor or hospital, the first thing they ask you is: "What's wrong?"

In the United States, the first thing they ask you is: "What kind of insurance do you have?"

NUMBER 14:

In Canada, the government negotiates drug prices so they are more affordable.

In the United States, under Obamacare, Congress made it specifically illegal for the government to negotiate drug prices for volume purchases. As a result, drug prices remain exorbitant and continue to skyrocket.

NUMBER 13:

In Canada, the government health care funds are not profitably diverted to the top 1 percent.

In the United States, under Obamacare, health care funds will continue to flow to the top. In 2017, the CEO of Aetna alone made a whopping $59 million.

NUMBER 12:

In Canada, there are no required copays or deductibles in inscrutable contracts.

In the United States, under Obamacare, the deductibles and copays will continue to be unaffordable for many millions of Americans. Fine-print traps are everywhere.

NUMBER 11:

In Canada, the health care system contributes to social solidarity and national pride.

In the United States, Obamacare is divisive, with rich and poor in different systems and tens of millions left out or with sorely limited benefits.

NUMBER 10:

In Canada, delays in health care are not due to the cost of insurance.

In the United States, under Obamacare, patients without health insurance or who are underinsured delay or forgo care and put their lives at risk.

NUMBER 9:

In Canada, nobody dies due to lack of health insurance.

In the United States, tens of thousands of Americans will continue to die every year because they lack health insurance or can't pay much higher prices for drugs, medical devices, and health care itself.

NUMBER 8:

In Canada, health care on average costs half as much, per person, as in the United States. And in Canada, unlike in the United States, everyone is covered.

In the United States, a majority supports Medicare for all. But they are being blocked by lawmakers and their corporate paymasters.

NUMBER 7:

In Canada, the tax payments to fund the health care system are modestly progressive—the lowest 20 percent pays 6 percent of their income into the system while the highest 20 percent pays 8 percent.

In the United States, under Obamacare, the poor pay a larger share of their income for health care than the affluent.

NUMBER 6:

In Canada, people use GoFundMe to start new businesses.

In the United States, fully one in three GoFundMe fundraisers are now to raise money to pay medical bills. Recently, one American was rejected for a heart transplant because she couldn't afford the follow-up care. Her insurance company suggested she raise the money through GoFundMe.

NUMBER 5:

In Canada, people avoid prison at all costs.

In the United States, some Americans commit minor crimes so that they can get to prison and receive free health care.

NUMBER 4:

In Canada, people look forward to the benefits of early retirement.

In the United States, people delay retirement to sixty-five to avoid being uninsured.

NUMBER 3:

In Canada, Nobel Prize winners hold on to their medal and pass it down to their children and grandchildren.

In the United States, a Nobel Prize winner sold his medal to help pay for his medical bills.

Leon Lederman won a Nobel Prize in 1988 for his pioneering physics research. But in 2015, the physicist, who passed away in November 2018, sold his Nobel Prize medal for $765,000 to pay his mounting medical bills.

NUMBER 2:

In Canada, the system is simple. You get a health care card when you are born. And you swipe it when you go to a doctor or hospital. End of story.

In the United States, Obamacare's 954 pages plus regulations (the Canadian Medicare Bill was 13 pages) is so complex that Nancy Pelosi, then the Speaker of the House, said before passage, "We have to pass the bill so that you can find out what is in it, away from the fog of the controversy."

NUMBER 1:

In Canada, the majority of citizens love their health care system.

In the United States, a growing majority of citizens, physicians, and nurses prefer the Canadian-type system—Medicare for all; free choice of doctor and hospital; everybody in, nobody out; and far less expensive with better outcomes overall.

It's decision time, America!

Big Pharma: Gouges, Casualties, and the Congressional Remedy!

AUGUST 7, 2019

Congress can overturn the abuses of Big Pharma and its "pay or die" subsidized business model for drugs.

Big Pharma's trail of greed, power, and cruelty gets worse every year. Its products and practices take hundreds of thousands of lives in the US from overprescriptions, lethal combinations of prescriptions, ineffective or contaminated drugs, and dangerous side effects. The biggest drug dealers in the US operate legally. Their names are emblazoned on ads and promotions everywhere. Who hasn't heard of Eli Lilly, Merck, Pfizer, and Novartis? Big Pharma revenues and profits have skyrocketed. In 2017, US consumers spent $333.4 billion on prescription drugs.

There are no price controls on drugs in the US as there are in most countries in the world. Senator Bernie Sanders just took a bus tour to a Canadian pharmacy where insulin cost patients one-tenth of what it costs them in the US. Yet, remarkably, drug companies, charted and operating in the US, charge Americans the highest prices in the world. This is despite the freebies our business-indentured government lavishes on Big Pharma. The FDA weakly regulates drugs, which are supposed to be both safe *and* effective before they can be sold. Who funds this FDA effort? The drug industry itself—required by a law it has learned to love.

The Big Pharma lobby doesn't always get what it craves. In the 1970s, Dr. Sidney Wolfe, director of Public Citizen's Health Research Group, produced two paperbacks for a wide television audience (e.g., he appeared on the *Phil Donahue Show*). They were titled *Pills That Don't Work* and *Over the Counter Pills That Don't Work*. Because of Dr. Wolfe's tireless efforts, hundreds of different pills were removed from the market, saving consumers billions of dollars and sparing them the side effects.

Big Pharma's greatest strength is its hold over Congress. That is where it gets its huge bundle of subsidies and monopolistic privileges. During George W. Bush's first term, the drug companies got the Republicans and some spineless Democrats to forbid Medicare from negotiating volume discounts with the drug companies, as the Pentagon and Veterans Affairs have done for years. Big Pharma had over 1,200 lobbyists swarming over Capitol Hill to get these handcuffs on Uncle Sam. Lobbyists, along with campaign cash donated by Big Pharma industry players, sealed the deal.

Your congressional representatives gave the drug giants much in return: lucrative tax credits to pay Big Pharma to do what they should do anyway—engage in research and development. Drug companies are profitable recipients of taxpayer-funded government research on developing new drugs—and then are given monopolies that enable them to impose sky-high prices, even when the purchaser is the very government that funded the invention of the new drugs in the first place.

The drug industry has also made sure there are no price controls on their drugs—whether gifted to them by the National Institutes of Health or developed by drug companies internally. The absence of price controls accounts for new "blockbuster drugs" going for $100,000 or higher per patient per year. Many drug prices generally increase faster than inflation.

Greed is infinite for Big Pharma. In addition to tax credits, free drug research and development (compliments of the federal government), and no price restraints, the drug companies have moved much production to China and India. No antibiotics are manufactured in the US—a clear national security risk to which the Pentagon and Trump should pay heed. Two new books, *China Rx* and *Bottle of Lies*, document the safety risks of poorly inspected labs in those countries that create pills that affect your body without your mind being made aware of "country of origin" on the label.

The great hands-on humanitarian organization Doctors Without Borders, operating in seventy countries, often in the midst of dangerous armed conflicts, lists "Six things Big Pharma doesn't want you to know," in its recent alert letter.

They are:

1. Costs of developing new medicines are exaggerated tenfold or more.

2. You're paying twice for your medicines—first as taxpayers and second as consumers or through your government programs.

3. Drug companies are not that good at innovation. About two-thirds of new drugs (called "me-too drugs") are no better, and may be riskier, than the ones already in pharmacies. But they are advertised as special.

4. Monopoly patents are extended by clever lawyers to block more affordable generic versions. This maneuver is called "evergreening."

5. Pharma bullies low and middle income countries like South Africa, Thailand, Brazil, Colombia, and Malaysia that try to curb its rapaciousness. These drug companies use trade rules and the US government toward their brutal goals.

6. In the 1990s, a small group of consumer advocates led by Jamie Love, Bill Haddad, and Robert Weissman persuaded Cipla, an Indian drug firm, and Ministries of Public Health to lower the price of AIDS medicines from $10,000 per patient per year down to $300 (now under $100). The US drug companies were quite willing to let millions die who couldn't pay.

7. Big Pharma always says they need large profits to pay for research and development (R & D) and innovation. Really? Why then do they spend *far more* on stock buybacks (one of the metrics for executive compensation) and on marketing and advertising than on R & D? Dr. Wolfe exposed this malarkey years ago.

Yet exposure has not stopped the worsening behavior of Big Pharma. Good books by Katharine Greider (*The Big Fix*) and Dr. Marcia Angell (*The Truth About the Drug Companies*) are devastating critiques of Big Pharma's practices. Despite this, the books reach small audiences and are brushed off by the drug giants. Big Pharma is able to ignore these books because it controls most of Congress—candidates rely heavily on the industry for campaign budgets.

But the American people outnumber the drug companies, and only the people can actually vote come election time. Focused voters mean more to politicians than campaign money. The August recess for Congress means your lawmakers are back home having personal meetings. Visit them and make known your demands against the "pay or die" industry. Tell them your own stories.

Or better yet, make them come to your town meetings. Remember: "It's your Congress, people!"

One galvanizing move by an enlightened billionaire could establish a twenty-person advocacy group on drug pricing, focusing on Congress and mobilizing citizens back home. Its effect would be decisive for taming the drug industry's gouging. Any takers? If so, contact Public Citizen at med-saccess@citizen.org.

Gross Hospital Negligence Does Not Exempt Celebrities

SEPTEMBER 26, 2018

Solid studies by physicians at leading medical schools have been warning of the huge casualty toll of preventable problems in hospitals. A 2016 peer-reviewed study by physicians at the Johns Hopkins University School of Medicine estimated that at least five thousand people a week in the US lose their lives due to such causes as hospital-induced infection, medical malpractice, inattentiveness, and other deficiencies. Media attention for the study lasted one day.

What will it take to make the powers-that-be outside and inside the government reduce what medical analysts call the third leading cause of death in America? Let that statement sink in—preventable problems in hospitals are the third leading cause of death in America after heart disease and cancer!

Indignation and frustration over the massive avoidance of action to save American lives and reduce even more preventable injuries and sicknesses prompted the issuance of an eye-opening, factual report by the Center for Justice and Democracy (lodged at New York Law School) titled "Top 22 Celebrities Harmed by Medical Malpractice." Surely in a celebrity culture, this documented report should have made headlines and prompted widespread commentary. Unfortunately, the report received little coverage from major news outlets.

Let's see if you agree that this compilation, written by Emily Gottlieb and conceived by Joanne Doroshow, the center's executive director, should have been newsworthy. Surveys cited in the report show that "four in ten adults have experience with medical errors, either personally or in the care of someone close to them," and "nearly three-quarters [73 percent] of patients say they are concerned about the potential for medical errors."

Tennis superstar Serena Williams was among them. She had to save her own life overcoming inattentive medical personnel "that initially dismissed her legitimate concerns about lethal blood clots following the birth of her child." That story made news. Other celebrities passed away without the public knowing the causes until lawsuits were filed and settlements were rendered. For the most part, the physicians have received reprimands or temporary suspensions but rarely lost their license to practice.

Joan Rivers, the longtime comedian, entered an endoscopy center in July 2014 for a routine throat procedure in New York. Her vital signs started failing, but her caretakers were "so busy taking cell phone pictures of their famous patient that they missed the moment her vital signs plummeted," according to her daughter, Melissa, who filed a successful lawsuit ending in a private settlement.

Celebrity doctors who "cater to 'the demands of wealthy and/or famous drug-seekers'" are overprescribing painkillers and other drugs. Reckless practices "led to the premature deaths of legendary entertainers like Elvis Presley, Marilyn Monroe, and Judy Garland, to name just three." More recently, overprescription of drugs has harmed or killed Michael Jackson, Prince, Anna Nicole Smith, and 3 Doors Down guitarist Matt Roberts, to name a few. These were not one-time prescriptions but rather deadly ministrations over time by physicians who knew the conditions and vulnerabilities of their famous patients.

Other tragedies recounted in the center's report, based on lawsuit evidence and/or a medical board sanction, include singer and actress Julie Andrews (destroyed her singing career); Jefferson Airplane cofounder and lead singer Marty Balin (destroyed his career); comedian Dana Carvey (led to "serious illness"); Bee Gees star Maurice Gibb (died in a Florida hospital); NASCAR champion Pete Hamilton (survived "horrendous surgical errors causing . . . multiple complications"); and Emmy award–winning actor John Ritter ("misdiagnosed and improperly treated at a hospital, where he died").

The great sports writer Dick Schaap died after routine hip replacement surgery, which was performed despite tests indicating that the procedure would be too dangerous due to his weakened lungs.

In 1987, the pioneering artist, director, and producer Andy Warhol underwent gallbladder surgery and died a day later when medical personnel put too much IV fluid into his body.

The center's report concludes by noting that "health care in the United States can be incredibly unsafe, and this is true even for well-known actors, singers, musicians, athletes, and other personalities . . . wealth and fame cannot shield someone from being victimized by a preventable medical error."

Safety and health reforms are long overdue in hospitals and clinics, astonishingly. The American Medical Association has not produced any calls to action with effective recommendations. State regulators are heavily compromised by conflicts of interest and low budgets. The federal government is AWOL. A minimum of five thousand lives lost a week, not counting the casualties in clinics and medical offices, is a serious health crisis. This ongoing epidemic should lead to public alarms and reforms long known but kept on the shelf. Contact your members of Congress and demand public hearings. The evidence cannot be ignored any longer.

If Only Your Body Could Speak
to Your Mind

FEBRUARY 26, 2016

For thousands of years humans have defended themselves from harm by others. But many have proceeded to regularly harm themselves. They have actively searched for substances to ingest, inhale, inject, and apply that may give them some immediate relief but damage or destroy their lives over time.

Why do these humans so beat up on their own bodies? Obviously they know that damaging behaviors have serious consequences, both immediately and in the long run. Why have health care professionals had such a hard time convincing people to "do no harm" to themselves? The persistence of partial self-immolation is unremitting.

What's different about recent centuries from prior millennia is that addiction, masochism, and slow-motion suicide have become a big business. Now there are huge profits to be made in seducing, tempting, or deceiving people at all ages to spend money to harm themselves.

The addictive industries—like tobacco, legal and illegal drugs, gambling, and excessive alcohol—are marketed with remarkably proficient psychological expertise ranging from the overt to the more subtle subliminal persuasions.

These vendors like to start with their victims (a.k.a consumers) when they are young. The tobacco industry has known this for generations. Hook 'em when they're ten or twelve and you'll have them for life. The junk fast-food business has also perfected ways to turn young tongues against young brains.

As former FDA commissioner Dr. David Kessler has written, including about himself, junk food has clear biologically addictive effects that drive cravings for more of the same. Obesity levels worldwide are hitting 13 percent and skyrocketing, reaching over 30 percent of adults in the US, triple the level of forty years ago.

The injurious consequences of marketing self-harm are the widely known diseases and traumas we read about—heart trouble, diabetes, cancer, lung and liver diseases, and more. Those are the inventories for another big business that diagnoses and treats with varying degrees of competence tens of millions of patients. The side effects of many treatments—hospital-induced infections, bad medicines, and surgeries—create more business for more treatments.

There is, of course, a wellness industry too, though it doesn't come close to the trillions of dollars of the addictive industries and their profitable collateral damage. Preventative health care—good diets, exercise, smoking cessation, drinking alcohol in moderation, adequate rest—is growing in acceptance. Pollution prevention and safer products and services are also beneficial.

Somehow the pro-health forces always seem to be confronted with new hazards coming on fast. The highly addictive opioid epidemic—for supposed pain relief—is now taking almost as many lives as those lost on the highways, which was over thirty-five thousand last year. The *New York Times* reports that fentanyl, the pain reliever that took the life of Prince, is thirty times more powerful than heroin. Self-medication is getting easier, and rising casualties mark this trend.

So does anyone have any ideas? With all the apps, websites, and blogs, is there any effective answer to the question of how to counter the self-harm that has plagued humankind forever? Would it be focused family upbringing? Sure. But obviously that leaves out many people who do not have that good fortune.

Oh, if only the vulnerable livers, kidneys, hearts, intestines, stomachs, cardiovascular systems, lungs, teeth, ears, and eyes could directly speak and admonish the recklessness of self-destructive practices coming from the brain!

An E. Coli's Last Message to President Obama

FEBRUARY 26, 2016

Deadly invisible pathogens are on the march. Ebola and now the Zika virus; the ongoing cholera epidemics; and the enormous casualties from tuberculosis, malaria, and varieties of avian influenza—all of these should be waking us up to the global spread of disease and the public health challenges of dealing with mutational virulence. Millions die every year. But the political leaders of nations don't seem to respect the warnings from our scientists. *Pandemic*, the important book by Sonia Shah, is a jeremiad, and should spark policymakers' public concern. Unfortunately, basketball and March Madness occupy more public attention by our political leaders.

A large US hospital has a bigger budget than the beleaguered World Health Organization, which is tasked, by nearly two hundred nations, with heading off epidemics and pandemics and trying to limit their spread.

Errant microbes are getting assistance from environmental upheavals, global travel, poor sanitation, and starved public health facilities, as well as political corruption and dense urbanization.

Yet the big money still goes into armaments, where the profits prosper. Presidents make speeches about terrorism and national security. Congress holds constant hearings, rubber-stamping military budgets. Have you heard these bacteria and viruses—those most certain terrorist perils—discussed in a nationally televised address by any president or brought up in major congressional hearings? Of course you haven't. There haven't been any.

Over the years I have tried mostly in vain to get this country's leadership to wake up to this looming century of pandemic threats. True, grants by big foundations and some public money have gone into reducing malaria and some other infectious diseases. But it has been too little and, for many men, women, and children, too late.

Frustration often leads to satire. Let me share with you an unanswered letter I wrote to President Barack Obama on June 3, 2011. I was told that some scientists at the Centers for Disease Control and Prevention were pleased with the message.

Dear President Obama:

My name is E. coli 0104:H4. I am being detained in a German laboratory in Bavaria, charged with being "a highly virulent strain of bacteria." Together with many others like me, the police have accused us of causing about twenty deaths and nearly five hundred cases of kidney failure—so far. Massive publicity and panic all around.

You can't see me, but your scientists can. They are examining me, and I know my days are numbered. I hear them calling me a "biological terrorist," an unusual combination of two different E. coli bacteria cells. One even referred to me as a "conspiracy of mutants."

It is not my fault, I want you to know. I cannot help but harm innocent humans, and I am very sad about this. I want to redeem myself, so I am sending this lifesaving message straight from my petri dish to you.

This outbreak in Germany has been traced to food—location unknown. What is known to you is that invisible terrorism from bacterium and viruses take massively greater lives than the terrorism you are spending billions of dollars and armaments to stop in Iraq, Afghanistan, and Pakistan.

Malaria, caused by infection with one of four species of Plasmodium, a parasite transmitted by Anopheles mosquitoes, destroys a million lives a year. Many of the victims are children and pregnant women. Mycobacterium tuberculosis takes over one million lives each year. The human immunodeficiency virus (HIV) causes over a million deaths each year as well. Many other microorganisms in the water, soil, air, and food are daily weapons of mass destruction. Very little in your defense budget goes for operational armed forces against this kind of violence. Your agencies, such as the Centers for Disease Control and Prevention, conduct some research but again nothing compared to the research for your missiles, drones, aircraft, and satellites.

Your associates are obsessed with possible bacteriological warfare by your human enemies. Yet you are hardly doing anything about the ongoing silent violence of my indiscriminate brethren.

You and your predecessor, George W. Bush, made many speeches about fighting terrorism by humans. Have you made a major speech about us?

You speak regularly about crushing the resistance of your enemies. But you splash around so many antibiotics (obviously I don't like this word and consider it genocidal) in cows, bulls, chickens, pigs, and fish that your species is creating massive antibiotic resistance, provoking our mutations so that we can breed even stronger progeny. You are regarded as the smartest beings on Earth, yet you seem to have too many neurons backfiring.

In the past two days of detention, scientists have subjected me to "enhanced interrogation," as if I have any will to give up my secrets. It doesn't work. What they will find out will be from their insights about me under their microscopes. I am lethal, I guess, but I'm not very complicated.

The United States, together with other countries, needs more laboratories where scientists can detain samples of us and subject us to extraordinary rendition to infectious disease research centers. Many infectious disease scientists need to be trained, especially in the southern hemisphere, to staff these labs.

You are hung up on certain kinds of preventable violence without any risk/benefit analysis. This, you should agree, is utterly irrational. You should not care where the preventable violence comes from except to focus on its range of devastation and its susceptibility to prevention or cure!

Well, here they come to my petri dish for some more waterboarding. One last item: You may wonder how tiny bacterial me, probably not even harboring a virus, can send you such a letter. My oozing sense is that I'm just a carrier, being used by oodles of scientists taking advantage of a high-profile infectious outbreak in Europe to catch your attention.

Whatever the *how*—does it really matter to the need to act now?

E-cologically yours,
E. coli 0104:H4 (for the time being)

Hillary Clinton Sugarcoating Her Disastrous Record

FEBRUARY 12, 2016

Bernie Sanders is far too easy on Hillary Clinton in their debates. Clinton flaunts her record and experience in ways that Sanders could use to expose her serious vulnerabilities and disqualifications for becoming president. Sanders responds to Clinton's points, but without the precision that could demolish her arrogance.

For example, she repeatedly says that Sanders has not leveled with people about the cost of *full* "Medicare for all," or single-payer. Really? In other countries, single-payer is far simpler and more efficient than our present profiteering, wasteful, corporatized health care industry. Canada covers all of its citizens, with free choice of doctors and hospitals, for about $4,500 per capita, compared to the over $9,000 per capita cost in the US system that still leaves tens of millions of people uninsured or underinsured.

Detailed studies in the *New England Journal of Medicine* show big savings from a single-payer system in our country.

It is Clinton who is not leveling with the people about the consequences of maintaining the spiraling costs of US drugs, hospital stays, and the highest insurance premiums in the world. The consequences include: the waste of well over $1 trillion a year; daily denials of coverage by the Aetnas of the corporate world; about forty thousand Americans dying each year, according to a peer-reviewed Harvard Medical School study, because they cannot afford health insurance to get diagnosed and treated in time; and daily agonizing negotiations over insurance company denials, exclusions, and bureaucratic paperwork that drive physicians up the wall.

Clinton hasn't explained why she was once for single-payer until she defined her "being practical" as refusing to take on Big Pharma, commercial hospital chains, and the giant insurance companies. She is very "practical" about taking political contributions and speaking fees from Wall Street and the health care industry.

As one eighteen-year-old student told the *New York Times* recently about Clinton, "Sometimes you get this feeling that all of her sentences are owned by someone."

This protector of the status quo and the gross imbalance of power between the few and the many expresses perfectly why Wall Street financiers like her so much and prove it by continuing to make large monetary contributions.

Clinton is not "leveling with the American people" when she keeps the transcripts (which she requested at the time) of her secret speeches (at $5,000 a minute!) before large Wall Street and trade association conventions. Her speaking contracts mandate secrecy. Clinton still hasn't told voters what she was telling big bankers and many other industries, from automotive to drugs to real estate developers, behind closed doors.

She has the gall to accuse Bernie Sanders of not being transparent. Sanders is a presidential candidate who doesn't take big-fee speeches or big donations from fat-cat influence-peddlers, and his record is as clean as the Clintons' political entanglements are sordid. (See *Clinton Cash* by Peter Schweizer.)

But it is in the area of foreign and military affairs that "Hillary the Hawk" is most vulnerable. As secretary of state, her aggressiveness and poor judgement led her to the White House, where, sweeping aside the strong objections of Defense Secretary Robert Gates, she persuaded President Obama to bomb Libya and topple its dictatorial regime.

Gates had warned about the aftermath. He was right. Libya has descended into a ghastly state of chaotic violence that has spilled into neighboring African nations, such as Mali, and that opened the way for ISIS to establish an expanding base in central Libya. Her fellow hawks in Washington are now calling for US Special Forces to go to Libya.

Whether as senator on the Armed Services Committee or as secretary of state, Mrs. Clinton has never met a war or raid she didn't like, or a redundant, wasteful weapons system she was willing to aggressively challenge. As president, Clinton would mean more wars, more raids, more blowbacks, more military spending, and more profits for the military-industrial complex that President Eisenhower so prophetically warned about in his farewell address.

So when Sanders properly chided her for having as an adviser Henry Kissinger, secretary of state under Richard Nixon, she bristled and tried to escape by asking Sanders to name his foreign-policy advisers.

In fact, Kissinger and Clinton do have much in common about projecting the American empire to brutal levels. Kissinger was the "Butcher of Cambodia," launching an illegal assault that destabilized that peaceful country into the Pol Pot slaughter of millions of innocents. She was the illegal "Butcher of Libya," an ongoing, unfolding tragedy whose "unintended consequences" are building by the week.

In a devastating recounting of Clinton's disastrous war-making, Jeffrey D. Sachs, professor of Sustainable Economies at Columbia University, concludes that Clinton "is the candidate of the war machine." In a widely noted article on *HuffPost*, Professor Sachs, an adviser to the United Nations on millennium development goals, called her record a "disaster," adding that "perhaps more than any other person, Hillary can lay claim to having stoked the violence that stretches from West Africa to Central Asia and that threatens US security."

The transformation of Hillary Clinton from a progressive young lawyer to a committed corporatist and militarist brings shame on the recent endorsement of her candidacy by the Congressional Black Caucus PAC.

But then, considering all the years of Clintonite double-talk and corporate contributions going to the Black Caucus PAC (according to FEC reports January through December 2015) and the Black Caucus charitable and political arms, why should anybody be surprised that Black Lives Matter and a growing surge of young African Americans are looking for someone in the White House who is not known for the Clintons' sweet-talking betrayals?

See Michelle Alexander's recent article in the *Nation*, "Why Hillary Clinton Doesn't Deserve the Black Vote," for more information on this subject.

Yours to Know: Worst Pills, Best Pills

JULY 17, 2015

When I cofounded the Public Citizen Health Research Group with Dr. Sidney M. Wolfe in 1971, he declared that this was his "last job." The drug industry might have been advised to quiver. For through his *Worst Pills, Best Pills* books, newsletters, and spectacular outreach via the *Phil Donahue Show*, he has exposed by brand name hundreds of drugs with harmful side effects (worst pills) compared to drugs without such an unfavorable risk-benefit profile (best pills). In the seventies, he and his associates successfully advocated that many totally useless prescription and over-the-counter drugs be taken off the market.

Saving lives and saving consumers' money—which the Food and Drug Administration (FDA) neglected to do so often—was the mission of Dr. Wolfe and his dedicated colleagues. Citizen dues and donations are what maintained this lean and efficient watchdog.

In the historic annals of consumer groups correcting the false or deceptive corporate assurances associated with consumer products, no one has done more to expose Big Pharma's mendacity. Wolfe and his Health Research Group team made countless such corrections regarding hundreds of pharmaceuticals, deploying hawk-like intensity and accuracy despite the drug companies' obstructions and false denials.

I'm making this point because this week I received, along with many thousands of people, what has to be considered the most phenomenal offer to subscribe to *Worst Pills, Best Pills News* to "protect you from unsafe or ineffective medications." At least 80 percent of all Americans take some kind of pills during the year. Many of them may be taking just the kind of medicines that are actually making things worse for their bodies and minds.

This alert mailing is not about generalities. One insert lists "20 Pills you Should Never Take" (but only after you inform and consult with your physician). Here are their names: Actos, Aricept, Avandia, Celebrex, Crestor, echinacea, glucosamine and chondroitin, Lunesta, Miacalcin nasal spray, Mobic, Qysmia, Relenza, Serevent, Singulair, Synephrine, Tricor, Tussionex, Ultram, Valium, Victoza, and eleven top-selling dietary supplements.

You may react by saying, "Why has the FDA approved these drugs instead of taking them off the market?" To put it mildly, it is because the FDA is always behind in its work and too often has high-level regulators sympathetic to the powerful drug industry whose lobbyists are always swarming around the agency and the members of Congress who do its bidding.

In the amazing Health Research Group mailing, there is an eight-page invitation that you won't be able to put down. Here is a sample:

> Some Drugs Are Not Dangerous By Themselves, But . . . they can be deadly in combination with other drugs. There are many dangerous combinations: insulin and INDERAL; PLAVIX and PRANDIN; TAGAMET and DILANTIN; DEMEROL and NARDIL; and CALAN SR and quinidine or LANOXIN, to name a few.

Here is more:

> We've also seen cases where one doctor was prescribing a medication to treat symptoms that were being caused by another medication prescribed by another doctor! You'd be surprised how many drugs cause symptoms that are similar to those in patients with Parkinson's Disease (CARDIZEM, amytriptyline, GEODON, HALDOL, PROZAC, REGLAN, chlorthalidone, and RISPERDAL are among them), and how often people taking those drugs are then given *other* drugs to treat the parkinsonism symptoms caused by the first drug!

Throughout the eight pages are statements by named patients regarding improvements in their painful symptoms after they got off these harmful medicines. Among some of the named medications was the notorious VIOXX, which Dr. Wolfe warned about years before the FDA took it off the market.

Now, here's the offer: for senior citizens, fourteen monthly issues of *Worst Pills, Best Pills News* for ten dollars, half of the regular price. (Made out to Pills News, PO Box 96978, Washington, DC 20090-0978.)

Does any of this sound like quack mailings we all get so often? Banish the very thought. This is the most accurate information you'll receive about your medicines. As the super-precise Dr. Wolfe guarantees: "If you are ever less than 100 percent satisfied with *Worst Pills, Best Pills News* . . . just cancel your subscription for a full refund of the subscription price."

I'm giving subscriptions now to ten older friends who are taking medications on the say-so of their prescribers. You know the saying "Trust, but verify." There is one that is better: "Do not trust, if you can verify."

The Havoc of the Unrestrained Drug Industry

SEPTEMBER 12, 2014

It is remarkable what very profitable drug companies—as they merge into fewer giant multinationals—continue to get away with by way of crony capitalism. Despite frequent exposure of misdeeds, the army of drug company lobbyists in Washington continues to gain political influence and rake in corporate welfare at the expense of taxpayers. The drug industry goes beyond crony capitalism when it then charges Americans the highest drug prices in the world.

Here is a short list of the honeypot produced by the lobbying muscle of the $300 billion-a-year pharmaceutical industry. It receives billions of dollars in tax credits for doing research and development that it should be doing anyway. Some companies reaped billions of dollars in revenue when they were granted exclusive rights to market a drug, such as Taxol, developed by the government's National Institutes of Health (NIH). These corporations turn around and gouge patients without any price controls or royalties to NIH. (See keionline.org for more information.)

The pharmaceutical industry spends far more on marketing and advertising to physicians and patients than what it spends on research and development. More drug industry funds go to influencing politicians to prevent the implementation of price restraints on its staggering markups.

As Dr. Marcia Angell, former editor of the *New England Journal of Medicine*, wrote in her book *The Truth About the Drug Companies*, "only a small fraction of [the industry's] drugs are truly new; most are simply 'me too' variations on older drugs." Dr. Angell charges that the industry is "primarily a marketing machine to sell drugs of dubious benefit . . . [it] uses its wealth and power to co-opt every institution that might stand in its way, including the US Congress, the Food and Drug Administration, academic medical centers, and the medical profession itself." By the way, the drug industry is required by law to fund a large portion of the FDA's drug review budget, which contributes to this weak regulatory oversight.

Katharine Greider points out in her book *The Big Fix: How the Pharmaceutical Industry Rips Off American Consumers* that "other countries move to control prices and sharply limit advertising." This does not happen in the US, where many patients confront a "pay or die" system.

In recent years, this stark choice has made headlines. New drugs, such as Sovaldi for treating hepatitis C, are costing consumers or taxpayers $84,000 for a full course of treatment, or $1,000 a pill per day! The same drug treatment, according to the *Washington Post*, costs "$57,000 in the United Kingdom and just $900 in Egypt." Other so-called "breakthrough" drugs are costing patients over $100,000 each per year and driving frantic health insurers and Medicaid managers up the wall.

Will competition bring prices down? Wall Street pharmaceutical analyst Tim Anderson, at Sanford C. Bernstein & Company, explains in a recent *New York Times* article that this is not the case. "[Anderson] said that drug companies, while not colluding, 'have all looked at each other and said, 'None of us needs to compete on price if we just hold the line.'" The cause of competition was not helped when the drug company lobbyists used their campaign contributions and influence on Congress in 2003 to brazenly *prohibit* Uncle Sam from negotiating prices for the gigantic Medicare drug benefit program.

The financial rip-offs aren't the only problems with the out-of-control drug industry. Federal law requires all approved drugs to be both "safe and effective." The actual record has been shocking. The Public Citizen Health Research Group published three books—*Pills That Don't Work* (1981), *Over the Counter Pills That Don't Work* (1983), and *Worst Pills, Best Pills: A Consumer's Guide to Avoiding Drug-Induced Death or Illness* (2005)— documenting hundreds of prescription and over-the-counter drugs that were not effective for their advertised purposes or had harmful side effects. Wide exposure to these findings, especially on the *Phil Donahue Show*, helped get many of these so-called medications off the market.

Over the years, the government has fined drug companies billions of dollars for pushing unapproved uses of drugs. More perilously, drugs get approved prematurely and result in mass sickness and fatalities. This human toll is an estimated hundred thousand deaths a year in the US from adverse effects of such drugs. For example, the drug Vioxx, sold by Merck & Co. as an anti-inflammatory drug, stayed on the market from 1999 to 2004 despite documented cardiovascular risks. According to the well-regarded medical journal *Lancet,* an estimated eighty-eight thousand Americans had heart attacks from taking Vioxx, and thirty-eight thousand of them died!

Pfizer's Bextra, another anti-inflammatory analgesic drug, was approved by the FDA in 2001, and was then removed in 2005 because of concerns about increased risk of heart attacks and strokes, as well as serious, sometimes fatal skin reactions.

Rezulin, made by Parke-Davis/Warner Lambert, was approved by the FDA in 1997 and withdrawn in 2000 because the drug caused liver toxicity, having been linked to sixty-three liver-failure deaths.

Meridia, a weight-loss drug sold by Abbott Laboratories, was withdrawn by the company after thirteen years of sales because studies demonstrated that it increased the risk of adverse cardiovascular episodes, such as heart attacks, strokes, and cardiac arrest.

These illustrations come from Public Citizen's Health Research Group, whose newsletter *Worst Pills, Best Pills News* has been reliably reporting these avoidable tragedies for many years.

There are other human and economic costs of the drug industry's relentless sales pressure. Antibiotic resistance has been building up for half a century due to massive overuse of antibiotics both in humans and in edible farm animals. As a result, there are now lethal infections for which existing antibiotics are ineffective. And inadequate warning labels have led to the misprescription of drugs and the use of drug combinations that have dangerous interactions.

Congress used to regularly investigate drug companies when senators like Estes Kefauver (D-TN) and Gaylord Nelson (D-WI) were on Capitol Hill. Silence is now the norm. Even the drug company practice—to seek even more profits—of importing about 80 percent of the ingredients in our medicines from China and India, where public inspection regulations can be weak and the FDA has few inspectors, does not command the attention of our congressional representatives. About 150 Americans died in 2008 from a contaminated blood thinner called heparin imported from China.

So, next time you hear the talking heads from corporatist think tanks such as the American Enterprise Institute or the Heritage Foundation or their corporate allies demand "deregulation," consider what an inadequately regulated drug industry has already inflicted on millions of Americans.

The Crime of Overbilling Health Care

AUGUST 29, 2014

Over twenty years ago, Pat Palmer, in her own words, "stumbled upon a $400 overcharge in a bill my father received for a routine medical procedure." That might have become the costliest "overcharge" that the gouging, overbilling health care industry ever inflicted on itself; it led Ms. Palmer— whom Steve Brill (author of the *Time* magazine cover story "Why Medical Bills are Killing Us," April 4, 2013) called "one of my earliest tutors as I tried to figure out the dysfunctional world of medical economics and billing"—to start a business investigating the overbilling of patients.

Located in Roanoke, Virginia, Medical Billing Advocates of America (MBAA) makes money by saving patients money. No savings, no charge. In twenty years, she has collected a multitude of cases of doctors, hospitals, and insurance companies overcharging. This evidence reflects routine, everyday overbilling in the many billions of dollars a year.

How extensive is this commercial crime wave? The nation's expert on computerized billing fraud, Malcolm Sparrow, who is an applied mathematician at Harvard, estimates medical billing fraud adds up to a minimum of $270 billion a year or at least 10 percent of all health care expenses. His classic book *License to Steal* showed that these rip-offs are not just clerical errors or computer malfunctions. The systemic fraud goes far beyond the organized criminal syndicates defrauding Medicare that the FBI raids once in a while. The frauds are designed with corporate interests in mind to filch your wallet directly or under the nose of unobservant insurers, from the very design of billing statements to the manipulation of codes.

Palmer is out with a paperback titled *The Medical Bill Survival Guide*, which is self-published by her firm, MBAA. She explained she almost gave up on "all the rules and regulations that no one is enforcing." It's a good thing she didn't. Instead, Ms. Palmer decided to rile up the patients and their families directly with her book by describing how outrageously brazen billing practices are (not just an aberration) and showing how people can become commonsense investigators if they receive these shocking bills.

Start with the fact that about 80 percent of all medical bills contain errors, with the average error being $1,300. Most of these overbillings favor, unsurprisingly, the sellers (euphemistically called "the providers"). Ms. Palmer says the situation has been getting worse. With the number of diagnostic codes growing from seventeen thousand to about sixty thousand under Obamacare—supposedly to improve efficiency—the system has become even more complicated, with hospitals knowing how to increase their profits by gaming or beating the system.

She lists many of the ways that medical bills are hugely inflated using the technique known as unbundling, when tests and procedures are broken down into their individual components, which allows for double or triple billing. Some hospitals also, by their own admission, incorporate their overhead in the itemized pricing of even simple items like twenty-dollar aspirins or fifteen-dollar disposable razors.

An example of double-billing technique is when a patient is charged thousands of dollars a day for being in an intensive care unit (ICU) and then also charged for the ventilator, which is already factored in to the cost of the ICU. Hospitals charge for their mistakes, as in the radiology departments misreading imaging and X-rays. Another example is when they charge, say, twelve dollars for each time a nurse brings you an Aspirin, even though you're paying for these hospital services in your room rate. Transporting that Aspirin is called an "oral administration fee." Gobbledygook names are omnipresent in these bills.

You can get these itemizations by refusing to accept a "summary bill," and ask, as is your right under state law, to receive an itemized bill, which sometimes will extend to multiple printed pages in inscrutable code that you can then demand an explanation for in ordinary English.

Hospital billings for similar services or items vary wildly and arbitrarily. Ms. Palmer found a hospital charging $444.78 for a ten-milligram vial of the neuromuscular blocking drug Norcuron. She then found another hospital "charging $17.90 for the very same ten-milligram vial."

In her book, she often refers to documented examples of massive overbilling on major surgeries, major medical equipment, and lesser items. People have been charged for phantom procedures, nominal physician visits, and hospital employees transporting specimens down a few floors to the labs. Patients are charged for omnibus services and products, then charged again and again for the pieces.

Now obviously there are variations as well in levels of honesty and fraud between institutions and practices. But overall, what Palmer and Sparrow are writing about is arguably our country's biggest commercial crime wave.

However, strangely, prosecutors reserve their few grand-jury indictments largely for the criminal underworld stealing from Medicare or other insurers. For the corporate establishment, there are always the easy ways out, such as confessing error but not intent when caught, or arguing reasonable industry practices. They quickly correct the specific bill of its offending bloat and satisfy the complaining patient, but nothing changes overall.

Clearly the current criminal laws do not adequately prevent such computerized theft and need to be amended to account for this fraud. Furthermore, if our nation followed the example of other countries and transitioned to a universal full "Medicare for all" system, this would end fee-for-service, and the Pat Palmers of the nation would be out of business (see singlepayeraction.org for more information).

The main point of Palmer's book is that if enough outraged or concerned patients can follow her clear roadmap and challenge the bilkers, maybe the law enforcers will get the message, and maybe the lawmakers will give the law enforcers the budgets to stop these widespread corporate crimes.

People Want Full Medicare for All

SEPTEMBER 26, 2013

Freshman senator Ted Cruz (R-TX), who somehow got through Princeton and Harvard Law School, is the best news the defaulting Democratic Party has had in years.

As the Texas bull in the Senate china shop, he has been making a majority of his Republican colleagues cringe with his bare-knuckle antics and language, such as his twenty-one-hour talkathon on the Senate floor demanding the defunding of Obamacare. His Nazi appeasement analogies and threats to shut down were especially embarrassing.

After listening to his lengthy rant on the Senate floor on Tuesday and Wednesday, one comes away with two distinct impressions: Cruz cannot resist inserting himself here, there, and everywhere. And nothing is too trivial for Senator Talkathon. He likes White Castle hamburgers; he loves pancakes; he talked about what he liked to read as a little boy, where he's traveled, what clothes he wears, and other trivia.

You'd think he would have used his time to talk specifically about the suffering that uninsured people and their children are going through, especially in the Lone Star State. Or about what could replace Obamacare other than his repeated "free market" solution, which is to say the "pay or die," profiteering, tax-subsidized corporate system.

It was puzzling why he never mentioned that during his two days of talking, over two hundred Americans died, on average, because they couldn't afford health insurance to get diagnoses and timely treatment. (A peer-reviewed study by Harvard Medical School researchers estimated about forty-five thousand die annually for lack of affordable health insurance every year.)

The other reaction to Senator Cruz was that many of his more specific objections to Obamacare—its mind-numbing complexity, the opposition by formerly supportive labor unions, and the fact that employers react by reducing worker hours to less than thirty a week to escape some of the law's requirements—are well-taken and completely correctible by single-payer health insurance, as provided in Canada. Single-payer, or full "Medicare for all," with free choice of physician and hospital, has been the majority choice of Americans for decades. Even a majority of doctors and nurses favor it.

Single-payer's advantage is that everybody is in, nobody is out. It is far more efficient, allows for better outcomes; saves lives; prevents injuries and illnesses; relieves people of severe anxieties and wasted time spent figuring out often fraud-ridden, inscrutable computerized bills; and allows for the collection of pattern-detecting data to spot harmful trends.

For example, in Canada, full Medicare covers everyone at half the per capita cost that Americans pay, even though fifty million Americans are still not covered. The US per capita figure is almost $9,000 a year, and over 17 percent of our total gross domestic product (GDP). In Canada, administrative costs are much lower.

Symbolically, the single-payer legislation that passed in Canada over four decades ago was thirteen pages long, compared to over nearly one thousand pages for Obamacare.

Critics of Canada's system charge it with delays for patients. For some elective procedures, provinces that were underinvesting experienced some delays until Ottawa raised its contributions. Canada spends just over 10 percent of its GDP on health care, by comparison.

But in the US, not being able to pay for treatment is the biggest problem. And who hasn't heard of delays in various areas of the US due to lack of primary care physicians or other specialties? I have many friends and relatives in Canada who have not complained of delays for routine, essential, or emergency treatments.

For those who prefer to believe hard-bitten businesspeople, Matt Miller, writing yesterday in the *Washington Post*, interviewed big-business executives—David Beatty, who ran the giant Weston Foods, and Roger Martin, longtime consultant to large US companies in Canada. They were highly approving of the Canadian system and are baffled at the way the US has twisted itself in such a wasteful, harmful, and discriminatory system.

Mr. Beatty wondered why US companies "'want to be in the business of providing health care anyway' ('that's a government function,' he says simply)."

Mr. Martin, an "avowed capitalist," who has experienced health care in the US and Canada, called Canadian Medicare "incredibly hassle-free" by comparison. (In Canada, single-payer means government insurance and private delivery of health care under cost controls.) Now dean of the business school at the University of Toronto, Mr. Martin told reporter Miller: "I literally have a hard time thinking of what would be better than a single-payer system."

So why is the US the only Western country without some version of a single-payer system?

Most concessionary Democrats, including Barack Obama and Hillary Clinton, have said in the past that they prefer single-payer, but that the corporate forces against it cannot be overcome. (They use phrases like "single-payer is not practical.")

But with the Cruz crew in Congress going berserk against Obamacare, now is the time to press again for the far superior single-payer model. Or at least get single-payer into the public discussion. Unfortunately, even some of the major citizen groups that are organized for single-payer and behind House Resolution 676 are keeping quiet, not wanting to undercut Obama and the congressional Democrats.

Go to singlepayeraction.org and connect with the movement that does not play debilitating politics and seeks your engagement.

What?! A Charismatic Manager of Public Drinking Water

In contrast to years of serious underinvestment in America's public drinking-water works—which has resulted in takeover drives by large corporations hustling city governments—George S. Hawkins, general manager of the District of Columbia Water and Sewer Authority, or DC Water for short, is leading a comeback in the nation's capital. A career environmentalist, Mr. Hawkins, in just nineteen months on the job, has brought immense energy and vision and ambitious, overdue plans to the forefront. Consequently, people are calling this public servant the rarest of names—a charismatic leader.

Start with his outreach programs that are underused by citizens. For starters, he reports in print or online to every residence what is going on with their water—from the intake of water from the Potomac through the Washington Aqueduct until it reaches home or business faucets.

Here is what Mr. Hawkins means when he speaks of "community outreach":

1. Water Conservation Program—a rolling water-conservation display for large community events (more than one hundred people) that shows ways to save water in your kitchen sink, shower, toilet, etc.

2. For a gathering of ten or more, there is a free DC Water Speakers Bureau with knowledgeable lecturers on various aspects of the water and sewer systems, from processing facilities to neighborhoods. Sometimes the speaker is George Hawkins.

3. There are environmental education programs for grades K–8 related to drinking water, water pollution, and wastewater treatment. These are available for various grade levels, class sizes, or time schedules. Most students in our country haven't the faintest idea where their water

comes from or where it is processed for distribution, much less their rights under the 1974 federal Safe Drinking Water Act.

I worked intensively to get that law enacted by Congress and in the process was appalled at the low status and support given to public drinking-water officials in city after city, especially in Cleveland and New Orleans.

Mr. Hawkins was interested in my suggestion that testing protocols for water contaminants be prepared for high school students taking lab courses in physics and chemistry. If this were applied around the country, high school students could be regularly testing their local drinking water, keeping officials on constant alert and water-drinkers informed.

DC Water has had children's water festivals to teach the value of water. There are two hundred DC locations for free water-bottle refills on the go. It runs an Emergency Command Center to be used during extreme weather events and complex water-main breaks and sewer repairs. It staffs National Drinking Water Week, World Water Monitoring Day, and the Earth Day Celebration in April, and is launching its very ambitious Green Infrastructure Design Challenge.

The green infrastructure challenge invites people and firms to enter a contest to design innovative green practices to absorb rainwater before it floods into the combined sewer system. What Mr. Hawkins would really like to see is the green approach become so widespread as to replace the presently planned, traffic-choking building of two giant storage tunnels to manage stormwater runoff before it goes into the Potomac, Rock Creek, or other waterways heading for Chesapeake Bay.

DC Water is looking for pilot projects to determine if there are enough permeable surfaces to meet the burden of large amounts of rain overflowing from sewers and going into basements, streets, or rivers.

DC Water is responsible for monitoring water quality in the distribution system. About ten years ago, long before Hawkins arrived, the department was exposed by the *Washington Post* for allowing impermissible levels of lead in drinking water. This scandal led to the department offering free filters to DC residents with lead water-services lines, as well as free testing for any resident. It also sparked an increase in bottled-water purchases by people who could afford the product.

In an interview with Mr. Hawkins, he said that public drinking-water systems get publicity only when things go wrong. He was determined to restore confidence in high-quality tap water, rebuild the system, and make good news the norm. Last year, DC Water, which maintains 1,300 miles of pipe for six hundred thousand people, conducted more than forty-one thousand tests on water samples from hydrants, commercial buildings, and household taps.

Many jurisdictions and departments in the greater DC area will have to agree about which green paths to take and who is going to pay what share of the rate increases. DC's antiquated water mains and sewers will cost at least $2.6 billion to repair or replace. "We foresee rate increases coming almost every year as far as we can see in the future," Hawkins says publicly. "So over ten years, you're seeing average bills double," he forthrightly predicts.

DC Water negotiated a preliminary partnership agreement with the Environmental Protection Agency (EPA) to explore rain gardens, green roofs, and permeable pavements as an alternative to the current expensive big-tunnel approach. If these projects can show the way to a green future, provide DC-area jobs, and persuade ratepayers that this groundbreaking path is in the nation's future, Mr. Hawkins may find himself one day moving to head the federal EPA. That is just how high a hurdle he has set for himself and his energetic colleagues.

In the meantime, "fill 'er up" with your reusable water bottle all over DC. It's your water. And don't hesitate to complain, if necessary, about the water or if your monthly bill is not accurate or understandable. DC Water can only do better when they hear from you.

Hernia Repair Vacation, Anyone?

JULY 17, 2013

Do you know anybody with a hernia problem who wants to repair it and have a vacation at the same time? Well, if you do, send them to Shouldice Hospital, right outside of Toronto, Canada, situated on twenty-three beautifully landscaped acres with greenhouses, walking paths, stables, a tennis court, and putting greens.

Over four days and twelve meals, you'll experience the finest, friendliest, safest surgical and postoperative recovery experience in North America. You'll pay from one-half to one-third less, with often far better outcomes, than you would for an outpatient operation for abdominal-wall hernias in the US.

I know this and more from personal experience—one so pleasant that from time to time I visit Shouldice to see how they're doing. They give me a quick, free examination. And this is not special treatment; this is standard care. Some years ago, they invited their "alumni" for annual reunions where up to 1,500 patients came from all over Canada and other countries to honor the staff and the institution. In addition to dinner and entertainment, they provided a free hernia examination. Any former patient dropping by can receive the same special welcome.

The Shouldice technique is known worldwide as the ever-improving "gold standard." Harvard Business School has a best-selling case study lauding the technique's amazing efficiency while producing a superior performance. Patients give it an evaluation that would be the envy of the best clinics in the US.

Over your four days at Shouldice, you are with eighty-eight other hernia patients in various stages of recovery. You dine with them, walk specially inclined stairs and walkways, and perform other exercises with them. You all have something in common to discuss. You are not immediately sent home to recover with only the help of your family, friends, or home care services. You recover at Shouldice with good food and new friends.

Shouldice, with very few exceptions, does not use general anesthesia and is proud of its dramatically lower recurrence and infection rates (compared with patients who get operations at general hospitals). General surgeons do, on average, less than one-tenth the number of hernia surgeries per year than the surgeons at Shouldice.

The ten surgeons at Shouldice perform 7,500 operations a year. All they do are hernia procedures. In their spare time they publish peer-reviewed articles in medical journals advancing the state of the art. Unfortunately, too many general surgeons and hospitals have on average over ten times the rate of recurrence and four times the rate of infection, and they often use expensive mesh both to replace lack of surgical skill and to speed up the operation. Plus they charge much more before they quickly say sayonara.

The Shouldice procedure is described by hospital officials as a "natural tissue repair that combines the surgical technique with the body's natural ability to heal" and takes, on average, forty-five minutes to complete. Except in rare circumstances, "the technique does not use artificial prosthetic material such as mesh because mesh can introduce unnecessary complications such as infections or migration, dramatically increasing the cost of the operation. Shouldice does not use laparoscopic technology because of the potential intestinal punctures and bladder and blood vessel injuries, which may lead to infection and peritonitis." Shouldice staff note that laparoscopic surgery also requires general anesthesia and hugely higher costs for disposable items per surgery than is the case at their hospital.

There are about one million abdominal-wall hernia operations yearly in the US. Hospitals and general surgeons for the most part do not use the Shouldice technique. Still, the deplorable "quick and dirty" that invites overuse of mesh—used on about 80 percent of the patients—has become a perverse incentive for higher billings in the United States. Superior talent is needed for the more natural procedure used by Shouldice.

At its annual convention, the American Hernia Society is cool to the Shouldice model, which has almost seventy years of experienced application. After all, at Shouldice, there is no fee-for-service practice. Ten physicians (licensed by the College of Physicians and Surgeons) are on the staff and make less than a $200,000 salary each year.

It is consumer-driven health care through superior competency where, before discharge, patients participate more actively in their own health care in a facility specially designed for their condition.

Shouldice director Daryl J. B. Urquhart makes a strong case for small, specialized hospitals that can deliver all-around superior outcomes. As Harvard Business School professor Earl Sasser says: "It's more than an operation, it's a total experience."

In the US, the health care industry's rocketing costs and inferior outcomes (especially for those without health insurance); its exclusion of tens of millions of Americans from coverage; its inability to learn from others; and its gouging, profiteering, and frequent subordination of patient well-being by insurance and drug companies, assure that superior procedures such as those used at Shouldice are largely ignored.

US Medicare does not cover Americans who go to Ontario's Shouldice, even though it would save money on all fronts. Still, for those of you with nonemergency hernias, sizable deductibles, or even those willing to go without Medicare coverage who just want an enjoyable, economical respite without risking more recurring visits for infections or failures—consider Shouldice Hospital at 855-328-3423 or go to shouldice.com.

Global Pandemics: Not If, but When

MAY 9, 2013

The deadly influenza virus H7N9 was first detected in China this March. "When we look at influenza viruses, this is an unusually dangerous virus for humans," said Keiji Fukuda, the World Health Organization's (WHO) assistant director-general for health security.

The new H7N9 avian influenza has infected more than 120 Chinese people and taken nearly 30 lives, so far as is known. This strain of the flu has never been detected in humans before. Although Chinese health officials have not located the virus's origins, they have determined that it comes from an assortment of birds—including domesticated ducks and chickens and migratory wild birds.

What is unique about H7N9 is that it does not seem to make the birds sick, so it is hard to track, unlike the 2003 H5N1 outbreak that killed chickens quickly and led investigators to the sources of the virus.

Another unsolved puzzle is why dead pigs and dead ducks in the thousands suddenly were seen floating down some of China's rivers in March. Historically, influenza viruses that have spread around the world have started with Chinese chickens, spread to pigs, and then, due in part to the close living proximity of humans with their farm animals, spread to humans in China and then spread to other parts of the world.

The US Centers for Disease Control and Prevention (CDC) is on high alert, receiving samples of the virus and beginning the process of preparing a vaccine. The CDC says that "influenza viruses constantly change, and it's possible that this virus could become able to easily and sustainably spread between people, triggering a pandemic."

So far H7N9 has only spread to one case in Taiwan—a man who returned from a trip to China.

The problem with the reported numbers of cases is that the Chinese government often delays reports and does not have sufficient experts all over the country to test and provide full and timely information to the world.

Nor does the US have adequate numbers of CDC specialists in China for early detection. The CDC informed us this month that they have "one US direct hire and three local employees dedicated to the influenza program in China." The agency added that it has a total of fifty-four staff members, including one assigned to WHO, adding that "apart from the influenza team, others on the staff have supported the H7N9 outbreak efforts in their area of expertise such as lab, epidemiology, communications, and assisting with the embassy's committee tracking the outbreak."

Given the immense stakes of the health of the American people, this is a tiny staff allocation—smaller than a normal Obama assassination team in a foreign country. The Influenza Epidemic of 1918–1919, involving the H1N1 virus, took 1.9 million lives in the US and, like many recurrent avian flu epidemics that experts believed started in China since then, the total loss of American life exceeds the loss of lives in all of America's wars.

Clearly we are now better prepared scientifically and logistically for such epidemics, but the facility of international travel is much greater now as well. Yet the budgets for detection and prevention of epidemics are much smaller than the bloated cost of a few F-35 fighter planes that Lockheed Martin is still mired in producing.

Some leading US health officials—such as Dr. Anthony Fauci, the great communicator and director of the National Institute of Allergy and Infectious Diseases—are properly worried that H7N9 is showing some adaptation to humans but doesn't kill the birds. Though it could mutate further, Dr. Daniel Jernigan, deputy director of the CDC's influenza division, says the virus is presently "somewhere in that middle ground between purely avian and purely human," which Dr. Fauci calls a red flag.

As if the looming presence of the H7N9 virus from China is not troubling enough, a deadly coronavirus has infected at least twenty-three people in Saudi Arabia, resulting in thirteen Saudi deaths and five more in neighboring countries—a high fatality rate. Earlier this year two cases were documented in the UK of people who were recent arrivals from Saudi Arabia. This week, a patient who was exposed to this coronavirus and suffering from acute respiratory illness has been reported in France.

WHO officials are urging all countries to report faster and more fully what they know about the spread of this virus in order to comply with international health regulations.

When all is said and done, the world is not devoting anywhere near enough resources to combat these viral and bacterial "terrorists." Governments are far more frightful of sporadic, anthropomorphic, human-based physical terror—whether stateless or state-sponsored—than the grim annual toll of epidemics and the informed warnings by infectious disease specialists of a potential pandemic. They all agree: it is not a matter of if, it is only a matter of when!

For many years, I have urged the White House to take greater action and make more substantial preparations regarding infectious diseases. President Bill Clinton declined to speak to the annual meeting of the American Society of Tropical Medicine and Hygiene in Philadelphia in 1998 when alarms over malaria and tuberculosis were rising. At the time, a traveling associate with Hillary Clinton told me that being at risk for such infections on the First Lady's journeys to developing countries was always foremost on their minds. Such concern did not materially change her husband's public health priorities while in office.

To get President Obama's attention, I sent him a letter from E. coli 0104:H4 warning about the "invisible terrorism from bacterium and viruses." He and his assistants never responded.

In many areas, our country needs to reset its priorities. Both the White House and Congress need more maturity regarding pandemic risks before it is too late.

Where's the War on Lethal Super-Bugs?

SEPTEMBER 5, 2012

What if two thousand US soldiers were losing their lives every week in Afghanistan? Would the peddlers of the electoral politics of trivia, distraction, and avoidance take notice? Of course.

Every week, two thousand Americans—or about a hundred thousand men, women, and children a year—die from mostly preventable hospital-acquired infections in the United States. The toll may even be higher (Centers for Disease Control updates its figures soon).

To put this deadly disaster into perspective, hospital-acquired infections kill more Americans per year than the combined fatalities from motor vehicle collisions, AIDS, fire, and homicides combined. Additional millions more survive infections. The pain and costs are enormous.

Why the silence about this silent violence? Every president, including Barack Obama, says over and over again that the safety of the American people is his top priority. They spend trillions of dollars to guard against and confront stateless terrorists in ways that seem to produce terrorist blowback in more countries. Yet the Washington lawmakers can't seem to adequately respond to the little-publicized yet dire warnings and casualty figures published by our leading scientists and public health officials about the big-time terrorists called lethal bacteria.

This year, our government is not even devoting the dollar equivalent of two unnecessary F-22 fighter jets to the fight against what the *Washington Post* calls "a global epidemic of hospital-acquired bugs that quickly grow resistant to the toughest drugs."

The story behind this colossal callousness toward innocent, trusting people taken to hospitals for care and healing starts with the drug company executives who do not see much profit from developing new antibiotics. After all, drugs for depression, high blood pressure, and "lifestyle" make huge profits. Only vaccines are lower on the profit totem pole than antibiotics. Remember the ever-changing superbugs keep challenging the heavily government-subsidized and tax-credited drug companies to invest in antibiotics research and development.

When the drug companies balked at spending money to discover anti-malaria drugs for our soldiers during the Vietnam War, the Pentagon opened its own research section at Walter Reed Army Medical Center and developed several effective medicines itself.

David Shlaes, a specialist in drug development, told the *Post* that only four of the twelve largest global drug companies are researching new antibiotics. The last company to drop out was Pfizer, closing its Connecticut antibiotics research center, laying off 1,200 employees, and moving operations to China. Some corporate patriotism!

All Congress has recently done is give drug companies five more years of patent monopolies for inventing new antibiotics. This is the case even though just about every person can tell you of neighbors, friends, or relatives who have caught serious infections in a hospital.

Last year (but unethically not disclosed until last month), the nation's premier clinical research hospital at the National Institutes of Health lost six patients to a superbug resistant to all known antibiotics. Moreover, resistant strains of tuberculosis are spreading in Eastern Europe and Asia, according to a new study published in the *Lancet*.

Beyond the slowdown in developing new antibiotics—thirteen new categories of antibiotics were discovered between 1945 and 1968, with just two new ones since then—is the massive overpromotion of antibiotics by physicians who should know better. In addition, the daily feed of domesticated chickens, turkeys, cows, and pigs is laced with antibiotics for disease prevention and growth enhancement. This reduces animals' natural immunity and leads to mutating resistant bacteria that can move into the human consumers of meat products.

As the *New York Times* reported, "Eighty percent of the antibiotics sold in the United States" go into these animals. Their producers "are not required to report how they use the drugs—which ones, on what types of animal, and in what quantities."

According to the *Times*, a small sampling by federal agencies found a "ferocious germ resistant to many types of antibiotics had increased tenfold on chicken breasts." The Food and Drug Administration says it is moving to require animal producers to get prescriptions from veterinarians for certain antibiotics that they now get over the counter.

Congress has not been helpful, cutting its own deals with agribusiness and drug lobbies in return for campaign cash and other niceties at the expense of public health. Show most members of Congress a few described human terrorists in the mountains of Afghanistan and they give open checkbooks to the Pentagon and the CIA. Such imbalanced priorities bespeak unstable mental health on Capitol Hill, especially since they and their families eat the same meat products and go to hospitals.

Henry Masur chief of NIH's Critical Care Medicine Department, told the *Post* that "six patients die[d] from the bacterium *Klebsiella pneumoniae* when even colistin, that old warhorse, stopped working." According to the *Post*, "doctors have resorted to such an old, dangerous drug—colistin causes kidney damage—[because of a] lack of new antibiotics coming out of the pharmaceutical pipeline even in the face of a global epidemic of hospital-acquired bugs that quickly grow resistant to the toughest drugs." People have to start asking, "why are Doctors routinely catering to patients with colds by prescribing unnecessary antibiotics without even knowing whether the affliction is viral or bacterial?" "The patients demand this; they think they are being neglected without a prescription," is the frequent frustrated response by physicians. Some hospitals are cutting their hospital-acquired infection rates by using disciplined checklists, getting tough on physicians and nurses washing their hands, and cracking down on general sanitation. This more rigorous application of medicine's famous injunction "do no harm" must be applied faster, deeper, and more regularly in all hospitals and clinics.

By the way, where are the cartoonists? Picturing these superbugs in their grisly roles while our leaders look the other way is a graphic approach to get people's serious attention. Start drawing for life, you guys!

4.

ON ENVIRONMENT, HEALTH, AND SAFETY

Dishonoring Earth Day 2022 with an Oil, Gas, Coal, and Nuclear Heyday

APRIL 22, 2022

Instead of championing solar, wind, and conservation energy, the GOP (Greedy Old Party) is championing the skyrocketing profits and prices for the omnicidal fossil fuel and atomic power companies.

Surging gasoline prices at the pump are not met with excess-profits tax on profit-glutted Big Oil. Rather, the GOP and the Democrats are suspending taxes on gasoline sales that are used to repair roads and bridges. An excess-profits tax could be used to provide rebates to consumers who are being gouged at the pump.

The case for an excess-profits tax is made in a new report, "Big Oil's Wartime Bonus: How Big Oil Turns Profits Into Wealth," released on April 5, 2022, by Bailout Watch, Public Citizen, and Friends of the Earth. Profits (and stocks) of companies like ExxonMobil and Chevron zoomed so much that Big Oil, not wanting to moderate its wholesale prices, has spent $45 billion of your money to buy back its stocks this past year and increase the compensation of its bosses.

Unleashing their lobbying forces in Washington, Big Oil and Gas are demanding, the report relates, "faster approval for natural gas pipelines . . . and increased drilling on public lands and waters." Biden is opening up more oil and gas leases on public lands even though he reported some nine thousand leases already granted are still not being utilized by the oil and gas companies.

The Biden administration is spending $6 billion to shore up aging nuclear plants that safety advocates say should be mothballed.

Washington is silent about using taxes on fossil-fuel price profiteering for more wind, solar, and the little-mentioned energy conservation retrofits of buildings throughout the US. The energy savings and renewable approach would be faster and cleaner, produce more jobs, and provide benefits more directly to Main and Elm Streets USA.

The becalmed Department of Justice and the Federal Trade Commission should swing into bold action under their anti-monopoly and consumer-protection authorities.

It shouldn't have taken Consumer Watchdog in California to sound the alarm on the price manipulation by the five big oil refiners that control 96 percent of the gasoline made in California, led by Chevron. Jamie Court, the dynamic president of Consumer Watchdog, declared: "With California taxes and environmental fees adding about 60 cents per gallon, Californians have long wondered where the extra $1.50 per gallon more they are paying than [other] US drivers (from 5 to 7 dollars per gallon) goes, and with [Senate Bill 1322] we will finally know. California has been an ATM for oil refiners for too long. SB1322 requires California oil refiners to document monthly how much they pay for the average barrel of crude oil they process into gasoline and how much they charge for the barrel of finished gasoline. At 42 gallons per barrel, we will then know how much they are making per gallon of gasoline sold in California, and be able to take back the excessive profits." That is, assuming the completely Democrat-dominated California state legislature enacts this legislation.

If Democrats do not stand tall in going after gasoline price inflation and other price gouging, the GOP will succeed in putting the blame on the Dems in the November elections. Washington is decades late in cutting our addiction to fossil fuels that are causing the climate crises.

On the first Earth Day in April 1970, over 1,500 demonstrations against air, water, and pesticide pollution were held on college campuses around the country. With the onset of the omnicidal, fossil fuel–driven climate catastrophes, leading to even more virulent wildfires, hurricanes, droughts, and floods, college campuses are now too silent, the streets too empty, and Congress too somnolent.

Congress is on another vacation this week, so citizens should be buttonholing their representatives back home and pressing them to take action to counter the fossil fuel industry's greed and to move toward a clean energy future.

Except for the far too small number of authentic advocates pressing decision-makers in government and industry to "follow the science," the country's officials appear too resigned, too attentive to short-term campaign money and political myopia, to be stewards of the people, the natural environment, or the planet.

If these power brokers need any more evidence of the ominous threat to humanity and its tiny planet, they should read the latest assessment by the Intergovernmental Panel on Climate Change, which said humanity has a "brief and rapidly closing window" to head off a hotter, deadly future. United Nations Secretary-General António Guterres warned that the world is "sleepwalking to climate catastrophe" as the COVID-19 pandemic, the war in Ukraine, and lack of political willpower undermine the necessity to cut greenhouse gas pollution by about half before 2030 and get rid of the carbon footprint by 2050.

It is not as if an abused nature is not warning *Homo sapiens* daily with unprecedented intensifications of its deadly outbursts and disruptions all around the world.

Once again, given the way our government is structured, it is Congress—with just 535 members—that can become the rapid engine of energy transformation to the readily known renewable solutions. Solar panels are now seen on rooftops, windmills on hillsides. Energy-efficient technologies are affordable and abundant. Unfortunately, the GOP blocked the infrastructure proposals for clean energy proposed by Biden and the Democrats. Will the voters remember in November?

You know the congressional switchboard number: 202-224-3121. Summon your representatives to your own town hall meetings and directly confront their desire for reelection in the fall. Tell them, for the sake of the world, their country, and their state, it is time to shake off whatever invisible chains are around them and do what they and most of America know has to be done. A clean energy future is better for the climate, the economy, and the health and consumer pocketbooks of *all the people*, regardless of their self-described political labels.

When it comes to the ravaging climate disruptions, all people bleed the same color. Summon your senators and representatives directly to your community. (See my book *Breaking Through Power: It's Easier Than We Think*, pages 144-145.)

New Auto Safety Report Demands Biden Strengthen Federal Programs Now

JANUARY 22, 2021

Today the *New York Times* rediscovered its previous auto safety news beat that blossomed in the 1960s after my book *Unsafe at Any Speed* (1965) caused an uproar in Detroit. Reporter Christopher Jensen told *New York Times* readers about a new report by a coalition of six automotive safety groups demanding that the new Biden administration recharge the moribund, industry-dominated National Highway Traffic Safety Administration (NHTSA) with strong leadership; adequate budget; and long-overdue, proven vehicle safety standards. See: Safer Vehicles and Highways: 4.2 million U.S. Lives Spared Since 1966, 55th anniversary of *Unsafe at Any Speed*.

Since its creation by Congress in 1966, NHTSA has had some bright moments that made motor vehicles more crashworthy and operationally safer, with less pollution and more fuel efficiency. Since then, over four million lives have been saved and many more injuries prevented. Property damage was diminished, and insurance premiums were lower than they would have been had the Wild West–style nonregulation and "style over safety" mania been allowed to continue. Laissez-faire runs amok.

In recent decades, however, under both Democratic and Republican administrations, NHTSA was degraded into more of a sporadic, meek consultant to the auto giants instead of a strong law-enforcement agency. Its administrators wafted sleepily in their few years at the helm and then retired to lucrative positions in the industry they failed to regulate.

To the extent that NHTSA did anything significant, it was due to a small band of gritty citizen safety advocates such as Joan Claybrook, the prime author of the aforementioned report; Clarence Ditlow of the Center for Auto Safety; and the insurance industry–funded Advocates for Highway and Auto Safety led until recently by Jackie Gillan and now Cathy Chase. These advocates used the tools of litigation and lobbying to protect all of us, receiving little recognition for their unsung and lifesaving endeavors.

Alas, for the most part at NHTSA, the routine was official inaction, not considered "news" by the mass media. Standards not issued nor strengthened, recalls not ordered, penalties not applied, data not compiled by make and model, safety-research vehicles not funded, and chronic secrecy by the auto companies and government not qualifying as "newsworthy." A few high-profile auto defect scandals, often exposed when manufacturers were sued by tort lawyers, were widely reported, but the news coverage rarely included NHTSA's inaction and institutional abandonment by Congress and the White House.

The revival of the federal government's motor vehicle safety, pollution, and fuel efficiency missions must start with congressional hearings for updated, stronger laws, including criminal penalties for refusal by auto companies to recall defective or noncompliant vehicles, legislatively mandated safety advances, and more capacity and funding for NHTSA's tiny budget, now far less than what is spent on military bands!

With distracted driving and ever more vehicles on more crowded highways, fatalities (including pedestrian casualties) started to increase pre-COVID.

The media, for its part, should not be distracted by the hype around a premature autonomous vehicle and supersmart highways. Every day, people are dying in the old-fashioned ways that could be prevented by long-ready, better-handling, and crash-protective vehicles.

Imagine the benefits of safer vehicles with far more environmentally benign engines, plus adequate funding for cost-effective public investment in new forms of public transit and upgrades to existing mass transit. Getting around on the ground should include many diverse forms of arriving at one's destination in a timely, safe, and environmentally preferable manner.

The Claybrook report, titled *Safer Vehicles and Highways: 4.2 million U.S. Lives Spared Since 1966*, is very specific about what needs to be done. New technical talent is needed at NHTSA in this era of electric cars, autonomous safety assists, and the computerization of motor vehicles vulnerable to hacking.

A tougher position on recalls is essential. Automakers "continue efforts to minimize expensive recall costs by delaying the recall, narrowing the scope of a recall, or denying the defect," declares the report.

Moreover, many of the safety features (child safeguards, for example) and performance levels in your vehicle have not been updated for years in practical, cost-effective ways long urged by the more innovative automotive suppliers.

It is time for the Biden people, under the new secretary of transportation, Pete Buttigieg, to catch up and end the soporific record of their predecessors, including that of those from the Obama/Biden administration. (See: "Jerry Cox, Steven Bradbury, and Why 30 Million Takata Airbags Are Not Being Recalled" in *Corporate Crime Reporter*.)

The French have a saying: "The more things change the more they stay the same." That applies to the auto company executive-suite culture. In their comfortable atriums, they arrange for deniability while they press for immunity from criminal and tort laws. They still preside over obscure financing and advertising deceptions. They still dangle before buyers of their less expensive vehicles overpriced options for long-amortized safety improvements that are standard equipment on higher-priced vehicles so as to pressure them to upgrade.

They still instruct their lobbyists to go to Congress with one message: "NO, NO, NO" to long-delayed improvements for motorists to reduce the casualty toll on the highway and the various economic costs associated with such stagnant corporate stubbornness.

Biden promises a "new day" from Trumpism. Let's see if he and his team can provide America with a new day of public safety from callous corporatism on the nation's roadways.

The Fiftieth Anniversary of OSHA

DECEMBER 29, 2020

Today is the fiftieth anniversary of the Occupational Safety and Health Administration (OSHA). President Richard Nixon signed the bill into law at a White House ceremony on December 29, 1970. Our citizen advocacy was central to its passage over the opposition of the business lobbies, but we were not invited to the White House signing. We [our staff and colleagues] worked on this legislation meticulously and obtained media coverage and labor support during its difficult path through the Senate and the House. Unsung heroes were Tony Mazzocchi, secretary-treasurer of the Oil, Chemical, and Atomic Workers Union (OCAW), and our lawyer, Gary Sellers, who worked closely with the great congressional champion for OSHA, Representative Phillip Burton (D-CA).

OSHA, whose mission is to save workers' lives and protect their health and safety, has come under fierce and unjust attack by industries with unsafe workplaces such as coal mines, chemical plants, agribusiness, and the construction industry. OSHA's funding has been tiny, its inspectors small in number, and its authority undermined by corporate-indentured members of Congress and pressure from the White House.

Given the terrible hazards that millions of frontline workers are experiencing during the COVID-19 pandemic, the mission of OSHA has never been more important or timely. Yet Donald Trump and his Trumpsters have refused to issue mandatory safety standards and protection for these workers and have virtually shut down OSHA's overall enforcement duties.

President-elect Joe Biden must revive OSHA's lifesaving mission with a strong nominee to head this agency and assure it is adequately funded. Presently its annual budget of about $500 million a year is what the Department of Defense spends each year on military bands. Almost sixty thousand workers lose their lives from workplace diseases and traumas every year.

Stopping Trump's Demonic Reversals of the Long-Term Benefits of the First Earth Day, April 22, 1970

APRIL 22, 2020

Earth Day, April 22, 1970, was the most consequential demonstration of civic energy in modern American history. Engaging nearly twenty million Americans participating in about thirteen thousand local events, this first Earth Day changed corporate and government policies through popular demands for clean air, water, soil, and food.

Senator Gaylord Nelson launched Earth Day, having tired of congressional inaction and the power of the corporate pollution lobby. Earth Day quickly became a grassroots educational and action-driven week of activities that aroused the country.

Even reactionary President Nixon quickly planted a tree on the White House South Lawn in recognition of the public support for environmentalism after he saw the huge turnouts at rallies and marches.

Imagine the environmental threats fifty years ago. Cities were choking with motor vehicle and factory pollution. Los Angeles was smogland. Air pollution caused respiratory disease and stung your eyes. The Cuyahoga River near Cleveland, slick with oil, would catch on fire. Steel mills in Birmingham, Alabama, turned the air into a brownish haze.

I spoke at several large rallies on the first Earth Day and during Earth Week alongside environmental leaders, including the great David Brower and dynamic professor Barry Commoner. The energy at the gatherings made indentured politicians nervous. Eleven thousand schools, colleges, and universities hosted events focusing on local deadly poison hotspots and challenging state governments and Congress.

Mass media coverage was spectacular. All the TV networks, the covers of *Time* and *Newsweek* (a big deal then), and the popular daytime TV talk shows (Phil Donahue, Merv Griffin, and Mike Douglas)—national and local media provided saturation coverage coast to coast.

There was a huge rally on the Mall in Washington, DC, which was very visible to a wary Nixon in the White House and lawmakers in Congress. Hearing the rumble of the people supported by scientists and health specialists, Nixon and members of Congress knew they had to enact environmental protections.

Within three years, Congress produced sweeping, unsurpassed landmark laws such as the Clean Air Act, Clear Water Act, and Endangered Species Act. New laws also created the Environmental Protection Agency, Occupational Safety and Health Administration, and the White House Council on Environmental Quality. New environmental groups (Greenpeace, Public Citizen, Friends of the Earth, National Resources Defense Council, and Environmental Defense Fund) joined the earlier organizations, such as the Sierra Club, to strengthen the civic bedrock for environmental advocacy and watchdogging.

Out of Earth Day came many of the young authors, filmmakers, and leaders of the next half century of environmental action. They included Denis Hayes, lead coordinator of Earth Day 1970; David Zwick of Clean Water Action; professor Paul Ehrlich; Selma Rubin, cofounder of Earth Day; and Dr. Brent Blackwelder. Later the environmental justice movement stressed that poor communities are exposed to the most lethal dumping grounds and deadly emissions.

Although constantly obstructed by corporate polluters, the air and water did become cleaner. There is far less lead in most, if not all, human bodies (note Flint, Michigan) and far less asbestos in your lungs. Both substances are banned from most consumer product uses.

Adam Rome, a University of Buffalo environmental historian, documented what happened on and after the first Earth Day in his book *The Genius of Earth Day*. He said the intensity of local organizers is largely missing from climate and environmental activism today.

Anybody doubting this observation should take note of how dangerous Donald and a supine Congress are failing to protect our environment. Trump is viciously unraveling the established protections to flood your families with more mercury, soot, coal ash, cancerous pesticides, dirty drinking water, and toxic workplaces. What Trump calls "deregulation" is increasing death, disease, and property damage in America by taking the federal cops off the corporate poison beat.

Dumb, disgraceful Donald still sneers at the oncoming climate catastrophe, calling it a hoax. His arrogant ignorance is scuttling federal programs and scientific research on climate, destroying restrictions on greenhouse gases produced by the fossil fuel giants and inviting them to further exploit federal wilderness lands and offshore areas. Despite the massive oil flooding of the Gulf by BP oil company ten years ago, disgraceful Trump is loosening restrictions on drillers imposed after the Deepwater Horizon disaster. The consequences for the fishing and tourist industry once again could be devastating.

The omnicidal Republicans controlling the Senate support Trump's reckless agenda regardless of the environmental harm done to their own families. The Democrats controlling the House complain about gridlock. Unfortunately, with few exceptions, they are not racing to again impeach Trump or demand his resignation, if only to rid the nation of his chaotic scapegoating and the egomaniacal, self-contradicting, colossal misman-agement regarding the coronavirus crisis. It is time to stop the further preventable loss of life caused by Trump's fibbing, flailing, and daily fail-ures to process reliable information and lead.

Trump's resignation should be the grassroots focus of today's Earth Day and become every day's popular demand for the sake of American lives and health.

Children's Moral Power Can Challenge Corporate Power on Climate Crisis

APRIL 16, 2019

The famous anthropologist Margaret Mead once said to me that children have a distinct moral authority to change some of their parents' habits or opinions. She gave the use of seat belts and smoking cigarettes as examples.

Indeed, most of us know instances when sons and daughters have looked into the eyes of their fathers and mothers and urged them to wear their seat belts or stop smoking. They say in their own plaintive way that they want Mommy and Daddy around for them. Many mothers and fathers have had such experiences.

Many parents and corporate executives are doing slow-motion dances around global climate disruptions, despite the scientific and brutally visual evidence of our climate crisis. The rising tide of worldwide protests in recent months by young students cutting classes to shake up their elders should be a wake-up call and a sign of more activism on the horizon. Earth Day on April 22 should give them another visible platform.

Last year the global youth climate strike manifested in Sweden, where it was started by then-fifteen-year-old Greta Thunberg. Every Friday she stood in silent protest outside the historic Swedish Parliament in Stockholm.

On March 15, an estimated 150,000 European students left school to protest. In Sweden, Germany, France, Britain, and other countries, these youngsters admonished adults, who have the power to urgently diminish greenhouse gases by cutting the use of coal, oil, and gas and expanding the use of renewables and energy conservation.

In India, demonstrations were about the suffocating air pollution. In South Africa, protestors spoke about the worsening droughts.

At a rally in Washington, DC, eight-year-old Havana Chapman-Edwards told protestors at the US Capitol: "Today we are telling the truth, and we do not take no for an answer," according to the *New York Times.*

Protestors already see the truth in the Pacific Ocean's rising sea levels and the Arctic Circle's melting ice.

These youngsters can argue their case with facts and figures, with stories of record-setting fires, floods, tornadoes, and hurricanes and species extinctions. But they are viscerally feeling the impact of climate crisis and fearing for their lives before reaching middle age.

As University of Maryland professor Dana Fisher told the *Times*, children are afraid of the tumultuous world they will inherit. Their elders are not protecting them.

Greta, the emerging spokesperson for this escalating youth agitation, put it wisely: "There [is] a crisis in front of us that . . . we will have to live with for all our lives, our children, our grandchildren, and all future generations." The movement has much more room to grow, but we are depending on them developing a strong, organized voice while retaining their individual spontaneity.

Not surprisingly, climate deniers took to social media to falsely declare that environmental groups were using the students. In fact, this outburst was quite commendably a result of students taking what they've learned seriously.

In England, students are insisting their government declare a state of emergency to highlight the severity of the threat. They want more material on global warming in their national school curriculum.

Some teachers and principals in the UK don't like students missing classes and are trying to block or penalize those who do. But many school leaders are approving such brief intermissions to help save the planet. Sixteen-year-old Bonnie Morely decried the politicians for being "asleep at the wheel. We have to wake them up, and I think thousands of kids on the streets will do just that."

How about millions of them! Their numbers are growing, with some demonstrations reaching tens of thousands. In France, over two million students signed petitions. Some politicians are chiding them about the costs of their demands, as if energy pollution and toxic waste are not costly to people, as if the costs of violent weather patterns aren't costing huge sums of money and lives already.

In Brussels, Belgium, eighteen-year-old Liam pointed to "a growing momentum," but he told a *Times* reporter maybe it should become more disruptive to attain more attention. "Maybe we should change the timing of the protests to rush hour."

The youngsters understand the problem and want solutions now to counter the current omnicidal lethargy. Although some companies get it—such as the sterling Patagonia and Interface corporations in the US—most large companies are either resisting, engaging in "greenwashing" lip service, or taking the smallest of steps for public relations purposes.

The people of our tormented planet must pull together as if there were an impending invasion from Mars. Fortunately, the urgent pathways to be pursued are full of favorable economic efficiencies and good jobs. Think of solar energy installations, weatherized homes and other buildings, modern public transportation, grants to speed up climate chaos mitigation, and economies moving to net-zero or even negative carbon impact. The known remedial technology is far ahead of its mandated applications by sluggish legislators and their myopic corporate paymasters.

Children can and do communicate with each other often and freely around their community, country, and globe. The faster that trivial text messages are replaced by texts calling for a relentless call to action, the better. Students taking to the streets and taking on legislators will advance the fight for a safer planet and a more just society.

Stay tuned! This is only the beginning of the world's children raising adults to a maturity that faces the awful, onrushing realities.

Who Will Displace the Omniciders?

MARCH 8, 2019

Citizens challenging the towering threat of climate crisis should never underestimate the consequences of our dependence on fossil fuel corporations. Real engagement with worsening climate disruption means spending more of our leisure hours on civic action. The fate of future generations and our planet depends on the intensity of these actions.

This was my impression after interviewing Dahr Jamail, author of the gripping new book *The End of Ice,* on my *Radio Hour.* Jamail wrote books and prizewinning articles as the leading freelance journalist covering the Bush/Cheney Iraq War and its devastating aftermath. For his latest book, Jamail went to the visible global warming hotspots to get firsthand accounts from victims of climate disruption. His gripping reporting is bolstered by facts from lifelong specialists working in the regions he visited.

Readers of *The End of Ice* are taken on a journey to see what is happening in Alaska, the mountain forests of California, the coral reefs of Australia, the heavily populated lowlands of South Florida, the critical Amazon forest, and other areas threatened by our corporate-driven climate crisis.

Jamail, an accomplished mountaineer, precisely illustrates the late, great environmentalist Barry Commoner's first law of ecology—namely, that "everything is connected to everything else." Jamail makes the connection between the rising sea levels and the untold catastrophes engulfing forests, mountains, and wildlife on land and in the sea. Jamail is not relying on computer models. What he is seeing, photographing, and experiencing is often worse than what the models show in terms of accelerating sea level rises and the melting ice of the glaciers.

Jamail's trenchant conversations with bona fide experts who have spent a lifetime seeing what mankind has done to the natural world present a compelling case of the threat the climate crisis poses to human survival.

Jamail, near the end of his narrative, writes: "Disrespect for nature is leading to our own destruction. . . . This is the direct result of our inability to understand our part in the natural world. We live in a world where we are acidifying the oceans, where there will be few places cold enough to support year-round ice, where all the current coastlines will be underwater, and where droughts, wildfires, floods, storms, and extreme weather are already becoming the new normal."

If you don't know that melting ice and permafrost is a big tragedy, then that is all the more reason to read this book and immerse yourself in its vivid prose.

His chapter on South Florida and its millions of residents exemplifies the one scenario that will bring an alarming message home to people in coastal communities worldwide: South Florida could be underwater in fifty years or less. Many of the houses, buildings, and structures are located only a few feet or yards above sea level. Engineers and some city officials see Miami Beach as doomed and say Floridians must prepare for evacuations.

There are other more imminent dangers. As Jamail writes: "One major source of concern is the Florida aquifer. Once that water is contaminated by saltwater, it's over."

Already, some banks will not provide thirty-year home mortgages for vulnerably located houses. Some home values along the ocean are starting to be adversely affected. Insurance companies are reluctant to publicize their projections, but their actuarial tables are not, shall we say, consumer-friendly.

Then there are the lethal storm surges during major hurricanes as sea levels and high tides rise relentlessly.

Most businesses, people, and municipalities are looking the other way. Two-term governor Rick Scott (a corporate crook) even prohibited state employees from uttering or writing the words "climate change" in any state documents. It is admittedly hard to face such catastrophe while the sun is shining and most normal life continues. In 2017, the Nuclear Regulatory Commission gave Florida Power & Light the go-ahead to build two new nuclear power plants (they're too expensive and won't be built) to join its aging plants on the beach. Shades of the Fukushima disaster in Japan eight years ago.

None of these warnings are recent. Climate scientists warned President Lyndon Johnson about the dangers associated with carbon release in the atmosphere in 1965. President Bill Clinton and Vice President Al Gore released a detailed, urgent report, with pictures and graphs, about climate disruption in 1993 to demonstrate that the clock was ticking. Unfortunately, in the following seven years, they mostly did what the auto industry wanted them to do—nothing.

Some of the most poignant passages in Jamail's book are the informed cries and worries of the onsite specialists he interviewed. People you have never heard of, but who should be heard all the time. One of them, Dr. Rita Mesquita, a biologist with the largest research institute in Brazil for the Amazon rainforest says, "We are not telling the general public what is really going on." While the general public is spending more time in virtual reality and, with growing urbanization, becoming estranged from nature, this ominous disconnect is widening.

The new president of Brazil, Jair Bolsonaro, has openly vowed to bolster more commercial development in the Amazon and on Indigenous tribal land.

How will India's billion-plus people get their water if its rivers dry up because the glaciers in the Himalayas have melted? How do you relocate thirty million people from Mumbai away from rising sea levels? How do you head off diseases that are spreading due to habitat destruction? Meanwhile, one hundred corporations (e.g., ExxonMobil, Shell, and state entities) continue to be the source of 71 percent of total global carbon dioxide emissions.

There are hundreds of cable channels in the US transmitting largely junk programs. How about 1 percent of them (six) being dedicated to the global stories and urgencies of climate catastrophes, and to how movements like Project Drawdown (of greenhouse gases) are succeeding in cutting these menaces (see *Drawdown*, edited by Paul Hawken) around the world?

Think about what we should be doing with some of our time for our descendants so as not to have them curse us for being oblivious, narcissistic ancestors!

We can start with instructing our Congress to deploy its transformative leverage over the economy. The only reason Congress has been an oil, gas, and coal toady instead of an efficient renewable energy force is because we have sat on the sidelines watching ExxonMobil be Congress's quarterback.

Boeing Mismanagers: Forfeit Your Pay and Resign: An Open Letter to Boeing CEO Dennis Muilenburg

APRIL 26, 2019

Dennis A. Muilenburg
Chairman, President, and Chief Executive Officer
The Boeing Company

Dear Mr. Muilenburg:

On April 4, 2019, you somewhat belatedly released a statement: "We at Boeing are sorry for the lives lost in the recent 737 MAX accidents." You added that a preliminary investigation made it "apparent that in both flights" the MCAS (Manuevering Characteristics Augmentation System) "activated in response to erroneous angle of attack information."

Your acknowledgement of the problems with the 737 MAX 8 somehow escaped inclusion in your messages to shareholders, the capital markets, and the Securities and Exchange Commission. It is now stunningly clear that your overly optimistic outlook on January 20, 2019—after the Indonesian Lion Air crash—was misleading. Whatever the public learns, day after day, about the troubles of your company, it is still far less than what Boeing knows will come out day by day, and not just about the deadly design of the 737 MAX 8.

Your narrow-body passenger aircraft—namely, the long series of 737s that began in the 1960s—was past its prime. How long could Boeing avoid making the investment needed to produce a "clean-sheet" aircraft and, instead, in the words of *Bloomberg Businessweek,* "push an aging design beyond its limits"? Answer: as long as Boeing could get away with it and keep necessary pilot training and other costs low for the airlines as a sales incentive.

To compete with the Airbus A320neo, Boeing equipped the 737 MAX 8 with larger engines tilted more forward and upward on the wings than prior 737s. Thus began the trail of criminal negligence that will implicate the company and its executives. The larger engines changed the center of gravity and the plane's aerodynamics. Boeing management was on a fast track and ignored warnings by its own engineers, not to mention scores of other technical aerospace people outside the company.

The MCAS software fix or patch, with all its glitches and miscues, is now a historic example of a grave failure of Boeing management. Yet you insist the 737 MAX 8 is still safe and that some alteration of the MCAS and other pilot advisories will make the aircraft airworthy. Aircrafts should be stall-proof, not stall-prone. Trying to shift the burden onto the pilots for any vast numbers of failure modes beyond the software's predictability is scurrilous. The Boeing 737 MAX 8 must never be permitted to fly again—it has an inherent aerodynamic design defect. Sell your Boeing 737NG instead.

No matter your previous safety record of the 737 series, Boeing doesn't get one, two, or more crashes that are preventable by adopting long-established aeronautical knowledge and practices. You are on the highest level of notice not to add to your already extraordinary record of criminally negligent decisions and inactions. Result: 346 innocent people lost their lives.

Boeing management's behavior must be seen in the context of Boeing's use of its earned capital. Did you use the $30 billion surplus from 2009 to 2017 to reinvest in R & D, in new narrow-body passenger aircraft? Or did you, instead, essentially burn this surplus with self-serving stock buybacks of $30 billion in that period? Boeing is one of the companies that *MarketWatch* labeled as "five companies that spent lavishly on stock buybacks while pension funding lagged."

Incredibly, your buybacks of $9.24 billion in 2017 comprised 109 percent of annual earnings. As you know, stock buybacks do not create any jobs. They improve the metrics for the executive compensation packages of top Boeing bosses.

To make your management recklessly worse, in December 2018 you arranged for your rubber-stamp board of directors to approve $20 billion more in buybacks now placed on pause.

After the Indonesian crash came the second software bomb that took away control from the pilots and brought down Ethiopian Airlines Flight 302 on March 10, taking the lives of 157 passengers and crew. At the time, you were way overdue with your new software allegedly addressing the avoidable risks associated with the notorious 737 MAX.

Don't you see some inverted priorities here? Don't you see how you should have invested in producing better aircraft? Instead, your top management was inebriated with the prospect of higher stock values and higher profits by keeping your costs lower with that "aging design" of the Boeing 737s. You guessed wrong—big-time—for your passengers as well as for your company.

Boeing is in additional trouble that reflects poor management. On March 22, 2019, the *Washington Post* reported that according to NASA administrator Jim Bridenstine NASA is considering sidelining the massive rocket Boeing is helping build because the project is far behind schedule.

"And now," the *Post* continued, "the agency is about to announce another major delay in a separate high-profile program: the spacecraft Boeing is building to fly astronauts to the International Space Station."

Then, on April 21, 2019, the *New York Times*—in a lengthy front-page story based on "internal emails, corporate documents, and federal records, as well as interviews with more than a dozen current and former employees"—reported that your South Carolina factory, which produces the 787 Dreamliner, "has been plagued by shoddy production and weak oversight that have threatened to compromise safety."

It is not as if you are receiving anything but top-dollar payments for these military (the Air Force tanker) and government contracts. You overpaid yourself at more than $23 million in 2018, which comes to about $12,000 an hour!

In the midst of these accusations, whistleblower lawsuits, and alleged retaliations by management, the *Times* reports your pace of production "has quickened" and that you are eliminating "about a hundred quality control positions in North Charleston [South Carolina]." Why?

Big corporations are run like top-down dictatorships where the hired hands determine their own pay and strip their shareholder *owners* of necessary powers of governance. Your board of directors should disclose what you told them about the 737 MAX 8 and when they knew it.

Already, corporate crime specialists are making the case for you and other top Boeing managers—those who refused to listen to the warnings of your conscientious engineers regarding the redesign of the 737 MAX 8—to face criminal prosecution. Note BP pleading guilty to eleven counts of manslaughter in the Deepwater Horizon oil spill case in 2013.

Glass Lewis urges removal of Boeing audit committee head Lawrence

Kellner for "failing to foresee safety risks with the 737 MAX 8 aircraft," reported the *Financial Times*, on April 16, 2019.

Consider, in addition, the statement of two Harvard scholars—Leonard J. Marcus and Eric J. McNulty (authors of the forthcoming book *You're It: Crisis, Change, and How to Lead When It Matters Most*):

> Of course, if Boeing did not act in good faith in deploying the 737 Max 8 and the Justice Department's investigation discovers Boeing cut corners or attempted to avoid proper regulatory reviews of the modifications to the aircraft, Muilenburg and any other executives involved should resign immediately. Too many families, indeed communities, depend on the continued viability of Boeing.

These preconditions have already been disclosed and are evidentially based. Your mismanagement is replete with documentation. Management was criminally negligent; 346 lives of passengers and crew were lost. You and your team should forfeit your compensation and *should resign forthwith*.

All concerned with aviation safety should have your public response.

Sincerely,

Ralph Nader

OPEN LETTER TO BOEING—Passengers First, Ground the 737 MAX 8 Now!

MARCH 12, 2019

I called Boeing's office in Washington, DC, about the new Boeing 737 MAX 8 crashes in Indonesia and Ethiopia, with over three hundred fatalities, to give them some advice. They were too busy to call back, so I'm conveying some measures they should take fast in this open letter.

Dear Boeing Executives:

You don't seem to see the writing on the wall. Your Boeing 737 MAX 8 is being grounded by more and more countries and foreign airlines. Airline passengers in the US are switching away their reservations on this plane, and there are signs of an organized boycott of this aircraft, which is used by the major US airlines.

It is only a matter of time before the bereaved families organize, before members of Congress start forcefully speaking out, as senators Ed Markey and Richard Blumenthal just did. Both senators are on the Senate aviation subcommittee.

Soon the technical dissenters in the reported "heated discussions" with the Federal Aviation Administration (FAA), the airline industry, the pilot unions, and your company will see some internal emails, memos, and whistleblowers go public. Technical dissent cannot be repressed indefinitely.

Your own lawyers should be counseling you that Boeing is on public notice. If, heaven forbid, there were a Boeing 737 MAX 8 crash in this country—if your arrogance again leads to algorithms overpowering the pilots—law enforcement could be moved to investigate potential personal criminal negligence.

Clearly, you run a company used to having its way. Used to having a patsy FAA, with its "tombstone mentality"; used to delaying airworthiness directives that should be put out immediately, and not diluted or delayed;

used to getting free government R & D; and used to avoiding state and federal taxes.

Stop digging in your heels. Tell the airlines to stop digging in their heels. Public trust in your Boeing 737 MAX 8 is eroding fast. Get ahead of the curve that is surely heading your way.

You see the Boeing 737 MAX 8 as being a large part of your passenger aircraft business. You've delivered over three hundred planes and reportedly have over three thousand orders. Over the years, your engineers have solved many technical problems brilliantly. The domestic safety record of the major airlines, using your equipment, has been very commendable for more than a decade. A lot of the credit goes to Boeing as well as to the airline pilots, flight attendants, traffic controllers, and mechanics.

But there is always a time when commercial dictates and a rush to get ahead of Airbus result in too many corners being cut. There is always a time when the proverbial rubber band, being stretched, suddenly snaps. This aircraft is not an old DC-9 being phased out. The stakes involved in your erring on the side of safety and letting your engineers exercise their "options for revision" affect the future of a good part of Boeing.

Tell the US airlines and other recalcitrant airlines overseas to ground their 737 MAX 8 planes, and then you should do what is necessary to restore the engineering integrity of your company. You did this before with the Boeing 787 in 2013.

Once an aircraft starts to carry a stigma in the minds of passengers, time is of the essence. You know all about branding's pluses and minuses. It is better to act now before being forced to act, whether by Congress, the FAA, a prosecution, or another aircraft disaster that could have been avoided.

For safety,

Ralph Nader
Coauthor of *Collision Course: The Truth About Airline Safety*

New Book about Ethics and Whistleblowing for Engineers Affects Us All!

DECEMBER 7, 2018

It's tough to be an engineering student these days, with so many new developments in modern technology and technological knowledge. The course curricula are more crowded than ever, and the impact of emerging technologies is monumental. Some engineering professors worry that their students' busy course schedules prevent them from adequately exploring the liberal arts. Without exposure to the liberal arts, engineering students will lack the broad context that will help them approach their work as a profession, not just a trade.

Pressed as they are now in their undergraduate and graduate courses, engineering students may not appreciate the pressures and challenges they will face in their work after graduation. More than handling the stress that comes from needing to meet commercial or governmental deadlines and standards, they will need to understand the ethical ramifications of their actions. Existing industry standards rarely measure up to the necessary health, safety, and reliability requirements in the workplace, marketplace, and environment. Moreover, the news media and social media create an environment that shines a spotlight on the personal responsibility of the engineering professions and the obligation to blow the whistle on misdeeds.

The core curriculum for engineering students must include courses and seminars that explore the ethical responsibility of engineering. Understanding economic and political pressures and, if necessary, whistleblowing obligations is an important matter for engineers. This is the subject of *Ethics, Politics, and Whistleblowing in Engineering* (CRC Press), a new book edited by Rania Milleron, PhD, and Nicholas Sakellariou, PhD (Rania, my niece, is a microbiologist at the Texas Department of State Health Services, and Nicholas is a lecturer at California Polytechnic State University).

One of the goals of *Ethics, Politics, and Whistleblowing in Engineering* is to make technologically inclined students realize at the very beginning of their careers that the best kind of engineering comes from a foundation in the applied sciences *and* the humanities. This engaging book—which will interest anyone who wants to know more about professionally applied ethics, regardless of field, is full of short renditions of individual engineers as heroes or bold advocates of changing hazardous procedures and ways of doing business.

The engineers featured in this book are professionals who cannot abide working in corporations where common candor has to be called courage. They demand the right to take their conscience to work.

There are sections in this book on whistleblowing around the world, and on the too-passive standards-setting roles of engineering societies (like the Society of Automotive Engineers or the Society of Mechanical Engineers). Novel interviews with deep thinkers and beloved, creative professors, such as Princeton's David P. Billington, who combined history and art in his rigorous courses, make a deep imprint on the reader.

Part I, titled "Engineering Leadership," is meant to stimulate engineering educators to experiment broadly and open-mindedly in liberal education curricula, to promote unpopular but fact-based viewpoints, and to encourage students to learn about the heroic roots of engineering.

Part II, "Daily Practice," recounts stories about engineers having to make excruciating decisions affecting their careers and public safety when they take on their profit-obsessed corporate bosses or government officials.

Part III, "Raising the Bar," "offers creative, concrete, and sustainable engineering solutions. In an age of designs generated by committees or computers . . . some think that technologists are losing their creativity and imagination."

The appendix offers abundant resources for engineering students and teachers. In the 1950s and 1960s, I was pushing the top executives of the auto companies to liberate their engineers to build lifesaving, cleaner, and more fuel-efficient motor vehicles. As I learned more about the industry, it became clear that engineering integrity was subordinate to short-term profit goals, frivolous styling, and excessive horsepower.

Providing a climate of conscientious engineering work, instead of the all-too-frequent self-censorship that comes from top-down or myopic dictates, can save corporations from serious trouble—litigation, public anger, and subsequent loss of sales. In the US auto industry, authoritarian corporate bosses presided over technological stagnation that resulted in shrinkage and bankruptcy.

The development of biotechnology, nanotechnology, and artificial intelligence industries has occurred without an effective legal or ethical framework. As a result, we are ever reliant on the first responders. Unfortunately, many engineers working on the front lines have abdicated their role as sentinels. Their long silence must end.

In the coming years, engineers will need a deep wellspring of professional self-respect. And our society will need to expand the laws and institutions to protect engineers when they do step up and speak out.

This unique book, for which I have written an introduction, argues in many intriguing and compelling ways that we cannot afford to neglect the ethical dimensions of engineering.

The stakes, from climate disruption to the military arms race to our public infrastructure to the health and safety of posterity and our planet, are so high. So must be the expectations accorded the engineering profession everywhere in our midst.

(There are feasts of abundant references in this book for any reader to dig deeper.)

For more information, visit ethicalengineering.org.

Driverless Cars: Hype, Hubris, and Distractions

JUNE 26, 2017

The hype and unsubstantiated hope behind the self-driving car movement continues unabated, distracting from addressing necessities of old "mobilities," such as upgrading inadequate public transit and highway and rail infrastructure.

At a conference on driverless cars sponsored by George Washington University Law School earlier this month, the legal landscape of unresolved problems and unasked questions was deliberated for a full day: What are the legal requirements that should be applied to the testing phase, the deployment phase, liability and insurance, impacts on displaced workers, cybersecurity, privacy, and antitrust? A takeaway from this gathering was the number of mind-numbing, unresolved systems awaiting this untested new technology.

First, a little background—car ownership and car sales are expected to flatten or decline due to ride-sharing and a new generation of consumers that is less inclined to purchase motor vehicles. How is the industry to react? By adding high-priced value to motor vehicles, already described as computers on wheels. Voilà, the race for the driverless car! The mass media took the bait and overreported each company's sensationalized press releases, announcing breakthroughs without disclosing the underlying data. The arrogance of the algorithms, among many other variables, bypassed simple daily realties, such as bustling traffic in cities like New York.

In the shadows were the daily tribulations of Americans just trying to get to and from work, especially the poor and those who don't own a vehicle.

Don't expect driverless cars to be taking over anytime in the next few decades. Autonomous vehicles do not exist in the autonomous contexts of daily life. Start with how to fit these futuristic vehicles in a sea of over 250 million driven vehicles in the US. It's easy to score driverless vehicles in well-orchestrated courses with minimum traffic over low mileage. Apply that controlled scenario to the scale and complexity of *actual* roads with *actual* drivers in *actual* conditions and the difficulties multiply enormously.

The industry—from Silicon Valley to Detroit—argues safety. Robotic systems do not get drunk, fall asleep at the wheel, or develop poor driving skills. But computers fail frequently; they are often susceptible to hacking—whether by the manufacturers, dealers, or deadly actors. Hacking is a driverless car industry's nightmare, and American motorists can see why. They like to remain in control and not have their engine stop, accelerate, or be turned in disastrous directions by remote interventions.

Already Volkswagen and other companies have been caught by law enforcement manipulating software emission controls on a gigantic scale.

Until that distant dream by the technocrats when all vehicles are driverless is realized, there may be less safety because of the mix of autonomous and human-operated vehicles.

On top of all this is the emerging demand to rewrite the rules so that there are fewer mandatory regulations (to be replaced by mere guidelines), less tort liability, less clear *contractual* responsibility between the many inputting companies, less openness for the data, far fewer privacy protections, and little attention to the awesome public investment needed for preparing highways and other facilities.

Already, Level Three—an autonomous vehicle needing emergency replacement by the surrogate human driver—is being viewed as unworkable by specialists at MIT and elsewhere. The human driver, lulled and preoccupied, can't take back control in time.

Modern mass transit has shown how drivers who choose to become passengers can relax and not have to drive. Why won't we concentrate on what can be improved and expanded to get safer, more efficient, less polluting mobility?

Over forty years ago Northwestern University transportation specialists developed a plan for "personalized public transit," meaning, for example, connecting your car to a monorail system for daily commutes!

The driverless car is bursting forth without a legal, ethical, or prioritization framework. Already asking for public subsidies, companies can drain much-needed funds for available mass transit services and the industry's own vehicle safety upgrades in favor of a technological will-o'-the-wisp.

For a clear, detailed look at the risks posed by driverless cars, read the new report, "Self-Driving Vehicles: The Threat to Consumers," by Harvey Rosenfield of Consumer Watchdog.

Federal Regulation Saves
Millions of Lives

SEPTEMBER 9, 2016

Fifty years ago this month (on September 9, 1966), President Lyndon Johnson signed into law the National Traffic and Motor Vehicle Safety Act that launched a great lifesaving program for the American people.

I was there that day at the White House at the invitation of President Johnson, who gave me one of the signing pens. In 1966, traffic fatalities reached 50,894, or *5.50 deaths* per 100 million vehicle miles traveled. By 2014, the loss of life was 32,675, or *1.07 fatalities* per 100 million vehicle miles traveled. A huge reduction!

This was an astounding success for the federal safety program, which included mandatory vehicle-safety standards (seat belts; airbags; better brakes, tires, and handling; among other advances) and upgraded driver- and highway-safety standards.

When the crashworthy standards were first proposed in 1967, Henry Ford II warned that they "would shut down the industry." Ten years later, on NBC's *Meet the Press*, he conceded, "We wouldn't have the kinds of safety built into automobiles that we have had unless there had been a federal law."

At the White House signing ceremony, I distributed a brief statement, requested the previous day by the *New York Times*, which said, "To translate potential into reality will require competent and vigorous administration of the laws and new manufacturing priorities by the auto industry."

Over the years, the political pressure of the almost always resistant auto industry stalled, slowed, and sometimes shut down National Highway Traffic Safety Administration (NHTSA) initiatives. Toady administrators taking orders from the auto companies' friends in Congress, such as Congressman John Dingell (D-MI) and the White House all slowed auto safety advances. Nonetheless, based on the comparative yardstick of fatalities per motor-vehicle miles traveled over the years, the Center for Auto Safety estimated 3.5 million lives saved between 1966 and 2014 in the United States.

Of course, the number of injuries prevented or diminished is even greater. The savings in hundreds of billions of dollars spent on crash consequences—such as property damage, medical expenses, wage losses, and less tangible costs such as family anguish and disruption are major additional benefits of rational regulation.

If the auto company bosses had liberated their own engineers and scientists and cooperated with the federal regulators, who early on were physicians and engineers, even more casualties would have been prevented.

Today, the challenges remain in the upgrading of the operational and safety aspects of motor vehicles, especially large trucks, improvements in highway infrastructure, and handling drivers distracted by cell phones or under the influence. Much is being written of futuristic autonomous vehicles. Don't be taken in by the hype or the arrogant reliance on algorithms. It will be many years, if ever, before the entire vehicle fleet is converted into unhackable driverless machines.

Meanwhile, modest semiautonomous braking systems, with drivers still at the steering wheel, are here and will improve. There will be other systems inviting the dependency of drivers, which will raise questions of ultimate control of a fast-moving vehicle.

Recent disclosures—the General Motors ignition-switch defect crime and Volkswagen's criminal manipulation of software regarding toxic emissions—demand the passage of a criminal penalty amendment to the 1966 safety law. Senators Richard Blumenthal (D-CT) and Edward Markey (D-MA) have introduced such a bill—S. 900—but it is blocked by soft-on-corporate-crime Republicans.

The consumer advocates' struggle to save lives on the highway, including those of pedestrians and motorcyclists, continues. Despite many innovations (see Rob Cirincione's report: *Innovation and Stagnation in Automotive Safety and Fuel Efficiency*) by the automotive suppliers, the bureaucratic auto companies still have that old "not-invented-here" syndrome bedeviling them.

Can a young person today, writing a book exposing an industry's chronic abuses, experience such a level of congressional action and recurrent media attention as was accorded me and my book *Unsafe at Any Speed*?

Very doubtful, without a brand-new Congress. Congress doesn't have enough senators or representatives like senators Warren Magnuson,

Abraham Ribicoff, and Gaylord Nelson and Congressman John Moss, who took on the auto giants and persisted until necessary legislation was enacted. There is less perceived rumble from the people than in the 1960s.

Also, a more corporate media gives us celebrity stories, sports, violent natural and man-made disasters, political horse races, and just plain fluff. News by citizen groups is not a media priority.

Democracy and its result—a more just society—is not a spectator sport. People have to organize to challenge the forces of injustice. As the great abolitionist Frederick Douglass said for the ages: "Power concedes nothing without a demand. Never has and never will."

Your Safety and Your Congress in 1965 and Now

DECEMBER 7, 2015

The fiftieth anniversary of my book *Unsafe at Any Speed*, which analysts associate with the launch of the modern consumer movement, prompts comparisons between 1965 and 2015.

The lifesaving impact of the book has been historic—it led Congress to pass highway and auto safety laws in 1966, creating an auto safety enforcement agency to lift up safety standards for motor vehicles. According to an analysis of deaths per mile driven by the Center for Auto Safety (CAS), "The 1966 federal laws, federal agency, and general measures they created have averted 3.5 million auto deaths over the past fifty years."

CAS executive director Clarence Ditlow declared that "3.5 million represents the difference between the number of deaths that there would have been if the death rate had stayed at 5.50 per 100 million VMT (vehicle miles traveled) in 1966 versus what it went down to in each subsequent year, falling to 1.07 by 2014. [Lives] have been saved by traffic laws (seat belt use, helmet and drunk driving laws), safer roads, vehicle safety standards and vehicle safety improvements spurred by consumer demand for more safety after *Unsafe at Any Speed*."

Of course, even more injuries were prevented or reduced in severity by these vehicle and highway safety advances.

How did this happen? As author and consumer advocate Mark Green writes, "The issue is not the size of government but how a smart democracy can successfully save millions of lives." It started with knowledge about the gap between cars, promoted for their style and horsepower, and what feasible safety devices were being left out of the vehicles by the auto industry bosses.

The more people knew, the more they questioned why their friends and relatives did not survive vehicle crashes. Congressional hearings, widely disseminated by the mass media, addressed this issue again and again. It was because the auto companies wanted to market anything but safety. It was also because there was no meaningful federal policy and program for highway safety, leaving it to the states, whose legislatures were uniformly under the control of industry lobbyists.

Unfortunately the insurance industry (with few exceptions, such as Liberty Mutual) focused on drivers and premiums but not getting safer vehicles on highways.

The winning combination included 1) Enough influential senior members of Congress, led by senators Abraham Ribicoff, Warren Magnuson, Gaylord Nelson, and Walter Mondale, along with Congressman John Moss; and 2) reporters such as the *Washington Post*'s Morton Mintz, *United Press*'s Patrick Sloyan, the *Detroit News*'s Bob Irvin, the *New Republic*'s James Ridgeway, and the *New York Times*' Walter Rugaber, all of whom stayed with the developing exposés week after week. There were also columns by the famous Drew Pearson that appeared in five hundred newspapers. Finally, there was President Lyndon Johnson and his chief of staff Joseph A. Califano, who encouraged Congress to act and then organized the signing ceremonies for the landmark auto safety legislation in the White House in September 1966.

It took only ten months between the appearance of *Unsafe at Any Speed* and the first regulation of the giant auto industry for safety and fuel economy.

All this movement to protect Americans from industry malfeasance would prove difficult today. Congress is a wholly owned subsidiary of big business. Reporters are not the same for lots of reasons beyond their control in the new-media business. Even after corporate crime and abuse is reported by leading newspapers, efforts in Congress to correct and reform sputter.

Congress has become the "graveyard" of our country's needed changes that are supported by a majority of the American people. Look at congressional deadlock on increasing the minimum wage; climate change; regulatory frameworks for biotechnology and nanotechnology; and infrastructure repairs of airports, bridges, and railways. Medical and hospital malpractice and overprescription of medication (including those that are antibiotic-resistant) and avoidable hospital-induced infections are together taking over a quarter of a million lives annually. Yet Congress does little to curb medical negligence. Both political parties are dialing daily for the same commercial dollars—not seriously championing advances in health and safety.

Yet it is still possible to make changes through Congress, which is made up of only 535 men and women who need your votes more than they need corporate lobbyists' money. One change after another long-overdue change can be achieved if the majority of the people want it. With this support, it takes 1 percent or less of the voters back home to organize and get Congress to do the people's bidding.

That 1 percent or less, sometimes far less, needs to spend a "hobby amount" of time each year (say three hundred to five hundred hours) organizing in every congressional district, and a "hobby amount" of money to maintain an office of three or four full-time advocates in each district.

How do I know this? First of all, it took less than that to make many important reforms and changes in American history. Second, our numerous citizen groups made changes in industry after industry—from coal to drug and food companies to the polluting chemical companies. And third, a handful of dedicated activists pushed Congress to create the Occupational Safety and Health Administration (OSHA) in 1970, to name just one of many small-group achievements.

So take heart, America! We have far more problems than we deserve and far more solutions on the shelf than we apply. That is the "democracy gap" that is being widened by the plutocrats and the oligarchs from Wall Street to Washington. A results-driven, democratic citizen resurgence would bring the best out of the American people, often with alliances between the left and right that are unstoppable. Visit nader.org for examples of what small numbers of activists with limited budgets have accomplished.

Enough! Stop More Giant Tractor-Trailers on Your Highways

JULY 2, 2015

Are you one of the millions of people in the United States who drives a car every day? How do you react to the trucking industry, whose lobbyists with ample campaign cash swarm over Congress, pressing for a rider to a transportation appropriations bill to be passed to overturn laws in thirty-nine states that currently ban unsafe *double thirty-three-foot* tractor-trailer combinations? What is your opinion of another provision in this bill to permanently increase truck-driver working and driving hours up to eighty-two hours per week, abolishing the "weekend off" for two nights of restorative rest? Or what is your view of various exemptions that allow current federal truck weight limits of 80,000 pounds to reach up to 129,000 pounds, further damaging roads and bridges already in need of repair? Or what about families whose loved ones are killed or suffer costly and disabling injuries only to discover that the truck or bus company responsible for the crash does not have enough insurance, because trucking industry lobbies, aided by their friends in Congress, are trying to freeze the absurdly low minimum insurance requirements? These assaults are being led by members of Congress who are owned by the trucking lobby that includes FedEx, UPS, and the American Trucking Associations with their ample campaign contributions.

Your replies, given polls going back twenty years, are likely to match the large majorities of people opposed to further unleashing more oversized, overweight trucks and tired truckers (see Parents Against Tired Truckers at trucksafety.org/tag/parents-against-tired-truckers) onto our roads.

Members of Congress owned by the trucking industry, such as Senator Susan Collins (R-ME) and Senator Richard Shelby (R-AL) (a states' rights advocate who should know better) pushed adoption of this rider in a Senate appropriations bill funding federal transportation and housing programs (HR 2577, which has already passed the House of Representatives) without any public input. Astonishingly, there have been no congressional hearings on the FedEx proposal to compel every state to allow double 33s! FedEx, UPS, the American Trucking Associations, and others are looking to attach the double 33s mandate to any legislation that has a chance of passing Congress in the next few weeks. The big trucking-industry lobbyists are now laser-focused on a truck safety bill that is being considered by the Senate Commerce, Science, and Transportation Committee next Wednesday, July 15. The truck safety bill will become part of the multiyear, multibillion-dollar highway and transit bill that Congress must act on before August 1, when highway construction funds are expected to run dry. Every bill moving through Congress is a target for attaching these antisafety provisions, so every member of Congress urgently needs to hear from constituents.

The Appropriations Committee chairman, Senator Thad Cochran (R-MS)—supported vigorously by Dick Hall, chairman of his state's Transportation Commission—voted against the trucking lobbies but lost the committee by one vote late in June. Fortunately, the Department of Transportation and President Obama oppose increasing truck hazards that affect other drivers and the highways themselves.

The fight to stop this highway space grab now goes to the Senate floor, where the Democrats and some Republicans will try to get this rider deleted. They have, led by senators Dianne Feinstein (D-CA), Richard Durbin (D-IL), and Tom Udall (D-NM), plenty of arguments. Listen to Jackie Gillan, president of Advocates for Highway and Auto Safety: "Over the past five years alone (2009–2013), fatalities from large truck crashes have increased by 17 percent, and injuries have increased by 28 percent. Every year, on average, there are four thousand people killed and one hundred thousand more injured in large truck crashes, which is equivalent to a major airplane crash every week of the year."

Imagine, the big trucking industry now wants to roll back protections in thirty-nine states, put longer double trailers on your roads, and cut back on giving truck drivers the rest they (and you) need.

Is there any limit on the supremacy of commercial greed over safety values? Go to these websites for details about what you can do and factual rebuttals of the freight industry's assertions that double 33s will result in fewer trucks on the road or that two trailer trucks are as safe as single-unit trucks:

http://saferoads.org/
http://trucksafety.org/tag/citizens-for-reliable-and-safe-highways/

In past battles with the powerful trucking industry and its insidious ally, the US Chamber of Commerce headed by Thomas Donohue (the former head of the American Trucking Associations), the railroads could be counted on to challenge the truck lobby. Solid freights using the railways make for safer roads and transport. Lately, however, the railroad interests have been less of a counter to the trucking industry, in part due to their investments in trucking operations.

So it's up to all of you who outnumber even the number of dollars spent each year on your members of Congress by the freight-industry coalition. Yes, there are far more automobile drivers than the mass of dollars that the trucking companies float on Capitol Hill. But unlike those corporations supplying campaign cash, you have power because you have the votes.

It should not take descriptions of grisly casualties in crashes with overturned cars and trailer trucks to motivate automobile drivers, the people whose lives are at stake when roads become less safe. You've driven by these dreadful roadside scenes, even if you haven't actually experienced them.

You can win this fight if you just spend a little time calling the senators and representatives who are advocating for the double trailers and weaker tired-trucker rules. Ask them either by telephone, letter, or email to send you a letter reporting how much money they have taken from the trucking companies and their allies over the past five years. They have to report this information to the Federal Election Commission.

Tell your members of Congress what kind of safety you want for you and your families by demanding safer, tougher rules for giant trucks and their loads, braking systems, and adequately rested drivers—not a rollback!

Call the congressional switchboard number (202-224-3121) and ask the always polite operator to transfer you to the senators or representatives whom you wish to admonish and advise. After all, if they are supposed to work for you, they need reminding that you'll remember in November.

Nuclear Power's Insanities—
Taxpayer-Guaranteed

SEPTEMBER 5, 2014

The Nuclear Energy Institute (NEI)—the corporate lobbyist in Washington, DC, for the disintegrating atomic-power industry—doesn't have to worry about repercussions from the negative impacts of nuclear power. For nuclear power is a government- and taxpayer-guaranteed boondoggle whose staggering costs, incurred and deferred, are absorbed by American taxpayers via a supine government regulatory and subsidy apparatus.

So if you go to work at the NEI and you read about the absence of any permanent radioactive waste storage site, no problem, the government and taxpayers are responsible for transporting and safeguarding that lethal garbage for centuries.

If your reactors experience ever-larger cost overruns and delays, as is now happening with two new reactors in South Carolina, no problem, the supine state regulatory commissions will just pass the bill on to consumers, despite the fact that consumers receive no electricity from these unfinished plants.

If these plants, and two others in Georgia under construction, experience financial squeezes from Wall Street, no problem, a supine Congress has already passed ample taxpayer loan guarantees that make Uncle Sam (you, the taxpayer) bear the cost of the risk.

If there were to be an accident such as the one that happened in Fukushima, Japan, no problem, under the Price-Anderson Act, the government and taxpayers bear the cost of the vast amount of damage from any nuclear power plant meltdown. To put this cost into perspective, a report by the Atomic Energy Commission about fifty years ago estimated that a Class 9 meltdown could make an area "the size of Pennsylvania" uninhabitable.

Why do we stand for such a doomsday technology all over America that is uneconomic, uninsurable, unsafe, unnecessary (it can't compete with energy conservation and renewable energies), unevacuable (try evacuating the greater New York City area from a disaster at the two Indian Point

plants thirty miles from Manhattan) and unprotectable (either from sabotage or earthquake)?

S. David Freeman, the famous energy engineer and lawyer, who has
run four giant utilities (the Tennessee Valley Authority; the Sacramento
Municipal Utility Department complex, where he closed the Rancho
Seco Nuclear Plant; the New York Power Authority, and the Los Angeles
Department of Water and Power) sums up the history of nuclear power
this way: "Nuclear power, promoted as too cheap to meter, turned out to
be too expensive to use, the road to nuclear proliferation, and the creator
of radioactive trash that has no place to go." Right-wing conservatives and
libertarians call it extreme "crony capitalism."

Nuclear power plants are shutting down. In 2013, four reactors shut
down: Crystal River 3, Kewaunee, San Onofre 2, and San Onofre 3. Now,
Michael Peck, a senior federal nuclear expert, is urging that the last nuke
plant left in California, Diablo Canyon, be shut down until the Nuclear
Regulatory Commission can demonstrate that the two reactors at this site
can withstand shaking from three nearby earthquake faults.

Meanwhile, the human, environmental, and economic disasters at
Japan's Fukushima Daiichi power plants keep metastasizing. Scientists are
producing studies that show serious biological effects (genetic damage and
mutation rates) of radiation on plant, insect, and bird life in and around
the large, cordoned-off, uninhabitable area surrounding these shut-down
reactors. The giant, politically influential electric utility company underestimated the likelihood of a powerful earthquake and tsunami.

In the early 1970s, the industry and its governmental patrons were
expecting one thousand nuclear plants—one hundred of them along the
California coast—to be operating by the year 2000. Instead, a little more
than a hundred reactors were built nationwide and, as of 2014, only a little
more than one hundred are operable reactors, many of which are beyond
their initial forty-year licensed periods.

The pitfalls are real and numerous. In addition to growing public opposition and lower-priced natural gas attracting electric utilities, there are
the ever-present, skyrocketing costs and delays of construction and repair
and the question of where to store nuclear waste. These costs are what
make Wall Street financiers turn their backs on nuclear power unless the
industry can ram tens of billions of dollars more into government and
taxpayer loan guarantees through Congress.

And what is all this nuclear technology, from the uranium mines to the nuclear plants to the still-absent waste storage dumps, for? To boil water!

These are the tragic follies when the corporate masters and their political minions, who are ready and willing to guarantee taxpayer funding, have no "skin in the game." This kind of staggering power without responsibility is indeed radioactive.

Congressman Dingell: Down on Motor Vehicle Safety

FEBRUARY 27, 2014

Congressman John Dingell (D-MI), the longest-serving member of Congress in history (fifty-nine years), did much good and much bad. Reports of his retirement stressed his work in championing Medicare, civil rights legislation, and several environmental laws. Less noticed was his vigorous oversight and investigations of federal departments and agencies that were lax, riven with conflicts of interest, or mistreated whistleblowers.

But Dingell had another, darker side to his otherwise liberal image. He was totally and cruelly indentured to the auto industry even though he was from an overwhelmingly safe Democratic district. More than any other lawmaker, Democratic or Republican, he fought to make sure that the auto Goliaths got their way in Congress and at the Environmental Protection Agency and Department of Transportation.

I observed his tenacity in delaying the issuance of the lifesaving airbag standard, in opposing noxious emission controls on motor vehicles, and, most irrationally, in freezing fuel-efficiency rules for many years. He did this with sheer stubborn willpower and by forging a mutually destructive alliance between the Big Three auto companies—General Motors (GM), Ford, and Chrysler—and the United Auto Workers (UAW).

In the greatest ironies of his lengthy career, he helped mightily in sheltering the technological stagnation of Detroit's auto barons from innovation-advancing regulation that eventually cost them massive market share to more fuel-efficient and higher-quality foreign imports from Germany and Japan. This also cost the UAW tens of thousands of jobs.

When, in recent years, the domestic auto industry's demise was finally clear to him, he began to relent on fuel efficiency, but it was too late to save the industry from its own mismanagement and illusions.

The resultant impact on the health and safety of the American people was his most lasting, devastating legacy. Year after year people breathed more vehicle emissions and lost their lives or were injured in less safe vehicles because of Mr. Dingell's huge presence on Capitol Hill. He upset the balance in his party and thereby made his Republican colleagues more powerful in their opposition to updating health and safety rules.

At his retirement announcement, Mr. Dingell described service in Congress these days as "obnoxious" because of "the acrimony and the bitterness" and the lack of productivity. Back in the 1970s, and after he took over the chair of the powerful House Energy and Commerce Committee in 1981 from the retiring great congressman John Moss (D-CA), other consumer advocates and I experienced his "obnoxious" and exclusionary dictatorial regime laced with exceedingly foul language directed to anyone who dared criticize him from the civic community.

Congressman Dingell knows politics, however. He is keeping his seat in the family. His wife Deborah Dingell will announce her candidacy to replace him very shortly and is considered a shoo-in. At age sixty, she could complete a full century of Dingells by 2033—John Dingell's father, a New Deal liberal and advocate of universal Medicare, was elected in 1933.

Deborah Dingell, a former GM lobbyist, is an irreverent soul, even chiding her often grumpy husband at public dinners when he did not hide his disdain for people in attendance. She may surprise us yet by tying her experience in politics, her contacts with high-ranking Democrats, and her independent personality to some good works.

Asked this week by the *Washington Post* whether the condition in Congress "is fixable," he replied fundamentally: "There's only one person that can fix it, and there's only one group of people that can answer that question, and that's the voters. If they want it to change, it will change."

Yes, Congressman Dingell, it will change, but only if we have a more competitive democracy with more choices of candidates and more voices for the voters.

(See competitivedemocracy.org and ballot-access.org for more information.) Party and candidate dynasties are not compatible with democratic elections.

Climate Disasters—Ending
Congressional Stupor Now!

FEBRUARY 8, 2014

Every year brings the world more climatological science showing that man-made climate change, or overall global warming, is chronically worsening.

Every year, from Antarctica to Greenland, from the Andes to Alaska, the ice is melting, the permafrost is melting, and very soon the Arctic may have an unprecedented ice-free season. Every year, more and more companies are speaking out on how climate change is damaging their businesses. Insurance companies were in the lead on sounding the alarm on global warming. Just a few days ago, Coca-Cola's vice president for environment and water resources, Jeffrey Seabright, told the *New York Times* that "increased droughts, more unpredictable variability, 100-year floods every two years" were affecting the supply of sugarcane and sugar beets, "as well as citrus for [Coca-Cola's] fruit juices."

Every year, companies quit the climate-denying US Chamber of Commerce and instead attend conferences for big businesses and politicians on the threat of climate change at places like the annual World Economic Forum in Davos, Switzerland.

Every year, more mainstream and conservative economists and companies declare their support for a carbon tax.

In Washington, Jim Yong Kim, president of the World Bank, has put climate change center stage for becoming what he said is a chief contributor to rising global poverty rates.

Every year, there are more demonstrations and marches of people and students around the world demanding action, conversion to renewable energies, and conservation efficiencies. University students are increasingly demanding their schools' divestment of stock from fossil fuel companies.

Every year, it seems records are being set for sea-level elevation, furious storm surges, heat waves, floods, typhoons, and droughts.

Yet every year one institution allows *no* change in its political climate; nothing is warming up our Congress of 535 legislators who are split between believers and disbelievers on the climate change crises. The result is worse than gridlock; it has become somnolence.

While people may become more frugal in their energy consumption and while businesses may use more renewable energy, a comprehensive national energy conversion mission, reflecting the urgency of action, *has to go through Congress.*

Omnicidal as it is, climate change has been taken off the table on Capitol Hill. Yes, there are some bills languishing in the hopper, some statements in the *Congressional Record*, but overall, for different Democratic and Republican reasons, Congress has gone AWOL since the energy bill was blocked in the Senate seven years ago.

The Republicans are aggressive climate-change deniers. Senator James Inhofe (R-OK) calls global warming a massive hoax and is willing to debate any Democrat. Meanwhile, by and large, most Democrats are concerned but unwilling to make it a campaign or electoral issue. They're even unwilling to take on Mr. Inhofe. Somehow, they've myopically convinced themselves— even those with grandchildren—that the fast-looming peril provides no net electoral or campaign-cash advantages.

This shocking congressional bubble has avoided the intense focus of the environmental lobby. Astonishingly, there are fewer than a half dozen scattered lobbyists in Washington, DC, working in personam and full-time on Congress and its role in blocking action regarding climate change.

To open up this critical Khyber Pass called Congress, we need, at minimum, a new hundred-person lobbying organization with laser-beam daily focus on every member of the Senate and the House of Representatives. This group would have the requisite scientific, legal, organizing, public relations, and political experience. Every day, the 535 members of our national legislature would feel the light, the heat, and the might of what these hundred advocates unleash directly and indirectly.

The Pentagon's study a decade ago—with its dire message that climate change is a national-security priority—would be brought to bear. The federal government's procurement budget would be steered toward renewable fuel and efficiency specifications for the energy it purchases. The protest activity at the grassroots, which now bursts mostly into the ether, would be sharply redirected to each member of Congress.

The congressional hearings would garner regular, intensive, and productive national attention. The electoral campaigns of both parties would not be allowed to sideline this giant backlash from nature so abused by humankind.

Where would the $25 million annual budget come from for such a lobbying group working to prevent trillions of dollars and millions of lives from being lost? The question is almost absurd were it not for the bizarre aversion to this focus by well-heeled and leading advocates of addressing climate change.

Megabillionaire Michael Bloomberg, just named the United Nations special envoy for climate change and cities, is already funding efforts to reduce coal usage and could write the check out of his hip pocket. Billionaire Tom Steyer, a proven environmentalist from California and a big-time opponent of the Keystone XL Pipeline from Canada, could also handily write the check.

Very wealthy Henry M. Paulson Jr.—former head of Goldman Sachs and US Treasury Department secretary, who is working with Bloomberg and Steyer to commission an economic study on the financial risks connected to climate change, region by region, across the US economy—could also write the check.

And don't forget Al Gore, the leading global publicist of what climatologist Lonnie Thompson of Ohio State University called a "clear and present danger to civilization." Former senator Gore—who received the Nobel Prize in 2007 for highlighting the perils of global warming and climate change—could also fund and lead such a group.

Why, readers may ask, am I suggesting a sum small enough that one person could foot the bill for such a portentous peril? Because small sums are better at shaming all those well-endowed institutions and individuals who know better but inexplicably have not transformed their concerns into really powerful, serious pursuits for the human race and its more vulnerable posterity.

The Fukushima Secrecy Syndrome—
from Japan to America

JANUARY 24, 2014

Last month, the ruling Japanese coalition parties quickly rammed through Parliament a state-secrets law. We Americans better take notice.

Under its provisions, the government alone decides what are state secrets, and any civil servants who divulge any "secrets" can be jailed for up to ten years. Journalists caught in the web of this vaguely defined law can be jailed for up to five years.

Government officials have been upset at the constant disclosures of their laxity by regulatory officials before and after the 2011 disaster at the Fukushima Daiichi Nuclear Power Plant, operated by Tokyo Electric Power Company (TEPCO).

Week after week, reports appear in the press revealing the seriousness of the contaminated water flow, the inaccessible radioactive material deep inside these reactors, and the need to stop these leaking sites from further poisoning the land, food, and ocean. Officials now estimate that it could take up to forty years to clean up and decommission the reactors.

Other factors are also feeding this sure sign of a democratic setback. Militarism is raising its democracy-menacing head, prompted by friction with China over the South China Sea. Dismayingly, US militarists are pushing for a larger Japanese military budget. China is the latest national security justification for our "pivot to East Asia," provoked in part by our military-industrial complex.

Draconian secrecy in government and fast-tracking bills through legislative bodies are bad omens for freedom of the Japanese press and freedom to dissent by the Japanese people. Freedom of information and robust debate (the latter cut off sharply by Japan's Parliament on December 5, 2013) are the currencies of democracy.

There is good reason why the *New York Times* continues to cover the deteriorating conditions in the desolate, evacuated Fukushima area. Our country has licensed many reactors here with the same designs and many of the same inadequate safety and inspection standards. Some reactors here are near earthquake faults with surrounding populations that cannot be safely evacuated in case of serious damage to the electric plant. The two aging Indian Point reactors that are thirty miles north of New York City are a case in point.

The less we are allowed to know about the past and present conditions of Fukushima, the less we will learn about atomic reactors in our own country.

Fortunately many of Japan's most famous scientists, including Nobel laureates Toshihide Maskawa and Hideki Shirakawa, have led the opposition against this new state-secrecy legislation with three thousand academics signing a public letter of protest. These scientists and academics declared that the government's secrecy law "threatens the pacifist principles and fundamental human rights established by the constitution and should be rejected immediately."

Following this statement, the Japan Scientists' Association and Japan's mass media companies, citizen associations, lawyers' organizations, and some regional legislatures opposed the legislation. Polls show the public also opposes this attack on democracy. The present ruling parties remain adamant. They cite as reasons for state secrecy "national security and fighting terrorism." Sound familiar?

History is always present in the minds of many Japanese people. They know what happened in Japan when the unchallenged slide toward militarization of Japanese society led to the intimidating tyranny that drove the invasion of China, Korea, and Southeast Asia before and after Pearl Harbor. By 1945, Japan was in ruins, ending with Hiroshima and Nagasaki.

The American people have to be alert to our government's needless military and political provocations of China, which is worried about encirclement by surrounding US-allied nations and US air and sea power. Washington might be better to turn its immediate attention to US trade policies that have facilitated US companies shipping American jobs and whole industries to China.

The Obama administration must become more alert to authoritarian trends in Japan that its policies have been either encouraging or knowingly ignoring—often behind the curtain of our own chronic secrecy.

The lessons of history beckon.

Fracking's Lure, Trap, and
Endless Damage

DECEMBER 13, 2012

Say what you will about Yoko Ono's art; there is no denying that she is unique. Who else would put several $100,000 full-page notices in the *New York Times* displaying only the word "Peace" or "Imagine Peace" in small type with the rest of the page blank? No elaboration, no examples of the ravages of war or mention of people "waging peace" around the country and world. Inscrutable, yes. Effective, who knows, except maybe Yoko Ono?

Well, in the December 10 issue of the *Times* there appeared a most un-Yoko-type message. And this one wasted no space with the headline "Governor Cuomo: Imagine there's no fracking." The ad, commissioned by her and her son, Sean Lennon, contained a graphic case against fracking designed to get New Yorkers to urge the governor to ban fracking and make permanent the moratorium first established by former New York governor David Paterson. The moratorium was in place pending further scientific studies regarding the environmental and health impact of drilling deep into the Marcellus Shale deposits underneath a large portion of the state.

The gas companies are putting heavy pressure on Governor Cuomo to join Pennsylvania, which is already suffering the ravages of fracking. Landowners in Pennsylvania and in other states where fracking is permitted now realize that their water was contaminated by chemicals used in the fracking process and leaked natural gas from fractured shale deposits.

There also exists a formidable coalition of government officials, physicians, scientists at Cornell, civic groups, farmers, and other diverse opponents fighting against this hydrofracking. The relentlessly factual Walter Hang, president of Toxics Targeting in Ithaca, New York, is one of the most effective environmentalists opposing fracking.

Of course, on the other side are the oil and gas industries pursuing profits, landowners seeking royalties (though the fine-print contracts may rise up to bite them), and upstate laborers hoping for employment. The

gas industry publicists, who exaggerate the benefits to the local economies, ignore the short-term nature of most of the jobs and the costly, toxic
air, water, and land destruction fracking leaves behind.

The fight against fracking in New York is like the recurrent struggle put
on by the taxpayer-subsidized fossil fuel and nuclear industries that want
to dominate energy policies in government and push the safer alternatives
out of the way because energy efficiency and renewable energy don't make
profits for them. As Yoko and Sean point out, through their new group
Artists Against Fracking, by insulating buildings, for example, they could
"save far more energy and create far more jobs than fracking [can pro-
duce], plus save consumers money forever."

Industry engineering manuals portray the immense complexity of fracturing technology, the huge amount of water used per well, the pipelines
and compressor stations, the congested truck traffic, the dozens of chemicals needed in the water to draw out the gas vertically and horizontally
under the surface of the land. These materials leave out the grim emerging
reality that is memorably portrayed in Josh Fox's documentary *Gasland*.

Hydrofracking, whose side effects haven't been fully vetted, is a new
industrial method for obtaining natural gas. Instead of seeking these
deposits, we should pursue alternative energy sources. Think of solar
energy—dutifully, naturally providing most of the energy needed, from
absolute zero, to make the Earth habitable. The rest is up to *Homo sapiens*—a species that must be giving Mother Sun the fits over not adapting
its energy for efficient, safe daily uses.

We need to remember Ben Franklin, our frugal forebear who coined the
phrase "a penny saved is a penny earned." Today he would say "a trillion
BTUs saved is a trillion BTUs earned." The problem is that reducing waste
is not encouraged by present perverse market and regulatory incentives.

Despite progress, we are far less energy-efficient than Western Europe
or Japan. Germany is way ahead of us in both energy conservation and
renewable energy. There, nuclear power is being phased out. And higher
prices discourage use of fossil fuels. There is growing support for a carbon
tax in the US, including among some leading corporate chieftains, but the
message hasn't reached the lawmakers in Congress. Too many of them are
marinated in oil.

Your tax dollars helped develop fracturing technology that, if not
stopped, will unleash its furies all over the world. There are hydrocarbons

everywhere. Methane, many times worse a greenhouse gas than carbon dioxide, will be released in excess, among other gases. The regulators are not keeping up.

But the sun is everywhere in many forms—solar thermal energy, photovoltaics, passive solar architecture, wind power, wave power, non-corn biomass that doesn't compete with food supplies or raise food prices. As I said years ago, "If Exxon owned the sun, we'd have solar energy very quickly."

Therein is the rub. What is best for a planet with a decentralized, job-producing, safe, efficient, inexhaustible form of energy (at least for three billion more years) does not yet have the political muscle to go to the top of the US's energy priority ladder. The concentrated profits and the limited energy infrastructure are in the grip of the Chevrons and the Peabody Energies.

But history is not on their side. Countries with minimal fossils fuels are leading the way with renewables. Post–Fukushima disaster, Japan is upping the ante on conservation and renewables. Climate changes and natural disasters will wake up the rest of the world. Let's act to make it sooner rather than later.

The latest bulletin from the indefatigable Walter Hang alerts people to protest that the New York State Department of Health review is now "being conducted in total secrecy without any public participation." He believes Mr. Cuomo will make his decision within three months and urges you to call the governor's office.

The Rise of Reuse

MAY 22, 2012

Last week I read that the glitzy world of digital reality created instant multimillionaires and several billionaires when Facebook went public selling shares.

Last week I also noted the important real-world problem of some 250 million tons of solid waste a year in our country alone.

Guess which "world" gets the most investment, status, fame, klieg lights, and attention of the skilled classes and the power structure?

Guess which world is more important for our well-being and that of the planet?

You've heard of CEO Mark Zuckerberg and Facebook's nine hundred million users exchanging gossip and other personal pleasantries or worries through a medium that inflates narcissism.

You've probably not heard of Ben Rose of the New York City Materials Exchange Development Program (NYC MEDP) or the equivalent organization in your community providing services to thousands of charitable nonprofit groups that promote the donation and reuse of materials to avoid incineration, landfilling, and recycling.

To grasp the enormity of modern society's waste products, Ann Leonard created a sparkling website, visited by millions of people (storyofstuff.org). She also recently published a popular book titled *The Story of Stuff* that details every aspect of your environment and physical being. Air, water, food, soil, and even your genes absorb the byproducts of processing mountains of stuff. The results are not pretty.

While recycling efforts in cities like San Francisco, Vancouver, and Los Angeles rise above 50 percent, New York City has been slipping behind its own 2002 level and is still struggling to reach 20 percent. New York City has been a leader in improving air quality and reducing greenhouse gas emissions, but it still has dreaded incinerators producing toxic air and toxic residues.

In the early nineties, pragmatic environmental scientist and professor Barry Commoner demonstrated in two operational pilot projects that the city could reach a residential recycling level of nearly 100 percent. Unfortunately, New York City missed a chance to become a world leader in recycling when its leaders, beginning with Mayor Rudolph Giuliani, declined to establish a citywide recycling program based on Professor Commoner's model.

New York City recycling still hasn't recovered from that devastatingly wrongheaded decision. But politicians and corporations cannot stop a superior environmental cycle, presently driven by charitable associations, which, in Mr. Rose's words, are "nimbly accepting, exchanging, and distributing thousands of tons of reusable material each year," as they have done for generations, "all the while contributing to the social, economic, and environmental fabric of New York City." Over the decades, the recipients have been communities in need, such as homeless shelters and poor populations.

The NYC MEDP now sees a great potential to "organize, grow, and advocate for the practice of donating and reusing materials for the benefit of all New Yorkers," creating local jobs and adding productivity without any tax dollars. They are rediscovering the past of a thrifty culture and expanding it mightily to contribute to the neighborhood and economic landscape.

Donating materials instead of trashing or recycling them enlarges the gifting culture and the beneficial human interactions that follow. As Ben Rose notes: "In contrast to recycling, where used materials are broken down into their raw elements to make new items, reuse takes useful products and exchanges them without reprocessing, thus saving time, money, energy, and valuable resources."

The obstacles are obvious. First, a throwaway economy of waste is profitable for sellers who want you to keep throwing away and buying. They plan product obsolescence and lure consumers with the convenience of disposable products. So we have to change habits: become more cunning about what manufacturers and vendors are up to and expand secondhand, reuse, and materials-exchange programs.

What are reusable materials? Just about everything you purchase that doesn't spoil or perish. Clothing, furniture, books, bicycles, containers, computers, tools, surplus construction materials, and things you buy or grow that you do not use. Reuse outlets include Goodwill or thrift stores, charitable book and clothing drives, ecology centers, and creative arts programs.

Nothing less than a new age for a burgeoning subeconomy of reusable products and materials is being envisioned by the collaborative likes of the New York City Sanitation Department and the City College of New York's civil engineering department. Collecting data that shows how much energy is saved, how many jobs can be created, how much better pricing systems can be, and how much solid waste can be prevented will elevate this subject and its social status within the zero-waste movement. We should aspire to use resources, in the words of author and activist Paul Hawken, "ten to one hundred times more productively."

Other countries are advancing in the reuse sector in ways we can learn from immediately. Holland is starting numerous "repair cafes" that are attracting increasing interest in "fixing" rather than dumping. These used to be called "fix-it shops" in the US before the advent of our throw-away-happy corporate culture.

For more information visit nycmedp.org.

5.

ON CORPORATE CRIME AND CORPORATE WELFARE

Repudiating the Myths of Market Fundamentalism and the Corporate Coercions It Masks and Enables

JANUARY 20, 2022

1. There can be no free market when companies engage in monopolistic or anticompetitive activity and systems.

2. There can be no free market when companies lie, cheat, and steal as a way of doing business (e.g., mortgage rackets and payday loans) and systematically engage in deceptive advertising (as described in *Pills That Don't Work*, by Dr. Sidney Wolfe, Public Citizen Health Research Group).

3. There can be no free market when companies demand and lobby for subsidies, handouts, giveaways, and bailouts (most notoriously, the bastion of self-styled free-market fundamentalism that is Wall Street). The New York Stock Exchange's own private regulations are far-reaching but do little to curb Wall Street excesses. The manipulation of cost/benefit formulas is legion, and exaggerated costs often go unrebutted!

4. There can be no free market when certain companies demand preferential tax avoidance treatment or engage in systematized tax evasion (as in the offshore rackets). Amazon received billions of dollars in benefits because of the unfair, competitive avoidance of sales taxes, while brick-and-mortar stores, including small businesses, had to pay 6–8 percent sales tax (plus property taxes). Only recently have some online sales been upheld by the Supreme Court. This politically lobbied unfair advantage helped mightily to create the multiheaded Amazon monster. Or shall we use the name Moloch?

5. There can assuredly be no free market when there is no freedom of contract for the consumer or buyer or franchisee. Herein lies the overpowering phenomenon of contract peonage or contract servitude known as the fine-print, standard-form contract, which is so coercively

tyrannical and so nonconsensual that a leading authority on contracts, Professor Margaret Radin, called them "torts" in her seminal book *Boilerplate*. These "mice-print contracts," in the words of Senator Elizabeth Warren, block use of the courts (compulsory arbitration), impose "unilateral modification changes by the vendor," waive constitutional rights such as trial by jury, and much more. Companies do not compete over fine print, further eliminating choice. (See the article "Land of the Lawless" in the Spring 2018 *Lapham's Quarterly*).

6. There can be no free market when there is systemic corporate crime, fraud, and abuse (see *Corporate Crime Reporter*). With Medicare being drained of some $60 billion in vendor fraud a year, Medicare is not really benefitting from the free market. This is a big area—corporate crime as a way of doing business over time (see Volkswagen, General Motors, and Toyota, whose recently concealed defects, along with the Takata airbag cover-up, are troubling illustrations of lawlessness). So are financial and insurance rackets and forced purchases (Wells Fargo) imposed by leading companies on and off Wall Street. Applied mathematician and Harvard professor Malcolm Sparrow estimates, at minimum, that computerized billing fraud and abuse in the so-called health care industry totals 10 percent of all sales on about $335 billion this year (see his book *License to Steal*). Then there is the massive matter of harmful diseconomies—environmental, occupational, and planetary damage to people, species, and the natural world.

7. Deliberate complexity to confuse, wear down, and deceive consumers is rampant and getting worse. Too many contrived choices, most of them trivial, lead to a cognitive dissonance by consumers who basically signal "I don't know, take me, I'm yours." This is also part of what is known as Chamberlain's theory of monopolistic competition (as with brand-name advertising). Complexity includes hiding the actual price and other terms of the transaction before the consumer clicks or signs on the bottom line.

8. Jurisdictional escapes—i.e., doing bad things but being outside the arm of the law or jurisdiction—are increasingly becoming common practice for foreign and domestic companies and their subsidiaries

(shell companies) that are located in permissive tax havens. This has become another discrediting element of free-market fundamentalism.

9. Free-market fundamentalists claim that they observe the laws of the land—they are not anarchistic; they play by the rules. Market actions powerfully make the rules through government (the campaign money, lobbying, the corporate state, tort deform). Moreover, there are large gaps of lawlessness, meaning there are deliberately no laws, or the laws are essentially dead letters. Recall the repeal of usury laws in almost all the states by corporate pressure during the 1970s. Nonstop coercive robocalling circumvents no-call-list enforcement and saturates people's phones.

10. There are many more corporate-bred distortions and destructions of free market operations. Theoretical free markets themselves can still be damaging and need boundaries (regulation when banks and insurers reject poorer people as a class).

Market fundamentalism's ideological tyranny keeps on metastasizing, afflicting the young, silencing politicians and hoodwinking the media as its propagandists avail themselves of the *free* public airwaves (talk about nonmarket pricing).

Done clearly, concisely, with illustrations and some galvanizing narratives as to the critical importance of displacing this fundamentalism *as a force*, both economically and politically, that perpetuates *controlling processes* and corporate propaganda, this gathering and the subsequent publications of its proceedings can plant many seeds for cultivation by realistic minds and provide consequential leverage!

Too many progressives don't have a handle on the arguments that must be made to counter market fundamentalism. (Consider the presently asserted "too much government regulation" or "deregulation" when it's really government-sanctioned corporate regulation, or "just too liberal for the congressional district" or "socialistic" uttered by corporate socialists etc.).

Watch the Destroying the Myths of Market Fundamentalism Conference from October 2018 here: https://www.c-span.org/video/?453260-3/center-study-responsive-law-conference-part-1&event=453260&playEvent.

Watch Out for Big Corporations and Dangerous Politicians Breaking Our Established Norms

AUGUST 12, 2022

Norms, in a society or culture, are the accepted ways of behavior we grow up observing and learning in our everyday lives. Norms are rarely backed up by laws, though when norms are grossly violated, calls for legislation may ensue.

In our country, voluntarily recognized fundamental norms have been breaking down. The chief impetus for this collapse is the ascending supremacy of commercial power over civic values. The surrender of the latter to the former in sector after sector has spelled the decline of our country as measured by its own promise and pretensions. Compared to seventy years ago, there are almost no commercial-free zones anymore. Almost everything is for sale—or should be, according to the minds of dogmatic free-market fundamentalists and free-market apologists like Milton Friedman and his disciples.

Let's be specific. When I was a schoolboy in the 1940s, the top CEOs of the largest Fortune 300 companies kept their pay at about twelve times the salary of the average worker in their business. If any CEO had sought to increase that ratio to fifty or three hundred times, he would be roundly condemned, from the pulpits to the boards of directors to civic and charitable groups. In those days, CEOs also did not want to arouse the anger of their industrial labor unions or encourage workers to demand more pay in response.

Now CEOs of major companies pay themselves, via a rubber-stamp board of directors, three hundred or more times the average worker's salary. Some are more extreme, such as Apple's CEO Tim Cook, whose pay package this year comes down to $833 a *minute* on a forty-hour week. Hardly a squeak of objection is heard from anyone. Hey, you didn't know? "Grab whatever you can get" is the mantra of greedy CEOs. Absent any laws on maximum income, toss modest pay equity out the window (see *The Case for a Maximum Wage*, by Sam Pizzigati, 2018).

By contrast, it used to be an unchallenged norm to pay women less for doing the same work as men. No more. In 1963 the Federal Equal Pay Act made it illegal to pay women lower wages than men.

It used to be against strict social norms for companies to sell directly to children, bypassing their parents to exploit youngsters' vulnerabilities. For one, little kids cannot distinguish between ads and programming. Now commercial marketing directly to children—junk food and drink, toxic medicines and cosmetics, harmful toys, violent entertainment videos, and more—is a business approaching a half trillion dollars a year. The iPhone doubles down as a gateway to this electronic child molestation.

The blasphemy of yesterday has become commonplace today.

Gambling used to evoke strong moral condemnation, thereby driving it underground to the back of newsstand stores, often called the "numbers racket." Now gambling is at your fingertips via your computer. State governments run lotteries. Business is moving big-time into sports gambling. Casinos are everywhere.

The norms against gambling were promoted by organized religion. When the churches started allowing Big Bingo in their basements, the defenses against aboveground, organized gambling (apart from Las Vegas) began to crumble. The gambling boosters claimed it would produce tax revenue and help the elderly. This deception was part of the pitch by the builders of the first casinos in Atlantic City, New Jersey. Now gambling casinos are described as economic development engines, however fraudulent that assertion is seen by economists.

Far from age-old stigmas, a failed gambling czar was selected (by the Electoral College) as US president in 2016. He broke more norms and laws daily than all previous presidents, and until recently has gotten away with these violations.

College sports stars have started selling their likenesses and other emblems—something that for years was verboten and cause for expulsion.

Historically, there have been cruel norms beyond avarice. Some were ensconced in law—such as legalized slavery before the Civil War.

Child labor in dungeon-like factories was not only legal, it was accepted as a norm. It has been illegal for almost a century since the law memorialized the new norm that youngsters should be going to schools instead of going to sweatshops.

It's good to think about norms—big and small—as yardsticks of what kind of society we want. Not doing so, over time, can result in deeply recognized norms, such as the protection of the personal privacies of the young and old being smashed to smithereens by Facebook, Instagram, and other internet barons who make huge profits by getting, for free, their customers' detailed personal information every day, which is then sold to advertisers.

Because of the unbridled political power of corporatism and other lawless forces, the rule of law cannot begin to catch up with protecting good norms or replacing cruel norms. This challenge first rests on us—on our reinvigorating civic and educational institutions, on our bar associations, our faith groups, and our family circles.

That is why it is so important for active citizens—those who strive to get, for example, health, safety, and economic protection standards made into law by petitions, lawsuits, marches, writings, or lobbying—not to despair when they so often lose these battles. For even if they do not prevail, they are keeping alive the public, decent, respectful, underlying norms of our society that can be advanced and ultimately provided with legal protections.

There must be some crucial norms you see being fractured or weakened. Speak up about them, otherwise you'll find them going, going, gone. It is time to reverse the lowering of expectations by people. Even big historic norms are under systemic assault, like the vendors' drive to reject cash or check as payment in favor of the incarcerating credit card payment-system gulag. Or the Trump GOP's massive lies about voter fraud in order for dangerous Republican extremists to enact legislation to obstruct voting and honest vote counting.

California Advocates Counterattack Corporate Crime and Control

FEBRUARY 18, 2022

Want to unite conservatives and liberals in the red and blue states? Just mention those unreadable computer-generated bills we all get online or in the mail. Overflowing with abbreviations and codes, they are inscrutable, especially health care bills.

If you call the vendors for an explanation, be prepared to wait and wait and wait for any human being to answer or call back, even after you've pushed all the required buttons to leave a voicemail message. The vendors are counting on you to surrender as you mumble that you've got better things to do with your time.

If you're lucky enough to get a human and you disagree about the bill, you know that if you persist against their assurances of accuracy, your credit score can go down. Algorithms can be made to work so impersonally.

A few months ago, Michelle Singletary, currently the syndicated consumer columnist for the *Washington Post*, tried to correct errors in her credit bureau's file. She described trying to get through to them as a "nightmare," a "journey to automation hell." Service by algorithm doesn't differentiate between ordinary and prominent customers. Everyone gets the same shaft.

One of the worst companies in not getting back to customer inquiries or complaints is the Bank of America. Sources tell us the bank has algorithms that measure how long they can keep customers waiting so as to have fewer workers needed to answer the calls.

The very design of computerized bills is a premeditated endeavor by the cheaters. The nation's expert, applied mathematician Malcolm Sparrow—a Harvard professor—wrote an entire book on this subject titled *License to Steal* in which he conservatively estimated that billing fraud in the health care industry makes up 10 percent of all expenses—or about $360 *billion* this year alone!

The anonymous cheaters, hiding behind the corporate web of complexity, keep getting bolder. They bill you for things you never bought or wanted. Wells Fargo Bank did this to millions of their customers over the years. The bank opened unwanted credit card accounts and billed for auto insurance, for example, imposing sales quotas on their employees. The media caught the bank, finally. Wells Fargo had to pay out money in fines and restitution. The company easily absorbed the payments as part of the cost of doing business. No executive was criminally prosecuted; a few resigned. The board of directors was not replaced. And Wells Fargo is flying high today, pretty much unscathed.

Many consumers don't even look at their bills anymore. They just give up and let the sellers, such as the utilities, get direct electronic payments from their bank accounts.

On July 30, 2014, Senator Jay Rockefeller's consumer subcommittee held hearings on "cramming." Here customers are charged for things on their telephone bill they never ordered by firms that somehow got the phone companies to add their charges. The testimony described what has to be seen as criminal billing. Members of Congress turned their backs on the proposed legislation to end this scam while keeping their pockets open to campaign contributions from the wrongdoers.

Credit scores, credit ratings, and grossly one-sided fine print contracts are resulting in the financial and contractual incarceration of the American consumer. In many instances, the corporate lawyers who create these contractual handcuffs make sure that you've "consented" to your "jailing," to your rip-offs, to your giving up your rights to go to court to challenge marketplace abuses. They point to some deeply buried sentence in these contracts that you have never even seen.

Maybe someday such deceit by these lawyers, who are deemed "officers of the court," will be considered legal malpractice.

Well, someone cares! In a groundbreaking report accompanied by a comprehensive proposed model act for state legislatures to enact, California consumer advocates Harvey Rosenfield and Laura Antonini document the thousand and one "nonstop thefts of our money, safety, time, and privacy."

If you read through the waves of documented corporate rip-offs, billing frauds, and deceptive promotions, you'll be nodding so much from your own experience that you may have to stop and rest your neck.

The authors don't just expose the fraudsters, however. They have drafted legislation to stop the corporate crooks and to protect and empower you in the perilous marketplace of corporate crime, fraud, and abuse.

Read the report (four years in the making) for yourself by visiting the Represent Consumers website. You will see how the eroded civil justice system can be toughened across the board to represent you.

Those of you who wish to listen to Harvey and Laura talk about their battle for American consumers, turn to the *Ralph Nader Radio Hour*, where their interview will be available as a podcast on Saturday, February 26, 2022.

You'll want to take your righteous fury straight to your state legislator with the model statute in hand.

Why Do Americans Give Away So Much Control to Corporations?

SEPTEMBER 18, 2020

The American people own most of the wealth—private and public—and most of the information in the country. The top 1 percent do not.

The American people have most of the power in the country. The top 1 percent do not.

These assertions may surprise you, because the top 1 percent and the giant corporations work overtime to *control* what you *own*. This means they do not have to seize what you *own* so long as their *control* provides them with both riches and power over you.

Let's spell this out with specifics. Our Constitution starts with the words "We the People"; it doesn't start with "We the Corporations" or "We the Congress" or "We the super-rich." The sovereign authority under the Constitution is *us*; we the people are the bosses. But we give our power away to the Big Boys who run the big companies that control most of our elected politicians. The politicians in turn proceed to corrupt our elections with campaign money, gerrymandering, deceitful ads, voter obstruction, and a totally dominant two-party duopoly. This corporate state destroys competitive democracy, which would give our votes meaning, choices, and effectiveness.

Shouldn't we be discussing why, when we own the vast federal public land (one-third of America) and the vast public airwaves, we give control of these resources to corporations every day of the year to profit from at our expense? We give the television and radio stations that block our voices free control and use of the airwaves, 24-7. We receive very little in royalties from the energy, mining, timber, and grazing companies extracting huge wealth from our federal lands.

We send our tax dollars to Washington, DC, and the federal government gives trillions of these dollars to companies in the form of subsidies and bailouts.

Trillions of dollars are devoted to government research and development

(R & D), which has built or expanded private companies. These include such industries as aerospace, pharmaceuticals, military weapons, computers, internet, biotechnology, nanotechnology, and containerization.

Our taxpayer-funded R & D is essentially given away free to these for-profit businesses. We the people receive neither royalties nor profit-sharing returns on these public investments. Worse, we pay gouging prices for drugs and other products developed with our tax dollars.

We have trillions of dollars in savings and retirement money placed in giant mutual and pension funds. The managers of these institutions make big profits by investing your money in the stock and bond markets. If you controlled these trillions of dollars in stocks and bonds that you own— that is, if there were real shareholder and bondholder power—you would control the ownership of all the big companies and turn the tables on the Big Bosses. Polls show a big majority of people think big business has too much power and control over us. Nonetheless, we regularly give these plutocrats control over what we own.

We own our personal information. Yet we give it totally free to the likes of Facebook, Google, Instagram, and YouTube etc. so they can make trillions of dollars selling data on what we buy, what we like, what we think, and what we're addicted to in the marketplace. The advertisers then pester us 24-7 and even betray our trust. Imagine Alexa eavesdropping in our homes and businesses. High-tech companies should not be privy to our personal information.

Unfortunately, giving companies our personal information, from which they profit immensely and gouge and penalize us profusely, started long ago. The moment we took out credit cards, for example, we began to lose control of our money and our privacy. With the internet, companies are generating new payment-system controls, with their dictatorial fine-print agreements and never-ending additional surcharges, driven by their greedy overreaches.

People spend lots of time just trying to get through to these companies for refunds, adjustments, corrections, and simple answers to their questions.

Why have we handed over the enormous assets we own to this expanding corporate state? Why have we surrendered to statism or corporate socialism? The corporate "Borg" is sucking the ready availability of the good life; decent, secure livelihoods assured by our collective self-reliance; and the freedom to shape our future out of our political economy.

Why are we allowing the United States—this rich land of ours—to have so many impoverished, powerless people, dominated by the few? With ever-greater concentration of powers under corrupt Trumpism and its corporate supremacists, control of our lives is getting worse.

It starts with us being indoctrinated into being powerless (civic skills and practice are not taught in schools). This leads to the people not taking control of Congress (only 535 of them). We are allowing elections and debates to ignore these basic democratic issues of who *owns* what and who should *control* our commonwealth.

David Bollier and his colleagues are working to have adults and students learn about the commons—owned by all of us—and the few examples of people sharing in our commonwealth. Through the Alaska Permanent Fund, every Alaskan gets about $2,000 a year from the royalties that oil companies pay for taking the people's oil from that state.

If you're interested in reading further about the "commons" we own but do not control, go to bollier.org and breakingthroughpower.org. It's in our hands!

Time for a Taxpayer Revolt Against Rich Corporate Welfarists

JUNE 10, 2022

It is time for an unusual but long-overdue revolt by the 150 million tax-withheld taxpayers. I'm not speaking of rates of taxation that the rich and corporations largely avoid because of the gigantic tax escapes, which they grease through Congress. Today I'm hoping to get your dander up by showing how corporatist politicians make you pay for big corporations to come to their corporate welfare–friendly state and make profits.

You've been required to subsidize these companies for them to make a profit, and you get nothing in return—silent partners pouring money indirectly into big-name corporations. They misleadingly call these subsidies "incentives," but they are really coerced entitlements.

Before getting into these recent tax breaks, a little history is needed to show that once upon a time, giveaways to these self-styled "capitalists" were not so easy.

In 1971, the Lockheed corporation was not doing so well. So its corporate lawyers went to Congress to ask for a $250 million loan guarantee so that banks would lend the company money and have no risk because of Uncle Sam's backing. The proposal created an uproar on Capitol Hill. The House and Senate held hearings, and extensive debate on the floor dissected all sides of this controversial, hitherto-unheard-of special privilege. The press covered it extensively.

The bill eventually passed, but not without a strong fight and amendments by its opponents.

Fast-forward to today, when $250 million is chump change. Do you have any idea of the sum total of outstanding loan guarantees for private businesses passed or authorized by Congress? You don't? Well, neither do any members of Congress. The data is not collected, though I'll guess it is over a trillion dollars, including big chunks for unfinished or suspended nuclear power plants. Government-guaranteed capitalism.

Congress hasn't even compiled data on how many of these loan guarantees have been called in by failing or mismanaged corporations.

213

Besides loan guarantees, there are a blizzard of other forms of corporate welfare at the federal, state, and local levels (see goodjobsfirst.org). There are property tax abatements and direct cash subsidies, as were extended to grossly mismanaged General Motors (GM) after it went bankrupt to get rid of its creditors and its wrongful-injury lawsuits.

There are federal taxpayer–paid research and development (R & D) programs, such as new government medicine research, given free to Big Pharma to sell without price restraints, and pioneering R & D break-through research for the computer, aerospace, biotech, nanotech, and agribusiness industries, to name a few recipients of government giveaways.

Bear in mind that these handouts and bailouts rarely come with any payback conditions. The rare instances are when the feds take stock in companies they rescue. This partial reciprocity occurred in the form of stock from the GM and Chrysler bailout of 2008. When the Treasury Department eventually sold this stock, the revenue did not come close to paying for the bailout.

Now, handouts, bailouts, and other subsidies are given to compa-nies as a matter of mindless routine. New York City mayor Eric Adams announced the other day that he was going to give the newly approved marijuana retailers about $4 million to help them get started. Hey, delica-tessens, fresh fruit, and vegetable markets, why not get in line? If there's tax money for getting people "high," surely Mayor Adams should have some of your taxpayer cash to advance "nutritional highs," especially for people in need.

However, it was up to Kathy Hochul, the unelected governor of New York (as lieutenant governor, she succeeded Andrew Cuomo after he resigned last year) to raise the corporate tax-break competition to unheard-of jackpot levels. The *$10 billion* tax break for chip-makers to locate in New York State, instead of any other state, was so brazen that the governor resorted to secrecy and legislative darkness.

As reported in the *Albany Times Union*, with no prior public exposure, her bill was passed without any public hearing by the state Senate on the final day of its legislative session. The state Assembly whisked it through, also without hearings, at eight in the morning on its last day, following twenty continuous hours of voting before adjourning.

The newspaper took note of "sleep-deprived lawmakers who were enduring the grueling schedule." (Republicans went along in both chambers).

John Kaehny, executive director of Reinvent Albany, told the *Times Union*: "This is like the ugliest of Albany. In this type of fog, the governor's office can misinform the Legislature, and do it all at the last second."

There is no reinventing the governor. Marinated in avalanches of corporate campaign money for her election bid this November, Hochul is addicted to heavily obligating taxpayers for years without their knowledge or the informed, open consent of their state representatives. This last point was raised by dissenting state senator Liz Krueger (who should be the state's governor).

Earlier this year, Hochul secretly negotiated an $850 million taxpayer subsidy for a new Buffalo Bills stadium. The owner of this NFL team, the Pegula family, is worth $5.8 billion, according to *Forbes*! She then rammed this entertainment giveaway through the Legislature, again without public hearings, as part of the state's budget.

Hochul is just getting started in her enormous giveaways to the super-rich and greedy. She is the plutocrats' governor. Public defenders are leaving their crucial positions in the state because they are paid so little that they can't meet their living expenses. Kathy Hochul has no interest in raising their salaries and securing their constitutional mission of justice for indigent defendants.

There is something seriously out of control with this reckless corporate welfare–disbursing governor. She even refuses to meet the press or return calls from civic leaders about her dictatorial giveaways to a very profitable semiconductor industry.

It gets worse. Every day since 1982, according to corporate tax expert and reform advocate Jim Henry (follow on Twitter @submergingmkt), the state is refunding electronically about $40 million every day collected from the financial transaction taxes on Wall Street trades in stocks, derivatives, and bonds. This is a miniscule sales tax (a fraction of 1 percent) in a state where consumers pay 8 percent sales tax on their purchases of essential goods.

With New York City's budget shaky and the state budget relying heavily on a one-time burst of federal monies, Hochul is refusing requests by numerous informed state legislators, such as Assemblyman Phil Steck, to simply keep the daily collected transaction tax. No way! She'd rather collect campaign money from her Wall Street contributors.

It's clearly time for a taxpayers' revolt. For starters, call Governor

Hochul to protest. Her office's phone number is 518-474-8390, and you can email her via mmgovernor.ny.gov/content/governor-contact-form. If you are not from New York State, her race to the bottom to grab some factories will pressure your state to offer the same tax breaks, on your back.

Commercial Defrauding of Uncle Sam—
Biggest Booming Business

MARCH 18, 2022

The biggest business in America is stealing from and defrauding the federal government, Uncle Sam, and you, the taxpayers. In terms of sheer stolen dollars, the total amount is greater than the annual sales of Amazon and Walmart over the past two years.

Before getting to the real big stuff, start with how much was stolen or not delivered by the contractors in Iraq and Afghanistan. Just in one program, John Sopko—Special Inspector General for Afghan Reconstruction (SIGAR), estimated that $30 billion of the $100 billion repairs project was purloined. Despite his many damning reports on what was also wasted—like the $40 million natural gas–powered fueling station (there were no natural gas–powered cars in Afghanistan)—no one was indicted, no one was fired, no one missed a promotion. This is according to author Andrew Cockburn, who interviewed Sopko extensively for his new book *The Spoils of War: Power, Profit and the American War Machine*. In fact, Cockburn told *Corporate Crime Reporter*, "They were giving bonuses to people for stealing our money."

Of the $360 billion in annual billing fraud by the health care industry, over $100 billion is fraud on Medicare and Medicaid.

Turning to the $6 trillion appropriated (without reversing the tax cuts by Trump on the super-rich) by both Trump and Biden since March 2020, government investigators and the media are seeing staggering thefts and frauds. Money was stolen outright by fake companies and fraudulent applications, or taken by profitable companies, law firms, and others that these programs were never intended to benefit.

One estimate has the trillion-dollar Paycheck Protection Program (PPP) delivering only 25 percent to the people for whom it was intended. Even people like the notorious antitaxer Grover Norquist, who is loaded with corporate donations, applied for and got a bundle of tax dollars.

From the beginning I called members of Congress to caution them to draft very tight language in the giant rescue and infrastructure programs in order to foresee and forestall the predictable giant heist. There were some provisions—expanding enforcement budgets and inserting certain general review obligations on government agencies. But it was massively too little and too late—and utterly inadequate for the volume of coming robberies.

Corporate lobbyists were already swarming over Capitol Hill to get their bailouts, grants, sweetheart contracts, and other benefits. The airlines got about $50 billion in bailouts, for example, after they had bought back $45 billion of their own stock from passenger revenues.

The mass media was also largely inattentive, spending far more time on the friction between politicians in Congress than the burning of taxpayer dollars. The inspectors general attached to each federal agency were timid, underbudgeted, and had weak authority. Moreover, several inspector general positions were vacant.

Professor Malcolm Sparrow at Harvard has shown how there are specific, proven ways to prevent thefts and frauds on government programs. Effective criminal law enforcement authority, adequate enforcement budgets, and plenty of investigators and auditors with higher-level political support are crucial.

Neither Congress nor the White House has met this challenge of titanic corruption, which should become a major campaign subject in the coming elections. Apart from a few perfunctory hearings, Congress has not held the intense, high-profile hearings that grab public attention—in part because both parties have culpability, though the GOP is worse.

Biden spoke briefly this month about this thievery in his State of the Union address and promised a chief prosecutor for pandemic fraud. This is a little late. And where was the mention of adequate budget and authority? Professor Sparrow recommends that the enforcement budgets for commercial crimes have to be at least 1 percent of the estimated theft or fraud. The Biden oversight isn't a tenth of that measure.

Finally, the *Washington Post* and the *New York Times* have started to investigate. The findings of their lengthy features are predictably staggering, especially regarding the Small Business Administration (SBA), which dispatched $343 billion in PPP loans over a fourteen-day period!

As recounted in the *New York Times* article by David Fahrenthold, a free-for-all robbery spree took hold. The SBA made classic, foreseeable blunders. First, it subcontracted out—without due diligence—to so-called nonprofits the job of distributing and monitoring the expenditures, giving them 15 percent of the overall disbursements to, for example, child-feeding programs. The blunder is not only an inappropriate delegation of governmental powers, but also a perverse incentive for the overseer to shovel out money to subcontractors.

Biden's Department of Agriculture arrogantly turned down Fahrenthold's request to interview officials there. This is another sign of unpreparedness, enabled by a Congress that astonishingly let the department "waive rules that had been put in place after previous scandals to make sure states watched the watchdogs," wrote Fahrenthold. (See his story "F.B.I. Sees 'Massive Fraud' in Groups' Food Programs for Needy Children.")

A longer exposé, by Tony Romm, appeared in the *Washington Post* with the headline "'Immense fraud' creates immense task for Washington as it tries to tighten scrutiny of $6 trillion in emergency coronavirus spending."

Romm's examples are about sheer theft. A person pleaded guilty to spending chunks of their $4 million loan on a Porsche, a Mercedes, and a BMW. A man was sentenced to prison for obtaining $800,000 for a business that did not exist. Fake or shell companies getting grants and unpayable loans illustrate that the guardrails were nonexistent in thousands of cases.

So minimal are the prosecutorial initiatives that the commercial criminals are still actively seeking huge sums in grants, loans, direct payments, and other forms of emergency assistance.

The SBA's diligent inspector general, Hannibal "Mike" Ware, has been producing report after report—incurring the hatred of Trump and his then-SBA administrator—and still not convincing Congress that without more enforcement funds, the corporate crime wave will prosper unabated. Even so, Romm points to evidence that dozens of criminal fraud cases were preventable with some more diligence from the SBA. It isn't reassuring that Romm reported that SBA officials turned down interview requests by the *Post*.

Recent efforts by a long-culpable Congress and a long-neglectful presidency are not close to catching up with current robberies, not to mention any chance of retrieving stolen monies. Ever since I requested in 1971 that President Richard Nixon set up a commission on corporate crime, the federal government has remained obstinately indifferent to the sheer scale of "crime in the suites." Consider the looted military contracting budget and the global level of corporate tax evasions up against the tepid responses from Washington. Too much discretion was delegated to the state and local governments without strict criteria. One New York Republican–controlled municipality is about to spend $12 million to renovate a baseball stadium.

Without a tradition of Congress requiring annual compliance reports from federal agencies, which would require securing regular data feedback flows, the government will continue to be caught flat-footed.

Why should the three-working-days-a-week Congress, with no skin in the game, really care? If it isn't the unorganized taxpayers paying for these massive thefts, the next generation of Americans will get the tab. Especially since the solons on Capitol Hill have refused to rescind the huge Trump tax escapes for the wealthy and giant corporations that have ballooned the federal deficit.

Ranking the Infinite Greed, Power, and Controls of Giant Corporations

AUGUST 6, 2020

The combination of greed and power often spins out of control and challenges the enforceable rule of law and the countervailing force of the organized civic community.

When greed and power are exercised by giant multinational corporations that escape the discipline of the nation-state, the potential for evil becomes infinite in nature. *Enough is never enough.*

Giant global companies, aided and abetted by their corporate attorneys and accountants, can literally decide how little taxes they are going to pay by shifting profits and expenses among different tax haven countries such as Ireland, Luxembourg, and Panama.

These same companies then proceed to lobby any nation, including most prominently the United States. Congress and the White House are pushed to cut formal tax rates, pack the tax laws with loopholes, and lower further the effective tax rate. The formal top tax rate for billions in company profits is now 21 percent, while the actual tax rate is lower—much lower—for banks, insurance companies, drug companies, and behemoth tech companies like Apple that master tax avoidance.

"Generous" is not a word one can associate either with Apple or its avaricious CEO Tim Cook. One of the first moves Tim Cook made—after replacing the cancer-stricken innovator and legendary Apple founder Steve Jobs in 2011—was to arrange a $378 million compensation package for himself and launch the biggest stock buyback in corporate history. Apple, which is worth $1.5 trillion, has spent $327 billion since 2013 to buy back 2.5 billion shares of stock. Yet Apple has done little to produce productive investments, remediate used and very toxic Apple products when discarded, or increase pay for the 350,000 serf-labor workers in China toiling under its merciless contractor Foxconn.

Apple made $104 billion in the last twelve months, puffed up by tax avoidance, tax cuts, and a no-tariff deal with Trump on its Chinese imports, yet Tim Cook has rejected pleas to spend a little over $2 billion (deductible) to award a full year's pay bonus to the 350,000 Foxconn workers who build Apple's iPhones and iPads.

Apple's massive stock buybacks have, however, increased the metrics to set compensation levels for Tim Cook and his executive sidekicks. Unfortunately, stock buybacks do little to tamp down excessive prices for Apple products. The massive stock buybacks also send a message that Apple's management has no other uses for its corporate cash—not for research and development, not for improving the nature and security of its workers' pensions, not for investing in curtailing the damaging side effects of Apple products on the environment, and not for reducing other offloaded damage to society.

Tim Cook and Apple are also stingy, given their vast wealth, with charitable contributions. So stingy that Apple's bosses do not even come close to the company's charitable deduction limit of 5 percent of adjusted gross income. In 2018 Apple gave $125 million to charities. Apple's net income for 2018 was $59.53 billion—so the charitable contributions were a tiny fraction of 1 percent!

Recently, the *New York Times* published articles showing how tiny the executive pay cuts were by the very few executives who announced and declared sympathy for their laid-off and impoverished workers. The media has also been reporting illicit maneuvers developed by corporate attorneys to help chain stores get relief payments that should have gone to legitimate small businesses. (Why isn't the National Federation of Independent Business speaking out against this abuse and avarice?)

Replacing some of their greed with generosity could be directed to the estimated $6 billion to $11 billion needed this coming school year to give low-income students full equipment and connectivity to the internet for remote learning during the COVID-19 pandemic restrictions. States and localities need $4 billion to assure the voting process will be fair and that all votes are counted and on time. The Republicans in the Senate are blocking the money needed to guarantee free and fair elections. Four billion dollars is peanuts for the profit-glutted Silicon Valley giants Facebook, Google, Apple, Amazon, and Microsoft. These high-tech digital giants could easily contribute the money needed to avert a widely predicted election-time disaster and weeks of understaffed counting after November 3. Imagine such a show of patriotism from these companies.

Then there are the matters of woefully inadequate supplies, facilities, and training programs to counter the spreading COVID-19 pandemic that is causing the economy to crumble. These companies, with their record-setting profits and soaring stock prices due to their monopolistic powers or consumer-gouging, should return some of Trump's giveaway tax cuts of 2017 and the burgeoning corporate welfare payments from crony-capitalistic Washington, DC, to help their afflicted or vulnerable fellow Americans. Many of these people are their own workers, friends, and relatives.

Economists should develop a "Hedonistic Index" to rank the "greed-with-power" status of the five hundred largest US corporations.

People have the right to know how CEOs and major corporations do on the "Hedonistic Index" of greed and power. After all, at the end of the day, we are all paying the price of the full measure of the infinite avarice spiraling from these corporate supremacists and their private governments of controls.

"Democratic Socialism"—Bring It On, Corporate Socialists!

FEBRUARY 15, 2020

Crooked Donald Trump, the erstwhile failed gambling czar and corporate welfare king, is assailing Bernie Sanders for his "radical socialism." How ludicrous given Trump's three-year giveaway of taxpayer assets and authorities to giant corporations—a perfect portrait of crony capitalism.

Others are joining the socialist labeling bandwagon, including corporatist right-wing radio talk show blowhards, themselves freeloaders, profitably using the public airwaves. This pack includes Lloyd Blankfein, former lawbreaking chairman of Goldman Sachs.

Bernie knows, of course, how to rebut this distorted interpretation of "democratic socialism." But will his rebuttals be enough given that the Biden-Bloomberg-Klobuchar wing of the Democratic Party is determined to label Bernie "unelectable" against the boastful Don the Con?

Some suggestions for Bernie and others to use in this upcoming back and forth on "democratic socialism" versus "corporate socialism" of the super-rich corporations:

1. Go after the corporate socialists who have invited Wall Street and big business to socialize the means of government against the people's necessities and freedoms. It is a government of, by, and for the dominant corporations. Such private power dominating our government in so many reported ways was called "fascism" in 1938 by President Franklin D. Roosevelt in a formal message to Congress. This is a fertile field for taking the offensive.

2. Democratic socialism is a political force in countries like Denmark, Sweden, Finland, Norway, the Netherlands, sometimes Canada, and others. In these places, it means all the people get their taxes returned in the form of improved livelihoods, economic security, and peace of mind. Democratic socialism means better pay, universal health care,

pensions, day care, family sick leave, vacations, tuition-free higher education, robust public transit and parks, and many other amenities backed by stronger unions, all of which are denied to the American people in the "land of the free and home of the brave." Since World War II, many European political movements were led by "social democratic" parties.

3. Back to our country. Corporatists and right-wing Wall Street Democrats are inferring that "democratic socialism" is un-American, ruinous for our economy. These demonizers argue that a self-proclaimed "democratic socialist" is a sure loser in the election against Donald Trump—a self-enriching crook and outlaw; a boastful, savage sexual predator; bigoted and racist in his policies; an inciter of violence; and a delusional serial liar. Trump, the Electoral College–selected tool of the super-rich and corporate powers, should be easy to defeat given his disgraceful presidency.

American people of all backgrounds like their public libraries; public, locally controlled water works; municipal fire departments; police precincts; and public schools. They seem OK with government highways, bridges, and public transit, and they want their taxes spent to repair and upgrade these vital pieces of our infrastructure. Taxpayers don't want our commonwealth being owned by tax-escaping, gouging corporations.

There are over one thousand municipal public utilities providing electricity. The "red" states of Tennessee and Alabama would fight any corporatization of the Tennessee Valley Authority, which eighty-seven years ago brought electricity to a large poor region that the private electric companies didn't think was profitable enough.

The unfairly maligned Department of Veterans Affairs brought free hospitals and health care to millions of veterans. Millions of Americans are favorably disposed to lifesaving Medicare and Medicaid and are economically saved by Social Security and unemployment compensation. Hey! There must be a lot of "democratic socialists" out there in blue and red states. New Hampshirites are mostly OK with revenue-producing hard liquor retail stores owned by the state.

At a meeting long ago with top medical officials at the Walter Reed Army Medical Center, I was told that after learning the second leading cause of hospitalization for US soldiers in Vietnam was malaria, the US Army asked the drug companies to develop remedies. The negative response was that developing medicines to deal with malaria wasn't profitable enough. In response, the Pentagon brought together skilled doctors and scientists and started its own "drug company" inside Walter Reed and Bethesda Naval Hospitals. For less than 10 percent of what the big drug companies say it costs, our government developed three out of four of the leading antimalarial drugs in the world and made them available everywhere without any patents producing Big Pharma–like profits.

If the political and corporate Trumpsters and the Clintonite Democrats snort at all this, tell them that they do agree on one thing. Those in both these camps have always been eager to have collapsing capitalism—as during the 2008 Wall Street dive—saved by reliable socialism, a.k.a. trillions of taxpayer dollars—via Washington, D.C.—funding the bailout of the reckless bankers and speculators.

Big Business Lies Taught a
Watchful Donald Trump

SEPTEMBER 12, 2019

For avalanche-level lying, deceiving, and misleading, megamimic Donald Trump need look no further than the history of the corporate advertising industry and the firms that pay it.

Dissembling is so deeply ingrained in commercial culture that the Federal Trade Commission (FTC) and the courts don't challenge exaggerated general claims that they call "puffery."

Serious corporate deception is a common sales technique. At times it costs consumers more than dollars. It has led to major illness and loss of life.

Take the tobacco industry, which used to sell its products in the context of health and facilitating mental concentration. Healthy movie stars and athletes were featured in print and on TV until 1970.

Despite studies showing that sugary soft drinks can damage health, increase obesity, and reduce life expectancy, the industry's ads still feature healthy, fit families in joyous situations guzzling pop. Fortunately, water has regained its first-place position as the most consumed liquid in the US.

Whether it is the auto industry falsely inflating fuel efficiency, the e-cigarette companies deceiving youngsters about vaping, the food industry selling sugary junk cereals as nutrition for children, or the credit banking companies misleading on interest rates, truth in advertising is oxymoronic.

To counter these "fake ads," the consumer movement pushed for mandatory labeling on food and other products. The FTC is a chief enforcer against deception in advertising, but it has waxed and waned over the decades. The FTC describes its duties to protect consumers from unfair or deceptive acts or practices as follows:

> In advertising and marketing, the law requires that objective claims
> be truthful and substantiated. The FTC does not pursue subjective

claims or puffery—claims like 'this is the best hairspray in the world.' But if there is an objective component to the claim—such as 'more consumers prefer our hairspray to any other' or 'our hairspray lasts longer than the most popular brands'—then you need to be sure that the claim is not deceptive and that you have adequate substantiation before you make the claim.

A few times, companies caught engaging in false advertising were compelled by the FTC to announce the correction in their forthcoming ads and apologize. Those days are long gone.

Another way consumers fought back is the spectacular success of Dr. Sidney Wolfe and his associates at Public Citizen's Health Research Group. They researched hundreds of prescription drugs and over-the-counter medications and found they were not effective for the purpose for which they are advertised. Relentless publicity on such dynamic mass media outlets as the *Phil Donahue Show* led to the withdrawal of many of these products, likely saving consumers billions of dollars and protecting them from harmful side effects (see Wolfe's book *Pills That Don't Work*).

When large companies are fighting regulation, their lies become "clear and present dangers" to innocent people. I recall at a technical conference in the early 1960s, a General Motors engineer warned that seat belts in cars would tear away the inner organs of motorists from their moorings in sudden decelerations, as in collisions. For the longest time, lead, asbestos, and a whole host of chemicals were featured as not just necessary but safe. All false.

Someone should write a book about all the prevarications by leading spokespeople of industry and commerce justifying the slavery of the "inferior races," arguing against the abolition of child labor in dungeon factories, and predicting that legislating Social Security would bring on communism.

Interestingly, corporations can lie vigorously and not lose credibility. Artificial corporate personhood comes with immunity from social sanctions that apply to real human beings.

In 1972, the People's Lobby in California, led by the impressive Ed and Joyce Koupal, qualified an initiative called "The Clean Environment Act." Corporations threw millions of dollars and made false claims to defeat the act. The corporate public relations firm, Whitaker and Baxter, put out a fact sheet reaching millions of voters. The oil companies declared that "lowering the lead content of gasoline would cause automobile engines to fail, resulting in massive congestion and transit breakdowns." They also claimed that reducing sulfur oxide emissions from diesel fuel "would cause the state's transportation industry to grind to a halt," with huge joblessness and "economic chaos."

Other companies said a moratorium on nuclear power plant construction would lead to "widespread unemployment and darkened city streets." Banning DDT (an insecticide) in California would "confront the farmer with economic ruin and produce critical shortages of fruits and vegetables" and more lurid hypotheticals.

The lies worked. Voters turned down the initiative by nearly two to one. All these reforms have since been advanced nationwide with no such disasters.

The media at the time did not distinguish itself by separating the lies from the truth. But later, in 1988, the media, led by the *Los Angeles Times*, did not let the auto insurance industry get away with lies about Prop 103, pushed by a $70 million television/radio buy. Prop 103 won and, as of 2013, saved California motorists over $100 billion, according to leading actuary and consumer advocate J. Robert Hunter (see consumerwatchdog.org/prop-103-california-insurance-reform).

Corporate fibbing pays monetary rewards. Informed consumers, their champions, and regulatory agencies at the national, state, and local level must continue to make these companies pay a price, especially over social media. Madison Avenue calls the effect of such pushback "reputational risk."

Society Is in Decay—When the Worst Is First and the Best Is Last

MAY 29, 2019

Plutocrats like to control the range of permissible public dialogue. Plutocrats also like to shape what society values. If you want to see where a country's priorities lie, look at how it allocates its money. While teachers and nurses earn comparatively little for performing critical jobs, corporate bosses—including those who pollute our planet and bankrupt defenseless families—make millions more. Wells Fargo executives are cases in point. The vastly overpaid CEO of General Electric left his teetering company in shambles. In 2019, Boeing's CEO got a bonus—despite the Lion Air Flight 610 737 MAX 8 crash in 2018—just days before a second deadly 737 MAX 8 crash in Ethiopia.

This disparity is on full display in my profession. Public interest lawyers and public defenders, who fight daily for a more just and lawful society, are paid modest salaries. On the other hand, the most well-compensated lawyers are corporate attorneys who regularly aid and abet corporate crime, fraud, and abuse. Many corporate lawyers line their pockets by shielding powerful violators from accountability under the rule of law.

Physicians who minister to the needy poor and go to risky regions, where Ebola or other deadly infectious diseases are prevalent, are paid far less than cosmetic surgeons catering to human vanities. Does any rational observer believe that the best movies and books are also the most rewarded? Too often the opposite is true. Stunningly gripping documentaries earn less than 1 percent of what is garnered by the violent, pornographic, and crude movies at the top of the ratings each week.

On my weekly radio show, I interview some of the most dedicated authors who accurately document perils to health and safety. The authors on my program expose pernicious actions and inactions that jeopardize people's daily lives. These guests offer brilliant, practical solutions for our widespread woes (see ralphnaderradiohour.com). Their important books usually go unnoticed by the mass media and barely sell a few thousand copies, while the bestseller lists are dominated by celebrity biographies. Ask yourself, when preventable and foreseeable disasters occur, which books are more useful to society?

The monetary imbalance is especially jarring when it comes to hawks who beat the drums of war. For example, people who push for our government to start illegal wars (e.g., John Bolton pushing for the war in Iraq) are rewarded with top appointments. Former government officials also get very rich when they take jobs in the defense industry. Do you remember anyone who opposed the catastrophic Iraq War getting such lucrative rewards?

The unknown and unrecognized people who harvest our food are on the lowest rung of the income ladder despite the critical role they play in our lives. Near the top of the income ladder are people who gamble on the prices of food via the commodities market and those who drain the nutrients out of natural foods and sell the junk food that remains, with a dose of harmful additives. Agribusiness tycoons profit from this plunder.

Those getting away with major billing fraud grow rich, while those people trying to get our government to do something about $350 billion in health care billing fraud this year—like Harvard professor Malcolm K. Sparrow—live on a college professor's salary.

Hospital executives, who each make millions of dollars a year, preside over an industry where about five thousand patients die every week from preventable problems in US hospitals, according to physicians at Johns Hopkins School of Medicine. The watchdogs who call out this deadly hazard live on a fraction of that amount as they try to save lives.

Even in sports, where people think the best athletes make the most money, the reverse is more often true. Just ask a red-faced Brian Cashman, the Yankees general manager, who, over twenty years, has spent massive sums on athletes who failed miserably to produce compared to far lesser-paid baseball players. Look at today's top-ranked Yankees, whose fifteen "stars" are injured while their replacements are playing spectacularly for much smaller compensation than their high-priced teammates.

A major reason why our society's best are so often last while our worst are first is the media's infatuation with publicizing the worst and ignoring the best. Warmongers get press. The worst politicians are most frequently on the Sunday morning TV shows—not the good politicians or civic leaders with proven records bettering our society.

Ever see Congressman Pascrell (D-NJ) on the Sunday morning news shows? Probably not. He's a leader who is trying to reform Congress so that it is open, honest, and capable and represents you, the people. Surely you have heard of Senator Lindsey Graham (D-SC), who is making ugly excuses for Donald Trump, always pushing for war and bloated military budgets, often hating Muslims and Arabs, and championing the lawless American empire. He is always in the news, having his say.

Take the 162 people who participated in our Super Bowl of Civic Action at Constitution Hall in Washington, DC, in May and September 2016. These people have been and are changing America. They are working to make food, cars, drugs, air, water, medical devices, and drinking water safer. Abuses by corporations against consumers, workers, and small tax-payers would be worse without them. Our knowledge of solutions and ways to treat people fairly and abolish poverty and advance public services is greater because of their courageous hard work (see breakingthrough-power.org).

The eight days of this Super Bowl of Civic Action got far less cov-erage than did Tiger Woods *losing* another tournament that year or the dismissive nicknames given by the foulmouthed Trump to his mostly wealthy Republican opponents on just one debate stage.

All societies need play, entertainment, and frivolity. But a media obsessed with giving one hundred times the TV and radio time—using our public airwaves for free—to those activities than to serious matters crucial to the most basic functioning of our society is assuring that the worst is first and the best is last. Just look at your weekly *TV Guide*.

If the whole rotted-out edifice comes crashing down, there won't be enough coerced taxpayer dollars anymore to save the plutocrats, with their limitless greed and power. Maybe then the best can have a chance to be first.

Unmasking Phony Values Campaigns
by the Corporatists

OCTOBER 17, 2018

Corporatist candidates like to talk up *values* without getting specific and without drawing attention to how their voting records put the interests of big financial backers against the interest of most voters. This election season is no exception, from Florida to Texas to California to Ohio to Wisconsin. In 2014, I wrote the following article for the Louisville *Courier-Journal* comparing Kentucky values to the starkly opposing record and behavior of Senator Mitch McConnell.

All current candidates for elective office who stand for "we the people" and believe that big corporations should be our servants, not our masters, may find this list of values applicable in their states. Corporatist opponents' voting records and positions, as well as their campaign contributors' interests, can be clearly compared with civic values and any other values voters and candidates wish to highlight. This kind of comparison can only help to turn out larger numbers of voters who want to elect candidates who will champion causes related to consumers, workers, children, and small taxpayers.

✝ ✝ ✝

From my travels throughout Kentucky, starting with the late-sixties campaign for coal miners' health and safety laws, I've observed that Kentuckians would like their politicians to be driven by Kentucky values. This election season, voters must be wondering: How has Senator Mitch McConnell lived up to key Bluegrass State commitments?

1. REWARDING HARD WORK

Kentuckians don't want handouts—they believe in working for a living. That's why they believe in a fair day's wage for a fair day's work.

Mitch McConnell is worth more than $27 million but has blocked efforts to prevent the minimum wage from seriously eroding due to inflation. He would rather allow McDonald's and Walmart to have taxpayers, through the earned income tax credit, pay for their workers' public assistance than raise the minimum wage to meet workers' basic needs.

2. HONORING YOUR ELDERS

Many Kentuckians follow the Fifth Commandment: Honor thy father and thy mother. They believe our elders, after a lifetime of work, deserve a decent living standard.

Mitch McConnell dishonors our fathers and mothers when he says that the government should cut funding for Social Security and Medicare, programs that give Kentucky elders, who paid into these safety nets, much-deserved security in their golden years.

3. PRACTICALITY

Kentuckians want politicians to have the same practical problem-solving spirit that they and their neighbors exhibit in daily life.

Mitch McConnell has called himself a "proud guardian of gridlock" in Washington and, as the *Washington Post* wrote, has "raised the art of obstructionism to new levels."

4. RESPECTING WOMEN

Kentucky women have made sure that respect and equality for women is a pillar of Kentucky culture.

Mitch McConnell has shown where he stands on disrespecting women: he has voted against helping mothers take leave for sick children, domestic violence victims seeking justice, and working women seeking fair pay.

5. BEING FORTHRIGHT

Kentuckians don't like politicians talking behind their backs—saying one thing to them in public and another in closed rooms full of fat cats.

Mitch McConnell does just that, meeting privately with the multibillionaire Koch brothers and promising even more Senate opposition to raising the minimum wage, extending unemployment benefits, and helping students pay for college.

6. RESPONSIBILITY

Kentuckians believe people should be held responsible for how they treat others. They believe corporations should be held responsible for the harm they cause to their workers.

Mitch McConnell has helped roll back safety measures that hold corporations responsible for worker safety. At the urging of business groups, he helped pass a resolution declaring that Clinton administration safety rules protecting against repetitive-stress injuries "shall have no force or effect." Bill Banig, legislative director of United Mine Workers of America, said McConnell has "not done anything to help us with mine safety."

7. LOVE THY NEIGHBOR

Kentuckians don't want their neighbors in hard times dying because they're struggling to make ends meet. That's why they don't want their neighbors subjected to "pay or die" health care, whether it is because of the staggering prices of drugs, operations, emergency treatments, or health insurance.

Mitch McConnell stands opposed to the most efficient health care system: single-payer, or full "Medicare for all": everybody in, nobody out, with free choice of doctor and hospital. He even campaigned vigorously against Kynect, which has helped hundreds of thousands of Kentuckians sign up for health care.

8. NO ONE BEING ABOVE THE LAW

Kentuckians do not believe anyone should be above the law. They want Wall Street crooks who crashed our economy and were bailed out by taxpayers to be prosecuted and put in jail.

Mitch McConnell is an avid Wall Street protector in Congress and takes campaign cash from Wall Street bosses who he works to keep above the law. He has pledged to "go after" Dodd–Frank financial protections and has been a vocal opponent to the law-enforcing Consumer Financial Protection Bureau. According to the Center for Responsive Politics, Wall Street was the number one contributor to McConnell's campaign committee from 2009 to 2014.

9. DEFENDING THE CONSTITUTION

Kentuckians defend the Constitution and especially believe in its first phrase: We the People. They believe that corporations are supposed to be our servants, not our masters.

Mitch McConnell has said that the "worst day" of his political life was when Congress passed the bipartisan McCain-Feingold campaign finance reforms aimed at limiting corporate influence on governance. He proudly told a group of billionaires that the *Citizens United* decision allowing floods of corporate money into elections was a victory for "open discourse."

10. PATRIOTISM

Kentuckians love the commonwealth and the nation. They honor our soldiers and the fallen for their loyalty to America.

Mitch McConnell has allied with disloyal, unpatriotic corporations that are abandoning America. He voted against laws that would help stop outsourcing and for tax breaks that perversely reward corporations for shipping American jobs overseas.

McConnell also voted in 2003 to defeat an amendment to provide $1 billion in lifesaving body armor for the National Guard in Iraq and later in 2005 voted against an amendment to provide $213 million for more Humvees to protect soldiers from roadside bombs in Iraq.

As Kentuckians head to the polls this November, I hope they keep these facts in mind about how McConnell has opposed these longstanding Kentucky values.

The Root of the Internet's Disrepute:
Online Advertising!

OCTOBER 4, 2018

In all the mounting media coverage of problems with the internet, such as invasion of privacy, vulnerability to hacking, political manipulation, and user addiction, there is one constant: online advertising. Online advertising is the lifeblood of Google, Facebook, and many other internet enterprises that profit by providing personal data to various vendors. Moreover, the migration of tens of billions of dollars from conventional print and broadcast media continues, with devastating impacts, especially on print newspapers and magazines.

But does online advertising work for consumers? The internet was once considered a less commercial medium. But today consumers are inundated with targeted ads, reviews, comments, friends' reactions, and other digital data. Unfortunately for advertisers, consumers are not intentionally clicking on online ads in big numbers.

Google's search ads tackle people when they search for a product or service. A controlled study by eBay research labs in 2014 concluded that Google was greatly exaggerating the effectiveness of such ads—at least those bought by eBay. Researchers at eBay concluded that "more frequent users whose purchasing behavior is not influenced by ads account for most of the advertising expenses, resulting in average returns that are negative." This is the "*I-was-gonna-buy-it-anyway* problem," says an *Atlantic* article, "A Dangerous Question: Does Internet Advertising Work At All?". The *Atlantic* notes:

> There's reason to wonder whether all advertising—online and off—is losing its persuasive punch. . . . Think about how much you can learn about products today before seeing an ad. Comments, user reviews, friends' opinions, price-comparison tools . . . [are] much more powerful than advertising because we consider them *information* rather than *marketing*. The difference is enormous: We seek information, so

we're more likely to trust it; marketing seeks us, so we're more likely to distrust it.

Some companies like Coca-Cola have cooled on using online advertising. But advertising revenues keep growing for Google, Facebook, and the other giants of the internet. These companies are racing to innovate, connecting ads to more tailored audiences, which tantalize and keep hope springing eternal for the advertisers. The internet ad-sellers also provide detailed data to advertise themselves to the advertisers, staying one step ahead of growing skepticism. This is especially a problem when there is inadequate government regulation of deceptive advertising. It is the Wild West! Online advertising revenues are the Achilles' heel of these big internet companies. Any decline will deflate them immensely, more so than public and congressional criticism of their intrusiveness, their massive allowed fakeries, their broken promises to reform, and their openings to unsavory political and commercial users. If they lose advertising revenue, a major revenue bubble will burst, and there goes their business model, along with their funding for ventures from video hosting to global mapping.

After reviewing the many major negatives attributed to the internet, the *New York Times'* Farhad Manjoo writes, "So who is the central villain in this story, the driving force behind much of the chaos and disrepute online? . . . It's the advertising business, stupid." He adds, perhaps optimistically, "If you want to fix much of what ails the internet right now, the ad business would be the perfect perp to handcuff and restrain."

Randall Rothenberg, who heads a trade association of companies in the digital ad business, urges advertisers to "take civic responsibility for our effect on the world." Then he shows his frustration by saying that, "Technology has largely been outpacing the ability of individual companies to understand what is actually going on." All of this even before artificial intelligence (AI) takes root. Meanwhile, Facebook, Google, and Twitter keep announcing new tools to make their ads "safe and civil" (Facebook), open, and protective of privacy. At the same time, matters keep getting worse for consumers. The backers and abusers keep getting more skilled too (see YouTube Kids).

In a recent report titled "Digital Deceit," authors Dipayan Ghosh and Ben Scott write:

The central problem of disinformation corrupting American political culture is not Russian spies or a particular media platform. The
central problem is that the entire industry is built to leverage sophisticated technology to aggregate user attention and sell advertising.

If so, why isn't more public attention being paid to this root cause?
The mass media (which is obviously too compromised), the Congress,
academia, and more of us need to address this problem before "We the
People" become the conditioned responders that Ivan Pavlov warned
about so many years ago.

Apple's CEO Tim Cook—Serf Labor, Overpriced iPhones, and Wasted Burning Profits

AUGUST 7, 2018

The *New York Times* screamed its headline—"Apple Is Worth $1,000,000,000,000. Two Decades Ago, It Was Almost Bankrupt," but in 1997 Apple was ninety days from going broke. On Thursday [Aug. 2, 2018], it became the first publicly traded American company to be valued at one trillion-dollars!

The boosters and commentators cheered, adding, "How High Could It Go?" In CEO Tim Cook's announcement, we learned that there was $20 *billion* more of the shareholders' money spent on wasteful stock buybacks. Stock buybacks enable fatter compensation metrics for Apple's bosses (see Steven Clifford's *The CEO Pay Machine*). Corporate managers love stock buybacks.

Earlier this year Apple executives dictatorially announced that the company was going to spend $100 billion to buy back its stock—without, of course, receiving the owners-shareholders' approval. The owners might have preferred that some of that amount be used to pay them greater cash dividends. More farsighted shareholders consider the presumably longer view: institutional shareholders might have recommended more productive and equitable uses for that vast sum.

Some suggestions: $2 billion (a mere 2 percent of that $100 billion) would double the wages of its 1.3 million serf-workers driven to the wall by Apple's China-based megafactory contractor. Another $2 billion would have made major improvements in the global recycling of the present deadly (to the environment and workers) handling of toxic discarded iPhones and computers. Some of that $100 billion could have gone to productive investments, research and development, shoring up Apple's pension plan, raising wages of Apple's employees, paying Apple's fair share of taxes or—consumers take note—lowering the prices of their overpriced phones and components.

Apple's media cheerleaders can only see blizzards of dollars. They don't see the damage that this touted "successful business model" is doing to Apple stakeholders.

Exceptionally, Mark Phillips, in his front-page *New York Times* story on Apple's report, takes note of the corporate concentration in business profits and markets. "Economists," he writes, "are starting to look into whether the rise of so-called superstar firms is contributing to the lackluster wage growth, shrinking the middle class and raising income inequality in the United States. The vast social and political influence wielded by their megacompanies has prompted lawmakers to demand more regulation to rein them in."

Apple's business model rests on utilizing low-wage labor in China and gouging iPhone consumers in the US. The federal cops on the corporate antitrust beat have been asleep for years—a somnolence well-recognized by Apple, Facebook, Amazon, and Google.

Phillips reports, "Apple and Google combined now provide the software for 99 percent of all smartphones. Facebook and Google take 59 cents of every dollar spent on online advertising in the United States. Amazon exerts utter dominance over online shopping and is quickly getting bigger, fast, in areas like streaming of music and videos."

The CEOs of these companies behave like "emperors," a designation leveled at ExxonMobil's CEO years ago by prominent shareholder advocate Robert A. G. Monks at the company's annual meeting. These new CEOs exude arrogance (sometimes with Zuckerberg-like false public humility). Once they hook their customers, the network costs for customers switching to a competitor become higher with time and also serve to discourage any new would-be competitor. Years ago, dominant Hertz car rental had Avis as a competitor. Who are the domestic noncollusive Avis equivalents to the aforementioned Big Four—Amazon, Apple, Facebook, and Google—today?

The big institutional shareholders like Vanguard, Fidelity, and giant worker pension funds better wake up. Tim Cook can ignore small shareholder complaints with impunity. The big institutional shareholders, with their skilled staff, can get his attention. They can take a longer, more responsible view and demand that he stop burning all their shareholder money with buybacks and give shareholders more in cash dividends and other important investments that create productive and equitable outcomes.

Concentration of market power in other fields feeds the likelihood of future instability through a domino effect. The top five megabanks in the US control about half of the deposits, compared to about one-fifth twenty years ago. Labor's annual share of the nation's wealth gains has been declining since the 1990s. Speculation on Wall Street, slowed after the great crash of 2008, is roaring ahead toward the inevitable cliffs of unbridled greed. More taxpayer bailouts?

Grave risk levels are signaling caution, yet incredibly, a Republican Congress and Trump have loosened regulation on Wall Street.

As for you the people, your next big chance to grab hold of Congress and slow down these corporate supremacists comes in November. Do a little homework and find out who is on your side. "Slogan voters" are suckers.

Public Cynicism Enables Costly
Political Hypocrisy

NOVEMBER 8, 2017

The political hypocrisy of crony capitalism—touting market capitalism while making taxpayers fund corporate welfare—is a rare and unfortunate case of bipartisan consensus. Republicans openly embrace it, but many Democrats also fall prey to government-guaranteed corporate capitalism when they believe it to be politically expedient.

Maybe these examples will get you steamed enough to tell your members of Congress "Enough already!"

Jeff Bezos recently launched a bidding war pitting cities against one another for Amazon's second headquarters. Imagine shelling out at least $7 billion (funded by taxpayers) in return for Amazon's unenforceable promise of fifty thousand jobs and $5 billion in capital investment.

The bidding frenzy with the taxpayers' money, without a taxpayer referendum, should be an embarrassment to the mayors who are bidding for Amazon's business. Mayor Jeff Cheney of Frisco, Texas (population 160,000), wants to build the city around Amazon and its taxpayer-funded entitlements. Philadelphia's officials have offered a slew of tax incentives for Amazon's empty promises. Never mind that existing businesses would continue to pay taxes that are waived for a giant company that is emptying out property tax–paying Main Street, USA.

So far, Amazon has managed to flim-flam local leaders across North America. G. T. Bynum, Tulsa's mayor, is doing somersaults. No problem with tax escapes. "Whatever it takes," he assures them. From the mayor of Washington, DC, to the mayor of Ottawa, Canada, cities are promising whatever it takes to bring this predatory-pricing Moloch to their city.

Egging them on before the October 19, 2017, deadline for submissions, Bezos's spokesman, Adam Sedo, imperiously declared: "We invited cities to think big, and we are starting to see their creativity."

Sam Liccardo, mayor of San Jose, California, said "No way." In a column printed by the *Wall Street Journal*, Liccardo wrote: "My city won't

244 + OUT OF DARKNESS

be offering incentives to Amazon. Why? Because they are a bad deal for taxpayers. With many subsidies, the jobs a company brings to an area don't generate revenues commensurate with public expenditures." He cites the cost to Boston's taxpayers for luring General Electric's headquarters from Connecticut to be $181,000 for every job promised. Iowa, he added, gave Apple $213 million in tax escapes to establish a fifty-job data center in Waukee, Iowa.

Besides, wrote the forthright Mayor Liccardo, the presence of a skilled workforce, good schools, and infrastructure "play a far larger role in determining boards' corporate location decisions."

"Why are they doing this whole dog and pony show?" asks Matthew Gardner, from the nonpartisan Institute on Taxation and Economic Policy. "They would like a package of tax incentives for something they were going to do anyway." Professor Art Rolnick of the University of Minnesota went so far as to call Amazon's bidding wars "blackmail."

Meanwhile, Emperor Jeff Bezos, the world's richest man, gets to sit back and watch his "candidates" fight it out.

A Taiwanese giant, Foxconn, the builder of Apple's iPhones in China, enjoys a similar advantage. To build a flat-screen plant, by sheer coincidence, in House Speaker Paul Ryan's district, Ryan's buddy, Wisconsin governor Scott Walker, compelled his Republican legislature to cobble together a $3 billion taxpayer-funded package for an unenforceable promise of thirteen thousand jobs (from an initial eight thousand jobs, after more taxpayer cash was assured).

The whole deal, repeatedly trumpeted by Trump, with a company notorious for not following through on previous deals elsewhere, was pushed on Wisconsin's elected officials by funding from the extreme right-wing Charles Koch Foundation and the Bradley Foundation.

Not to be outdone, Trump's energy secretary, Rick Perry, is pushing $3.7 billion in loan guarantees to the failing, long-delayed, red-ink-doused Vogtle nuclear power plant in Georgia. Add this sum to the $8.3 billion already extended in taxpayer-guaranteed loans to this "boondoggle," and still the *Washington Post* reports that these guarantees "might fall short of what will be required to complete the costly reactors."

These corporate interests see American taxpayers as a limitless honeypot for their giant, bungling, conniving businesses. At the same time, Trump's director of management and budget, Mick Mulvaney, constantly justifies ruthless cuts to important public programs by citing taxpayers' rights. Apparently, these rights are not applicable to protecting taxpayers from predatory big-business executives hungry for the corporate welfare that gets Mulvaney's regular approval.

Public cynicism allows the costly hypocrisy of politicians to thrive. So watch out for the "pox on both your houses" public sentiment. Beware of crony capitalism—it turns politicians against the taxpayers they allegedly represent in favor of unaccountable corporate interests. Don't let the "welfare kings" pick your pockets by letting Congress wallow in cash-register politics, misusing the very power you have delegated to it.

For more information on accountability in sustainable economic development, see goodjobsfirst.org.

How Big Corporations Game Our Democracy into Their Plutocracy

OCTOBER 4, 2017

A major chapter in American history—rarely taught in our schools—is how ever larger corporations have moved to game, neutralize, and undermine the people's continual efforts to protect our touted democratic society. It is a fascinating story of the relentless exercise of power conceived or seized by corporations, with the strategic guidance of corporate lawyers.

Start with their birth certificate: the state charters that bring these corporate entities into existence, with limited liability for their investors. In the early 1800s, the Massachusetts Legislature chartered many of the textile manufacturing companies. These charters could be renewed on good behavior because lawmakers then viewed charters as privileges contingent on meeting the broad interests of society.

Fast-forward to now. The charter can be granted online in a matter of hours; there are no renewal periods, and the job is often given over to a state commission. Over the decades, corporate lobbyists have had either the legislatures or the courts grant corporate entities more privileges, immunities, and concentration of power in management, rendering shareholders—their owners—increasingly powerless. The same corporate fixers work for corporations and their subsidiaries abroad to help them avoid US laws and taxes and escape disclosures.

Remarkably, the artificial creation called the "corporation" has now achieved almost all of the rights of real people under our "We the People" Constitution that never mentions the words "corporation" or "company."

Corporations cannot vote, at least not yet; only people can. That *was* seen as a major lever of democratic power over corporations. So what has happened? Commercial money to politicians started weakening the influence of voters because the politicians became increasingly dependent on the corporate interests that bankrolled their campaigns. The politicians use their ever-increasing corporate cash to saturate voters with deceptive political ads and intimidate any competitors who have far less money but may be far better representatives of the public good.

To further shatter the principle of voter sovereignty, corporations have rewarded those politicians who construct restrictive political-party rules, gerrymander electoral districts, and obstruct third-party candidate ballot access. By concentrating political power in fewer and fewer hands, corporate influence becomes more deeply entrenched in our democratic society. Politicians quickly learn that political favors will attract more corporate campaign cash and other goodies.

Institutions that are supposed to represent democratic values, such as Congress and state legislatures, are meticulously gamed with the daily presence of corporate lawyers and lobbyists to shape the granular performance of these bodies and make sure little is done to defend civic values. These pitchmen are in the daily know about the inner workings of legislative bodies long before the general public. They often know who is going to be nominated for judicial and executive branch positions that interpret and administer the law and whether the nominee will do the bidding of the corporate bosses.

Then there is the press. Thomas Jefferson put great responsibility on the newspapers of his day to safeguard our democracy from excessive commercial power and its runaway political toadies. Our history certainly has some great examples of the press fulfilling Jefferson's wish. For the most part, however, any media that is heavily reliant on advertisements will clip its own wings or decide to go with lighthearted entertainment or fluff rather than dig in the pits of corruption and wrongdoing.

What of the educational institutions that purport to convey facts and the lessons of history and not be beholden to special interests? The corporate state—the autocratic joining of business and government—exerts its influence all the way down to the state and local levels, not just in Washington. It works through boards of education and trustees of colleges and universities, drawing heavily from the business world and its professional servants in such disciplines as law, accounting, and engineering.

Moreover, the most influential alumni—in terms of donations, endowments, and engagements—come from the business community. They know the kind of alma mater they want to preserve. The law and business schools are of particular interest, if only because they are the recruiting grounds for their companies and firms.

Their subversion even extends to the sacrosanct notion of academic freedom—that these institutions must be independent centers of knowledge. For example, Monsanto, General Motors, Exxon, and Eli Lilly are only a few of the companies that have pushed corporate, commercial science over academic, independent science through lucrative consultantships and partnerships with professors.

The unfortunate reality is that the wealthy and powerful are driven to spend the necessary time and energy to accomplish their raisons d'être, which are profits and the relentless pursuit of self-interest. Citizens, on the other hand, have so much else on their minds as they just try to get through the day and raise their families.

The path forward is to learn from history how citizens, when driven by injustice, organized, raised the banners of change, and concentrated on the ways and means to victory. These initiatives require civic self-respect and an understanding that the status quo is demeaning and intolerable.

The requisite to such an awakening is the awareness that our two precious pillars of democracy—freedom of contract and freedom to use the courts—are being destroyed or seriously undermined by corporate influence. The indentured servitude of fine-print contracts, signed or clicked on, is the basis of so many of the abuses and rip-offs that Americans are subjected to with such regularity. Add this modern peonage to the corporate campaign to obstruct the people's full day in court and right of trial by jury guaranteed by our Constitution. The plutocrats have succeeded, gravely, in doing just that. The court budgets are tighter, jury trials are less frequent, and the number of wrongful injury lawsuits filed keeps going down to case levels well under 5 percent of what justice requires.

Some fundamental questions are: Will we as citizens use our constitutional authority to reclaim and redirect the power we've too broadly delegated to elected officials? Will we hold these officials accountable through a reformed campaign finance system that serves the people over the plutocrats? Will we realize that a better society starts with just a few people in each electoral district and never requires more than 1 percent of the voters, organized and reflecting public opinion, to make the corporations our servants, not our masters?

Big Institutions—Immunities, Impunities, and Insanities

SEPTEMBER 26, 2017

One of the first times I used the phrase "institutional insanity" was in 1973 to describe the behavior of scientist Dixy Lee Ray, chairperson of the presumed regulatory agency the Atomic Energy Commission (AEC). I pointed out that her personal and academic roles were quite normal. But her running of the AEC was a case study in "institutional insanity": pressing for a thousand nuclear plants in the US by the year 2000 (there are ninety-nine reactors left in operation now) and going easy on a deadly, taxpayer-subsidized technology that lacked a place to put its lethal radio-active wastes and was privately uninsurable, a national security risk, and replete with vast cost overruns, immunities, and impunities shielding culpable officials and executives should a meltdown occur and take out a city or region (all to boil water to produce steam to make electricity).

Both the AEC and its successor, the Nuclear Regulatory Commission (NRC), captured by the atomic energy industry, operate that way to this day, no matter the near misses, the spills, the growing corporate welfare outlays, or the inadequate maintenance of aging nuclear power plants.

Our moral and ethical codes and our civil and criminal laws were originally designed to hold individuals accountable. The kings of yore operated under a divine right of being above the laws.

With the rise and proliferation of ever more multitiered governmental and corporate bureaucracies, methods of immunity, impunity, and secrecy were built into these structures to shield them from moral and ethical codes and laws. Increasingly, we are ruled by no-fault big corporations and their no-fault toady governments.

Some comparisons are in order. If your neighbor entrusted you with her savings and paid you a fee for holding these funds then you purchased stocks for her account while you were selling them for your account, deceiving the cheated neighbor in the process, would you escape the law? That is just some of what the Wall Street barons did on a massive scale about ten years ago. No one was prosecuted and sent to jail for this corporate crime wave.

Suppose you hired a security person for your defense who, at the same time, wasted your money and couldn't account for your payments because his books were un-auditable. Would you keep doing business with him? Wouldn't you demand an audit? Well, on a much larger scale, this is the Pentagon contracting system and your tax dollars. Why not demand that the defense department stop violating federal law, as it has since 1992, and provide Congress with auditable information so that its accounting arm, the Government Accountability Office (GAO) can audit the notoriously porous Pentagon books?

Suppose the head of your neighborhood association kept sugarcoating problems, kept lying to you, kept describing conditions that weren't so, and kept doing things that would enrich himself in conflict with his duties. Would you keep supporting him in that position? Probably not. Well, that is your president, day after day.

What if your neighbor kept dumping polluted water and solid-waste pollutants on your lawn and all around your house? Would you demand that your town or city stop this contamination, or would you sit quietly and accept this abuse because you don't believe in regulation? Well, Trump's EPA wrecker, Scott Pruitt, is busily going around weakening environmental protections and even taking away investigators of environmental crime and forcing them to be his personal security guard.

Let's say your farmers' market vendors sensed that you were very dependent on the food they provide and they proceeded to triple the prices—it's not difficult to predict your reaction. Yet that is what the drug companies have done with many of your important medicines over the past ten years. Yet where are the outraged demands for the government to have the power to negotiate volume discounts, facilitate generics, restrain prices for drugs rooted in your taxpayer-funded research by the National Institutes of Health, and allow imported competition from Canada?

You get into a bus or cab and the driver regularly cheats you into paying several times more than you should pay and then covers it up. When you find out about it, all hell breaks loose next time you confront him. What about Wells Fargo bank—they knowingly created unauthorized, false credit card and auto insurance accounts, wrongly billing customers millions of times. Imagine: no criminal prosecutions yet, no wholesale resignation of the well-paid board of directors, and very few customers are leaving the bank. Wells Fargo keeps reporting great profits while hassling victims into settlements. What's one takeaway? The bigger the crook, the bigger is our surrender. Too big to fail or jail!

The neighbor in charge of the communal drinking-water well on rural land knows it's being contaminated by his previous employer, and he expects to be hired back by his old boss. Children as well as their parents are at risk. Well, welcome to Trump's deregulations of food, drugs, auto pollution, and workplace investor safety. The regulators come from the industries' payroll and expect to go back to their former employers with a big raise.

There are just a few contrasts between individual and institutional crimes and wrongdoing and our different responses to them. Facebook, Google, and Equifax can misuse your personal information to your perceived disadvantage and repeatedly get away with it.

The White House under Bush/Cheney can unconstitutionally ignite wars and lie to the people about the reasons, produce millions of casualties and untold destruction of innocent people's homelands, get reelected, and later retire with huge speech fees without being chased by the "sheriffs."

It is doubtful whether you would allow your hamlet's political leaders to get away with such violent assaults, even if they wanted to do so.

If our moral, ethical, and legal codes cannot reach up to the tops of these institutions on behalf of wronged, injured individuals and communities and societies, we'll get what we've been getting, which is worse and worse immunities and impunities with each passing decade.

Isn't this a fault/no-fault paradox worth thinking about?

Detecting What Unravels Our Society—
Bottom-up and Top-down

JULY 19, 2017

The unraveling of a society's institutions, stability, and reasonable order does not sound alarms to forewarn the citizenry, apart from economic yardsticks measuring poverty, jobs, wages, health, savings, profits, and other matters *economic*.

However, we do have some signs that we should not allow ourselves to ignore. Maliciousness, profiteering, and willful ignorance on the part of our political and corporate rulers undoubtedly contribute to worsening injustice. Let's consider some ways that we as citizens, far too often, collectively allow this to happen.

1. Democracy is threatened when citizens refuse to participate in power, whether by not voting, not thinking critically about important issues, not showing up for civic activities, or allowing false emotional appeals and flattery by candidates and parties to sway them on important issues. Without an informed and motivated citizenry, the society starts to splinter.

2. If people do not do their homework before Election Day and know what to expect of candidates and of themselves, the political TV ads and the plutocrats' campaign cash will take control of what is on the table and what is off the table. This leads to the most important changes ending up on the floor, despite the majority of Americans wanting them.

3. Too often, you have a grievance as a consumer, worker, taxpayer, or citizen and you hit the wall trying to reach someone who should be helping you. Robots on the telephone, either nonhuman or human, are of little help. Repeated failure to productively voice one's grievances leads to alienation, anxiety, and withdrawal rather than resurgence to demand remedy.

4. When a majority of people think their government doesn't work for them but instead serves the rich and powerful, they begin to forget the good that government and honest civil servants at all levels do, or can do (see Jacob Hacker and Paul Pierson's 2016 book *American Amnesia*), thereby disregarding their crucial watchdog role as citizens. In the process, they passively surrender control of government to the plutocrats and oligarchs—leading to a corporate state defined by crony capitalism. The military-industrial complex and the corporate welfarists know how to extract dollars for boondoggles from our government, which is all too willing to turn its back on taxpayers.

5. When people make up their minds about an ideology or politician without the facts and relinquish any willingness to hear alternative views, societies become polarized. People are stereotyped, the marketplace of ideas goes bankrupt, and instances of incivility and dehumanization increase.

6. When people constantly consume media fueled by violence, political insults, crime, and celebrity misbehavior rather than giving voice to the good that people do every day in civil society or to important points of agreement between liberals and conservatives, the way we relate to news and each other becomes needlessly skewed. This problem has increased exponentially in recent years.

7. If people of all backgrounds feel powerless, they will be powerless. This self-perception stifles democracy and often results in people turning their blame against one another and ignoring the power structures at the root of the problem.

8. Readers think; thinkers read. That includes learning from the mistakes of societies throughout history that wrongly believed that they were impervious to crumbling from within. In our culture of virtual reality and Twitter-length propaganda, we all too often forget the valuable lessons of past mistakes. History is a great teacher, as anyone can attest who has studied how the bloody World War I was triggered by a teenager assassinating an archduke in Sarajevo or how a few rulers of autocratic nations, without institutional civic and political

resistance, caused the deaths of approximately sixty million people in World War II.

9. At this point, some readers may be wondering about the powerful people who comprise the Wall Street and Washington supremacists. Aren't they heavily responsible for the disintegration of our society's economic and political health? Of course. But we citizens, day after day, let them get away with actions that embolden them further through what they see as our habitual passivity.

10. Supporting good candidates who so often lose to silver-tongued bad candidates would be a start. Given what people think of Washington politicians, tens of millions of voters are choosing bad candidates. The voters may want to ask themselves whether the candidates and rhetoric they bond with are hiding cruel records and votes against the voters' own interests. The Washington Republicans' current effort to take away or make less affordable health insurance, even of Trump voters, is a case in point.

For a top-down analysis, read Peter Wehner's searing column "Declaration of Disruption" in the July 4, 2017, issue of the *New York Times*, regarding how the rulers at the top are now leading our country "toward chaos, disarray and entropy."

Half of democracy is showing up at community gatherings, marches, meetings, and elections with your fellow citizens. No one can stop you from saying yes to your neighbors, near and far, when they send you their kind invitations to meet new people, hear new ideas, and be urged to pull together for a better community, state, nation, and world.

Democracy and its blessings work, but only if we don't drop out, and only if we recommit ourselves to securing these blessings for our posterity. It's easier than we think!

The Destructive Power Trips of Amazon's Boss

For his smallish stature, Amazon boss Jeff Bezos has a booming, uproarious laugh. Unleashed during workdays, its sonic burst startles people, given it comes from as harsh and driven a taskmaster as exists on the stage of corporate giantism.

Is Bezos's outward giddiness a worrisome reflection of what Bezos is feeling on the inside? Is he laughing at all of us?

Is Bezos laughing at the tax collectors after having avoided paying most states' sales taxes for years on all the billions of books he sold online, thereby giving him an immediate 6–9 percent price advantage over brick-and-mortar bookstores, which also paid property taxes to support local schools and public facilities? That and being an early online bookseller gave Bezos his crucial foothold, along with other forms of tax avoidance that big companies utilize.

Is Bezos laughing at the bureaucratic labor unions that somehow can't get a new handle on organizing the tens of thousands of exploited blue-collar workers crying for help in Amazon warehouses and other stress-driven installations? With a net worth over $80 billion at the time of this writing, why should he worry?

Is Bezos laughing at the giant retailers, who are closing hundreds of stores because their thin margins cannot withstand Amazon's predatory pricing?

Is Bezos laughing at the Justice Department's Antitrust Division which, before Trump, was studying how old antitrust laws could be used to challenge monopolizing Molochs such as Amazon in the twenty-first century? It is time for antitrust officials to explore new regulatory actions and modern legislation to deal with today's conglomerates.

Is Bezos laughing at Main Street, USA, which he is in the process of hollowing out, along with nearby shopping malls that can't figure out how to supersede the convenience of online shopping with convivial ground-shopping experience?

Is Bezos laughing at Walmart, bestirring itself, which is starting to feel like giant Sears Roebuck did before Walmart's relentless practices caught up and crushed what is now a shrunken, fragile Sears?

Is Bezos laughing at the United States Postal Service, to which he has given—for the time being—much business for shipping Amazon's packages? Bezos has no intention of this being a long-term arrangement. Imagine Amazon with its own fleet of driverless vehicles and drones. Amazon is already using part-time workers to deliver its wares.

Is Bezos laughing at the *Washington Post*, which he bought for a song in 2014 while he was holding down a large contract with the CIA and other government agencies?

Is Bezos laughing at Alibaba, the huge (bigger than Amazon) Chinese online seller that is trying but failing to get a toehold in the US market? It is hard to match Amazon's ruthlessness on its home turf.

Is Bezos laughing at people's manipulated susceptibility for convenience, hooking them with ninety-nine dollars a year for free shipping? Ordering from their computer or cell phone for speedy delivery to sedentary living, Amazon's customers are robbed of the experience of actively going to local businesses where they can personally engage with others, get offered on-the-spot bargains, and build relationships for all kinds of social, civic, and charitable activities.

Is Bezos laughing at many millions of Amazon customers who think temporary discounts and minor shipping convenience can make up for the billions of tax dollars Amazon has learned to avoid and the thousands of small-business competitors whose closures shrink the local property tax base that supports schools and other essential public services?

As Amazon spreads around the world selling everything and squeezing other businesses that use its platform, is Bezos laughing at humanity? His ultimate objective seems to be to preside over a megatrillion-dollar global juggernaut that is largely automated except for that man at the top with the booming laugh who rules over the means by which we consume everything, from goods to media to groceries. Crushing competitors, history shows, leads to monopolizers raising prices.

Consumers, workers, and retailers alike must be on higher alert and address this growing threat. You have nothing to lose except Bezos's tightening algorithmic chains. To start the conversation, you can wait for Franklin Foer's new book out this September, titled *World Without Mind: The Existential Threat of Big Tech*. Until then, a good substitute is his 2014 article in the *New Republic*, "Amazon Must Be Stopped."

Vanishing the People's Wealth to Make the Bosses Richer

JULY 11, 2016

Imagine you are a shareholder in a big company and the top executives are sitting on huge amounts of cash and are not interested in putting it to work through productive capital investments, research and development, reducing company debt, or paying employees a higher wage. What would you want done about it? Since you and other shareholders are the owners of the company, you'd likely say, "Give us back our money in cash dividends."

"No way," say your hired hands, the company managers, who have spent a staggering $2.1 trillion of your money in the last five years on stock buybacks allegedly to increase the company's earnings per share ratio instead of increasing shareholder dividends. Over time, this tactic has not worked except to make the corporate bosses richer, which is the real reason for many buybacks.

What is the incentive for this cash-burning frenzy? According to University of Massachusetts scholar William Lazonick, in 2012 the five hundred highest-paid executives received 52 percent of their remuneration from stock options and another 26 percent from stock awards.

Call it self-interest or conflict of interest with their shareholder-owners—they continue to get away with this massive heist, this clever transfer of wealth. They do not need to get the approval of their owners—the stockholders—under what is called the "business judgement rule" (BJR). Developed by corporate attorneys and adopted with few boundaries by the Delaware courts—the state where corporate bosses go for pioneering leniency—the BJR strips a corporation's owners of meaningful control over company executives and the board of directors other than to sell their stock, thereby leaving the rascals in charge.

Here is the definition of the BJR by the Delaware courts: "The business judgement rule . . . is a presumption that in making a business decision the directors of a corporation acted on an informed basis, in good faith, and in the honest belief that the action taken was in the best interests of the corporation."

How's that for a legally entrenched entitlement during a growing, decades-long corporate crime wave that largely goes unprosecuted by politically and budgetarily strapped enforcement agencies? A crime wave that in 2008 brought a criminally speculative, self-enriching Wall Street down, draining trillions of dollars in pension-fund and mutual-fund assets—the very institutions that owned the most shares on the major stock exchanges!

Making matters worse, as *Business Insider* concludes, "all the evidence shows that—in recent years—[stock buybacks have] not actually helped boost stock values at all." The bosses are eating the company's seed corn. Indeed, before 1982, when the obeisant Securities and Exchange Commission (SEC) opened the floodgates for this executive rampage, buybacks were illegal. They were considered *insider trading* by the top company executives.

How do these trillions of dollars of inert money accumulate? From conniving management that doesn't know how or want to deploy it to increase the value of the company and its stakeholders. The money flows from consumers and taxpayers (corporate welfare) and from the sacrifices of workers whose needs and increased productivity could be rewarded with better pay and pensions.

Walmart's buyback binge brings the impact closer to Hometown, USA. The company, whose controlling stock is held by the super-rich Walton family, has spent *$70 billion* in stock buybacks since 2004. Its poorly paid laborers, often without full-time hours, have a high turnover rate and cannot make ends meet for their families, not to mention a harsh paucity of benefits.

Looking at Costco and other big competitors that pay better and experience lower turnover and higher worker morale, Walmart has inched its workers toward a minimum of ten dollars an hour in the past two years. How much family anguish and deprivation would have been avoided over the years if Walmart's bosses did not waste tens of billions of dollars and instead followed founder Sam Walton's practice of "retain and reinvest" that built the company's model?

Warren Buffett, in his letter to shareholders back in 1999, declared that "all too often," repurchases of stock are made for an "ignoble reason: to pump or support the stock price." Only now it's mostly not even working for that narcissistic objective.

Since the mid-1980s, massive stock buybacks have bizarrely resulted, declares Mr. Lazonick, in corporations "fund[ing] the stock market rather than vice versa. Over the past decade net equity issues of non-financial corporations averaged [negative] $376 billion per year." So much for stock markets raising investment capital.

In 2009, President Barack Obama pushed through Congress a modest $831 billion stimulus bill spread over a decade. The money was allocated to federal tax incentives, infrastructure, education, and expansion of social welfare benefits such as unemployment compensation.

Republicans in Congress hit the ceiling, attacking the bill as wasteful government spending. In a private-enterprise, free-market economy, they say it is not the government's business to create jobs. Apparently, their big corporate paymasters believe that it's not the business of business to use trillions of dollars of profits to create jobs either.

Uncontrollable—Pentagon and Corporate Contractors Too Big to Audit

MARCH 17, 2016

The Reuters report put this colossal dereliction simply: "A law in effect since 1992 requires annual audits of all federal agencies—and the Pentagon alone has never complied."

All $585 billion and more—e.g., for the Afghanistan and Iraq conflicts—of your money not just un-audited, but, in the sober judgement of the Government Accountability Office (GAO) of Congress, this vast military budget is year after year *un-auditable*. That means that the congressional auditors cannot obtain the basic accounting data to do their job on your behalf.

Auditing the Department of Defense (DOD) receives support from the left and right, from Senator Bernie Sanders (I-VT) to Senator Ted Cruz (R-TX).

HR 942, the "Audit the Pentagon Act of 2014," is supported by both Democrats and Republicans in the House of Representatives. In the statement announcing this legislation, the sponsors declared, "In April the Government Accountability Office reported the Pentagon's financial house remains in disorder, finding more than 1,000 weaknesses relating to accounting standards, management oversight and compliance with laws. 'Funds control weaknesses have prevented DOD from reporting reliable financial information, including information on the use of public funds, results of operations, and financial statements, and put DOD at risk of overobligating and overexpending its appropriations,' the GAO said."

Republican right-winger representative Mike Conaway (R-TX) used to be a CPA in private life. At a congressional hearing in 2011, he told Defense Secretary Robert Gates: "I go home to folks in West Texas, and when they find out the Department of Defense can't be audited, they are stunned." His constituents may be more stunned to learn that their congressman also voted for all bills that would expand defense budgets, which is why HR 942 is going nowhere unless the people rally to make auditing the Pentagon a presidential-election issue.

Secretary Gates and his successor, Secretary Panetta, agree with Representative Conway's observations. Yet it has seemed that the military—this huge expanse of bureaucracy, which owns twenty-five million acres (over seven times the size of Connecticut) and over five hundred thousand buildings in the US and around the world—is beyond anybody's control, including that of the secretaries of defense, the military's own internal auditors, the president, tons of publicly available GAO audits, and Congress. How can this be?

Enormous scandal after enormous scandal is reported by newspapers such as the *New York Times*, the *Washington Post*, and the *Wall Street Journal* and by news services such as Reuters, the Associated Press, and ProPublica. Citizen groups from the left and right excoriate this runaway budget, including the National Taxpayers Union, the Project On Government Oversight, and Taxpayers for Common Sense. TO NO AVAIL!

Have you heard of the $43 million natural gas station in Afghanistan that was supposed to cost $500,000? Do you know about the $150 million villas that were built for corporate contractors in Afghanistan so they could spend another $600 million advising Afghans about starting private businesses in that war-torn country?

Or how about the billions of dollars spent on spare parts because the Army or Air Force didn't know the whereabouts of existing spare parts in forgotten warehouses here and there? What about the $9 billion the Pentagon admitted could not be accounted for in Iraq during the first several months of the invasion?

The list goes on, together with massive cost overruns by the private contractors that are rewarded with more contracts. Soldiers get dirty drinking water, bad food, inadequate equipment, and security breaches by these contractors. No matter.

President Eisenhower's farewell warning about the "military-industrial complex" becomes ever more of an understatement as it devours over half of the entire federal government's operating budget.

Mike McCord, the Pentagon's chief financial officer, has some startling explanations for why the DOD is not ready for an audit. It's not the DOD's "primary mission," he says, which is "to defend the nation, fight, and win wars." He continues: "We're too big to just sort of blow up all our systems and go buy one new, gargantuan IT system that runs the entire department."

Where are the accounting-standards groups when we need them to speak up?

Mr. McCord certainly knows how to enhance his job security. Why no Pentagon audit? Too big to audit? No. Just too many scandals, too much waste, gigantic weapon-system redundancies, overlaps between military branches, and many sinecures in bloated, inflexible bureaucracies, so often condemned by commanding generals in the field.

McCord himself has pointed to the areas in which he prefers to cut costs in order to save money: congressionally opposed base closures, retiree costs, and consolidating "its Tricare health system."

In the final analysis, the principal culprits, because they have so much to lose in profits and bonuses, are the giant defense companies like Lockheed Martin, Boeing, General Dynamics, Raytheon, Northrop Grumman, and others that lobby Congress, congressional district by congressional district, for more, more, more military contracts, grants, and subsidies. They routinely hire ex-Pentagon specialists and top brass who know how to negotiate the ways and means inside of the government.

President Eisenhower sure knew what he was talking about. Remember, he warned not just about taxpayer waste, but a Moloch eating away at our liberties and our critical domestic necessities.

Monsanto and Its Promoters versus
Freedom of Information

OCTOBER 2, 2015

Next year, the federal Freedom of Information Act (FOIA) will celebrate its fiftieth anniversary as one of the finest laws our Congress has ever passed. It is a vital investigative tool for exposing government and corporate wrongdoing.

The FOIA was championed by Congressman John E. Moss (D-CA), who strove to "guarantee the right of every citizen to know the facts of his Government." Moss, with whom I worked closely as an outside citizen advocate, said that "without the fullest possible access to Government information, it is impossible to gain the knowledge necessary to discharge the responsibilities of citizenship."

All fifty states have adopted FOIA statutes.

As the FOIA approaches its fiftieth year, it faces a disturbing backlash from scientists tied to the agrichemical company Monsanto and its allies. Here are some examples.

On March 9, three former presidents of the American Association for the Advancement of Science—all with ties to Monsanto or the biotech industry—wrote in the pages of the *Guardian* to criticize the use of state FOIA laws to investigate taxpayer-funded scientists who vocally defend Monsanto, the agrichemical industry, the use of pesticides, and genetically modified food. They called the FOIA requests an "organized attack on science."

The super-secretive Monsanto has stated, regarding the FOIA requests, that "agenda-driven groups often take individual documents or quotes out of context in an attempt to distort the facts, advance their agenda, and stop legitimate research."

Advocates with the venerable Union of Concerned Scientists (UCS) do worry that the FOIA can be abused to harass scientists for ideological reasons. This is true; for example, human-caused global warming deniers have abused the FOIA against climate scientists working at state universities, such as Michael Mann of Pennsylvania State University.

Among other suggestions, UCS recommends the following:

- Universities should clarify their policies and procedures with regard to open records requests, ensure that their employees understand these policies, and make sure they have considered how they will respond when overly broad requests are used to harass their researchers. . . .

- Legislators should examine their open records laws and ensure that they include appropriate exemptions that will protect privacy and academic freedom without compromising accountability.

- The National Academy of Sciences and other research organizations should provide guidance to legislators and universities on what should be disclosed and what should be protected.

For more on the UCS positions see: ucsusa.org/resources/freedom-bully.

The proper response to abuses of the FOIA is not, however, to advocate blocking citizens or reporters from using the FOIA.

There are countless government and corporate scandals that have been revealed by the FOIA, but here are just two from this year.

In February, Justin Gillis and John Schwartz of the *New York Times* used documents obtained by Greenpeace and the Climate Investigations Center through the FOIA to expose the corporate ties of climate change–denying scientist Wei-Hock "Willie" Soon, who received over $1.2 million from the fossil fuel industry over the last ten years. Soon even called his scientific papers "deliverables" to his corporate donors.

Another area of risk to food and health was revealed by FOIA requests. There are legitimate concerns about the environmental and health-related perils of genetically engineered crops and food. And the concerns are mounting. For example, in March, the World Health Organization's International Agency for Research on Cancer (IARC) classified the herbicide glyphosate—which is sprayed as Roundup on many genetically engineered crops—as "probably carcinogenic to humans."

On August 20, in the *New England Journal of Medicine*, Philip J. Landrigan and Charles Benbrook wrote that "the argument that there is nothing new about genetic rearrangement misses the point that GM crops are now the agricultural products most heavily treated with herbicides and that two of these herbicides may pose risks of cancer." Another study published on August 25 in the journal *Environmental Health* suggests that very low levels of exposure to Roundup "can result in liver and kidney damage" in rats, "with potential significant health implications for animal and human populations."

US Right to Know, a nonprofit consumer group staffed by consumer advocates, is conducting an investigation of the food and agrichemical industries, including companies like Monsanto, and how they use front groups and taxpayer-funded professors at public universities to advance their claims that processed foods, artificial additives, and GMOs are safe, wholesome, and beyond reproach.

Based on documents that US Right to Know obtained through the FOIA, two-time Pulitzer Prize winner Eric Lipton wrote a front-page *New York Times* article about how Monsanto, and the agrichemical industry as a whole, use publicly funded scientists to lobby and promote their messages and products. For example, Lipton reported on a $25,000 grant from Monsanto to University of Florida professor Kevin Folta, who had repeatedly denied having ties to Monsanto: "'This is a great 3rd-party approach to developing the advocacy that we're looking to develop,' Michael Lohuis, the director of crop biometrics at Monsanto, wrote last year in an email as the company considered giving Dr. Folta an unrestricted grant."

One thing is clear: food safety, public health, the commercialization of public universities, corporate control of science, and the research produced by taxpayer-funded scientists to promote commercial products are all appropriate subjects for FOIA requests.

The use of the FOIA by citizens, journalists, and others to expose scandals is essential to ensure honest scientific inquiry and is critical to developing protective public health and environmental standards. Scientific research should not be contaminated by the inevitable biases and secrecy that come with corporate contracts at public universities.

The FOIA is a valuable tool to help citizens uncover corruption and wrongdoing, and to vindicate our right to know what our own governments are doing.

General Motors: Homicidal Fugitive from Justice

SEPTEMBER 18, 2015

Yes, it's official. General Motors engaged in criminal wrongdoing for long knowing about the lethal defect in its ignition switch that took at least 174 lives and counting, plus serious injuries. At least 1.6 million GM cars—Chevrolet Cobalt and other models—hid this danger from trusting drivers, according to the Center for Auto Safety (autosafety.org). Corporation executives who lie to or mislead the federal government violate Title 18 of the federal code and risk criminal penalties.

But the long-mismanaged automaker was not required by the Department of Justice (DOJ) to plead guilty at all. Preet Bharara, the US attorney for New York's Southern District, and US attorney general Loretta Lynch did not indict either General Motors or known culpable officials in GM, including top GM lawyers and safety directors, who participated in the cover-up year after year while lying to federal officials and not reporting these defects.

The DOJ fined GM a modest $900 million, which the *Wall Street Journal* called a "lower-than-expected financial penalty." The government also agreed to a notorious three-year "deferred prosecution" deal, which corporate crime expert and law professor Rena Steinzor called "a toothless way of approaching a very serious problem." Three years of compliance while watched by a federal monitor, and then the DOJ dismisses the charges.

The "problem" is a fast-maturing enforcement doctrine—under George W. Bush and Barack Obama—that can be called crimes without criminals. This turns criminal jurisprudence on its head. There is one standard for big corporations shielding their individual criminals with immunity. There is another standard for street criminals who can be imprisoned for many years for forging checks or burglarizing buildings without harm to humans.

At a press conference to announce the hoisting of this sweetheart deal, US attorney Preet Bharara weakly excused the absence of indictments by asserting: "We apply the laws as we find them, not the way we wish they might be." Former NHTSA administrator Joan Claybrook asked Mr. Bharara whether he would urge Congress to meet his wishes. Mr. Bharara dodged the question. He argues that his prosecution was restricted because of "complex structures" in corporations. A multimillion-dollar prosecution budget, with many subpoenas, interviews with GM officials, and engineers should have penetrated the "corporate veil," especially since Mr. Bharara waxed eloquent about how GM cooperated and opened itself up for inquiry.

Professor Steinzor, author of *Why Not Jail?: Industrial Catastrophes, Corporate Malfeasance, and Government Inaction*, rebutted, saying these excuses "are contradicted by their own creative and aggressive behavior in other cases" involving some small, criminal companies. In one case, against a peanut company, the DOJ got felony convictions, and a former owner is facing a life sentence under the federal sentencing guidelines.

University of Virginia law professor Brandon Garrett, author of *Too Big to Jail: How Prosecutors Compromise with Corporations*, pointed out that "individuals were even wrongly convicted of vehicular manslaughter, having been driving defective [GM] cars. A case this serious should result in a criminal conviction for the company and many criminal convictions for the individuals involved."

In short, as noted by the *Corporate Crime Reporter*: "GM did the crime, the drivers do the time." A former top DOJ prosecutor and current University of Michigan law professor David Uhlmann said that the deferred prosecution agreement with GM "demonstrated how badly the Justice Department has lost its way with regard to corporate crime. . . . There is no excuse for the Department agreeing to dismiss its criminal case against GM if the company pays a large fine and cleans up its act."

The industry is now heavily lobbying the House and Senate to keep a provision for criminal penalties out of the pending highway bill being championed by Senator Richard Blumenthal (D-CT) and Senator Edward Markey (D-MA). But since 1966, brazen GM and the auto industry have spent millions of dollars to make sure there is no specific criminal penalty, even for willful violations of safety standards that take lives, in the auto safety law.

Unfortunately, these giant companies have Congressman Fred Upton (R-MI) and Senator John Thune (R-SD), the respective committee chairs, wrapped around their dollar-spinning fingers.

Senators Blumenthal and Markey severely criticized the DOJ's concession: "Knowing and willful violations of the vehicle safety statutes—deception[s] that literally kill American consumers—should be a criminal violation, as we have proposed in the Motor Vehicle Safety Act of 2015 and in the Hide No Harm Act." They should also demand no more deferred prosecution malarkey in dealing with corporate crime generally.

The mass media has given significant coverage to the sixty-four million cars recalled by the likes of Toyota, Honda, GM, Chrysler, and other auto manufacturers, along with the huge debacle by Takata over its airbag cost cutting. So the politicians on Capitol Hill, having conducted tough-talk public hearings in the past two years, know they are in the spotlight.

Please help the hundreds of victims and their families, such as Laura Christian, who lost her sixteen-year-old daughter, Amber Marie Rose, and is still fighting to bring GM and its culpable officials to justice.

Call Senator Blumenthal's office at 202-224-0335 or Senator Markey's office at 202-224-2742 for further information.

"King Obama," His Royal Court, and the Trans-Pacific Partnership

JUNE 25, 2015

The Trans-Pacific Partnership (TPP)—a global corporate noose around US local, state, and national sovereignty—narrowly passed a major procedural hurdle in Congress by gaining "fast-track" status. This term, fast-track, is a euphemism for your members of Congress—senators and representatives—handcuffing themselves so as to prevent any amendments or adequate debate before the final vote on the Trans-Pacific Partnership, another euphemism that is used to avoid the word "treaty," which would require ratification by two-thirds of the Senate. This anti-democratic process is being pushed by "King Obama" and his royal court.

Make no mistake. If this was only a trade treaty—reducing tariffs, quotas, and the like—it would not be so controversial. Yet the corporate-indentured politicians keep calling this gigantic treaty with thirty chapters—of which only six relate to traditional trade issues—a "trade agreement" instead of a "treaty." The other twenty-four chapters, if passed as they are, will have serious impacts on your livelihoods as workers and consumers, as well as on your air, water, food, and medications.

The reason I call President Obama "King Obama" in this case is that he and his massive corporate lobbies (royal court), have sought to circumvent the checks-and-balances system that is the very bedrock of our government. They have severely weakened the independence of the primary branch of our government—Congress—and fought off any court challenges with medieval defenses, such as "no American citizen has any standing to sue for harm done by such treaties" or "the subject is a political, not judicial, matter."

Only corporations, astonishingly enough, are entitled to sue the US government for any alleged harm to their profits from health, safety, or other types of regulations; these cases are then carried out not in open courts but in secret tribunals that operate as offshore kangaroo courts.

President Obama has weakened two branches of our government in favor of the third, which is currently his executive branch that has secret negotiations with eleven other nations, some of which are brutal regimes.

Allowing foreign investors (a.k.a. corporations) to bypass our courts and sue the US government (a.k.a. the taxpayers) for monetary damages before secret outside tribunals is considered unconstitutional by many, including Alan Morrison, a constitutional law specialist and litigator now at George Washington University Law School.

In the mid-nineties, I opposed the creation of the North American Free Trade Agreement (NAFTA) and the World Trade Organization (WTO). President Obama and some members of Congress say that the TPP will be different from NAFTA and the WTO, but I doubt they have read the entire draft of the TPP. They're relying on summary memos by the US Trade Office and corporate lawyers who, for example, represent drug companies that sugarcoat the complex monopolistic extension of pharmaceutical patents and how this will result in higher prices for your medications.

I challenge President Obama to state publicly that he has read the entire TPP. Even a benign monarch would do this for their trusting subjects.

Inside these hundreds of pages of cross-references and repeals of conflicting existing laws is the central subversion, which subordinates our protective laws for labor, consumers, and the environment (impersonally called "nontariff trader barriers") to the supremacy of international global commercial traffic.

One very recent example—by no means the worst possible—just occurred. After Congress passed a popular "country of origin" labeling requirement on meat packages sold in supermarkets, Brazil and Mexico, both exporters of meat to the US, challenged this US law in a secret (yes, literally secret in all respects) tribunal in Geneva under the WTO Treaty. Brazil and Mexico won this legal challenge.

"Many Americans will be shocked that the WTO can order our government to deny US consumers the basic information about where their food comes from and that if the information policy is not gutted, we could face millions in sanctions every year," said Lori Wallach, director of Public Citizen's Global Trade Watch. "Today's ruling spotlights how these so-called 'trade' deals are packed with nontrade provisions that threaten our most basic rights, such as even knowing the source and safety of what's on our dinner plate." A May 2013 survey by the Consumer Federation of America found that 90 percent of adult Americans favored this "country of origin" requirement.

Fearing billions of dollars in penalties, the US Congress is racing to repeal its own law. See how the noose works: foreign countries trying to pull down our higher standards can take conflicts to secret tribunals with three trade judges, who also have corporate clients and can say to the US, "Get rid of your protections or pay billions of dollars in tribute."

The same noose can choke efforts by the US to upgrade our health, safety, and economic rights. Had airbags been proposed by the US Department of Transportation under today's global trade *über alles* regimes, the proposal would have had to go to a harmonization committee of the WTO's signatory countries that would sandpaper or reject this lifesaving technology. Or if the US went it alone, it would expose itself to "repeal or pay" demands by car-exporting nations.

For ten reasons why the TPP is a bad idea for our country and the world, see my recent *HuffPost* column titled "10 Reasons the TPP Is Not a 'Progressive' Trade Agreement."

If this all sounds so outrageous as to strain credulity, go beneath the tip of this iceberg and visit: https://www.citizen.org/topic/globalization-trade/. Then, get ready for the battle over the TPP itself in late autumn. The following are three examples of how to build resistance to an international problem in your local communities.

First, send the legislators who supported the fast-track handcuffs a citizen's summons to appear at a town meeting where you, not they, present the agenda. If the lawmakers think five hundred or more determined people will show up, it is very likely they will relent and meet with you. The unions and other groups working to stop the TPP around the country can get their people to attend these town meetings. August is the congressional recess month. The senators and representative will have no excuse to avoid a town meeting with their constituents. For a list of those legislators who need to be focused on, visit stopfasttrack.com.

Second, hustle together some modest money from groups and individuals, rent an empty storefront, plaster the windows with large signs, and start a rumble of civic resistance in all directions. Politicians sometimes shrug off the warnings of losing contributions from unions. What politicians do fear is their inability to control groups of resurgent voters indeterminately expanding from inside their district or state.

Since opposition to TPP reflects a left-right alliance in Congress and back home, storefronts spell real worry for politicians. They should worry because they chose not to do their homework for their home country.

Third, hold rallies designed to attract, collectively, hundreds or thousands of people around the country. These rallies could have an array of high-profile speakers and entertainers, as well as workers who have been harmed by past so-called trade agreements. Rallies can bring in new people and start the process of galvanizing them about the many problems with the TPP.

Remember, a majority of Americans oppose Congress giving the president fast-track authority to advance the TPP. People know what these "pull down," misnamed trade agreements have done in their own communities. Start organizing today to win tomorrow!

Billionaire Hanauer Hammers
Stock Buybacks

MARCH 13, 2015

Self-made billionaire (meaning he didn't inherit it) Nick Hanauer is not one to mince words, especially when they are backed by facts and principles of fairness. The Seattle entrepreneur, author, and venture capitalist (he was the first nonfamily investor in Amazon), is known for vocally championing Seattle's staggered increase of its minimum wage to fifteen dollars an hour as good for workers and the economy. Any contrary corporatist to debate him on this subject would lose big.

Mr. Hanauer is speaking before business and political groups, including the Democratic senators at their recent Baltimore retreat, about a favorite cause of mine—the utterly damaging waste of massive corporate profits known as stock buybacks. Stock buybacks are so massive—$6.9 trillion worth since 2004—that it justifies Mr. Hanauer's description of them as "the biggest scam bankrupting business and the middle class."

Hear him out: "Our crisis of income inequality wasn't principally caused by the rich not paying enough tax, even though we don't. Rather, it is largely the product of the $1 trillion a year that once went to wages, but now goes to corporate profits. And this demand and investment-killing trillion-dollar-a-year transfer of wealth from the bottom 80 percent of households to the top 1 percent is the direct result of the economic and regulatory policies both Republicans and Democrats have imposed since the dawn of the trickle-down era." That was in 1982, when President Reagan loosened the rules that had made stock buybacks a form of illegal stock manipulation, he adds.

Between 2003 and 2012, stock buybacks amounted to an astounding 54 percent of corporate profits, which could have gone to "higher wages or increased investments in plants and equipment or in public investment," such as infrastructure, all of which would have increased consumer demand—the engine of economic growth, he notes.

Leading shareholder-rights advocate and author Robert A. G. Monks has pointed out that stock buybacks reflect a serious failure of management. Corporations have not used this money for productive purposes and labor well-being, but rather for a paper increase in the earnings per share (EPS) to elevate the value of already-skyrocketing executive compensation packages.

Mr. Hanauer adds to the growing realization by business writers of how harmful stock buybacks, driven by executive greed, can be with this example from Walmart, which recently announced giving its lowest-paid workers a billion dollars more a year in wages:

"[Over ten years], Walmart has spent more than *$65.4 billion* on stock buybacks—about 47 percent of its profits. That's an average of more than $6.5 billion a year in stock buybacks, enough to give each of its 1.4 million US workers a $4,670-a-year raise. It is also, coincidentally, an amount roughly equivalent to the estimated $6.2 billion Walmart costs US taxpayers every year in food stamps, Medicaid, subsidized housing, and other public assistance to its many impoverished employees. In this context, how can stock buybacks be either morally or economically justified?"

James Montier, an asset allocation manager, has documented how a generation of stock buybacks has contributed to reduced business investments and increased inequality.

Jeff Reeves, a MarketWatch contributor, says that stock repurchases are a "clever trick among Wall Street sharks . . . to buy back stock to maximize the value of stock awards to top executives." In an article on March 12, 2015, he listed six giant companies that engaged in mega-cap stock buybacks in 2014 but didn't succeed in increasing their shares' prices. They are ExxonMobil, IBM, Caterpillar, Boeing, McDonald's, and AT&T. He concluded that "massive buyback plans cannot change the fundamentals of a business and turn a stock in a tough spot into a good investment."

Harvard Business Review writers William Lazonick and Matt Hopkins just wrote an article criticizing GM's $5 billion stock buyback, titled "GM's Stock Buyback Is Bad for America and the Company," a few years after US taxpayers had put up $49.5 billion to bail out the company from a self-inflicted, fast-approaching bankruptcy. They quote former top GM executive and auto designer Bob Lutz as saying that stock buybacks are "always a harbinger of the next downturn . . . in almost all cases, you regret it later."

If all the above reflects Mr. Hanauer's views, why does he declare that he too has "done stock buybacks" for his public companies? Well, "virtually all public companies do it. In this era of short-term-focused activist investors, it is nearly impossible to avoid," he acknowledged.

In an interview with me he elaborated. Both major activist shareholders and institutional shareholders, such as leading mutual funds like Fidelity, put "enormous pressure on the company CFOs," he said. They use the argument "Well if you don't believe enough in your stock to buy it back, why should *we* buy your shares?" When he resisted this "artificial inflation of the stock price," saying "we shouldn't be doing this," he "lost every time."

There has been considerable discussion about the misallocation of public budgets toward bloated military expenditures and corporate welfare subsidies, giveaways, bailouts, and extreme tax escapes. Get ready for another public spotlight on the misallocation of record-breaking corporate profits by their executives and boards of directors. Making both of these cruel power plays into major political issues during the next presidential campaign could be a very healthy antidote to an otherwise tedious, vapid, rhetorical exercise through the long primaries and general-election days.

Corporate Destruction of
Free Markets Rules Us

OCTOBER 30, 2014

The ruling dogma of our political economy is corporatism. Corporatism claims to draw legitimacy from the free-market theory that all vendors who do not meet market demands will go under. Corporatism uses this illusion to exert power over all aspects of our political economy.

Free markets, corporatists believe, are the best mechanism to allocate resources for the exchange of goods and services. They believe markets free of regulation, taxation, and competition from government enterprises produce the best results. Their favorite metaphor is Adam Smith's "invisible hand" that produces the greatest good for the greatest number of people by the exertions of many willing sellers and many willing buyers (Adam Smith, they neglected to add, favored public works, public education, and social safety nets like decent wages and public welfare as needed).

Many things intrude on free-market theories, including military expenditures, wars, taxation, public infrastructure, health and safety regulation, and governments' emergency duties. What financier George Soros has called "market fundamentalism" is opposed to any interference with free markets. Yet corporatism makes massive exceptions that rig markets and tilt the seller-buyer balance heavily in favor of the former, which become bigger and bigger global corporations.

Market critics call this hypocrisy. Corporations push for larger military budgets, which have concentrated power in ever fewer military contractors. Other interferences with free markets are less recognizable and more part of the culture of acceptance. Corporate power has entrenched these interferences so deeply that they are rarely part of any political or election-time debate.

Let this point be made in the form of questions rarely asked and therefore rarely answered.

Can there be a free market without freedom of contract? Corporatism has stripped consumers of freedom of contract with fine-print standard-form contracts that become more dictatorial every decade. They now often take away consumers' rights to go to court for their grievances via compulsory arbitration clauses. They stipulate that the vendors can change the contract any way they want—called unilateral modification—which takes away the last vestiges of consumer bargaining power. An example is the unilateral changes in what you have to pay in penalties, late fees, or any hundreds of fees hidden in the fine print. And you can't shop around, because companies don't compete over the fine print. (See faircontracts. org.)

Can there be a free market if workers cannot join together to bargain with large employers whose investors have expanding freedom to form companies, holding companies, subsidiaries, joint ventures, and partnerships to advance their bargaining power? Moreover, in comparison with the freedom of investors, workers are besieged with union-busting intimidations, lockouts, and a system of corporate-driven labor laws that present far more obstacles to go through than is the case with the labor laws of other Western nations.

Can there be a free market without strong and comprehensive antimonopoly, anticartel, and other laws against the myriad of anticompetitive practices that Adam Smith alluded to back in 1776 when he warned of the motives when businessmen gather together?

Today, the antitrust laws are weak, dated, and little-enforced, with puny budgets.

For example, thousands of joint ventures between direct competitors are being formed without concern for the moribund antitrust police. There is globalization of businesses without globalization of law enforcement. Big companies can leverage the differences between nations in a race to the bottom to unfairly gain market power against buyers, workers, and small businesses.

Can there be a free market without a free market of retaining lawyers to pursue wrongful injuries and fraud by both direct negotiation with the perpetrators or resorting to open, public courts? In our country, such private disputes are not socialized by government. They are given over to a market system of legal and other supplementary services. Yet corporatism strives strongly to block or limit, through captive legislators, access to the courts, or it ties the hands of judges and juries, the only people who see, hear, and evaluate the evidence in each case.

Can there be a free market when corporatists produce crony capitalism or torrents of corporate-welfare tax escapes, subsidies, handouts, and bailouts that rig markets against other smaller businesses that are playing by the rules of the market?

Can there be a free market when corporate-managed trade agreements, such as the North American Free Trade Agreement (NAFTA) and the World Trade Organization (WTO), subordinate civic efforts to secure better labor and environmental and consumer treatments to the supremacy of commercial trade? (See citizen.org/trade.)

Finally, can there be a free market when the banks fund and control the powerful, secretive Federal Reserve that tightly regulates interest rates and can buy trillions of dollars in bonds (a.k.a. quantitative easing) to juice the stock markets and the banks, while tens of millions of savers receive less than half of 1 percent in interest on their savings? Libertarians, to their credit, have noted this abuse by this corporate government more clearly than have many liberals.

There are other corporate controls against the free market, such as politically extending already lengthy patent monopolies to ward off competition by, for instance, generic drug producers.

Suffice it to say that the American people have enough evidence to abandon the ideological hypocrisy that corporatism uses to control them.

Corporatism, in reality, is the corporate state—a tyranny, greased by big money in elections—never envisioned by the framers of our Constitution when they started its preamble with "We the People."

Wake up call, anyone? (See citizen.org for more information.)

The Incarceration of the
American Consumer

OCTOBER 3, 2014

How do corporate attorneys sleep at night considering that with the power of their large corporate clients, they often crush the freedoms of workers, consumers, and small communities who are trying to break out of a complex web of shackles?

These highly paid power lawyers expertly weave an intricate system of controls into one-sided contracts enforced by laws garnished with the muscle of big business to wear down all but the most intrepid shoppers.

I am not referring only to the mass-marketing scams, crams, deceptions, and hidden frauds. Who can keep track of this proliferation in the credit, lending, insurance, cell phone, car, health care, home repair, and mortgage businesses? Every year, books and manuals come out to show consumers how they can smartly protect themselves and their money. They are written in a clear, detailed, and graphic manner, but they almost never become bestsellers.

Vendors are trained to rip people off from a distance and make them feel good at the same time. That is one of the purposes of advertisements and packaging. Ripping off consumers is made easier because elementary and high schools neglect this subject. After twelve years of education, millions of students are unequipped with the necessary knowledge that can enable them to make astute purchases and pursue remedies if they are cheated.

We need to focus on the incarcerating infrastructure that corporate attorneys build year after year to insulate their corporate paymasters from structural accountability under the rule of law.

Take the two main pillars of American law—contracts and torts. For half a century, power lawyers, backed by corporate campaign cash for legislators, have hacked at the roots of the legal protections for shoppers and for wrongfully injured people. Fine-print contracts—called "mice print" by Senator Elizabeth Warren—block consumers from going to court and mandate compulsory arbitration. Other fine print lets the vendors change the contract at any time without getting specific consent of the buyers. Internet fine print amounts to simply "clicking" and being instantly bound by a matrix of contract peonage. This victory for corporate lawyers is a defeat for the American people who lose their freedom of contract—a servitude that should arouse conservatives and liberals alike.

The other freedom to have safe products, services, and environments is stripped away by "tort deform," euphemistically called tort reform by the insurance lobby and its corporate clients. Tort law is supposed to award adequate compensation for negligently or intentionally inflicted injuries upon innocent people. Shrinking by the decade in favor of the wrong-doers, tort law has been twisted to block the courtroom door for the most vulnerable of our population.

Corporate lobbyists have swarmed over state legislatures to pass rules that require courts to limit compensation by an arbitrary cap, restrict the evidence that juries can weigh, pulverize class actions, and tie up the judges and juries who are the only ones actually receiving and evaluating the evidence.

An added burden is created by the domination of the credit economy, which harnesses the rights of consumers by the unbridled controls known as secret credit ratings, the iron collar of credit scores, and the very personal information collected on people in the computer age.

The credit economy also undermines people's control of their own money, thus facilitating an array of penalties and fees imposed by credit firms, banks, and payday loan shops, along with growing charges for services unasked-for and unused by consumers, known as cramming.

As if these and other controls over consumers are not enough, corporate lawyers are the architects of the notorious trade agreements such as the North American Free Trade Agreement and the General Agreement on Tariffs and Trade, which created the World Trade Organization (WTO). Americans are learning that these transnational autocratic forms of governance subordinate their labor, consumer, and environmental rights to the supremacy of international commerce. The WTO bypasses our domestic courts and agencies by processing disputes between nations before secret tribunals in Geneva, Switzerland (see citizen.org/trade for more information).

So if consumer safety or labeling standards in the US are viewed as restrictive of trade by nations that export such nonconforming products to the US, they can bring the case to Geneva, where we will likely lose. Instead of going after the nations that sell unsafe products, these "pull down" trade agreements punish those nations that treat their workers fairly, safeguard their environments, and protect their consumers.

The patsy US government under President Clinton even went along with allowing foreign companies to sue our government to compensate them for regulations such as chemical standards that might reduce their sales and profits.

The mounting privilege and immunities of giant global corporations go well beyond tax escapes, loan guarantees, and other abuses using our government to rig the market. Right-wingers condemn these actions and refer to them as "crony capitalism." For example, patients pay higher drug prices because companies rig patent extensions through Congress or bring harassing lawsuits against competitors.

The political power of the "military-industrial complex" leads to sweetheart, single-source contracts and the wholesale and expensive outsourcing of what were once governmental functions, such as feeding soldiers and providing health insurance under contract.

Corporations have succeeded in blocking, delaying, or diluting long-overdue regulation of corporate crime, fraud, and abuse. They have made Congress keep law enforcement budgets so paltry, for example, that billing fraud in the health care industry alone amounts to about $270 billion a year, according to fraud expert Malcolm Sparrow of Harvard University (author of *License to Steal*).

It is the external infrastructure—trade agreements, credit scores, credit ratings, and the privatization of contract law and weakened dispute resolution—that strips consumers of control over their own money and purchases and makes it difficult for such consumers to fight back in court.

Stay tuned. It is only going to get worse unless consumer groups rethink and regroup to move systemic shifts of power from sellers to buyers through community-based economies, group buying, cooperatives, and political power leading to updated law and order. (See yesmagazine.org, faircontracts.org, and ilsr.org for more information.)

Encouraging schools to adopt experiential instruction in detecting consumer fraud and using small-claims court to secure inexpensive justice is an easy first step on the long march to consumer justice.

Corporations Spy on Nonprofits
with Impunity

AUGUST 22, 2014

Here's a dirty little secret you won't see in the daily papers: corporations conduct espionage against US nonprofit organizations without fear of being brought to justice.

Yes, that means using a great array of spycraft and snoopery, including planned electronic surveillance, wiretapping, information warfare, infiltration, dumpster diving, and so much more.

The evidence abounds.

For example, six years ago, based on extensive documentary evidence, James Ridgeway reported in *Mother Jones* on a major corporate espionage scheme by Dow Chemical focused on Greenpeace and other environmental and food activists.

Greenpeace was running a potent campaign against Dow's use of chlorine to manufacture paper and plastics. Dow officials grew worried and eventually desperate.

Ridgeway's article and subsequent revelations produced jaw-dropping information about how Dow's private investigators, from the firm Beckett Brown International (BBI), hired:

- an off-duty DC police officer who gained access to Greenpeace dumpsters at least fifty-five times;

- a company called NetSafe Inc., staffed by former National Security Agency employees expert in computer intrusion and electronic surveillance;

- a company called TriWest Investigations, which obtained phone records of Greenpeace employees and contractors. BBI's notes to its clients contain verbatim quotes that they attribute to specific Greenpeace employees.

Using this information, Greenpeace filed a lawsuit against Dow Chemical; Dow's PR firms, Ketchum and Dezenhall Resources; and others, alleging trespass on Greenpeace's property, invasion of privacy by intrusion, and theft of confidential documents.

Yesterday, the DC Court of Appeals dismissed Greenpeace's lawsuit. In her decision, Judge Anna Blackburne-Rigsby notes, "However Greenpeace's factual allegations may be regarded," its "legal arguments cannot prevail as a matter of law" because "the common law torts alleged by Greenpeace are simply ill-suited as potential remedies." At this time Greenpeace has not decided whether to appeal.

The court's opinion focused on technicalities, like who owned the trash containers in the office building where Greenpeace has its headquarters and whether the claim of intrusion triggers a one- or three-year statute of limitations. But whether or not the court's legal analyses hold water, the outcome—no legal remedies for grave abuses—is lamentable.

Greenpeace's lawsuit "will endure in the historical record to educate the public about the extent to which big business will go to stifle First Amendment protected activities," wrote lawyer Heidi Boghosian, author of *Spying on Democracy*. "It is crucially important that organizations and individuals continue to challenge such practices in court while also bringing notice of them to the media and to the public at large."

This is hardly the only case of corporate espionage against nonprofits. Last year, my colleagues produced a report titled *Spooky Business*, which documented twenty-seven sets of stories involving corporate espionage against nonprofits, activists, and whistleblowers. Most of the stories occurred in the US, but some occurred in the UK, France, and Ecuador. None of the US-based cases has resulted in a verdict or settlement or even any meaningful public accountability. In contrast, in France there was a judgment against Électricité de France for spying on Greenpeace, and in the UK there is an ongoing effort regarding News Corp/News of the World and phone hacking.

Spooky Business found that "many of the world's largest corporations and their trade associations—including the US Chamber of Commerce, Walmart, Monsanto, Bank of America, Dow Chemical, Kraft, Coca-Cola, Chevron, Burger King, McDonald's, Shell, BP, BAE, Sasol, Brown & Williamson, and E.ON—have been linked to espionage or planned espionage against nonprofit organizations, activists, and whistleblowers."

Three examples:

- In 2011, the US Chamber of Commerce, its law firm Hunton & Williams, and technology and intelligence firms such as Palantir and Berico were exposed in an apparent scheme to conduct espionage against the Chamber's nonprofit and union critics.

- Burger King was caught conducting espionage against nonprofits and activists trying to help low-wage tomato pickers in Florida.

- The *Wall Street Journal* reported on Walmart's surveillance tactics against anti-Walmart groups, including the use of eavesdropping via wireless microphones.

Here's why you should care.

This is a serious matter of civil liberties.

The citizen's right to privacy and free speech should not be violated by personal spying merely because a citizen disagrees with the actions or ideas of a giant multinational corporation.

Our democracy can't function properly if corporations may spy and snoop on nonprofits with impunity. This espionage is a despicable means of degrading the effectiveness of nonprofit watchdogs and activists. Many of the espionage tactics employed appear illegal and are certainly immoral.

Powerful corporations spy on each other as well, sometimes with the help of former NSA and FBI employees.

How much? We'll never begin to know the extent of corporate espionage without an investigation by Congress and/or the Department of Justice.

While there is a congressional effort to hold the NSA accountable for its privacy invasions, there is no such effort to hold powerful corporations accountable for theirs.

Nearly fifty years ago, when General Motors hired private investigators to spy on me, it was held to account by the US Senate. GM president James Roche was publicly humiliated by having to apologize to me at a Senate hearing chaired by Senator Abraham Ribicoff (D-CT). It was a memorable but rare act of public shaming on Capitol Hill. GM also paid substantially to settle my suit for compensation in a court of law (*Nader v. General Motors Corp.*, 307 N.Y.S.2d 647).

A public apology and monetary settlement would have been a fair outcome in the Greenpeace case too.

But in the intervening half-century our Congress has been overwhelmed by lethargy and corporate lobbyists. Today, Congress is more lapdog than watchdog.

Think of the Greenpeace case from the perspective of executives at Fortune 500 companies.

They know that Dow Chemical was not punished for its espionage against Greenpeace, nor were other US corporations held to account in similar cases.

In the future, three words may well spring to their minds when contemplating whether to go after nonprofits with espionage: go for it. Unless the buying public votes with its pocketbook to diminish the sales of these offending companies.

The Myths of Big Corporate Capitalism

Large corporate capitalism is a breed apart from smaller-scale capitalism. The former can often avoid marketplace verdicts through corporate welfare, strip owner-shareholders of power over the top company bosses, and offload the cost of their pollution, tax escapes, and other "externalities" onto the backs of innocent people.

Always evolving to evade the theoretically touted disciplines of market competition, efficiency, and productivity, corporate capitalism has been an innovative machine for oppression.

Take productive use of capital and its corollary that government wastes money. Apple Inc. is spending $130 billion of its retained profits on a capital return program, $90 billion of which it will use to repurchase its own stock through 2015. Apple executives do this to avoid paying dividends to shareholders and instead strive to prop up the stock price and the value of the bosses' lucrative stock options. The problem is that the surveys about the impact of stock buybacks show they often do nothing or very little to increase shareholder value over the long run. But they do take money away from research and development. And consumer prices rarely, if ever, drop because of stock buybacks.

Apple's recent iPhone is produced by three hundred thousand low-paid Chinese workers employed by the Foxconn Technology Group. They are lucky to be paid two dollars per hour for their long work weeks. It would take $5.2 billion a year to pay these Chinese iPhone workers about ten dollars per hour.

If the $130 billion from Apple's capital return program was put into a foundation, it could pay out, at 4 percent interest, $5.2 billion year after year. Compare $130 billion of "dead money" to the $1 billion in "live money" Tesla Motors has spent on research and development to produce its revolutionary electric cars.

Forget marketplace competition when it comes to the abuse of the monopoly patent system for medicines, steeped in taxpayer-funded basic research, and its obsolete rationale for encouraging innovation. Welcome to the $1,000 pill—yes, that's the price of Gilead Sciences' latest drug, Sovaldi, which is used to treat hepatitis C, a liver-destroying virus. It is said to have fewer side effects and a higher cure rate than its counterparts. Taken daily at a cost of $1,000 a pill, the twelve-week treatment that is recommended for most patients costs $84,000, and a twenty-four-week course of treatment for the hard-to-treat strain costs $168,000.

Use of this drug is beginning to break the budgets of the insurance-company payers. Representatives from Doctors Without Borders have said that a twelve-week course of treatment should cost no more than $500. Gilead did not sweat out the research and development of this drug. Gilead simply bought Pharmasset—the company with the patent on this drug. Not surprisingly, Gilead stock has surged upward, oblivious to surging public criticism.

Some overseas countries are not so submissive to the "pay or die" corporate edict. The nonprofit group I-MAK (Initiative for Medicines, Access, and Knowledge) has filed a challenge to the patent, claiming that Sovaldi is based on "old science" with "a known compound," thereby not meeting India's stringent requirements for patentability.

Additionally, economist Jamie Love has developed an alternative to such "pay or die" patent monopoly prices while keeping rewards for true innovations (keionline.org).

Another example of corporate greed and waste is the astounding story of the White House trying to procure the replacement of its aging presidential helicopter fleet, which further undermines the myth that big corporations are more efficient than government. Under the George W. Bush administration, the Navy put in an order for twenty-three new helicopters from AgustaWestland, working with Bell Helicopter and Lockheed Martin. The price in 2005 was to be $4.2 billion. Three years later the price of the contract zoomed to $11.2 billion, or nearly $500 million per helicopter (about the price of an Air Force One 747).

Congress's Government Accountability Office (GAO) and the Air Force criticized the contractors and their subcontracting practices. As is usual, Lockheed complained that the cost overruns were due to government modifications.

In June 2009, the Navy terminated the contract after spending $4.4

billion and taking delivery of only nine of these (VH-71) helicopters. By December 2009, the White House and Department of Defense officials washed their hands of this debacle. By that time, the projected cost had risen to $13 billion. In total, the bungled enterprise wasted $3.2 billion, and this presidential procurement effort has to start all over again.

By comparison, $3.2 billion is greater than the combined budgets of Americorps, Public Broadcasting Service, public housing (Choice Neighborhoods), the arts (National Endowment for the Arts), the humanities (National Endowment for the Humanities), the Peace Corps, and the worker safety programs of the Occupational Safety and Health Administration (OSHA).

Imagine if there were similar squandering of those budgets—there would be indignation roaring from Congress! When it comes to the defense industry, well, that's just business as usual, complete with the golden handshakes with the Pentagon for the almost certain cost overruns.

Big corporations should not be allowed the myths of competitive, productive, efficient capitalism—unless they can prove it.

(For many more examples, see my book *Getting Steamed to Overcome Corporatism*, Common Courage Press, 2011.)

Corporate Contractors' Heavy Burdens on Taxpayers

JUNE 5, 2014

Next time you hear federal officials say that there is no money to repair or build necessary public facilities in your community, ask them why there always seems to be money to greatly overpay for government projects that are routinely outsourced to corporate contractors.

It is important to understand why incomplete projects have gone way over budget—projects such as the proposed campus-like Department of Homeland Security in Washington, DC; the "cleanup" of the biggest repository of radioactive waste in the US at the Hanford nuclear reservation in southeastern Washington State; the ballistic missile defense program; and the pie-in-the-sky fusion reactors. They are either behind schedule or without any clue for completion or cessation.

First, the dismal scenes: According to the *Washington Post*, "The construction of a massive new headquarters for the Department of Homeland Security (DHS) . . . is running more than $1.5 billion over budget, is 11 years behind schedule and may never be completed, according to planning documents and federal officials. . . . The entire complex was to be finished as early as this year, at a cost of less than $3 billion."

Only one of the buildings for the Coast Guard has opened.

Second, at Hanford, more than $30 billion has already been spent for the "cleanup," under the Tri-Party Agreement between the US Department of Energy (DOE), the US Environmental Protection Agency (EPA), and the Washington State Department of Ecology. Started in 1989, the effort had a proposed thirty-year timetable. Instead, Hanford officials say they are decades and tens of billions of dollars from completion of this admittedly sprawling brew of atomic-weapons waste in 177 giant underground storage tanks and nine nuclear reactors.

Third, the much-ballyhooed DOE's Fusion Energy Science program has been receiving federal funding since 1951 (declassified in 1957) and has not yet had a replicable successful discovery from which to generate affordable energy. It is a boondoggle annuity for contracting university physicists and companies who once in a while issue a news release announcing a presumed partial step forward as to keep hope alive for awe-struck science writers.

Late physicist Norman Milleron, a critic, who worked at the Lawrence Livermore Lab, was wont to say: "Why not focus on the best fusion reactor we'll ever have—the sun?

Fourth, for thirty years the ballistic missile defense pork barrel has fed the likes of Raytheon and the insatiable corporate lobby that has grown up to feed off the tens of billions of dollars already spent (over $9 billion this year, almost as much as the EPA's budget). Unfortunately, the test results show ballistic missile defense systems don't work. Nor will they likely ever have substantial success. The proposed weapon is too easy to decoy, and even if it did function 100 percent, it is easy to bypass with other more lethal weapons through our ports and other modes.

So dubious is this endless program that years ago the American Physical Society delivered the ultimate denunciation: the mission was unworkable. The leading opponent, MIT professor Theodore Postol, continues to dissect its stumbling, deceptive history and how Congress continues its annual deceptions as it writes gigantic taxpayer checks.

The aforementioned cannot compare to the tens of billions of dollars in cost overruns on the F-35 and F-22 fighter planes, whose Pentagon orders from Lockheed Martin keep being reduced because of the skyrocketing cost of each plane (the F-35 is now at $115 million each; the F-22's last plane in 2009 cost $137 million—which is equivalent to $151 million in 2014 after inflation). The F-35 is still in early production after decades of trouble.

What gives here? How could the remarkable P-38 of World War II come in at $1.3 million a plane, inflation-adjusted, and be produced so quickly in 1944? How could Bechtel Corporation sign a contract in March 1942 with the Navy, drain a swampy area, and construct major buildings before the end of the year? By October 27, 1945, with a workforce of seventy-five thousand people at its peak, the company built ninety-three ships!

Well of course there are lots of reasons and excuses. Different urgencies. Unforeseen situations emerged. Or Congress didn't appropriate enough money each year to keep these projects on schedule, which has led to an increase in costs. Or the planning was unrealistic from the outset. Or corporations knowingly submitted unrealistic budgets ("lowballing") to win federal contracts and funding of these projects instead of opting for adequate, more feasible and frugal alternatives.

There is self-censorship by officials and others who were skeptical of the necessity of these projects, as the deferential Government Services Administration people were regarding the site for the DHS. And of course, the dysfunctional Congress voted to perpetuate pork barreling.

Least noticed are the detailed terms of the contracts themselves. Tighter contracts could have held the government's and contractors' feet to the fire in a variety of ways that could be culled from the history of past successful projects that came in on time and budget. Contract terms could include putting named compliance officers in the hot seat.

Some roads to good performances include automatic disclosure to the public of the full texts of the contracts, including their observance over time; more breaking points to penalize and/or jettison contractors; and better oversight of the early planning process by congressional committees.

Referring to the DHS construction, Representative Jeff Duncan (R-SC) said: "Sometimes you just have to drop back and punt. At what point in time does the government just cut its losses and look for a better way of doing things?" Apparently this will only happen when there is no powerful special interest lobby pushing for sweetheart deals. That is why the only one of the above projects that is likely to be scrapped for alternatives is the DHS project. It has no constituency, according to former DHS secretary Michael Chertoff. The other aforementioned projects will continue to waste taxpayers' dollars. This crony capitalism is disgraceful.

Maybe in all the miasma, there is one clarifying principle, which if observed can greatly correct these chronic, vastly over-budget delays, screw-ups, and incompletions. Nassim Nicholas Taleb elaborated on this topic in inimitable ways—historical and otherwise—within his under-appreciated recent book *Antifragile* (2012), which is actually six books in one. He writes about the importance of having "skin in the game," noting that Roman engineers had "to spend some time under the bridge they built—something that should be required of financial engineers today."

From all pertinent directions regarding a project, the supposedly responsible people need to have skin in the game. It does wonders for focusing attention. It starts with the people who conceive, plan, and find projects. And it doesn't leave out the lawyers who draft those porous contracts filled with escape clauses.

The Cruel and Shameless Ideology
of Corporatism

FEBRUARY 21, 2014

Like ravenous beasts of prey attacking a weakened antelope, the forces of subsidized capital and their mercenaries sunk their fangs into the United Auto Workers (UAW) and its organizing drive at the Volkswagen factory in Chattanooga, Tennessee. The UAW narrowly lost—712 to 626—and the baying pack of plutocrats exalted, as if they had just saved Western civilization in the anti-union, lower-wage South.

The days preceding the vote were a corporatist frenzy with corporatist predators bellowing, "The sky is falling." VW, which sensibly stayed neutral but privately supported the UAW's efforts and its collateral "works councils" (an arrangement that had stabilized and made their unionized, higher-paid workers in Germany more productive), must have wondered on what planet they had landed.

First out of the growling caves were the supine politicians, who always offer those proposing a factory big taxpayer-subsidized bucks to bring crony capitalism to their region. Senator Bob Corker (R-TN) who, without citing his source, warned "I've had conversations today and based on those am assured that should the workers vote against the UAW, Volkswagen will announce in the coming weeks that it will manufacture its new midsize SUV here in Chattanooga." VW immediately denied that cause-and-effect claim.

No matter—Senator Corker then assailed the UAW and its negotiated wages and work rules for bringing down Detroit, along with the Big Three auto companies—GM, Ford, and Chrysler. That's strange because for decades the UAW lifted up industrial labor while the auto companies made record profits. Apart from the mistake the UAW made years ago when they sided with the auto bosses in lobbying Congress against fuel efficiency standards, which would have made domestically produced vehicles more competitive with foreign imports, the responsibility for the auto industry's collapse lies with management. It was all about "product,

product, product," as the auto writers say, and Detroit's products fell behind the Japanese and German vehicles. The J.D. Power ratings, year after year, had US cars bringing up the rear. The foreign car companies rated higher on fit and finish, other quality controls, and fuel efficiency, while, as one former Chrysler executive told me about his industry, "We were producing junk."

Add these losses of sales to the speculative binge of the auto companies' finance subsidiaries, like Ally Financial Inc., previously known as General Motors Acceptance Corporation, which got itself caught in the huge Wall Street downdraft in 2008 and 2009. The result was that the auto giants rushed to demand a huge taxpayer bailout from Washington, which they were given.

Business associations warned of a UAW invasion of other Southern states if the union organized the VW plant.

Nevertheless, the big lie the corporatists tell is that it was all the UAW's fault for getting decent wages for its workers, who face more than a few occupational hazards.

Then something strange happened. In jumped antitax leader Grover Norquist, with a new group that went by the Orwellian name of Center for Worker Freedom (CWF), to put up thirteen billboards in Chattanooga accusing the UAW of supporting Obama and "liberal politicians." Perhaps Mr. Norquist thought this would influence a majority of the factory's workers, who are Republicans.

The CWF's website also made ludicrous postings such as "UAW wants your guns." Was all this anti-unionist Grover Norquist's bizarre way of promoting the idea of cutting tax revenues by keeping wages down?

It gets stranger. Powerful Republican state legislators joined with the local state senator, Bo Watson, who said that if workers vote to join the UAW, "I believe any additional incentives from the citizens of the state of Tennessee for expansion or otherwise will have a very tough time passing the Tennessee Senate." He was referring to a continuation of the $577 million already granted (in state and local subsidies) to the existing VW plant to locate there, with an additional bonanza of $700 million more in taxpayer funds should VW open up a new line of SUVs.

This is big-time corporate welfare, which Grover Norquist has repeatedly said he is adamantly against. How to reconcile? Who knows? He dominates congressional Republicans with his no-tax pledge, but Norquist may be spreading himself too thin when he takes on the livelihoods of American industrial and commercial workers.

There is another anomaly operating here. As Jay Bookman, the *Atlanta Journal-Constitution* politics writer, observes, these legislators and Governor Bill Haslam "are clearly threatening to use tax subsidies to punish VW for what it believes to be a good business decision."

What were the factors among the 89 percent of the workers who voted in the union election?

The no-voters felt that VW was paying them wages and benefits equivalent to what workers get at other UAW or organized factories, following the union's major concessions in recent years. So why should they pay monthly union dues? They also took in the warnings of the politicians that a possible extension of the plant may not be given "tax incentives."

The "yes" voters, on the other hand, wanted a collective voice through the "works councils," which, under US law, require a union. Such a combination has worked in all other European VW plants. Plant worker Chris Brown said it helps efficiency. He explained that "on the assembly line, the process changes each year because [of] new models. A voice in the company would help smooth the process from year to year."

The nonunion foreign transplants, as they are called, have to-date opposed the UAW's unionizing efforts, including Nissan, Toyota, and Honda. But the UAW will keep trying.

It's not the end of the world for the union that Walter and Victor Reuther built, which in the 1930s lifted up exploited, voiceless auto workers to a decent living standard with benefits, at the same time as the auto industry was expanding enormously.

As the two-tier auto industry wage system moves more workers to the lower tier, the appeal of a unified labor voice will become clearer.

Corporatizing National Security:
What It Means

JUNE 20, 2013

Privacy is a sacred word to many Americans, as demonstrated by the recent uproar over the brazen invasion of it by the Patriot Act–enabled National Security Agency. The information about dragnet data-collecting of telephone and internet records leaked by Edward Snowden has opened the door to another pressing conversation—one about privatization, or corporatization of this governmental function.

In addition to potentially having access to the private electronic correspondence of American citizens, what does it mean that Mr. Snowden—a low-level contractor—had access to critical national security information not available to the general public? Author James Bamford, an expert on intelligence agencies, recently wrote: "The Snowden case demonstrates the potential risks involved when the nation turns its spying and eavesdropping over to companies with lax security and inadequate personnel policies. The risks increase exponentially when those same people must make critical decisions involving choices that may lead to war, cyber or otherwise."

This is a stark example of the blurring of the line between corporate and governmental functions. Booz Allen Hamilton, the company that employed Mr. Snowden, earned over $5 billion in revenue in the last fiscal year, according to the *Washington Post*. The Carlyle Group, the majority owner of Booz Allen Hamilton, has made nearly $2 billion on its $910 million investment in "government consulting." It is clear that "national security" is big business.

Given the value and importance of privacy to American ideals, it is disturbing how the terms "privatization" and "private sector" are deceptively used. Many Americans have been led to believe that corporations can and will do a better job handling certain vital tasks than the government can. Such is the ideology of privatization. But in practice, there is very little evidence to prove this notion. Instead, the term "privatization" has become a clever euphemism to draw attention away from a harsh truth. Public functions are being handed over to corporations in sweetheart deals, while publicly owned assets such as minerals on public lands and research and development breakthroughs are being given away at bargain-basement prices.

These functions and assets—which belong to or are the responsibility of the taxpayers—are being used to make an increasingly small pool of top corporate executives very wealthy. And taxpayers are left footing the cleanup bill when corporate greed does not align with the public need.

With this in mind, let us not mince words. "Privatization" is a soft term. Let us call the practice what it really is—corporatization.

There's big money to be made in moving government-owned functions and assets into corporate hands. Public highways, prisons, drinking water systems, school management, trash collection, libraries, the military, and now even national security matters are all being outsourced to corporations. But what happens when such vital government functions are performed for big profit rather than the public good?

Look to the many reports of waste, fraud, and abuse that arose out of the overuse of corporate contractors in Iraq. At one point, there were more contractors in Iraq and Afghanistan than US soldiers. Look to the private prisons, which make their money by incarcerating as many people as they can for as long as they can. Look to privatized water systems, the majority of which deliver poorer service at higher costs than public-utility alternatives.

Visit privatizationwatch.org for many more examples of the perils, pitfalls, and excesses of rampant, unaccountable corporatization.

In short, corporatizing public functions does not work well for the public, consumers, and taxpayers who are paying through the nose.

Some right-wing critics might view government providing essential public services as "socialism," but as it now stands, we live in a nation increasingly comprised of corporate socialism. There is great value in having public assets and functions that are already owned by the people, to be performed for the public benefit, and not at high profit margins and prices for big corporations. By allowing corporate entities to assume control of such functions, it makes profiteering the central determinant in what, how, and why vital services are rendered.

Just look at the price of medicines given to drug companies by taxpayer-funded government agencies that discovered them.

(Autographed copies of my new book *Told You So: The Big Book of Weekly Columns* are available from Politics and Prose, an independent book store in Washington, DC.)

What about Some Corporate Patriotism!

What would happen if we asked the executives of the giant US corporations, whose products constantly surround us, to show some *corporate patriotism?*

After all, General Electric, DuPont, Citigroup, Pfizer, and others demand that they be treated as "persons" under our Constitution and our laws. And they expect unfiltered loyalty from American workers, even to the point of blocking the organization of unions that would allow workers to band together for collective bargaining.

Moreover, many of these corporations expect to be bailed out by American taxpayers when they are in trouble, and they regularly receive a covey of direct and indirect government subsidies, giveaways, and complex handouts.

Some of them pay no federal income taxes year after year, and a few game the tax laws to receive additional money back from the US Treasury. Historically, the US Marines and other US armed forces have risked their lives to protect these corporations' overseas interests by invading or menacing numerous countries.

So it is reasonable for the American people to expect some *reciprocity* from these immense corporate entities that were born in the US and rose to their economic prowess on the backs of American workers. The bosses of these companies believe they can have it both ways—getting all the benefits of their native country while shipping whole industries and jobs to communist and fascist regimes abroad that keep their workers in serf-like conditions.

The first test as to whether these US companies have any allegiance to the US and its communities is to demand that CEOs stand up at their annual shareholder meetings and pledge allegiance in the name of their corporation, not their board of directors, "to the flag of the United States of America," ending with that ringing phrase, voiced by millions of Americans daily, "with liberty and justice for all."

More than seventy years ago, a famous Marine general, the two-time congressional Medal of Honor awardee Smedley Butler, said his Marines were ordered to make sure the flag followed US companies from Central America to Asia. In the past, the lack of allegiance was shockingly callous. DuPont and General Motors worked openly with fascist Germany and its companies before World War II and did not sever all dealings when hostilities started.

About fifteen years ago, I sent letters to the CEOs of the top one hundred largest US-chartered corporations asking that they pledge allegiance to our country in the name of their company at their annual shareholder meetings. Their responses were instructive. Many said they would review the request; others turned it down while some were ambiguous, misconstruing the request as being directed to their board of directors instead of their US-chartered corporate entity.

Walmart replied that they would "give it every consideration." Federated Department Stores expressly thought it was a good suggestion. Citicorp (now Citigroup) wrote that it is "not our practice to respond."

Time for an update. I've just sent letters renewing the request for the pledge to twenty of the largest US-chartered companies. They include ExxonMobil, Walmart, Chevron, General Motors, General Electric, Ford Motor, AT&T, Bank of America, Verizon Communications, JPMorgan Chase, Apple, CVS Caremark, IBM, Citigroup, and Cardinal Health.

Imagine the CEOs of General Motors (or ExxonMobil, Citigroup, Bank of America, etc.) pledging allegiance "to the Flag of the United States of America, and to the Republic for which it stands, one Nation under God, indivisible, with liberty and justice for all."

You may wish to contact these companies and urge their CEOs to take the pledge. This effort needs your participation as consumers, workers, taxpayers, and/or shareholders. It opens up a long-overdue discussion about corporate patriotism and what it all should mean.

As conservative author Patrick Buchanan wrote some years ago: "If they [large US corporations] cannot pledge loyalty to America, why should Americans be loyal to them?. . ."

Corporate Pledge of Allegiance Letter

JUNE 22, 2012

Dear CEO,

Corporations and their attorneys like to be judged as "persons" under our constitutions and laws. So it is entirely appropriate to judge the character of a US-chartered corporation by the measure of corporate patriotism—especially if it is operating worldwide. Here is a start.

Do you think it desirable to have you and your president at your annual shareholder meetings stand up on the stage and, in the name of your company (not your diverse board of directors), pledge allegiance to our flag that is completed by the ringing phrase "with liberty and justice for all"?

Over the past fifteen years, Americans have wondered about where US companies, who grew to success with American workers and were given bailouts and subsidies from American taxpayers, stood on this cardinal issue of corporate patriotism. Too many American jobs and industries have been sent abroad to dictatorial regimes and oligarchic societies to dispel the impression of abandoning America for greater profits and greater license in these "serf-labor," anti-independent-trade-union nations.

Having due regard to millions of loyal, hardworking American workers—who have lost a great deal, if not everything, in this global economy—is long overdue. Their sense of betrayal is palpable. It would be an expression of respect to assert an allegiance to the country of your company's birth and the laborers who made your company into an economic power.

Please respond to the bracketed question above, as soon as possible, at any of the contact points below. We are going to release all of the responses and nonresponses on the Fourth of July.

"With liberty and justice for all."

6.

ON VOTING AND THE 2012, 2016, AND 2020 ELECTIONS

Lessons for Democrats in 2024

NOVEMBER 18, 2022

Once again, the congressional Democratic Party leaders are claiming a victory of sorts in an election where the Dems should have won in a landslide against the most corrupt, cruel, and lying Republican Party in history. The Dems lost the House of Representatives and once again narrowly won the Senate, flipping only the Pennsylvania seat (even though the Dems had fourteen seats up for reelection compared to twenty seats up for the Republicans).

In the 2024 Senate race, the odds will not favor the Dems. There will be twenty-three Democratic senators up for reelection (including two independents who vote with the Democrats), compared to only ten Republican senators. All the Republican seats are in red states.

Given these numbers, the Democrats face a certain loss of the Senate in 2024 unless they look at themselves in the mirror and start, as Lincoln said, "thinking anew." The lessons from the near-total loss of Congress this year are manifest and visible. Here are a few suggestions for the Dems in 2024:

1. Start investing now in a ground game. Commit to rejecting wasteful television-ad megabuys. Convey Democratic policies and records that connect with people where they live, work, and raise their families. We all bleed the same color. Abstract ideologies and fabricated GOP distractions matter less when candidates focus on people's livelihoods and specific justice.

   Since the Republicans can't shake their corporate paymasters' greed, even to support basic social safety-net protections, long established in other Western countries, the Democrats will have this field to themselves. That is, if they choose to be strongly on the side of labor, consumers, children, women, and the small taxpayers. Remember, the GOP regularly loots the Treasury to increase corporate welfare.

2. Recruit working-class candidates, whether urban, suburban, or rural. The victory of Marie Gluesenkamp Perez in the state of Washington's Third Congressional District—beating a Trump-endorsed election-denier and Fox News regular, Joe Kent—should be a case study for the Dems. Given only a 2 percent chance of winning the Republican-leaning district by FiveThirtyEight's final forecast, this young mother, who co-owns an auto repair shop with her husband in rural Skamania County, scored a campaign victory.

   New York Times columnist Michelle Goldberg described how Perez brought her life experiences to voters on the campaign trail. Perez spoke of building their hillside house because they couldn't get a mortgage to buy one. She spoke of bringing her young son to work because they couldn't find childcare. She turned the theme of "freedom" powerfully against the authoritarian-minded Kent.

   Representative-elect Gluesenkamp Perez listened to herself and to her voters. Her underdog race wasn't encumbered by corporate-conflicted political media consultants whose long grip on so many Democratic campaigns has hamstrung the party into avoidable defeat after defeat.

3. Dems should start listening to the progressive civic advocates and leaders who have been at the center of many popular changes for the better in our country. About two dozen of them offered their ideas for winning votes in a Zoom conference for Democratic candidates and their staff in July (see winningamerica.net).

   Most of the candidates wouldn't or couldn't break through the usual force field that the highly paid, control-freakish consultants create to exclude input from authentic reformers. Too bad, since any one or two of the many suggestions from this Zoom conference would have tipped the House's closest races in favor of the Democrats.

   The big loser in the race for governor of Texas against a truly mean Republican Greg Abbott was Beto O'Rourke. He managed to campaign in every county without absorbing the ways to campaign in rural areas from the state's best communicator—Jim Hightower (see hightowerlowdown.org/).

   Just totaling up unreturned calls by progressive leaders. such as by Hightower to Democratic candidates, would reveal the deadly insularity of campaigns that measure their progress by whether they can out-dial the GOP for campaign dollars.

4. The Democratic Party better join up with National Popular Vote (see nationalpopularvote.com), designed to expand the interstate compact of states that pledge to give their Electoral College votes to the presidential candidate who wins the national popular vote. Launched by entrepreneur Steve Silberstein, this movement has persuaded states with a total of 195 Electoral College votes to pass legislation that prevents presidential votes from being canceled out at the state level. Once states totaling 270 Electoral College votes adopt the National Popular Vote bill, the Democrats would be spared a third presidential loss. (The Democrats won the popular vote but lost the presidency in 2000 to George W. Bush and in 2016 to Donald J. Trump.) Since the Dems picked up four new governorships, there is a chance to reach 270 by 2024.

5. It is time for a new group of Democratic Party managers, coaches, and trainers to replace entrenched apparatchiks who over the past thirty years have lost so many winnable state and national elections or won others by such narrow margins as to limit progress.

Americans who vote for the Democrats need fresh language—no more scapegoating of small third parties—and a revival of "on-your-side" policies and messaging domestically. Waging peace abroad to replace the empire-driven two-party consensus that is boomeranging and devouring our domestic priorities, such as abolishing poverty (see *Washington Post* article "Universal Basic Income Has Been Tested Repeatedly. It Works. Will America Ever Embrace It?"), would also be a fresh start for the war-prone Democratic Party.

Aroused citizens may wish to convey their thoughts about expanding the effort initiated by those civic advocates' presentations at winningamerica.net by sending an email to info@winningamerica.net.

Suggestions for Successful Elections in 2020 at All Levels

OCTOBER 9, 2020

The following are eleven suggestions, with useful links, for getting out more progressive voters to the polls in the approaching elections at the local, state, and national levels. For a variety of reasons and causes, tens of millions of eligible Americans do not vote. These ideas can spark interest and participation by these citizens and regular voters in shaping a more productive and fair democratic society. Spread the word.

The following items were assembled before COVID-19, which means that some of them need to be altered accordingly, while the majority are not significantly affected:

1. Corporatist right-wingers prefer to campaign on "values" and not on their voting records. They cannot answer the question "Which side are you on?" in ways that appeal to voting families. Right-wingers will describe deceptively a law they voted for, such as the tax cut for the rich and corporations (2017), but for the most part, they block or oppose votes to provide necessities for the people. Right-wingers prefer campaigning about "values" and abstractions. Consequently, in 2014 when Senator Mitch McConnell was up for reelection, I drafted a list of "Kentucky Values" and compared them to the contrary positions and votes of McConnell. The latter were clearly contrary to broad Kentucky values. A member of Congress hand-delivered to McConnell's opponent this list of values in the context of McConnell's votes. McConnell's opponent declined to use this approach in the campaign. The *Louisville Courier-Journal*—the state's largest newspaper—thought enough of the message to print it as an op-ed by me.

    Of course, every state—Texas, Georgia, Wisconsin, Minnesota, etc.—can be seen as having similar broad and appealing values. Comparing an incumbent's vague embrace of values to the incumbent's specific votes and positions is powerful and can motivate voters to look beyond campaign slogans and platitudes. It makes the "values rhetoric" clash with the reality of the incumbents' actions. No more using abstractions as camouflage for the misdeeds on the ground. It makes the politician's *record* matter.

2. Getting out the vote by telephone banks, postcards, or door-knocking is important but has several limitations. It doesn't work very well with non-voters or people who do not see that the election matters to them where they live, work, and raise their families (the "pox on all your houses" people). This memo [https://nader.org/wp-content/uploads/2020/10/Get-Out-the-Vote-Civic-Initiative-Memo.pdf]—*pre-COVID-19*—emphasizes the importance of early person-to-person conversations and developing relationships in neighborhoods, organized and staffed by full-time organizers and local "influencers." The memo suggests transportation options and then postelection celebrations to solidify voter participation and future civic and electoral action. The price tag is half of what Mr. Bloomberg spent to end up winning American Samoa in the Democratic presidential primary. Adjustment here needs to be made for much greater mail voting.

3. The theme of *corruption* must be prominent and continually restated. No matter the polls or the country, when people are asked what they dislike the most about government and politicians, corruption is almost always near or at the top of their concerns. The Trump administration is the most deeply overt, covert, and varied *corrupt* regime in US history— think of the daily impeachable offenses such as spending unauthorized money, also a federal crime under the Antideficiency Act, and defying scores of congressional subpoenas that reflect corrupt Trumpian practices. *Corruption* is a word that sticks in people's minds. Use it, repeat it, exemplify it to strike home.

4. Make the voting record of the incumbent—and the positions taken— specific and personal to voters. Here is one approach (call it a "Voter Self-Help Guide—Where Do You Stand?") On one side, the voters can answer yes or no questions on several important issues. On the other side, voters can then compare candidate answers with the positions of their opponents and with the voter's own views. Of course,

there can be different designs, including ones suited to social media. But the goal should be to show that the incumbent *disagrees* with the voter and the challenger *agrees* with the voter.

The many bad votes of the adversary need to be publicized for a deep imprint. It is remarkable how little attention is given to this strategy. The aggregate votes show that the whole is larger than the sum of its parts. On television or in social media, this aggregate list can be broken down into a serial rendition—showing a string of votes over days. This will be both dramatic and compelling and will have a deep imprint, unlike a conventional thirty-second ad.

5. Millions of Americans who work the *midnight shift* are keeping the country going while we are sleeping. These include health care workers, nursing home staff, police, firefighters, security guards, and other all-night workers at convenience stores, fast-food restaurants, gas stations, retail stores (e.g., drugstores and grocery stores), factories, and more. The candidates can issue a one-page press release describing the categories of workers and thanking them. These workers are not part of campaign events, and they know they are marginalized by candidates. Candidates can show these workers how valued they truly are. Candidates that campaign for X number of nights, starting at the midnight shift at the largest hospital in your district or state, will see the benefit of visiting workers from midnight until 3:00 a.m. or so, especially with likely news coverage and social media outreach. Candidates as "midnight campaigners" will be much appreciated, and word of mouth will spread the news of the "midnight" candidate's concern for the forgotten workers.

6. Winning elections without *mandates* will leave a cynical trail among voters. Empty ads violate the principle that *policy* precedes *message*. Candidates need to persuade people that they want to win with mandates from the people, that they know where they came from and won't forget the specifics on which they campaigned. Campaigning on mandates will produce supportive feedback for campaigns from tens of thousands of active people. Mandates mean postelection accountability and preelection contrast with one's opponents.

7. Trump has shown the power of his *nicknames*. Why? Because, astonishingly, the mass media keeps repeating them over and over again
(including during the 2016 campaign) without offering the target of
his pejorative nicknames a chance to reply. Ordinarily, candidates do
not use nicknames, and principled candidates don't want to descend to
his level. But as a top Trump campaign official gleefully said on NPR:
they work, why not use them? Nicknames *in return* blunt Trump's
nicknames from working. Giving a bully his own medicine, including
circulating millions of buttons, signs, and posters, will either help get
equal time or stop the initiator from engaging in this branding tactic.

8. In Florida, ex-felons, owing a few hundred dollars in unpaid prison
fees, court costs, etc. still may be obstructed from voting despite Florida
overwhelmingly passing a constitutional amendment allowing them
to vote. With the governor opposed and the courts still in process, it
is worth expanding on LeBron James's $100,000 down payment to the
Florida Rights Restoration Project to start paying off the debts, with
more money to come from his new More Than A Vote organization.
But will it not be enough? A Michael Bloomberg–level contribution
is needed for the hundreds of thousands of ex-felons who know the
specific amount owed. Others await notice of the amounts due. It is
a mess but very worth addressing, given how close and consequential
Florida elections have turned out to be.

9. Candidates running for Congress or for the governorship of a state
need better coaching for candidate debates. There are times while
watching these debates when it is difficult to distinguish between the
positions of Democrats and Republicans. Too many Democrats have
lost when they should have easily won given the voting record and/
or public stances by the Republicans. The Democrats too often come
across as tentative, cautious, defensive, and seemingly unwilling to
let the audience really know the difference between them and their
opponents (answering the perennial question "Whose side are you
on?"). Why? Because they often don't really know who they are—and
because they are coached by dim or conflicted consultants. Democratic candidates also don't seem to know how to reply and gain the
momentum. Democrats should end their responses to questions with

attack themes that put their opponents on defense. The questions asked by debate moderators and reporters are part of the problem. More attention needs to be paid to training candidates to propose consequential questions during debates. There are reasons why the Democrats have lost four of the last five House elections to the worst, most vicious antiworker/consumer, corporate cronyism party in GOP history.

10. Debate content, timing, and techniques need to be the subject of national training sessions. The ads that will follow can present powerful themes and be worth their price because they will be more memorable for word-of-mouth communications.

11. In 2018 the Democrats could have won four more Senate seats had Democratic candidates not tried to sound like Republicans—and talked about what families and young voters really need and want from the most powerful (under the Constitution) branch of government (e.g., advancing livelihood protections that elaborate the disgraceful status quo).

12. Candidates need to develop *powerful uniform themes*, grouped as a highly visible "commitment to voters," that attract more left/right support from people who have household and neighborhood conditions on their minds, *writ small* and *writ large* (living wage, health care costs, and access to job-intensive infrastructure projects in their community—to cite three of many). Focus on what the perceived necessities and injustices are by families, regardless of the political labels they place on themselves. (See this excerpt [https://nader.org/2014/04/27/unstoppable-25-proposals/] from my book *Unstoppable: The Emerging Left-Right Alliance to Dismantle the Corporate State.*)

There are many issues bringing left/right voters together just waiting for elaboration and authentic candidate stands. Put simply, a left/right approach nationalizes the election and recognizes that conservatives, liberals, and progressives are all getting ripped off by companies and exposed to toxic pollution, crumbling public services, the many controls of big companies, and health and safety hazards—and most have a surplus of *anxiety, dread, and fear* about the future. The Democratic

Party can take command of agendas and reforms that Republicans will not support, cannot be blurred or credibly denied, and are on most people's minds.

One such long-overdue, nonblurrable issue is raising the federal minimum wage from its long-frozen level of $7.25 per hour to $15.00 an hour. The party needs to make its existing support more vocal and visible and repeat it in many human-interest contexts. The party should accelerate its implementation and not wait for five years, as did the House-passed bill. Over twenty-five million workers will benefit in intangible ways. The message must be authentic, vivid, front and center, and not just seen as the political rhetoric from past years.

13. An authentic and well-publicized *contract with America* needs to be drafted and widely disseminated by all Democratic candidates after Labor Day. Veteran politicians have told me people do not know what the Democratic Party stands for—its agenda is too piecemeal. Look at their weak slogans. Even with the Republicans blocking the next massive relief bill, already passed by the Democrats last May, the contrasting message of what the Democrats stand for is not getting through to the majority of the voters. If the message, in its granularity, was getting through, the polls would be plummeting for the GOP, not merely sliding.

Big Campaign 2022 Issue: The GOP's Cruelty to Children

SEPTEMBER 30, 2022

Republican Party leaders didn't have a platform in 2020.

Their Senate leader, Senator Mitch McConnell (R-KY), presently tells reporters inquiring about the GOP agenda if the Republicans regain a congressional majority: "I'll let you know when we take it back."

Pretty smug and arrogant.

But the GOP's actions speak louder than its words. In no Western democracy is there such a party that so slams its own country's children. Wasting no time, the GOP starts right at birth with opposition to adequate neonatal and maternal care; opposition in GOP-controlled states seeking available Medicaid coverage for poor families; opposition to universal health insurance for all children; opposition to paid family leave, maternity leave. and childcare; opposition to federally increasing the minimum wage now frozen at $7.25 per hour. All other Western democracies meet these basic necessities.

The Republican Party's rulers go deep with their viciousness. Had they not, in 2017 under Trump, radically cut taxes for the wealthy (including Trump and McConnell's family) and giant corporations, the tax revenues from the 1 percent undertaxed super-rich would have paid for vital services and protections for all Americans, regardless of the political labels.

Moreover, beginning in 2011, the GOP in Congress deliberately kept the Internal Revenue Service's budget so low year after year that the agency, according to its Trump-appointed director, cannot collect about $1 trillion in uncollected taxes a year! The Democrats can fairly accuse the GOP on Capitol Hill of actively aiding and abetting massive tax evasion.

Madcap McConnell openly calls himself the "Grim Reaper" and "the Guardian of Gridlock," brazenly declaring that he wished he could obstruct more. Kentucky voters, wake up! The Reaper goes after you too. Hundreds of thousands of your children (plus fifty-eight million children nationwide) are, since January 2022, no longer receiving the benefits of the $300 a month child tax credit because the congressional Republicans *blocked its extension.*

The GOP knew this one benefit reduced overall child poverty by one-third! They could not care less.

Every day the Democrats should be exposing such child abuses by the GOP.

The GOP, ignoring their human benefits, keeps saying all these programs increase the deficit. Yet by cutting to a new low the taxes of the rich and corporate, and by their support of hundreds of billions of dollars in annual corporate welfare—subsidies, giveaways, and bailouts—they are creating this harsh deprivation for our children. We know their drill, year after year.

Historically and presently, the Republican Party has placed corporate greed over children's need. Even greed that radically undermines parental supervision and directly markets health-harming products like junk foods and violent programming to children. Under Trump, the callous Republicans even pressed to have more junk food in school lunch programs. (See Susan Linn's new book, *Who's Raising the Kids? Big Tech, Big Business, and the Lives of Children.*)

This corporate GOP, this fossil fuel party, this enabler of the corporate assault against family interests, has pushed for corporate antifamily policies as a routine, predictable way of infesting Congress.

The Democrats have piecemeal gone after their Republican opponents on their family-impact cruelty. But they haven't clustered the egregious assaults into a major, daily-articulated campaign drive for November. Such a unified compilation has much greater impact. This platform would reach Republican parents who are concerned with real conditions, not distracting ideologies and slogans, when it comes to protecting their family where they live, work, and raise their children.

The challenge in this election was put very well last July by law professor Robert Fellmeth, director of the effective Children's Advocacy Institute at the University of San Diego School of Law (sandiego.edu/cai):

> Children, of course, are our legacy. They're what we leave behind and what should be a leading frame in this year's campaigns. We prize our forebears who risked everything for us in the Eighteenth century. How are people 200 years from now going to view us? That's what all

the candidates should be talking about. "We've got the future of our children and country at stake here."

But that future apparently doesn't matter to the GOP, which is taking big campaign money from the likes of the oil (ExxonMobil, Chevron, Axis), gas, and coal profiteers. Republican politicians are working overtime to block congressional policies directed against fossil fuel–driven climate disruptions, including massive storms battering their own GOP-controlled Southern states. Talk about not caring about the future of our children.

As children march and demonstrate for a faster transition toward renewable energy (solar, wind, etc.), they make this repeated, poignant plea to adults: "We are children and you are not protecting us."

To the Democratic candidates, I say: Go on the offensive against the daily fake rhetoric and lawless behavior of the GOP. Make this last stretch of the November campaign a vibrant commitment to protect and nurture our children against the corporate-tied Republican Party trafficking in *anxiety, dread, and fear.* (See winningamerica.net/notes for examples of how to counter the cruel GOP.)

Democrats: To Win in November, Listen to the Messages of Citizen Groups

SEPTEMBER 9, 2022

Prospects for Democrats winning in November in the House and Senate have picked up recently. Nonetheless, political pundits are still not counting on the Democrats to win the House of Representatives. Candidates have eight weeks to refine their policies, messages, and strategies to energize and mobilize voters.

If they break through the force field of their political and media consultants—often conflicted by corporate clients and 15 percent commissions for TV and radio ads—and tap into the experience of citizen advocacy groups, they can win a comfortable margin in Congress.

Astonishingly, citizen leaders for years have been marginalized to their and the Democratic politicians' disadvantage. The Republicans do not make such mistakes. Witness the roles and influence of right-wing advocacy groups such as the Heritage Foundation, the Cato Institute, and the National Taxpayers Union.

Most political campaigns get tired and repetitive. Each day is like the previous day—think Bill Murray in the movie *Groundhog Day*. Candidates need fresh language and issues and tough rebuttals to the neofascist GOP, which doesn't even bother to camouflage its antidemocratic missions or its takedowns of Social Security, Medicare, Medicaid, and other government programs for the people. Republicans boast about long-range plans, which they falsely call "populist," but they are driven to put the plutocrats and oligarchs in full predatory charge of our federal and state governments.

Above all, Democrats need to give voters from all backgrounds practical motivations to register and get out to vote in record-setting numbers. Setting a voter turnout record is not hard. With predictions of 130 million eligible voters not voting, getting ten million of these Americans voting in the swing states could produce a working Democratic majority in Congress.

Citizen advocates know what it takes to make a more just society for all

Americans—all workers, all consumers, all patients, and all communities. With no axe to grind, civic leaders have learned how to speak plainly, authentically, and persuasively, for they know that is the way to succeed in making life better, safer, and fairer. They also can't stand bullies.

Recently, over two dozen of these leaders placed their specialized knowhow and clear ways of communicating what they know—that reach people where they live, work, and raise their families—at the disposal of the Democrats. Some have run referendums and have developed sensible, often unused ways to get people to vote. Others have honed effective language such as "Go vote for a raise, you've earned it and it is long overdue," or talk about "investing in public works," not "spending." Builders of factories say they are investing, not spending, don't they?

It's "climate violence," not "climate change." Taxpayers should demand: "We want our tax dollars used to benefit our communities and families, not used for reckless corporate welfare or taken by corporate looters defrauding government programs like Medicare or the Pentagon."

Civic leaders know how to win debates, how to urge cracking down on corporate crooks, and how to expose waste, fraud, and other abuses that rile up people who often feel powerless. Above all, civic leaders are all about empowering you or, better said, "We the People." Remember, the Constitution placed the basic sovereign power in our republic and in the hands of the citizenry.

More specifically, if Democrats want access to the pathways that used to lead to a bright future, children's rights, superior health care, elevated livelihoods for workers and retirees, racial and gender equality, an economy for all of us, neighborhood renewable energy, affordable housing, a redefined national security, and engaged voters, they need to start returning calls made to their campaign offices.

Let me repeat: start returning calls by the citizen community from which nearly all the blessings of justice and liberty in our nation's history have emerged.

Candidates that are kept so busy that they don't have time to adjust, readjust, and reinvigorate their campaigns in the real, not the virtual, world are at a disadvantage. You win by developing your own escalator, not by paying minders to place you on a media treadmill that eats up campaign contributions without energizing voters.

See winningamerica.net for more information.

Ginsburg Institute for Justice Needed for Our Depleted Democracy

OCTOBER 2, 2020

Jean Monnet, a founder of the European Union, once said: "Nothing is possible without men, but nothing is lasting without institutions."

I'm reminded of his observation each time our country loses a "just" Supreme Court justice. So, what will follow after the few days of prominent encomiums at memorial events and editorial praise of Justice Ruth Bader Ginsburg?

Historians will record her decisions, writings, and advocacy. Many people will celebrate her groundbreaking contributions to equal rights for women and other civil rights. Justice Ginsburg's fervent admirers, however, should look not only at past accomplishments but to creative ways to build on a great and enduring legacy.

Several years ago, I tried to interest some of Justice John Paul Stevens's former law clerks (many of whom became successful lawyers) to enlist their colleagues in establishing a "John Paul Stevens Institute for Justice." In 2014, retired Justice Stevens, at age ninety-four, had just published another book—*Six Amendments: How and Why We Should Change the Constitution*. This book was then the latest product in his vigorous retirement period of writings and addresses.

I wrote to Justice Stevens urging him to give a nod to his hundred or more clerks, many of whom were wealthy attorneys. He was too modest. A few former clerks showed interest, but not to the point of initiating action.

A similar attempt to persuade supporters of Justice Sandra Day O'Connor fell flat. At the time, she was pressing hard for full legal aid for poor people seeking justice and real civic education in the nation's elementary and secondary schools.

After she retired from the court, she criticized the 2010 Supreme Court decision—*Citizens United v. Federal Election Commission*—that opened the floodgates for corporate campaign cash. Her former clerks did not envision an "Institute for Justice" in honor of their adored mentor. Justice

O'Connor was also honest enough to publicly acknowledge regret about her vote in the 5–4 decision to install George W. Bush as president.

Was I just engaging in fanciful dreaming about adding these new institutional oak trees for justice to replenish our depleting democratic forest? Not at all. A vibrant Brennan Center for Justice has been on the ramparts for justice since 1995. Located at New York University Law School, it was founded by the family and former law clerks of Supreme Court Justice William J. Brennan Jr., who was nominated to the court by President Eisenhower.

With an annual budget of $26 million, the tough Brennan Center for Justice has produced a remarkable output on ways to advance improvements in criminal justice, electoral procedures, and broader public participation in the circles of power.

The Center has been described as "part think tank, part public interest law firm [that litigates] and part communications hub," working to advance "equal justice for all."

It started when one former law clerk stepped up, followed by more who joined the effort to create this institutional tribute to Justice Brennan. Together they raised the seed money, and this new institution was launched to implement the law as if people mattered first and foremost.

The same kind of institution can be created quickly, should Justice Ginsburg's hundred-plus law clerks, from her many years as a federal circuit court judge and as an associate justice of the Supreme Court, heed Jean Monnet's words.

Given the immense goodwill and unprecedented fame of Justice Ginsburg, especially among women, as a pioneering lawyer and jurist, raising the basic funding should be easy. Moreover, foundations would line up to back this initiative and its projects.

For this to happen, the energy from the huge outpouring of accolades since her passing on September 18, 2020, needs to be promptly transformed into an operating vision and not left as a nostalgic memory.

Some of the former law clerks who could form the core group are Amanda L. Tyler, professor of law at the University of California, Berkeley; Kelsi Corkran, who heads the Supreme Court practice at a large law firm; Ruthanne Deutsch, an appellate litigator; Elizabeth Prelogar, a Supreme Court and appellate litigator; Trevor W. Morrison, dean of New York University School of Law; Neil S. Siegel, professor of law and political science at Duke University School of Law; Paul Schiff Berman, professor of law at George Washington University Law School; and many others who revered and were so inspired by the feisty, resilient, kind Ruth Bader Ginsburg.

I'm sure that the Brennan Center's president, Michael Waldman, would be pleased to share his experience in furthering such a noble and lasting mission.

Is there any better way to compliment Justice Ginsburg's legacy and carry forward her foundational work for the American people? It is really entirely in the hands of Justice Ginsburg's admirers to accomplish this worthy goal.

Perhaps the creation of the Ginsburg Institute for Justice will jump-start the now influential former clerks of Justice Stevens and Justice O'Connor to follow the example of Justice Brennan's clerks. It is never too late for more institutional infusions toward a just society.

Only Civic-Driven Voter Turnout
Can Defeat Tweeter Trump

JULY 26, 2019

Does the Democratic Party know how to defeat the foul-mouthed, bigoted, self-enriching crony capitalist Donald Trump? Trump pretends to be a populist. In reality he does the bidding of Wall Street instead of Main Street and weakens or repeals governmental health and safety programs.

Defeating corrupt, disgraceful, disastrous Donald should be easy. He is, on many documented fronts, the worst and most indictable president in US history. Moreover, Trump is personally obscene and is a walking tortfeasor against women. He is a politician who doesn't read and doesn't think. He doesn't know anything about government and doesn't care about the rule of law. All he seems to know how to do is stoke the war machine with taxpayer dollars and shut down law enforcement agencies designed to protect the health, safety, and economic well-being of citizens from today's big business robber barons.

Dumb as he is on matters of public policies, Trump is a cunning schemer and a master of deflection. For Trump, every day is a reality show, in which he must dominate the news cycle with his destructive personal politics of distraction. The mass media, looking for ratings and readers, can't get off its Trump high. He even taunts them with this conceit.

In our autocratic two-party duopoly, the country is left with the anemic, corporatized Democratic Party establishment to save the country. Every day the Democratic National Committee (DNC) feverishly calls big donors. Most candidates are addicted to the narcotic of campaign money and think their pathetic political consultants will solve their electoral problems.

Then there are the twenty or so Democratic presidential candidates exhausting themselves by trying to stand out from one another while fitting into the straitjacket of the DNC's rules and debate format. Some are advancing major changes and reforms, such as Elizabeth Warren and Bernie Sanders. The DNC apparatchiks, however, would rather have Joe Biden.

Even so, some party bosses worry that his age, gaffes, and past record could make him a Hillary redux should his current makeover not stick.

None of the presidential candidates are taking on Trump directly. A few glancing ripostes, sure, but most Democratic candidates think attacking Trump is a distraction from their proposals for America. They don't seem to be listening to viewpoints such as those stated by Ana Maria Archila, of the Center for Popular Democracy: "Don't just condemn the racism and the language but use it as an opportunity to argue for a vision of the country in which we can all be included." In reality, the Democratic candidates all fear taking Trump on daily in this way because of his intimidating personal smear tactics supinely reported by the mass media, which rarely allows rebuttals to Trump's trash talking.

Now comes the possible crucial third factor in the race: well-funded, vigorous voter-turnout drives in ten states that are driven exclusively by the civic community. Freed of the shackles of the serial loser DNC, this independent civic drive can easily turn the tide in these key electoral swing states. Based on past elections, there will be 120 million *nonvoters* in 2020. Bringing out 10 million nonvoters in states like Florida, Pennsylvania, Ohio, Michigan, Wisconsin, Missouri, Arizona, Colorado, and Montana could swamp Trump, who is stuck with greasing his minority base of frenzied supporters. Getting out the voters who stayed home four years ago is also a priority.

An independent civic initiative, funded by small and large donations, can also jettison Republican control of the Senate and end the Republican stacking of the federal judiciary with corporate right-wing ideologues. The DNC can help ensure a Democratic Senate by convincing some tractionless presidential candidates to return to their states and run for the Senate. Governor Steve Bullock of Montana will be more valuable in the Senate than clinging to the debate stage.

Then there is the prospect of Trump defeating himself. He never recognizes any boundaries and is convinced that he can get away with anything because he always has. He is a repulsive loudmouth and has been a serial fugitive from justice since his years as a shady businessman.

Trump knows that the Democrats don't want to get down in the mud with him. So he makes the mud their quicksand, with the media dittoheads replaying his reality TV show monologues. If there are any Democratic Party activists who know how to goad Trump regularly, they had better step forward. The sum of Trump's electoral strategy is lying by the hour, creating false scenarios, false achievements, and phony promises conveyed by relentless intimidation. His Achilles' heel is being goaded by mockery and accusations symmetrical to what he is dishing out. That's the way overreaching bullies are brought down.

His vanities are the roadmap. He is sensitive to charges of having a "low IQ"; of his presidency being characterized as a "disaster"; of being anything other than "a stable genius"; of being nicknamed; of having a snarling visage with unattractive, bulging body parts; of being a racist, a tool of Wall Street, wasteful of taxpayers' money; and of not creating infrastructures, jobs he promised. The Trump presidency has brought us the first-ever reduction of life expectancy in the US, the stagnation of wages, and an avalanche of cancerous particulates in the water and air of our country. Including in that of his coal-country base!

He gives his crowds verbal "red meat" while giving Washington away to the big bankers and the "greed hounds" of big business. He is a flatterer and flummoxer of people who let their emotions displace what is best for the communities where they live, work, and raise their children. People are being battered by intense, record-breaking heat, storms, floods, tornadoes, and droughts, and Trump tells them the climate crisis is a hoax. All while his programs worsen the situation.

It is time to persuade a large majority of voters that Trump is the Fake President destroying the best of America and bringing out the worst. But he has to be directly confronted on all fronts. No more free rides for the Tweeter.

Don't be Flattered, Fooled, or Flummoxed in Tomorrow's Election

NOVEMBER 5, 2018

Let's face it. Most politicians use the mass media to obfuscate. Voters who don't do their homework, who don't study records of the politicians, and who can't separate the words from the deeds will easily fall into traps laid by wily politicians.

In 2002, Connecticut governor John Rowland was running for reelection against his Democratic opponent, Bill Curry. Again and again, the outspent Curry informed the media and the voters about the corruption inside and around the governor's office. At the time, the governor's close associates and ex-associates were under investigation by the US attorney. But to the public, Rowland was all smiles, flooding the television stations with self-serving, manipulative images and slogans. He won handily in November. Within weeks, the US attorney's investigation intensified as they probed the charges Curry had raised about Rowland. Rowland's approval rating dropped to record lows, and impeachment initiatives and demands for his resignation grew. He was prosecuted, convicted, and imprisoned. Unfortunately, enough voters were flattered, fooled, and flummoxed to cost Bill Curry the race.

In 2004 Tom Frank, a Kansas author, wrote: "The poorest county in America isn't in Appalachia or the Deep South. It is on the Great Plains, a region of struggling ranchers and dying farm towns, and in the election of 2000, George W. Bush carried it by a majority of greater than 75 percent." Inattentive voters are vulnerable to voting against their own interests. They are vulnerable to voting for politicians who support big business and ignore their interests as farmers, workers, consumers, patients, and small taxpayers. Big business will not spur change in a political system that gives the fat cats every advantage. Change must come from the voters, and here's how:

President Donald Trump and the Republicans in Congress are masters at flattering voters and lying about their positions on issues ranging from health care to the minimum wage. Before you vote, rid yourself of all preconceived, hereditary, ideological, and political straitjackets. Use two general yardsticks for candidates for elective office: are they playing fair and are they doing right?

Stay open-minded. Avoid jumping to conclusions about candidates based solely on their stance on your one or two top issues. Pay attention to where these politicians are on the many other issues that profoundly affect you and your family. If you judge them broadly rather than narrowly, you will increase your influence by increasing your demands and expectation levels for public officials. There are numerous evaluations of their votes, easily available on the internet.

Know where you stand. A handy way to contrast your views with those of the incumbents and challengers is to make your own checklist of twenty issues, explain where you stand, and then compare your positions with the candidates' votes and declarations. Seeing how their positions or their actual record matches up to your own positions makes it harder for politicians to play you. Compare candidates' actions and votes with their declarations.

Ask the tough questions. There are many issues that politicians like to avoid, including questions about whether candidates are willing to debate their opponents and how often, why they avoid talking about and doing something about corporate power and its expanding controls over people's lives, or how they plan specifically to shift power from these global corporate supremacists to the people. After all, the Constitution starts with "We the People" not "We the Corporations." The words "corporations" and "company" are never mentioned in our Constitution!

Ask candidates to speak of solutions to the major problems confronting our country. Politicians often avoid defining solutions that upset their commercial campaign contributors. Ask about a range of issues, such as energy efficiency; livable wages; lower drug prices; massive government contractor fraud; corporate crimes against consumers, workers, and investors; reducing sprawl; safer food; and clean elections.

Ask members of Congress to explain why they keep giving themselves salary increases and generous benefits and yet turn cold at doing the same for the people's frozen minimum wage, health insurance, or pension protections.

All in all, it takes a little work and some time to become a *supervoter*, impervious to manipulation by politicians who intend to *flatter, fool,* and *flummox*. But this education can also be fun, and the pursuit of justice can offer great benefits to your pursuit of happiness.

Such civic engagement will help Americans today become better ancestors for tomorrow's descendants.

Where Is the Democrats' Contract with America 2018?

SEPTEMBER 13, 2018

What does the Democratic Party stand for? The big question persists! Typical of the Democrats, they delegated this question to political consultants who came up with the vapid slogan "A Better Deal." The specifics under that moniker are too general and, as a result, too easily dismissed by the public.

The Democratic operatives need to take a page out of Newt Gingrich's playbook when he toppled an anemic Democratic House of Representatives in the stunning 1994 elections and became Speaker of the House.

During the 1994 congressional campaign, Gingrich's party released a "Contract with America." It was so anti-American that comedians called it a "Contract *on* America." For example, the "Contract with America" attacked the fundamental right of having your full day in court, based on falsely asserting there was an "endless tide of litigation." That was only one of the ways Gingrich pleased the big corporations.

House Democratic leader Nancy Pelosi and her deputy, Steny Hoyer, just can't put forward a compelling agenda. They seem unable to speak assuredly and concretely about how their agenda will improve people's lives.

Congressman Hoyer returned from a listening tour of the US where he only listened to himself. In his summation speech, Hoyer declined to put forward numbers and specifics about raising the minimum wage or expanding health care. Moreover, his tour seemed to ignore the multiple devastations that unaccountable global corporations are causing in this country.

Fortunately there are a few dozen insurgents in the Democratic Party who are winning congressional primaries and are addressing progressive specifics. But their numbers need to grow.

Unfortunately the old guard still dominates the Democratic Party. Maybe this November election will change this. If the Democrats wish finally to prevail over the worst, cruelest, most corrupt, warmongering, Wall Street–toady Republican Party in history, they need to be clear in their convictions. The Democrats need a resounding declaration of what they stand for with major news conferences, political ads, get-out-the-vote materials, and speeches before large audiences.

A Democratic Party "Contract with America" should include a $15.00-per-hour federal minimum wage—up from the present frozen $7.25 an hour. It should endorse a Medicare-for-all system that emphasizes preventive care, cost controls on drug companies, and prevention of criminal or immoral overcharging. Serious attention should be paid to saving lives and preventing injuries and diseases. Preventable problems in hospitals are taking at least five thousand lives per week (see Johns Hopkins's May 2016 report: https://hub.jhu.edu/2016/05/03/medical-errors-third-leading-cause-of-death/).

A Democratic "Contract with America" should commit to what more than 83 percent of the American people want—tough law enforcement on corporate crime, fraud, and abuse. Consumers, workers, and small taxpayers would understand such a pledge. Much of the anxiety, dread, and fear in people's hassled daily lives is caused by lawless or abusive companies. Taxpayers would relish cracking down on businesses that defraud Medicare, Medicaid, and military contracts and almost always get away with it.

The Contract should include an empowering agenda and also a commitment to democracy—shifting power from the few to the many workers, consumers, and voters. The Democrats know how to overcome Republican voter suppression and how to make it easier for Americans to band together to defend themselves, through labor unions, consumer cooperatives, taxpayer watchdog associations, and open access to the courts.

It is also time to launch a long-overdue dedication to major public works and infrastructure projects that will produce millions of good-paying jobs—paid for by restoring corporate and super-rich taxes, along with decreasing the bloated, wasteful military budget that exceeds half of the entire federal government's operating expenditures.

The Democratic Party should reverse course and tell taxpayers they will oppose all those massive corporate-welfare (crony capitalism) subsidies, handouts, and bailouts that embody the hypocrisy of so-called corporate capitalists right down to those stadiums and ballparks that taxpayers pay for without even getting naming rights!

Democrats, frantically dialing for corporate campaign dollars, have become anemic, fuzzing their campaigns with weak rhetoric and losing so much of the people's trust. They have joined with the Republicans on waging boomeranging wars instead of waging peace and engaging in treaties protecting workers, consumers, and the environment.

The Democrats should convey crisp clarity, repeated again and again in believable ways and means in the coming weeks, so when the words "Democratic Party" are spoken, millions of voters would know what it stands for so they can hold candidates specifically accountable should there be any postelection betrayals.

So, Democratic National Committee Chairman Tom Perez, where is the Party's "Contract with America"? Send him a message at tomperez. org/contact-1 (site discontinued).

Universal Voting Dissolves the Obstacles Facing Voters

JULY 11, 2018

When will the authoritarians and their political henchmen stop harassing American voters and let all citizens vote? No other Western country comes close to imposing so many obstructions for certain categories of people to keep them from the voting booth. In Canada, England, France, Germany, Norway, Sweden, and Denmark, it is very easy to vote.

Voter suppression is real and getting worse. Voter fraud is virtually nonexistent, but this spurious claim is used as the excuse for unnecessary restrictions. Voter turnout, not surprisingly, is lower than in any other Western country.

According to the *New York Times*, the state of Alabama is obstructing voters in specific ways. This former plantation/slavery state doesn't overtly keep people of color, especially Black people, from voting. That would clearly violate the federal civil rights laws. No, instead of *race*, Alabama electoral tyrants use *class* as a proxy for racial bias.

In 2014, the Supreme Court's usual corporatist 5–4 majority lifted the federal oversight of the Voting Rights Act for misbehaving states like Alabama and paved the way for voter suppression and obstruction. Here are seven ways Alabama continues to do this:

1. Alabama requires photo identification to vote. Studies have found that "among registered Alabama voters, blacks and Hispanics were more likely than whites to lack photo identification."

2. In 2015, Alabama started the process of closing thirty-one driver's license offices in the state—places where people could get photo IDs. The reason given was "budget cuts" (this from a state that is overly reliant on corporate welfare). The impact was clearly racial when one sees where the majority of closures occurred.

3. Alabama wanted "to require proof of citizenship to vote in state and local elections," which is not required in federal elections. The US Court of Appeals for the District of Columbia Circuit blocked that move in 2016.

4. Alabama tried to suppress voters by closing polling places. By November 2016, Alabama had closed sixty-six polling places, with a clear racial impact that likely also affected lower-income white rural voters.

5. Alabama bans money transfers from one political action committee to another—ostensibly to ward off corruption. The main impact, however, was on the Alabama Democratic Conference (ADC), which is a Black get-out-the-vote endeavor. Not having rich patrons, the ADC has to rely heavily on other entities for contributions.

6. Alabama has also purged rolls of voters who haven't voted for four years or more. That's a clever disincentive. If voters show up after "verifying their registration details," some can cast "provisional ballots."

7. Finally, in 2017, Alabama governor Kay Ivey "signed legislation re-enfranchising thousands of people convicted of felonies. . . . But [Secretary of State and fellow Republican John Merrill] refused to use state resources to publicize it, or to automatically register people who were turned away before it passed."

Citizens in Florida have a referendum on the state ballot to reenfranchise 1.7 million ex-felons, many of them nonviolent offenders, who have served their time. In 2000, Florida's secretary of state hired a consulting firm that somehow wrongly misidentified people as ex-felons and took thousands of voters off the rolls. That number was far greater than the vote difference between Bush and Gore (537 votes), before Justice Scalia's Supreme Court majority conducted their treasonous judicial coup d'état and stopped the statewide recount ordered by the Florida Supreme Court.

There are still many states with antagonistic election laws and regulations that allow state officials to take away people's right to or their facility in voting.

States have long obstructed ballot access for third-party or independent candidates, thereby depriving voters of more choices and voices. Fortunately, in the past fifteen years many court challenges have gotten rid of a number of petty obstacles. But many states still require independent or third-party candidates to collect more signatures than Republicans or Democrats to get on the ballot. Texas and California require more signatures by far from independent and third-party candidates than any single entire Western European country (*Ballot Access News*). There is a simple solution. It's called universal voting. In Australia and a few other nations, voting is a duty, overwhelmingly accepted by the public. That makes obstruction of voters a serious crime. Australia's turnout in federal elections is over 95 percent. No candidates or parties there have to spend bundles of money to persuade people to vote.

Some libertarians object to universal voting. If, however, voters can write in their choice, vote for themselves, or vote for a binding none-of-the-above option, that ought to take care of the civil liberties issue. Jury duty is a civic responsibility and the only constitutionally mandated duty.

It is a legal duty to obey the laws enacted by our legislative bodies whose authority comes from us. Doesn't it make sense that we should have a legal duty to vote?

At the very least, isn't universal voting worthy of a national debate in the coming election period? Get your candidates and parties to take a stand on this taboo subject one way or another.

The Devastating Cost of
Monetized Elections

JANUARY 21, 2016

Corporatized and commercialized elections reach a point where they stand outside of and erode our democracy. Every four years the presidential and congressional elections become more of a marketplace where the wealthy paymasters turn a civic process into a spectacle of vacuous rhetorical contests, distraction, and stupefaction.

The civic minds of the people are sidelined by the monetized minds of a corrupted commercial media, political consultants, pundits, and the purveyors of an evermore dictatorial corporate state.

The dominance of influence money by the plutocracy and now of big-business political action committees (PACs), such as that of the super-rich Koch brothers, is just the beginning. The monetized minds don't just rely on their "quid pro quo" checkbooks. They foster the gerrymandering of electoral districts so that politicians indentured to them pick the voters instead of a legitimate congressional district's voters picking a candidate. And the debates now are more ratings inventory for Big Media than a discussion of major issues that remain off the table.

Presidential debates are controlled by a Commission on Presidential Debates (CPD)—a private corporation—created by the Republican and Democratic parties and funded by beer, auto, telephone, and other corporations whose patronage includes lavish hospitality suites. Thus, through the cover of CPD, the two big parties control the number of debates, who is invited to participate, and which reporters ask the questions before an approved audience.

This year, the monetized minds went further. Now a commercial-cable or network-television company decides the formats and who is in tier one or tier two or not included at all. The Big Media sponsors (Fox, CNN, NBC, and others) decided that Mark Everson, who was the first candidate to go to all of Iowa's ninety-nine counties and who dropped out in November, should be excluded from the competition because he does not have a PAC sponsor and hasn't raised enough money. Yet he is the only Republican presidential candidate with executive-branch experience. Under George W. Bush, he was head of the IRS and deputy commissioner of the Immigration and Naturalization Service.

Monetizing elections has predictable consequences. Dittohead reporters, obsessed with tactics and gaffes, never ask about corporate crime, corporate welfare, the American empire with its un-auditable Defense Department, the over $300 billion a year in computerized billing fraud in the health care industry, or why corporations are given free exploitation of our public property—such as gold and silver mines on public land, the public airwaves, and the trillions of dollars of federal research given away to big business in such industries as drugs, aerospace, computers, biotech, and information.

Commercializing elections leads to an astonishing similarity among reporters traveling with candidates or those asking questions during so-called debates.

For example, Donald Trump always brags about his business prowess as an asset for his presidential run to "Make America Great Again" but is not pressed by reporters to voluntarily release his thousands of pages of annual tax returns to see whether his boasts are justified.

The pretentious Marco Rubio—fresh from the Florida legislature and now an absentee US senator still getting his pay—repeatedly flaunts his difficult previous experience with student loans and living paycheck to paycheck. No reporter asks why then he is opposed to raising the inflation-gutted minimum wage and has no proposal to deal with the massive yoke of $1.3 trillion in student loans, with very high interest rates.

The brazen, PAC-created senator Ted Cruz now tells his audiences that the time for rhetoric is over, and that the focus should be on a candidate's record. Meanwhile, he gets away without having to explain one of the zaniest, most hateful, corporatist, empty presences in the US Senate.

The monetized minds running our elections also make sure that our civic culture and its many intelligent civic advocacy groups are sidelined when it comes to informing the voters about important issues. This is just about the most amazing exclusion of them all. Nonpartisan civic leaders and specialists—people who know the most about energy, the environment, and the health industry; about militarism abroad and public budget abuses at home; about taxation and electoral reforms; about law enforcement regarding corporate crime and the prison industrial complex—are rarely given a voice by the media, including PBS and NPR.

Look at the Sunday-morning network news shows. Pundits and politicians fill the stages. The real experts don't get interviewed; they have trouble getting into the op-ed pages of the print media and are rarely drawn on by the candidates who are too busy dialing for commercial dollars that conflict with seeking out those who work with facts, for truth and justice.

Consequently, shorn of any participating civic culture, the political culture is ready for hijacking by the commercial interests and the corporate state.

The politicians ride merrily on a torrent of words and opinions without having to explain their record, so often different or at odds with what they are bloviating. Hillary Clinton gets away with her illegal war on Libya (against the advice of Secretary of Defense Robert Gates) and the resultant chaotic bloodshed spilling over into other African countries.

None of the candidates are asked whom they would consider as their White House advisers and cabinet secretaries. This information would give voters an idea of the likelihood of broken promises.

In 2008 Barack Obama campaigned repeatedly for "hope and change." Then, after his election, he gathered for a surprise photo opportunity with Clinton retreads like the bailout-taking, self-enriching banker Robert Rubin and others known for anything but "hope and change."

Voters, you can change all this rancid defilement of our republic and its democratic dreams. Do your homework on the parties and the candidates, form local groups to demand debates and agendas that you preside over, push for more choices on the ballot, make votes count over money. The internet can help speed up such efforts.

You outnumber the politicos and their entourages everywhere. You are the ones who keep paying the price for letting politics remain a deadly form of distracting entertainment with a mainstream media obsessed with the horse race rather than the human race.

The One Question Reporters Never Ask Candidates

NOVEMBER 20, 2015

Candidates for public office, especially at the state and national levels, are never asked this central question of politics: "Since the people are sovereign under our Constitution, how do you specifically propose to restore power to the people in their various roles as *voters, taxpayers, workers,* and *consumers?*"

Imagine that inquiry starting the so-called presidential debates of both the Republican and Democratic presidential candidates. I'm not sure any of the candidates—so used to saying "I will do this" and "I propose that"—would even know how to respond. Regardless of their affiliation with either of the two dominant parties, politicians are so used to people being spectators rather than participants in the run-up to Election Day that they have not thought much about participatory or initiatory democracy. Too many of them, backed by the concentrated wealth of plutocrats, have perfected the silver-tongued skills of flattery, obfuscation, and deception.

Many voters oblige candidates by not doing their homework about the candidates, their records, and the issues they want addressed. Such passivity lowers expectations of what voters should demand from the elected officials who, after all, are supposed to hold their delegated power in trust and not sell it to big-money donors.

Let's begin with *voters.* How could elected officials empower the people they represent?

Power to the voters would mean eliminating the private money financing public elections. Big commercial interests nullify votes and turn most elections into low-grade ditto days of tedious repetition. Well-promoted voluntary checkoffs up to, say, $300, can make public financing of elections into a more politically acceptable reform. But to strengthen the power of voters there must also be more voices and choices on the ballot lines; the Electoral College should be abolished; and state legislators must stop gerrymandering districts that ensure seriatim one-party domination. Same-day voter registration and a binding none-of-the-above choice can give more voters significant leverage as well. Voters themselves must demand that legislative votes by their representatives be immediately put on their public website with their justification.

Taxpayers lack the tools and resources to challenge the many hundreds of billions of federal tax dollars that each year are used illegally or corruptly or are shockingly wasted. Taxpayers have no standing, under our laws, to sue to stop such abuses. They are rendered weak and meek by this exclusion. When will voters hear a candidate pledge to give them their day in court? Another way to increase taxpayer power is to provide for a voluntary checkoff on the 1040 tax return that makes it easy for taxpayers to voluntarily contribute funds and band together with a full-time staff of watchdogs focused on the government's waste, fraud, and abuse. Big-time leverage is likely with this taxpayer searchlight.

Workers are empowered when they demand that candidates stand for the repeal of the notorious Taft–Hartley Act of 1947—the most handcuffing law obstructing union organizing and union rights in the Western world. Enforcing fairer labor standards that are already on the books, protecting pensions from looting by corporate management (pensionrights. org), establishing full improved "Medicare for all" (singlepayeraction.org), and lifting the minimum wage (timeforaraise.org)—all of these initiatives increase the power of workers.

Finally, how can it be that "the customer is always right" when the *consumer* has no might? Consumers are becoming serfs in many ways—deceived and tied up by fine-print contracts that exclude them from the courts, even if wrongfully injured, and allow vendors, using the same fine print, to unilaterally change contract terms whenever they want. Consumers have no way to easily band together either for collective bargaining or collective justice, such as negotiating away those fine-print contracts and restoring the exercise of trial by jury.

Corporate power, led by the cruel US Chamber of Commerce in Washington, DC, is stripping consumers of class-action remedies, imposing severe penalties and fines in the marketplace, and intimidating them to prevent them from complaining for fear of lowering their credit ratings and credit scores. Add to this the gouging prices for drugs and health care, malpractice, near-zero interest rates on their savings, high rates on credit cards, and vulnerability to unregulated foreign imports of food, medicines, and other products, and you have a compelling case for a power shift from vendors to consumers.

Inserts in billing envelopes or online required by vendors—such as electric, gas, and water utilities; banks; and insurance companies—inviting consumers to band together in nonprofit advocacy organizations, with full-time champions, can be a great step forward in getting consumers seats at the tables of power.

Consider how much of your money and assets the government spends to facilitate business organizations—with subsidies, handouts, bailouts, and giveaways; with tax credits and deductions; and with privileged bankruptcy laws to give mismanaged or reckless companies second and third chances.

Consumers and taxpayers pay for all these goodies. Where is the reciprocity; where is the modest payback for all these exactions? Let consumers have easy ways to organize, with full-time advocates, as bank customers, insurance policyholders, car owners, energy and credit users, and those simply wanting food that is safe to eat. When enough consumers can organize, through easy checkoffs, they can defend themselves and make for an efficient and equitable economy.

The appeal of these power shifts is that they come at little or no cost to citizens. No more than the equivalent of one week of the Pentagon's budget would comprise the aggregate costs of all of these resets for a functioning democratic society. By their own accomplishments, they would save consumers, workers, taxpayers, and voters more dollars than the entire Pentagon budget. Not to mention the quality of life, peace of mind, and lifesaving justice that cannot be measured just in dollars.

Meet your candidates; ask your candidates the question never asked!

Compare the 1912 Elections with the 2012 Elections

DECEMBER 31, 2012

Before the electoral year of 2012 slinks into history, it is worth a comparative glance back to the electoral year of 1912 to give us some jolting perspective on how degraded our contemporary elections, voter performance, and election expectations have become.

One hundred years ago, workers were marching, picketing, and forming unions. Eugene Debs, the great labor leader and presidential candidate that year, spoke to outdoor labor rallies of one hundred thousand to two hundred thousand workers and their families gathered to protest low wages and unsafe working conditions.

Farmers were flexing their muscle with vibrant political activity in progressive parties, organizing farm cooperatives through their granges, and pushing for proper regulation of the banks and railroads.

On the presidential ballot were Republican incumbent William Howard Taft, Democrat Woodrow Wilson, and the Progressive "Bull Moose" Party's choice, former president Theodore Roosevelt. Taft would be repudiated for being far too populist and too critical of corporations by today's Republican Party. He favored national, not state, charters for "national corporations."

The Democrats were committed to their platform of 1908, which asked, "'Shall the people rule?' is the overshadowing issue which manifests itself in all the questions now under discussion." The context was shaped by the giant corporations (called "the trusts") and their lobbies in Washington, which had to be curbed. The Supreme Court in 1911 had just ruled to break up the giant Standard Oil trust.

Women's suffrage; abolition of child labor; workers' compensation; states adopting the initiative, referendum, and recall; the eight-hour work day; minimum-wage laws (Massachusetts was the first in 1912); taxing corporate profits; and the "inheritance of fortunes" were some of the many hot issues of 1912.

Taft, Wilson, and Roosevelt fought over who was the most progressive. In an August 1912 speech, Theodore Roosevelt declared, "Behind the ostensible government sits enthroned an invisible government owing no allegiance and acknowledging no responsibility to the people. To destroy this invisible government, to befoul the unholy alliance between corrupt business and corrupt politics is the first task of the statesmanship of the day."

Meanwhile, Wilson repeatedly said that the country's salvation required the dissolution of the evil partnership between the government and the trusts.

Apart from how deeply these candidates believed in what they said, they repeated their campaign pledges again and again because the people were rising and breathing down their necks with demands.

Fast-forward to 2012 to the far greater grip of big business on government and elections. So much so that both major parties offer no solution to the "too big to fail" perch of the giant banks and additional corporate behemoths, other than to continue bailing them out with taxpayer dollars and underregulating them to boot.

Entrepreneur, lawyer, shareholder advocate, and author Robert A. G. Monks said recently that American corporations today enjoy an absolute reign. They and they alone have the power to control the rules under which they function. Corporations, and the most powerful CEOs acting through them, have "have effectively captured the United States: its judiciary, its political system, and its national wealth, without assuming any of the responsibilities of dominion."

Was corporate domination the theme of the recent Republican and Democratic conventions? Only to the extent to which hospitality parties put on by the drug, banking, insurance, energy, and other industries had the best booze, food, and other allurements.

The conventions and their scripted speeches off the PAC-greased election trails were congealed BS.

The leader of the AFL-CIO, Richard Trumka, was trotted out for a few minutes before a nationwide television audience to ignore mentioning both his own priority of legislating "the card check" for union organizing and the needs of thirty million American workers making less than workers made in 1968, inflation-adjusted, due to a frozen minimum wage. Eugene Debs, one of Trumka's heroes, not only made establishing the minimum wage one of his clarion calls, but also indefatigably ran for president in 1912 on the Socialist Party ticket, garnering nine hundred thousand votes (equal to about five million votes today) and pushing the major candidates and parties from the grassroots.

In 2012, third-party candidates were blocked from the debates, given virtually no media, obstructed from access to the ballots, and otherwise harassed by officialdom.

The two major parties were like corporate lapdogs fed daily with corporate cash to shut up about corporate crime; corporate tax evasion; corporate control of government; corporate abuses of consumers; toxic chemicals and fossil fuels jeopardizing air, water, soil, and the climate; corporate abandonment of American labor to fascist and communist regimes abroad, facilitated by global trade agreements and drafted by their corporate lawyers; corporate corruption of electoral campaign integrity; corporate fine-print contract servitude; corporate closing of courtroom doors to individuals wrongfully harmed; and the draining, corporate-bred military-industrial complex that President Eisenhower warned about in his farewell address.

The Democrats, from Obama to the congressional leadership and candidates, took corporate oaths; they wouldn't even raise the minimum-wage issue to "catch up to 1968" for thirty million Americans and their impoverished families laboring for Walmart, McDonald's, and other low-wage companies.

Meanwhile, the clenched-teeth Republicans with their vacuumed brains nominated Mitt Romney, who for years led the Bain Consulting Group to, in Monks's words, "reap untold millions in profits by using borrowed capital to buy companies, then sucking them dry, leaving the remains for bankruptcy referees to sort through, and stashing vast profits in offshore tax havens." In 1912, such an aspiring oligarch *would have been laughed away.*

Let's face it, our country is in crisis, and wallowing in disgust, discouragement, and despair won't turn it around. Nor will apathy, accepted powerlessness, or preoccupation with those weapons of mass distraction we hold in our hands or watch on our screens just about everywhere.

Only together can we make the difference, with far better modes of communication and transportation than our poor forebears, who still managed to rise up and show up more than one hundred years ago to make their country better for them and us. See seventeensolutions.com for my take on this patriotic mission of immediate renewal as well as respect for future generations.

7.

ON THE MEDIA

To the *New York Times*—
"We Thought We Knew Ye"

In 1980 we produced a report titled *How to Appraise and Improve Your Daily Newspaper: A Manual for Readers*, authored by David Bollier, one of our precocious interns, who had just graduated from Amherst and went on to become an expert on the Commons (see bollier.org). I thought about this past initiative to empower readers/consumers while contemplating what is happening in recent months to the print edition of the *New York Times*.

The editors call it a historic revamping in the digital age that is absorbing a growing, aliterate younger generation. I call it a frantic overreach replacing serious content with excessive photography and graphics slouching toward stupefaction. (The digital *Times* is doing very well.)

I spend serious time reading the *New York Times* in print—marking up at least thirty selections daily and sending them to a variety of advocates, scholars, and groups. I started reading this august newspaper at the age of ten.

Until the Internet Age of verbal incommunicados, I extended my reading experience by speaking frequently with *New York Times* editors, reporters, and opinion writers. Many a story idea flowed from these conversations. Many a change for a better country resulted.

What, why, and how the *New York Times* has moved so heavily into a vast visual mix of magazine styles and supplemental entertainment for its various sections are open questions. There is a daily Arts section but not a single weekly section devoted to civic activities, which should invite an extensive assessment by journalism critics and serious journalists.

Also useful would be an evaluation of the many other *New York Times* commercial ventures—launched by the desperate management to make up for the loss of print advertising (space and classified) revenue.

However, here I wish to register an objection to the very recent, unseemly, inexplicable collapse of the *Times*' historic editorial and op-ed pages that are arguably the most significant two pages in all of our country's mainstream journalism.

The implosion of these pages started some months ago when I noticed that

343

op-eds were displacing the previously sacrosanct space for the *Times*' daily editorials. From the usual three editorials taking up the left half of the page (the rest of the page was reserved for letters to the editor) emerged op-eds such as the tepid exchanges between professed "liberal" Gail Collins and "conservative" hawk Bret Stephens (whose earlier *Wall Street Journal* writings argued for illegal wars and imperial armed violence overseas). Now, in addition to each having a weekly column, they engage in strained exchanges in the weekly opinion feature The Conversation. What is the point of using precious space in the *New York Times* to showcase Bret seeking agreement on current news topics with the more moderate Gail, especially compared to featuring vibrant, fresh columns the editors could be seeking from more freelance contributors? (See some little-covered subjects listed on Reporters Alert: reportersalert.org).

The pages are getting more exclusive. Preference for the remaining space not occupied by regular columnists now goes to writers who have been signed up for New York Times podcasts and newsletters. This paper is pointing toward a journalistic monoculture, keeping out of its pages knowledgeable, experienced writers on many important, ignored subjects and positions.

It keeps getting worse. In the last week or so the former editorial space was taken up with a long demand for New York City to teach children how to swim (important, but belonging to another section). The entire editorial page was recently an artistic portrayal of the headline "The Choices My Mother Could, and Couldn't, Make" (good for another section). And just this August 3, 2022, another full-page article titled "Liz Cheney is Prepared to Lose Power, and It Shows" replaced editorials with a gigantic picture of the legislator's face.

Is it not enough that photographs and graphics have taken up huge spaces (in the Business section and in the various Sunday sections) where paying readers used to receive content? The editorial and opinion pages that used to be a haven of print, with no photographs taking up space for precious content, are now also losing space to gratuitous graphics—art over function.

To be sure, this is a visual age. But there is such a thing as much too much. Visuals have replaced the incisive Sunday Business section articles by Gretchen Morgenson, consumer features by Joe Sharkey, and others. Now there are photographic/print articles that have some serious readers shaking their heads and asking what they are doing in the *Times* Business section.

Page two of the daily *Times* often has reporters explaining how they got their breakthrough stories, including glimpses up front and personal. I may have missed it, but no such explanations were printed giving the real reasons for thinning down the editorial and op-ed pages.

I never thought that the *Washington Post*—owned by Jeff Bezos—would ever overtake the *Times* in presenting serious content. The *Post* has indeed overtaken them, especially comparing its Sunday Outlook section with its remodeled counterpart, the *Times* Sunday Opinion section. The *Post* readers still receive three editorials a day. The *Post* also devotes a full page on Saturday to letters to the editor, unlike the *Times*.

As for editorials, I noticed one, just one, in a recent six-day period, demurely tucked in the lower quarter of the opinion page. Whatever happened to the dozen or more full-time editorial writers who robustly championed serious issues? Have they been laid off, reassigned, or what?

The *Times* still produces remarkable, pioneering features, such as its spectacular series on the illegal predations and burning of the critical Brazilian Amazon rainforest. It publishes other domestic muckraking stories so good that they beg the formation of a citizen group just to extend this newspaper's exposure of wrongdoing and to push for reforms.

But there are also bizarre forays, such as the eleven full biographical pages on Fox's Tucker Carlson (which he used as a promotion).

There have been many other strange journalistic misadventures, filled with over-visualizations surrounding puzzling choices of subject matter. For instance, the *Times* is hung up on narrative features about little-known extreme right-wing groups and ventures. The subjects love it. They raise money off this coverage, becoming a big act for their followers. Readers are left wondering whether anything is happening on the progressive side of the political ledger in this election year.

What should be done? Open a couple of pages for longtime readers, who have a comparative perspective, to express their opinion of these changes. Have the editors give us the reasons for these changes, beyond self-reinforcing surveys.

Of course, the *Times* needs to react to what the new generations of readers *want* to read (hopefully elevating the quality of its many such pages). Nonetheless, its most basic mission is to offer the readers what they *need* to know about this tormented world of ours in the far fewer print pages they are allocating for that purpose.

Years ago, it used to be said: "You can always tell a *Times* man, but you can't tell him much." Please reverse your slide toward mediocrity and recover a sense of your own special significance in an unceasingly deteriorating journalistic culture of print, radio, television, and social media.

Two Conventions: Profiles in Decadent Cowardliness

SEPTEMBER 12, 2012

The Republican and Democratic Conventions are mercifully over, but their corrosive impacts on our democracy persist.

First, did you know that taxpayers helped fund these conventions at a level of $100 million for logistics and police sequestrations of demonstrators in Tampa and Charlotte, and an additional $18.2 million *each* for general convention expenses?

The two-party duopoly obviously controls the honeypot in Congress. That corporate welfare is what they enacted in spite of the fact that the party's convention committees are private corporations that should pay for their own big political party and their many smaller social parties with plentiful food and drink. No third party—Green, Libertarian, or others—received any taxpayer money for their conventions this year.

Second, the Republican and Democratic conventions have jettisoned their original purposes, which were to resolve the contest for the presidential nomination and work up a platform. Both functions are now decided beforehand, setting the stage for a choreographed theatrical event of political pomposity and braggadocio. On the periphery are the omnipresent corporate lobbyists and their parties of free food and drink.

Did they ask you, the taxpayers, to foot so much of this bill? Silly question for an oligarchy greased by a plutocracy.

Taking these conventions at face value, one is shocked by how they are scripted right down to every line of every speech vetted by the politicos. Clint Eastwood's spontaneity that so angered the GOP operatives was the exception.

The Republicans put three themes in just about every speech. Tell your personal story, recount your humble beginnings, and describe how you pulled yourself up by your own bootstraps. Show the people you're human or at least humanoid, not corporatist. Keep heralding small business so you don't have to talk about big business, which has bad vibrations these days around the country. Also, praise, praise, praise Mitt Romney and Paul Ryan as family men with family values. Imagine Republicans telling the press that the convention was to "humanize" Romney and give the voters a warm, fuzzy feeling about their candidate so as to forget that his campaign is a clenched-teeth mouthpiece for big business.

The Democratic Convention evokes pity. They too had similar scripts at the podium—narrate your humble, hardworking family lines, talk incessantly about jobs so you won't have to talk about wages. Especially muzzled was the willing Richard Trumka, head of the AFL-CIO, who, since 2009, has been given the back of Obama's hand on "card-check organizing rights" and on an inflation-adjusted minimum wage. His staged remarks even withheld any mention of a ten-dollar minimum wage (See HR 5901, the "Catching Up To 1968 Act of 2012") and the raiding of worker pensions by corporate raptors.

The repetitive, overwrought praise of *el presidente* in every speech became mawkish, reminding one of the "politics of personalism," present in many countries with underdeveloped political institutions. Michelle Obama found no time for mentioning the Obama family and America's mission to grow and consume nutritious food and keep fit to avoid the ravages of obesity. She was too occupied gushing over her aggressive drone commander's touching nightly reading of letters from Americans about their problems.

The mass obeisance ended when the commander-in-chief himself sprung onto the stage to speak the language of hope, meanwhile avoiding addressing the number of undesirable conditions that need his attention at this singular opportunity.

Conservative *New York Times* columnist David Brooks, trying to be sympathetic, was looking for some significant specificity:

> What I was mostly looking for were big proposals, big as health care was four years ago. I had spent the three previous days watching more than 80 convention speeches without hearing a single major policy proposal in any of them. I asked governors, mayors and legislators to name a significant law that they'd like to see Obama pass in a second term. Not one could. At its base, this is a party with a protective agenda, not a change agenda.

Fortifying Brooks's observation was Obama's recounting of the differences between the Democrats and Republicans. They are almost all defensive in nature. Defend Social Security, Medicare, and abortion from the Republican offensive. The Democrats are not on the offensive—not getting tough on corporate crime, consumer gouging, bank abuses, corporate tax avoidance, and evasions. They are not on the offensive fighting for worker safety and labor rights or minimum-wage increases or helping the poor earn more and pay less.

Even when Obama mentioned climate change—a recent no-no in the Democrats' lexicon—his words were defensive, namely "climate change is not a hoax," and he did not elaborate.

This defensive attitude against the cruelest, most ignorant, corporate-indentured, antiworker, warmongering Republican Party in history is also seen in the debates and programs of Democratic congressional and state candidates.

Being on the offensive with an agenda standing for and with the people—who are being driven economically, along with their country, into the ground by unpatriotic global corporations and their political minions—should be easy. Unless, that is, the Democrats want to continue dialing for the same corporate campaign dollars.

Playing defense explains why veteran Democrat members of the House of Representatives tell me that the party is going to lose the House again to the likes of John Boehner and Eric Cantor. The Democrats cannot even defend the country from Republicans who think Ronald Reagan was too moderate and unelectable today.

Eight New Year's Resolutions for NPR to Consider Now

JANUARY 14, 2022

The reasons Congress created National Public Radio (NPR) under the Nixon administration were to fill the yawning gaps of commercial radio in local, national, and international news coverage and to give voice to the people, without ads. It was to be publicly funded by taxpayers. Almost fifty-one years later, NPR is now funded heavily by national corporations, with its local affiliates soliciting local business advertisements.

RESOLUTION ONE: Apart from excellent features around the country and the world, NPR should give voice to what civic groups are doing to improve our country locally and nationally. NPR is heavy on entertainment and entertainers and needs to fill some of that airtime with news of the bedrock civic community in America. The imbalance is serious, from the national to the local.

RESOLUTION TWO: NPR features many reports and interviews on *race* but needs far more focus on *class*. Class exploitation by the rich and powerful corporate supremacists feeds into racial discrimination. The euphemism used is "inequality," but corporate-bred crime, fraud, and abuse affects *all people indiscriminately*, which often disproportionately harms minorities. A result of the gross imbalance of time devoted to race and not to class is that *indiscriminate injustice* is mostly ignored.

Over sixty million very poor whites in our country, if they even bothered to listen to NPR, might ask: "What about us?"

Focusing on racial plights without considering their sources in commercial greed, redlining, exploited tenants, lower pay, poverty, substandard health care, rampant overcharging of the poor (recall the book *The Poor Pay More: Consumer Practices of Low-Income Families*, by David Caplovitz), greater difficulty getting loans, and discrimination against upward mobility to corporate executive ranks are some examples of systemic commercialism fueling systemic racism.

NPR's collateral benefit from this inattention is that business advertisers large and small love NPR and its affiliates. This is especially the case for corporations with bad records. NPR should reject ads from disreputable or criminal corporations.

RESOLUTION THREE: Stop mimicking commercial radio. NPR's three-minute news segments on the hour often don't even match the quality of CBS Radio's choice of topics. For example, why are tennis star Novak Djokovic's visa problems in Australia at the top of NPR news day after day? As for commercials, NPR stretches the envelope, airing, with its affiliates, as many as thirty ads per hour! Imagine the audience irritation. How many times do we have to hear each hour "NPR is supported by this station"? NPR gives such abundant, repetitive ad time to the same few advertisers—Progressive Insurance, C3 AI, etc.—that one wonders whether they are assured of exclusivity vis-à-vis competitors. Moreover, NPR starts the evening program *Marketplace* with ads, which the commercial networks do not do.

Your listeners want you to decongest your ads, and some may want to know why you have given up on reversing the relative decline of congressional appropriations. You give ample time to loud right-wingers and right-wing causes. Why aren't you gaining bipartisan support for more congressional funding?

RESOLUTION FOUR: Compress the weather forecasts. Back in 1970–71, Congress knew that commercial radio stations gave plenty of time to weather, traffic, sports, and music. That is still true. So why does Albany's WAMC, an NPR local affiliate, have such lengthy forecasts, some starting with the West Coast, with ludicrous repetition for adjacent areas? With its full-time staff, WAMC is above average in covering local and state governments and candidates for public office.

RESOLUTION FIVE: NPR should reevaluate its music policy. NPR takes its weekends seriously, so much so that they take off right at 6:00 p.m. on Saturday and Sunday evenings. "Let them hear music" for the rest of the time, as if the world stops then. Also, musical intervals are often too long, inappropriate for their context, and foolishly interjected. NPR's evening program *Marketplace*, anchored by jumping-jack Kai Ryssdal, illustrates these observations. Even while he is rapidly giving the stock-market numbers, there is background music loud enough to be considered foreground.

RESOLUTION SIX: Reconsider the formulas shackling your reporters. They respond to the anchor's inquiry with a zigzag between their sound bites and corroborating sound bites from consulting firms, think tanks, and academic commentators. This model has a tedious staccato ring to it, especially since the reporters often, by way of their introduction, repeat what the interviewees are going to say.

RESOLUTION SEVEN: Correct or explain your major faux pas. NPR staff need tutorials on the constitutional authority of Congress. NPR needs to explain to its listeners why, with all that staff in Washington, DC, it took about ninety minutes (or until about 3:30 p.m.) to start telling its affiliates about the violent assault on Congress on January 6. Commercial CNN and other commercial media started reporting no later than 2:00 p.m. that fateful day. "And that's not the only time NPR has messed up," said one reporter for WAMC (that annually pays NPR a million dollars for NPR programming).

RESOLUTION EIGHT: Give your public editor, Kelly McBride, a regular public time slot to discuss her insights, presently communicated mostly internally, and to address serious feedback from your listeners about NPR's broadcasting flaws. (Local affiliates invite political opinions, personal development, and how-to questions on related shows.)

Ms. McBride could share the program with NPR's CEO—a position more remote from the NPR public every decade. Hear ye, John Lansing! Among other benefits, you'll get good suggestions for important, little-told news stories (see reportersalert.org).

Congress should hold long-needed public hearings in both the Senate and the House of Representatives to ascertain whether the original missions accorded public radio and public broadcasting are being pursued both qualitatively and quantitatively, and whether these networks and their affiliates have steadily strayed from those missions, due in part to the absence of mechanisms for public evaluations and congressional oversight.

There is so much to learn regarding NPR's and PBS's relations with American Public Media, the BBC, and other connections, to make them better and raise the expectations of their listening audience.

It's hard not to be complacent when you have so little competition from the commercial stations that for decades have debased our publicly owned airwaves, free of charge.

Unleashed Graphic Designers—
Art Over Function

FEBRUARY 27, 2019

Many readers object to illegible print in contemporary print newspapers and magazines. In today's print news, legible print is on a collision course with flights of fancy by graphic artists.

Admittedly, this is the golden age for graphic artists to show their creativity. Editors have convinced themselves that with readers' shorter attention spans and the younger generation's aversion to spending time with print publications, the graphic artists must be unleashed. Never mind what the ophthalmologists or the optometrists may think. Space, color, and type size are the domain of liberated, gung ho artists.

There is one additional problem with low expectations for print news-readers: even though print readership is shrinking, there will be even fewer readers of print if they physically cannot read the printed word.

I have tried, to no avail, to speak with graphic design editors of some leading newspapers about three pronounced trends that are obscuring content. First is the use of background colors that seriously blur the visibility of the text on the page. Second is print size, which is often so small and light that even readers with good eyesight would need the assistance of a magnifying glass. Third is that graphic designers have been given far too much space to replace content already squeezed by space limitations.

Function should not follow art. Readers should not have to squint to make out the text on the page. Some readers might even abandon an article because of its illegible text! One wonders why editors have ceded control of the readability of their publications to graphic designers. Editors cannot escape responsibility by saying that the graphic designers know best.

I am not taking to task the artists who combine attention-getting graphics with conveyance of substantive content. A good graphic provides emotional readiness for the words that follow.

However, in the February 17, 2019, Sunday edition of the *New York Times*, the page one article of the Sunday Review section was titled "Time to Panic," a piece by David Wallace-Wells about global climate disruption. He is the author of the forthcoming book *The Uninhabitable Earth: Life After Warming*. The editors wanted to strike fear in readers to jolt their attentiveness to such peril through two giant, lurid fingers with a human eye in between. A dubious attempt. Taking up the entire first page of the precious Sunday Review section (except for a hefty slice of an ad for the Broadway play "To Kill a Mockingbird"), smattered by three paragraphs of small, almost unreadable white text on a dark pink background, is counterproductive. Less graphic license and clearer type would have had art following function.

Many graphic artists seem to have lost their sense of proportion—unless, that is, the editors are pushing them to bleed out more and more valuable space with their increasingly extravagant designs. It is bad enough that print publications have been shrinking due to diminished ad revenue. It is time for better editorial judgment and artistic restraint.

Unfortunately, there is no sign of such prudence. In that same Sunday edition of the *Times*, over *80 percent* of page one of the Business section was devoted entirely to a graphic of a presumed taxpayer smothered by flying sheets of the federal tax return—it rendered the page devoid of content. At the bottom of this front page, there was a listing of five articles under the title "Your Taxes 2019." I can only imagine *Times* reporters gnashing their teeth about having their prose jettisoned from being featured on this valuable page of the Business section. That wasn't all. The artists ran amok on the inside pages with their pointless artistry taking up over half of the next three pages of this section.

Think of all the additional articles on other pressing business topics that never reached readers. Gretchen Morgenson's prize-winning weekly column exposing corporate wrongdoing used to be on page one of the Business section. She is now at the *Wall Street Journal*.

This is happening in, arguably, the most serious newspaper in America—one that is trying to adjust its print editions to an internet age that, it believes, threatens the very existence of print's superiority for conversation, impact, and longevity for readers, scholars, and posterity alike.

I first came across run-amok graphic design at the turn of the century in *WIRED* magazine. Technology has dramatically reduced the cost of multicolored printing. I could scarcely believe the unreadability and the hopscotch snippets presented in obscure colors, and small print nestled in degrading visuals. At the time, I just shrugged it off and did not renew my subscription due to invincible unreadability.

Now, however, the imperialism of graphic designers knows few boundaries. Many graphic designers don't like to explain themselves or be questioned by readers. After all, to them, readers have little understanding of the nuances of the visual arts and, besides, maybe they should see their optometrists.

Well, nearly a year ago, I wrote to Dr. Keith Carter, president of the American Academy of Ophthalmology, and Dr. Christopher J. Quinn, president of the American Optometric Association, asking for their reactions (enclosing some examples of designer excess). I urged them to issue a public report suggesting guidelines with pertinent illustrations. After all, they are professionals who should be looking out for their clients' visual comfort. Who would know more?

Dr. Carter responded, sympathizing with my observations but throwing up his hands in modest despair about not being able to do anything about the plight of readers. I never heard from anybody at the Optometric Association.

Of all the preventable conditions coursing across this tormented Earth, this is one we should be able to remedy. It is time to restore some level of visual sanity. Don't editors think print readers are an endangered species? One would think!

The Realized Temptations of
NPR and PBS

FEBRUARY 13, 2019

Recently an elderly gentleman asked me about my opinion on NPR and PBS, knowing of my vigorous support in the 1960s for these alternatives to commercial radio and television stations.

Here is my response:

Congress created NPR and PBS to provide serious programming, without any advertisements, for the American people. Former media executive Fred Friendly and others worried that the commercial stations were not meeting the 1934 Communications Act requirement that they operate for the "public interest, convenience and necessity."

In 1961, before a shocked convention of broadcasters, the new chairman of the Federal Communications Commission (FCC), Newton N. Minow, called commercial television "a vast wasteland."

Over the decades, NPR and PBS have produced some good programming—original features (among the best coming from Boston affiliate WGBH) and interviews. NPR has the largest radio audience in the country. David Brancaccio, the bright host of *Marketplace Morning Report*, has a daily listening audience of eleven million.

However, over the years, without regular critiques by liberal and progressive groups, both NPR and PBS have bent to the continual right-wing antagonism in Congress that decreased public budgets. PBS started to allow advertisements ("support for X station or X PBS network program comes from Y corporation"). These ads have become more frequent and can be as long as fifteen seconds.

During the 8:00 to 9:00 a.m. hour, WAMC of Albany recently aired twenty-eight such "support from" commercials. That is almost one "ad" every two minutes!

The omnipresence of the ads hour after hour has irritated many NPR listeners around the country. By way of comparison, a major commercial station in Hartford—WTIC—clocked eighteen advertisements in that 8 a.m. slot—albeit they were longer than the NPR ones.

It seems that NPR and PBS, often by their omissions and slants, bend over backward in order not to offend right-wing lobbies and corporations. They invite guests on air who ideologically oppose public broadcasting—that's fine, but then they minimize the appearances by leading progressives.

Occasionally I speak with the NPR and PBS ombudsmen. The purpose of the ombudsman is to maintain proper standards and ethics as well as to consider audience complaints. A while back, an NPR ombudsman volunteered to me that NPR was giving far more time to representatives of conservative evangelical groups than to representatives of liberal religious organizations.

Charlie Rose on PBS had many more CEOs on his program than civic leaders. During a rare appearance by me on his show with Jim Hightower and William Greider in 1998, the audience reaction was robust. The response from around the country was so pronounced that in an internal email, which was inadvertently sent to my office, a Rose staffer complained that we might have been encouraging the positive response. Absurd and false, but revealing nonetheless.

Rose, by the way, set the stage for PBS and NPR by interviewing his two favorite reporters again and again instead of active specialists or scholars in various fields. For example, Judy Woodruff, the ultracautious, exclusionary anchor of *PBS NewsHour*, interviewed reporters on complex tax legislation instead of authentic experts such as the longtime director of the well-regarded Citizens for Tax Justice, Robert McIntyre, often invited by her predecessors.

In 2016 we convened for eight days in the largest gathering ever brought together of civic leaders, doers, and thinkers of reforms and redirections. They made over 160 presentations in Constitution Hall (see breakingthroughpower.org). Although we advanced this remarkable Superbowl of Civic Action directly to NPR and PBS producers, their reporters never showed up. Certainly they have not treated right-wing conventions in Washington, DC, in that manner.

There are other practices of public broadcasting and its syndicated talk shows that its audiences should know about to understand how much broader coverage they have been denied. One is that the amount of time devoted to music and entertainment pieces goes well beyond the intent of the legislators who created NPR and PBS (both created by the Public Broadcasting Act of 1967). Members of Congress knew that entertainment was adequately taken care of by the thousands of commercial stations.

Moreover, even commercial network radio would not use its weekday 6:00 p.m. hour for music, as one NPR station does in Washington, DC. Nor does commercial network TV news in the evening start their programs with several advertisements, as does *PBS NewsHour* and Kai Ryssdal's jazzy, drumbeat-driven, breathless NPR evening show *Marketplace*.

Recently, I discovered another woeful transformation. Wondering why I could not get calls back from the statewide NPR stations in Minnesota and Wisconsin, I sent them written complaints. These stations had venerable programs that used to interview me and other civic leaders on consumer, environment, and corporate crime topics.

Minnesota Public Radio politely wrote back, regretting that they had not called me back, and explained that they now adjust their programming to react or expand on "what is in the national conversation." Since Trump et al. command the heights (or the depths) of the news agenda, very important subjects, conditions, and activities *not* part of this frenzied news feed are relegated to far less frequent attention.

These are just a few of the issues that should be analyzed by print journalists who cover the media full time, such as the estimable Margaret Sullivan of the *Washington Post*, formerly the "public editor" of the *New York Times*. But then, she also doesn't return my calls.

The slide toward commercialism and amiable stupefaction will continue on PBS and NPR until enough people review public broadcasting's history, raise their expectation levels consistent with why PBS and NPR were created, and insist on adequate public funding (a truly modest amount compared to giant corporate subsidies by taxpayers). These redirections would enable public broadcasting to fulfill better its serious statutory public-interest missions.

Questions, Questions—Where Are the Answers?

SEPTEMBER 18, 2018

In an oft-reported exchange between Gertrude Stein, an American widely known for her wisdom and glittering 1920s Parisian literary salon, and one of her earnest admirers, the admirer asked her, "What are the answers, Madame Stein?" She replied "What are the questions?"

Within our media/political/corporate culture of self-censorship and taboo topics, we should restate Ms. Stein's rejoinder—what are the questions of gravity and relevance that are chronically unasked?

Here are some questions that should be asked until answered!

1. Why are Supreme Court nominees, including Judge Brett Kavanaugh, not asked by the Senate Judiciary Committee about corporate crime; tyrannical, one-sided fine-print contracts; weakened tort law; and US violations of constitutional and international law affecting all Americans?

2. Why do reporters and elected and regulatory officials decline to ask questions about peer-reviewed studies concluding a minimum of 250,000 Americans are losing their lives every year due to preventable problems in hospitals? (See Johns Hopkins University School of Medicine's May 2016 report.) Five thousand fatalities a week on average, plus many more preventable injuries and illnesses, should be an ongoing subject of urgent inquiry for action.

3. Computerized billing fraud is rampant. Last year in the health care industry alone, computerized billing fraud amounted to about $350 billion. The leading expert, Harvard's Malcolm Sparrow, and a congressional Government Accountability Office report estimate at least 10 percent of all health expenditures are a result of fraudulent billings. Why aren't the TV networks, PBS and NPR, and the major newspapers all over this massive, ongoing heist?

4. Sanctions imposed on foreign agencies and personnel are flying out of Washington. What are these sanctions, how are they enforced, are they legal under international law, is there any due process to protect the innocent or indirect victims, and how are they countered? There are regular stories about the US government announcements of sanctions, but no follow-up questions about this burgeoning unilateral foreign policy.

5. The Taliban is composed of no more than thirty thousand to thirty-five thousand fighters without an air force, navy, or heavy ground armor. Why are they holding down for over a decade US forces and their allies many times their number, with advanced weaponry, and enlarging their territorial control? Is it because expelling foreign invaders motivates their astonishing determination? And who are all those suicide bombers and what is motivating them to stand in line waiting for the call?

6. Why has the congressional scrutiny of the wasteful, *un-auditable* military budget crumbled as never before, with the Democrats voting for more money than even Trump initially asked for in the last funding cycle? Over 50 percent of federal government operating expenses goes to defense. Both parties act as if adequate money for infrastructure repair in this country is nowhere to be found.

7. Why aren't the hundreds of full-time reporters who cover Congress demanding to know why members, or their staff, routinely do not reply to substantive letters, calls, or emails without constant hammering by citizens? The exception is if you are a campaign donor. Why are congressional offices often so unavailable during working hours? If you are lucky you can leave a message on the office voicemail. Inside the heavily guarded Russell Senate Office Building, Senator Rand Paul (R-KY) even locks the door to his suite of offices.

8. Similar unresponsiveness holds true with government agencies in the executive branches at the federal and state levels. A group of citizens, including me, has been waiting for months to get a reply from the Justice Department about their request for the department's posi-

tion on starting a long-needed corporate-crime database. One would think that newspapers, begging for readers, would do regular, random surveys of these agencies who, after all, work for the people they are shutting out. It's a small wonder that citizens are turned off government when they can't get through to get answers to their critical inquiries.

9. When I manage to get through to them, I tell newspaper, radio, and TV reporters and editors about agencies that do not respond (corporations are another dark void of obstruction); they invariably say that this would be a good service story for their readers, viewers, and listeners. Yet somehow, they never do such surveys of agencies, perhaps because as newspeople they have an easier time getting through.

Have you had a serious personal or critical inquiry put to your US senator or representative that has gone unanswered? Send us your ignored letter or email or telephone request by October 1, and we'll try to get you an answer from your hired hands on Capitol Hill.

Be Aware of the Dark Side
of Sports Media

NOVEMBER 28, 2017

The sports pages of major newspapers, such as the *Washington Post,* are thriving while other sections of newspapers such as business sections or book-review pages struggle to survive.

That doesn't mean that the sports pages allow the fans, the consumers, the taxpayers, and many of the players to have their say. Over the years, the sports sections have been neglecting the dark sides of organized sports as a deliberate practice, not as an oversight.

Ken Reed, author of several books and weekly columns—and the sports policy director for our League of Fans (leagueoffans.org)—is arguably the leading contemporary essayist of sports at their best and at their worst. Ever hear of him? Probably not. His truth-telling rarely makes it onto radio, television, or sports pages, or into sports publications such as *Sporting News,* because he writes about the greed, the covered-up dangers, the exploitation of youngsters by greedy owners and coaches, and the ways in which sportsmanship is most often pushed to the sidelines—all issues that the sports industry works tirelessly to suppress and squelch.

Probably no segment of journalism makes censorship so central a part of its craft and yet receives so little criticism for its failings; no segment of journalism so arrogantly continues to exclude vast regions of crucial reporting from its pages. In his new book, *Ego vs. Soul in Sports: Essays on Sport at Its Best and Worst,* Reed systematically tackles the most neglected and underreported territories of the athletic world.

And he knows what he's talking about. He holds a doctorate in sport administration with an emphasis in sport policy. He has taught sports, played sports, worked in sports marketing, and has a regular blog for *HuffPost.* But mostly, he can't crack the sports media because he is on to too many serious topics affecting sports—from middle school to the NFL, MLB, NBA, and NHL—that the giant profiteering sports business doesn't want to reach you, so as to preserve sports fantasies.

Reed summarizes the driving ethics of organized sports as "win-at-all-costs" (WAAC) and "profit-at-all-costs" (PAAC). Reed writes about the hidden injury epidemics (early on to concussions and how to detect and minimize them); about sports participation for all (not just spectator sports); on the serious decline in physical education in elementary and high schools and how it is connected to the rise of obesity; on the harm of encouraging specialization at age ten in sports; on athletes' right to protest; on women athletes still being shortchanged under Title IX; on Division I of the NCAA with its corruption, cheating, and exploitation of student athletes; on the need for creating a national sports commission, as other Western countries have done; on taxpayer and consumer rip-offs in the subsidized construction and operation of stadiums, arenas, and ballparks; on the need for oversight that can lead to the benching of tyrannical coaches; on how television and aggressive advertising are not good for sports; on deliberate, brutal fighting in NHL games; on overcommercialization and why it's time "the fans ran the show"—to name a few of these engrossing essays in Reed's book.

Year after year, Reed works relentlessly to sound the alarms and urge our society to get the best out of sports. He gives many examples of efforts that are sidelined by sports media reporters in favor of gratuitous slime and reporting on petty behaviors that they revel in sensationalizing—often without denouncing the roots of the behavior itself. Why *should* they be critics? Get fewer favors and freebies? Get fewer doors opened to the thrilling inner sanctums of the sports owners and high-dollar players?

Most sports pages have either no sections for letters to the editor—or they devote very little space to letters to the editor. Why should they allow letters that might expose their incompetence, their sacred-cow managers and players, their refusing to give the fans—the source of all their profits—consistent voices, beyond some selected ones calling into sports talk-radio shows with rapid-fire comments on that day's teams, tactics, and strategies? ESPN Radio, for example, needs to think about these exclusions.

Earlier this year I sent a letter to Joe Torre, the former general manager of the New York Yankees and current chief baseball officer for Major League Baseball, detailing the incessant in-game advertisements ("this is an X company call to the bullpen," "that's an X company double play," etc., breaking the spirit of the action). The letter was also sent to sports reporters and columnists, some of whom I notified in advance. Not a word came in response. Not a reply came from anyone to this longtime Yankees fan since the time of Joe DiMaggio.

People I know, who are inveterate fans, often get brushed aside with no responses to their well-thought-out emails, and they are screened out when trying to make calls to talk-radio hosts.

Some impartial observers of contemporary sports trends believe that self-destruction lies ahead for most high school football (concussions, etc.), for unpaid big-time college athletes, and for pushing the commercialistic envelope too far (staggering ticket prices and other extortions) in big-time sports.

We'll see how much spectator fans will take before they demand that the tax dollars and priorities go toward neighborhood recreational athletic facilities so that sport becomes a pleasurable way of life for tens of millions of presently sedentary adults and youngsters.

If you'd like to read Ken Reed's book, you can order a copy at Xlibris.com.

Copps's Plea for You and Me

MAY 13, 2016

The plainspoken, public-spirited former FCC commissioner Michael Copps is indignant—and for good reason: the Federal Communications Commission is not enforcing the law requiring the dark-money super PACs and other campaign cash conduits to reveal, on the air, the names of the real donors behind all political advertisements, which are now flooding the profitable radio and television airwaves.

It is bad enough that political ads far overwhelm political news stories. One study of the 2014 election campaign found Philadelphia stations gave forty-five times more airtime to political ads than they devoted to their news stories that were designed to inform viewers about the candidates. Political ads have become a huge cash cow for the television and radio stations that use *our* public airwaves free of charge. We citizens, who are the owners of the public airwaves, receive no rent payment from these tenants (thanks to a corrupted Congress!).

As Mr. Copps has written, viewers watching these ads are provided a nice-sounding name, such as "Paid for by Citizens for Amber Waves of Grain," and "nothing else, no hint of who put up the money; no clue as to the real agenda behind the message." They could be chemical companies polluting our water, big arms manufacturers wanting more overpriced government contracts, or banks that are opposed to proper regulation of their consumer-gouging tactics and their risky speculation.

Years ago the FCC declared that audiences "are entitled to know by whom they are being persuaded." So why isn't the FCC enforcing the clear-cut, unambiguous Section 317 of the Communications Act of 1934? After all, the mass media is regularly writing about dark money, secret money, and bought-and paid-for politicians without being able to supply the names of the donors. The FCC could be the agency that gives the voters their right to know.

Earlier this year, the FCC voted to require that cable and radio stations maintain a public file on political advertising. In 2012 the agency required such a public file for broadcast television stations to maintain a database.

But still, there are no requirements for disclosing the "true identity" of people, corporations, or other entities paying for the ads.

This is what 170 House Democrats demanded the FCC do in a letter released on January 20, 2016.

Such a demand, and even the knowledge that voters would overwhelmingly approve such openness, are not enough for cautious FCC chairman Tom Wheeler. His agency has been sitting on petitions to require disclosure under Section 317 for years. In December 2015, the Sunlight Foundation, Common Cause, and the Campaign Legal Center filed formal complaints against eighteen television stations in four states, asking the FCC to order the stations to comply with this law. Former commissioner Copps wonders what else the FCC needs before it enforces the law that its five commissioners have sworn to uphold. Billions of dollars of dark money in this campaign year need to be brought into the sunlight.

Well, as Michael Copps writes, "Broadcasting and cable companies fear that honest ads might lead to fewer ads and less in their coffers. Corporate and dark-money interests hide in the shadows of anonymous attacks. Even our major newspapers shy away from covering this issue, perhaps looking more toward their bottom-line interests than the public interest. Some of them own other media properties."

Apart from recent exertions on net neutrality, the FCC has been subservient to big media companies and their docile congressional allies who don't want to properly enforce the Communications Act of 1934, which stipulates that radio and television broadcasting companies adhere to the legal standard of the "public interest, convenience and necessity" in presenting programming. That standard implies a fair balance between serious content and entertainment/advertisements. The FCC, mercilessly harassed into slumber by members of Congress, has been AWOL from its legal duties.

On the bigger picture Copps writes, "Big money is corrupting our electoral process, strangling our civic dialogue, and endangering American self-government. The agency, the FCC, should respond to the petitions and complaints that have been filed, and indicate if it is going to live up to its obligations or not." Law and order, anyone?

Interested citizens may weigh in with their views by contacting FCC chairman Tom Wheeler (as many did effectively on net neutrality).

The overall subject of media responsibility will be the subject of day two (May 24, 2016) of the Super Bowl for Civic Action at Constitution Hall in Washington, DC: Breaking Through Power.

For the Conference on the Israel Lobby—
Press Blackout at the Press Club

APRIL 17, 2015

Following the heavy coverage of the American Israeli Public Affairs Committee's (AIPAC, the virulently pro-Israel government lobby) annual multiday Washington convention in March, the mainstream media might have been interested for once in covering alternative viewpoints like those discussed at the April 10 conference "The Israel Lobby: Is It Good for the US? Is It Good for Israel?" (Israellobbyus.org [site discontinued]). Fairness and balance in reporting should produce at least some coverage of such an event.

Organized by the *Washington Report on Middle East Affairs*, which was launched about thirty years ago by a British army officer who served in World War II and two retired US ambassadors to countries in the Middle East (wrmea.org), the daylong program at the prestigious National Press Club should have been intriguing to reporters. After all, are they not interested in important, taboo-challenging presentations on a critical dimension of US foreign and military policy?

The presenters were much more newsworthy than most of the speakers at the AIPAC convention, who redundantly restated the predictable AIPAC line. "The Israel Lobby: Is It Good for the US? Is It Good for Israel?" had presenters including the courageous, principled columnist Gideon Levy, of Israel's best and most serious newspaper, *Haaretz*; Richard Falk, Princeton professor emeritus of international law and former UN Special Rapporteur on the situation of human rights in the Palestinian territories; former members of Congress Paul Findley (R-IL) and Nick Rahall (D-WV); Mike Peled, author and son of an Israeli general; Dr. Jack Shaheen, the award-winning author documenting stereotypes of Arabs and Arab Americans in Hollywood and the US media; and even former AIPAC supporter M. J. Rosenberg (mjrosenberg.net), who witnessed the power of AIPAC money as both a congressional staffer and later as an AIPAC senior staffer in the 1980s.

Gideon Levy, the dean of Israeli journalists, who knows firsthand the situation on the ground in Israel and occupied Palestine, referred to Israel's intensely intrusive pressure on the US during Iranian nuclear negotiations. He offered the phrase "United States of Israel" and said, "Many times when someone looks at the relations between Israel and the United States, one might ask, who is really the superpower between the two?"

Mr. Levy described Israel as a society that "lives in denial, totally disconnected from reality" and that "lost connection with the reality in its backyard; it totally lost connection with the international environment."

The veteran journalist stunned the packed audience when he said that "the two-state solution is dead." With the Israeli occupation going "deeper and deeper," he pointed to the "systematic dehumanization of the Palestinians," Israelis presenting themselves as occupying victims, and the belief by many Israelis that they are "the chosen people" and "have the right to do what [they] want" as the basis for the occupation.

The serious, continuing breaches over decades of international law by Israel and its backer, the US government, were described by Richard Falk, who, during his six-year term as the UN Rapporteur, felt the brunt of these powers just for connecting the facts to the laws and noting widely acknowledged continuing violations of UN resolutions and the Geneva Conventions.

Former congressman Paul Findley spoke of politicians cowering before AIPAC because of the "anxiety over being accused of anti-Semitism." AIPAC is a leading anti-Semitic organization against the Arab peoples and the thousands of innocent civilian Palestinians and Lebanese children and adults slaughtered by the US-armed Israeli forces. (See Dr. James Zogby's remarks about "The Other Anti-Semitism," delivered at Hebrew University in Israel in 1994.)

AIPAC, knowing that the Israeli military was engaged daily as brutalizing occupiers, has never openly disavowed its support for such destruction of innocent humans and human rights, even when the videotaped devastation horrified the civilized world. AIPAC was conspicuously silent during the illegal US invasion and violent sociocide of Iraq—a nation that did not threaten the US.

A surprise speaker was the just-defeated thirty-eight-year veteran of the House of Representatives, former congressman Nick Rahall. Apparently, now extricated from AIPAC's congressional clutches, he is now free to stand tall for human rights and speak openly in describing congressional obeisance to the Israel lobby from the inside.

Unfortunately, there was no panel representing either US taxpayers, who foot the bill for the billions of dollars spent yearly, or the US soldiers who have been sent to kill or be killed in military invasions and other attacks backed by this self-defeating Israel–US government alliance that just worsens the insecurities in the Middle East, spreads into savage sectarian struggles, and portends more boomerangs against peace and justice in the world.

So, where were the reporters of the mainstream media? Where was C-SPAN during a week when Congress was on a holiday and its cameras were not preoccupied by Capitol Hill activities—its foremost priority? Apparently the American people were only to see and hear the extreme views of AIPAC that do not even command the support of a majority of American Jews, who do favor a two-state solution, along with a majority of Arab Americans.

It is true that a few members of the mainstream media RSVP'd to attend this conference, but they did not show up or write anything about it before or after.

Nonetheless, thanks to the internet, you can see the entire one-day conference online [https://www.youtube.com/playlist?list=PLqnzB-dOyKbnY_yD-_ogEw6DqZNKrBIH2q].

In the meantime, how about a little retrospective evaluation, by those so authorized, in the *New York Times*, the *Washington Post*, the *Wall Street Journal, Associated Press,* and *Reuters* to make better judgements about providing balanced news the next time around? As for the absentee "fair and balanced" Fox News—well, what do you expect?

Mainstream Media: Who Gets on
and Who Does Not

JANUARY 30, 2015

Over the years, discussions about whom the mainstream media gives voice to and whom it excludes are far too general. Editors bristle at the notion that they are anything but fair and objective. Sure, they concede that reporters miss stories, but appearances of bias or censorship, they say, are more likely due to laziness.

Well, let's climb down the abstraction ladder and make some observations. William Kristol, an editor at the *Weekly Standard*, and Newt Gingrich, long retired as Speaker of the House of Representatives (apart from his 2012 presidential campaign), have received in the past fifteen years more national newspaper ink and more television exposure over more media outlets than all of the following public intellectuals, advocates, and writers—who work on very important national subjects—put together.

1. Robert Fellmeth is a law professor and prolific author. He is arguably the nation's leading specialist and litigator on legal protections for children.

2. Karen Ferguson, Esq., is the head of the Pension Rights Center in Washington, DC, the only public interest group on pensions and retirement security since the mid-seventies. She is also a coauthor of *Pensions in Crisis*.

3. Jim Hightower is a former Texas commissioner of agriculture, author, advocate for progressive agendas nationwide, and editor of the *Hightower Lowdown* publication, which has a circulation twice that of Mr. Kristol's the *Weekly Standard*.

4. Edgar Cahn, who with Jean Cahn conceived of and lobbied through Congress the National Legal Services Program for the poor, founded

the Antioch School of Law and is the most creative, hands-on expert on poverty in the US and how to enlist the poor in ending it. He is a prolific author, most notably of the groundbreaking *Time Dollars*, which he coauthored.

5. S. David Freeman, energy expert extraordinaire, is an engineer and lawyer who ran three major public utilities: the New York Power Authority, the Sacramento Municipal Utility District, and the Los Angeles Department of Water and Power. He also stopped the construction of some nuclear power plants while serving as chairman of the Tennessee Valley Authority, and he served as an adviser to Lyndon Johnson, Jimmy Carter, and Jerry Brown.

6. Professor Rena Steinzor, corporate crime specialist, is the president of the Center for Progressive Reform, a large group of academic experts on regulation and deregulation. She is the author of the new book *Why Not Jail?* and a specialist in regulatory matters.

7. Paul Hawken, industrialist, is widely published on the nexus between industry and ecology and the economic and environmental necessity of conversion to a green economy. His book *The Ecology of Commerce* inspired the leadership of Ray Anderson, the CEO of Interface Global at the time, in breaking new ground by combining pollution reduction and corporate efficiencies. He was named by *Esquire* magazine as one of the best 100 People of a Generation.

8. Joel Rogers is a law professor at the University of Wisconsin, where he serves as director of the Center on Wisconsin Strategy (COWS), a nonpartisan social change organization. Rogers is a frequent author and consultant on national labor issues and public economic policies. He is extremely knowledgeable and articulate on politics and democratic reforms and is the founder of ALICE, a foil to corporate-backed ALEC.

9. Tom Devine of the Government Accountability Project is a top expert on whistleblower rights, disclosures, and the role of the judiciary in this regular front-burner subject. He is the author of *The Corporate Whistleblower's Survivor Guide*.

10. Robert McChesney has written numerous books on old and new media, including his 2014 title, *Digital Disconnect*.

11. Bill Black is a former government official in the Justice Department, author, and law professor. Black is a leading expert on corporate crime, corruption, negotiated settlements, and obstructions to reform—topics in the news every day.

12. Lori Wallach, director of Global Trade Watch, specializes in the trade agreements NAFTA and GATT and the politics of the forthcoming Trans-Pacific Partnership before Congress and should be the go-to person on this important topic.

13. Danielle Brian is the executive director of the Project On Government Oversight (POGO), where she focuses on both the big picture of national security and intricacies of topics including military contracts and the Pentagon budget.

14. Colman McCarthy has been a long-standing peace advocate; he started the Center for Teaching Peace that inspired high schools and colleges across the nation to adopt peace-related courses. Through his prolific articles, he has repeatedly made the case that waging peace trumps waging war for our national and global security again and again.

15. Robert McIntyre, director of Citizens for Tax Justice, is the leading expert on unfair tax breaks, tax havens, and the overall dysfunction of our tax system. He is a leading go-to for reporters searching for specific company and industry data, but rarely makes national TV or print media.

16. Lois Gibbs got her start in community activism protecting her hometown, Love Canal. Her movement grew to become the country's largest grassroots antitoxics movement, with hundreds of neighborhood groups working to protect their families from the silent violence of toxic chemicals. She founded and directs the Center for Health, Environment & Justice.

17. Patrick Burns is the codirector of the Taxpayers Against Fraud Education Fund, which applies knowledge of experts and whistleblowers to enforce federal and state false claims acts.

18. Tom Geoghegan is a nationally recognized labor union specialist and author of *Which Side Are You On?* and his latest, *Only One Thing Can Save Us*. Few can speak so knowledgeably, as a scholar and practitioner, to give workers a collective voice vis-à-vis multinational corporations.

19. Sheldon Krimsky, a longtime Tufts University professor, is a historical and contemporary specialist on science, ethics, conflicts of interest, and the deceptions and perils of genetically modified food. He is the coeditor of *The GMO Deception*.

20. Ramsey Clark, former attorney general under President Lyndon Johnson, has devoted decades to conflict prevention, conflict resolution, and opposing criminal wars of aggression.

21. Steffie Woolhandler and David Himmelstein are scholars and practicing physicians who have taught at Harvard Medical School and have written pioneering reports on the failures of the health care system and the need for full "Medicare for all."

22. Ted Postol, an MIT engineering professor, is by far the leading technical critic of the over $7 billion a year Ballistic Missile Defense System.

23. Amory Lovins and Peter Bradford both decry fossil fuels and nuclear energy in favor of solar renewables and efficient technologies, and reject the all-of-the-above policy of Washington. Lovins is a physicist, author, and consultant to utilities and government agencies, and Bradford is a former member of the Nuclear Regulatory Commission.

24. Arthur Rosenfeld, a prominent Berkeley physicist and adviser to state and federal governments, is the nation's leading specialist on massive energy conservation opportunities.

25. Jerry Mander of the International Forum on Globalization, a former advertising executive, has become an incisive published critic of globalized economies and what new technology is doing to damage localism.

The above knowledgeable, thoughtful, articulate Americans, mostly blocked out of the mainstream media and, for the most part, national public television and national public radio, demonstrate the media's obsession with the tedious punditry of the well-connected corporatist and militaristic "opinion oligopoly" in Washington and New York. It is always the same old talking heads uttering the predictably same old oligarchic commentary.

It is the independent media, such as the Pacifica stations, community radio, and sometimes C-SPAN, that search for people who know the realities and reforms that resonate so often with majoritarian opinion and the public's well-being.

People own the public airwaves. Shouldn't they be pressing for broader and deeper uses of their property on television and radio?

Serious News: In Low Supply from Mainstream Media

FEBRUARY 1, 2013

On January 30, 2013, an unusual front-page story appeared prominently in the *Washington Post* about a small DC charity called Martha's Table that serves meals to 1,100 people a day, has early-childhood and after-school programs, and provides other community-enriching programs. Among its distinctions is a giant volunteer corps of, according to the *Post*, "10,000 school kids, poor people and the occasional president who chops vegetables and builds sandwiches." Fascinating!

The only reason for the *Post* writing and front-paging the article is that the new, full-time, volunteer president is Patty Stonesifer, ex-Microsoft megamillionaire, ex–chief executive of the Bill & Melinda Gates Foundation, and ex-chairperson of the Smithsonian Institution's board of regents. Amazing!

The *Post*'s million readers also got to see Ms. Stonesifer say, "I was amazed at how there is a city within a city here. This idea that the District [of Columbia] has so much child hunger, it's mind-boggling."

The *Post*, local television stations, and cable shows often do not showcase the District's big dirty secret. That, alongside its glittering affluent class (mostly shorn of *noblesse oblige*), half a dozen major universities, and governmental departments, there is widespread, deep poverty; unhealthy and afflicted children; and higher rates of cancer and diabetes, for example, than most states.

What is important to the *Post* and other local media are local professional sports, local entertainment, visiting celebrities, and endless gossip or other permutations of such page- and time-fillers. The *Post* obviously believes that the injured knee of rookie sensation Robert Griffin III and its impact on the Redskins' organization are too big for its sport pages, thus requiring multiple front-page stories since RGIII injured himself during playoffs in January.

The *Post* has been cutting back—ending its separate daily Business section and its separate Sunday Book Review section. But its (spectator) sports section remains large with numerous reporters, columnists, feature writers, editors, and gossipmongers frantically scurrying around.

The *Post*'s front page features an article by sports columnist Sally Jenkins, but not one by their recently retired, superb business columnist Steve Pearlstein, who tells readers how and why their living standards are being mauled by big business. I doubt that readers would be upset were Ms. Jenkins to have written that column back in the sports pages instead.

When one of America's leading newspapers decides to lighten up or stupefy—take your pick—its content at a time of grave developments and degradations in our society—local, regional, national, and international—"We the People" need to be part of the conversation. It is not sufficient to be told vaguely about the illusive "surveys" of reader opinion that do not convey the availability of real choices.

Space and time for serious matters are also increasingly limited in other news outlets. Over 90 percent of commercial radio is music and advertisements. Commercial TV entertainment and ads are not far behind. There are fewer examples of serious, compelling programming by the national afternoon entertainment shows than there were in the Phil Donahue, Mike Douglas, and Merv Griffin shows. These shows found some time to inform readers about auto safety, unsafe medicines, and other consumer and environmental subjects. Now it is nonstop sadomasochism, reality-show family drama, or other similar kinds of cheating and betrayals in relationships. Forget about local television shows—most are long gone, having been displaced by these syndicated shows.

Bear in mind, much of this modern Sodom and Gomorrah is conducted on our public airwaves used by broadcasters for free. When I called Rush Limbaugh and Sean Hannity, the leading bloviating soliloquists on the radio, "corporate welfare kings," they were nonplussed, as if profitably using our public airwaves without payment is their birthright.

This week, the media buildup is for the Super Bowl. Endless articles, features, and gossip, with huge photographs, swarm superficially over the pages and airwaves and cable networks. There is simply no such restraint. Enough is enough! Soon the buildup will be for Hollywood's Oscars on February 24, and all the "players" will be profiled and psychoanalyzed.

In the meantime, valiant Americans are striving to reduce or prevent the pain, anguish, and costs of preventable tragedies—poverty, repression, marginalization, exclusion, and the chronic indifference to posterity in favor of vested pressures for instant gratification. The press releases, reports, accomplishments, and testimonies of those striving for justice receive very little coverage from the mass media.

Groups with compelling causes come from around the country to the National Press Building for well-prepared news conferences, only to find no one there from the press except an occasional indie reporter. NPR and PBS do not come close to wanting to fill some of this void.

Without media coverage, the civic community cannot, even if it demonstrates in the streets and squares, expand its audience of concern. Citizen morale struggles to persist in the face of powerful opposition. Gone is the wisdom of famed newspaper publisher Joseph Pulitzer, who, quoting humorist Finley Peter Dunne, advised his reporters "to comfort the afflicted and afflict the comfortable."

People in the colony of the District of Columbia march, protest, and host important news conferences to press for statehood so that they can have a voting representative and senator(s) in Congress. They regularly get shut out of the local media. After all, it's only electoral democracy they're working to install.

Maybe a blend is necessary. How about Robert Griffin III becoming the full-time chair of the DC statehood association in the offseason? Or would that give the editors of the *Post* too much cognitive dissonance?

Growing Doubts about Advertising

JULY 17, 2012

Ask yourself when you last saw any of those tiny ads on Google and Facebook and rushed to buy the products or services. For that matter, ask yourself whether any radio or television advertisements prompted you to go out and buy the product.

Sure, the newspaper ads announcing short-term sales for clothes or household goods may get you to the market, along with the supermarket specials for foodstuffs. But generally speaking, you must wonder what the business community gets for its tens of billions of dollars annually pouring out of their advertising budgets.

I can almost hear the chuckles from Madison Avenue reacting to this skepticism about whether ads are worth their price. Such doubts are almost never publicly discussed. One reason has its roots in the musing of pioneering department-store magnate John Wanamaker, of Philadelphia. About a century ago, he said he thought that half the money he spent on advertising was wasted but didn't know which half.

Another reason is that advertisements sell moods, feelings, exciting images about the product—selling the sizzle along with the steak, as the saying goes. These feelings connect to corporate branding strategies and are hard to measure.

But they are believed by the "hidden persuaders," to use Vance Packard's famous phrase, to be very effective, precisely because they are emotional rather than rational. And never before has the technology of inducing these emotions—with visuals, colors, sounds, and their synergies—been more hypnotic. It isn't for nothing that trademarked slogans and names are expensively valued.

Recently, however, it was General Motors, of all companies, that said very publicly what many companies have been thinking for a long time. In May, stunning the advertising and internet industry, the world's largest vehicle manufacturer announced that it would pull $10 million in ads from Facebook because they are not effective. A few days later, GM pulled out of the Super Bowl advertising frenzy—commercials for Super Bowl XLVII are now going for $4 million per thirty seconds—on the grounds that it "simply could not justify the expense." This is another way of saying the ads didn't sell enough cars.

The mass media, which carries such exorbitant commercial messages, plays large corporate competitors, as in the auto and computer industries, against one another. "You don't want to be left out of the Super Bowl, with its III million viewers, do you?" Of course, given the multiple distractions of family, dogs, cats, bathrooms, opening beer bottles, and laughing at each other's remarks, far fewer millions actually see the hyperkinetic ads that bleed into one another before viewers even catch a logo.

Those managers arguing for ever-larger ad budgets convey a "you gotta believe" mentality. It takes lots of myth, hope, gambling, and reliance on the artistry and cleverness of the copywriters and ad designers to bring about the blockbuster breakthrough ad that arouses its beleaguered, saturated audience, enmeshed in a blizzard of sequential ads, and induces a memorable recollection of the product or service offered.

Most telling, of course, and most ignored in the experts' evaluation of an ad's excellence, is the prevailing absence of useful information for the consumer, including comparative information or information describing function, quality, reliable price, performance, safety, and the like. Granted, on television and radio there is little time for a litany, but how about just one fact relating to usage or repair or disposal. Nah, say the faithful copywriters, that would break the emotional flow.

Some fifteen years ago, I discussed comparative pricing of auto insurance with my Princeton classmate, Progressive Insurance's CEO, Peter Lewis. It wasn't long before decisive Peter instituted the pioneering television ad that invited customers to submit their specifications to get the comparative price of equivalent policies by Progressive and its three or four competitors in a region. It seemed to work well for Progressive and certainly got people's attention and generated word of mouth.

There is one organization that doesn't lose any sleep over the question "Do advertising dollars work or are they largely wasted?" Consumers Union—through its monthly magazine, *Consumer Reports*, and its website services, consumerreports.org—gives you just the facts derived from its wide-ranging, honest testing programs. With over five million print magazine subscribers and three million online subscribers, more and more Americans are getting it the rational way.

By the way, *Consumer Reports* has never carried advertising in its seventy-five-year history.

8.

ON IMPERIAL POWER
AND THE MILITARY

Weaning the State Department from War-Making to Peaceful, Robust Diplomacy

JULY 22, 2022

Other than being an adjunct booster of overseas Pentagon military operations and refortifying its vulnerable embassies, what does the US State Department stand for and do anymore?

Sometimes it's hard to see much difference between the State Department and the much larger Department of Defense (DOD). Its more belligerent statements or threats since Bill and Hillary Clinton's days have made the DOD sound almost circumspect.

Recall it was "Generalissima" Hillary Clinton, secretary of state under Obama, who, against the opposition of Secretary of Defense Robert Gates, pressed the president in 2011 to unlawfully overthrow the Libyan regime, unleashing chaos, violence, and mayhem in Libya and in neighboring African nations that still prevail today. (Later, Obama said it was his biggest foreign policy regret.)

Our country's founders established the State Department in 1789 to conduct diplomacy (plus consular duties). Its charter explicitly instructs its function to be peaceful relations with other nations.

We now have Secretary of State Antony Blinken, who comes from the Hillary Clinton school of routine: unconstitutional and unlawful adventures overseas. He is ignoring the arms-control treaties, especially with Russia, that have either expired, are about to expire, or are violated by both Russia and the US and other nations—such as the Treaty on the Non-Proliferation of Nuclear Weapons.

Then there are the treaties signed by one hundred or more countries to which the US State Department has scarcely made a move for Senate ratification. These include the Convention on the Rights of Persons with Disabilities, the International Criminal Court, the Anti-Personnel Mine Ban Treaty, the Convention on Cluster Munitions, and the Convention on the Rights of the Child.

Waging peace and conflict resolution should be the State Department's main mission. There is a lot of inherited work for Antony Blinken and a revived foreign service corps to engage big-time. Mr. Blinken could press aggressively for cease-fires, for example, as with Russia's war in Ukraine.

In 2019, former president Jimmy Carter called the United States "the most warlike nation in the history of the world," adding that only 16 years out of our nation's 242 years were times of peace.

Washington and its "military-industrial complex" (President Eisenhower's words) have set records toppling foreign governments that were duly elected by the people, and propping up right-wing dictatorships in Latin America, Africa, and Asia, so long as they obey us and our corporations. (See: *War Is a Racket*, by General Smedley D. Butler, 1935.)

Against this militaristic mania, you may wish to know about the Veterans for Peace (VFP) organization of which I am a member. VFP is embraced by veterans from all our wars going back to World War II. Its members have written, spoken, picketed, and pursued nonviolent disobediences against the recent wars of the US empire. VFP has highlighted the immense harm done to millions of innocent victims in these countries, speaking out against the injuries and illnesses of returning US soldiers. VFP advocates for robust peace missions and enforceable arms-control treaties.

I found VFP's short report on the connections between militarism, environmental destruction, and climate violence especially noteworthy. (See veteransforpeace.org.)

Veterans for Peace challenges the proliferating impact of militarism and the vast, bloated, un-auditable military expenditures throughout our political economy, culture, and educational institutions.

With the leadership of Executive Director Garett Reppenhagen, VFP is planning a major expansion of its activities. Membership is open to nonveterans, and the organization welcomes donations. In particular, very wealthy elderly people who are looking for a universal cause to recognize might envision what a new future of peace and social justice looks like for our posterity. They can call Mr. Reppenhagen at 314-899-4514 or email at reppenhagen@veteransforpeace.org.

Perhaps the State Department can host a meeting with Veterans for Peace to remind itself of its original mission.

US–China Policy: A Perilous Arms Race Instead of Waging Critical Cooperation

JULY 11, 2022

Did the Biden officials know what they were doing when they announced a broad expansion of *export controls* on China? China is the world's second-largest economy, which is intricately intertwined with the economy of the US and other nations. This is mainly due to US multinational companies exporting huge slices of our manufacturing economy to China for its cheap labor.

What are the White House and the Department of Commerce thinking? China is not Venezuela nor is it Russia, a weak and dependent economy with a gross domestic product smaller than Italy. Do these brazen Bidenites realize the consequences of a grand list of technologies and know-how being barred from China?

As the dominant imperial world power, the US is struggling to understand how to deal with an aggressive rising power like China building spheres of influence around the world through exports, loans, development contracts, and technical assistance. It's OK that we have military bases in over one hundred countries whose leaders know the US as the premier overthrower of elected governments that have policies displeasing to Washington and Wall Street.

As a result, the Bidenites are unleashing export controls, arrived at through administrative secrecy, that will surely invite black markets, high-tech smuggling, and retaliation to make these controls a nightmare to enforce.

Provoking China to play its own cards is not smart. China, thanks to the greed of coddled and subsidized US drug companies, produces many of our pharmaceuticals. These companies have left America, for example, with no domestic production of antibiotics—certainly a national security priority!

China possesses critical minerals and rare earth metals and produces technology crucial to our own defense and high-tech industries. Its government allows US factories to be built in China on the condition of a flow of the latest "technology transfers." Ask General Motors.

How are export controls—based on asserted national security grounds—going to work, other than to accelerate a new arms race? "We need to ensure that the US retains technological overmatch," declared head of the Commerce Department's Bureau of Industry and Security, Alan Estevez. Gina Raimondo, the Commerce Secretary, said that export controls "are at the red-hot center of how we best protect our democracies." Tell that to the mass victims of the next round of viruses from China due to our minuscule, weak public health programs and early detection systems, while we spend more than two and a half times as much as China on our military budget, having had a huge head start in past years.

The *New York Times* reports that US officials also don't like China's deep surveillance of its people. It is as if surveillance capitalism (See, *The Age of Surveillance Capitalism: The Fight for a Human Future at the New Frontier of Power* by Professor Shoshana Zuboff) and the National Security Agency's dragnet violations of the Fourth Amendment are chump change.

China is already in the front ranks of artificial intelligence, biotechnology, and quantum computing. As a Commerce Department official said, to declare a cold war on China's access to technologies "that advance the country's scientific advancement," including on foreign companies that use some US products, is ludicrous. Aren't they aware of the traditional open exchange between scientists all over the world, not to mention China's own allies or collaborators in this regard?

What is also well-known but not uppermost in people's minds is that China, Russia, and the US have embedded malware in each other's cyber worlds that if triggered could cause catastrophe. The concern about China's tens of billions of dollars invested in US Treasury bonds should also be an issue for Mr. Biden.

Another calculation underweighted is the quiet opposition to export controls by US companies that salivate over the present and future profits with Chinese trade—Apple CEO Tim Cook (who, by the way, makes $833 a *minute* on a forty-hour week) got a special waiver treatment from Trump, continued by Biden, for importing tens of billions of dollars annually of iPhones and computers from its Chinese contractors without tariffs.

This is another way of noting that export controls invite both raw corruption and special lobbying for waivers. They were tried by the US against the old USSR, which developed elaborate circumventions.

So here we go again. Of course, certain lethal products need to be embargoed by all countries protective of their people. The US is expanding its so-called "entity list," cutting off hundreds of foreign companies and groups from certain US technologies unless US suppliers get licenses to sell goods to them. Don't these government officials know that blacklisted companies can mutate through other corporations chartered in tax havens or dictatorships abroad?

US belligerence will be met with more Chinese belligerence and vice versa as the perils and risk increase.

William Hartung (see the Center for International Policy) points out that a far brighter future would come from intense US and China cooperation on the climate crises, averting pandemics, ocean preservation, and international arms accords, including cybersecurity. Wage peace and pursue mutual self-interest as if our children and grandchildren matter.

Where is our Department of Peace, once advanced by Congressman Jim McGovern (D-MA) and former congressman Dennis Kucinich (D-OH), when we need it?

Relations between major nations are shaped by momentum in one direction or another. Both US political parties have chosen a militant path without an exit strategy—one that must please Lockheed Martin and the rest of the military-industrial complex.

The forces for muscular peace and cooperation must show there is an alternative path to secure the common interests of the two nations. That's called robust diplomacy in this era of recurring pandemics, expanding ransomware, bloated military budgets, and interconnected economies.

Audit the Outlaw Military Budget Draining America's Necessities

MAY 23, 2018

Top military, diplomatic, and political leaders have exposed, warned of, and condemned our runaway, un-audited military budgets for decades, to no avail. (For many examples, see *America's War Machine: Vested Interests, Endless Conflicts,* by James McCartney, with Molly Sinclair McCartney.) They usually come to the same desperate conclusion: that only organized citizens back in their congressional districts can make Congress stop this spending spree. Only *us*, Americans!

From President Dwight D. Eisenhower's 1953 "Cross of Iron" speech before the American Society of Newspaper Editors to full-length addresses by President Obama's secretary of defense, Robert Gates, the warnings about unrestrained military spending have not been addressed. The military budget—now at about a trillion dollars when you add up all costs—is spiraling out of control and draining the public budgets for rebuilding America's public infrastructure and services. Now both major parties go along with uncritical rubber-stamping.

Even the strict Pentagon budget of about $700 billion is now over 50 percent of the entire federal government's operational budget that includes the other departments and agencies. President Eisenhower said:

> Every gun that is made, every warship launched, every rocket fired signifies, in the final sense, a theft from those who hunger and are not fed, those who are cold and are not clothed. This world in arms is not spending money alone. It is spending the sweat of its laborers, the genius of its scientists, the hopes of its children.

The oft-repeated phrase of "waste, fraud, and abuse" describing the Pentagon's contracts with the giant defense industry rarely quantifies the toll of the outrageous waste of taxpayer dollars. Too many way-over-budget weapons systems that are not needed, such as the F-35 boondoggle. Too many nuclear-equipped *missiles, submarines,* and *bombers* (referred to as the nuclear triad) are maintained at too-expensive levels.

Former generals, such as presidents Gerald Ford's and George H. W. Bush's national security adviser Brent Scowcroft, have called for scrapping two of the triad. Doing so would still leave plenty of dispersed, globally destructive power to act as a sufficient nuclear deterrent. But the war machine of Lockheed Martin, General Dynamics, Boeing, Raytheon, and other big corporations is forever hungry for more and ever-bigger contracts. While warmongering neocons and so-called think tanks like the American Enterprise Institute keep looking for enemies to exaggerate, the weapons-industry lobbyists swarm over Capitol Hill demanding new military spending. The Trump administration is pushing a new arms race calling for spending at least $1.2 trillion over the next thirty years to allegedly upgrade existing nuclear weapons (see the Project On Government Oversight, "New Documents Raise Questions about Increased Nuclear Spending").

Former Secretary of Defense Gates made pointed reference to the vastly excessive firepower of our too-many submarines and other delivery systems compared to all other countries in the world combined.

With Trump throwing more money at the Department of Defense (DOD), the excessive Pentagon spending Gates described is much worse today. What to do? Start with requiring a fully and authentically audited military budget, a provision already required by federal law since 1992.

The Pentagon has been in violation of that congressional directive since 1992 but keeps promising Congress's Government Accountability Office (GAO) that an audit is coming.

At a House Armed Services Committee hearing in January, DOD comptroller David Norquist promised an audit later this year. To illustrate his sincerity, Norquist said his office had already discovered two stunning situations: "The Army found 39 Black Hawk helicopters that had not been properly recorded in its property system. The Air Force identified 478 buildings and structures at 12 installations that were not in its real property system."

The comptroller did not go into the fraud and waste minefield that has lost taxpayers trillions of dollars since 1992. Not all this comes from the Pentagon. For years, the DOD has wanted to close dozens of costly, obsolete military bases in the US. Various members of Congress, who view the military budget as a jobs program, have blocked these closures.

There is some light. Fifty-three members of the House of Representatives have signed on to HR 3079, which would reduce the budget of the department (subject to emergency presidential waivers) by .5 percent if the Pentagon's financial statements do not receive an audit OK by the GAO. HR 3079 is a stirring in the body politic, however weak the pulse.

Obtain a copy of HR 3079 and its named sponsors to see whether your representative is on board. If not, demand to know why. All of Connecticut's representatives have ducked cosponsoring this bill.

No such bill has been introduced in the Senate.

What more support do they need from the Pentagon than its own specialized audits, the GAO's famous investigations, and a quote from Secretary Gates inserted right in Section 3 (10) of HR 3079, from a speech given on May 24, 2011:

> The current apparatus for managing people and money across the DOD enterprise is woefully inadequate. The agencies, field activities, joint headquarters, and support staff functions of the department operate as a semi-feudal system—an amalgam of fiefdoms without centralized mechanisms to allocate resources, track expenditures, and measure results relative to the department's overall priorities.

This legislation needs immediate public hearings in Congress. Full annual audits will reveal the costs of empire. This is your money that could be used in your own community for jobs to repair and upgrade your public transit, roads, bridges, schools, drinking water and sewage systems, and other crumbling infrastructure and facilities.

At a recent gathering focused on auditing the annual military budget, citizens from sixteen congressional districts agreed to organize that pressure to make Congress work for *us*. Stay tuned.

The Hour Is Late—Speak Out, Stand Tall, Ex-Officials

APRIL 11, 2018

As a failed businessman, saved by business bankruptcies—which he called a "competitive advantage"—Donald Trump believed in chaos as a strategy. Unfortunately, chaos and foreign policy don't mix. Chaos may bring war. And tragically, military aggression can explosively boomerang back to the US mainland.

On April 3, Trump declared he was going to pull soldiers out of Syria. After the recent alleged chemical attack on Syrian civilians outside of Damascus, Trump threatened his friend Vladimir Putin, saying he will pay a price, and that the military response will be "very, very tough."

Being deliberately unpredictable and keeping your adversary off-balance may work for real estate deals in New York, but for potentates and armed groups it is a formula for quickly accelerating, uncontrollable disasters.

This flailing approach—implying the use of military violence—may please super war hawk and madman John Bolton, Trump's unconfirmed national security adviser yet to receive a top-secret security clearance from the FBI, but it appalls many retired military, national security, and diplomatic officials who served in high positions under both Republican and Democratic presidents.

Why don't more ex-officials speak up? It is simple patriotism to forewarn the American people about the gathering storms of military interventions. We are fortunate that a few patriots—such as retired colonels Larry Wilkerson and Andrew Bacevich—stand tall and speak out about the unwarranted or unwise use of military force. But where are James Baker, Brent Scowcroft, Colin Powell, and a slew of former Obama administration officials who are silently tearing their hair out over the daily news reports?

There is a strange tradition in our country of former public officials shutting up when they shouldn't.

I call this tradition an indulgence America cannot afford. Our country needs former public officials to stand up and speak out. Barack Obama, Joe Biden, and the dozens of former Senate-confirmed cabinet and sub-cabinet officials need to publicly challenge Trump's autocratic attacks on proven practices benefiting people under the rule of law. Our country is seeing rollbacks of rights and protections while the rich and powerful play with its seized riches and misappropriated delegated powers, which belong to the sovereign people.

Recently, several former Environmental Protection Agency (EPA) heads from previous Republican and Democratic administrations have protested against EPA marauder Scott Pruitt's unleashing toxic pollutants into the bodies of America's children, women, and men.

Recently David Shulkin, the fired head of Veterans Affairs, took Trump to task on TV and in an op-ed in the *New York Times*. There have been other modest displays of resistance to a few of Trump's depredations by some ex-officials. By and large, however, the widespread silence among them is shameful. Former leaders should know better. Whether they retire, resign, or are fired from their positions, these experienced and aghast Americans dwell in a self-imposed state of vanquishment.

I call on them—mostly well-off, with available time—to return to the fray and band together on the matters related to their know-how and know-who. Taxpayers have invested much in their shelved expertise and judgment.

Call them ex-Obamaites and reformed ex-Trumpsters. They can raise funds to open full-time advocacy offices in Washington that reach out to the country. Trump is wreaking havoc on the American people as workers, consumers, buyers of medicine, breathers of air, and drinkers of water; as taxpayers against waste and spreading corruption; and as children in serious need. These outrages must be counteracted by people who can get their calls returned, get on the mass media, and mobilize the caring public into sturdy citizen challengers of our hijacked federal government before the November elections.

This entreaty is to people who need no mind-changing about the Trump regime. They know what is happening, where the destructive trajectories are heading, and they dislike it intensely. I've heard enough about their expressions of private dread to urge former public servants to stand up for their country's well-being—nothing less is at stake!

Democracies die in many ways. But in the nineteenth century, political philosopher John Stuart Mill delivered a warning for the ages: "Bad men need nothing more to compass their ends, than that good men should look on and do nothing."

If any retired high officials wish to discuss the above plea on my weekly radio show, the *Ralph Nader Radio Hour*, please use the contact sheet provided on the website.

The Losing Warfare State

MAY 11, 2017

The USA is still bogged down in Afghanistan (the sixteen-year-old occupation is the longest in American history) and in Iraq (since the unconstitutional, illegal invasion of the country fourteen years ago).

With about 30,000 poorly equipped fighters, the Taliban has held down an Afghan army, equipped and trained by the US, that has eight times the number of soldiers, plus US forces—fluctuating from 100,000 at its peak to 8,500 now, plus contractors—with advanced air, sea, and land weaponry that is second to none.

Moreover, the Taliban has been advancing, controlling 30 to 40 percent of the country and a third of the population, according to the *Wall Street Journal.*

In Iraq, the US had hundreds of thousands of soldiers and contractors during the Bush years. Yet today the country is still in the throes of a civil war, where a previously nonexistent threat, ISIS—with less than fifteen thousand fighters—has been successfully resisting a huge Iraqi army backed by US trainers and Air Force.

How can this be? "We are vulnerable," writes military author William Greider, "because our presumption of unconquerable superiority leads us deeper and deeper into unwinnable military conflicts."

Jim Fallows asserts in *The Atlantic* that our military "is the best-equipped fighting force in history. . . . [It is] also better trained, motivated, and disciplined than during the draft-army years." Nonetheless, he concludes: "Yet repeatedly this force has been defeated by less modern, worse-equipped, barely funded foes. Or it has won skirmishes and battles only to lose or get bogged down in a larger war."

It gets worse. Less than three thousand ISIS fighters took sudden control in 2013 of Mosul, Iraq's second-largest city, which has over a million residents. Notwithstanding being vastly outnumbered by the Iraqi military and police—who fled—ISIS went on to control over a third of Iraq's land area. Iraqis and US forces are now destroying west Mosul in order to save it from a few hundred remaining ISIS fighters.

Fallows quotes former military intelligence officer Jim Gourley as saying, "It is incontrovertibly evident that the US military failed to achieve any of its strategic goals in Iraq."

Setting aside the fundamental questions about why we invaded Iraq and continued to occupy Afghanistan long after 9/11, Americans are entitled to question how continued American occupations across the Middle East serve any kind of vital national interest and why they continue to fail.

In his analysis, military historian Thomas E. Ricks writes that "an important factor in the failure" is that no one gets "relieved by the military brass for combat ineffectiveness." But there are other reasons all the way up the chain of command. Cargo planes ship hundred-dollar bills in bulk to Kabul airport as part of an extensive bribery/extortion system that weakens the opposition to the Taliban, whose appeal to the masses, despite their harsh rule over them, is to drive out the foreign invaders. That is a very powerful motivation, one that is lacking among Afghan forces and politicians, whom the people of Afghanistan view as puppets of the US and its Western allies.

Retired admiral Mike Mullen makes another point concerning "the growing disconnect between the American people and our military." He observes that "fewer and fewer [American citizens] know anyone in the military. It's become just too easy to go to war."

The ease at which we embrace military interventions is in large part due to a gross dereliction of duty on the part of Congress, which allows the White House to commence wars, large and small, without legal authority. Congress is the only branch of government constitutionally authorized to declare war and appropriate funds for war. The Libyan war, which was pushed by Hillary Clinton and Barack Obama (and opposed by Secretary of Defense Robert Gates) was waged without seeking either legal authority or funds from the legislative branch. The Obama administration took monies from the un-auditable Pentagon budget to start that continuing disaster in Libya and neighboring African countries.

Listening to the House and Senate Armed Services Committee hearings, one finds a sycophancy and level of questioning by the lawmakers of Pentagon officials that would embarrass a mediocre high school student.

But the senators and representatives have their reasons. They simply do not want the responsibility for military action except to provide a virtual blank check from taxpayers for the Department of Defense and its avaricious, wasteful contractors who fund their campaigns. Second, members of Congress see the military expenditures as a jobs program back in their states and districts. Finally, members of Congress are not getting any heat from the detached, indifferent voters (with few exceptions), either during or between elections. Notice there is never a debate by candidates on the military budget—how it is used or misused financially and strategically (yet candidates regularly pledge ever-increasing dollars for the defense budget).

As a final cruel insult to our children and grandchildren, Congress, by refusing to fund the wars as they persist, has built up a huge deficit for future generations of Americans to pay.

Retired colonel Andrew Bacevich has written, "A people untouched (or seemingly untouched) by war are far less likely to care about it. Persuaded that they have no skin in the game, they will permit the state to do whatever it wishes to do."

But, collectively, we all have skin in the game. Look at the unmet needs in our country; crumbling infrastructure, toxic environments, and corrosive costs of corporatism escaping law enforcement that would protect consumers and workers.

It is the members of Congress who have no skin in the game. Very few of their children are in the armed forces. Were the American people to demand enactment of a one-page bill that requires drafting all able-bodied children and grandchildren of members of Congress anytime they or the White House plunges our country into war, you would see a very attentive Congress that pays attention to its constitutional duties and responsibilities.

Why not ask your senators or representatives to put such a bill in the hopper?

Hillary's Latest Bow to AIPAC

MARCH 25, 2016

It is well-known to Washington political observers that politicians invited to speak at the giant annual American Israeli Public Affairs Committee (AIPAC) convention ask for suggested talking points from this powerful pro-Israeli government lobby. Hillary Clinton's pandering speech must have registered close to 100 percent on AIPAC's checklist.

Of course, both parties pander to AIPAC to such depths of similar obeisance that reporters have little to report as news. But giving big-time coverage to sheer political power is automatic. Compare it to the sparse attention given to the conference on the Israeli lobby a few days earlier at the National Press Club featuring scholars, authors, and the well-known Israeli dissenter Gideon Levy of the respected *Haaretz* newspaper (see israellobbyus.org).

But Mrs. Clinton's speech was newsworthy for its moral obtuseness and the way in which it promised unilateral White House belligerence should she become president. A reader would never know that her condemnation of Palestinian terrorism omitted any reference to the fact that Israel is the occupier of what is left of Palestinian lands—colonizing them, seizing their water and land, brutalizing the natives, and continuing the selective blockade of Gaza, the world's largest gulag ever since Israel closed its last colony there in 2005.

Clinton emphasized her condemnation of Palestinian children being taught "incitement" against their Israeli oppressors and the recent deplorable knife attacks against Israeli soldiers and civilians. She neglected to point to massive, daily Israeli incitement backed up by US-supplied deadly weapons that over the last decade have caused four hundred times more Palestinian fatalities and serious injuries to innocents than the defenseless Palestinians have caused their Israeli counterparts. One of Prime Minister Netanyahu's coalition partners from the Jewish Home Party, for example, called for the slaughter of all Palestinians. "Otherwise," the partner said

397

(in an English-language translation from the Hebrew), "more little snakes will be raised there."

Clinton did not mention any of these brutalities, though they are components of what is an illegal occupation under international law and the United Nations charter. The Yale Law graduate simply chooses not to know better. Instead, she told her wildly applauding audience of her support for increasing the amount of US taxpayer spending for the latest military equipment and technology to over $4 billion a year. For the record, Israel is an economic, technological, and military powerhouse that provides Israelis with universal health insurance and other social safety nets that are denied the American people.

In an obvious slap at President Obama, whose name she never mentioned (even Netanyahu thanked Obama in his address to AIPAC), Clinton almost shouted out: "One of the first things I'll do in office is invite the Israeli prime minister to visit the White House." This was a thinly veiled reference to Netanyahu's trip to a joint session of Congress, where he tried to undermine President Obama's negotiations with Iran in what was an unprecedented interference by a foreign leader. Not surprisingly, Obama did not ask Netanyahu over to visit the White House for a drink before the prime minister headed back to Israel.

High on AIPAC's checklist is to insist that all speakers condemn what Clinton called the "alarming boycott, divestment, and sanctions movement known as BDS." She then twice slanderously associated this modest effort (in which many Jews are active participants) to get Israel to lift some oppression from the occupied Palestinian territories with anti-Semitism. However, by totally erasing any nod, any mention, any compassion toward the slaughter of Palestinian children, women, and men in their homes, schools, and hospitals, Hillary Clinton makes a mockery of her touted Methodist upbringing and her declared concern for children everywhere.

For repeated applause at AIPAC's convention and its associated campaign contributors, she has lost all credibility with the peoples of the Arab world. Moreover, such hostility in her words registers "the other anti-Semitism," to cite the title of an address by James Zogby before an Israeli university in 1994.

With all her self-regarded experience in foreign affairs, Mrs. Clinton could pause to ponder why she is backing state terrorism against millions of Arab Palestinians trapped in two enclaves, surrounded by walls and military outposts, and suffering from deep poverty, including widespread diseases and severe anemia among Palestinian infants and children.

Unlimited is her militant animosity toward Iran, bragging about crippling sanctions that she spearheaded (which caused untold harm to the health and care of civilians), and threatening military force "for even the smallest violations of this [nuclear] agreement." Yet for decades Israel has violated numerous UN resolutions to withdraw its occupation and repression of Palestinians without a murmur from Secretary of State Clinton, who as a candidate opposes a role for the UN Security Council (over which the US has an often-used veto) in the peace process.

There were some restraints. She repeated her support for a Palestinian state but wondered whether the Palestinian leadership was up to the negotiations. Also, she resisted going along with recognizing the shift of Israel's capital from Tel Aviv to Jerusalem.

Her very oblique reference to illegal, expanding Israeli settlements did not amount to anything more than a wink, foreshadowing no action on her part to stop the expansion of colonies in the occupied territories should she reach the White House.

Near the conclusion of her deferential remarks, she stated, "If you see bigotry, oppose it. If you see violence, condemn it. If you see a bully, stand up to him." Some courageous Israeli human rights groups, such as B'Tselem, who defend Palestinian human rights, might view her words as applicable daily to how they perform their noble work.

Netanyahu, the Other Israelis,
and Bobby Burns

MARCH 6, 2015

Apart from inadvertently making the case for equal time by his Israeli pre-election opposition, the spectacle of Benjamin Netanyahu's wild diatribe at the joint session of Congress amidst the feral cheers of his congressional yahoos will be remembered as a textbook case of propaganda unhinged from reality.

Starting from his preposterous premise that Iran—a poor country of seventy-seven million people with an economy nearly the size of Massachusetts's—is planning a caliphate to conquer the world, Mr. Netanyahu builds his case on belligerent words by Iranian leaders, who believe they are responding to Israeli belligerence backed by its ultramodern, US-equipped military machine and its repeated threats of preemptive attacks against Tehran.

Unwilling, unlike his Israeli opponents, to subject himself to questions before congressional committees, this three-time soliloquist at joint congressional sessions (1996, 2011, and 2015) was received with hoopla quite different from his reception in a much more critical Knesset. The prime minister's forty-two-minute speech was punctuated by twenty-three standing ovations and sitting applauses that took up ten minutes.

The US Israel lobby has made Congress a rubber stamp for lopsided policies in the Middle East.

Only about fifty Democrats boycotted his address.

It is as if Iran is not frightened of Israel, which has two hundred nuclear weapons and rejected the Nuclear Non-Proliferation Treaty, whose international inspections are required for all other signatory nations on Earth, including Iran.

It is as if Israel has not threatened Iran with annihilation, sent spies to sabotage and slay Iranian scientists, and worked with its Arab allies to undermine the Iranian regime.

It is as if Iranians do not remember that the United States overthrew their popularly elected Prime Minister Mossadegh in 1953 to reinstate the shah's dictatorship for twenty-six years.

It is as if the Iranians do not mourn the loss of hundreds of thousands of soldiers and civilians killed by Saddam Hussein's brutal invasion of their country from 1980 to 1988 with the military, intelligence, and diplomatic support of the United States.

It is as if Iranians are not frightened into thinking they're next when George W. Bush named Iran as part of the "axis of evil" (along with Iraq and North Korea) and proceeded to destroy Iraq and surround Iran with US armed forces that are still in place to this day.

It is as if the Iranian people are not suffering from economic boycotts that, by disproportionately impacting civilian health and safety there (see Public Citizen's *Health Letter*) violate international law.

It is as if Iran should accept a wide sphere of influence by the US and not try to expand its sphere of influence for its own defense.

It is as if Iran had not proposed a serious plan to George W. Bush over ten years ago to settle disputes and establish a nuclear-weapons-free zone in the Middle East, which Mr. Bush completely ignored.

It is as if Iran is not, in the words of former Obama adviser Vali R. Nasr, carrying "most of the weight" in the "battles on the ground" against ISIS in Iraq, thereby saving the US from again committing US soldiers to averting a complete rout of those left behind after our deadly debacle in Iraq since 2003.

It is as if Iran is not claiming it is building nuclear power plants for electricity (a foolishly dangerous move for its own people) and not building an atomic bomb, has not been in full compliance with the Geneva interim agreement (November 2013) with the P5+1 countries, as these parties, led by the United States, strive to conclude a complete agreement this year.

It is as if Israel has not illegally occupied, colonized, and stolen Palestinian land and water over the decades (including regularly invading a blockaded Gaza, invading Lebanon five times, and attacking other nearby countries preemptively) and caused hundreds of thousands of civilian casualties.

It is as if Israel, while complaining about Iranian behavior, does not continue their Palestinian policies that violate several United Nations resolutions, while goading the US toward war against Iran.

It is as if the Arab League, with twenty-two member nations, has not offered repeatedly since 2002 a comprehensive peace treaty, which was also rejected by Israel, in exchange for Israel returning to its 1967 borders.

It is as if Iran has forgotten the shooting down of a scheduled Iranian civilian Airbus by the US Navy in 1988 with a loss of 290 innocent lives, including 66 children.

It is as if Iran, a country that hasn't invaded another country for over 250 years, should remain cool in the face of such attacks, threats, infiltrations, boycotts, and the US Navy in the Persian Gulf and not engage in any military alliances.

And it is as if Iran's authoritarian leaders are not preoccupied enough with pressures inside their country that are both internally and externally driven without also planning to conquer the world.

The pop-up lawmakers in Congress on Tuesday did not show any interest in their own government's causal responsibility for Iranian animosities. The priority for many in Congress is marching to the drumbeat of whatever the US Israel lobby wants from the Pentagon, the State Department, and the American taxpayers. (Some members of Congress have spoken up in the past, notably Republican congressmen Ron Paul and Paul Findley and senators Chuck Percy and James Abourezk.)

Why does a large majority of Congress block the viewpoints and policies that could lead to peace as advocated by many former chiefs of Israel's security, intelligence, military, and political institutions? They have spoken up repeatedly in Israel but are never allowed to testify before congressional committees. This entrenched anti-Semitism on Capitol Hill against the "other Israeli" Jews needs to be challenged by peace- and justice-loving Americans who want to avoid future blowbacks and war quagmires for our soldiers.

A way to clarify jingoistic biases in foreign policy is to ask the questions: Who was the initial aggressor? Who is the invader, the occupier, the ever-hovering armed drone operator? Who has backed and armed dictators to repress their people who want no more such nation-building by the US?

For a century, is it we, with the British and French, who have been over there or is it they who have been over here? Brutish conditions breed brutish behavior in all directions.

The poetic wisdom of the great Scottish poet Bobby Burns teaches crucial empathy: "O would some power the giftie gie us to see ourselves as others see us."

Senate Report Condemns
Government Torture Abroad

DECEMBER 13, 2014

The 528-page Senate Intelligence Committee report on CIA torture may come as a shock to many, but would not have surprised the late senator Daniel Patrick Moynihan (D-NY). In 1991 and again in 1995, fed up with his dealings with this agency, he introduced a bill for its abolition. Too much secrecy that amounted to a blanket institutionalized cover-up, too much bad or inadequate information leading to blunders, tragedies, and failures to anticipate events like the collapse of the Soviet Union. Moynihan believed that secret government breeds disaster and shreds democratic societies.

Despite the bill not being put to a vote, Senator Moynihan's criticisms proved justified after 9/11 when the CIA became more imperial, more secretive, more violently operational, and more of a "government within a government"—a phrase used by then senator Daniel Inouye (D-HI) during the Iran–Contra affair under President Reagan.

Outwardly, the CIA claims its "enhanced interrogation methods" (a.k.a. torture) have blocked plots and saved lives. Asked to document these claims, the agency automatically hides behind its secret curtain. When a federal agency claims what it is doing is legal and constitutional, it better back this up beyond general assertions of secret legal memos from the Justice Department and knowledge and approval from the war criminals (e.g., invasion of Iraq) President George W. Bush and Vice President Dick Cheney, the generic prevaricator.

The CIA's bureaucratic environment assured this kind of searing and specific criticism of this type of torture. After a five-year investigation, the Senate Intelligence Committee's report, delivered by its chairperson, Senator Dianne Feinstein (D-CA), revealed torture, cover-ups, lying, and a failure to achieve its objectives.

With a very ample, secret multibillion-dollar budget, near-zero independent congressional oversight, and the omnipresent sheen of protecting "national security," the CIA can never answer the old Latin question "Quis custodiet ipsos custodies?" ("Who will guard the guards themselves?") No rule of law or externally independent monitoring can contain this rogue agency driven by internal conviction and righteousness.

During the Bush years, the CIA's unbridled forays were commonly marked by dictatorial secret wars, secret prisons, secret courts, secret evidence, secret law, and dragnet illegal surveillance.

In addition, there were no criminal or civil prosecutions of any culpable bureaucrats either by the Bush or Obama administrations—with one exception. The only person prosecuted, under Obama no less, was the truly patriotic John Kiriakou—a well-regarded CIA interrogation specialist who accurately blew the whistle on illegal CIA torture. He is serving a thirty-month jail term—having copped a plea on a minor, questionable charge to spare his wife and five children from an even longer, financially breaking ordeal defending himself from vengeful prosecutors with endless budgets.

To prevent the Senate Intelligence Committee from finally redeeming its history of passivity and complicity exhibited by its "look the other way" tradition, the CIA tried to obstruct the committee staff in numerous ways. They blocked the staff from proper access to documents, leaked false information to the press, hacked into the committee's computers, and even urged the Justice Department to criminally prosecute the Senate's valiant investigators. When all that failed, the CIA delayed and delayed the issuance of the report, while it pored over its contents and secured so many redactions that readers would wonder what else they could possibly be hiding. (See for yourself: nytimes.com/interactive/2014/12/09/world/cia-torture-report-document.html.)

Well, how about six thousand more pages of the committee's work product, kept secret by CIA demands, describing in stomach-wrenching detail the various forms of torture and their uselessness, especially compared to other friendlier methods, described by former CIA interrogators such as Ali Soufan.

All of this "spook business" creates a tight-knit brotherhood of self-reinforcing admiration that belies or suppresses significant dissent inside spy agencies. Indeed, as the *New York Times* just reported, "In January 2003, 10 months into the Central Intelligence Agency's secret prison program, the agency's chief of interrogations sent an email to colleagues saying that the relentlessly brutal treatment of prisoners was a train wreck 'waiting to happen and I intend to get the hell off the train before it happens.' He said he had told his bosses he had 'serious reservations' about the program and no longer wanted to be associated with it 'in any way.'"

No wonder the *Times* headlines summed up the Senate Intelligence Committee's work with these words: "Report Portrays a Broken C.I.A. Devoted to a Failed Approach." So broken that the CIA contracted out torture to two psychologists who promptly formed a company that received $81 million in taxpayer money—to add to what one CIA official quoted in the report called "useless intelligence."

The bigger story in this sordid mess is that there will be no prosecution against the top government officials responsible, starting with Bush and Cheney. Senator Mark Udall (D-CO) framed this accountability issue on the Senate floor: "Director [John] Brennan and the CIA today are continuing to willfully provide inaccurate information and misrepresent the efficacy of torture. In other words, the CIA is lying." He urged the president to purge the agency leadership, including Mr. Brennan. "There can be no cover-up. If there is no moral leadership from the White House helping the public understand that the CIA's torture program wasn't necessary and didn't save lives or disrupt terrorist plots, then what's to stop the next White House and CIA director from supporting torture?" he concluded.

The response from the White House was President Obama expressing "complete confidence" in CIA director John O. Brennan, and Mr. Brennan calling all his subordinates "patriots." The circle has closed once again.

The even larger consequence of the increasing disclosures of how Bush/ Cheney and Obama have responded in their "war on terror" is the millions of innocent children, women, and men who were killed, injured, or sickened; millions more refugees in Iraq and Afghanistan; the loss of American life and limb; and the trillions of dollars in public funds that could have been used to rebuild America's crucial infrastructure to save lives and provide needed facilities and jobs.

The criminal gang that struck on 9/11 had no second-strike capability. Bush's gigantic overreaction—blowing apart whole countries and societies year after year—has only enormously spread the al-Qaeda forces into a dozen countries through affiliates and offshoots such as ISIS.

Fighting stateless terrorism with massive state terrorism and torture that strengthens the former creates a deadly boomerang. It destroys our priorities, mutes the waging of peace, and corrodes our democracy with its purported rule of law. It also obscures the century-long history of the West intervening violently in the East's backyard; carving up its colonies; and backing local, brutal dictatorships with US arms, money, and diplomatic cover.

The Senate Intelligence Committee's first step should arouse Congress to its constitutional duties and stop the destruction of the separation of powers by an overweening White House executive. Certainly the left- and right-leaning members of Congress should agree on that principle. It helps if we the people, who pay the price, give them constant nudges in that direction.

Damaging Our Country from Wars of Choice

SEPTEMBER 18, 2014

The drums of war are beating once again with the vanguard of US bombers already over Iraq (and soon Syria) to, in President Obama's words, "degrade and destroy" ISIS. The Republican Party, led by war-at-any-cost senators Lindsey Graham and John McCain, wants a bigger military buildup, which can only mean US soldiers on the ground.

Here they go again. Another result of Bush's war in Iraq. Washington has already expended thousands of American lives, hundreds of thousands of American injuries and illnesses, and over a million Iraqi lives. The achievement: the slaying or capture of al-Qaeda leaders—but with that came the spread of al-Qaeda into a dozen countries and the emergence of a new al-Qaeda on steroids called the Islamic State of Iraq and Syria (ISIS) which has nominal control over an area in Syria and Iraq larger than the territory of Great Britain.

Still, no lessons have been learned. We continue to attack countries and side with one sectarian group against another, which only creates chaos, sets in motion the cycle of revenge, and sparks new internal strife. So if slamming a hornet's nest propels more hornets to start new nests, isn't it time to rethink this militarization of US foreign policy? It only increases the violent chaos in that region with the risk of a blowback affecting our country, such as suicide bombers attacking heavily populated public spaces. This kind of attack is very hard to stop, as we have seen thousands of times overseas in Iraq and Afghanistan.

According to Richard Clarke—former White House antiterrorism adviser to George W. Bush—Osama bin Laden wanted Bush to invade Iraq so that more Muslims would take up arms against the US and more Muslims would hate our country for its destruction of their land and people. Similarly, ISIS would like nothing better than to embroil the US and our soldiers in a ground war so that it can rally more people to expel the giant US invader.

Then there is the massive overreaction by our government and its ever-willing corporate contractors. Political turmoil ensues, and our democratic institutions, already weakened in their defense of liberty, due process, and the rule of law, are further overwhelmed by the policing dictates of a profitable national security state.

Randolph Bourne, a hundred years ago, wrote an essay with these words about war:

> It automatically sets in motion throughout society those irresistible forces for uniformity, for passionate cooperation with the Government in coercing into obedience the minority groups and individuals which lack the larger herd sense. . . . Other values, such as artistic creation, knowledge, reason, beauty, the enhancement of life, are instantly and almost unanimously sacrificed.

Benjamin Franklin understood this collective panic when he said that people who prefer security to liberty deserve neither.

The fundamental question is whether our civil society can defend our institutions that are critical to maintaining a democratic society.

Will our courts fold before the overreaching panic by the executive branch and its armed forces?

Will our Congress and state legislatures stand firm against sacrificing our liberty and our public budgets that serve our civil society's necessities in the face of a police/military state's overreacting ultimatums?

Will our media resist hyperfocusing on the "war on terror" and give us other important news about ongoing American life?

Will our government pay more attention to preventing the yearly loss of hundreds of thousands of American lives from hospital infections, medical malpractice, defective products, air pollution, unsafe drugs, toxic workplaces, and other domestic perils?

Not likely. The aftermath of the 9/11 atrocities resulted in brutal reaction. In devastating two countries and their civilians, far more American soldiers were injured and killed than those lives lost on 9/11, not to mention the trillions of dollars that could have been spent to save many lives here and repair, with good-paying jobs, the crumbling public works in our communities.

Sadly, our democratic institutions and civil resiliency are not presently prepared to hold fast with the forces of reason, prudence, and smart responses that forestall a national nervous breakdown—one which happens to be very profitable and power-concentrating for the few against the many.

Consider what our leaders did to our democracy during their "war on terror": secret laws, secret courts, secret evidence, secret dragnet snooping on everyone; un-auditable, massive secret spending for military quagmires abroad; secret prisons; and even censored judicial decisions that are supposed to be fully disclosed! Government prosecutors often have made shambles of their duty to show probable cause and respect habeas corpus and other constitutional rights. Thousands of innocent people were jailed without charges and detained without attorneys after 9/11.

The al-Qaeda leaders wanted not only to instill fear about public safety in America but also weaken us economically by tying us down overseas. Why are our rulers obliging them? Because, in a grotesque way, power in Washington and profit on Wall Street benefit.

Only the people, who do not benefit from these wars, can organize the exercise of their constitutional sovereignty to shape responses that promote safety without damaging liberty.

One percent of the citizenry, diversely organized in congressional districts and reflecting the "public sentiment," can turn around, perhaps with the funding support of an enlightened billionaire or two, Congress, and the White House. Are you up to this challenge?

Hillary-the-Hawk Flies Again

AUGUST 15, 2014

"Hillary works for Goldman Sachs and likes war, otherwise I like Hillary," a former Bill Clinton aide told me sardonically. First, he was referring to her cushy relationships with top Wall Street barons and her $200,000 speeches with the criminal enterprise known as Goldman Sachs, which played a part in crashing the US economy in 2008 and burdening taxpayers with costly bailouts. Second, he was calling attention to her war-hawkish foreign policy.

Last week, Hillary the Hawk emerged, once again, with comments to *The Atlantic* attacking Obama for being weak and not having an organized foreign policy. She was calling Obama weak despite his heavy hand in droning, bombing, and intervening during his presidency. While Obama is often wrong, he is hardly a pacifist commander. It's a small wonder that since 2008, Hillary the Hawk has been generally described as, in the words of *New York Times* journalist Mark Landler, "more hawkish than Mr. Obama."

In *The Atlantic* interview, she chided Obama for not more deeply involving the US with the rebels in Syria, who themselves are riven into factions and deprived of strong leaders and, with few exceptions, trained fighters. As Mrs. Clinton well knows from her time as secretary of state, the White House was being cautious because of growing congressional opposition to intervention in Syria as Congress sought to determine the best rebel groups to arm and how to prevent this weaponry from falling into the hands of enemy insurgents.

She grandly told her interviewer that "great nations need organizing principles, and 'Don't do stupid stuff' is not an organizing principle." Nonsense. Not plunging into unconstitutional wars could have been a fine "organizing principle." Instead, she voted for the criminal invasion of Iraq, which boomeranged back into costly chaos and tragedy for the Iraqi people and the American taxpayers.

Moreover, the former secretary of state ended her undistinguished tenure in 2013 with an unremitting record of militarizing a department that was originally chartered over two hundred years ago to be the expression of American diplomacy. As secretary of state, Hillary Clinton made far more bellicose statements than Secretary of Defense Robert Gates did. Some career foreign service officers found her aggressive language unhelpful, if not downright hazardous to their diplomatic missions.

Such belligerency translated into her pushing both opposed Secretary of Defense Robert Gates and reluctant President Obama to topple the Libyan dictator Muammar Gaddafi. The Libyan dictator had given up his dangerous weapons and was reestablishing relations with Western countries and Western oil companies. Mrs. Clinton had no "organizing principle" for the deadly aftermath, when warring militias carved up Libya and spilled over into Mali, which resulted in violent disruption in Central Africa. The Libyan assault was Hillary Clinton's undeclared war—a continuing disaster that shows her touted foreign policy experience as just doing more "stupid stuff." She displays much ignorance about the quicksand perils for the United States of postdictatorial vacuums in tribal, sectarian societies.

After criticizing Obama, Mrs. Clinton then issued a statement saying she had called the president to say that she did not intend to attack him and anticipated "hugging it out" with him at a Martha's Vineyard party. Embracing opportunistically after attacking is less than admirable.

Considering Hillary Clinton's origins as an anti–Vietnam War youth, how did she end up such a war hawk? Perhaps it is a result of her overweening political ambition and her determination to prevent accusations of being soft on militarism and its imperial empire because she is a woman.

After her celebrity election as New York's senator in 2000, she was given a requested seat on the Senate Armed Services Committee. There, unlike her warlike friend Republican senator John McCain, she rarely challenged a boondoggle Pentagon contract; never took on the defense industry's waste, fraud, and abuse; and never saw a redundant or unneeded weapons system (often criticized by retired generals and admirals) that she did not like.

The vaunted military-industrial complex, which President Eisenhower warned about, got the message. Hillary Clinton was one of them.

Energetically waging peace was not on Secretary of State Clinton's agenda. She would rather talk about military might and deployment in one geographic area after another. At the US Naval Academy in 2012, Generalissima Clinton gave a speech about pivoting to East Asia with "force posture," otherwise known as "force projection" (one of her favorite phrases), of US Naval ships, planes, and positioned troops in countries neighboring China.

Of course, China's response was to increase its military budget and project its own military might. The world's superpower should not be addicted to continuous provocations that produce unintended consequences.

As she goes around the country with an expanded, publicly funded Secret Service corps to promote the private sales of her book, *Hard Choices*, Hillary Clinton needs to ponder what, if anything, she as a presidential candidate has to offer a war-weary, corporate-dominated American people. As a former member of the board of directors of Walmart, Hillary Clinton waited several years before coming out this April in support of a restored minimum wage for thirty million American workers (a majority of whom are women).

This delay is not surprising considering Hillary Clinton spends her time in the splendors of the wealthy classes and the Wall Street crowd, when she isn't pulling down huge speech fees pandering to giant trade association conventions. This creates distance between her and the hard-pressed experiences of the masses, doesn't it?

See Progressives Opposed to a Clinton Dynasty for more information.

To Kerry: Get Israeli Peace Leaders Before Congress

MAY 30, 2013

The new secretary of state, John Kerry, taking four trips to the Israel/Palestine region in the past two months means yet another US effort for a negotiated peace process between the Palestinians (under ruthless occupation) and the very dominant Israelis. Why should the prospects be any better than the failed attempts by the esteemed former senator George Mitchell and his predecessors?

As a senator with a "grade A" from the powerful pro-Israeli government lobby American Israel Public Affairs Committee (AIPAC), Secretary Kerry has forged a coalition of Israeli and Palestinian businessmen behind a $4 billion economic assistance plan for the West Bank and Gaza. He is also tapping into the significant Israeli public opinion behind a two-state solution.

Israeli prime minister Benjamin Netanyahu is outwardly going through the motions of supporting peace negotiations but demands preconditions and no cessation of expanding Israeli colonies in Palestine. Netanyahu knows how to play the US government like a harp. He talks about negotiations for peace but remains intransigent.

Back in 1996, he told an applauding joint session of Congress that Israel's mature economy would no longer need US foreign aid. Today, Israel is a bigger, more prosperous economy but is still receiving US foreign aid.

Kerry's trump card is recognizing the long-neglected specific peace offer by the twenty-two-member Arab League in 2002. These Arab countries have renewed and updated their proposal to make it easier for Israel to accept. It includes a comprehensive peace treaty with all Arab nations and Israeli recognition of a Palestinian state within the 1967 borders, with minor land swaps. Netanyahu has given this offer the back of his hand despite its highly publicized reiteration in the ensuing years. But this year, Israeli president (an honorific post) Shimon Peres highlighted the verbal Israeli government endorsement of a two-state solution and urged that "a broad structure of support be created for making progress."

The problem is that almost nobody in Israel—hawks, peace advocates, or those in the middle—believes anything will come out of Kerry's shuttle diplomacy.

Here are some reasons why. There is no pressure on Netanyahu's governing coalition to wage peace. As Ethan Bronner, longtime *New York Times* reporter in Israel, wrote this past Sunday: "Israel has never been richer, safer, more culturally productive or dynamic." He might have added that, with huge natural gas finds offshore, Israel is about to be both self-sufficient in fossil fuels and a net exporter.

Nor is there any pressure that Netanyahu recognizes from the Palestinian/Arab side. Palestinians are continually subjugated, impoverished, divided internally, and on the losing end of the casualty toll by a ratio exceeding four hundred to one. Israel can strike targets in Palestine at will.

Arab nations are internally preoccupied with civil wars, sectarian conflicts, and, except for the Gulf countries, weak economies. Israel, with the most modern military—heavily furnished by the United States—and scores of ready nuclear bombs, stands astride the Middle East as a giant colossus.

The main reality in Israeli domestic politics is that, if it weren't for external threats, however exaggerated, the Israeli government and society would have to face very deep divisions inside Israel between secular and ultraorthodox populations. Because of differences on expanding the colonies in Palestine, strict religious rituals and social mores, exemptions from military service, the place of women, and the treatment of Israeli Arabs, there are two Israels ready to erupt were peace to break out with Palestine and Arab neighbors.

Faced with this harrowing prospect of domestic civil strife, Netanyahu's government feels no urgency for peace, according to Bronner. The regional status quo is under control of its iron fist.

Many out-of-power Israeli politicians, such as former prime minister Ehud Olmert, and former deputy prime minister Dan Meridor, have all argued for vigorously pursuing a two-state solution to head off Israel becoming a state that, in a few decades, contains more Palestinians than Israelis. The militarists, however, are the ones running the government.

Moreover, Kerry cannot expect any pressure from Washington on the Israeli government, because Washington, especially Congress, always goes along with the Israeli government, to such a degree that it astonishes opposition parties in the Israeli Knesset.

Make no mistake about Netanyahu. He is and has long been an extreme vintage hardliner against any Palestinian sovereignty. In 1989, after the Tiananmen Square massacre in China, Netanyahu, then Israeli deputy foreign minister, told students at Bar-Ilan University that "Israel should have exploited the repression of the demonstrations in China, when world attention focused on that country, to carry out mass expulsions among the Arabs of the territories."

Eviction and the expropriation of what is left of the original Palestine has long been the dogma of Israeli militarists and leaders of the expansionist Likud Party, including Ariel Sharon.

The award-winning Israeli documentary *The Gatekeepers* presents six retired leaders of the Shin Bet—the Israeli FBI—speaking with remarkable candor about how rational actions, including those toward peace, were continually overruled by politicians who exploited the Israeli–Arab conflict for their own domestic advantage.

So, what is our secretary of state to do? Kerry should propose that these men and other prominent, outspoken retired leaders from the military, security, and elected office, together with well-known writers and scholars, testify at length before the US House and Senate. AIPAC cannot stop them from testifying. Congress and the American people will be given an opportunity to hear these experienced, persuasive voices for a peace settlement.

After all, peace in the Middle East is more in the US national interest and security than ever before. Americans are paying too hefty a human and financial price to allow a muzzled Congress to stay on bended knee, supporting whatever the Israeli government wants.

Such a breakthrough on Capitol Hill will also enhance the Israeli peace and human rights movement, which reflects the moral dimension for ending the occupation and colonization of Palestine.

In a recent pamphlet by Americans for Peace Now and its counterpart in Israel, Rabbi Michael Melchior, a former Israel deputy foreign minister and member of the Knesset, declared that "to occupy and control the lives of millions of Palestinians living in Judea and Samaria, and to negate their right to create their own state and future in peace, side by side with the State of Israel, is not just, is not moral, and is not Judaism." (See info at peacenow.org.)

In May 2004 Senator Kerry told me "I have many friends in the Israeli peace movement." It is time for him to begin the mission for peace in his old haunt, the US Congress, without which he will share the decades-long failure of those who came before him in both Republican and Democratic administrations.

Two Obamas, Two Classes of Children

APRIL 11, 2013

An Associated Press photograph brought the horror of little children lying dead outside of their home to an American audience. At least ten Afghan children and some of their mothers were struck down by an airstrike on their extended family household by order of President Barack Obama. He probably decided on what his aides describe as the routine weekly "Terror Tuesday" at the White House. On that day, Mr. Obama typically receives the advice about which "militants" should live or die thousands of miles away from drones or aircraft. Even if households far from war zones are often destroyed in clear violation of the laws of war, the president is not deterred.

These Obama airstrikes are launched knowing that very often there is "collateral damage," a form of "so sorry" terrorism. How can the president explain the vaporization of a dozen preteen Afghan boys collecting firewood for their families on a hillside? The local spotter-informants must have been disoriented by all those hundred-dollar bills in rewards. Imagine a direct strike killing and injuring scores of people in a funeral procession following a previous fatal strike that was the occasion of this processional mourning. Remember the December 2009 Obama strike on an alleged al-Qaeda training camp in Yemen, using Tomahawk missiles and—get this—cluster bombs, that killed fourteen women and twenty-one children? Again and again, "so sorry" terrorism ravages family households far from the battlefields.

If this is a war, why hasn't Congress declared war under Article 1, Section 8, of the US Constitution? The 2001 congressional Authorization for Use of Military Force is not an open-ended authorization for the president. It was restricted to targeting only nations, organizations, or persons that are determined to have been implicated in the 9/11 massacres, or harbored complicit organizations or persons.

For several years, White House officials, including retired general James Jones, have declared that there is no real operational al-Qaeda left in Afghanistan to harbor anyone. The Pakistani Taliban is in conflict with the Pakistani government. The Afghan Taliban is in brutal conflict with the Afghan govern-ment and wants to expel US forces—which their members view as occupying invaders—just as their predecessors did when they expelled the Soviet invaders. The Taliban represent no imminent threat to the US.

President Obama's ambassador to Pakistan, Cameron P. Munter, used to complain to his colleagues about the CIA's drone attacks, saying "he didn't realize his main job was to kill people." He knew how such attacks by whining drones, hovering 24-7 over millions of frightened people and their terrified children, produce serious backlashes that fester for years.

Even a loyalist such as William M. Daley, Mr. Obama's chief of staff in 2011, observed that the Obama kill list presents fewer and fewer signifi-cant pursuits. "One guy gets knocked off, and the guy's driver, who's No. 21, becomes 20?" Daley said, describing the internal discussion. "At what point are you just filling the bucket with numbers?"

Yet this unlawful killing by a seemingly obsessed Obama continues and includes anyone in the vicinity of a "suspect" whose name isn't even known (these are called "signature strikes"), or mistakes, like the recent aerial killings of numerous Pakistani soldiers and four Afghan policemen—con-sidered our allies. The drone kill list goes on and on—over three thousand is the official fatality count, not counting injuries. The Friends Committee on National Legislation, is critical of signature strikes, "in which people are targeted not because of militant status, but because of their confor-mance to a profile of certain suspicious behaviors (such as age or gender), is particularly disconcerting, as it fails to adequately distinguish between combatant and civilian."

In a few weeks, the *Nation* magazine will issue a major report on US-caused civilian casualties in Afghanistan that should add new information.

Now switch the scene. The president, filled with memories of what his secret drone directives as prosecutor, judge, jury, and executioner have done to so many children, in so many places, traveled on Monday to Newtown, Connecticut, for the second time. He commiserated with the parents and relatives of the twenty children and six adults slain by a lone gunman. Here he became the compassionate president, with words and hugs.

What must be going through his mind as he sees in that day's *New York Times* the rows of ten little Afghan children and their parents blown apart? How can the president justify this continued military occupation for what is a civil war? No wonder a majority of the American people want out of Afghanistan, even without a close knowledge of the grisly and ugly things going on there in our name that are feeding the seething hatred of Obama's war.

Sometime after 2016, when Barack Obama starts writing his lucrative autobiographical recollections, there may be a few pages where he explains how he endured this double life ordering so-called precision attacks that kill many innocent children and their mothers and fathers while he mourned domestic mass killings in the US and advocated gun controls. As a constitutional law teacher, he may wonder why there have been no "gun controls" on his lawless, out-of-control presidency and his reckless attacks that only expanded the number of al-Qaeda affiliates wreaking havoc in Iraq, Yemen, Somalia, Mali, North Africa, and elsewhere.

Al-Qaeda of Iraq is now merging with an affiliate called al-Nusra in Syria that will give Obama more futile exercises on Terror Tuesdays. The CIA calls the reaction to such operations "blowback" because the unintended consequences undermine our long-term national security.

Obama is not like the official criminal recidivist, former vice president Dick Cheney, who misses no chance to say he has no regrets. Obama worries even as he greatly escalates the aerial attacks started by George W. Bush. In his State of the Union speech, he called for a "legal and policy framework" to guide "our counterterrorism operations," so that "no one should just take my word that we're doing things the right way." Granted, this is a good cover for his derelictions, but it probably reflects that he also needs some restraint. Last year he told CNN it was "something you have to struggle with."

Not that our abdicatory Congress would ever take him up on his offer for such legal guidance should he ever submit a proposed framework. Nor would Congress move to put an end to secret laws, secret criteria for targeting, indefinite imprisonment, lack of due process (even for American citizens), or secret cover-ups of illegal outsourcing to contracting corporations and go on to enact other preventive reforms.

Mr. Obama recognized in his CNN interview that "it's very easy to slip into a situation in which you end up bending rules thinking that the ends always justify the means. That's not who we are as a country."

Unfortunately, however, that's what he has done as a president.

Unless the American people come to realize that a president must be subject to the rule of law and our Constitution, our statutes, and treaties, every succeeding president will push the deficit-financed lawlessness further until the inevitable blowback day of reckoning. That is the fate of all empires.

The Sociocide of Iraq
by Bush/Cheney

MARCH 21, 2013

Ten years ago, George W. Bush and Dick Cheney, as war criminals, launched the sociocide of the people of Iraq—replete with embedded television and newspaper reporters chronicling the invasion through the Bush lens. That illegal war of aggression was, of course, based on recognized lies, propaganda, and cover-ups that duped or co-opted leading news institutions such as the *New York Times* and the *Washington Post*.

Wars of aggression—this one blowing apart a country of twenty-five million people ruled by a weakened despot surrounded by far more powerful adversaries—Israel, Turkey, and Iran—are major crimes under international law and the UN Charter. The Bush/Cheney war was also unconstitutional since it was never declared by Congress, as then senator Robert Byrd eloquently pointed out at the time. Moreover, many of the acts of torture and brutality perpetrated against the Iraqi people are illegal under various federal statutes.

Over one million Iraqis died due to the invasion, the occupation, and the denial of health and safety necessities for infants, children, and adults. Far more Iraqis were injured and sickened. Birth defects and cancers continue to set lethal records. Five million Iraqis became refugees, many fleeing into Jordan, Syria, and other countries.

Nearly five thousand US soldiers died. Many other soldiers died by suicide. Well over 150,000 Americans were injured or sickened, far more than the official Pentagon underestimate that restricts nonfatal casualty counts only to those incurred directly in the line of fire.

So far, the Iraq War has monetarily cost taxpayers about $2 trillion. Tens of billions more will be spent for veterans' disabilities and continuing expenses in Iraq. Taxpayers are shelling out over $600 million a year to guard the giant US Embassy and its personnel in Baghdad, more than what our government spends for the Occupational Safety and Health Administration, the task of which is to reduce the number of American workers who die every year from workplace disease and trauma—currently about fifty-eight thousand.

All for what results? Before the invasion there was no al-Qaeda in Saddam Hussein's secular dictatorship. Now a growing al-Qaeda in Iraq is terrorizing the country with ever-bolder car bombings and suicide attacks, taking dozens of lives at a time and spilling forcefully over into Syria.

Iraq is a police state with sectarian struggles between the dominant Shiites and the insurgent Sunnis who lived together peacefully and inter-married for centuries. There were no sectarian slaughters of this kind before the invasion, except for Saddam Hussein's bloodbath against rebellious Shiites. The Shiites were egged on by President George H.W. Bush, who promptly abandoned them to the deadly strafing of Saddam's helicopter gunships at the end of the preventable first Gulf War in 1991.

Iraq is a country in ruins with a political and wealthy upper class raking off the profits from the oil industry and the occupation. The US is now widely hated in that part of Asia. Bush/Cheney ordered the use of cluster bombs, white phosphorous, and depleted uranium against, for example, the people of Fallujah, where infant birth deformities have skyrocketed.

As Raed Jarrar, an Iraqi American analyst observed: "Complete destruction of the Iraqi national identity" and the sectarian system introduced by the US invaders in 2003, where Iraqis were favored or excluded based on their sectarian and ethnic affiliations, laid the basis for the current cruel chaos and violence. It was a nasty, brutish form of divide and rule.

The results back home in our country are soldiers and their extended families suffering in many ways from broken lives. Phil Donahue's gripping documentary *Body of War* follows the pain-wracked life of one soldier returning in 2004 from Iraq as a paraplegic. That soldier, Tomas Young, nearing the end of his devastated life, has just written a penetrating letter to George W. Bush, which every American should read.

The lessons from this unnecessary quagmire should be: first, how to stop any more wars of aggression by the Washington warmongers—the same neocon draft dodgers are at it again regarding Iran and Syria. And second, the necessity to hold accountable the leading perpetrators of this brutal carnage and financial wreckage who are presently at large—fugitives from justice earning fat lecture and consulting fees.

In the nine months running up to the March 2003 invasion of Iraq, at least three hundred prominent retired military officers, diplomats, and national security officials publicly spoke out against the Bush/Cheney drumbeats of war. Their warnings were prophetically accurate. The dissenters included retired generals Anthony Zinni and William Odom and retired vice admiral Jack Shanahan. Even Brent Scowcroft and James Baker, two of President George H.W. Bush's closest advisers, strongly opposed the invasion.

These outspoken truthsayers—notwithstanding their prestige and experience—were overwhelmed by a runaway White House, a disgraceful patsy mainstream media, and an abdicatory Congress. Multibillionaire George Soros was also courageously outspoken. Unfortunately, prior to the invasion, he did not supply a budget and secretariat for these men and women to provide continuity and to multiply their numbers around the country, through the mass media, and on Capitol Hill. By the time he came around to organizing and publicizing such an organized effort, it was after the invasion, in July 2003.

Nine months earlier, I believe George Soros could have provided the necessary resources to stop Bush/Cheney and their lies from stampeding the government, and country, into war.

Mr. Soros can still build the grassroots pressure for the exercise of the rule of law under our Constitution and move Congress toward public hearings in the Senate designed to establish an investigative arm of the Justice Department to pursue the proper enforcement against Bush/Cheney and their accomplices.

After all, the Justice Department had such a special prosecutors' office during the Watergate scandal and was moving to indict Richard Nixon, who had resigned, before President Ford pardoned him.

Compare the Watergate break-in and obstruction of justice by Nixon with the horrendous crimes coming out of the war against Iraq—a nation that never threatened the US but whose destruction takes a continuing toll on our country.

Generalissima Clinton Expanding the Empire

FEBRUARY 8, 2013

Hillary Clinton has completed her four-year tenure as secretary of state to the accolades of both Democratic and Republican congressional champions of the budget-busting "military-industrial complex" that President Eisenhower warned about in his farewell address. Behind the public relations sheen—the photo opportunities with groups of poor people in the developing world—an ever more militarized State Department operated under Clinton's leadership.

A militarized State Department is more than a repudiation of the department's basic charter of 1789, for the then-named Department of Foreign Affairs, which envisioned diplomacy as its mission. Secretary Clinton reveled in tough, belligerent talk and action on her many trips to more than a hundred countries. She would warn or threaten "consequences" on a regular basis. She supported soldiers in Afghanistan, the use of secret Special Forces in other places, and "force projection" in East Asia to contain China. She aggressively supported or attacked resistance movements in dictatorships, depending on whether a regime played to Washington's tune.

Because Defense Secretary Robert Gates was openly cold to the drumbeats for war on Libya, Clinton took over and choreographed the NATO ouster of the dictator, Muammar Gaddafi, long after he had given up his mass-destruction weaponry and was working to rekindle relations with the US government and global energy corporations. Libya is now in a disastrous, warlord-run state of chaos. Many fleeing fighters have moved into Mali, making that vast country into another battlefield drawing US involvement. Blowback!

Time and again, Hillary Clinton's belligerence exceeded that of Obama's secretaries of defense. From her seat on the Senate Armed Services Committee to her tenure at the State Department, Hillary Clinton sought to prove that she could be just as tough as the militaristic civilian men whose circle she entered. Throughout her four years it was Generalissima Clinton, expanding the American empire at large.

Here is some of what the candid camera of history will show about her record:

1. A Yale Law School graduate, she shared with President Obama, a former Harvard Law Review president, a shocking disregard for the law and separation of powers, be it the Constitution, federal statutes, or international treaties. Her legal adviser, former Yale Law dean Harold Koh, provided cover for her and Obama's "drone ranger" (to use Bill Moyers's words), John O. Brennan, Obama's counterterrorism adviser. Brennan gave the president weekly opportunities (White House aides called decision day "Terror Tuesdays") to become secret prosecutor, judge, jury, and executioner. Imagine thousands of push-button deaths and injuries of internal resisters and civilian bystanders, who presented no threat to the US, in Pakistan, Afghanistan, Yemen, and elsewhere.

The war on Libya, which Clinton spearheaded for Obama, was conducted without a congressional declaration of war, without even a war resolution or a congressional authorization or appropriation. She and her boss outdid Cheney and Bush on that score.

2. Although touting "diplomacy" as a priority, Clinton made little attempt to bring the United States into a community of nations by signing or ratifying international treaties that already had over a hundred nations as signatories. As a former senator with bipartisan support, Clinton didn't use much of her capital on climate change agreements.

Human Rights Watch reports that chief among the unratified treaties are "international conventions relating to children, women, persons with disabilities, torture, enforced disappearance, and the use of anti-personnel landmines and cluster munitions." The last two treaties are designed to save thousands of lives and limbs of the children and their parents who are major victims of these atrocious concealed weapons. Clinton has not gone to bat against the advocates for those "blowback" explosives that the Pentagon still uses.

When the Senate recently failed to ratify the treaty on disabilities, Clinton, with former senator and injured veteran Robert Dole on her side, still didn't make the maximum effort of which she is capable.

3. Secretary Clinton had problems heralding accurate whistleblowers. A foreign service officer for twenty-four years, Peter Van Buren spent a year in Iraq running two of the State Department's Provincial Reconstruction Teams. He exposed State Department waste and mismanagement along with the Pentagon's "reconstruction" efforts using corporate contractors. Unlistened to, Van Buren, true to his civil-service oath of office, went public. Clinton fired him. (See wemeantwell.com.)

4. Possibly the action most revealing of Clinton's character was her ordering of US officials to spy on top UN diplomats, including those from our ally, the United Kingdom. Shockingly, she even ordered her emissaries to obtain DNA data, iris scans (known as biometric data), and fingerprints along with credit card and frequent flier numbers.

The disclosure of secret State Department cables proved this to be a clear violation of the 1946 UN convention. Clinton included in this crude boomeranging personal espionage the secretary general of the UN, Ban Ki-moon, and his top officials all around the world. As befits these lawless times, there were no congressional hearings, no accountability, and no resignation by the self-styled civil libertarian secretary of state—not even a public apology.

5. Clinton led a dangerous expansion of the State Department's mission in Iraq. As reported in the *Wall Street Journal* on December 10, 2011, "In place of the military, the State Department will assume a new role of unprecedented scale, overseeing a massive diplomatic mission through a network of fortified, self-sufficient installations."

To call this a diplomatic mission is a stretch. The State Department has hired thousands of private security contractors for armed details and transportation of personnel. Simply guarding the huge US embassy in Iraq and its personnel costs more than $650 million a year—larger than the entire budget of the Occupational Health and Safety Administration (OSHA), which is responsible for reducing the yearly loss of about fifty-eight thousand lives caused by workplace-related traumas and sicknesses.

Another State Department undertaking is to improve the training and capability of Iraq's police and armed forces. Countless active and retired foreign service officers believe expanded militarization of the State Department both endangers them overseas and sidelines their experience and knowledge in favor of contractors and military people.

Blurring the distinction between the Pentagon and the State Department in words and deeds seriously compromises Americans engaged in development and diplomatic endeavors. When people in developing countries see Americans working to advance public health or clean drinking water systems within their countries, they now wonder if these are front activities for spying or undercover penetrations. Violent actions, fueled by this suspicion, are already jeopardizing public health efforts on the border areas of Pakistan and Afghanistan.

Clinton's successor, former senator and war veteran John Kerry, says he wants to emphasize peace, human rights, and antipoverty endeavors. He doesn't have to prove his machismo should he strive to demilitarize the State Department and promote peaceful, deliberative missions in the world, from which true security flows.

Reining in Obama and His Drones

NOVEMBER 30, 2012

Barack Obama, former president of the *Harvard Law Review* and a constitutional law lecturer, should go back and review his coursework. He seems to have declined to comport his presidency to the rule of law.

Let's focus here on his major expansion of drone warfare in defiance of international law, statutory law, and the Constitution. Obama's drones roam over multiple nations of Asia and Africa and target suspects, both known and unknown, whom the president, in his unbridled discretion, wants to evaporate for the cause of national security.

More than 2,500 people have been killed by Obama's drones, many of them civilians and bystanders, including American citizens, irrespective of the absence of any "imminent threat" to the United States.

Justin Elliott of ProPublica wrote that "only 13 percent" of those killed under Obama "could be considered 'militant leaders'—either of the Pakistani Taliban, the Afghan Taliban, or Al Qaeda." The remaining fatalities, apart from many innocent civilians, including children, were people oppressed by their own harsh regimes or dominated by US occupation of their country. Aside from human rights and the laws of war, this distinction between civilian and combatant matters because it shows that Obama's drones are becoming what Council on Foreign Relations fellow Micah Zenko calls "a counterinsurgency air force" for our collaborative regimes.

The "kill lists" are the work of Obama and his advisers, led by John O. Brennan, and come straight from the White House, according to the *New York Times*. Apparently, the president spends a good deal of time being prosecutor, judge, jury, executioner, and concealer. But he does so quietly; this is no dramatic "thumbs-down" emperor.

Mr. Brennan spoke at Harvard Law School about a year ago and told a remarkably blasé audience that what he and the president were doing was perfectly legal under the law of self-defense. Self-defense that is defined, of course, by the president.

It appears from recent statements on *The Daily Show* that President Obama does not share the certitude boldly displayed by Mr. Brennan. On October 18, President Obama told Jon Stewart and his audience that "one of the things we've got to do is put a legal architecture in place, and we need congressional help in order to do that, to make sure that not only am I reined in but any president is reined in terms of some of the decisions that we're making."

So in the absence of "a legal architecture" of accountability, do presidents knock off whomever they want to target (along with bystanders or family members), whether or not the targeted person is actually plotting an attack against the United States? It seems that way, in spite of what is already in place legally, called the Constitution, separation of powers, and due process of law. What more legal architecture does Mr. Obama need?

Obviously what he wants is a self-contained, permanent "Office of Presidential Predator Drone Assassinations," to use author, scholar, and litigator Bruce Fein's nomenclature. According to the *New York Times*, President Obama wants "explicit rules for the targeted killing of terrorists by unmanned drones, so that a new president would inherit clear standards and procedures." Mr. Fein notes that "clear standards and procedures without accountability to the judiciary, Congress, or the American people" undermine the rule of law and our democracy.

Indeed, the whole deliberation process inside the Obama administration has been kept secret, a continuing process of morbid overclassification that even today contains secret internal legal opinions on targeted killings. The government refuses even to acknowledge that a drone air force operates over Pakistan—a fact that everybody knows, including the hundreds of injured and displaced Pakistanis. This drone air force uses what the *New York Times*—citing the CIA—called "'signature strikes' against groups of suspected, unknown militants."

Predictably, these strikes are constantly terrorizing thousands of families, who fear a strike anytime day or night, and are causing a blowback that is expanding the number of al-Qaeda sympathizers and affiliates, from Pakistan to Yemen. "Signature strikes," according to the *Times*, "have prompted the greatest conflict inside the Obama administration." Michael V. Hayden, former CIA director under George W. Bush, has publicly questioned whether the expansion in the use of drones is counterproductive and creating more enemies and the desire for more revenge against the US.

428 + OUT OF DARKNESS

Critics point out how, many times in the past, departments and agencies have put forth misleading or false intelligence, from the Vietnam War to the arguments for invading Iraq, or have missed what they should have predicted, such as the fall of the Soviet Union. This legacy of errors and duplicity should restrain presidents who execute by ordering drone operators to push buttons that target people thousands of miles away, based on secret so-called intelligence.

Mr. Obama wants, in Mr. Fein's view, to have "his secret and unaccountable predator drone assassinations become permanent fixtures of the nation's national security complex." Were Obama to remember his constitutional law, such actions would have to be constitutionally authorized by Congress and subject to judicial review.

With his attorney general, Eric Holder, maintaining that there is sufficient *due process* entirely inside the executive branch and without congressional oversight or judicial review, don't bet on anything more than a more secret, violent, imperial presidency that shreds the Constitution's separation of powers and checks and balances.

And don't bet that other countries of similar invasive bent won't remember this green-light on illegal unilateralism when they catch up with our drone capabilities.

9.

ON MONEY, BANKING, AND CLASS

Governor Cuomo: Avoid Budget Cuts by Not Rebating Stock Sales Tax to Wall Street!

JUNE 5, 2020

New York governor Andrew Cuomo is basking in the popularity of his meticulous COVID-19 news briefings and simultaneously predicting a pandemic-driven $61 billion state deficit over four years. Astonishingly, the governor electronically rebates an existing tiny stock-transfer sales tax back to Wall Street. This stock-transfer sales tax, bringing in an estimated $13 billion to $16 billion a year, would reduce forthcoming budget cuts in health, education, transportation, and other safety nets.

No governor in the country has the luxury of simply keeping very significant tax revenues that are already collected to avoid cutting necessities of life. Yet Governor Cuomo has supported these rebates for the past ten years, as have previous New York state governors all the way back to 1981, when this early-twentieth-century tax stopped being retained in the state's treasury. Nearly $250 billion, a staggering amount, has been immediately returned to the stockbrokers over that time period.

Bear in mind, a fraction of 1 percent of this tiny sales tax is paid by the investors buying stocks and bonds and engaging in massive volumes of derivative speculation. Since the great bulk of trading is conducted by upper-income people and large companies, this sales tax, unlike the regressive 8 percent sales tax ordinary New Yorkers pay when they buy from stores, is progressive in its impact.

So why hasn't the media taken this eminently timely and newsworthy story to the people? I've been talking about this surrender to Wall Street for years. Most recently, given its timeliness, I've been calling up reporters and columnists of major press outlets, but to no avail, with the exception of the *Buffalo News*. This indifference is inexplicable. After all, Governor Cuomo regularly talks about drastic budget cuts.

Well, a new factor may change this equation. Blair Horner, a prominent longtime director of the New York Public Interest Research Group, an influential university college student–funded civic advocacy group, is now on the case.

On May 28, 2020, Mr. Horner held a virtual news conference in Albany, where he presented a letter signed by over fifty labor, consumer, women's, educational, minority, health, taxpayer, elderly, and justice organizations—all calling on the governor to keep the many billions of dollars from the stock-transfer tax. The number of New York groups supporting this proposal will only grow. Attentively advanced by the seasoned Horner and his team, a detailed news release was distributed, and several speakers, including me, briefly spoke. At question time, only a *Newsday* reporter asked about Wall Street's reaction.

A half hour later, no reporter asked Governor Cuomo during his long daily briefings about keeping the collected revenues. The next day there was no media coverage of this event or the benefits the revenue could have for communities whose members will be bearing the brunt of avoidable service cuts and job losses.

Every day New York State rebates about $40 million to an economic upper class, already further enriched by Trump's 2017 tax bonanza. And these privileged plutocrats have not shared, via a wealth tax, a fraction of the sacrifice of New York's 2.2 million frontline COVID-19 workers. Shameful!

Bills mandating the retention of this stock sales tax are already in the state legislature. A prime sponsor, Assemblymember Phil Steck, believes that there will be overwhelming bipartisan support in the polls.

However, the legislature's leaders await the signal from Governor Cuomo, thus far reluctant. But not, I suspect, for long.

With Wall Street's Robert Rubin and Michael Bloomberg coming out for a financial transaction tax (thanks probably to the Bernie Sanders movement), can the son of Mario Cuomo be much far behind?

See the coalition release, letter to Governor Cuomo, and the New York State Assembly and Senate bills to stop the rebate of the stock-transfer tax at nader.org/ny-stock-tax.

The Federal Reserve Dictatorship Runs
Amok Against Savers

MARCH 18, 2020

If you are a saver in a money market account or in a bank, you've already noticed your dwindling interest income, as interest rates have been at their lowest in modern American history. Well, brace yourself. Your savings account has just become little more than a lockbox, thanks to the supreme dictatorship of the Federal Reserve.

On Sunday, March 15, the Federal Reserve announced that it would cut interest rates to "near zero."

After ignoring the largely unproductive spiral in corporate debt, now a staggering $9.3 trillion, the risk of a domino effect from underwater "zombie companies" is pushing the Fed toward an orgy of printing money for an anticipatory bailout of profitable corporations—not of depleted savers.

The Federal Reserve is our version of what other countries call a central bank. The Fed is not funded by Congress; its budget comes primarily from interest on government securities and fees from financial institutions. Bankers influence who gets appointed to its board of governors. Bankers can also elect three directors directly to the Fed's regional boards.

The Fed decides in secret the fate of the monetary policy, which includes the interest rates paid on your savings. There are no public hearings or open dockets for submission of views. No real explanations by the Fed, just dictates. It is a government of its own inside our government—the epitome of corporate socialism.

The president nominates members to the board of governors, and they have to be confirmed by the Senate. This is almost an automatic process by a supine Senate. These nominated "governors" and Chairman Jerome H. Powell have allowed themselves to be publicly bullied by Trump who, as a failed lifelong debtor, wants zero-interest rates.

The Fed has no regard for the hundreds of billions of dollars in interest payments taken from one hundred million unorganized savers who have their savings in Treasury bonds, banks, and money market accounts. Now trillions of dollars' worth of interest rates are getting "near zero." What a blow by the Trumped Fed, reducing interest rates from about 2.25–2.5 percent to near zero in five dictatorial steps over the past fourteen months.

The big Fed fib is that this cut in interest rates will stimulate a shaken economy buffeted by the coronavirus pandemic. How? By reducing mortgage rates and other costs of borrowing. Well, the last interest rate cut by the Fed actually saw mortgage rates increase. Moreover, the Fed's move doesn't affect the sky-high credit card interest rates on unpaid balances, the horrifically gouging "payday loan" and "rent-to-own" rackets, and the towering interest rates charged by lenders for student loans. There is no Fed regulation of usurious interest rates by profiteering lenders.

What harms the economy is reduced interest income for savers that in turn cuts down on consumer demand.

So what is the Fed up to? Juicing the stock market and big finance is the narcotic offered to the executive-suite speculators. To enhance further its credentials as the aider and abettor of crony capitalism, the Fed is buying $700 billion in government securities and will be increasing "its holdings of Treasury securities by at least $500 billion and its holdings of agency mortgage-backed securities by at least $200 billion" (see: Federal Reserve issues FOMC statement, March 15, 2020). At the same time, the Fed is reducing bank reserve requirement ratios to zero percent and letting banks tap into the Fed's discount window at ridiculously tiny interest rates. The average interest on millions of student loans is 5.8 percent.

On Sunday, when no one was looking, the Fed imperiously announced its decision to hold interest rates near zero until it is "confident that the economy has weathered recent events and is on track to achieve its maximum employment and price stability goals." That is a very nebulous standard. Congress doesn't establish any standards for the Fed except the vague mission of advancing employment and maintaining a stable monetary system.

The Fed has its own inscrutable language. "Quantitative easing" is jargon for printing trillions of dollars in liquid money to lift stock markets and big banks. What the Fed doesn't want to explain is how boosting the "paper economy" and tolerating trillions of dollars in unstable corporate debt—some incurred for unproductive stock buybacks—helps the common worker.

Pension funds, conservatively invested, can't begin to earn the interest rates called for by the actuarial tables for payouts. So, backed up against the wall, pension funds dive into riskier stock investments and derivatives for higher returns, which bring their own perils in case of stock market collapses.

The Fed has lots of explaining to do for the public in plain language. But why bother? As described by William Greider in his classic book *Secrets of the Temple: How the Federal Reserve Runs the Country*, the Fed can do pretty much what the financial industry wants it to do. For all the help the Fed gives to the unrepentant speculative financial industry, it does not ask for anything in return for the huge bailouts that would help the common folk. "Reciprocity" is outside of the Fed's self-defined dictionary.

After all, the Fed does nothing about rampant speculation and staggering debt until it sees a "liquidity problem" (a.k.a. "the greedy big boys got themselves into a fix"), and then it rushes to inject massive sums of liquidity into the economy as relief. And the self-inflicted cycle of government-guaranteed corporate greed and abuse of power starts all over again.

Remarkably, groups like Consumers Union and the Consumer Federation of America are not fighting for the one hundred million small and midsize savers who are being taken to the cleaners and have no voice whatsoever in the Fed dictatorship.

The Contented Classes—When Will They Rebel?

MAY 9, 2019

For all the rhetoric and all the charities regarding America's children, the US stands at the very bottom of Western nations, and some other countries as well, in terms of youth well-being. The US's exceptionalism is clearest in its cruelty to children. The US has the highest infant mortality rate of comparable Organization for Economic Cooperation and Development countries. Not only that, but 2.5 million American children are homeless and 16.2 million children "lack the means to get enough nutritious food on a regular basis."

The shamelessness continues as the youngsters increase in age. The Trump regime is cutting the SNAP food program for poor kids. In 2018, fewer children were enrolled in Medicaid and CHIP than in 2017. To see just how bad Trump's war on poor American children is getting, go to the websites of the Children's Defense Fund (childrensdefense.org) and the Children's Advocacy Institute (caichildlaw.org).

Trump brags about a robust economy—still, however, rooted in exploitation of the poor and in reckless Wall Street speculation with people's savings.

Trump's pompous promises during his presidential campaign have proved to be a cowardly distraction. He claimed he would take on the drug companies and their price gouging. The hyperprofiteering pharmaceutical Goliaths are quietly laughing at him. Worse, Trump continues their tax credits and allows them to use new drugs developed with taxpayer money through the National Institute of Health free of charge—no royalties. Even though he talks tough, Trump lets these companies sell imported medicines manufactured in China and India with inadequate FDA inspections of foreign plants.

Torrents of Trump tweets somehow overlooked HP Acthar Gel, a drug produced by Mallinckrodt to treat a rare infant seizure disorder, which increased in price from $40 per vial to $39,000 per vial! Other drug prices are booming cruelly upward while Trump blusters but fails to deliver on his campaign promises.

For years our country's political and corporate rulers have saddled college students with breathtaking debt and interest rates. Student debt is now at $1.5 trillion. Both corporations and the federal government are profiting off of America's young. In no other Western country is this allowed, with most nations offering tuition-free higher education.

On May 2, 2019, the *New York Times* featured an article titled, "Tuition or Dinner? Nearly Half of College Students Surveyed in a New Report Are Going Hungry."

When you read the stories of impoverished students, squeezed in all directions, you'd think they came out of third-world favelas. At the City University of New York (CUNY), 48 percent of students had been food insecure in the thirty days prior to the article.

Kassandra Montes, a senior at Lehman College, lives in a Harlem homeless shelter. Montes "works two part-time jobs and budgets only $15 per week for food. She . . . usually skips breakfast in order to make sure that her 4-year-old son is eating regularly." Montes said: "I feel like I'm slowly sinking as I'm trying to grow."

When you don't have a living wage, have to pay high tuition, are mired in debt, and live in rent-gouging cities, where do you go? Increasingly, you go to the community college or college food pantry. In a nation whose president and Congress in one year give tens of billions of dollars more than the generals asked for to the Pentagon, it is unconscionable that students must rely on leftover food from dining halls and catered events, SNAP benefits, and whatever food pantries can assemble.

The CUNY pantries are such a fixture in these desperate times that they are now a stop on freshman orientation tours.

As long as we're speaking of shame, what about those millions of middle- and upper-middle-class *informed, concerned bystanders*. They're all over America trading *tsk-tsks* over coffee or other social encounters. They express dismay, disgust, and denunciations at each outrage, from giant corporations' abuses to the White House and Congress's failings. They are particularly numerous in university towns. They *know* but they do not *do*. They are unorganized, know it, keep grumbling, and still fail to start the mobilization in congressional districts of likeminded citizens to hold their senators and representatives accountable.

Congress, the smallest yet most powerful branch of government, whose members' names we know, can turn poverty and other injustices around and help provide a better life for so many Americans. These informed, concerned people easily number over 1 percent of the population. They can galvanize a supporting majority of voters on key, long-overdue redirections for justice. Redirections that were mostly established in Western Europe decades ago (for more details, see my paperback *Breaking Through Power: It's Easier Than We Think*).

These informed, concerned people—who don't have to worry about a living wage, not having health insurance, being gouged by payday loans, and having no savings—were called "the contented classes" in *The Culture of Contentment,* a book by the late progressive Harvard economist John Kenneth Galbraith. His main point: until the contented classes wake up and organize for change, history has shown, our country will continue to slide in the wrong direction. He said all this before climate disruption, massive money-corrupting politics, and the corporate crime wave had reached anywhere near their present destructive levels.

The question to be asked: who among the contented classes will unfurl the flag of rebellion against the plutocrats and the autocrats? It can be launched almost anywhere they please. A revolution can start the moment they decide to prioritize the most marginalized people in this country over their comfort.

John C. Bogle: Renaissance Money Manager for the People and More

JANUARY 24, 2019

The accolades were uniformly respectful for the honest, innovative, and unyielding defender of shareholder/investor rights—the late John C. Bogle—the founder of the now giant Vanguard Group of mutual funds. Writers took note of his pioneering low-cost, low-fee investing and mutual funds tied to stock-market indices. Index funds, tied to such indices as the S&P 500, now total trillions of dollars.

Bogle abhorred gouging by the money managers. He would add up their fees—seemingly small at less than 1 percent a year—and show how over time they could cut the cumulative return by 50 percent or more. That's why he set up Vanguard in 1974, which by holding down costs and fees has begun to push the rest of the smug industry to be more reasonable. Vanguard now has over $5 trillion in managed assets.

He could have become as rich as Edward Johnson III—his counterpart at Fidelity Investments—who is worth over $7 billion. Instead, Bogle organized Vanguard as a *mutual* firm, not a stock firm, owned by its investors. Bogle's fortune, at the time of his passing last week, was estimated at $80 million after a lifetime of giving away half of his annual adjusted gross income to charitable and educational groups.

In the admiring words of Warren Buffett, Bogle's work "helped millions of investors realize far better returns on their savings than they otherwise would have earned. He is a hero to them and to me."

The *Philadelphia Inquirer* described the local giant of the investing world, based in Malvern, Pennsylvania, as "motivated by a mix of pragmatism and idealism. Mr. Bogle was regarded by friends and foes alike as the conscience of the industry and the sheriff of Wall Street." It was hard to be his foe. Bogle, a father of six children, was calm, gregarious, and amicable. He connected his irrefutable rhetoric with unassailable evidence. He was Mr. Fair Play, the go-to wise man for his judgment on whether the torrent of financial services and offerings were, as he put it, "all hat and no cattle."

He unraveled the sweet talk and complex camouflage of the financial services industry with analytic precision and explained it with clear language.

He would call out the corporatists whenever he saw "rank speculation," reckless debt, "obscene" executive pay, or the disgraceful, unearned golden parachutes handed to bosses who tanked their own companies. For Bogle, there were serious economic differences between "speculation" and "investment" with "other people's money."

His admirers were so numerous they organized themselves as "Bogleheads," two of whom wrote the book *The Bogleheads' Guide to Investing.* Right up to his passing at the age of eighty-nine, after surviving six heart attacks and a heart transplant, Bogle was still humble, approachable, and writing memorable articles.

He was responsive and kind. In May and September of 2016, we held four days of the Super Bowl of civic activities in Washington, DC. I invited Mr. Bogle to speak on the topic of "Fiduciary Duties as if Shareholders Mattered." His voice sounded weary from being overscheduled and from other responsibilities. Yet he said, "Yes, I'll take the train down from Philadelphia." (You can watch his presentation here: https://breakingthroughpower.org/.)

We were fellow Princetonians, and he often told me about his 1951 Princeton senior thesis where he laid the basis for his career emphasizing a "reduction of sales loads and management fees."

His family business—American Can—crashed in the Depression, so he grew up poor, working as a newspaper delivery boy, waiter, ticket seller, mail clerk, cub reporter, and a pinsetter in a bowling alley, and, as he described, "growing up the best possible way." The cheerful champion of the *fiduciary* rule between sellers of financial advice and their client pension funds, insurance policyholders, and other buyers/investors wanted fiduciary responsibility to be the law, not just a principle. He urged the large institutional investors—mutual, pension, and university endowment funds—to end their passivity and exercise their ownership rights as shareholders in giant companies (ExxonMobil, Bank of America, Pfizer, General Motors, etc.), including specifically challenging their political activities and campaign contributions.

Ever the contrarian, in a November 29, 2018, *Wall Street Journal* article, Bogle warned about the index mutual funds—an industry he started—having too much power! The big three—Vanguard, Black Rock, and State

Street Global—dominate the field with a collective 81 percent share of index fund assets. He wrote: "If historical trends continue, a handful of giant institutional investors will one day hold voting control of virtually every large US corporation . . . I do not believe that such concentration would serve the national interest."

Rick Stengel, former managing editor of *Time* magazine and former president of the National Constitution Center when Jack Bogle was the board chair, described him as "the last honorable man, a complete straight shooter." In his 2008 book, *Enough: True Measures of Money, Business, and Life*, Bogle ranged far beyond index funds and shareholders.

The *Philadelphia Inquirer* put it well: he was "less interested in counting than in what counts. . . . He revered language, history, poetry and classical wisdom, and frequently amazed and delighted people by reciting long passages of verse. . . . He was a social critic, civic leader, mentor and philanthropist." He was also very courteous—striving to return calls and respond to letters, which makes him unique these days.

A devoted father and husband, Jack Bogle declared that "the essential message is, stop focusing on self and start thinking about service to others."

Now is the time for his family, friends, and Bogleheads to plan a series of living memorials to this great and resourceful man, so that his legacy is not just a memory but an ongoing foray into the future that he so fervently wanted to become reality.

Savers Alert: Tens of Billions of Higher-Interest Dollars are Yours for the Asking

JULY 26, 2018

American bank customers are losing billions of dollars in higher-interest payments because they're not being "frugal shoppers" and making a telephone call or sending an email to compare interest rates. If they did, they would find out that the Federal Reserve's three years of gradual interest-rate increases have finally pushed the banks—traditional and online—to make ten times more in interest payments to savers than millions of bank customers are now receiving.

There is over $10 trillion in bank savings-deposit and money-market accounts at places like Fidelity or State Street. In the past four years, such institutions have been reluctant to pass on the benefits of higher interest rates to their trusting savers. However, about a year ago, the interest-rate spread between the interest that banks charge borrowers and the interest that banks pay savers became too glaring to ignore. Prodded by more competitive online banks with little overhead, and by the widening spread between short-term CDs and plain savings accounts, modestly alert savers can collect up to 2.25 percent in interest on minimums of $25,000 or less, depending on the institution.

Example: one person I know was keeping about $100,000 of life savings in a local saving bank at the rate of .02 percent. This was an undisturbed nest egg for years. A conversation with a neighbor led her to call the bank and ask for a better deal. Sure enough, she didn't know that she could get a twelve-month CD paying 2.25 percent interest. (She opted for the better interest rate.)

She didn't know about the better offerings because her bank, like most financial institutions, does not believe in affirmative action to inform their trusting customers of the better deals available to them. Consequently, inattentive Americans are literally leaving tens of billions of dollars on the table, which the banks happily scoop up into their record quarterly profit reports. The same is true for giant mutual funds like Fidelity, which has historically lagged behind its more successful competitor, Vanguard.

Absent personal friendships, very few bank officials contact their savings depositors and tell them they can make thousands of dollars more a year in interest payments with similar accounts. Typical conditions associated with higher interest–paying accounts include: maintaining a minimum balance, limiting savers to a few withdrawals a month, and tying up one's money for several months or even a year. If you want to shop around online, you'll find recent offerings by banks for a one-year CD with no minimum deposit at a rate of 2.5 percent. Smart savers can ask their bank to match these rates. And with the Fed saying it will raise rates two more times this year alone, these deals are only going to get better.

Savings are federally insured by the Federal Deposit Insurance Corporation up to $250,000 per account.

The worst interest rates are often from the giant banks—deemed too big to fail—that are flush with cash and enjoying lucrative tax breaks. They are staying put, offering ridiculous 0.01 to 0.02 percent interest rates. They won't match smaller bank rates. In short, you've been given little more than a lockbox.

One would think that national and local television and radio stations would leap to get more money so easily for their viewers and listeners. Well, banks and mutual funds advertise on these stations.

One would think that the federal and state bank regulatory agencies would inform consumers to be alert and check for the unnoticed available accounts with higher interest rates. Maybe they're too busy promoting banks, checking solvency indicators, and talking deregulation in the age of the Trumpsters (Trump likes to appoint deregulators straight from the banking industry).

We could take a lesson from video entrepreneurs like Eugene Jarecki, whose successful 2010 video "Move Your Money" urged customers to vote with their feet by leaving misbehaving banks for more reputable community banks or credit unions. (Mr. Jarecki is now busy promoting his new documentary, *The King*, on Elvis as a broad metaphor for Trump's America, rampant materialism, and self-indulgence).

Large consumer organizations—such as Consumers Union (CU), with millions of subscribers, and the Consumer Federation of America (CFA), with scores of institutional members, including consumer groups and unions—have a role to play. Come on, CU and CFA—move some of the billions of retained bank dollars into higher-interest-rate payments for hard-pressed Americans. They and other middle-class savers will thank you.

How about going full blast with eye-catching news releases and social media? Add some dramatic news conferences and mass media interviews to make this a grand party of immediate benefits. Let's go, Marta Tellado (CU president) and Jack Gillis (CFA president)!!! Why should the barons of finance keep laughing all the way to the bank?

The Serious Price of the Hyperconvenient Economy

NOVEMBER 11, 2017

Apart from sensual appeals, the chief marketing wave in our country is selling convenience. It has reached a level of frenzy with companies like Amazon and Walmart racing your order to your doorstep (with Amazon now wanting the electronic key to your house).

Ever since the industrial revolution, when the division of labor between consumers and producers widened and deepened, the convenience of not having to grow your own food, weave your own clothes, and build your own shelter has become a given of economic progress. Expert specialization has tended to make products better and more standardized as well.

But, in recent decades, vendors have added tiers of conveniences and touted them in their television, radio, and print advertisements but rarely mentioned the downsides.

For example, consider the fast-food industry. Fast food was sold to the American consumer as convenient, tasty, and always available. For these shallow advantages, many consumers chose to give up homemade and nutritious meals for those with heavy doses of fat, sugar, and salt—all deadly when taken in such excessive amounts by tens of millions of children and adults. Food that "melts in your mouth" and "tastes great" usually comes with additives that turn your tongue against your brain and bodily health.

There is the convenience of credit and debit cards. It started in the 1950s when a businessman found it inconvenient in restaurants to have to make sure he had enough cash. Why not sign restaurants up to take the Diners Club card? Before long, the question became: Why not take it all the way to enable massive impulse buying, massive invasion of privacy, revolving debt traps, bankruptcies, and the iron collar of unilaterally determined credit-score ratings? Why not deliberately overextend credit and turn consumers into hooked supplicants who won't complain to their car dealers, insurance agencies, or landlords for fear of a complaint lowering scores and ratings?

What could be more convenient than signing on the dotted line of fine-print contracts or click-on agreements? You don't have to read, understand, bargain, or reject. It's easy, if you don't mind having your rights taken away on page after page as fees, penalties, and other overcharges—plus closed courtroom doors—plunge you into contract servitude or peonage.

Like any steps of "progress," convenience taken too far induces dependency; ignorance of the product and service; and more loss of voice, self-determination, and self-reliance. Today, rampant advertising and telemarketers tell you to sign up to have your groceries be home-delivered. For some people with disabilities, this can be a plus, if you get what you ordered. For most people, the price is a loss of sociability, of going to markets where real people have meaningful interactions with and learn from one another.

The promotion of touted quick-fix drugs—when successful, less invasive treatments are available with fewer deadly side effects (note the opioid epidemic that will take sixty thousand American lives this year)—is accelerating beyond tranquilizers and sleeping pills. The advance of biologics could make Aldous Huxley's *Brave New World* (1932) an understatement of silent manipulation and mind control.

How about the convenience of online gambling, payday loan rackets, and cosmetic surgery—all loaded with their unpublicized and underreported costs—or the "convenience" of outsourcing your judgement and self-control to omnipresent apps?

But surely the "free" Facebook and Google do not come with such costs, do they? In return for this "free" service, you surrender your most personal information, which they turn into massive profits without giving you a share. Then they data-mine your buying profile for in-house use or outside sale; they select the news you get and expose you to anonymous and often fraudulent solicitations and propaganda. If these violations are invasive and omnipresent for you, just consider how it will affect your children and grandchildren.

Technology driven by narrow commercial interests needs to provoke us into asking, "What's all this convenience doing over the long run? What kind of community and society is coming out of this unassessed marketing?" For a better future, we must mobilize, community by community, for some inconvenient thoughts and organization. Unless, that is, the corporate future doesn't need us.

To get started, encourage your friends and neighbors to sign up for Jim Hightower's *Hightower Lowdown* newsletter.

The Savings and Stability of Public Banking

APRIL 11, 2017

As a society obsessed by money, we pay a gigantic price for not educating high school and college students about money and banking. The ways of the giant global banks—both commercial and investment operations—are as mysterious as they are damaging to the people. Big banks use the Federal Reserve to maximize their influence and profits. The federal Freedom of Information Act provides an exemption for matters that are "contained in or related to examination, operating, or condition reports prepared by, on behalf of, or for the use of an agency responsible for the regulation or supervision of financial institutions." This exemption allows financial institutions to wallow in secrecy. Financial institutions are so influential in Congress that Senator Dick Durbin (D-IL) says "[The banks] frankly own this place."

Although anti-union, giant financial institutions have significant influence over the investments of worker pension funds. Their certainty of being bailed out because they are seen as "too big to fail" harms the competitiveness of smaller community banks and allows the big bankers to take bigger risks with "other people's money," as Justice Louis Brandeis put it.

These big banks are so pervasive in their reach that even unions and progressive media, such as the *Nation* magazine and Democracy Now!, have their accounts with JPMorgan Chase.

The government allows banks to have concentrated power. Taxpayers and consumers are charged excessive fees and paid paltry interest rates on savings. The bonds of municipalities are also hit with staggering fees, and public assets like highways and drinking water systems are corporatized by Goldman Sachs and other privatizers with multidecade sweetheart leases.

Then there are the immense taxpayer bailouts of Wall Street, such as those in 2008 and 2009 after the financial industry's recklessness and crimes brought down the economy, cost workers eight million jobs, and shredded the pension and mutual fund savings of the American people.

Standing like a beacon of stability, responsiveness, and profitability is the ninety-eight-year-old state-owned Bank of North Dakota (BND). As reported by Ellen Brown, prolific author and founder of the Public Banking Institute (Santa Clarita, California), "The BND has had record profits for the last 12 years"—avoiding the Wall Street crash—"each year outperforming the last. In 2015 it reported $130.7 million in earnings, total assets of $7.4 billion, capital of $749 million, and a return on investment of a whopping 18.1 percent. Its lending portfolio grew by $486 million, a 12.7 percent increase, with growth in all four of its areas of concentration: agriculture, business, residential, and student loans."

North Dakota's economy is depressed because of the sharp drop in oil prices. So the BND moved to help. Again, Ellen Brown:

> In 2015, it introduced new infrastructure programs to improve access to medical facilities, remodel or construct new schools, and build new road and water infrastructure. The Farm Financial Stability Loan was introduced to assist farmers affected by low commodity prices or below-average crop production. The BND also helped fund 300 new businesses.

All this is in a state with half the population of Phoenix or Philadelphia.

A California coalition is forming to establish a state-owned bank for California. Coalition organizers say a California State Bank will cut the state's long-term financing costs in half compared to what avaricious Wall Street is charging. The nation's largest state (equivalent to the world's sixth-largest economy) can free itself from massive debt accumulation, bid-rigging, deceptive interest-rate swaps, and capital appreciation bonds at 300 percent interest over time.

What assets does the state have to make this bank fully operational? California has surplus funds that total about $600 billion, including those in the Pooled Money Investment Account, managed by the state treasurer, that contains $54 billion earning less than 1 percent interest.

Money in these funds is earmarked for specific expenditure purposes, but they can be invested—in a new state bank. To escape from a Wall Street that is, in Brown's words, "sucking massive sums in interest, fees, and interest rate swap payments out of California and into offshore tax havens," a state bank can use its impressive credit power to develop infrastructure in California.

Huge state pension funds and other state funds can provide the deposits. Each $1 billion capital investment can lend $10 billion for projects less expensively and under open stable banking control by California. Presently, California and other states routinely deposit hundreds of billions of dollars in Wall Street banks at minimal interest, then turn around and borrow for infrastructure construction and repair from the Wall Street bond market at much higher interest and fees.

This is a ridiculous form of debt peonage, a lesson Governor Jerry Brown has yet to learn. He and other officials who are similarly uninformed about how the state of California can be its own banker should visit publicbankinginstitute.org and read Ellen Brown's book *The Public Bank Solution*.

Legislation for public banks is being pursued in the states of Washington, Michigan, Arizona, and New Jersey, as well as the cities of Philadelphia and Santa Fe. Look for county commissioners and state treasurers to come on board when they see the enormous safeguards and savings that can be secured through "public banks" in contrast to the convoluted casino run by unaccountable Wall Street gamblers and speculators.

A longtime backer of public banking, retired entrepreneur Richard Mazess hopes that national civic groups like Public Citizen, Common Cause, People for the American Way, and Consumer Watchdog can get behind the proposal. "Public, not private, infrastructure is essential for an equitable economy," he says.

California already has a public infrastructure bank called the IBank. Mr. Mazess and others believe that expanding the *existing* IBank into a depository institution would be more likely to pass through the California legislature. The deposits would come from public institutions and NGOs (not from private persons). These pension funds and other public deposits would become reserves and serve as the basis for safely leveraged loans to public projects at a conservative tenfold multiplier. No derivatives or other shenanigans allowed.

Before that proposal can be enacted, however, there needs to be much more education of state legislators and the public at large.

Such enlightenment would illuminate the enormous savings, along with the restoration of state sovereignty from the absentee, exploitative grip of an unrepentant, speculating, profiteering Wall Street that believes it can always go to Washington, DC, for its taxpayer bailouts.

Hillary's Hubris: Only Tell the Rich for $5,000 a Minute!

AUGUST 19, 2016

There is a growing asymmetry between the media's mounting demands for Donald Trump to release his tax returns (Hillary has done so) and their diminishing demands that Hillary Clinton release the secret transcripts of her $5,000-per-minute speeches before closed-door banking conferences and other business conventions.

In its August 18 issue, the *Washington Post*, an endorser of Clinton, devoted another round of surmising as to why Trump doesn't want to release his tax returns—speculating that he isn't as rich as he brags he is, that he pays little or no taxes, and that he gives little to charity. Other media outlets endorsing Hillary have been less than vociferous in demanding that she release what she told business leaders in these pay-to-play venues.

When asked last year about her transcripts on *Meet the Press*, she said she would look into it. When the questions persisted in subsequent months, she said she would release the transcripts only if everybody else did. Bernie Sanders replied that he had no transcripts because he doesn't give paid speeches to business audiences. Nonetheless she continues to be evasive.

We know she has such transcripts. Her contract with these numerous business groups, prepared by the Harry Walker Agency, stipulated that the sponsor pay $1,000 for a stenographer to take down a verbatim record, exclusively for her possession.

The presidential campaign is moving into a stage where it will be harder for reporters to reach her. Except for a recent informal gathering with some reporters, Hillary Clinton, unlike all other presidential candidates, has not held a news conference since last December. This aversion to media examination does not augur well should she reach the White House. Secrecy is corrosive to democracy.

Why wouldn't Hillary tell the American people, whose votes she wants, what she told corporations in private for almost two years? Is it that she doesn't want to be accused of double-talk, of "gushing" (as one insider told the *Wall Street Journal*) when addressing bankers, stock traders, or corporate bosses? On the campaign trail Hillary only mimics Bernie Sanders's tough, populist challenges to Wall Street. The Clintons are not known for answering tough questions or participating in straight talk. Dodging and weaving is what they do, and too often they get away with it.

Hillary is the clear reported choice for president, and not just by the Wall Street crowd. The champions of the military-industrial complex love her variety of extreme hawkishness, which rings the cash registers for ever more military weapons contracts.

As the Sanders uprising dims, Hillary can be seen already returning to her former militarized foreign policy. On the last day of the Democratic Convention, the stage's military presence foreshadowed her return to militarism. Her supporters shouted "USA, USA" to drown out the Sanders shoutouts for peace and justice. Hillary's supporters sounded like the jingoistic Republicans. She's been endorsed by numerous retired Pentagon, CIA, and NSA officials who find Trump's "Why can't we get along with Russia and China?" statements disturbing to their worldviews.

Where Trump's White House is seen as utterly unpredictable, Hillary's White House is utterly predictable: more Wall Street, more military adventures. As senator and secretary of state she has never seen a weapons system or a war that she didn't support. Remember her singular pressure to attack Libya over the objections of then secretary of defense Robert Gates, who asked, "What happens after the regime is overthrown?"

Hillary's judgement and experience regarding Libya resulted in an ongoing, spreading disaster of violence and chaos in that war-torn country and its neighboring countries to the south.

It is bad enough that monetized politicians and the mass media reduce voters to the status of spectators, excluded from injecting their issues and their perceived injustices into the electoral campaigns. Now people are told to stop complaining when candidates such as Hillary Clinton tell the gilded few what she and they don't want many of us to hear.

Big Union Leaders Betray
Sanders and Workers

APRIL 8, 2016

Around a conference table inside the large Washington headquarters of the AFL-CIO, a furious exchange occurred between labor union presidents. It was late February, and up for decision by the executive council was whether the country's principal labor federation was going to make a primary-season endorsement of Hillary Clinton as favored by the leaders of the largest unions.

According to insiders, tempers flared when smaller unions challenged the Hillary-endorsing big unions such as the American Federation of State, County and Municipal Employees (AFSCME), the American Federation of Teachers, the National Education Association, the Service Employees International Union (SEIU), and the United Food and Commercial Workers International Union (UFCW). These large unions came out for Clinton in late 2015 and early 2016 before they sensed the growing rank-and-file workers' preference for lifetime advocate for workers and union backer Bernie Sanders.

Listening to the nurses' union head speak out for Sanders's strong pro-labor history, Lee Saunders, president of AFSCME, interrupted her, exclaiming: "I will not allow you to do a commercial for Sanders." She retorted, "You mean for the only candidate who has a 100 percent labor record?"

A union leader of postal workers charged the unions backing Hillary as being "completely out of touch with their workers." AFL-CIO president Richard Trumka then cut off their microphones.

All over the country, the observation by the postal workers' leader rings true. Even as Lee Saunders read the names of the Democratic presidential contenders at a large Washington State AFSCME membership meeting last October, "only Sanders's name brought loud, sustained applause," according to Bloomberg News.

Few union leaders allow a worker referendum to make the endorsement decisions. The seven-hundred-thousand-member Communication

Workers of America (CWA) does, and the result was a "decisive endorsement of Sanders," reported Rafael Návar, the union's political director. Whether it is the level of enthusiasm, campaigning to get out the vote, or talking up their candidate's record on such issues as minimum wage increases, abolition of public university and college tuition, full "Medicare for all" (single-payer system), and credibility in standing up to Wall Street, Hillary's votes and statements do not come close to respecting the working families of America compared to Bernie's consistent thirty-year record.

Based entirely on her lawless record as a pro-war senator (Iraq), as a war-making secretary of state (Libya), and her $5,000-a-minute speeches before closed-door big-business gatherings (in addition to millions in big-money campaign contributions), Clinton will continue to be the sponsor of war and Wall Street.

The volunteer Labor for Bernie grassroots drive is not just growing rapidly but cutting across all union categories and gaining support with nonunion workers. There is a potentially massive pool of American workers supporting Senator Sanders as he wins primary after primary, leading up to the April 19 contest in New York—the adopted state base for the Clintons, who are backed by all their monied interests.

This unaffiliated labor awakening bears watching, especially by the long-entrenched, affluent big-union leaders. First, Labor for Bernie is fomenting defections by local unions defying their Hillary-endorsing national organizations. So far, over eighty of these union locals have endorsed Bernie Sanders.

Typical of this exodus is Northern California Food and Commercial Workers Local 5, whose executive board voted 30–2 for Sanders, reflecting the views of most of its twenty-eight thousand members. Local 5's Mike Henneberry said, "For us it was not a very difficult decision. Compare an individual who's been supporting workers since he was mayor of Burlington [Vermont] with someone who's been on the board of Walmart."

The Service Employees Local 1984 (SEIU), New Hampshire's largest public-sector union, disagreed with its national union and came out for Sanders in November.

The big-union leaders don't smell revolt yet, but they must be worried. If the Clintons continue to play dirty tricks with the big unions, as was suspected in Iowa and Nevada against the Sanders campaign, the seeds of challenges within the ranks of these unions will be planted. Should Hillary become president and come out for antiworker trade treaties, return to her former coolness on a living wage and other labor issues, and cater to Wall Street, the insurrection could congeal against the big unions who will have taken credit, of course, for her victory, without having delivered a mandate for a labor agenda.

It is the AFL-CIO's practice of endorsing Democrats without demanding before and insisting after the election that candidates champion "card check," revision of trade treaties, repeal of anti-union labor laws, and stronger job-safety regulation. The Democratic Party treats the mostly shrinking labor unions as having nowhere else to go. And most union leaders meekly oblige by their chronic submissiveness.

The man to watch is strategist and former labor union insider Larry Cohen. He was for many years the president of the CWA that has endorsed Sanders. He's going all over the country helping the Sanders campaign, urging major labor unions that are still undecided, like those of the steel, auto, firefighters and electrical workers, to come out for Bernie.

But Mr. Cohen is looking beyond the elections to take the energy from the Sanders campaign and politically mobilize tens of millions of non-unionized workers behind a new Congress, furthering a new economy as if workers mattered.

Time is of the essence. When will workers again have such a scandal-free, consistent labor champion as Bernie Sanders seriously going for the presidency inside the Democratic Party? Had Sanders had two more months without this big-union opposition, his current momentum could have allowed him to overtake Clinton by now.

Facing a possible four or eight years of the corporatist and militarist Clinton, coupled with US multinational corporations exporting whole industries, not to mention accelerating labor-replacing automation, the hurdles for Americans believing in democracy, justice, and peace become far, far greater.

So the time for preventive civic and worker engagement with all electoral contests is now!

For America's Unbanked: Reestablishing the Postal Savings Bank

NOVEMBER 13, 2015

Fact: Tens of millions of Americans do not have a bank account. As a result, many of these Americans spend a reported $89 billion annually in interest and fees by using predatory services, such as those for payday loans and check cashing. It's a perpetuating cycle of poverty in which the poor get poorer just by accessing their own money. Fortunately, there is an ideal solution staring us in the face. An important voice driving the conversation is professor Mehrsa Baradaran of the University of Georgia Law School. Her excellent new book, *How the Other Half Banks: Exclusion, Exploitation, and the Threat to Democracy*, describes how, for decades, big banks have shed their social contract with the American public and transformed themselves into modern monstrosities that serve corporations and the wealthy and exploit or avoid the less affluent members of our society. Setting the stage with this historical context, Professor Baradaran makes a compelling case for a postal banking system that would greatly benefit millions of struggling "unbanked" Americans.

Predatory payday loan companies and check-cashing services soared like hawks in the 1980s to take advantage of communities where community banks and credit unions were displaced by the creep of large banking institutions. The payday lending industry now has more storefronts than McDonald's and Starbucks combined. These alternative "fringe banks" charge outrageous interest rates and fees, and millions of Americans turn to them each year, which allows the banks to bring in $40 billion a year in high-interest loans.

Where are the so-called large conventional banks? They are increasingly closing up shop in low-income areas. According to *Bloomberg*, from 2008 to 2013, "banks . . . shut 1,826 branches . . . and 93 percent of closings were in postal codes where the household income is below the national median." If you are living in a low-income neighborhood, just finding a bank is difficult. In 1993, we released a detailed report offering strong evidence that forty-nine major mortgage lenders had engaged in racial redlining in violation of federal Fair Lending laws in sixteen major US cities. Redlining occurs when banks and other mortgage lenders either exclude minority neighborhoods from their "effective lending territories" or substantially underserve such neighborhoods.

The unbanked now pay up to 10 percent of their income just to use the money they have already earned. To put it into real-world terms, an American family without a bank account, earning $25,000 a year, spends about $2,400 of that income on interest and fees. To put it even more bluntly—that's more than they spend on food! (This statistic includes the chance of unpredictable financial emergencies in which those in need turn to payday lenders to bail them out at huge interest rates—50 percent of Americans need to borrow money for emergencies costing over $400.)

In her book, Professor Baradaran gives some real-life examples: Tanya Burke, a single mother of two, racked up more than $2,000 of debt in fees and interest by taking out $600 from a payday lender to cover rent and unexpected medical costs for her son. Thelma Fleming, a mother and grandmother, took out a $300 loan to cover costs after losing one of her jobs. Forced to take out other loans to buy herself time, she ended up paying $2,500 over the course of ten months to pay back that initial $300 loan. These stories are far too common in America.

Until the 1970s and '80s, usury laws were in place to protect consumers by capping the maximum amount of interest that could be levied. Due to financial industry lobbying efforts, many states now have no usury caps (or there are ways around them). This deregulation gave way to the enormous growth of the payday loan industry.

Another telling example from Professor Baradaran deals with a high-wage earner who experiences a different borrowing outcome. "Steven" made some bad investments and could no longer afford his daily expenses. Luckily, he found a "miracle lender" who gave him very generous loans with low interest rates, saving him from financial ruin. "Steven" is, of course, America's big banks. When the reckless banking industry was under financial duress, it received a sweetheart deal when the American taxpayers bailed it out. Millions of struggling Americans, like Tanya Burke and Thelma Fleming, are not afforded that same luxury—and the banks have not repaid the goodwill forward by respecting their needs.

This brings us to postal banking, which could help break the cycle of madness that keeps millions of Americans in financial quicksand.

From 1911 until 1967, the Postal Savings System offered simple savings accounts to Americans who preferred an alternative to a private bank. It was a successful system until the bank lobby forced its cessation. (In many foreign countries, post offices still offer simple savings accounts with no fees and reasonable minimum-balance requirements.)

The United States Postal Service (USPS), which unlike the banks has an obligation to serve all communities, has more than enough retail locations to serve all of these underserved consumers. Last year, the office of the USPS inspector general released a report detailing the ways in which postal banking would be beneficial to both the public and the USPS itself, which has been made to endure an unprecedented advanced payment of $103.7 billion by 2016 to cover future health benefits of postal retirees for the next seventy-five years. No other government or private corporation is required to meet this unreasonable prepayment burden.

While the USPS already offers some financial services such as money orders and international fund transfers, it could expand to include paycheck cashing, prepaid debit cards, bill payments, ATMs, savings accounts, and small-dollar loans. The introduction of these services would offer millions of Americans a local, reliable, and affordable alternative to managing their finances. With over thirty thousand locations, USPS branches are everywhere in America.

A notable supporter of postal banking is Senator Elizabeth Warren (D-MA), who has been a leading advocate on this issue. Presidential candidate Bernie Sanders also supports it, recently stating in an interview that "the postal service, in fact, can play an important role in providing modest types of banking service to folks who need it."

The time is ripe to implement postal banking. What is needed is a rising rumble from the people focused on Postmaster General Megan Brennan— who has the authority to act now on implementing surcharge-free ATMs, payroll check cashing, bill-paying services, and electronic money transfers—and on Congress to allow loans and other new services. For more on the issue and to find out how easy it is to get active and involved, visit campaignforpostalbanking.org (site discontinued).

Republicans Support Massive Tax Evasion
by Starving IRS Budget

JULY 31, 2015

Representative Jason Chaffetz (R-UT)
Representative Ron DeSantis (R-FL)
Representative Jim Jordan (R-OH)

Dear Representatives Chaffetz, DeSantis, and Jordan,

The taxpayers elected you—and therefore pay your salary—with the expectation that you would be responsible legislators, but your behavior as committee and subcommittee chairs, along with that of House Speaker Boehner, regarding the IRS has been wholly irresponsible.

Following the example of Representative Darrell Issa (R-CA), you have made mountains out of molehills in regard to the charges of Internal Revenue Service (IRS) bias against tax-exempt right-wing political groups. These charges have been rebutted item by item by the IRS inspector general, congressional witnesses who have no political ax to grind, and by Representative Issa's counterpart, Representative Elijah Cummings (D-MD), most recently on July 27, 2015.

Remember that when these 501(c)(4) PACs have overtly politically partisan names and rhetoric, whether from a Tea Party or progressive viewpoint, the IRS should give them closer scrutiny.

In this letter, I wish to address your constituents about your utter ignorance or hypocrisy—you choose—in complaining about government deficits while strip-mining the already small tax collection budget of the IRS, which is supposed to collect over $3 trillion for all three branches of the federal government. Cutting the IRS budget to the bone means it cannot adequately address and collect more of the roughly $300 billion in tax evasions each year.

When the Republicans' yearly reductions in the IRS budget anger someone like conservative economist Jerry Jasinowski, who served as the president of the National Association of Manufacturers for fourteen years and was a frequent witness at congressional hearings, you'd better listen.

Mr. Jasinowski says that cutting the IRS budget for five consecutive years by a total of $1.2 billion and lowering the budget to $10.9 billion—its lowest level, adjusted for inflation, since 1998—"promotes cynicism [and] encourages cheats."

He continues: "As a result, the IRS has lost 13,000 employees, 11 percent of the total [employees]"; initiated "19 percent fewer criminal investigations than the year before"; and completed "46,000 fewer audits." Consequently, billions of dollars will, of course, go uncollected every year.

People cannot reach the IRS with their questions. There are not enough IRS agents to answer the phones; millions of calls go unanswered. You have helped cause this mass irritation and waste of time for the people back home.

The increased complexity of the tax laws and the surging number of identity thefts are putting more burdens on the diminishing number of IRS staff, who are resorting to spending their own money on office supplies in order to keep things running. (The Affordable Care Act alone has generated many questions for the taxpayers.)

Mr. Jasinowski charges that "Congress is undermining that trust [known as voluntary compliance], shortchanging the treasury and encouraging illegal behavior. This is a serious mistake."

It is more than a mistake. Republicans are to blame here because they are running Congress and passing these cuts despite the opposition from the Democrats. They are knowingly and willfully making it impossible to have the IRS crack down on big corporate tax evasion and large individual violators. No doubt some of these tax cheats are gratefully contributing to the campaign coffers of the Republicans.

It gets worse. While the Republicans are calling for the impeachment of the capable turnaround expert John Koskinen, the commissioner of the IRS, these same Republicans have fashioned a tax code that allows dozens of major corporations, like General Electric and Verizon, to pay no income taxes at all on billions in yearly profits in the US (see ctj.org for more information).

Republicans do not hesitate when taking money from commercial interests in return for providing tax laws with so many lucrative loopholes that the rich and powerful can become legal tax *avoiders* instead of remaining illegal tax *evaders*. The tax code has been wholly shaped by political influence. Fewer tax dollars are being collected even though our country has a huge federal deficit, leaving taxpaying Americans to ultimately pay the price for the flaws in the tax code.

How can you collect your sizable paycheck with that kind of grotesque performance? Try disagreeing with Mr. Jasinowski, who accuses Congress of presiding over an indecipherable tax code that results in "big time tax cheats . . . getting off scot free."

The rumble from the people gets louder and louder in left-right alliances. The gerrymandering of single-party congressional districts that allows members of Congress to avoid the consequences of these actions is ripe for change. Your day of reckoning is approaching. You will be held accountable for your ruinous actions.

Meanwhile, enact President Obama's partially restored IRS budget to slightly over $12 billion next year—still less expensive than the cost of the latest redundant aircraft carrier.

Sincerely,

Ralph Nader

Large Foundations: Rethink Your Priorities

FEBRUARY 9, 2015

The number of large foundations has been consistently increasing. Some of these foundations are bulging with billions of dollars in assets that could be contributed to nonprofit "good works." It is potentially the golden age of philanthropy, but unfortunately many areas of recognized need are too often ignored by foundation boards and their executives. Organizations with track records of effective advocacy and accomplishment stand ready to take on neglected problems of our society. Unfortunately, these groups lack adequate foundation support.

When foundations do donate to important areas, such as energy policy, they often award grants to the same organizations that are not original, motivating, or making necessary waves. Year after year, these bland organizations are seen as the "safe choice" for donors who are timid about new ideas and groundbreaking approaches. Cushy relationships, as have been demonstrated in the energy/environmental field, often amount to an annuity of contributions for lackluster studies and reports from the same old recipients futilely running over the same old ground.

What author and philanthropist Peter Buffett called—in a widely discussed op-ed in the July 26, 2013, *New York Times*—the "charitable-industrial complex" is in need of serious introspection. Is the "charitable-industrial complex" just treading water or, in Buffett's words, immersed in "a crisis of imagination" and not thinking "foundation dollars should be the best 'risk capital' out there"?

After decades of observing effective groups with untapped potential suffering from a dearth of funding, I can point to fifteen specific missed opportunities by indifferent foundations. Even funders who acknowledge the importance of the problems these groups are grappling with almost always reply to funding requests by saying the proposals "do not fit within our guidelines."

I say "almost always" because there were a number of pioneering moves by large foundations that serve as compelling contrasting examples. About forty-five years ago, Ford Foundation funded the startup of public interest law firms. Little more than a decade ago, the Rockefeller Foundation, followed by the Ford and MacArthur foundations, funded controversial nongovernmental organization efforts, already underway, to break monopolies for pharmaceutical drug treatments for HIV/AIDS, which lowered prices from more than $30 per day to less than $1 per day, leading to the inclusion of nearly ten million people from developing countries.

Here is my short list of areas where funding is needed, but lacking:

1. The area of pension rights and the shredding of pension assets by Wall Street machinations involves trillions of dollars and receives miniscule support from foundations (pensionrights.org).

2. Pressing for action regarding corporate governance; corporate welfare; and corporate crime, fraud, and abuse is largely underfunded. Years ago, a study by Archibald Gillies found less than 5 percent of foundation donations go to nonprofit groups working in this massive arena.

3. Over $500 billion a year is spent on all federal government purchasing of goods and services from corporations, including weapons systems, health care, energy, paper, and more. In 1988 we hosted The Stimulation Effect: A National Conference on the Uses of Government Procurement Leverage to Benefit Taxpayers and Consumers. This successful symposium dealt with one aspect of this largely ignored subject.

4. Freedom-of-information advocacy and litigation receives a pittance but should be an easy grant focus. Information is the currency of democracy. Past and present advocacy has proven to be extremely cost-beneficial. Foundations that want to reduce chronic government secrecy should take a close look here.

5. Racial redlining is the practice whereby mortgage lenders figuratively draw a red line around minority neighborhoods and refuse to make mortgage loans available there. Mortgage and insurance redlining leads to the deterioration of communities. In 1993 we produced orig-

inal geographic information system (GIS) maps with detailed data on financial institutions that were redlining minority neighborhoods in cities all over the country. Yet our researcher, Jonathan Brown, could barely scrape together financial support from foundations ostensibly committed to confronting racial discrimination and related poverty.

6. Auto, railroad, aviation, and bus safety are terra incognita for foundation grantmakers who undoubtedly use these forms of transportation. One aviation safety group of long-proven merit, the Aviation Consumer Action Project, had to close down, while another, the Center for Auto Safety, has worked wonders, but on a tiny budget. Furthermore, advocacy groups for railroad and bus safety are rarely seen in Washington, DC.

7. The indifference to occupational health and safety is astonishing. Foundations may think labor unions should be bearing the load in this field. Unfortunately, the AFL-CIO has very few people monitoring the weak Occupational Safety and Health Administration (OSHA). Protecting worker health and safety would be a good project for a consortium of foundations to fund. Imagine—advocacy organizations focused on the companies that produce mayhem on workers. There are over fifty-four thousand workplace-related fatalities each year. The number of injuries and illnesses is much greater.

8. Hospital-acquired infections take over two hundred lives a day in the US! Only recently have some foundations shown an interest in funding civic associations that work on this largely preventable tragedy.

9. Legendary foundation critic Pablo Eisenberg makes a strong case that these tax-exempt institutions should be doing far more about poverty in America (see "Helping the Poor Is No Longer a Priority for Today's Nonprofits" in *HuffPost*).

10. Advocacy for tax reform is much-needed considering there are hundreds of billions of avoided and evaded tax dollars every year. You can count the number of national citizen tax reform groups on one hand. This is another of the "starvation fields" for worthy groups suffering

from foundation indifference. (See what one group has done—Citizens for Tax Justice, ctj.org.)

11. Wars can often be prevented. The Iraq invasion might not have occurred if a well-staffed secretariat had been funded to organize retired prominent military, security, and diplomatic officials who had openly opposed that reckless war of choice. Requests for funding for such an initiative in 2002 and 2003, prior to the unlawful Iraq War, were ignored.

12. Some foundations avidly favor civic engagement. What better illustrates civic engagement than the hundreds of little local groups training themselves to successfully fight toxic environments, facilitated by Love Canal activist-turned-national-leader Lois Gibbs? Gibbs is now the director of the Center for Health, Environment and Justice and has had to lay off workers because of insufficient foundation grant support.

13. Encouraging consumer cooperatives, as does the National Association of Student Cooperatives (NASCO), should be an easy one for foundation support. This organization does many things right on college campuses and provides materials on the advantages of co-ops.

14. Organizing alumni classes to advocate for justice has been pioneered by Princeton University's class of 1955 and the Harvard Law School class of 1958. The motivating affinity group known as the alumni class—out of school, over thirty-five years—is an exciting model that foundations should eagerly support. Yet funding to stimulate such groups has received very little foundation support in the last twenty-five years.

15. The tumultuous technologies known as genetic engineering and nanotechnology receive less annual civic funding for ethical and safety monitoring than the annual salaries of one giant foundation's executive suite. There are only three small national civic groups with a focus on questioning genetic engineering and fewer focused on the invisible nanotech industry. Nanotech and genetic engineering research has

been heavily funded by taxpayers. But holding government and cor-porate researchers accountable is almost impossible because of a lack of funding.

Consider the beneficial impact when foundation funding enabled, starting in the early seventies, new environmental groups to perform their historic work or the significance of foundation funding for the "real news" of independent media. More creative and bold philanthropy is needed across the spectrum of our faltering democracy; more foundations need to be interested in the justice of prevention.

Remember, increased justice lessens the need for charity. It's time for an introspective symposium.

Ten Reasons Why I Don't
Have a Credit Card

DECEMBER 5, 2014

At a recent American Antitrust Institute (AAI) symposium in Washington, DC, I asked the presenters about the ability of cash and checks to compete with the credit card industry and its strict controls on merchants. This obvious point becomes less obvious when one takes into account the expanding exclusion of cash/check payments due to the overwhelming expansion of goods and services that you cannot buy unless you have a credit card or a friend with one whom you can reimburse.

When sending some types of express mail; renting a car; or paying for the services of airlines, trains, or hotels, you either cannot pay with cash/check or it is a real hassle of inquiries and conditions. The overall trend is to limit more and more what legal tender can actually buy in America because of exclusionary fine-print contracts (see faircontracts.org).

For many people, the convenience of a credit card and potential for rewards justify their preference to forgo cash. Moreover, lower-income consumers want a brief extension of credit, however expensive. Credit card carriers are given "points" such as frequent flyer miles, but often the consumer pays in other hidden ways for these "freebies."

Notwithstanding the above obstacles, I still do not have a credit card or a signature-based debit card. There are ten relevant reasons for my preferring cash or checks over plastic.

1. Plastic lays the groundwork for massive daily *invasions of privacy*. Personal purchasing data now floats around the world without controls. The data-mining industry is everywhere, and both government and hackers can get into people's files. As Facebook and Google demonstrate, it is almost impossible to keep up with the sharing of your personal information.

2. Once you enter the credit economy, you fall under the controls of arbitrary credit-rating and credit-scoring merchants. So if you com-

466

plain strenuously to an auto dealer or insurance company, if you are a victim of false information in your credit file, or even if you have too many credit cards, your credit can suffer so that you pay more or are denied loans.

3. The credit card economy, with its anticompetitive no-surcharge rules, etc., is inflationary and negatively affects consumer purchasing power as well as lower savings rates.

4. Credit cards encourage *impulse buying*. The industry knows this very well. Swiping a plastic card rather than opening a wallet and directly taking cash out creates a disconnect between the purchase and the loss of money to the consumer.

5. Credit card terms—what Senator Elizabeth Warren calls "mice print"—are mostly inscrutable and nonnegotiable. You sign on the dotted line, shut up, and shop. Companies rarely compete over fine-print terms that favor the consumer. Compare, with a suitable microscope, the standard-form contracts of Visa, Mastercard, and Discover; or General Motors, Ford, and Toyota; or Bank of America, Citigroup, and Wells Fargo. Consumers have been driven into a choiceless contract of peonage or servitude.

6. Using cash/check encourages consumers to live *within their means* and not get caught in an ever-deeper cycle of debt. For instance, if you are out shopping with cash and set a budget for yourself, it is impossible to overspend if you simply do not bring more than has been allocated for your purchases.

7. Paying by cash/check avoids the gouging of fees, penalties, termina- tion charges, and, of course, sky-high interest rates for consumers. Corporations, on the other hand, enjoy low interest rates across the board. (Remember, however, checks have a fee if they bounce.)

8. Paying by cash/check—say, in a restaurant—saves time and follow-up monitoring for errors. Furthermore, it prevents the addition of any fraudulent charges to the bill.

9. Paying by cash/check prevents having to give away your personal property to the likes of internet companies that turn around and very profitably sell this free information to advertisers with such specificity that the latter knows what ailment or craving you have.

10. Credit card issuers often approve consumers for credit cards with maximum spending limits that are too high considering their salary or lack thereof.

Apple is now out with a payment system that does not require signing or clicking. You can regularly fall into the credit penitentiary with a mere swipe. What's next, the evocation of brain waves?

There is a strong case for giving cash discounts to consumers, as is done by many gas stations. This would pass along the savings that the vendor would make by bypassing the credit card companies to benefit the consumers, a win-win situation. In addition, there should be no discrimination against consumers based on their choice of legal tender; vendors should have to accept all methods of payment.

What a Destructive Wall Street Owes Young Americans

MARCH 14, 2014

Wall Street's big banks and their financial networks that collapsed the US economy in 2008 and 2009 were saved with huge bailouts by the taxpayers, but these Wall Street gamblers are still paid huge money and are again creeping toward reckless misbehavior. Their corporate crime wave strip-mined the economy for young workers, threw them on the unemployment rolls, and helped make possible a low-wage economy that is draining away their ability to afford basic housing, goods, and services.

Meanwhile, Wall Street is declaring huge bonuses for their executive plutocrats, none of whom have been prosecuted and sent to jail for these systematic devastations of other people's money, the looting of pensions, and destruction of jobs.

Just what did they do? Peter Eavis of the *New York Times* provided a partial summary—"money laundering, market rigging, tax dodging, selling faulty financial products, trampling homeowner rights and rampant risk-taking—these are some of the sins that big banks have committed in recent years." Mr. Eavis then reported that "regulators are starting to ask: Is there something rotten in bank culture?"

The "rot" had extended long ago to the regulators whose weak laws were worsened by weak enforcement. Veteran observer of corporate criminality, former Texas secretary of agriculture, and editor of the *Hightower Lowdown* newsletter Jim Hightower writes:

"Assume that you ran a business that was found guilty of bribery, forgery, perjury, defrauding homeowners, fleecing investors, swindling consumers, cheating credit card holders, violating US trade laws, and bilking American soldiers. Can you even imagine the punishment you'd get?

"How about zero? Nada. Nothing. Zilch. No jail time. Not even a fine. Plus, you get to stay on as boss, you get to keep all the loot you gained from the crime spree, and you even get an $8.5 million pay raise!"

Hightower was referring to Jamie Dimon of JPMorgan Chase, the "slick" CEO who has "fostered a culture of thievery during his years as a top executive at JPMorgan, leading to that shameful litany of crime."

Shame? Dimon doesn't know how to spell it. "I am so damn proud of this company. That's what I think about when I wake up every day" he said in October 2013.

Millions of young Americans (called millennials, between ages eighteen and thirty-three) should start agitating through demonstrations, demand petitions, and put pressure on the bankers and members of Congress. First the plutocrats and their indentured members of Congress should drop their opposition to a transaction tax on Wall Street trading. A fraction of a 1 percent sales tax on speculation in derivatives and trading in stocks (*Businessweek* called this "casino capitalism") could bring in $300 billion a year. That money should go to paying off the student debt which presently exceeds $1 trillion. Heavy student debt is crushing recent graduates and alarming the housing industry. For example, people currently between the ages of thirty and thirty-four have a lower percentage of housing owner-ship than this age group has had in the past half century.

A Wall Street transaction tax was imposed in 1914 and was more than doubled in 1932 to aid recovery from the Great Depression, then was repealed in 1966. But the trading volume then was minuscule compared to now with computer-driven trading velocity. A tiny tax—far less than state sales taxes on necessities—coupled with the current huge volume of trading can free students from this life-misshaping yoke of debt.

Some countries in Europe have a securities transaction tax, and they offer their students tuition-free university education to boot. They don't tolerate the same level of greed, power, and callous indifference to the next generation expressed by the monetized minds of the curled-lip Wall Street elders that we do.

What about young people who are not students? The Wall Street tax can help them with job-training and placement opportunities, as well as pay for tuition for technical schools to help them grow their skills.

A good many of the thirty million Americans stuck in a wage range lower than the minimum wage in 1968, adjusted for inflation, (between $7.25 and $10.50) are college-educated, in their twenties and thirties, and have no health insurance, no paid sick leave, and often no full-time jobs.

A youth movement with a laser-beam focus, using traditional forms of demonstration and connecting in person, plus social media, must come down on Wall Street with this specific demand. Unfortunately, while Occupy Wall Street started an important discussion about inequality, they did not advance the transaction tax (backed vigorously by the California Nurses Association) when they were encamped near Wall Street and in the eye of the mass media in 2011. A missed opportunity, but not a lost opportunity. Fighting injustice has many chances to recover and roar back.

It is time for young Americans to act! Push Congress to enact a Wall Street speculation tax to help roll back your student debt and give you additional opportunities that are currently denied to you by the inside bank robbers who never had to face the sheriffs. They owe you.

As William C. Dudley, the eminent president of the Federal Reserve Bank of New York, recently said of Wall Street: "I think that they really do have a serious issue with the public." Yes, penance and future trustworthiness enforced by the rule of law.

Young America, you have nothing to lose but your incessant text messages that go nowhere.

Start empowering yourselves, one by one, and then connect by visiting Robin Hood Tax [https://www.nationalnursesunited.org/sites/default/files/nnu/documents/0522_TaxOnWallStreet_RHT_Federal_FactSheet.pdf].

Penny Brigade, Assemble!

DECEMBER 11, 2013

Shareholders are the majority owners of many of the world's largest, most powerful corporations. Despite this fact, the muscle of shareholder ownership is often far too soft to affect the actions of greedy corporate decision-makers. Shareholders are relatively powerless to protect their share values from decline under questionable or outright poor corporate management.

This is something that must change!

Imagine if a substantial group of shareholders banded together and pledged just one cent per share they own—per year—to fund an independent watchdog operation that was laser-focused on the vital interests of shareholders? This organization's full-time staff would directly answer to each company's contributing shareholders group. A real human's time, talent, and attention would be trained on the interests of corporate shareholders and would hold corporate feet to the fire when those interests were abused.

Company by company, a shareholder watchdog could effectively bolster the power of shareholders to a whole new level of constancy.

A mere ten billion shares, out of trillions of outstanding shares, self-assessed one cent per share, would hire a full-time watchdog for each of the top five hundred corporations in the country.

Shareholders of all political leanings must arise and form such a penny brigade. They have nothing to lose and everything to gain by protecting their share values from decline or collapse. It's time for shareholders to take hold of the companies they own and fight for their rights as owners.

To join the penny brigade or for more information, send an email to shareholders@nader.org.

The Democratic Party Sleeps on FDR's Legacy

AUGUST 8, 2012

Calling Obama, Pelosi, Reid, and the rest of the Democratic Party, elected officials, political operatives, and labor leader Richard Trumka. Thirty million American workers want and need a federal minimum wage of ten dollars per hour, which is slightly less than their predecessors got in 1968—yes, 1968—adjusted for inflation. What will it take for you to make this a priority?

Of course you all would like to see these desperate workers get an additional $2,000 to $4,500 a year for the barest necessities of life for themselves and their children. Sure, it is easy to be on the record and not on the ramparts for a higher minimum wage. What about the trust that your voters and your rank and file invested in you?

Imagine mobilizing Congress to have workers catch up with 1968, when worker productivity was about half of what it is today.

What would President Franklin Delano Roosevelt, who signed the first minimum wage law in 1938, say about today's pathetic Democrats (with few exceptions, such as the more than twenty representatives who signed on to Representative Jesse Jackson Jr.'s HR 5901 bill to raise the minimum wage to ten dollars per hour)? Remember how FDR pushed his Democrats in the 1930s? He would not have tolerated today's Democratic Party of caution, cash, and cowardliness.

Were the Democrats—from the White House to Congress to Richard Trumka and the major labor unions—to immediately make the ten-dollar minimum wage a frontline national issue, which they certainly could if they wanted, here are the arguments they could make:

1. Such an overdue raise is an economically and morally necessary initiative. The US has the lowest national minimum wage ($7.25 per hour) among major western nations, by a lot. France is over $11.00, and in Canada, the minimum wage ranges from $9.40 to $11.00; plus, Canadians

have a superior social safety net. Meanwhile, the US has the highest-paid CEOs, by far, in the world.

2. Over the years, poll after poll shows that 70 percent of the people support having the minimum wage keep up with inflation. That number includes many conservatives and Republicans. Even Rick Santorum and Mitt Romney, over the years, stood for this principle, even though Romney has hemmed and hawed in recent months.

3. Are there any economists saying that our shaky economy does not need more consumer demand? A ten-dollar minimum wage quickly releases billions of dollars in new spending by the poor. Poor! The single word the cowering Democrats, including presidential candidates, have refused to use since Jimmy Carter. NPR's Tavis Smiley on his poverty tour challenges Barack Obama: "Poor. Say it, Mr. President, say it. Poor!"

4. More income for the poor means less child and family poverty, which means less reliance on federal outlays for the poor to survive. The big companies, for example, take advantage of this by steering some of their employees to programs such as Medicaid. As Terrance Heath recently noted in an op-ed for NationofChange: "So all of us are subsidizing the wealthy owners and executives of Walmart, McDonald's, and Target."

5. A new report by the respected National Employment Law Project (NELP) titled "Big Business, Corporate Profits, and the Minimum Wage," said that "the majority (66 percent) of low-wage workers are not employed by small businesses, but rather by large corporations." The fifty largest of their employers are mostly "in strong financial positions." And note this finding by NELP: "Top executive compensation averaged $9.4 million last year at these firms." This means that the bosses, before taking a lunch on January 2, made more money than a minimum-wage worker makes in a year. Talk about the corrosive effects of inequality, which have been fed by the top 1 percent taking 93 percent of the income growth in 2010, according to Holly Sklar of Business for a Fair Minimum Wage.

6. Enlightened business leaders are ready to support the Democrats on this ten-dollar minimum-wage initiative. Jeff Long, vice president of Costco, gives the obvious reasons that the retrograde corporatists ignore: "At Costco, we know good wages are good business. We keep our overhead low while still paying a starting wage of eleven dollars an hour. Our employees are a big reason why our sales per square foot is almost double that of our nearest competitor. Instead of minimizing wages, we know it's a lot more profitable for the long-term to minimize employee turnover and maximize employee productivity and commitment, product value, customer service, and company reputation."

7. 7. A ten-dollar minimum wage will create jobs because sales will increase. Businesses, having lunched off the windfall of a falling real minimum wage since 1968, should be willing to recognize this greater good. The leading scholar refuting the net job loss propaganda is Alan Krueger, who is now head of Obama's Council of Economic Advisers. Certainly the people of Santa Fe, New Mexico, are not seeing job losses there, where the city minimum wage has been $9.50 per hour.

8. The corporate oligarchy has no moral standing whatsoever. Many of the nation's corporate giants pay no income tax or very little, far less than a cab driver. Last month, Ford Motor Company paid no federal or state income taxes despite registering nearly $9 billion in profits. It is hard for companies making record profits and paying executives record pay to have much credibility on this subject. Further, small business has received seventeen tax breaks under Obama.

August is the congressional recess month. Members of Congress are back home campaigning. Go to their public meetings and ask them directly whether they will vote for a ten-dollar minimum wage when they return to Washington, DC, after Labor Day, or call their office. One worker went up and asked this question of his representative, Bill Young (R-FL), who gave him the curled lip—"Why do you want that benefit? Get a job." This snarl made news all over the country.

Ask "the question," Americans, again and again until Labor Day. By then, maybe Mr. Trumka and the AFL-CIO will bestir their political muscles and march with the low-wage workers and recognize what they do for all of us.

If you want more information and would like to sign the petition for a ten-dollar minimum wage, please visit timeforaraise.org.

Don't Thirty Million Workers Deserve 1968 Wages?

JUNE 7, 2012

Thirty million American workers, arise—you have nothing to lose but some of your debt!

Wednesday morning, Representative Jesse Jackson Jr. (D-IL) introduced the "Catching Up To 1968 Act of 2012" (HR 5901)—legislation to raise the federal minimum wage to $10.00 per hour. The present minimum wage is $7.25, way below the unrealistically low federal poverty definition of $18,123 per year for a family of three. Adjusted for inflation, the 1968 minimum wage today would be a little above $10.00 per hour.

Together with representatives John Conyers (D-MI) and Dennis Kucinich (D-OH), as well as Robert Weissman, president of Public Citizen, I was pleased to be with Representative Jackson at a news conference to explain this long-overdue necessity for millions of hard-pressed working Americans of all political persuasions.

The policy behind the minimum wage, first enacted in 1938 under President Franklin Roosevelt, was to provide a minimally livable wage. This implied at least keeping up with inflation, if not with new living expenses not envisioned seventy-five years ago. While businesses like Walmart and McDonald's have been raising their prices and executive compensation since 1968, these companies have received a windfall from a diminishing real minimum wage paid to their workers.

The economics behind the Jackson bill are strongly supportive of moral and equitable arguments. Most economists agree that what our ailing economy needs is more consumer demand for goods and services, which will create jobs. Tens of billions of dollars flowing from a ten-dollar minimum wage will be spent by poor families and workers almost immediately.

Historically, polls have registered around 70 percent of Americans favoring a minimum wage keeping up with inflation. That number includes many Republican workers who can be consoled by learning that both Mitt Romney and Rick Santorum, during their political careers, have supported adjusting the minimum wage.

Were the Democrats in Congress to make this a banner issue for election year 2012, their adversaries, Speaker John Boehner (R-OH) and Senator Mitch McConnell (R-KY), would not be able to hold 100 percent of their Republicans on this popular issue. That means the bill's backers could override these two rigid ideologues—so-called public servants—who make nearly $200 per hour plus luscious pension, health insurance, life insurance, and other benefits.

President Obama, who has turned his back on many worker issues, can champion his promise in 2008 to press for a minimum wage of $9.50 by 2011 as well as benefit his campaign by helping people who have lost trust in government and their enthusiasm over Obama's "hope and change." Getting the attention of thirty million potential voters can change the dynamics of a tediously repetitive Obama versus Romney campaign.

A debate over the minimum wage throws a more acute spotlight on the gigantic pay of the big corporate bosses who make $11,000 to $20,000 per hour! Their average pay was up another 6 percent in 2011 along with record profits for their companies.

If the Democrats want intellectual heft to rebut the carping, craven objections of the corporatist think tanks and trade associations, headed by bosses making big-time pay themselves, they cannot do better than to refer to Alan Krueger, the former Princeton professor and now chairman of the White House Council of Economic Advisers to President Obama, who is the leading scholar behind inflation-adjusted minimum wages producing net job growth.

Moreover, there is no need to offset an inflation-adjusted minimum wage with lower taxes on smaller business. Since Obama took office there have been seventeen tax cuts enacted for small businesses.

Many organizations with millions of members around the country are on the record, if not on the ramparts, as favoring an inflation-adjusted increase in the federal minimum wage. They include the AFL-CIO and member unions, especially the nurses' union, the NAACP and La Raza, and the leading social-service and social-justice nonprofits.

In 2007 at the "Take Back America" conference, then senator Obama delivered a ringing oration making "the minimum wage a living wage

[tied] to the cost of living so we don't have to wait another ten years to see it rise." Even Ontario, Canada's minimum wage is $10.25 per hour.

So why aren't all these supporters of the minimum wage inside and outside of Congress making something happen? Because they're either out of gas and need to be replaced, or they are waiting on each other to make the first move.

The nonprofits and the labor unions are waiting on a signal from senior Representative George Miller (D-CA). Minority Leader Nancy Pelosi and the House Democratic Caucus are also waiting for Miller, who has not introduced a bill increasing the minimum wage since Obama took office (the Fair Minimum Wage Act of 2007 was the last, with increases to $7.25 ending in July 2009). Of course, in turn, Obama is waiting on the Democratic leadership in Congress who, though firmly behind the increase, are waiting on Obama and, of course, Miller, who hails not from Dallas, Texas, but from the progressive San Francisco Bay area of California. Go figure.

So maybe this cycle of insensitive lethargy by the Democratic Party can be broken by the congressional stalwarts who have joined with Representative Jesse Jackson Jr. in supporting his proposal (HR 5901) for a modest increase in the minimum wage to help tens of millions of downtrodden workers catch up with 1968!

10.

HEROES

Donald K. Ross (1943–2022): Activist and Builder of Democratic Institutions Extraordinaire!

MAY 20, 2022

It was a marathon day of thirty-minute interviews in 1970. Little did I think we were selecting recent law school graduates who would become, over a lifetime, civic leaders of historical significance in producing major changes for a more just and safe society.

Ten minutes into my interview with Donald K. Ross—fresh out of New York University Law School after two years of teaching in Nigeria with the Peace Corps—I knew he was someone very special. It wasn't about any charisma or galvanizing rhetoric. It was his steady, focused, mature explanations that he gave for his qualifications and desire to engage in the work of bringing people together to create strong foundations for a better society.

Donald and two other recruits spent two months assessing the temper of campuses north and south, after which Donald and I traveled to colleges and universities meeting with active students to start their own full-time public interest research groups (PIRGs). After some disappointments, we got PIRGs going in Oregon and Minnesota. Our early groundwork helped Donald persuade students on numerous campuses to persevere and form a total of thirteen statewide student public interest research groups. There are now over twenty such groups, run by student boards, with full-time staff advocates. PIRGs have canvassed millions of households in their states to move forward with legislation on environmental, consumer, and other causes for *all* the people.

It is hard to exaggerate how difficult the process was to stay on course and negotiate with university administrations for funding to establish and keep these PIRGs going. It took Donald's immense stamina, diplomacy, and foresight to mediate student conflicts and advise students on the organizational details of their civic start-ups. These efforts overcame many a stumble and drawback before such unique, wonderful civic training and civil justice organizations got underway.

During his nearly three years with us, Donald wrote, with me, *Action for a Change: A Student's Manual for Public Interest Organizing*, to guide students in starting or running PIRGs. In 1973, he wrote *A Public Citizen's Action Manual*, which was full of projects that today still retain their importance for "public citizens" to use in their communities.

Over the next fifty years, Donald demonstrated the remarkable range and depth of his skills to strengthen our democratic society. In 1973 he became the head of the New York PIRG (NYPIRG), and over the next decade built this student-funded and student-run nonprofit into the largest state-based research and advocacy organization in the country, with offices all over the state, including in its capital, Albany. NYPIRG pushed for government accountability and advanced political reforms. Donald and his NYPIRG colleagues also challenged the banks, insurance companies, utility companies, drug companies, and toxic polluters.

Students received course credit for turning their ideals into practice through legislation, litigation, or rigorous citizen monitoring, such as the Straphangers Campaign that Donald and his colleagues set up to improve the New York City subways.

This bold, friendly, humble civic giant, adored by scores of younger colleagues he mentored, had an uncanny sense of civic opportunity. After the Three Mile Island breakdown in 1979, Donald achieved the impossible task of organizing, in three weeks, a giant "No-Nukes" rally of 100,000 people in Washington, DC, followed a few months later in September by a 250,000-person rally on the sands of the Battery Park City landfill in New York City.

He was hard to keep up with, so methodical and diverse were his projects. His work with Rockefeller Family Fund expanded the horizons of what philanthropy could do to advance justice. He cofounded and helped manage the Environmental Grantmakers Association, which has grown to two hundred member foundations around the world. He expanded the impact of the Tortuga Foundation, which advances efforts to protect public lands and the environment, including the priceless Tongass National Forest in Alaska.

Together with one of his former student organizers Arthur Malkin, he started a large public relations firm (M+R Strategic Services) and a public interest law and lobbying firm (Malkin & Ross). They represented the interests of nonprofit organizations, most of whom hitherto had little muscle with lawmakers at the state and federal levels. He led fights against Big

Tobacco, Big Oil, and the Defense Department's toxic contamination of its military reservations and its contiguous environments and communities.

From 2009 to 2017 he undertook the improbable task of uniting Republican and Democratic state legislators in the passage of about two hundred bills regarding juvenile justice reform in nearly forty states. To do this he traveled incessantly with the support of the John D. & Catherine T. MacArthur Foundation, with whom he conceived the campaign.

A father of three, Donald always had time to travel, including a memorable trip with his wife, Helen, throughout rural China and his well-known "treks" with close friends up the Himalayas.

I was fortunate to discover such an unsurpassed superstar citizen organizer and builder of sustainable democratic institutions. He had an extraordinary civic personality of resilient stamina, motivated others by self-disciplined example, and had a relentless focus on results.

Millions of people who benefited from his proliferating projects never knew this modest man's name.

He was too authentic, too productive, and too generous in crediting others to warrant any media coverage. (His hometown newspaper, the *New York Times,* would do well to do more reporting on the civic community.)

Those Harvard professors who wrote the recent book *How Democracies Die* should now study the life and lasting achievements and institutions of Donald K. Ross to show how democracies can live. They would learn how much he has to teach them and millions of other Americans presently sinking into paralyzing discouragement and inaction in the face of Trump-driven fascism.

America lost a frontline champion of democracy and justice in action with the passing of Donald K. Ross on May 14, 2022. His legacy—the forces he put into motion—will continue to nourish what he and his collaborators fought for during the last half century. For more information about Donald K. Ross visit: donaldkross.org).

The Other 1 Percent

MAY 22, 2015

As a high school student, I came across an observation by Abraham Lincoln, who said that "with public sentiment, nothing can fail; without it nothing can succeed." Today "public sentiment" would be called "public opinion."

Over the years, I have been astonished at how less than 1 percent of the citizenry, backed by the "public sentiment," have changed our country for the better by enacting reforms to protect the people from abuses of power, discrimination, and deep neglect.

Specifically, if 1 percent or fewer people were to dedicate a modest amount of their time and money working together for much-needed changes that are overwhelmingly supported by public opinion in each congressional or state legislative district, they would prevail against the government and corporate power structures.

There are obstacles, such as a corporate influence over city hall and wavering politicians who insincerely pledge support but defer and delay action. But, if people work together, almost any problem can be solved.

History shows that it only takes a dedicated few to gain the momentum from many more to enact change. The major drives to give women the right to vote, workers the right to form unions and secure numerous protections, and farmers regulation of railroads and banks did not require more than 1 percent of seriously active champions. Those in power understood that there was overwhelming support for these reforms by affected populations.

Even the abolition movement against slavery was well underway in our country before Fort Sumter and did not involve more than 1 percent of the people, including the slaves who fled via the Underground Railroad. By 1833, the British Empire, including Canada, had already brought slavery to an end.

More recently, the breakthrough laws in the late sixties and early seventies regarding auto and product safety, environmental health, and occupational safety drew on far less than 1 percent of seriously engaged supporters. The air and water pollution laws were supported by widespread demonstrations that did not require a large burden of time by the participants. These air and water pollution laws, not surprisingly, were very popular when introduced, and the public made its support known to lawmakers with numerous phone calls and letters. Other reforms (auto safety, product safety, and occupational safety measures) were pushed through with far fewer than 1 percent of engaged citizens, as was the critical Freedom of Information Act of 1974.

Along with the small full-time advocacy groups, a modest level of visible activity around the country aroused the media. The more citizen power the media observed, the more reporting, and this in turn led to greater public awareness.

Lately this pattern can be seen in the efforts to enact civil rights for the LGBTQ community and to pass a substantially higher minimum wage for tens of millions of workers being paid less now than workers were paid in 1968, adjusted for inflation. The latter has become a front-burner issue at the city, state, and congressional levels, with picketers in front of McDonald's, Burger King, Walmart, and other giant low-paying chains over the past two years. Those pushing for higher wages number less than the population of Waterbury, Connecticut (approximately 110,000). The Service Employees International Union, some think tanks, organizers, writers, and economists rounded out this less-than-1-percent model of action for justice.

It is important to remember that the active 1 percent or less, with the exception of a handful of full-timers, are committing no more time than do serious hobbyists, such as stamp and coin collectors, or members of bowling leagues and bridge clubs, or birdwatchers.

Why is all this important? Because in a demoralized society full of people who have given up on their government and on themselves, and who are out of the public civic arena, learning about the 1 percent model can be decisive, can be hugely motivational and encouraging, especially with emerging left-right alliances. Prison reform, juvenile justice, crony capitalism, civil liberties, unconstitutional wars, and sovereignty-shredding and job-exporting trade treaties that threaten health and safety protections are all ripe for left-right action (see my recent book *Unstoppable: The Emerging Left-Right Alliance to Dismantle the Corporate State*).

Youngsters grow up exposed to numerous obstacles that tell them they "can't fight city hall" or the big corporate bosses. Unfortunately, they are not taught to reject being powerless, because they learn myths, not reality, and they graduate without civic skills and experience. Small wonder why so many of them could easily be members of a Society of Apathetics.

But lawmakers want to retain their jobs. Companies want to keep their customers. On many issues that could so improve livelihoods and the quality of life in America, it is important to bring to everyone the history and current achievements of the 1 percent who stood tall, spoke, and acted as the sovereign people our Constitution empowers them to become.

Send more 1 percent examples to info@nader.org.

Morton Mintz Turns 100—Investigative Nemesis of Corporate Criminals

JANUARY 25, 2022

"Hi Mort," began my calls to Morton Mintz, who would invariably answer his phone promptly at the *Washington Post*, "I've got a story," to which Mintz would respond warily: "Tell me about it." And so it went for nearly twenty years between Mort and me and lots of other citizen advocates, whistleblowers, and congressional committee staff. More than any other reporter, Mintz broke open the walls surrounding the media's noncoverage of serious consumer, environmental, and worker harms and rights.

The big advertisers and corporate lawyers, such as Lloyd Cutler, kept complaining to the *Post* publisher, Kay Graham, about his exposés and relentless stories that nourished congressional investigations, lawsuits, and prosecutions.

Mintz was not deterred, even from championing the *Post*'s union troubles with management. In 1978 the *Post* assigned him to cover the Supreme Court, making him an "official-source journalist," which he intensely disliked. (Official-source journalists rely on government officials or corporate executives as sources and often fail to quote activists or even academic experts.) After two years he went back to reporting, but by then Reagan was president, the Democrats' hold on Congress was weaker, and Washington was closing down on the citizenry in favor of the corporate supremacists.

Soon after Mintz joined the *Post* in 1962, from his job at the *St. Louis Globe-Democrat*, he broke the story about Thalidomide—a drug used as a sedative and to treat morning sickness that was given to pregnant mothers, causing thousands of children, mostly in Europe, to be born without arms or legs or sometimes no limbs at all. Fortunately, an alert scientist at the Food and Drug Administration (FDA), Frances Oldham Kelsey, spared America by refusing to approve Thalidomide. Mintz also wrote numerous stories about inadequate FDA tests for the birth control pill. His various probes into the drug industry led to his first book published in 1965, *The Therapeutic Nightmare*.

I met Mintz during the General Motors detective scandal in 1965. GM's detectives were hired to "get dirt" on this young lawyer challenging the auto industry's unsafe motor vehicles that put style and horsepower over saving lives with proven safety devices. Together with Jim Ridgeway, then at the *New Republic*, Mintz broke the story of a GM gumshoe following me into a Senate office building. The private detective mistook Bryce Nelson, a *Washington Post* reporter, for me. The following excerpt from the documentary *An Unreasonable Man* captures this bit of history:

BRYCE NELSON: I was walking to the old Senate office building, underground corridors that they used, and one of the Capitol policemen said to me, "You'd better get out of here; there are a couple of detectives following you." And I said, "What you do mean?" "There are two guys following you." He said, "Didn't you write a book on auto safety?" I said, "No."

MORTON MINTZ: It was February of '66, a Saturday afternoon, when Ralph Nader told me he'd been followed the previous day. Well, you can't write a story saying somebody says he's being followed when there's absolutely no evidence of it.

BRYCE NELSON: I felt that I better tell somebody in case I wound up face down in the Potomac or Anacostia rivers. I mean, something strange was going on, so I told my editor, the national editor of the *Washington Post*, Larry Stern.

MORTON MINTZ: And then Larry Stern, my boss, told me that another *Post* reporter who has white skin and black hair had told him something very similar.

BRYCE NELSON: Because we were so tall, thin, dark . . . dark hair.

MORTON MINTZ: I was, you know, astonished to have this confirmation.

A special attribute of Mintz is that he stayed with the story; he wasn't interested in a major one-time feature. That steadfastness helped consumer advocates and congressional staffers, such as Michael Pertschuk, immensely in their step-by-step drive to regulate corporate outlaws.

What made him stay on the story was not just his professionalism and his regard for the readers, but his passion for justice for the underdogs. He epitomized the aphorism "information is the currency of democracy."

Mintz's corporate critics were many. They knew of his commitment and told his editors that his emotions made him biased. Whether exposing the tobacco companies, the asbestos industry, or the medical device and pharmaceutical business, the corporatists tried to trip him up. He was just too factual, too full of evidence, and too aware of not going beyond the boundary of accuracy to fall prey to the corporate drive to silence or discredit him.

No matter how tense or explosive the subject, Morton had the softest tone of voice. He had a logical, linear, disarming way of interrogating industry people and others who did not believe in the public's need to know.

If he had a complaint, it was that he couldn't get enough space in the paper for his fact-packed reporting. To augment his reporting, he joined with lawyer Jerry S. Cohen in writing *America, Inc.* and *Power, Inc.* to overwhelmingly and devastatingly detail the abusive power of big business over America.

He was keen on mentoring younger reporters about journalistic standards and independence. No one felt the brunt of commercial advertisers more than this inexhaustible reporter of what was going on in the dark recesses of corporate systems. In 1985, he wrote the deadly story of the criminal A.H. Robins Company in his book titled *At Any Cost: Corporate Greed, Women, and the Dalkon Shield.*

The *Post* publishers and editors liked the journalistic prizes that Morton Mintz received, but they did not give him the cachet accorded to flashier journalists on the staff. Sometimes, the editors were downright irritated at how his exposés upset the business side of this large corporation registered on the New York Stock Exchange.

At a social gathering at Kay Graham's home, to which I was invited, she amiably asked "How's your Morton Mintz?" As if anyone could induce him to ever write a story that didn't hold up, or that didn't merit the high standards of newsworthiness the reading public deserved.

About the time he was leaving the *Post* in 1988, Mintz wanted to write a book about the American Association of Retired Persons (AARP) and its entanglements with the health insurance and other industries. Touted as an organization of elderly consumers, AARP was also a seller of services. It contracted out its huge membership for "Medigap" coverage and auto insurance to giants such as United Health Insurance and auto insurers, from which it took a large share for its budget. Unfortunately, he couldn't find a publisher. It is noteworthy that many years later no one picked up where he left off to write such a book.

In a 1996 *Washington Monthly* article, Mintz, who was troubled by reporters' namby-pamby questions to political candidates, prepared a list of twenty-seven serious questions whose answers would have probed the candidates' positions or lack thereof on such topics as corporate influence, campaign contributions, ethics, labor, military spending, and consumer policies. Needless to say, his dittoheaded colleagues largely ignored this veteran reporter's attempt to give them more professional significance and make news.

Full of quiet energy (except on the tennis court) Mintz even managed to coauthor books with his daughter, Margaret (*Quotations from President Ron*, 1987), and with his beloved late wife, Anita (*President Ron's Appointment Book*, 1988).

I had lunch with Morton when he turned ninety-five. I recall his utter astonishment at being informed that most email-driven *Washington Post* reporters do not return telephone calls to learn about scoops, leads, reactions, or corrections the way he used to.

Happy hundredth birthday (January 26), Morton. May your example reach the next generation and may they be energized by your impeccable career as a reporter.

We Honor What We Value—
Entertainers Over Saviors

MAY 6, 2020

"We honor what we value" goes the old saying. In our hedonistic culture we value most those who can put a ball in a hole. We ignore those who save lives through civic action.

The sports champions—golf, basketball, football, and baseball—receive riches and accolades from the masses. They are inducted into halls of fame and are the subjects of biographies, documentaries, and feature films. As for the mass lifesavers—few even know their names, much less their dramatic victories against overwhelming odds.

I was reminded of this contrast by a major *New York Times* sports feature on Tiger Woods and his comeback win in the 2019 Masters Tournament, which was watched breathlessly by millions of golf fans around the world. Praises poured in on social media, and many articles, features, and editorials covered every nuance of this golf match.

Barack Obama tweeted, "To come back and win the Masters after all the highs and lows is a testament to excellence, grit, and determination."

What about the excellence, grit, and determination of economist James Love? In the midst of the horrendous HIV epidemic, Love brilliantly organized, argued, wrote, and traveled the world before he found Dr. Yusuf Hamied and Cipla, an Indian company that took down Big Pharma's $10,000 price for HIV drugs per African patient per year to $300 per patient. Neither Love nor his allies William Haddad and Robert Weissman were the subjects of features in major media outlets.

Others in the unsung circle of self-motivated stalwarts are David Zwick, Clarence Ditlow, Dr. Sidney Wolfe, and Joan Claybrook. Zwick helped write the Clean Water Act of 1972 and then started Clean Water Action, which canvassed tens of millions of homes, distributing materials sparking local citizen action and nationally lobbying against water pollution for over four decades.

Engineer and lawyer Clarence Ditlow ran the Center for Auto Safety in Washington, DC, and over forty years caused the recall of millions of defective cars. He also got the states to enact "lemon laws" to give voice to new-car owners getting justice when their new car turned out to be a "lemon." Over roughly the same time span, Joan Claybrook repeatedly blocked the auto giants' constant efforts to weaken or stop federal safety regulation that protected motorists.

As for Dr. Wolfe, with his small team, he produced three major books: *Worst Pills Best Pills, Pills That Don't Work: A Consumers' and Doctors' Guide to Over 600 Prescription Drugs That Lack Evidence of Effectiveness,* and *Over the Counter Pills That Don't Work,* reaching millions of consumers through mass audience outlets such as the *Phil Donahue Show.* Dr. Wolfe also persistently pushed the FDA and drug companies to remove hundreds of ineffective and/or dangerous drugs from the market, thus preventing health-threatening side effects and saving consumers billions of dollars. Those are just a few of the successes of Dr. Wolfe's Public Citizen Health Research Group.

In 1971 three scientists spun off from our organization to start the Center for Science in the Public Interest (CSPI). Still turning its pistons nearly fifty years later, its longtime leader, Dr. Michael Jacobson, went after the junk food and drink industry and the deadly amount of high-salt, high-fat, and high-sugar content in processed foods with scientific rigor and persistence. CSPI publishes the very popular health newsletter *Nutrition Action* and uses litigation and regulatory interventions to educate the public. CSPI arguably changed the nutritional habits of millions of people and exposed the slick and deceptive ads and crude direct marketing to children by the fast-food chains and the cereal manufacturers. These companies are heavily responsible for the childhood obesity epidemic and its ongoing malignant health consequences.

Then there are Karen Ferguson and Karen Friedman running the Pension Rights Center in Washington, DC. They provide members of Congress and labor unions with technical advice on pension policy, inform the press, and help thousands of pensioners who are being ripped off by employers. Only trillions of dollars are at stake.

For these and many other long-term fighters for justice up against cruel or reckless corporations and their political toadies, there are few accolades, almost no recognition, and no citizen Hall of Fame. (See breakingthrough-power.org.)

It is time for foundations or the enlightened super-rich to start an annual Citizen Academy Awards to correct this imbalance of recognition and offer the mass media some inspiring content. This big-time dramatic event would elevate our priorities as a society and showcase motivating role models for our youngsters. Perhaps Barack Obama could be the first MC for this authentic reality event.

To put the spectator mania for professional sports in perspective, we can listen to the words of the great all-around Hall of Fame superstar, the late Al Kaline of the Detroit Tigers. At his peak in the 1960s, he told *New York Times* reporter Ira Berkow: "Sometimes I wonder what I'm doing, if I've wasted my time all these years. And sometimes I think I have. I would like to have more to contribute to society. I don't know, maybe a doctor. Something where you really play an important part in people's lives."

Al Kaline was one humble, great athlete compared, with some luminous exceptions, to the "me, me, me" narcissism of too many sports stars today. Sports superstars could easily direct more support and attention to those little-recognized citizen advocates who protect the serious necessities of life on shoestring budgets.

Moreover, in these critical times, the selfless dedication of the nurses, doctors, grocery store clerks, postal workers, sanitation laborers, and other truly essential workers should spark long-overdue recognition of these valiant heroes and their critical contributions to our lives beyond the stage or stadium. ESPN has just broadcast a ten-part series about Michael Jordan and the Chicago Bulls' triumphant years of putting balls in holes for championships. Someday a network may produce a *ten-part series* on how citizen leaders historically built the justice safeguards that benefit us all. We should make it happen as owners of our public airwaves.

S. David Freeman: Seven Decades of Participating in Power for All of Us

MAY 28, 2020

If the planet Earth were animate, it would have shuddered at the news that S. David Freeman passed away this month. Freeman was that important to Earth's future. In his ninety-fourth year, he inspired all he met with his burning passion, relentless energy, and keen intellect.

Freeman, an engineer and a lawyer, knew where decisions were being made or ignored regarding our energy future. He mocked the foolish embrace of fossil fuels and warned all who would listen about the deadly impact of coal, oil, and natural gas consumption on our environment. This humble son of an immigrant umbrella repairman made the most of his formidable talents over seven decades and helped steer mankind toward renewables and energy efficiency. Freeman worked to prevent the perilous use of fossil and nuclear fuels.

Freeman was one of the first environmentalists to warn us of the dangers posed by fossil fuels, and he was one of the first to offer practical remedies. He started his career in the 1950s as an engineer with the Tennessee Valley Authority (TVA) before holding a series of positions with the Federal Power Commission and the Johnson White House. In 1974 Freeman authored the Ford Foundation's groundbreaking report *A Time to Choose: America's Energy Future*. He was an adviser to President Jimmy Carter, who appointed him chairman of the giant TVA in 1978.

At the TVA, Freeman managed with a no-nonsense, down-to-earth, results-focused approach to reform. Using what he learned at TVA, Freeman became known for turning around giant hidebound utilities that were unable to process evidence that was contrary to their wasteful ways and environmental destructiveness. The tenacious Tennessean had no patience for self-serving talk that avoided obvious solutions. Freeman was a serious advocate who used humor, wit, and charm to make his case in the court of public opinion and the corridors of power. "Mother Nature doesn't care what we say; Mother Nature only cares about what we do," he would remind bloviators!

Freeman shut down or suspended construction of half a dozen nuclear reactors at the TVA, scoring them as dangerous, uneconomical, and unnecessary. He liked "free" sources of energy, such as solar and wind, instead of lethal coal, gas, oil, and uranium that had to be ripped perilously from the bowels of the Earth. As for vast opportunities afforded by energy-efficient sources, he paraphrased Benjamin Franklin, saying a megawatt of energy that isn't wasted is a megawatt you don't have to produce.

In between his clearheaded impact on conferences around the world—advising presidents, governors, members of Congress, and parliaments—and many cogent writings, Freeman ran three other giant utilities (other than TVA, Freeman ran utilities in California, Texas, and New York). At Sacramento Municipal Utility District (SMUD), he implemented a public vote against the troubled Rancho Seco Nuclear Generating Station, replacing its energy with conservation and renewables.

In the decades I knew David, he always made the changes he implemented look easy because he so deftly and honestly used evidence, facts, and economics—sometimes to rectify his previous positions. He used his knowledge to serve the public that was too often shoved aside by bureaucratic and corporate vested interests.

Freeman had that unparalleled combination of managerial experience, scholarly knowledge, and programmatic urgency in confronting the climate crisis. We would invite him for brown-bag lunches with younger leaders working on energy transition. He would "out-urgent" them, mocking dilatory cap-and-trade ideas while demanding mandatory reduction in fossil fuels and ending nuclear power, and replacing them with job-producing energy conservation, retrofitting homes and buildings as solar and wind ramp up. Freeman said, "We need to pass a law that says that every utility in this country must reduce their greenhouse gas emissions by 5 percent of 2020 emissions every year, starting now, and until we get down to zero."

You may be wondering why you haven't seen Freeman on television or read about his urgent proposals, as a doer, covering the crisis of climate and regular air, water, and soil safeguards from ruinous extractive fuels.

Certainly, the mass media has devoted many hours and pages to these subjects, interviewing far lesser and often conflicted people on NPR, PBS, commercial networks, and major newspapers. I made many calls to energy and environmental reporters about David's availability, but to no avail.

Was it ageism? Which is rampant. Was it his free-thinking challenges to named influential corporations? Was it that he was seen as no longer an adviser to powerful officials? At age ninety-three he was flying to California to negotiate the closure of the last nuke plant there with Pacific Gas Electric. He coauthored a book, *All-Electric America: A Climate Solution and the Hopeful Future,* with Leah Y. Parks in 2018, and his human-interest memoir, *The Green Cowboy: An Energetic Life,* in 2016. Recently he was meeting with the pro–Green New Deal members of Congress. But the media wasn't calling. Until, that is, David's "energetic" life came to an end and the obituary pages gave him his due in the *Washington Post,* the *New York Times,* and other outlets. Unlike celebrity entertainers and athletes, however, he didn't make page one. But his prescient legacy is an enduring example of how we can save our green planet and brighten our future. Biographers may wish to wrap their minds around this functional, enlightened life of such immense productivity.

They Don't Make Republicans Like the Great Paul Findley Anymore!

AUGUST 22, 2019

They don't make congressional Republicans like Congressman Paul Findley anymore. Not even close!

In his twenty-two years in Congress (1960–1982), Paul Findley achieved a sterling record for fundamental positions, proposals, and breakthroughs that revealed a great man, pure and simple. He never stopped learning and applying his knowledge to advance the right course of action, regardless of political party, ideology, or pressure from various groups.

Findley, a courteous, kindly World War II Navy veteran, passed away earlier this month at the age of ninety-eight in his hometown of Jacksonville, Illinois. The district he represented was the one Abraham Lincoln was elected from for his one term in the House of Representatives. Findley was a student of Lincoln's life, and embraced Lincoln's view that "a politician should be willing to reject outmoded ways of thinking that no longer fit the times."

Findley was a thoughtful, studious legislator with a superb sense of justice. He was an early civil rights champion. His opposition to runaway presidential war-making was reflected in his leading support for the War Powers Resolution of 1973, though he wanted stronger curbs on the White House's unilateral militarism.

Having been a journalist and owner of a small-town newspaper, the *Pike Press*, before going to Congress in 1960, Findley used his writing skills to explain issues regarding agricultural policies, a foreign policy of diplomacy and peace, and nuclear arms controls. He was an outspoken early opponent of the Vietnam War and a critic of the Pentagon's chronically wasteful spending. He was not a "press-release" legislator, staking out his opinions and leaving it at that. He worked hard and smart to lead, to persuade, to get down to the minute details of coalition-building, lawmaking, and legislating.

Back in Jacksonville, after his congressional career ended in 1982, Findley wrote books and articles and lectured around the country. He courageously defended Americans of the Islamic faith after 9/11 from bias, exclusion, and intimidation. He did his civic duties with local associations. He also started the Lucille M. Findley Memorial Foundation, in memory of his beloved wife—an Army nurse—whom he met in wartime Guam. They had two children. He always found time to be helpful, to serve others both locally and nationally. He also played tennis daily into his mid-eighties.

Findley possessed more than a streak of Midwest populism. Agricultural subsidies disproportionally going to a few wealthy landowners upset him greatly. He got through the House, after years of rejection, and over the objections of the Republican leadership, a $20,000 yearly limit of such subsidies per farm. The measure failed in the Senate.

Once again, in 1973, he bucked his party and introduced an impeachment resolution against Nixon's vice president Spiro Agnew, who later resigned in disgrace over a bribery scandal.

It was Findley's interest in US policies and operations in the Middle East—following his successful 1973 effort to obtain the release of a constituent from South Yemen—that showed his moral courage, his belief in dialogue between adversaries, and his commitment to the treatment of all people with dignity and respect. It also led to his defeat by Democrat Dick Durbin, now Illinois's senior senator.

Findley learned that the dispossessed and occupied Palestinian people were being treated unfairly and deprived of their human rights and self-determination. He visited refugee camps in the region. He met with Yasser Arafat, head of the Palestine Liberation Organization (PLO), and urged peaceful diplomatic resolution of that conflict. For this sensible though rare outreach by a congressional lawmaker, he earned the immense enmity of US partisans of the Israeli government. How dare he speak out on behalf of Palestinians even though he continued to vote for foreign aid to a prosperous, militarily advanced Israeli superpower?

As the *New York Times* reported: "He became convinced that the influential pro-Israel lobby known as Aipac, the American Israel Public Affairs Committee, had a stranglehold on American politicians that prevented the establishment of a Palestinian state and prevented rational dealings with Arab leaders in general."

AIPAC activists, nationally and with their local affiliates, openly mobilized to defeat Findley in the 1980 election. They failed to do so. In 1982, they tried again, helping his Democratic opponent, Richard Durbin, to end Findley's congressional career by a margin of less than 1,500 votes. AIPAC took credit for the win, raising over 80 percent of Durbin's $750,000 in campaign funds from around the country. AIPAC's executive director told a gathering in Texas: "We beat the odds and defeated Findley."

Three years later, in 1985, Findley wrote and published his bold book *They Dare to Speak Out*, which described his efforts at peaceful advocacy for a two-state solution, now supported by many Israelis and Jewish Americans. In his book, he profiled other Americans who dared to speak out, and who endured intimidating slander and ostracism. Findley's documentation of the suppression of their freedom of speech was an early precursor of what is going on now.

It was acceptable for the early patriots to boycott British tea, for civil rights leaders to boycott certain businesses in the South, for opponents of South Africa's apartheid to launch a worldwide economic boycott. But some state governments impose sanctions on their contractors if they merely speak out in favor of the call to boycott, divest, and sanction Israel's illegal and brutal occupation of Palestine and its millions of Palestinians. (Today, Palestine is only 22 percent the size of the historical Palestine.)

Findley wrote his autobiography in 2011. But it will take a fuller biography to place him—this modest lawmaker, public citizen, and wager of peace over unlawful wars and rampant militarism—in the conforming context of his times. His career contrasts with the present GOP of big business, Wall Street over Main Street, and militarism, and shows that the Republican Party didn't always demand rigid unanimity.

To his credit, Senator Durbin eulogized Paul Findley as "an exceptional public servant and friend." He added that the man he defeated was "an elected official who showed exceptional courage in tackling the age-old controversies in the Middle East."

Senator Durbin could not say this about a single Republican in either the Senate or the House today, nor of over 95 percent of the Democrats.

Herb Kelleher of Southwest Airlines—
One of a Kind!

JANUARY 9, 2019

When Herb Kelleher, the joyous, fun-loving founder and retired CEO of Southwest Airlines, soared past permissible flight levels for passenger aircraft on his way to heaven last week, the accolades in the exuberant obituaries were also sky-high.

Listen to former American Airlines CEO Bob Crandall: "He was a man of great imagination. He was a man of diligence. He paid careful attention to the details. And he was a man of integrity. I think we will look back on Herb Kelleher as an example of the kind of people who ought to be our leaders."

Herb (everyone called him Herb), was much more than a super-successful creator of a low-fare, no-frills, high-pay, unionized, constantly profitable airline (since 1973) that never laid off any workers, with consistently high customer-approval ratings and the most solid financial stability in a boom-bust, highly-regulated industry. In overturning the stagnant, brusque customs of the industry, he overcame its cartel-like ways, with four Boeing 737s in 1971 flying between Dallas, San Antonio, and Houston. After beating back numerous lawsuits by other airlines trying to stop his fledgling enterprise, he rewrote the book on management for a large company.

For starters, he put employees, not consumers, first. That seemed ineffective to me at first. But then came his explanation. You treat employees well in all ways, occupationally and personally, they'll treat airline passengers well and safely, which makes the airline prosper for the shareholders. He did all three, having fun along the way. More than a few of his pilots, attendants, and other staff became—as workers/shareholders—millionaires.

Making money was not his personal first priority. Making work pleasurable and exciting and giving employees discretion to bring the best from themselves—not playing rigidly by rule books—gave him the most professional gratification.

After a while it probably did not surprise him that his wealth grew and grew to an estimated $2.5 billion.

His way of doing business, motivating people, and relieving their anxieties should invite many diverse living memorials to him. It is easy to think of many ways to recognize business practices that could be established in his same joyously productive fashion.

I've made no secret that Southwest is my favorite domestic airline. There is no second. When I step from the Jetway onto the plane, I invariably say to the flight attendants and pilots "the best airline in America," often adding that it reflects the pioneering ways of Herb Kelleher.

Once I called him to say that he is such a critical asset to the airline that shareholders should pass a resolution demanding that he stop his five-pack-a-day smoking habit.

His successor, CEO Gary Kelly, captured the full breadth of Kelleher's lifelong contributions. Kelly said: "His legacy extends far beyond our industry and far beyond the world of entrepreneurship. He inspired people; he motivated people; he challenged people—and he kept us laughing all the way."

Born in Camden, New Jersey, in 1931, young Herb worked in a soup factory where his father labored, later calling it his best education (including his time at Wesleyan and New York University Law School) because it taught him how to interact with and understand all kinds of people—and "how to produce results, not just paper."

He attributed to his mother an outstanding influence. In one of his many writings, he described why: "She had a very democratic view of life. She had enormously wide interests in politics and business, so it was very educational in that respect, just talking with her. We'd sit up and talk to two, three, and four o'clock in the morning when I was quite young about how you should behave, the goals that you should have, the ethics you should follow, how business worked, how politics can join with business."

When you fly Southwest and order refreshments, the flight attendant brings you the drink and a napkin emblazoned with the airline's motto: "In a world full of no, we're a plane full of yes."

To make such an expectation a reality, Kelleher put in place a recruiting priority that placed "temperament" above talent and skill. He would say, "We could change skill levels through training. We can't change attitude."

Southwest ate the lunches of their stodgy competitors by doing business differently: no first-class seats, no seat assignment, more leg room, lower fares, fast turnaround for its efficiently used aircraft (a record-breaking fifteen minutes), a great safety record, no fees for changing reservations or checking two bags, using less congested, near-to-cities airports (e.g., Chicago, Dallas), flying only one class of airplane—the Boeing 737—to reduce maintenance and training costs and avoid the "hub and spoke" inconvenience for travelers. Southwest engaged in fuel hedging that locked in prices and then won the bet, saving hundreds of millions of dollars over their competitors when fuel prices soared. It also, until recently, answered the phones immediately with a human being. Its global mileage-reward program rejects termination dates. It is now the nation's largest domestic airline, conveying 120 million passengers last year to over a hundred destinations.

"We market ourselves on the personality and spirit of ourselves," Kelleher told an interviewer. That's why some flight attendants love to tell jokes during the pretakeoff announcements, which gets passengers to either chuckle or roll their eyes in mirth.

Kelleher was a many-splendored human being. He and his wife, Joan Negley, raised a family of four children. He had a robust, quirky side to him, riding motorcycles and engaging in amusing stunts that have become legendary in both family and company history.

With his fifty-eight thousand productive employees, Kelleher, in the words of airline industry analyst Robert Mann, "literally brought air travel to the masses on a scale that was unimaginable." Small wonder that Herb immediately approved my suggestion that Southwest's mantra should be "We do not imitate!"

His self-deprecation was consistently funny. One sample: "Because I am unable to perform competently any meaningful function at Southwest, our employees [they were also shareholders] let me be CEO."

No one has been able to imitate Kelleher's super-successful management philosophy, hands-on behavior, or authenticity. They may install cut-rate fares, but unfortunately for the people, Kelleher stands as one of a kind.

Warner Slack—Doctor for the
People Forever

JULY 18, 2018

Warner Slack was a humble, multifaceted, great American physician at Harvard Medical School's affiliated hospitals. Yet after he passed away last month at age eighty-five, Dr. Slack did not receive the news coverage accorded numerous late entertainers, athletes, writers, and scoundrels. In fact, his life was ignored by the *New York Times* and the *Washington Post*.

Dr. Slack, in his pioneering, brilliant, humane work, always focused on the lives of the American people, whom he served in the millions, directly and indirectly.

It has been said that in a celebrity culture, we honor whom we value. Along the way the most important human beings who give us the blessings of liberty, justice, health, safety, knowledge, and overall well-being mostly are missed or slighted by the priorities of a commercially driven culture. These people lift up our society every day on their largely anonymous, selfless shoulders.

In his final days, struggling with pulmonary fibrosis, I called Dr. Slack to express my deepest admiration and said: "For all your adult life, Warner, you have been a physicians' physician, a patients' physician, a students' physician, a citizens' physician, and a champion of peace and justice." This gentle, many-splendored medical doctor achieved such excellence in an age of specialization and amorality.

Dr. Sidney Wolfe, the nationally known longtime director of Public Citizen's Health Research Group, called Warner "a hero of mine."

Just what did Warner Slack do to receive such encomiums? First, he was an early vocal medical practitioner who supported universal health insurance when few were urging such humanity. He was among the first physicians in the world to see and apply the potential of computers in health care delivery but declared that advances mattered only if they advanced patients' well-being. He insisted on patients being informed and empowered, and he led the way from his clinical practice in ending the absurdity of prohibiting patients from accessing their own medical records. Over the opposition of most of his profession and hospitals, he pressed on until this basic patient right was enacted as part of the Health Insurance Portability and Accountability Act.

Dr. Slack founded the Division of Clinical Computing from which flowed many professional articles and studies, including prescient warnings about how computers, when misused, can invade patients' privacy and waste a ton of taxpayer money. He also pointed out that mindless converting from paper records to digital records might ill-serve the patients.

Once in a rare while, we meet relentlessly honest and courageous people who instinctively and cognitively see through the ruses, the snares, the delusions, and the profiteering propaganda that harm innocent, trusting people in so many grave ways.

Unlike many innovators who bask in the limelight of praise, Dr. Slack humbly kept at it, pressing for how his breakthroughs could actually benefit patients and not be hijacked for the almighty dollar. Human beings were never to be reduced to numbers.

As his son, author Charlie Slack, wrote:

> [Warner Slack's] article "The Patient's Right to Decide," published in the British journal *The Lancet*, put forth a then-radical idea of "patient power"—encouraging patients and physicians alike to overturn the traditionally paternalistic nature of healthcare. Patients, Dr. Slack believed, should play a crucial part in determining their own care. Their insight, he often said, was "the least utilized resource in healthcare."

As an original thinker, a visionary, and a rigorous conveyer of medical ethics and responsibility to the hundreds of young clinicians he mentored or trained, Dr. Slack maintained his steadfastness with a remarkable congeniality and the human touch.

In pain and hospitalized for weeks, he never complained. His demeanor and continual regard for the orderlies, nurses, and physicians who took loving care of him revealed his authentic character.

An early defender of the underdog, he was among the first physicians to publicly oppose the Vietnam War, to go down South to help injured civil rights marchers, even working to help ease the integration of the University of Wisconsin football team. While in his seventies, he twice went to Honduras to provide medical assistance to residents of impoverished remote villages.

A Princeton classmate of mine, Warner and I got to know each other better in 1980 when he and our Center for Study of Responsive Law independently issued tough critiques of multiple-choice standardized testing (SATs, etc.). As the author or coauthor of many articles, book chapters, newspaper op-eds, and books, such as *Cybermedicine: How Computing Empowers Doctors and Patients for Better Health Care*, Warner was very aware of phony studies, deceptive statistics, and other technical ways to manipulate people.

Together with his colleague Douglas Porter, he authored, in the *Harvard Educational Review*, the myth-busting article "The Scholastic Aptitude Test: A Critical Appraisal." They demonstrated that, contrary to Educational Testing Service's defiant assertions, aptitude was not frozen, and test scores could be raised by studying and training for the tests. They also showed that SAT scores are poor predictors of college academic performance compared with high school grades.

Our study "Reign of ETS: The Corporation that Makes Up Minds" added that nonquantifiable traits, such as diligence, creativity, stamina, and even motivational idealism, can be more important as predictors of college performance.

This year, Warner's critiques were further vindicated by the news that, joining some other colleges, the University of Chicago has dropped these standardized tests as a requirement for admission.

Warner managed his interests and professional activities and duties without sacrificing being with his wife, Carolyn; their three children; and seven grandchildren. He relished these gatherings where he expressed his limitless curiosity about the world and continued to be, in Charlie's words, "a person defined mainly by his youthfulness."

Someone once said that "the only true aging is the erosion of one's ideals." No one who knew and worked with Warner viewed him as "elderly." He couldn't have been more contemporary and forward-looking with his classmates whenever they gathered for meetings regarding their unique alumni class organization—Princeton Project 55, which placed Princeton undergraduates and graduates with systemic civic groups around the country.

Dr. Slack was as complete a brainy, humane, down-to-earth, big-picture human being as you could ever meet.

He left this life in Carolyn's arms on the morning of their 62nd wedding anniversary.

His legacy is strong, deeply rooted in his many students and colleagues, and is lastingly conveyed in his writings and exemplary career, under pressure and controversy.

A biography of Warner Slack and his times needs to be written.

Donations may be made to the Warner Slack Scholarship for Clinical Informatics. In order to donate, select the aforementioned scholarship under "gift designation."

Needed: An Educational Institute to Extend Dick Gregory's Legacies

SEPTEMBER 6, 2017

On hearing about the loss of Dick Gregory, at age eighty-four, political analyst and former White House counselor Bill Curry said, "He was the first successful black comedian who insisted on having opinions."

Until Dick Gregory—with his pioneering, satiric, audacious humor on stage and on national TV, which made white audiences laugh their way into reality. Author Mel Watkins told the *Washington Post* that "Mr. Gregory broke the mold among black comedians by employing political satire at a time when audiences expected black performers to do minstrel skits in baggy pants and outsize shoes and use slapstick humor." Breaking through the national media in the early 1960s—from *Time* magazine to the famous Jack Paar's TV show, *Tonight*—Dick Gregory showed America that he could connect comedy with a myriad of important social justice causes, even at the expense of his career.

Watkins describes Gregory well: "He was sharp. He was urbane. He smoked a cigarette onstage. He was very calm in demeanor but very outspoken in what he said. . . . He brought in current political and social issues into his comedy—which was astounding to most white Americans at that time. It was during a time when blacks were considered incapable of doing this."

Before an audience of white Southern business executives, he hit at segregation, saying, "I know the South very well. I spent twenty years there one night." Unruffled by hecklers shouting racial epithets at one nightclub, he responded calmly that his contract with the club stipulated a fifty-dollar bonus each time someone used "the N-word," and he invited the audience to keep on saying it. Moreover, he titled his 1964 memoir *Nigger: An Autobiography*—coauthored with Robert Lipsyte—so that every time the slur was spoken, it was advertising the book, which became a bestseller.

In a 2000 interview with NPR, a serious Dick Gregory said this about "the N-word": "Let's pull it out of the closet, let's deal with it, let's dissect it. It should never be called 'the N-word.'"

One of his classic jokes that showed his wit, timing, and imagery went like this: He walks into a restaurant in the segregated South where a wait-ress declares, "We don't serve colored people here." Mr. Gregory replies: "That's alright, I don't eat colored people. Just bring me a whole fried chicken."

But the former high school and college track star, Army veteran, and father of eleven children was much, much more than a searing comedian whose humor exposed deeper truths behind inhuman conditions around the country and the world. No one showed up at more rallies, demon-strations, or pickets; conducted more fasts; was arrested for nonviolent protests more times—sometimes beaten and spat upon—over half a cen-tury than this wiry, bearded advocate for a world without malice and hate.

The last time I saw Dick Gregory was in 2014. We were participating in a rally for DC statehood with Mayor Vincent Gray. I came to the stage and tapped him on the shoulder saying, "Mr. Gregory, is this your first protest?" He turned around and, for an instant, gave me a quizzical, speechless expression before we both broke out laughing.

In a long front-page obituary recognizing his impact, the *New York Times's* Clyde Haberman writes: "There seemed few causes he would not embrace. He took to fasting for weeks on end, his once-robust body shrinking at times to 95 pounds. Across the decades, he went on dozens of hunger strikes, over issues involving the Vietnam War, the failed Equal Rights Amendment, police brutality, South African apartheid, nuclear power, prison reform, drug abuse and American Indian rights." His com-mitment to civil rights did not keep him from being an opponent of all injustices, such as mass hunger and lack of universal access to health care.

Indeed, Mr. Gregory battled on all possible fronts. In 1967 he ran for mayor of Chicago to challenge longtime mayor Richard J. Daley for his harsh crackdown on peaceful protesters. A year later he traveled the country running for president against Richard Nixon. He joined causes with John Lennon, and in 1980 he went to Tehran to try and free the US Embassy officials being held by the new revolutionary regime that toppled the US-backed dictator. He fasted down to ninety-seven pounds before being compelled to leave the country.

Amidst increasingly trivial and frivolous (and not just a little ageist) mass media, his formerly publicized fasts were increasingly ignored, as were his other activism and actions. Unfazed, Dick Gregory became a popular five-day-a-week presence on the college campus lecture circuit and continued putting out albums and writing books.

Along with the white comics Lenny Bruce and Mort Sahl, Mr. Gregory was all about breaking taboos, defying stereotypes, and combating entrenched modes of oppressive power.

Unlike other high-profile comedians, Dick Gregory refused to deliver profanities or obscenities to get his points across or to provoke his audience's attention. He was unique, using current events and social tensions to fuel his incisive imagination.

He still has millions of fans, most of them now over forty-five and some with ample discretionary income, not to mention the affluence of the leading comics for whom he paved the way. Can a determined core of Gregory devotees organize to start a center or institute in his name to extend his examples of civic courage, remarkable communication skills, and the combination of humor and steadfast seriousness that induces people to listen and open their minds? Our tense, manipulated society needs the kind of clean, contemporary new satire that such an institute, among other purposes, can engender with a new generation of comedians showing that "in humor there is truth."

George H. Haddad—Unsung Excellence in Medicine

JANUARY 24, 2017

Ever wonder about the people who make our health care system work at a time when reports of greed, fraud, profiteering, and harmful malpractice are rampant and remedies are not advanced?

I was recently reminded how hard these proficient and caring physicians, nurses, and physician assistants are working day after day and how their commitment to patients and their profession receives so little recognition. The sad occasion for these reflections was the passing this month of Dr. George H. Haddad, an alert 101-year-old surgeon who had worked for many years in New York City's public hospitals.

Growing up in Egypt, he graduated from the American University of Beirut Medical School and returned home to serve poor farmers in a small village in the Nile Delta. Later he would say that was one of the most fascinating experiences in his life.

He came to New York City in 1947 and began a life of singular commitment to patients. He believed profit-seeking should be taken out of medical practice as much as possible. He certainly practiced what he preached as a staff physician who worked long hours for modest remuneration. Soon after his arrival in New York, fellow physicians and nurses noticed his drive toward perfection; his keeping up with developments in surgery; his quiet, reassuring bedside manner; his unfailing courtesy and mentoring of staff; and his readiness, as a bachelor, to take the place of other doctors wanting to spend holidays with their families.

He took the hard cases in emergency rooms where victims of crimes flowed into highly pressurized situations. One year he conducted more surgeries than any other physician in New York City. During these procedures, he noticed that many surgeons could not easily differentiate between the wounds that penetrated into the abdominal cavity from those that did not. As a result, the customary procedure was to operate into the abdominal cavity, which was often excessively invasive. Drawing on the medical literature and his experience, he was instrumental in introducing surgical techniques to save patients from unnecessary operations, an improvement that, since the late sixties, has spread all over the world.

Dr. Haddad also knew a great deal about the waste, redundancy, and gouging in the health care economy. He favored a reorganization of medical care where primary care would be very local and the more technologically intensive care would be in regional centers. He saw the increasing corporatization of his beloved profession as interfering with professional judgments, leading to profitable overdiagnosis, overtreatment, and higher prices resulting in patients without universal health insurance not being able to afford to pay for basic health care.

Inasmuch as he was my second cousin, I would often call and ask him for specialists to help friends and associates. He had an uncanny sense of who the best physicians in many fields were, not just in their skills, but also for their character and personality.

He viewed the profession of medicine as one where self-renewal was critical, where prevention was the first duty and availability for treatment was to be maximized. He was always willing to be on call and ready for any emergency.

I would frequently query him whether any public official would ask for his advice on improving the health care industry, about which he knew so much, or whether anybody in the media ever wanted to interview him in place of the usual bloviators or hucksters. He would smile and shake his head no.

As far as disputes over medical behavior, he wished for lawyers not to be just adversarial but also technically informed. In that pursuit, he wrote a meticulous chapter in the encyclopedia *Proof of Facts* on foreign items left inside patients during operations and ways to avoid such damaging malpractice.

George Haddad's self-effacing, honest, generous lifetime work for sick and injured people evokes the observation by the ancient Greek philosopher Aristotle. The sage wrote, "We are what we repeatedly do. Excellence, then, is not an act, but a habit."

Would that there were more public recognition of such regular, consistent, and faithful excellence, if only to provide an exemplary legacy for future generations.

Ken Bossong—"Favorite Sun"

OCTOBER 14, 2016

If Mother Sun were to select a *favorite son* on Planet Earth, Ken Bossong would be high on the list. Operating for over forty years on a tiny budget from a tiny office in Takoma Park, Maryland, the unsung solar energy advocate has been a one-man informing and organizing machine.

He founded the Sun Day campaign in 1992 to, in his words, "aggressively promote sustainable energy technologies as cost-effective alternatives to nuclear power and fossil fuels."

With renewables like solar and wind energy becoming the fastest-growing sources of new energy in many areas of the world, Bossong is now seeing his long and often frustrating battles against the traditional corporate skeptics increasingly vindicated. The doubters—often fueled by vested interests in oil, gas, coal, and atomic power—called solar unreliable, too diffuse, said that energy from solar couldn't be stored and that it was too expensive to produce.

I recall in the seventies, nuclear engineers at the Hanford Reservation in Washington State said derisively that solar power was just "sophisticated plumbing"—unworthy of the attention of skilled technical talent.

Notwithstanding their rhetorical dismissals, the fossil fuel and nuke companies saw solar as bad for more parochial reasons. Solar could put them out of business or at least cut into their sales. Solar could be produced in a decentralized manner that would disrupt monopolies; solar was a suitable vehicle for small businesses and homeowners to seize control away from the centralized power of the Big Energy giants. Solar also has the advantage of being safer, more abundant everywhere, and environmentally benign.

The visual contrast could not be clearer. On the one hand there are the oil spills and air pollution, the pipeline problems of natural gas with its deadly methane and greenhouse gas releases, the vast destruction of coal—strip mines and subsidence, blown-away mountains, dirty air, and millions of coal-worker casualties from lung disease and coal-mine collapses over the past 130 years. On the other hand, solar panels, solar thermal, solar photovoltaics, and wind power draw a stark contrast. If wind power locations cause some controversies, they pale in comparison to the unsafe, uneconomic, uninsurable, stalled nuclear technology that now has to rely on a 100 percent taxpayer guarantee for any expansion. Moreover, it would be impossible for people near most nuclear power plants to evacuate in the event of serious nuclear power accident.

Steadfast and serious, Ken Bossong calmly steeps himself in the startling statistics put out by the Federal Energy Regulatory Commission and the US Energy Information Administration, which are showing that "nuclear power is rapidly losing the race with renewable energy sources."

Consider three data sets from six months in 2016 by these two agencies. In *energy production*, renewable sources (biofuels, biomass, geothermal, hydropower, solar, and wind) accounted for 5.242 quadrillion Btus (quads) of domestic energy production. By comparison, nuclear power provided only 4.188 quads. That is, renewables outpaced nuclear by more than 25 percent.

In total, available installed *generating capacity* in the US, from the combination of utility-scale renewables, has grown to 215.82 gigawatts or 18.39 percent of total generating capacity, while nuclear power's installed capacity is only 107.06 gigawatts or 9.12 percent of the total.

However, reports Bossong, actual electrical generation by nuclear plants for the first seven months of 2016 is 19.9 percent of total generation. This has been steady for many years and is still higher than that provided by renewable sources which contributed 15.8 percent (a figure which does not include electricity produced by distributed renewables such as rooftop solar).

These figures are rarely reported in the mainstream media. Instead the newspapers and radio and television companies are taking millions of dollars in advertisements from the Nuclear Energy Institute—a lobbying arm of the atomic power industry—declaring that the safe, clean power of the atom is the wave of the future. There is no mention of aging plants, earthquake risks, the recent shutdown of several nukes, nor the cessation of new construction due to extreme costs. The latest disaster at Fukushima in Japan dissolved the nuke industry's mantra that risks of meltdowns are "vanishingly small."

The political power of the fossil fuel and nuclear lobbies is much greater than the renewables lobby. Over the decades, they have forged tight relationships with federal and state lawmakers and executive agencies. Many of their officials are well-placed in government positions. And fossil fuel fat cats like the Koch brothers are busy pumping money into election campaigns.

Yet look around you. Installers are placing solar panels on homes and other buildings all over the country. Wind turbines are being erected on hillsides everywhere. Geothermal energy's nascent promises are finally coming to fruition. Major companies like Google are moving toward renewables and are even investing in their generation.

A long-distance runner, Ken Bossong continues to press his Sun Day campaign. Sign up for Sun Day campaign alerts by sending an email to sun-day-campaign@hotmail.com. Twitter: follow @SunDayCampaign. Ken Bossong is another example of one person making a serious difference.

Twelve People Who Made a Difference
(And You Can Too!)

JANUARY 8, 2016

Can one person truly make a difference in the world?

Far too many people think not, and thus they sell themselves far too short. A wave of pessimism leads capable people to underestimate the power of their voice and the strength of their ideals. The truth is this: it is the initiatives of deeply caring people that provide the firmament for our democracy.

Take a sweeping look at history and you will discover that almost all movements that mattered started with just one or two people—from the fight to abolish slavery to the creations of movements for the environment, trade unions, consumer protection, and civil rights. One voice becomes two, and then ten, and then thousands.

It's fitting that this time of year marks the seventy-ninth anniversary of the sit-down strike in Flint, Michigan, in which thousands of workers sat down in a General Motors factory to fight for recognition of the newly formed United Auto Workers (UAW) union. On February 11, 1937, General Motors conceded to raising wages and labor standards and recognizing the UAW, a major win for unionization in the United States.

This is an aspect of the American story that most people love and celebrate, yet sadly are quick to dismiss as being improbable in today's partisan, corporate-dominated world. But as I often say, real change is easier than you think.

The following twelve men and women maximized their power as citizens to improve the lives of millions of people in real, tangible ways. Let their stories serve as an inspiration to you in the coming year.

1. **LOIS GIBBS.** Lois lived with her family in the Love Canal neighborhood of Niagara Falls, New York, when news of the toxic contamination beneath their feet made local headlines. Lois organized her neighbors into what was known as the Love Canal Homeowners

Association. Her movement grew to become the country's largest grassroots antitoxic movement. She later founded the Center for Health, Environment & Justice.

2. **RALF HOTCHKISS.** I first met Ralf at Oberlin College over forty years ago; he was majoring in physics and moving about the campus in a wheelchair after a high school bicycle accident that had rendered him paraplegic. Recognizing a need for low-cost, sustainable, and versatile wheelchairs, he started Whirlwind Wheelchair to teach people around the world how to manufacture their own wheelchairs in small-shop facilities.

3. **CLARENCE DITLOW.** Once described by the *New York Times* as "the splinter the [auto] industry cannot remove from its thumb," Clarence Ditlow is an engineer, lawyer, and the executive director of the Center for Auto Safety. He has been responsible for car companies initiating millions of lifesaving recalls and was instrumental in the passage of "lemon laws" in all fifty states, which compensate consumers for defective automobiles.

4. **AL FRITSCH.** A Jesuit priest and PhD, Al Fritsch was the environmental consultant at Center for the Study of Responsive Law in Washington, DC, before returning to his roots in Appalachia to start the Appalachia Center for Science in the Public Interest. Using applied science and technology, Al Fritsch is a driving force for sustainability and maintaining a healthy planet.

5. **RAY ANDERSON.** The late Ray Anderson was founder and CEO of Interface, the world's largest modular carpet manufacturing firm based in Atlanta, Georgia. Disturbed by the hugely damaging effects of industry on the environment, he shifted his company's directive to "make peace with the planet." With the ultimate goal of zero pollution and 100 percent recycling for his company, he managed to move toward these objectives while reducing expenses year after year and increasing profits. Why aren't more CEOs following his example?

6. **ANNIE LEONARD.** With her widely successful Story of Stuff project, Annie Leonard scoured the world for the stories that tell the

tale of where our throwaway economy is leading us (hint: it doesn't have a happy ending). Her imaginative twenty-minute *Story of Stuff* film has been watched and shared online by millions, and was turned into a book and an ongoing website. She is now the executive director of Greenpeace.

7. **WENONAH HAUTER.** As the founder and director of Food & Water Watch, Wenonah has fought tirelessly for the future of our food, water, energy, and environment. A relentless organizer, author, and activist, she is a champion in getting citizens involved in issues that matter most—the things we put in our bodies.

8. **DR. WILLIAM J. BARBER.** The Reverend William Barber walks with a cane, but he is making big strides for justice and equality through his organizing of "Moral Mondays" protests, which first started in North Carolina. The protests started as a response to the "mean-spirited quadruple attack" on the most vulnerable members of our society. In the tradition of the Reverend Martin Luther King, Reverend Barber is fighting restrictions on voting and for improvements in labor laws. In addition to his work as a minister, Reverend Barber is the president of the North Carolina National Association for the Advancement of Colored People.

9. **MICHAEL MARIOTTE.** For over thirty years, Michael Mariotte has been a leader in successful movements against nuclear power in the United States. As the president of the Nuclear Information and Resource Service, Michael has testified before Congress and spoken in countries around the world against the dangers of nuclear power and its radioactive byproducts.

10. **DAVID HALPERIN.** David is a tenacious advocate and tireless worker for justice who has launched several advocacy organizations and projects such as Progressive Networks, the American Constitution Society, and Campus Progress. Nothing gives him greater joy than thwarting those with positions of power in our society who seek to profit from unjust practices. Most recently, Attorney Halperin has focused his considerable talents on exposing the predatory and deceptive practices of for-profit colleges.

11. **SID WOLFE.** Sidney M. Wolfe and I started the Public Citizen Health Research Group in 1971 to promote good health care policy and drug safety. Dr. Wolfe, through his *Worst Pills, Best Pills* books, newsletters, and outreach via the *Phil Donahue Show*, has exposed by brand names hundreds of ineffective drugs with harmful side effects, which were then removed from the marketplace.

12. **DOLORES HUERTA.** A legendary activist, Dolores Huerta cofounded the United Farm Workers union with Cesar Chavez in the 1960s and has a long history of fighting for social change, workers' rights, and civil justice. She was rightfully awarded the 2011 Presidential Medal of Freedom, among many other awards and recognitions.

Our country has more problems than it should tolerate and more solutions than it uses. Don't allow cynicism to silence your voice—people matter, *you* matter, and systemic change will only happen when citizens speak out, gather, and believe in themselves and their ideals.

The Activist Awards

FEBRUARY 12, 2014

The annual Academy Awards gala, viewed by one billion people world-wide, is scheduled for the evening of March 2, 2014. Motion pictures and the people who act in and produce them are center stage. Apart from the documentaries, this is a glittering evening of "make believe" and "make business."

Now, suppose our country had another Academy Awards gala for citizen heroes—those tiny numbers of Americans who are working successfully full-time in nonprofit groups to advance access to justice; general operations of our faltering democratic society; and the health, safety, and economic well-being of all citizens.

This must sound unexciting in comparison to the intensity of the world of film—until you see what these unsung people do in your local communities, your state, and your country. Then let's see if you think what my choice of civic heroes do every day isn't exciting. They are selected because they work in groups associated either directly or indirectly with me over the course of several decades.

1. **CLARENCE DITLOW.** Clarence was the director of the Center for Auto Safety and an engineer and lawyer. Mr. Ditlow has forced the auto companies to recall millions of defective motor vehicles, has brought auto companies to justice on many occasions in courts of law, and puts out volumes of information to inform elected representatives and the public about the need for stronger federal regulation of the resisting auto industry.

2. **JAMES LOVE.** James is the director of Knowledge Ecology International. As a mere high school graduate, he stunned specialists with the brilliance of his written analysis of energy subjects in Alaska. Mr. Love has been on the move all over the world challenging the tax-sub-

sidized, highly profitable drug companies to stop gouging millions of patient-victims with "pay or die" marketing schemes. Big Pharma endured a rare defeat in 2001 when Mr. Love convinced Dr. Yusuf Hamied, head of India's Cipla pharmaceutical company, to break the $10,000 per patient per year drug treatment for AIDS and bring the cost down to $300 per year (fireintheblood.com).

3. **DR. MICHAEL F. JACOBSON.** Michael was a young PhD student in biochemistry at MIT when I interviewed him for a position with us. I told him we were looking for long-termers. He nodded. Nearly forty-five years later, Dr. Jacobson, having started the Center for Science in the Public Interest, has done more than anyone to document and brightly publicize enjoyable nutritional diets with less salt, sugar, and fat. His center knows how to communicate. *Nutrition Action* goes to 900,000 subscribers. He sends messages to your stomach in order to stimulate your mind.

4. **AL FRITSCH.** Another scientist PhD, Al joined us at the same time as did Michael Jacobson. He didn't spend much time in Washington before he returned to his home region of Appalachia, where he started the Appalachia Center for Science in the Public Interest. Applied science and technology, as if people mattered most, was his credo. He pioneered simple, old, and new ways—for example, to preserve the land and forest, make the drinking water safe, and grow more food—that he conveyed to local people of all ages who then became community scientists creating their own innovations.

5. **LOIS M. GIBBS.** Lois started as a mother and housewife until she saw what the chemicals seeping through the ground of her middle-income housing project in Niagara Falls were doing to residents, especially children. She then became unstoppable, moving from protesting for a cleanup to starting the Center for Health, Environment, and Justice in 1981 with chapters and activists all over the country taking on and often winning the battle against the silent violence of reckless industries.

6. **DR. SIDNEY M. WOLFE.** Sidney founded with me the Health Research Group of Public Citizen. Do you want to see what a small

group of half a dozen people can accomplish in getting rid of hundreds of prescriptions and over-the-counter drugs that don't work? Or do you want to learn how Dr. Wolfe has kept the Food and Drug Administration's feet to the fire and held many doctors accountable to professional standards? Or how about investigating scores of harmful conditions bred by the avarice or incompetence of the medical/hospital/drug industry complex? (See: citizen.org/healthletter.)

7. **JOAN CLAYBROOK.** Joan went from heading our immense Congress project—which issued magazine-size profiles of every member of Congress going for reelection in 1972—to running the National Highway Traffic Safety Administration for President Jimmy Carter, and then to the presidency of Public Citizen for nearly thirty years, without missing a beat. The auto companies called her the "Dragon Lady." A fixture on Capitol Hill, she roared down the corridors on behalf of safety protections for millions of Americans.

8. **KAREN FERGUSON.** Karen started, a few years out of Harvard Law School, with my help, the Pension Rights Center (PRC) in 1976. Karen and her staff dedicated themselves completely to being a watchdog of Congress, the Department of Labor, and a myriad of corporations, proposing legislative and regulatory changes and responding to the growing crisis of declining or looted traditional pensions for millions of workers. One of the biggest economic injustices in our economy is the loss or shredding of defined benefit pensions, which either aren't being replaced or are replaced by exploitable 401(k)s. Trillions of dollars and millions of families are affected—luckily, the PRC and Ms. Ferguson are there year in and year out.

9. **ROBERT C. FELLMETH.** In 1970 Robert brought hundreds of eager law students from Harvard and other law schools to work with us. In a short time, he authored or coauthored three large books, then went to California to become a prosecutor, then combined a career as law professor, litigator, and leading public advocate for children through his Children's Advocacy Institute. No one can ever outwork or outproduce Fellmeth. His example has prompted his associates to coin the word "Fellmethian." His emphasis on children—protection,

legislation, lawsuits, exposés, and a unique annual California Children's Budget only provide a glimmer of this creative civic giant's prodigious successes.

10. **ROBERT G. VAUGHN.** When his mid-twenties, Robert chose our Center for Study of Responsive Law's project on federal civil servants. His work became a book titled *The Spoiled System* (1975). Over forty years later he teaches at American University Washington College of Law in Washington, DC; is an expert on civil-servant law; and is the world's leading authority on whistleblowing in dozens of countries (see *The Successes and Failures of Whistleblower Laws*, Edward Elgar Publishing, 2012). He has inspired hundreds of law students to treat law as justice and practice along that pathway.

11. **JOHN RICHARD.** John has worked with us since 1978, becoming a peerless networker and adviser for citizen groups, their leaders, and staff on all kinds of subjects. In his thirty-five years, he has participated in more gatherings and action meetings on more topics than anyone. This has nourished the wisdom of his assistance to scores of civic advocates who seek his help. Mr. Richard avoids taking any credit, but his daily low-key pushing forward of the train of justice speaks for itself.

These people of significance, and many more stalwarts who labor in the vineyards of a better life for all Americans, receive far less public attention than cartoon characters, misbehaving entertainers and athletes, and carousing politicians.

The more difficult, despairing, and overburdened are the livelihoods of millions of hard-pressed Americans, the more they spend time becoming spectators of mass entertainment and sports as a distraction and relief from their painful and desperate situations.

A drama-filled activist award night for civic courage and creativity will inspire millions of viewers to try their hand at operating the levers of power for the good of our society. And what is more dramatic than real-life struggles and successes for justice against the bullies, the greedhounds, and the authoritarians who presently make up the few who rule the many?

Dare it be said that the more people immerse themselves in learning about these heroics, the more compelling will be their civic interest and passion. Certainly there is more meaning to their daily lives than watching make-believe or someone putting a ball in a hoop or into the ground.

Where is the enlightened billionaire who can launch such a televised national activist awards evening for the greatest work of humans on Earth—which is advancing justice?

The Other Buffett Takes on Hunger

JUNE 25, 2014

He could have chosen an easier path in life. After all, Howard G. Buffett is the son of brainy investor Warren Buffett. Instead, he chose to become a working farmer in Decatur, Illinois, and launch a serious effort to fight world hunger in poor countries and in the United States (where fifty million humans are food insecure) with self-sustaining, locally rooted solutions.

In so doing, he has made substantive visits to over 120 countries, some of which were in the most dangerous, chaotic regions of the world, including Eastern Congo, South Sudan, and violent areas of Afghanistan. He interacts with local farmers on the most minute aspects of soil, water, and seeds, plus the problems of credit, transportation, and finding local markets.

You see, Howard Buffett is a determined empiricist and a self-taught agronomist. He wants to know what is working well with the land and what can be improved, sometimes with the help of his foundation but always with the real changes coming from the local cultures and local famers.

His group has experimental farms in Arizona and South Africa to analyze, test, and improve the diverse chains of food production for the nearly one billion adults and children in the world who suffer from chronic hunger and its lifelong physical and developmental burdens. From all this constant traveling deep into the afflicted places where subsistence farmers live, "his body has taken a terrific beating," in the words of one knowledgeable person who has been with him on a few of these trips.

Years ago (he is fifty-nine years old) Howard Buffett started his travels as an experienced photographer of endangered species, such as the cheetah and the mountain gorilla. These adventures in wilderness habitats and the "experiences of the poor" introduced him to his more recent calling to take on world hunger.

I know this from reading his fascinating, critical, encouraging, often anthropological new book *40 Chances* (Simon & Schuster, 2013) which recounts, with his own photographs of the young and old, the Howard G. Buffett Foundation's efforts to help get things underway and make a difference in places where people are suffering the most. He is not reluctant to admit mistakes; he learns from them and starts fresh.

His father wrote these words in the foreword of *40 Chances*: "Howie's love of farming makes his work particularly helpful to the millions of abject poor whose only hope is the soil. His fearlessness has meanwhile exposed him to an array of experiences more common to adventurers than philanthropists."

This is a book with great empathy and little ideology. Mr. Buffett opposes hedge funds being able to purchase large tracts of agrarian land in Africa, as this has a long-lasting, damaging impact on the people of those countries.

Howard Buffett writes that "we need to act with urgency. People are dying and suffering *today*." He quotes his father's advice: "Concentrate your resources on needs that would not be met without your efforts. . . . Expect to make some mistakes; nothing important will be accomplished if you make only 'safe' decisions."

Throughout the book, it is clear that Buffett believes in advancing solutions that are localized and lasting, rather than putting forth charity that is temporary, external, and induces dependency, or worse, becomes an inducement for corrupt seizure of food by local powers.

The book is rich with engrossing details. Buffett believes in utilizing or rediscovering old knowledge from these rural areas as well as using appropriate modern technologies that are affordable. "We can't use Western thinking to solve African challenges," he writes. Still, he is big on no-till techniques and cover crops.

Buffett's poignant chapter on hunger in Illinois brought forth his admission that he hadn't realized how "widespread and yet hidden it was," there and around our country.

He has visited and been impressed by the Rodale Institute's work on organic food in Pennsylvania. Yet he uses and believes GMO crops are necessary to meet the growing demands of the world's hungry. I look forward to the empiricism of the open-minded Mr. Buffett as he receives reports from scientists and field analysts here and abroad whose opinions differ from his, among them being the increasing evidence of resistance by mutating weeds and insects that will require ever more powerful and costly herbicide and pesticide applications (see genewatch.org).

I recommend his 411-page book for immersion reading, especially for urban and suburban people who have little understanding of what has to be done to get food to people who cannot casually drive to the local super-market and stock up.

And stay tuned to the widening efforts (such as helping East Congolese "make soap from palm nut oil") of Howard Buffett and his widening arc of informed self-starters on four continents. They are serious about imple-menting workable solutions. As long as he does not go too hard on himself personally and can avoid being "too busy" to achieve more, I believe that the best of Howard G. Buffett is yet to come.

Pete Seeger—Character, Personality, Intuition, and Focus

JANUARY 31, 2014

After ninety-four years, on January 27, 2014, the world lost Pete Seeger. The world is the lesser for that loss. The accolades for this giant of folk songs and herald of all just causes are pouring in from around the world. He is celebrated for regularly showing up at mass protests, for singing songs so transcendent ("This Land is Your Land"; "We Shall Overcome"; "Where Have All the Flowers Gone") they are sung in many foreign languages all over the Earth, and for his mentoring and motivating of millions of people and children.

Pete Seeger overcame most of his doubters and adversaries. On his famous five-string banjo, he inscribed the slogan, "This machine surrounds hate and forces it to surrender."

No less than the *Wall Street Journal*, after reprinting an ugly commentary on Seeger's earlier radicalism, wrote: "troubadour, rabble rouser, thorn in the side of the bloated and complacent, recipient of the National Medal of Arts, American idealist and family man, Seeger maintained what Mr. Springsteen called his 'nasty optimism' until late in life."

At a Madison Square Garden songfest for Seeger's ninetieth birthday, Springsteen added: "Pete Seeger decided he'd be a walking, singing reminder of all of America's history. He'd be a living archive of America's music and conscience."

I met and spoke to Pete Seeger a few times and can attest to his steady determination and uplifting spirit. All the above are measures of this authentic man and his rare traits of character, personality, intuition, scope, and focus.

The man's character shone when he was subpoenaed before the powerful House Un-American Activities Committee (HUAC) in August 1955; along with other outspoken entertainers and actors, he refused to take the easier way out and invoke the Fifth Amendment against self-incrimination. Instead, he made himself vulnerable to later prosecution by pleading the First Amendment and his right to free speech, petition, and assembly.

After rejecting the committee's probe about whom he associated with politically and his beliefs, he suggested that they discuss the music that the committee members found so objectionable. He offered unsuccessfully to sing his songs, then and there, before the startled, clenched-jaw politicians.

"I think," he told them, "these are very improper questions for any American to be asked, especially under such compulsion as this." In those days, that was an astounding act of courageous character.

He paid the price when he was prosecuted and convicted before winning his appeal. In those years of witch hunts of "commie symps" by McCarthyite zealots, his career nearly collapsed. Television networks banned him for over a decade; record companies shunned him; concerts dwindled. So what did he do? He continued recording, touring among everyday people around the country, learning music from them and singing on street corners, at union halls, churches, schools, and what he called "hobo jungles."

He quit a popular band he formed—The Weavers—after it did an advertisement for Lucky Strike cigarettes. More recently—according to his producer, Jim Musselman, and record label, Appleseed Recordings—he turned down an offer by BP of $150,000 to use one of his songs in a commercial, even though he could have given the money to charity.

Complementing this sterling character, Seeger possessed a stunningly functional personality. His resilience in overcoming setbacks, ideological adversaries, and smear specialists was legendary. That was because he never let his ego get in the way and wear him down and he recognized the big picture of social change and how he could use his stardom to amplify the people's efforts for peace, justice, the environment, and other necessities of the good life. It helped mightily that he was married to the stalwart Toshi for seventy years.

"The key to the future of the world," he remarked in 1994, "is finding the optimistic stories and letting them be known." In 2009, he said his task was "to show folks there's a lot of good music in this world, and if used right it may help to save the planet." He placed his greatest hope in women wisely teaching their children. Three years ago, he won a Grammy for his album *Tomorrow's Children*.

His connection with audiences of all kinds, here and abroad, was uncannily attuned to getting them to participate and sing. For Mr. Seeger, it was not about the song or the singer—these were the means—it was about the audience's own experience.

He disliked the overwhelming sound of rock that blotted out the lyrics. The lyrics, he believed, were what needed to be communicated and therefore had to be heard, sung, and understood. That is one reason he avoided electric guitars and other electrified instruments.

In his biography, by David Dunaway, titled *How Can I Keep from Singing: Pete Seeger*, Mr. Seeger spoke about rural traditions. "I liked the strident vocal tone of the singers, the vigorous dancing. The words of the [folk] songs had all the meat of life in them. Their humor had bite, it was not trivial. Their tragedy was real, not sentimental."

Arlo Guthrie, son of the great Woody Guthrie, a mentor of Seeger's, played with Pete for nearly fifty years. He spoke to *Time* magazine about his magic in getting audiences to "relax and sing along with him. My eyes just opened up and I couldn't believe what was happening in front of me. He would just wave his hand, and you could hear people singing. . . . Someone who has not [seen him] will find it hard to believe. It was almost as if he had some extra sense that allowed that kind of response. There's no one else I have ever seen in my life that has had that, on any country, on any continent or in any city. Nobody came close."

His intuition was augmented by a vast knowledge of American history, astonishing memory, and what one reporter called "a vast repertoire of ballads, spirituals and blues songs."

Seeger's scope covered just about every social justice cause that arose from the people and some that he helped ignite, such as opposing wars and cleaning up rivers. He knew what he was singing about, such as when he focused on his beloved Hudson River. He launched his famous 106-foot sloop, the Clearwater, whose journey with musicians up and down the Hudson unleashed civic and litigation energies that have greatly reduced the pollution of that storied river. Again and again, the Clearwater would take adults and children on these trips so they could appreciate the river, learn, sing, and resolve to combat the polluters, such as General Electric and its dumping of PCBs, or polychlorinated biphenyls. The children, recounted Musselman, would go home knowledgeably motivated and urge their parents to act. The work done on the Clearwater is now a model for cleanup efforts in other rivers.

This man, who led sing-alongs and gave benefit concerts for the downtrodden and the defiant, would bring his audience to silence and then joyous singing. Imagine today's domineering, ear-splitting, flashing bands jetting their fans into frenzied, uproarious, sweaty reactions with the sounds drowning out the lyrics. That was never Seeger's vision. Thank goodness he leaves behind hundreds of hours of music that both stimulates the ears and sweetens or alerts the mind.

Musselman related a powerful example of how Pete Seeger communicated at gatherings. He quotes Seeger as saying, "Nelson Mandela went from prison to the presidency of his country without a shot being fired. The Berlin Wall came down without a shot being fired. And did anybody think there would be peace in Northern Ireland? There is always hope when it comes to unlikely social change."

"Pete planted many seeds all over the world," Musselman concluded. That is why Pete Seeger lives on.

The Jolting Peter Lewis— a CEO Who Mattered

DECEMBER 5, 2013

Insurance, art, architecture, civil liberties, auto safety, think tanks, peace, free thinkers, political candidates, marijuana, his alma mater Princeton University—these and other varied interests drove the inspiring career of the late Peter Lewis, chairman of the board of Progressive Insurance, who passed away at age eighty last month.

He interacted with many people who sparked his sense of the "unconventionally possible" as he built Progressive into the nation's fourth-largest auto insurer and made himself into one of the nation's leading philanthropists.

Peter was my classmate at Princeton. More than twenty-five years ago, I suggested he equip his company cars with air bags, both to prevent costly crash injuries to his employees and also to set an example for other insurance companies to give meaning to their "loss prevention" rhetoric. At lunch, he grasped the suggestion immediately and agreed. When I called for a progress report, he casually said it was done, as if to say, what else did you expect?

I never expected much in talking to corporate chiefs about what they should do in their own and the public's interest. In my experience, they had difficulty listening to anything not on their bureaucratic wavelength. With Peter it was different, and not because of any Princeton connection.

For example, he heard about my remarks that insurance companies were not engaged in meaningful competition. On a trip to Washington, DC, we had lunch and he said that the big auto insurers compete like crazy. "What do you mean?" he asked.

I replied that State Farm, Allstate, Geico, Progressive, and other insurance companies competed against each other in ads, marketing, sales incentives, and imagery, but not directly for the consumers' benefit. I explained that it was almost impossible for the average customer to compare policies and prices between the various companies. His eyes lit up. It wasn't long before the famously successful Progressive ads were offering free competitors' rates, including Progressive's, even if the latter was higher than one or more of the other auto insurers.

Other proposals he thought about and turned down. One that he considered too complicated was for Progressive to build a few prototype safety cars in order to push the auto companies to liberate their engineers and build more crashworthy vehicles with better handling and therefore fewer claims. This idea stemmed from the pioneering Liberty Mutual Insurance project in the 1950s when it rebuilt a much safer Chevrolet.

However, in the early nineties, Peter made sure Progressive was a financial supporter of the effective new group Advocates for Highway and Auto Safety.

Another proposal was to fund organizers who would convince coalitions in major cities across the country to demand that presidential debates come to their communities in 2012. This would break the grip of the three "debates" choreographed by the Republican and the Democratic parties via their creation, the Commission on Presidential Debates (CPD). CPD is a private nonprofit that picks the reporters, invites only candidates from its two patron parties, and solicits corporate donations for its budget. Peter "loved the idea," but after considerable back and forth concluded it was not possible to pull it off.

Peter was deeply serious about civil liberties and worried about invasions of privacy, repression of dissenting views, and government snooping in the aftermath of 9/11. He became the largest individual donor to the American Civil Liberties Union, with a record-breaking endowment gift of $7 million. He hated President George W. Bush's invasion of Iraq, which he called "a disaster in all ways," and funded civic opposition, including ours, to this worsening, brutal quagmire.

As a prominent Democrat, he supported John Kerry's presidential campaign with many millions of dollars. After Bush's reelection and Kerry's wishy-washy performance in 2004, he told me he was pretty much turned off of political campaigns.

He became more focused on building the institutions that will facilitate and support progressive policy for years into the future. As was his wont, he went beyond by helping launch Media Matters and the Center for American Progress, and was the founder of the Management Center, which conducts seminars to help nonprofits be more efficient and effective.

Once Peter joked that before joining the Princeton University Board of

Trustees, the due diligence report called him a "functional pothead." Yet to my knowledge, he was known for promptly returning calls. He suffered pain—his leg was amputated below the knee due to chronic infection and poor circulation—but rarely exclaimed it. Instead he responded by becoming physically fit.

As a major patron of the arts from his hometown in Cleveland to New York City and elsewhere, he believed an artist's purpose was to make people view their surroundings through innovative, irreverent eyes. At Progressive's headquarters, he hung Andy Warhol's portraits of Mao and relished the anger of some employees, noting that at least they were stimulated.

Whenever I asked him how business was, he would talk about how "terrific" his successor—New Zealander Glenn Renwick—was as CEO, before noting some new approach like "instant claims service."

Occasionally he expressed disappointment about his and other charitable and political contributions not getting results. "I'm at the edge of despair" about the state of the country, he confessed several years ago.

That disappointment, bordering on resignation, seemed to come forth during a discussion I arranged at the New York Public Library with Peter and Ted Turner, two of the protagonists in my book *Only the Super-Rich Can Save Us!*—a work of political fiction that could inspire real-world change. He began to doubt whether any major proposals for change could break through.

But Peter had so many irons in the fire that he always found sources of resiliency. And he liked to shock people out of their comfort zone. Earlier this year, he relayed a conversation that he'd had with the new president of Princeton, Christopher L. Eisgruber, wherein he urged the Princeton football program be dropped. Even though Peter is Princeton's largest benefactor in the modern era ($220 million), he may have stepped out of bounds on that one. Which is just what the boundary-breaker expected— to turn silence now into conversation later.

Peter Lewis put so many forces in motion that his beloved extended family need not wonder about a legacy. They grieve through the enlivening presence, future, and memories he gave them. He leaves behind a candid forthcoming autobiography that should show how he kept evolving and renewing himself to the benefit of many people.

The Cashiering of Helen Thomas

JULY 20, 2013; JUNE 15, 2010

There will never be another Helen Thomas. She shattered forever one anti-woman journalistic barrier after another in the Washington press corps and rose to the top of her profession's organizations. Helen Thomas asked the toughest questions of presidents and White House press secretaries, and over her sixty-two-year career took on sexism, racism, and ageism. She endured prejudice against her ethnicity—Arab American—and her breaking the taboo regarding the rights of dispossessed Palestinians. She also made many friends in journalism and spoke to audiences all over the country about the responsibility of journalists to hold politicians accountable with tough, probing questions that are asked repeatedly until they are either answered or the politician is unmasked as an unaccountable coward. That is the example she set as a journalist and the recurrent theme in her three books.

Her free spirit, her courageous belief that injustice must be exposed by journalists, her congenial personality, and her relentless focus (she asked former president George W. Bush and his press secretary Ari Fleischer dozens of times: "Why are we in Iraq?") will be long remembered. Her tenacious, forthright approach to journalism stands as a stark contrast to the patsy journalism of too many of her former self-censoring White House press colleagues.

The remarkable combination of skills and perseverance will distinguish Helen Thomas as one of the giants of American journalistic history.

✝ ✝ ✝

The termination of Helen Thomas' sixty-two-year career as a pioneering, no-nonsense newswoman was swift and intriguingly merciless.

The event leading to her termination began when she was sitting on a White House bench under oppressive summer heat. The eighty-nine-year-old hero of honest journalism and women's rights, the scourge of dissembling presidents and White House press secretaries, answered a passing visitor's question about Israel with a snappish comment worded in a way she didn't mean; she promptly apologized in writing (see http://www.democracynow.org/2010/6/8/veteran_white_house_reporter_helen_thomas). Recorded without permission on a hand video, the brief exchange, which included a defense of dispossessed Palestinians, went viral on Friday, June 7.

By Monday, Helen Thomas was considered finished, even though she embodied a steadfast belief, in the praiseworthy words of *Washington Post* columnist Dana Milbank, "that anybody standing on that podium [in the White House] should be regarded with skepticism."

Over the weekend, her lecture agent dropped her. Her column syndicator, the Hearst company, pressed her to quit "effective immediately," and it was believed that the White House Correspondents' Association, of which she was the first female president, was about to take away her coveted front-row seat in the White House press room.

Then Helen Thomas announced her retirement on Monday, June 10. No doubt she's had her fill of racist, sexist, and ageist epithets hurled her way over the years—the very decades she was broadly challenging racism, sexism, and, more recently, ageism.

Although the behind-the-scenes story has yet to come out, the evisceration was launched by two pro-Israeli war hawks, Ari Fleischer and Lanny Davis. Fleischer was George W. Bush's press secretary who bridled under Helen Thomas's questioning regarding the horrors of the Bush/Cheney war crimes and illegal torture. His job was not to answer this uppity woman but to deflect, avoid, and cover up for his bosses.

Davis was the designated defender whenever Clinton got into hot water. As journalist Paul Jay pointed out, Davis is now a Washington lobbyist whose clients include the cruel corporate junta that overthrew the elected president of Honduras. Both men rustled up the baying pack of Thomas-haters during the weekend and filled the unanswered narrative on Fox and other facilitating media.

Then, belatedly, something remarkable occurred. People reacted against this grossly disproportionate punishment. Ellen Ratner, a Fox News contributor, wrote—"I'm Jewish and a supporter of Israel. Let's face it: we all have said things—or thought things—about 'other' groups of people, things that we wouldn't want to see in print or on video. Anyone who denies it is a liar. Give [Helen] a break."

Apparently, many people agree. In an internet poll by the *Washington Post*, 92 percent of respondents said she should not be removed from the White House press room. An NPR listener, R. Carey, emailed: "DC would be void of journalists if they all were to quit, get fired or retire after making potentially offensive comments."

Listen to Michael Freedman, former managing editor for United Press International: "After seven decades of setting standards for quality journalism and demolishing barriers for women in the workplace, Helen Thomas has now shown that most dreaded of vulnerabilities—she is human. . . . Who among us does not have strong feelings about the endless warfare in the Middle East? Who among us has not said something we have come to regret? . . . Let's not destroy Ms. Thomas now."

Katrina vanden Heuvel, editor and publisher of the *Nation*, wrote: "Thomas's remarks were offensive, but considering her journalistic moxie and courage over many decades, isn't there room for someone who made a mistake, apologized for it and wants to continue speaking truth to power and asking tough questions? . . . Thomas was the only accredited White House correspondent with the guts to ask Bush the tough questions that define a free press."

Last week, in front of the White House, people calling themselves "Jews for Helen Thomas" gathered in a small demonstration. Medea Benjamin, cofounder of Global Exchange, declared, "We are clear what Helen Thomas meant to say, which is that Israel should cease its occupation of Palestine, and we agree with that." Another demonstrator, Zool Zulkowitz, asserted that "by discrediting Helen Thomas, those who believe that Israel can do no wrong shift attention from the public relations debacle of the Gaza flotilla killings and intimidate journalists who would ask hard questions about the Israeli occupation of Palestine and American foreign policy."

Helen Thomas, who grew up in Detroit, is an American of Arab descent. She is understandably alert to the one-sided US military and foreign policy in that region. Her questions reflect concerns about US policy in the Middle East by many Americans, including unmuzzled retired military, diplomatic, and intelligence officials.

In 2006, when George W. Bush finally called on her, she started her questioning by saying, "Your decision to invade Iraq has caused the deaths of Americans and Iraqis. Every reason given, publicly at least, has turned out not to be true." Or when she challenged President Obama last month, asking "When are you going to get out of Afghanistan? Why are we continuing to kill and die there? What is the real excuse?"

Asking the "why" questions was a Thomas trademark. Many self-censoring journalists avoid controversial "why" questions, thereby allowing evasion, dissembling, and just plain BS to dominate the White House press room. She rejected words that sugarcoated or camouflaged the grim deeds. She started with the grim deeds to expose the double-talk and officialdom's chronic illegalities.

What appalled Thomas most is the way the media rolls over and fails to hold officials accountable. (British reporters believe they are tougher on their prime ministers.) This is a subject about which she has written books and articles—not exactly the way to endear herself to those reporters who go AWOL and look the other way so that they can continue to be called upon or to be promoted by their superiors. She did not engage in the despicable deeds committed by so many littering the Washington political scene.

The abysmal record of the *New York Times* and the *Washington Post* in the months preceding the Iraq invasion filled with Bush/Cheney lies, deception, and cover-ups is a case in point. As usual, she was proven right, unlike the celebrated reporters and columnists deprecating her work, including the *Post*'s press critic, Howard Kurtz.

Thomas practiced her profession with a deep regard for the people's right to know. To her, as Aldous Huxley noted long ago, "facts do not cease to exist because they are ignored."

Lastly, there is the double standard. One offhand, "ill-conceived remark," as NPR ombudsman Alicia Shepard stated in praising Ms. Thomas, ended a groundbreaking career. Meanwhile, enhanced careers and fat lecture fees are the reward for ultra-right-wing radio and cable ranters and others, like columnist Ann Coulter, who regularly urge wars, mayhem, and dragnets based on bigotry, stereotypes, and falsehoods directed wholesale against Muslims, including blatant anti-Semitism against Arabs. (See adc.org/education/educational-resources and Jack Shaheen's book and companion documentary about cultural portrayal of Arab stereotypes, *Reel Bad Arabs*.)

Ms. Thomas's desk at the Hearst office remains unattended a week after her eviction. One day she will return to pack up her materials. She can take with her the satisfaction of joining all those in our history who were cashiered ostensibly for a gaffe, but really for being too right, too early, too often.

Her many admirers hope that she continues to write, speak, and motivate a generation of young journalists in the spirit of Joseph Pulitzer's advice, quoting Finley Peter Dunne, to his reporters a century ago—that their job was to "comfort the afflicted and afflict the comfortable."

Toward a Living Legacy for Nelson Mandela Now

JULY 9, 2013

Nelson Mandela's exceptional and exemplary life has and will produce worldwide celebrations of his extremely unique blend of character, personality, and resolve for broad-gauged justice. To truly memorialize his contributions, however, requires grand actions.

Taking immediate recognition of the deep wellsprings of respect, affection, and sorrow over the loss of his leadership to the people of South Africa and the world, leaders from various nations can come together to establish the Nelson Mandela Institute for Global Human Rights with an endowment of $1 billion. The founders must be possessed of a vision that includes posterity's rights to peace and justice, to freedom and opportunity compatible with the survival of the planet.

To be perceived as impeccable for this specific noble mission, the founders must select themselves so as to define a unanimity of purpose, resolve, and expeditiousness. To turn the powerful spirit of Nelson Mandela into a powerful vision and proliferate his ideals and actions, his courage and humanity, his uncanny sense of what it takes to move the immovable and inspire the shameless to higher levels of human possibilities, a combination of seasoned knowledge and material resources will be required.

The founders need not be angels, need not be pure in background or without "baggage." They need only to be lawful and capable in creating a well-funded institute and engaging with substantive experienced and innovative people in human rights, research, communication, and advocacy to carry forward Mandela's work. Most immediately, the founders need to come together with all deliberate speed. At the outset they need not be representative of the world. That will come later. The immediate need is for a critical mass of individuals with foresight who can create the Mandela Institute.

By way of nonexclusive suggestion, suppose a quartet of Bishop Desmond Tutu, Congressman John Lewis, Warren Buffett, and former president Bill Clinton initiated a conversation between themselves. Here is what could happen forthwith:

Bishop Tutu brings his friendship and alliance with Nelson Mandela, together with the respect of his country's people and human rights advocates around the world with whom he has worked tirelessly.

Congressman John Lewis brings his ground-level valor in the US civil rights movement of the sixties and the widespread nonpartisan high regard for his undeterred principles and moral values.

Warren Buffett brings a core of multibillionaires who have pledged to give at least half their estate to good works (See givingpledge.org). They are looking for good collaborative ideas.

Bill Clinton brings his unrivaled Rolodex of establishment achievers and leaders who come to his annual conference to discuss commercial and charitable ways to improve the world.

Besides the memorial vision, nothing gathers attentive support more than the availability of material resources. Mr. Buffett (who modestly tells friends that at least he gets his calls returned) can draw on over one hundred (and growing) pledgers from the US and other countries. Their combined reported net worth is $504 billion. An average of $10 million from each pledger for this grand institution would take the fundraising over the $1 billion level. This can occur before major foundations decide on significant founding contributions. As the proposal moves into organization and substantive phases, the organizers of the institute do have to be impeccable, pure of heart, and results-oriented, without the conflicting or distracting personal ambition that self-censors their worthiest traits and ideals.

The fine details of the institute's leadership and activities, so as to maximize its great potential, are, of course, important. But they are not immediate. For now it is the guiding light, work, and principles of Nelson Mandela that can assure that he lives through the coming generations both in deed and via grassroots leaders who reflect his courage and humanity.

The Greatest Environmentalist of the Twentieth Century

OCTOBER 9, 2012

Dr. Barry Commoner, equipped with a Harvard PhD in cellular biology, used his knowledge of biology, ecosystems, nuclear radiation, public communication, networking scientists, political campaigning, and community organizing to become the greatest environmentalist in the twentieth century. He died on September 30 at the age of ninety-five, deeply involved in challenging conventional dogmas in the field of genetic engineering.

The range and depth of his work flowed from an integrative public philosophy of what makes the world work or not work in the interaction between what he called "the technosphere" and "the ecosphere." His best-selling books were brilliant, clear, and motivating.

In all the years I've known him, he maintained his methodical approach to analyzing problems and recommending superior strategies to achieve superior solutions. He kept his composure even in the most raucous public gatherings where others were arguing or shouting at one another. The mainstream media liked his calm demeanor, which conveyed a searing evaluation that went to the root causes of what and how we produce. He made the cover of *Time* magazine, as a symbol of the first Earth Day's activities nationwide in April 1970; was a frequent guest of network TV shows; and wrote for major publications such as the *New York Times*.

A fundamental inquirer, Commoner took on his fellow scientists who seemed indifferent to the nuclear arms race with the Soviet Union and the radioactive fallout from A-bomb testing. While working as, in the *Times*' words, a "brilliant teacher and a painstaking researcher into viruses, cell metabolism and the effects of radiation on living tissue" at Washington University, he sparked the St. Louis Citizen's Committee for Nuclear Information, which in turn mobilized enough scientists around the country to push for the nuclear test ban treaty that President John F. Kennedy proposed in 1963.

One of his "laws of ecology" is that "everything is connected to everything else," and he wasn't just referring to natural systems. Wars, corporate power, greed, injustice, discrimination, and poverty connect to what makes people sick and die.

He declared that prevention, rather than wrangling over piecemeal regulation, was the most effective way to protect our air, water, soil, and food. He pointed to lead in gasoline that was prohibited at long last, not gradually regulated. The banning outright of vinyl chloride was another example of prevention.

He told *Scientific American*: "What is needed now is a transformation of the major systems of production. . . . Restoring environmental quality means substituting solar sources of energy for fossil and nuclear fuels; substituting electric motors for the internal-combustion engine; substituting organic farming for chemical agriculture; expanding the use of durable, renewable and recyclable materials—metals, glass, wood, paper—in place of petrochemical products that have massively displaced them."

He told me in the 1980s that he wanted to write a book about the necessity and practicality of replacing the petrochemical industry. Commoner urged the Department of Defense in detail to use solar technologies for economic and environmental reasons and thereby jump-start an expanding civilian market for solar. The Navy, for which he served in World War II, did install thousands of photovoltaics at remote locations to save money and cut pollution. Procurement by government is a great stimulus to innovation and avoids the regulatory delays by corporate lobbyists.

Pollution in the workplace attracted his expertise when we needed it in pressing for the Occupational Safety and Health Act of 1970. When he brought poverty into his focus, he showed how impoverished racial minorities were exposed to higher intensities of pollution where they lived, due to their powerlessness. This "laid the groundwork for what later became known as the environmental justice movement," as professor Peter Dreier of Occidental College recently wrote.

Always the practical modern Renaissance man, Commoner helped start the Citizens Party in 1979 and was chosen as the party's presidential candidate. He knew how third parties are structurally marginalized in the US, as compared with the Green Party in Germany, but he wanted to enlarge the public consciousness to connect causes and consequences. He later joked about the time a reporter in New Mexico asked him: "Dr. Commoner, are you a serious candidate, or are you just running on the issues?" Too bad the media didn't heed his clarion calls to action.

Unperturbed, Commoner applied his knowledge in many other directions, including a pioneering pilot recycling program in New York City, to show how most trash could actually be reused or recycled.

Today's younger environmental activists hardly know of Commoner and his three great books—*The Closing Circle* (1971), *The Poverty of Power* (1976), and *Making Peace with the Planet* (1992), all of which remain unsurpassed and timely in their integrative frameworks for understanding and leveraging action.

I called Barry to congratulate him on his ninetieth birthday. "It happens," he replied wryly. For the people, flora, and fauna on planet Earth, it is a great gift that Barry Commoner "happened."

His students, supporters, and some wealthy benefactors in this nation should extend his broad-gauged approach ("the finely sculptured fit between life and its surroundings") by establishing an institute of thought and action in his name. Those interested in donations in Barry's name can make them out to the Center for the Biology of Natural Systems, sent to Sharon Peyser, Queens College—CBNS, Remsen 311, 65-30 Kissena Boulevard, Flushing, NY 11367.

Harry Kelber Challenges the AFL-CIO

AUGUST 29, 2012

"Why should I listen to anything Harry Kelber says?" exclaimed a visibly indignant Richard Trumka, president of the AFL-CIO (American Federation of Labor and Congress of Industrial Organizations).

Maybe because Kelber, ninety-eight years young, has been honestly fighting for labor rights as a worker, union organizer, pamphleteer, author, professor, and overall hairshirt of the moribund organized labor movement for seventy-eight years—or fifteen years before Trumka, the former coal miner and United Mine Workers president, was born.

Kelber writes and speaks about what is on the minds of millions of union workers and nonunion workers. Why aren't leaders of organized labor more aggressive in addressing the plight of American labor by challenging big companies and their political allies? Why didn't the AFL-CIO leadership hold Barack Obama in 2009, 2010, and 2011 to his specific 2008 promises to press Congress for a $9.50 federal minimum wage by 2011 and, when under control of the Democrats, get Congress to pass the "card check" that would give millions of workers a chance to organize at Walmart, McDonald's, and other companies that employ low-wage labor and provide few benefits?

How can the AFL-CIO's "policy of silence and secrecy . . . serve the interest of union members?" Kelber criticizes the federation for its top-down control, its aversion to any democratic process for its elections, and for not taking full advantage of the Wall Street crash, the taxpayer bailouts, and US corporations sending jobs to repressive dictatorships abroad.

Kelber wants the AFL-CIO and its member unions to fight against this strip-mining of the American economy and work closely with labor unions from other countries with the same corporate employers.

In truth, to outsiders, Trumka's labor federation appears a defeated giant in its great white headquarters on Sixteenth Street in Washington, DC, across from the White House. To be sure, it confronts formidable external trends, which include a declining union membership, right-wing governors attacking its pensions, faster automation, corporate globalization, huge corporate slush funds to buy or rent politicians, and antiworker laws such as the notorious union-blocking Taft–Hartley Act of 1947, now in its sixty-fifth year of damage.

The old saying, however, is that when the going gets tough, the tough get going. That is not happening. Trumka delivers "give 'em hell" speeches against corporate abuses, but gives the cowardly Democratic Party and its elected officials a pass. Consequently the Democrats take campaign money from unions and, led by a president who would not have been elected president without them, take the AFL-CIO support for granted.

Recently, Representative Jesse Jackson Jr. and other representatives introduced HR 5901 (the "Catching Up To 1968 Act of 2012") to enact a $10.00 minimum wage to benefit thirty million workers languishing between the present $7.25 minimum wage and $10.00. So far the AFL-CIO hasn't put any muscle or part of its multimillion-dollar television ad buys behind it.

Inside an AFL-CIO's executive council meeting one day, Trumka criticized President Obama and incurred the displeasure of one labor baron who said there should be no criticism, even in their private meeting. Trumka objected to that request for self-censorship.

Meanwhile, the corporate barons in the nearby US Chamber of Commerce building go after Obama with hammer and tongs, even though the president has gone out of his way to coddle them, to walk over and speak to them last year—something he has not done to his AFL-CIO neighbors.

Worse, Obama appointed Jeffrey Immelt—CEO of the net job-exporting, no-federal-tax-paying, anti-union, very profitable General Electric—head of the President's Council on Jobs and Competitiveness. Mr. Trumka sits with him and never urges the repeal of Taft–Hartley while he listens to the corporatists demand more and more deregulation, tax breaks, subsidies, and other forms of corporate welfare.

Kelber has pointed out the financial distress enveloping the AFL-CIO itself. So strapped is the AFL-CIO budget that it is selling its affiliate's visionary forty-seven-acre labor campus in suburban Maryland where it is reportedly losing about $6 million a year. Why? The federation is not about to explain its budgetary priorities to its rank and file.

There are good people inside the labor headquarters. They are muzzled.

Trumka will say he has his hands full with the heads of member unions who, he has implied, are not exactly progressive or aggressive for change. Here he has a point. While Trumka and Jon Hiatt control the staff, he has to deal with a fractious group of member unions, most of which want to stay beneath the radar and avoid notice.

Unless they have nothing to hide, union leaders generally avoid the spotlight. They remember too many prosecutions of their forbears. Don't rock the boat. Even on Labor Day, they do not come forward prominently to dominate the news with major events and announcements. The Labor Day parades are either extinct or a diluted shadow of their earlier years.

Yet, this upcoming Labor Day, as I wrote to President Obama, there is a great opportunity for collaboration between him, union leaders, workers, and social justice organizations to take a stand for the ten-dollar minimum wage that is favored by 70 percent of the people. It would be a leading media event that is the long-overdue right thing to do, both morally and economically.

Even Rick Santorum and Mitt Romney, until the latter waffled earlier this year, have long favored a minimum wage keeping up with inflation. Isn't it time for thirty million hard-pressed American workers to receive what workers got in 1968? Obama has not replied to my suggestion. Nor has the AFL-CIO. Kelber is right. It is time for a new labor federation of, by, and for the workers. See Kelber's laboreducator.org and participate. He vigorously welcomes you and your views.

"Public Justice"—Standing Forty Years Against Brutish Corporate Power

MAY 6, 2022

It is not often that one speech urging the creation of a national public-interest law firm, driven by seasoned trial lawyers, would move from word to deed, from oratory to action.

That is just what happened following my address in June 1980 to the Michigan Trial Lawyers Association. I spoke of a gap in trial practice that needed to be filled. There was a pressing need to bring cases against the many corporate abuses, which included nonenforcement of regulatory laws. Without the prospect of a contingent fee after a successful outcome, trial lawyers were unlikely to take on these uncertain cases or structural reform cases on behalf of tenants, farm workers, or cruel prison conditions.

I noted the assault by corporations on "the biosphere [and] personal injury law from trauma to toxics." The corporate lobby was blocking legislative proposals to strengthen class-action consumer rights, digging deeper for unconscionable corporate welfare payments and funding corporatist politicians. To challenge these damaging corporate power plays, I suggested a full-time core of public-interest attorneys supported by a sabbatical program for trial lawyers who wanted to take a year off from their regular practice and come to Washington, DC, to advance justice and refresh themselves.

It turned out that there were some leading trial lawyers—Scottie Baldwin, J.D. Lee, Bill Colson, and Dean Robb—who were dissatisfied with the slow pace of the American Trial Lawyers Association (ATLA), then controlled by a small clique of smug members. They took this proposal to the ATLA convention and convened a meeting of like-minded attorneys. With the determined assistance of Joan B. Claybrook, who was with Public Citizen, the nonprofit Trial Lawyers for Public Justice (TLPJ) was born.

In the ensuing forty years, TLPJ, renamed Public Justice in 2007, has shown that there are opportunities for widespread justice successes as long as the people's advocates are on the field of action.

Public Justice has taken on a wide range of cases, from going up against mountain-top removal and the coal industry's poisoning of fresh water in West Virginia, to fighting industrial agriculture's toxic contaminations, to making sure Title IX is enforced to open wide the doors for women participating in intercollegiate athletics.

Today, led by Paul Bland, Public Justice is celebrating its fortieth anniversary. The firm has a $7 million annual budget (which is about three and a half weeks' pay for the miserly Tim Cook, CEO of Apple), twenty-three staff on its legal team, and a total staff size of forty-six.

Look at Public Justice's docket of lawsuits (See: publicjustice.net/what-we-do/access-to-justice/). They have challenged court secrecy and fought compulsory arbitration, federal preemption of good state laws, and the weakening of class actions. Students subjected to harassment and discrimination have found a champion in Public Justice, as have consumers cheated in so many ways by devious commercial thieves.

Special is Public Justice's stand against what it calls the Debtors' Prison Project. Here governments try to cash in by imposing fees on charged defendants, trapping them in cycles of poverty, with Public Justice arguing that "no one should lose their freedom because they lack the means to pay a fine."

A large vacuum is filled by Public Justice in its Worker Justice project. Giant agribusiness, Public Justice asserts with abundant evidence, "has always capitalized on the exploitation of workers, since its origins in plantation agriculture that relied on the forced labor of enslaved Africans. Today, meatpacking workers are subject to some of the most brutal working conditions in the labor market."

When COVID-19 came to America, Public Justice went to the defense of food-system workers who were not given protection and care, causing their industry facilities to "quickly [become] epicenters of outbreaks."

Paul Bland and his colleagues teamed up with other public interest groups on some cases, including Toward Justice and the Heartland Center for Jobs and Freedom.

Within today's right-wing, corporatist judicial system, Public Justice still wins cases, deters wrongdoing because companies know it is on watch, and even raises the visibility of issues when they lose.

Like any forty-year-old institution, it must remain alert to becoming too settled, too risk-averse, and instead continue to be a pioneering organization and break new ground with bold causes of action as if there is no tomorrow. Hear that, younger attorneys? Your burden is to keep your unique law firm as fresh as a cool mountain breeze caressing a gushing mountain brook. For more information visit the Public Justice website: publicjustice.net.

Tomas Young's Last Letter
to Bush, Cheney

NOVEMBER 14, 2014

The courageous journey of seriously wounded Iraq War veteran Tomas Young ended this past Monday, nearly eleven years after he was ambushed in a wholly exposed military truck. He passed away in Seattle while being lovingly cared for by his wife, Claudia.

Tomas did not go quietly, despite his being paralyzed from the chest down, excruciating pain, comas, and reliance on caregivers. He became an antiwar peace activist, addressing convocations and responding to as many interview requests as his agonized condition could tolerate.

I learned about Tomas when his mother, Cathy Smith, called from Walter Reed Army Hospital in 2004, where her son was under care. She said Tomas liked to read and wanted me to visit him. I called legendary talk show host Phil Donahue and asked him to join me in bringing Tomas a box filled with some thirty books. We learned that he enlisted in the Army two days after the 9/11 attacks because he wanted to help bring the perpetrators of those attacks to justice and also acquire some savings for a college education. Instead, he was sent to Iraq, which had no connection to 9/11 or to any national security threat to the US. In his words, "We were used. We were betrayed. And we have been abandoned."

Phil was so taken with all that had happened to Tomas that he stayed in close touch with Tomas and his family and helped him spread his story. With Ellen Spiro, Phil Donahue produced the gripping documentary based on Tomas's story, *Body of War*, in 2007. It detailed the excruciating experiences of Tomas Young, who managed to travel to some film screenings to support soldiers "speaking out against this war."

One of the most memorable clips from *Body of War* showed George W. Bush joking and looking around for weapons of mass destruction (his omnicidal fabrication) at the Radio and Television Correspondents' Dinner in 2004.

Another memorable scene, one that uplifted the human spirit, was the personal exchange between Senator Robert Byrd (D-WV) and Tomas while a recording of Tomas and Senator Byrd reading the list of the senators who voted against the invasion of Iraq played in the background. Senator Byrd deemed these lawmakers "the immortal twenty-three."

After he received the call that he had been dreading for ten years, Phil told me that Tomas's body and mind "took every hit," but he fought to live for over a decade. Phil committed himself to that heroic decade of survival, helping him along the way to get better health care and rehabilitation, encouraging him to keep going, and facilitating Tomas Young's voice and place in recorded history. This friendship that developed from such a dire circumstance is a book in itself.

It was on the tenth anniversary of the Iraq War that, near death and in hospice, Tomas Young sent a "last letter" to George W. Bush and Dick Cheney. Here are some of his searing words from that letter, which, of course, neither the two war criminals nor their taxpayer-funded staff bothered to even acknowledge:

> I write this letter on behalf of husbands and wives who have lost spouses, on behalf of children who have lost a parent, on behalf of the fathers and mothers who have lost sons and daughters and on behalf of those who care for the many thousands of my fellow veterans who have brain injuries. . . . I write this letter on behalf of the some 1 million Iraqi dead and on behalf of the countless Iraqi wounded. I write this letter on behalf of us all—the human detritus your war has left behind, those who will spend their lives in unending pain and grief.
>
> I write this letter, my last letter, to you, Mr. Bush and Mr. Cheney. I write not because I think you grasp the terrible human and moral consequences of your lies, manipulation and thirst for wealth and power. I write this letter because . . . I want to make it clear that I, and hundreds of thousands of my fellow veterans, along with millions of my fellow citizens, along with hundreds of millions more in Iraq and the Middle East, know fully who you are and what you have done. You may evade justice but in our eyes you are each guilty of egregious war crimes, of plunder and, finally, of murder, including the murder of thousands of young Americans—my fellow veterans—whose future you stole.
>
> Your positions of authority, your millions of dollars of personal wealth, your public relations consultants, your privilege and your power cannot mask the hollowness of your character. You sent us

to fight and die in Iraq after you, Mr. Cheney, dodged the draft in Vietnam, and you, Mr. Bush, went AWOL from your National Guard unit. Your cowardice and selfishness were established decades ago. . . . You sent hundreds of thousands of young men and women to be sacrificed in a senseless war with no more thought than it takes to put out the garbage.

I joined the Army two days after the 9/11 attacks. . . . I wanted to strike back at those who had killed some 3,000 of my fellow citizens. I did not join the Army to go to Iraq, a country that had no part in the September 2001 attacks and did not pose a threat to its neighbors, much less to the United States. I did not join the Army to "liberate" Iraqis or to shut down mythical weapons-of-mass-destruction facilities or to implant what you cynically called "democracy" in Baghdad and the Middle East. . . . I especially did not join the Army to carry out preemptive war. Preemptive war is illegal under international law. And as a soldier in Iraq I was, I now know, abetting your idiocy and your crimes. The Iraq War is the largest strategic blunder in US history. . . .

I would not be writing this letter if I had been wounded fighting in Afghanistan against those forces that carried out the attacks of 9/11. . . .

We were used. We were betrayed. And we have been abandoned. You, Mr. Bush, make much pretense of being a Christian. But isn't lying a sin? Isn't murder a sin? Aren't theft and selfish ambition sins? . . .

My day of reckoning is upon me. Yours will come. I hope you will be put on trial. But mostly I hope, for your sakes, that you find the moral courage to face what you have done to me and to many, many others who deserved to live. I hope that before your time on earth ends, as mine is now ending, you will find the strength of character to stand before the American public and the world, and in particular the Iraqi people, and beg for forgiveness.

In the annals of military history, moral courage is much rarer than physical courage, in part because of the long-lasting sanctions against dissenters and those who speak truth to power about the faults in our own society. Tomas Young had both moral and physical courage. His example should be heeded by young soldiers in the future who are ordered by their gravely flawed politicians to make the ultimate sacrifice for their leaders' illegal follies and ambitions.

11.

ON THE LAW AND
CORPORATE POWER

Think Big to Overcome Losing
Big to Corporatism

JANUARY 7, 2022

The progressive citizen groups—which in the sixties and seventies drove through Congress the key environmental, worker, and consumer legislation, since unmatched—must feel nostalgic. Those were the years when legislation throwing cruel companies on the defensive was signed by arch-corporatist President Richard Nixon because he read the political tea leaves.

These bills included the creation of the Environmental Protection Agency and environmental laws, the establishment of the Occupational Safety and Health Administration for worker health and safety, the Consumer Product Safety Commission, the Freedom of Information Act, and worker pension protection, among others.

Alas, Richard Nixon was the last Republican president to be afraid of liberals. When B-grade actor Ronald Reagan flew into Washington, he opened all doors to big business. A cruel man with a smile, Reagan gave an actor's cover to the greatest collapse into the corporate power pits in American history.

Here is a checklist showing the takeovers of our government at all levels by the corporate supremacists for whom enough is never enough when it comes to profits and power.

1. Regulatory agencies curbing corporate ravages were essentially shut down. Reaganites thought companies should regulate themselves when it comes to the health, safety, and economic well-being of the American people; which is to say, the corporate rule took over the rule of law.

2. Labor unions were weakened by timid leadership, antilabor policies, acceleration of job exports, and the major shift by the Democratic Party to solicit money from rapidly expanding corporate political action committees.

3. Congress abandoned its role of checks and balances and gave much of its constitutional power to the imperial, autocratic presidency. This concentration of power and secrecy in the White House seriously weakened the power of civic groups that had been able to start their reform drives in Congress.

4. The consequences of corporatizing Congress allowed the tax system to be filled with escapes and lower rates for the super-rich and global corporations. It allowed presidents to get corporatist judges confirmed to dominate the courts. It permitted total inaction on the necessity of strengthening our federal corporate criminal laws, including anti-trust enforcement and laws, so out of date that they slipped out of the minds of the supposed enforcers in the executive branch.

5. A spineless Congress fell to its knees before the military-industrial complex so much so that the bloated, un-audited "defense" budget zoomed over 50 percent of discretionary spending by the federal government. The military empire grew without congressional oversight.

6. Meanwhile, the corporate giants became dominant in weakening the private pillars of American law. They turned freedom of contracts into fine-print consumer servitude, while coercing consumers into also giving up key rights and remedies under the law of torts should they incur wrongful injuries.

7. A manipulated credit economy took away consumers' control over their own money, subjecting them to penalties, ultimatums, and punitive credit scores.

8. Without challenge to their marketing, corporations commercialized childhood, directly selling to kids junk foods and junk drinks that set off the deadly obesity epidemic and its health-damaging results. They sold violent programming and exploited the weaknesses of children, circumventing parental authority and discipline.

9. In the Internet Age, corporations can be described as raising our children—getting their personal information for free and selling this

collected data to advertisers. They are trapping these youngsters in the peonage of click-on contracts they never see through in their daily screen hours.

10. Whether in reality or virtual reality, corporations have become electronic child molesters with few pursuing sheriffs.

11. Corporate globalization has erected mechanisms such as corporate-managed trade agreements that operate to pull down our standards for workers, consumers, and the environment to the lower levels of developing countries, many of them under dictatorial regimes.

12. Decades after warnings by scientists of rising global warming, the fossil fuel giants, while on the defensive, still have the economy in their clutches, slowing their substitutes of conservation and renewable energy.

13. Corporate welfare is larger, more varied, and more automatic than ever. Subsidies, handouts, giveaways, and bailouts are now routinely enacted by little-challenged, government-guaranteed capitalism at the federal and state levels!

14. Big corporations even control the wealth owned by the people, such as the public lands, public airwaves, and trillions of dollars in pension and mutual funds.

15. Voting rights and electoral accuracies are being undermined in many states by legislation.

16. Medicare is being corporatized (over 40 percent of elderly beneficiaries are under corporate plans). Billing fraud is greater than ever (reaching $360 billion in 2021 just in the health care industry). Traditional defined-benefit pension plans are disappearing, with the unstable 401(k) as a replacement if workers are lucky enough to have any retirement savings plans at the workplace.

Clearly the situation in our political economy is getting worse by the year. To be sure, progressive groups have maintained some successes, such as the near abolition of most uses of deadly asbestos, lead out of paint and gasoline, safer cars, better labeling, more recalls, removals of unsafe or ineffective drugs, and reduction of air and water pollutants. Civil rights and child protection laws still have some teeth. But civic groups are winning some skirmishes while losing the battle and the war to the entrenched corporate state. As Franklin Delano Roosevelt told Congress in 1938: whenever private power takes control of the government, that is fascism.

These citizen groups and their supporters must now step back and develop a ten-year plan to overpower the corporate state with a democratic state. The people, however passive now, are largely on their side. Originally, in the state-chartering days of the early nineteenth century, corporations were expected to be our servants, not our masters. The reverse is now true.

This plan will require thousands of new organizers, lobbyists, strategists, and all the skills used by big corporations. It will also require systematically connecting with enlightened billionaires, already worried about our country's slide into the abyss, for a budget of at least $10 billion over ten years.

Otherwise, ongoing skirmishes will continue to lower the expectations by progressive civic groups to a point of self-delusion.

The Continuing Damages from Corporate-Managed, So-Called "Free Trade"

JUNE 24, 2022

The great progressive Harvard economist and prolific best-selling author John Kenneth Galbraith wrote, "Ideas may be superior to vested interest. They are also very often the children of vested interest." I wished he had written that assertion before I took Economics 101 at Princeton. One of the vested ideas taught as dogma then was the comparative advantage theory developed by the early-nineteenth-century British economist David Ricardo. He gave the example of trading Portuguese wine for British textiles, with both countries coming out winners due to their superior efficiencies in producing their native products.

Ricardo's theory drove policy and political power for two centuries, fortifying the corporate and conservative proponents of alleged "free markets" (see: "Destroying the Myths of Market Fundamentalism," https://www.youtube.com/watch?v=5687cmbf9L4) and "free trade." The theory's endurance was remarkably resistant to obviously contrary empirical evidence. Whether Ricardo envisioned it or not, "free trade" became an instrument of colonialism, entrenching poor nations in the extraction and exportation of natural resources while becoming almost totally dependent on western nations' value-added manufactured products. "Iron ore for iron weapons," as one observer summed it up. Tragically, too often, the weapons came with the invaders/oppressors.

Fast-forward to today's supply chain crisis disrupting the flow of commerce. Why does the world's largest economy and technology leader have a supply chain problem forcing businesses and consumers to helplessly wait for simple and complex goods to arrive at our shores? Why did we find ourselves in March 2020 desperately waiting on an Italian factory to sell us simple protective equipment to safeguard patients, nurses, and physicians to address the pandemic's deadly arrival? Answer: the touted theory of comparative advantage embedded in so-called "free trade."

In reality, there is no such thing. It is corporate-managed trade under the guise of "free trade." As Public Citizen attorney Lori Wallach asked her audiences, while holding up heavy volumes of NAFTA and WTO trade agreements: "If it's free trade, why are there all these pages of rules?" Because they are corporate rules often having little to do with trade and everything to do with the subordination of labor, consumer, and environmental rights and priorities.

The officials who arrived at these agreements in secret made sure that they *pulled down* higher US standards in these areas instead of having them *pull up* serf labor, polluting factories, and consumer abuses in authoritarian nations. Corporate-managed trade leads to inherently dangerous dependencies, such as no antibiotics being produced in the US, which imports these and other critical drugs from unregulated Chinese and Indian laboratories. The supply chain enchains.

A remarkable takedown appeared in a lengthy essay titled "The Idea of a Local Economy" twenty-one years ago by the agrarian wise man Wendell Berry, who used a larger framework to take apart so-called "free trade," which was under monetized corporate control of the government, a clueless media, and academics still indentured to Ricardo theory. He didn't go after the obvious—that imported products from serf-labor countries are corporate opportunities to make even more profits by keeping prices high. Other than textiles, note the high prices of Asian-made computers, iPhones, electronic toys, Nike shoes, and foreign motor vehicles sold to American consumers. This imbalance allows Apple's boss Tim Cook to pay himself $833 a minute or $50,000 an hour. The markups on these products are staggering, but not as staggering as the plight of Apple's one million serf laborers in China.

Berry opens up new horizons on the deception called "free trade"; to wit,

> Unsurprisingly, among people who wish to preserve things other than money—for instance, every region's native capacity to produce essential goods—there is a growing perception that the global "free market" economy is inherently an enemy to the natural world, to human health and freedom to industrial workers, and to farmers and others in the land-use economies; and, furthermore, that it is inherently an enemy to good work and good economic practice.

The farmer-thinker Berry listed numerous erroneous assumptions behind corporatist global trade. A few follow:

1. "That there can be no conflict between economic advantage and economic justice."

2. "That there is no conflict between the 'free market' and political freedom; and no connection between political democracy and economic democracy."

3. "That the loss of destruction of the capacity anywhere to produce necessary goods does not matter and involves no cost."

4. "That it is all right for a nation's or a region's subsistence to be foreign-based, dependent on long-distance transport and entirely controlled by corporations."

5. "That cultures and religions have no legitimate practical or economic concerns."

6. "That wars over commodities—our recent Gulf War, for example—are legitimate and permanent economic functions."

7. "That it is all right for poor people in poor countries to work at poor wages to produce goods for export to affluent people in rich countries."

8. "That there is no danger and no cost in the proliferation of exotic pests, weeds, and diseases that accompany international trade and that increase with the volume of trade."

A common theme in Berry's warnings is that monetized corporations, in their ferocious search for profits, destroy or undermine far more important nonmonetized democratic values of societies. That, in turn, leads to the suppression of impoverished societies on the ground where people live, work, and raise their families.

That is why limitless greed, unbridled, whether formed from empires or by domestic plutocrats, eventually produces convulsions that devour their mass victims and themselves.

Website: Destroying the Myths of Market Fundamentalism: https://csrl.org/destroying-the-myths-of-market-fundamentalism-forum/.

Website: The Idea of a Local Economy by Wendell Berry: https://orion-magazine.org/article/the-idea-of-a-local-economy/.

Going for Tax Reform Big Time

MARCH 11, 2022

What if $10 billion were raised over ten years to transform Congress and make it do what it should be doing for the people? (See page 573: "Think Big to Overcome Losing Big to Corporatism," January 7, 2022.) In a more recent column, "Facilitating Civic and Political Energies for the Common Good," February 2, 2022, I outlined how $1 billion per year could be spent lobbying Congress for a people's agenda.

The first $100 million per year would be used to get through Congress long-overdue legislation such as full "Medicare for all," a living wage, preventing corporate abuses, and more. The second $100 million would be devoted to creating facilities that make it easy for people to band together in their various organized roles (e.g., workers, consumers, patients, savers) so they could counter corporate bosses who unite their investors and many lobbying trade groups.

Now I wish to suggest the third $100 million per year be used to make Congress change the disgracefully unfair, wasteful, and inefficient tax laws.

Start with Congress providing the Treasury Department with adequate funds to crack down on tax evasion—estimated to be between $600 billion and $1 trillion a year! Republicans in Congress, since 2011, have strip-mined the Internal Revenue Service (IRS) budget, especially in the area of *enforcement* against tax evasion by the Big Boys and the big global corporations.

The GOP has cut the IRS budget by 20 percent of its 2010 level, inflation-adjusted. Thousands of skilled IRS auditors, investigators, and accountants could not be retained. Audits of large companies plunged by 58 percent between 2010 and 2019. Congress was turned into a recidivist enabler of massive tax evasion—which if done by ordinary people would constitute a crime.

Last year, fifty-five large corporations made $40 billion in US profits and paid *no* federal income tax. Other companies paid less than 10 percent. To give you an idea of the size of yearly uncollected taxes, the lowest estimate is $600 billion, which is $168 billion less than the entire $768 billion military budget approved last year. The current IRS commissioner, Charles P. Rettig, says the sum of uncollected taxes last year was $1 trillion!

When super-rich individuals and corporations escape taxes, either middle-class taxpayers have to pay more or there are fewer government services or the federal deficit gets bigger. The last two results are the ones usually favored by Congress.

Turning to tax reform, there are lists and lists of proposals to get rid of grossly unfair tax loopholes, the parking of money in overseas tax havens, unjustifiable commercial tax deductions, arbitrary deferrals of income, rapid depreciation, shell corporations, and other complex travesties cooked up by corporate tax lawyers.

There is the notorious "carried interest" tax escape, condemned by Warren Buffett and just about every impartial tax expert. This is where private equity, and hedge funds in particular, get their no-risk net services for investors taxed at a much lower capital gains tax rate instead of higher ordinary income rates.

These legal tax escapes are called "tax avoidance" and are carved out by commercial-interest lobbyists who wine, dine, and give campaign cash to many of the 535 members of Congress. Some of these "avoidances" have existed for years, while others are quietly pushed through at the end of many congressional sessions. If people only knew more specific examples of what profitable freeloaders are getting away with, their ire would spark indignation and civic action. Think tax deductions for extravagant entertainment or paying wrongfully injured people and so forth.

Spending $100 million a year could fund hundreds of skilled people's lobbyists on Capitol Hill and back home in congressional districts. These advocates would make tax reform front-page news, push for revelatory public hearings, and encourage disclosures by whistleblowers. They would also propose specific airtight legislation. These and other initiatives would make "tax reform" a top-ranked election issue.

For years, all kinds of fair tax proposals have been developed by law professors and public interest groups, such as the Citizens for Tax Justice and its former director Robert McIntyre. But no legislative muscle has been applied to Congress to counter the relentless corporatist assault on fair and proper tax laws.

Some reformers are concluding that giant corporations are moving the tax code toward *de facto* tax exemption for themselves. David Cay Johnston, author of many articles and books on this subject, has concluded that corporations, using global tax escapes, can now decide what to pay, when to pay, and where to pay their dwindling taxes. He thinks unenforceable federal income taxes for corporations should be scrapped in favor of a much simpler, more collectible corporate tax system.

Western European nations rely heavily on "value-added taxes," a cascading form of sales tax starting with mining to manufacturing to wholesale and retail levels. Sales taxes are usually easier and quicker to collect.

Other tax reform advocates urge that we start first with taxing pollution ("tax what we burn before taxing what we earn"), corporate crime, and financial transaction taxes on Wall Street trades and speculation.

Doubters of much success in Congress, take note. There are no more than a tiny handful of full-time advocates doing this work. Not a single full-time person, for example, is lobbying to end the "carried interest" tax escape. Similar voids exist for any one of hundreds of such unconscionable and indefensible schemes.

Why would you expect anything to happen with nobody on top of Congress? With $100 million a year a corps of savvy experts, publicists, and communicators could decisively take on Capitol Hill.

For now, Congress must pass the Biden administration's restorative funding to the depleted IRS to make the Big Boys pay up.

Who is Raising Our Children? Liberating Tweens from Corporate Tentacles

SEPTEMBER 17, 2022

Consider the harmful, grasping tentacles of corporations around the bodies and minds of youngsters through relentless direct marketing that bypasses parental authority. Now comes my sister Claire Nader's new book *You Are Your Own Best Teacher!: Sparking the Curiosity, Imagination, and Intellect of Tweens.*

The corporate creep started out in the movies and early kids' television, such as Mickey Mouse and Donald Duck cartoons. Then these cartoons expanded to include ads for sweets and soft drinks. Then the marketeers promoted diets exploding with sugar, salt, and fat, documented in detail by the Center for Science in the Public Interest (see: *NutritionAction*—cspinet.org/page/nutrition-action). This resulted in obesity, diabetes, and predispositions to other diseases. The TV stations would not air counter ads to defend vulnerable children.

Meanwhile, outside middle and high schools' premises, vendors for the carcinogenic tobacco companies were passing out free cigarettes. Hook them at age twelve and you've got them for life was the savage Big Tobacco strategy.

In recent decades, the open floodgates of direct marketing of anything and everything to kids has become a half-trillion-dollar annual business. Every mode of seduction, manufactured peer pressure, and minute psychological profiling is delivered by highly paid promoters, packagers, and influencers.

Then about 2007 came the iPhone and other "smart" phones that plunged preteens and teens into the addictive Internet Gulag. Predatory practices were planned to the nth degree by the likes of Facebook, Instagram, and others right down to click-on, fine-print contract peonage. But that's not enough for Mark Zuckerberg and Tim Cook, who are eagerly planning a deeper Metaverse quicksand and so-called "augmented reality" (read: depthless virtual reality). Already, many kids are staring at iPhones and computer screens six to seven hours a day. Violent video games have become hyperaddictions interfering with schoolwork and convulsing family life.

Although parenting columns, recent actions by the Federal Trade Commission, and an overwhelming bipartisan vote in the California legislature to address the serious mental health consequences of the internet on youngsters are raising alarms, the corporations are digging ever deeper into young psyches. Profits are kings not to be dethroned. As James U. McNeal put it in his 1992 book *Kids as Customers: A Handbook of Marketing to Children*, there is always "Needed: New, New Product Strategies that Really Target Kids."

Over the years, Claire has been observing these merciless, cruel exploitations and wondering about our society's failure to protect the young generations. As a response to this commercialization of childhood ("tearing apart the fabric of childhood," as former Arizona governor Bruce Babbitt phrased it), she has written on fifty-four topics speaking directly to nine- to twelve-year-olds (tweens) and, unlike the profiteers, connecting tweens to families, communities, and nature through various elevated conversations and experiences.

Call the book an antidote, like no other, to liberate young, innately curious, imaginative, practical idealists from the commercial pressures coming down on them every day.

She doesn't talk down to tweens. Instead, she guides them toward raising their own sense of significance (giving examples of accomplished tweens) and realizable achievements.

You Are Your Own Best Teacher! recounts many motivating stories, from history to the present, that make Claire's nudges toward self-educational experiences exciting. She introduces them to young Benjamin Franklin, young Frederick Douglass, and young Helen Keller to illustrate their profound self-awareness and discipline. She takes them on a tour of the print dictionary, highlighting concepts such as justice, freedom, peace, wisdom, and gratitude.

By addressing tweens' self-consciousness, the book takes youngsters on explorations about "being smart" to learn about their own bodies, and encourages them to press for more physical activity, to eat smartly, to control their time, and to avoid hours glued to hypnotic screens. Explaining the importance of "learning to unlearn" and asking questions such as

"What if?" and "Why?" regarding the outside world, she encourages tweens to teach themselves to distinguish fact from fiction, thinking from just believing, and respect from self-respect, all of which will prepare them for the realities they will face as they mature.

Claire has long believed that if you have low expectations for tweens, they will oblige you, but if you have high expectations, they will surprise you. Her book offers suggestions for communing with nature, enriching family discussions, appreciating the wisdom of the ancients, and using proverbs to extend the ability of children to concentrate.

Teachers understand the benefits of self-education that enhances the vitality of their classrooms. Self-teaching to build tweens' confidence is also heartening for parents who feel they have lost control over raising their own children to the stupefying seductions of video-driven hucksters. This book is for the whole family!

The main thrust of her effort, however, is to directly speak to tweens, with a calming sense of humor, about their futures as active young citizens, skeptical shoppers, and lifelong learners. This means anticipating how to better handle their turbulent adolescent years and later apply their talents to further the common good and protect posterity.

Of the many encomiums bestowed on this transformative book, one stood out for me from law professor and author Robert Fellmeth, who wrote: "All in all, this book is full of wisdom—more than any other I have read in my 76 years on this earth. . . . I wish I could have read it to my two sons. None of us would fall asleep and all of us would grow wiser."

To obtain *You Are Your Own Best Teacher!* go to inspiringtweens.com. It makes an important gift for tweens, parents, and local libraries.

The New Corporate Dictators—
Super-rich & Superimmune

MAY 13, 2022

Ever since East India Trading Company (1600) and Hudson's Bay Company (1670) were incorporated by English royal charters, there have been corporate dictators. Their range and actions have varied widely, however. Today's new corporate dictators shatter past restraints.

John D. Rockefeller ruled the Standard Oil Company monopoly until the trustbusters from Washington broke up its giant price-fixing and predatory practices into several companies.

Andrew Carnegie was the ruler of the giant Carnegie Steel Company (which became U.S. Steel Corporation). Carnegie violently broke up strikes, such as the 1892 Homestead strike, before he left the company to be a major philanthropist building libraries and universities.

In the post–World War II years, the CEOs of General Motors and Ford had immense power but still had to contend with a strong United Auto Workers union and later with jolting consumer advocacy leading to federal safety and emissions regulation.

Today's corporate dictators are like no others, with unparalleled wealth towering over that held by Rockefeller and Carnegie (adjusted for inflation).

Consider the sheer unchallenged power of Mark Zuckerberg, CEO of Facebook (Meta); Tim Cook, CEO of Apple; the wannabe CEO of a going-private Twitter, Elon Musk (unless the sinking Tesla stock ends the debt-deep acquisition price); and Sergey Brin and Larry Page, still in control of Google. Despite recent stirrings, there are no companywide unions at these companies, and the prospect for such is still in the distant future.

These CEOs snap their fingers, and their patsy boards of directors sign off on huge optimally priced stock options and other goodies. These CEOs don't have to worry about their shareholders, because, like Zuckerberg, with a large portion of the shares, they have rigged their even larger control of voting shares, giving them an unassailable shareholder majority.

They are hauled before congressional committees, appearing humble, and afterward they must be breaking open the champagne because after the public posturing by the lawmakers, no effective regulation is ever enacted. Antitrust action year after year doesn't materialize, other than some weak consent decrees against Facebook, which for a decade it violated while paying laughable civil fines.

No corporate monopolist comes close these days to being prosecuted for jail time. Under both the Democratic and Republican parties, the Department of Justice cuts sweetheart "deferred prosecution agreements" (see *Corporate Crime Reporter*: corporatecrimereporter.com) with the corporate entity and lets off the bosses. Boeing, after its two criminal 737 MAX 8 crashes, is the latest example (See: *Flying Blind: The 737 MAX Tragedy and the Fall of Boeing*, by Peter Robison, November 30, 2021).

The dictatorship over consumers is most unprecedented. Whereas the old dictatorial bosses—pre-unions—had control over workers' lives at the workplace, today's corporate dictators can ply their power 24-7. They can get into the minds of people to addict them and have their personal lives invaded and their personal information offered for sale all over the globe. The old bosses used child labor until the early twentieth century, but then kids were largely off limits.

Today's dollar dictators have fused children's hands with their iPhones and incarcerated them in their vast, gluttonous, nasty, violent internet world to which they become addicted. For six to ten hours a day, their screen time has become their lifetime—families begone!

Not only do these bosses' avaricious clutches have no "quit time," the little ones are now being lured into the metaverse gulag, equipped with three-dimensional goggles to distance themselves further from daily reality.

Although circumvented, millions of parents are at their wits' end, trying to recover their children from their screens and their video games and their digital fantasy worlds at all hours. Although there have been dozens of exposé books, documentaries, and newly formed citizen groups focusing on these corporate child molesters, the hijacking of little America by these internet barons continues unabated.

Suing these commercial dictators for whom enough is never enough has gone nowhere. Judges don't recognize offered causes of action. Moreover, under a special exception (Section 230 of the Communications Decency Act) from federal communications law, media like Twitter and Facebook are largely immune from suits no matter how violent, defamatory, or false the anonymous hate messages traversing their corporate portals.

The contrast between the old and new corporate dictators is that the latter use, for free, your personal data for a fantastically profitable sale. The profit margins flowing from turning free "products" into big-time cash are so high as to stun old-time economists who are used to margins under 10 percent, not over 50 percent.

Perhaps a bottom line in the differences between the old and new corporate dictators is twofold. Year after year, there is no number two really challenging their tight controls—no Avis to take on Hertz, as the old phrase went.

Second, the workers in these old industries felt and knew the oppressors or dictators ruling them. They were deep in this corporate reality. They could organize themselves because they knew their coworkers, and this proximity gave birth to the union movements that led to fair labor standards and other regulations protecting workers (still much to be done here).

How do the users organize to overcome transaction costs (as with Facebook, Google, and Twitter) when they never see each other? It's a one-way gold mine ether out there. When Facebook users formed a group for enhanced bargaining several years ago, Facebook sued for trademark infringement and blocked that nascent effort.

As long as Silicon Valley behemoths continue to rule Washington, DC, and state capitals, get ready for more refinements of commercial tyranny.

Consumer Protection Progress and Regress—
from the Sixties to Now

APRIL 15, 2022

I'm often asked whether consumers are better or worse off since the modern consumer movement took hold in the 1960s.

Let's look at the record. Motor vehicles are much safer, less polluting, and more fuel-efficient now, but not nearly what they should be. Today, consumers have warranty rights, recall rights, and equal credit opportunity rights they did not have back then. Labeling has also improved. There is no more lead in gasoline and paint, though lead water pipes still contaminate some drinking water systems. Deadly asbestos is out of most products.

From being King Tobacco over fifty years ago, cigarette companies are more regulated, and daily tobacco smoking is down from 45 percent of adults to less than 15 percent of adults. But now there is vaping.

Solar energy and wind power are growing, even though energy company propaganda smeared them as Buck Rogers science fiction over fifty years ago.

Nutritional, organic, and ethnic foods are more widely available.

Nuclear power plants are closing and no new ones are under construction, except for the massive Georgia boondoggle projects costing taxpayers and ratepayers billions of dollars in cost overruns. Heating, lighting, and air-conditioning technologies are more efficient but nowhere near what they could be.

Clothing is cheaper due to production being taken to horrific polluting sweatshops abroad, leaving empty factories here (see *Fashionopolis: The Price of Fast Fashion and the Future of Clothes* by Dana Thomas, September 3, 2019).

Now look at the dark side. Housing is less affordable and homelessness is greater. Hunger is still a shameful plague in a land of plenty, with some fifteen million children going to bed hungry. We have pandemics instead of epidemics. Highway congestion and the paucity of mass transit are probably comparatively worse, despite some new investments in public transit since the sixties.

The profit-driven opioid pandemic taking over a hundred thousand American lives a year didn't exist in the 1960s. Drug prices are sky-high, even with large government subsidies and free research and development from the National Institutes of Health.

Corporate crime escaping accountability is more diverse, brazen, and massive. Big-time corporate crime pays. Over *$350 billion* is lost in computer billing fraud every year just in the health care industry. There are very few prosecutions. Since computer use has grown, it has been much easier for corporations to cheat, fine, penalize, and overcharge consumers and commit automated billing fraud. With the repeal of state usury laws in the 1970s, payday rackets and rent-to-own swindles have fewer restraints.

Fine-print contracts keep reaching new levels of coercion unheard of in the 1960s. This is due to the endless opportunities created by the incarcerating credit card economy, which has taken away consumers' control over their own money. Over 80 percent of consumers do not use cash or checks as they did in the sixties.

It is hard to exaggerate the massive controls over consumers that come from loss of freedom of contract and coercion by companies with threats to worsen consumer credit scores and credit ratings, especially if they dare to persistently complain about a lemon car or a callous landlord. Fine-print contract companies—just about every major corporation selling to you—are now taking away your right to go to court and have a trial by jury if you are wrongfully injured and want to hold wrongdoers accountable for damages.

Working only three days a week when they are not in extended recesses, Congress holds fewer investigative public hearings on issues affecting consumers such as monopolies or oligopolies that plague one industry after another. There are far fewer full-time consumer reporters at newspapers and radio or TV stations. Wells Fargo Bank creates fictitious credit card accounts, auto insurance, and other sales for millions of their nonrequesting customers for years and then, when caught, its top bosses escape jail time. Where was the preventative oversight?

What would have been incredible in the 1960s is the relentless drive by companies such as Amazon, rental car giants, and others to get rid of purchasing by cash or check. Many companies want to coerce everybody into the credit/debit penitentiary so they can charge your account for their dictatorial fees and other abuses (see my column on page 480, "Ten Reasons Why I Don't Have a Credit Card," December 5, 2014).

Companies can charge you an outrageous fee or so-called penalty. They control your money through access to your credit card and deduct their bilk. What if instead they had to send you a bill to pay by check? They would probably decide to revise their business model, because you would be more outraged if you had to consciously pay them instead of being passively debited.

Finally, the marketing to children is out of control. Companies are circumventing parental authority selling directly to kids harmful junk food, junk drink, and violent programs and games. These avaricious corporations are electronic child molesters. Direct-marketing to kids and pushing to hook them with credit cards at an early age are both tactics that pull them into the addiction industries and create intense family turmoil—especially with children's omnipresent iPhones as the delivery vehicles.

Now comes Facebook's murky "metaverse" that sucks in these youngsters far beyond the cruel seductions of today's internet, further distancing this generation from the realities of life and communion with their families and the natural world.

We need hundreds of new consumer protection organizations, from the local to the national and international levels, making tough demands on lawmakers and pushing for wider access to justice for aggrieved people.

Big corporations have meticulous strategic plans for humans, including robotic replacement of workers and of human-to-human contact. It is time for a new consumer revolution and new consumer rules for a just, safe, and consumer-sovereign economy.

Alexa can't help you with this portentous mission.

Students, Campuses, and Dominant Corporate Power

JULY 16, 2022

When it comes to corporate power and control over their lives, now and into the future, today's college students are perilously dormant. When it comes to putting pressure on Congress to counter the various dictates of corporatism, there is little activity other than some stalwarts contacting their lawmakers on climate violence.

Much of campus activity these days focuses on diversity, tuition, student loans, "politically correct" speech demands, and conforming conduct.

This campus environment is strangely oblivious to the corporate abuses of our economy, culture, and government. This indifference extends to the endless grip of corporate power over the educational institutions that the students attend.

Companies see universities and colleges as profit centers.

Corporate vendors influence or control the food students eat on campus, down to the junk in vending machines, along with their credit cards, iPhones, very expensive textbooks, and, of course, student debt.

College boards of trustees are dominated by corporate executives or corporate-affiliated people. Corporate science—as from drug, biotech, military weapon, and fossil fuel companies—is coopting, corrupting, or displacing academic science, which is peer-reviewed and unencumbered by corporate profiteering (see professor Sheldon Krimsky's books: sites. tufts.edu/sheldonkrimsky/books).

Corporate law firms dominate law schools with few exceptions, seriously distorting the curriculum away from courses on corporate crimes and immunities and courses that show how corporations have shaped public institutions such as Congress, state legislatures, and the Pentagon along with state and federal regulatory agencies.

Business schools, except for a few free-thinking professors, are finishing schools for Wall Street and other businesses. They operate in an empirically starved environment regarding what is really going on in the world of global corporate machinations, while feeding their students' dogmatic free-market fundamentalism.

Engineering departments narrowly orient their students toward corporate missions without educating them about the engineering profession's ethical and whistleblowing rights and duties. (See *Ethics, Politics, and Whistleblowing in Engineering*, by Nicholas Sakellariou and Rania Milleron, CRC Press, 2018.)

Social science courses are largely remiss as well. There are very few courses on plutocratic rule and the ways uncontrolled big business gets commercial values to override civic values. Teachers may be wary of raising such taboo topics, but the enthusiastic student response to professor Laura Nader's course on "Controlling Processes" at UC Berkeley over the years might indicate deep student interest in courses on top-down power structures.

Active students in the 1960s and '70s took their environmental and civil rights and antiwar concerns directly to Congress. They, with other citizen groups, pushed Congress and got important legislation enacted.

Students in about twenty states created lasting full-time student advocacy groups called Public Interest Research Groups or PIRGs (see studentpirgs.org).

Today the PIRGs are still making change happen in the country (see: the Right to Repair project: uspirg.org/feature/usp/right-repair). However, few new PIRGs have been established since 1980. Students need to embrace how important, achievable, and enduring independent nonprofit PIRGs can be. With skilled advocates continuing to train students in civic skills and provide students with extracurricular experiences for a lifetime of citizen engagement, the PIRGs create a vibrant reservoir for a more functioning democracy.

As leading European statesman Jean Monnet said decades ago: without people nothing is possible, but without institutions nothing is lasting.

Students need to think about the civic part of their years ahead and focus on building the pillars of a democratic society that dissolve the concentrated power of giant corporations and empower the citizenry as befits the "We the People" vision in our Constitution.

What Are Torts? They're Everywhere!

FEBRUARY 20, 2019

What exposed the tobacco industry's carcinogenic cover-up? The lethal asbestos industry cover-up? The General Motors deadly ignition-switch defect cover-up? The Catholic Church's pedophile scandal? All kinds of toxic waste poisonings?

Not the state legislatures of our country. Not Congress. Not the regulatory agencies of our federal or state governments. These abuses and other wrongs were exposed by lawsuits brought by individuals or groups of afflicted plaintiffs using the venerable American law of torts.

Almost every day, the media reports on stories of injured parties that use our legal system to seek justice for wrongful injuries. Unfortunately, the media almost never mentions that the lawsuits were filed under *the law of torts*.

Regularly, the media reports someone filing a *civil rights* lawsuit or a *civil liberties* lawsuit. When was the last time you read, heard, or saw a journalist start their report by saying "so and so today filed a tort lawsuit" against a reckless manufacturer or a sexual predator, or against the wrongdoers who exposed the people of a town like Flint, Michigan, to harmful levels of lead in drinking water? Or tort lawsuits against Donald Trump for ugly defamations or sexual assault?

I was recently discussing this strange omission with Richard Newman, executive director of the American Museum of Tort Law and a former leading trial attorney in Connecticut. He too was intrigued. He told me that when high school students tour the museum, their accompanying teachers often admit that they themselves have never heard of tort law!

Last fall, a progressive talk show host who has had many victims of wrongful injuries on her show visited the museum. While walking through the door, she too declared that she didn't know what tort law was. She certainly did after spending an hour touring the museum. (See tortmuseum.org.)

Public ignorance about tort law should have been taken care of in our high schools. Sadly even some lawyers advised us not to use the word "tort" in the museum's name because nobody would know what it meant.

"Tort" comes from the French word for "a wrongful injury." Millions of torts involving people and property occur every year. Bullies in schools, assaults, negligent drivers, hazardous medicines, defective motor vehicles, toxic chemicals, hospital and medical malpractices, occupational diseases, and more can all be the sources of a tort claim.

Yes, *crimes* are almost always *torts* as well. When police officers use wildly excessive force and innocent people die, families can sue the police department under tort law and recover compensation for "wrongful deaths."

American law runs on the notion that "for every wrong, there should be a remedy." When Americans get into trouble with the law, they are told by judges that "ignorance of the law is no excuse" and that "you are presumed to know the law." In that case, why then don't we teach the rudiments of tort law (or fine-print contract law, for that matter) in high schools?

After all, youngsters are not exempt from wrongful injuries in their daily street and school lives. Just recently, scores of schools' drinking water fountains were found to contain dangerous levels of lead. That is a detectable, preventable condition and would be deemed gross negligence invoking tort law.

Most remarkably, the insurance industry has spent billions of dollars over the past fifty years on advertising and demanding "tort reform," meaning restricting the rights of claimants who go to court and capping the compensation available to injured patients no matter how serious their disability. Still, the public's curiosity was never quickened to learn more about tort law and trial by jury. The right to trial by jury is older than the American Revolution, is protected by the Seventh Amendment to our Constitution, and is available to be used by injured parties to help defend against or deter those who would expose people and their property to wrongful harm or damage.

One way to educate people is to do what a physician friend of mine did at a conference of ear, nose, and throat (ENT) specialists. He walked in wearing a Tort Museum T-Shirt, causing raised eyebrows and provoking discussion.

There are, of course, more systematic ways to inform Americans about tort law. Bring the high school curriculums down to earth and educate students about this great pillar of American freedom. Devote one of the six hundred cable channels in America to teaching citizens about the law and how to use it to improve levels of justice in our country.

From social media to traditional media, the law of torts needs to be illustrated with actual case studies showing its great contribution and even greater potential to provide compensation for or deterrence of all kinds of preventable violence.

Artists and musicians should use their talents to convey many of these David and Goliath battles in our courts of law. Oh, for a great song on the delights of having a jury bring a wrongdoer to justice.

The powerless can hold the powerful accountable with a contingent-fee attorney. Tort law remains vastly underutilized—though it is before us in plain sight. The plutocrats must be happy that so few people know about or use the remedies available through tort law.

Hear this, practicing plaintiff lawyers—wherever you are, you number sixty thousand strong in the US. If you each speak to small groups—classes, clubs, reunions, etc.—totaling some one thousand people a year, that is sixty million people receiving knowledge central to their quality of life and security. Every year! Fascinating human interest stories full of courage, persistence, and vindication of critical rights will captivate and inspire your audiences. What say you, "officers of the court"?

Shernoff, Bidart, and Echeverria—Wide-Ranging Lawyers for the People

FEBRUARY 14, 2018

I first heard about William M. Shernoff in the mid-seventies when he was pioneering a field of law known as insurance bad faith litigation. That "bad faith" occurs when insurance companies deny legitimate claims or try to use deceptive fine-print clauses to escape policy coverage. He was starting to collect both compensation for his clients and large punitive damages when the evidence showed insurance companies were imposing these abuses on many thousands of their customers.

One day I called Attorney Shernoff and said that if he would match my $25,000 donation, we could start the National Insurance Consumer Organization (NICO) headed by the former federal insurance commissioner J. Robert Hunter, a pro-consumer actuary who served under both presidents Ford and Carter.

NICO's Bob Hunter thereafter became the single greatest advocate for consumers against the insurance giants that those companies have ever encountered. He knew their fraudulent complexities, translated those complexities into plain English, and brought his expertise and pleasing personality to legislatures, courtrooms, and agencies in all fifty states. During the mid-eighties he visited all the states in a little over one year, rebutting the savage industry attack on a wrongfully injured person's right to have their day in court. The insurance lobbyists have never seen such a whirlwind for justice who defeated them time and time again.

Bill Shernoff was instrumental in putting Bob Hunter, a force of nature, in motion. But this low-key attorney from Claremont, California, was just getting underway. He blazed the trail for rejected insurance consumers and became a feared private regulator of claim-denying insurers by winning cases before judges and juries. He won multimillion-dollar verdicts for a roofer whose disability payments were cut off, for a Samoan government involving hurricane damage, and for a paraplegic Marine whose insurance company rejected his physician on the medical necessity of his 109-day hospital stay. He secured a bad faith settlement on behalf of Northridge, California, earthquake victims and even a $50 million settlement in 1981 for Southern California Physicians over a malpractice insurance policy that overcharged on premiums.

Not wanting to be a lone ranger, Shernoff went around the country conducting seminars training attorneys to bring insurance bad faith lawsuits. It became a movement of sorts, filling in for the notoriously weak state regulation of insurance.

But Shernoff was interested in more than representing specific aggrieved clients. He was an educational leader who furthered consumer education by writing, lecturing, and appearing in mass media. Besides coauthoring a legal textbook on his specialty, he wrote books like *How to Make Insurance Companies Pay Your Claims: And What to Do If They Don't, Payment Refused,* and *Fight Back and Win: How to Get HMOs and Health Insurance to Pay Up.*

One day he called me up and said he wanted to start a consumer law clinic at his alma mater—the University of Wisconsin Law School. The clinic is in its twenty-seventh year and has trained scores of students in consumer advocacy law. Its students represent real clients fighting unfair debt collection, repossession, home improvement fraud, credit fraud, and other unscrupulous business practices. There are also William Shernoff Health and Consumer Law Fellowships to work for health care reform.

This small law firm of Shernoff, Bidart, and Echeverria welcome their responsibilities as "officers of the court" as well as their broader duties to build institutions of justice that provide powerless people ever more access to justice. They are major contributors to Consumer Watchdog, a leading California advocacy association, and to Public Justice, a large public interest nonprofit law firm. They are also major contributors to the American Museum of Tort Law, which as a volunteer I established as an educational institution dedicated to informing the public about the law of wrongful injuries.

Whenever there are insurance industry–indentured legislators—state or federal—pressing for cruel laws to stifle wronged Americans from their day in court or before regulatory agencies, chances are this firm is there either in person or with donations to fight them or overrule them with statewide referendums. One victory was Proposition 103 in California that regulated the property/casualty insurance companies thirty years ago, which has saved California consumers over $100 billion since that voter revolt.

Of course, there are still many obstacles to the exercise of consumer rights and remedies, such as the Federal Employee Retirement Income Security Act pension law's massive preemption of tort claims. But if there were more firms doing what Shernoff's firm does, millions of people would be receiving judicial or regulatory justice for their costly injuries or illnesses.

My best guess is that not more than twenty-five plaintiff personal injury firms are sharing, training, and helping to build consumer protection institutions either in their state or nationally. However, proportionate to their relative size, few of them have packed the continual wallop of Shernoff's law firm.

How do Shernoff, Bidart, and Echeverria do it? For starters, they have the right sensitive and generous values that are necessary for the work. Moreover, they recognize that they have to be both *attorneys* for clients and *lawyers* for the broader institutional advances of justice so that more people can use the laws meant for them.

How do they get underway? They make calls and *above all return calls*—a practice over 90 percent of their peers have not deigned to do when citizen groups want to initiate ways and means for a more just rule of law, as if people matter first.

Around the country plaintiff lawyers vary in their resolve to push back the corporate predators who want to repeal the American Revolution and its subsequent Bill of Rights for the people, especially the Constitution's Seventh Amendment securing the right of trial by jury. For instance, the repeated failure of the major Texas trial lawyers to ward off the tort "deformers" contrasts with efforts by their counterparts in New York to hold the fort in Albany.

Years ago, Dr. Sidney Wolfe of Public Citizen's Health Research Group published the popular, widely used book *Worst Pills, Best Pills*. All these drugs were licensed by the Food and Drug Administration, but some had bad side effects and others were much safer. Maybe it is time to have a list of the "Worst Lawyers, Best Lawyers." All of these lawyers would be licensed to practice, but widely differ in their commitment to defend, preserve, and expand the civil justice system, under relentless attack by the corporate lobbies, that they and their forebears built.

The Rule of Power over
the Rule of Law

NOVEMBER 15, 2017

Me Too is producing some results. At long last. Victims of sexual assault by men in positions of power are speaking out. Big-time figures in the entertainment, media, sports, and political realms are losing their positions—resigning or being told to leave. A producer at *60 Minutes* thinks Wall Street may be next.

Sexual assaults need stronger sanctions. Only a few of the reported assaulters are being civilly sued under the law of torts. Even fewer are subjects of criminal investigation so far.

Perhaps the daily overdue accounting regarding past and present reports of sexual assaults will encourage those abused in other contexts to also blow the whistle on those abuses. Too often there are rewards instead of penalties for high government and corporate officials whose derelict and often illegal decisions directly produce millions of deaths and injuries.

A few weeks ago, former secretaries of state Madeleine Albright and Condoleezza Rice shared a stage at the George W. Bush Institute, reflecting on their careers to widespread admiration. What they neglected to mention were the devastated families, villages, cities, communities, and nations plunged into violent chaos from the decisions they deliberately made in their careers.

In a 1996 interview, Lesley Stahl of CBS *60 Minutes* asked Madeleine Albright, then secretary of state under Bill Clinton, about the tens of thousands of children in Iraq whose deaths were a direct result of Clinton-era sanctions designed to punish Baghdad. Ms. Stahl asked whether it was worth it (at that time, Ms. Stahl had just visited these wasting children and infants in a Baghdad hospital). Secretary Albright replied in the affirmative.

Condoleezza Rice, secretary of state under George W. Bush, pushed for the criminal and unconstitutional invasion of Iraq, which resulted in over one million Iraqi deaths, millions of refugees, a broken country, and sectarian violence that continues to this day. She has said she often thinks about this mayhem and feels some responsibility. Yet one wonders, as she collects huge speech fees and book advances from her position at Stanford University, whether she might consider donating some of her considerable resources to charities that support those Iraqis whose lives were destroyed by the illegal interventions she advocated.

Then there is lawless Hillary Clinton, who, against the strong advice of Secretary of Defense Robert Gates and without any congressional authorization, persuaded Barack Obama to support a destabilizing regime overthrow in Libya—which has since devolved into a failed state spreading the death, destruction, and terror in Libya to its neighboring countries. Clinton, who is at large touting her new book and making millions of dollars in book royalties and speech fees to applauding partisan audiences, should also consider making donations to those who have been harmed by her actions.

Relaxing in affluent retirement are George W. Bush and Dick Cheney, the butchers of millions of innocent Iraqis and Afghans. They too are raking it in and receiving ovations from their partisans. No prosecutors are going after them for illegal wars of aggression that were never constitutionally declared and violated our federal laws, international treaties, and the Geneva Conventions.

As these ex-officials bask in adulation, the American people are not being shown the burned corpses, charred villages, and poisoned water and soil created by their "public service." Nor are they exposed to the immense suffering and broken hearts of survivors mourning their deceased family members. Americans never hear the dreaded 24-7 whine of the omnipresent drones flying over their homes, ready to strike at the push of a button by remote operators in Virginia or Nevada. Nor do they hear the screams and sobs of the victims of unbridled military action, fueling ever-greater hatred against the US.

Corporate executives also get rewarded for the mayhem they unleash by selling dangerously defective cars (e.g., General Motors, Toyota, and Volkswagen recently) or releasing deadly toxins into the air and water or presiding over preventable problems in hospitals that a Johns Hopkins School of Medicine study reported are taking five thousand lives a week in this country.

What's the difference? There is a great distance in time and space between the cause and effect of officials pushing lethal politics, openly carried out with massive armed forces (the Nuremberg principles after World War II, which included adherence by the US, addressed this problem). They lather their massively violent, unlawful actions with lies, cover-ups, and deceptions, as was the case in 2002 and 2003 in Iraq. They wrap the flag around their dishonorable desecrations of what that flag stands for and the lives of US soldiers whom they sent there to kill or die.

These officials overpower the rule of law with the rule of raw power—political, economic, and military.

For centuries patriarchal mayhem has exploited women in the workplace or the home. Raw power—physical, economic, and cultural—regularly overpowers the legal safeguards against wrongful injury, rape, and torture, both in the household and at work.

Sporadic assertions of a punishing public opinion will not be enough in either sphere of humans abusing humans. That is why the rule of law must be enforced by the state, and through private civil actions.

Why Harvard Law School Matters:
A New Critique

OCTOBER 26, 2017

Harvard Law School celebrates its two hundredth anniversary on October 26 and 27 with two days of events attended by hundreds of alumni and some law students, led by Pete Davis ('18), are inviting the law school community to engage in extraordinary introspection as it looks toward its third century.

Mr. Davis, after two years of observation, participation, conversation, and research, has produced a major report titled *Our Bicentennial Crisis: A Call to Action for Harvard Law School's Public Interest Mission.* Over the past sixty years, many of the beneficial changes at the law school were jolted, driven, or demanded by a small number of organized students calling for clinical education, for women and minorities to be admitted as students and faculty, for more affordability, for more realism in their legal education, and for more intellectual diversity among the professors (the critical legal studies scholars obliged them up to a point). Over time, the law school administration, with faculty persuasion, responded.

The bicentennial report by Pete Davis asks important questions about the law writ large, square in the context of the law school's long-declared mission statement: "To educate leaders who contribute to the advancement of justice and the well-being of society."

Out there in the country, the rule of law and justice is relentlessly overwhelmed by concentrated, unjust power. Just consider the stark reality that our profession's legal services are unaffordable to most Americans and, as retired Supreme Court justice Sandra Day O'Connor has been tirelessly arguing, legal aid resources for access to justice are consistently pathetic.

But the reality of raw economic, political, and technological power over a just legal order has broader consequences. From the lawlessness of presidential war-making exercised daily abroad, to the plutocrat-shaped and dominated corporate state, to stifling the fair usage of our two pillars of private law—contracts and torts—there is an undeniable crisis outside of Harvard Law School that Davis factually and normatively contends is aided and abetted by the culture, incentives, and practices at our alma mater.

The underlying moral basis of law has been supplanted by the commercial motivations and their tailored analytic skills. For most students, Harvard Law has long been a finishing school—a farm team, if you will—for lucrative corporate law practice in service to ever larger global corporations. The corporate attorneys weave strategies that mature the authoritarian corporate state (recall President Eisenhower's warning about the military-industrial complex as one example) to undermine a weakening democratic society and support corporate supremacy.

As institutionalized lawlessness robs our country of its potential and promise, the opportunities for Harvard Law, a well-endowed, proud historic law school, to be a leading institution for justice become ever more significant and urgent. The civic jolt, as always, comes from the rising of the deprived, denied, excluded, and disrespected citizenry; from an informed and motivated student body—seeking higher estimates of their own significance in contemporary history and drawing on their forebears' finest initiatives; and from a faculty that lifts its horizons beyond its specializations and moves from knowledge to action—as a few Harvard professors have done. It helps to nourish a media that recognizes law schools as heavily underutilized but very important national resources. In short, law schools need a constant dose of demands and invitations that come from higher public expectations.

Looking at HLS 200: HLS in the World—Friday's numerous sessions—one wonders about key subjects left out, such as corporate crime, consumer protection, and the role of large corporate law firms, and about who was invited and not invited to participate based on knowledge, record, and something to say.

Our Bicentennial Crisis was written by Pete Davis to be discussed, analyzed, and amplified by the Harvard Law School community, including its alumni and the affected public at large. Copies will be distributed to all the law schools in the country and other civic and public organizations.

The law school administration, so historically adept at waiting out its student and alumni critics, would do well to engage with an open and sensitive mind. With John Manning taking the helm as dean, a fresh attitude, unencumbered by past decisions, can encourage constructive engagements in the coming weeks. Our country's crises are worsening, the needs are great, and the existing capacities at HLS should rise to meet, in the words of Oliver Wendell Holmes Jr., "the felt necessities of our times."

Restricting People's Use of Their Courts

FEBRUARY 21, 2017

In not-so-merry old medieval England, wrongful injuries between people either were suffered in silence or provoked revenge. Cooler heads began to prevail, and courts of law were opened so such disputes over compensation and other remedies could be adjudicated under trial by jury.

Taken across the Atlantic to the colonies, this system—called tort law or the law of wrongful injuries—evolved steadily to open the courtroom door until the 1970s. It was then that the insurance industry and other corporate lobbies began pushing one restriction after another through state legislatures—not restrictions on corporations' rights to sue, but restrictions on the rights of ordinary people to have their day in court.

Lawmakers, whose campaign coffers were stuffed by corporate lobbyists, were not concerned about advancing their passing rules that arbitrarily tied the hands of judges and jurors—the same judges and jurors who were the only people to see, hear, and evaluate individual cases in their courtrooms. Legislation imposing caps on damages—as with California's $250,000 lifetime cap on pain and suffering—was especially cruel for those victims of medical malpractice who were young, unemployed, or elderly and thus did not have significant enough wage losses to receive sufficient damages.

In recent decades, the nonsense about our society being too litigious (except for business-versus-business lawsuits) has become even more extreme. We file far fewer *civil lawsuits* per capita than in the 1840s, according to studies by University of Wisconsin law professors, and jury trials have been declining in both federal and state courts, with trials down by 60 percent since the mid-1980s.

My father used to say that "if people do not use their rights, they will over time lose their rights." This truism brings us to a new book by University of Connecticut law professor Alexandra Lahav, with the title *In Praise of Litigation* (Oxford University Press). The title invokes the necessity of legal recourse in a society where ordinary people are being squeezed out of their day in court, being denied justice, and becoming cynical enough to want to get out of jury duty—a right that our forebears demanded from King George III.

Professor Lahav makes the point we should have learned in high school, or at least college. The right to litigate is critical to any democratic society. Imagine living in a country where no one can sue powerful wrongdoers or the government. We have names for countries like that. They're called dictatorships or tyrannies.

Here is author Lahav's summary: "Litigation is a civilized response to the difficult disagreements that often crop up in a pluralist society. The process of litigation does more than resolve disputes; it contributes to democratic deliberation. This is the key to understanding what this process is supposed to be about and what should be done to improve it. By appreciating the democratic values people protect and promote when they sue—enforcement of the law, transparency, participation, and social equality—reformers can work toward a court system that is truly democracy promoting."

It would be reassuring if more judges reflected those words. Were that the case, they would be fighting harder to expand the shrinking court budgets (about 2 percent of state budgets) that are increasingly causing civil trials to be deferred or courtrooms to be temporarily closed. Tighter budgets lead judges to excessively pressure lawyers to settle or go to arbitration. The latter is a malicious inequity between consumers, workers, and other people unequal in power vis-à-vis big corporations like Wells Fargo, ExxonMobil, Pfizer, and Aetna, which force consumers to sign fine-print contracts that limit people's rights to use the courts.

The usual sally against praising civil litigation is the claim of too many frivolous suits. Whenever Richard Newman, the executive director of the American Museum of Tort Law, hears that asserted, he asks for examples. They are not forthcoming. For good reason. Litigation is expensive; lawyers have to guard their reputations, and judges, who largely lean to the conservative side, are in charge of their courtrooms. They are quite ready to approve motions to dismiss a case or summary judgments.

We have to take a greater interest in our courts. They are open to the public for a reason. Students need to visit them and understand what the burdens are on courts, and how our civil justice system can be improved.

When I ask assemblies of students if they have ever visited a court as a spectator, hardly one in ten raises a hand.

Courts should not be places of case overloads and long delays. They should be welcoming temples of justice where judge and jurors engage in reasoned deliberation for the advancement of justice as part of a functioning democracy. The demands for justice are such in our country that courts should have more judges, more juries, and more trials.

As the great judge Learned Hand wisely wrote: "If we are to keep our democracy, there must be one commandment: Thou shalt not ration justice."

Harvard Lawless School and You

JULY 18, 2016

Harvard Law School professors love to use hypotheticals in their classes. So let's try one that they have not subjected their students to in the school's two hundred years of storied history. What if the law school split itself into two parts—each with different professors and students—on its crowded campus in Cambridge, Massachusetts? One half would retain the name Harvard Law School, while the other half would be called Harvard Lawless School. How would the courses differ?

Well, the Harvard Law School curriculum would remain pretty much the same, accepting the law as is; working its interpretation by courts, regulators, and legislatures; and speculating a little about how it could be clarified and improved.

Harvard Lawless School would be more grounded in grim realities, where there are no operating laws to discipline raw power or where the laws are so violated as to be systematically inoperative over a large range of activities.

Lawlessness, the kind that is considered as factual noncompliance with existing law, is often far more widespread than the studied phenomenon known as compliance.

I am reminded of the long history of this duality by a 1932 review by Daniel James of *The Modern Corporation and Private Property*—a famous book by Adolf A. Berle Jr. and Gardiner C. Means that documented the split between *ownership* (the shareholders) and *control* (by the corporate executives). He wrote then what is worse now, that "there is a paper government for corporations and there is an actual government. The one is embodied in constitutional provisions, statutes, charters, by-laws, decisions; the other has its being in the conduct of men who control corporate activity. . . . With them as with all human institutions there is a divergence of the *intended* and the *realized*, the *ought* and the *is*."

The "is," declared Mr. James, is "made up of blunt, realistic facts," which is what Harvard Lawless School would teach and take off from.

What's all this got to do with you? Just about everything. If you cannot use the law to pursue your rights—say, health coverage—under fine-print contracts or gain adequate compensation for your wrongful injuries, you are being strapped by lawlessness through the design of the power elites. They, of course, live under their own rules—monetarily greased through their plunder of the political economy—and, not surprisingly, use these special rules to their advantage in ways that disadvantage you and most other people.

Business crooks get away with over $300 *billion* a year just in computerized billing fraud and abuse in the health care industry, despite the existing laws against fraud. Starvation enforcement budgets for the federal cops on the corporate crime beat are allocated by an indentured Congress. Thus, a routinely vast area of theft and harm drives a political climate of lawlessness and exacerbates crime in the suites.

When Congress cuts the IRS's budget year after year, the agency cannot collect what it estimates is over $450 billion a year in "uncollected taxes." Add additional massive sums of "avoided taxes" by corporate lobbyists driven through a greased Congress and you end up paying more taxes, or receiving fewer public services or incurring larger government deficits. Huge sums of money are outside the tax laws.

As the protections of tort law—the law of wrongful injuries—are diminished, millions of Americans are left outside the civil justice system—unable to hold perpetrators accountable. The forced underutilization of consumer, environmental, and worker protection laws by their supposed beneficiaries against violators is overwhelmingly the norm.

Expanding areas of lawlessness flow wildly from existing laws. Criminal wars of choice, mass government surveillance, the tortures and the licenses accorded military contractors, are examples of rampant lawlessness. Wars of aggression (Iraq, Libya) are not declared, the Fourth Amendment to the Constitution is violated routinely, torture and unlawful imprisonment (euphemistically called "detention") are the stuff of media exposés that go nowhere.

Domestically, using the law itself as an instrument of oppression, institutionalized dimensions of lawlessness include prosecutorial abuses, police and prison lawlessness, and entrenched procurement violations between vendors and governments. There are unconstitutional laws that need amendment or repeal.

Who enforces the legal boundaries on the Federal Reserve, whose widening unaccountable penumbras of lawless indiscretion are worrying the right and left in this country? Then-secretary of the treasury Henry Paulson told the *Washington Post* that he had "no authorities" to engage in his serial bailouts of Wall Street, but somebody had to do it.

There are no international laws regarding ongoing, growing cyber warfare; no laws governing tumultuous nanotechnology; few rules that can contain the spread of migrating, untested biotechnology.

When at least 250,000 Americans can die yearly (about 700 a day!) because of medical malpractice, medical error, hospital-induced infections, and misprescription of medicines and their lethal side effects, there clearly is no "rule of law" applicable in this realm of preventable mass violence—at least not a rule of law with any quantitative significance.

This short introduction to a hypothetical curriculum at Harvard Lawless School only scratches the surface of the "blunt, realistic facts." Students, professors, and courses at this kind of law school would not be mired in what professor Jon Hanson has called "the illusion of law."

Hypotheticals can spark the imagination to connect law to justice in thought and practice. Who knows what the future holds for an imaginative Harvard Law(less) School?

What about Starting Stevens and O'Connor Institutes for Justice?

APRIL 23, 2014

What do retired justices of the Supreme Court of the United States do with their time and reputation?

One of them—Justice Paul Stevens, age ninety-four—just published another book, *Six Amendments: How and Why We Should Change the Constitution.* This new work adds to his vigorous postretirement writings and addresses.

Another—Justice Sandra Day O'Connor, age eighty-four—has been busy making people miss her swing vote on the court. She has cast doubt on the wisdom of her vote in *Bush v. Gore* and the unlimited corporate campaign cash allowed by the *Citizens United* decision issued after she left the court. Her addresses declaring existing legal services for the poor as grossly inadequate and arguing that our country needs more pro bono services by lawyers and supervised law students are among the most specific and eloquent ever delivered on that shame of the legal profession. She promotes increasing civic education in our schools and the "merit selection for judges" in place of forcing our judges to grub for campaign cash from specific interests.

It seems ripe for these vibrant human civic assets to be the inspiration for permanent institutes in their names—say the Stevens Institute for Justice and the O'Connor Institute for Justice.

Given their long tenure on the high court, Justices Stevens and O'Connor each have had at least one hundred law clerks to assist them. Many clerks are now wealthy, successful attorneys, while others are law professors and judges. They could organize themselves and launch these institutions with a solid funding base that could attract endowments, especially if the two justices support this idea. In a short time, the depleting forest of American democracy—law and justice—could be replenished by two solid oak trees.

Am I just dreaming? Not at all. An effective model exists at New York University Law School called the Brennan Center for Justice. It was founded in 1995 by the family and former law clerks of Supreme Court Justice William J. Brennan. With an annual budget of $10 million, the Brennan Center has a remarkable output for preserving and strengthening our democracy as if people matter first. It is described as "part think tank, part public interest law firm, and part communications hub" working for "equal justice for all."

The Brennan Center uses instruments of education, power through the courts and legislature, and networking with grassroots groups and public officials to give strength to citizens who desire to participate in government decision-making and elections.

The Brennan Center dives into the messiest of our plutocratic politics—the corruption of political money, the obstruction of voters and candidates, the rigging of elections through redistricting, the costs of mass incarceration and racially biased enforcement—and always focuses on solutions. Going where few go, the Brennan Center for Justice has taken to court unlawful actions by presidents and exposed the New York State Legislature as being "the least deliberative, most dysfunctional state legislature in the nation." The *New York Times* reported that "the two men who control the Legislature—[the] Assembly Speaker . . . and the Senate majority leader . . . have almost total power over which bills they will allow their members to vote on, and a wide range of sticks and carrots to help them keep their members in line." The Brennan Center is pressing for a set of ethics reforms, an independent redistricting commission, and a public financing system for state elections that could be applicable to other states' lawmakers.

Imagine going to a law school where students as interns are given an experiential role with the full-time staff in achieving both procedural and substantive justice—what Senator Daniel Webster called the great work of humans on Earth. (See brennancenter.org for more information.)

I have not spoken to Justices Stevens and O'Connor about their willingness to give their names and backing to such institutes. But Jason Adkins, chair of Public Citizen, had a conversation with Justice Stevens on this subject in which the justice responded favorably. Mr. Adkins gets things done, so look for some activity among Justice Stevens's legions of admirers soon.

As for Justice O'Connor, she actively responds to invitations to address law reforms at educational conferences and serves as a trustee of the

National Constitution Center in Philadelphia and of the group Justice at Stake. She started Our Courts America, a website that offers interactive civics lessons to students and teachers. Therefore it is not hard to imagine the huge groundswell of supporters for such an institute furthering her goal of wider access to justice.

The motivation to develop these institutes can begin with the former clerks of Justices Stevens and O'Connor, who spent a year or two working in close proximity to these jurists and the court. Who among them will step forth to start the process of extending the careers and spirit of these famous justices to the benefit of posterity?

If we can do anything to help spark these initiatives, contact us at info@nader.org.

The Majesty of the Law Needs Magisterial Lawyers: Remarks by Ralph Nader on the occasion of receiving the Connecticut Bar Association Distinguished Public Service Award

JUNE 17, 2013

Today, we gather as both attorneys and lawyers to contemplate our privileged profession. The many specialized workshops today are largely designed to better our role as "attorneys"—as attorning for our clients. Permit some words on our role as "lawyers" urged by our ethical canons and codes to strive for justice, to enlarge the people's access to justice, and to improve the administration of justice. Of the nearly one million licensed members of the bar nationwide, the bulk of our time obviously is devoted to being "attorneys" as compared with our time spent exercising wider duties as "lawyers."

Yet if we profess to be a *profession*, invested with monopolistic authority, instead of a *trade*, we should address the three distinctions between a profession and a trade. Unlike a trade, a profession has:

1.   A learned tradition;

2.   An institutional independence; and

3.   A spirit of public service.

Indeed, a careful reading of our canons perceives these characteristics both explicitly and implicitly. They are not simply idealistic principles good for placement on our office walls. For they represent important public interests that we are uniquely empowered, free, and expected to render operational. Should we not give meaning to the words "officers of the court"—a quasi-official status that could properly mean both being sentinels and guardians for the just rule of law?

The world is becoming exponentially more complex; so is the law. Yet the enduring purpose of the law remains as critical as ever—to restrain,

599

redirect, discipline, at times displace abusive power completely, and facilitate the civic and political energies of the people. Serious failings in these roles allow the supremacy of raw power over the law, either to enact legislation that serves the few rather than the many, or to take existing legal systems and distort them into instruments of unfair advantage or injustice against their presumed beneficiaries. That is what happens when the few (plutocrats and oligarchs) control the many to benefit the few. It is what Justice Louis Brandeis meant when he said: "We may have democracy, or we may have wealth concentrated in the hands of a few, but we can't have both." This is what Judge Learned Hand meant when he wrote: "If we are to keep our democracy, there must be one commandment: Thou shalt not ration justice."

Today those insights bear application. We have a serious continuing problem of tens of millions of Americans unable to afford legal representation. Existing legal services and public defender resources are grossly inadequate and relatively on the decline—a deplorable condition criticized repeatedly by former Supreme Court justice Sandra Day O'Connor. Court budgets are being cut back harmfully, as prison budgets loom so much larger.

The national-security government has given us secret law, secret courts, secret evidence, surveillance of attorney-client communications, un-auditable secret expenditures for quagmires abroad, even redacted published judicial decisions and secret prisons. It has shunted aside probable cause and habeas corpus and upended the other bulwarks of due process, such as through indefinite imprisonment without charges and dragnet snooping. An unaccountable executive, breaking constitutional, statutory, and treaty restraints and condoned by abdicatory legislative and judicial branches, is a recipe for tyranny that was foreseen by the framers of our Constitution.

The two pillars of our legal system—the laws of contract and tort—are incrementally ravaged by powerful corporations advised by power attorneys. Corporate privileges and immunities deepen as fine-print contracts and tort deforms both strip-mine the rights of defrauded and wrongfully injured people and destroy deterrence. Corporatism—the blending of big business and big government—produces massive corporate welfare bailouts, subsidies, handouts, outsized tax escapes, and other giveaways, and it locks in the purpose of commercial campaign contributions.

Where are the lawyers? Where are the sentinels and the guardians?

They are here and there. We know them, don't we? Shall we call them the brave 1 percent? The ones who have knowledge in their brain and fire in their belly. There are nowhere near enough of these brothers and sisters in law. Far greater numbers of their peers know what they know or could know. They need to join with them and also arouse the overvocationalized law schools and the underchallenged bar associations, who need more active members.

They need, in a variety of institutional ways, to organize our profession. We are underorganized as "lawyers," as compared with how intricately organized we are as "attorneys."

With a higher estimate of our significance, we must respond to the silent cries of the people for justice—what Senator Daniel Webster called, nearly two centuries ago, "the great interest of man on Earth. It is the ligament which holds civilized beings and civilized nations together."

Thank you.

Law Day, the ABA, and Addressing Reality

MAY 1, 2013

In case you did not know, May 1 is Law Day! Initiated by the American Bar Association (ABA), established by President Dwight D. Eisenhower, and made official by Congress in 1961, Law Day was seen as a counterweight to May Day, which celebrates the workers of the world within socialist and communist countries.

For Law Day, the ABA prepares materials and encourages events in communities and schools to inspire reflection about the importance of equality under the law and of our nation's guaranty of freedom for all. Local bar associations are urged to observe Law Day "to commemorate the rule of law, the judiciary and its place in American society."

These are obviously important generalities. But unless they are tested in the realities of our times, they become important delusions. Bringing these legal values down their abstraction ladder provides a jolting reminder that our country is in the grips of chronic law-breaking from government officials, starting with the president and extending to managers of giant corporations, whose dedicated goal is either to write the laws for themselves via the corporate government in Washington and state capitals or violate the laws with impunity due to their raw power and wealth.

One only needs to read the leading newspapers and see the regular documentation of the scofflaws that have turned the rule of law into an instrument of oppression directed at the weak and for the advantage of the strong. Whether in the pages of the *New York Times*, the *Washington Post*, or the *Wall Street Journal*, or in Associated Press stories, big corporations such as the banks, oil companies, and drug firms are shown to be, in the words of one concise prosecutor, "lying, cheating, and stealing."

A corporate crime wave is running amok, eroding people's savings, pensions, jobs, health, and safety! Corporatism is becoming the law of the land as enforcement budgets and political will shrink before the torrent of abuses.

Freedom is, partly, being left alone. But pollution doesn't leave you alone; invasion of your privacy in a digital credit/debit economy doesn't leave you alone; rip-offs don't leave you alone.

Official lawlessness has reached new depths of decay. It is no longer just the usual graft of public officials, the violations of the for-profit prison-industrial complex, the arrogant greed of many government contractors, especially in the areas of militarism, natural-resource grabs, corporate-welfare subsidies, or the various ways of bribing elected officials. Increasingly, presidents of the US regularly violate our Constitution, laws, and treaties under the pretext of their own definition of national security and their own role as prosecutor, judge, jury, and executioner.

After all, it was the ABA itself, in a rare and great expression of professional duty, that sent three reports in 2005 and 2006 to President George W. Bush concluding that he was violating the Constitution. Then ABA president Michael Greco called those years a period of very dangerous legal crisis for our republic.

Welcome to the encore under President Obama and his "rule of man" superseding the rule of law. His tenure has marked the most extreme and chronic violations of separation of powers, of seizing the exclusive war-declaring power (Article 1, Section 8, Clause 11) from Congress, and, in the case of the Libyan war, even dispensing with the authorization and appropriations authority of Congress.

Freedom must include, as Marcus Cicero wrote, "participation in power." Do people have any of that in the way our government makes major decisions? People can't even have their day in court, as long delays and court budget cutbacks nullify, in practice, constitutional rights for the accused.

Shut out as citizens, people are finding ever greater obstacles in gaining access to justice for their civil grievances. Former conservative Supreme Court justice Sandra Day O'Connor has written eloquently on the absence of legal representation for tens of millions of low-income Americans. She described the real effects this has on their lives, health, safety, and property, as well as the basic problem of not being told of their rights.

The ABA knows all this and more about the failing rule of law, worsening inequality, and shredded freedoms. But the largest organization of lawyers in the world is heavily populated by corporate attorneys whose clients in the plutocracy reward them generously.

As Wesley Smith and I noted in our book *No Contest: Corporate Lawyers and the Perversion of Justice in America*, they, as "officers of the court" (as are all licensed attorneys), have difficulty dropping their attorney/corporate client hats and donning their "lawyer/professional" hats while on duty at the ABA's far-flung network of committees.

Given their embedded retainer/astigmatism, these big-firm lawyers have aggressively fostered regimes over the people of one-sided fine-print contracts (see faircontracts.org), weakened tort law for wrongfully injured persons, and, most brazenly, even lobbied and litigated to place insuperable procedural obstructions before real people's access to the courts. (See Arthur R. Miller's "Simplified Pleading, Meaningful Days in Court, and Trials on the Merits: Reflections on the Deformation of Federal Procedure.")

So, here is my advice to the ABA for future Law Days: Get a grip on the real crises in the law and its uses, misuses, and hypocrisies. Convey that to the folks on Main Street so that lawyers and laborers, students and scholars, can be given real reforms to ponder instead of deceptive illusions highlighted by annual presidential proclamations (see Obama's 2013 Law Day proclamation).

Obama at Large: Where Are the Lawyers?

MAY 30, 2012

The rule of law is rapidly breaking down at the top levels of our government. As officers of the court, we have sworn to "support the Constitution," which clearly implies an affirmative commitment on our part.

Take the administrations of George W. Bush and Barack Obama. The conservative American Bar Association sent three white papers to President Bush describing his continual unconstitutional policies. Then and now civil liberties groups and a few law professors, such as the stalwart David Cole of Georgetown University and Jonathan Turley of the George Washington University, have distinguished themselves in calling out both presidents for such violations and the necessity for enforcing the rule of law.

Sadly, the bulk of our profession, as individuals and through bar associations, has remained quietly on the sidelines. They have turned away from their role as "first responders" tasked with protecting the Constitution from its official violators.

As a youngster in Hawaii, basketball player Barack Obama was nicknamed by his schoolboy chums as "Barry O'Bomber," according to the *Washington Post.* On Tuesday, May 29, the *New York Times* published a massive page-one feature article by Jo Becker and Scott Shane that demonstrated just how inadvertently prescient was this moniker. This was not a newspaper scoop leaked by an adversary. The article had all the signs of cooperation by the three dozen current and former advisers to President Obama and his administration who were interviewed. The reporters wrote that a weekly role of the president is to personally select and order a "kill list" of suspected terrorists or militants via drone strikes or other means. The reporters wrote that this personal role of Obama's is "without precedent in presidential history." Adversaries are pulling him into more and more countries—Pakistan, Yemen, Somalia, and other territories.

The drones have killed civilians, families with small children, and even allied soldiers in this undeclared war based on secret "facts" and local grudges (getting even). These attacks are justified by secret legal memos claiming that the president, without any congressional authorization, can without any limitations other than his say-so target far-and-wide assassinations of any "suspected terrorist," including American citizens.

The bombings by Mr. Obama, as secret prosecutor, judge, jury, and executioner, trample proper constitutional authority, checks and balances, and separation of powers and constitute repeated impeachable offenses. That is, if a pathetic Congress ever decided to uphold its constitutional responsibility, including and beyond the war-declaring powers of Article I, Section 8.

As if lawyers needed any reminding, the Constitution is the foundation of our legal system and is based on declared, open boundaries of permissible government actions. That is what a government of law, not of men, means. Further, our system is clearly demarked by independent review of executive branch decisions—by our courts and Congress.

What happens if Congress becomes, in constitutional lawyer Bruce Fein's words, "an ink blot," and the courts beg off with their wholesale dismissals of constitutional matters on the grounds that an issue involves a "political question" or that parties have "no standing to sue." What happens is what is happening. The situation worsens every year, deepening secretive dictatorial decisions by the White House—and not just regarding foreign and military policies.

The value of the *New York Times* article is that it added ascribed commentary on what was reported. Here is a sample:

- The US ambassador to Pakistan, Cameron P. Munter, was quoted by a colleague as complaining about the CIA's strikes driving American policy, commenting that he "didn't realize his main job was to kill people." Imagine what the sidelined Foreign Service is thinking about greater longer-range risks to our national security.

- Dennis Blair, former director of national intelligence, calls the strike campaign "dangerously seductive." He said that Obama's obsession with targeted killings is "the politically advantageous thing to do—low cost, no US casualties, gives the appearance of toughness. It plays well domestically, and it is unpopular only in other countries. Any damage it does to the national interest only shows up over the long term." Blair, a retired admiral, has often noted that intense focus on strikes sidelines any long-term strategy against al-Qaeda, which spreads wider with each drone that vaporizes civilians.

- Former CIA director Michael Hayden decries the secrecy: "This program rests on the personal legitimacy of the president, and that's not sustainable," he told the *Times*. "Democracies do not make war on the basis of legal memos locked in a [Department of Justice] safe."

Consider this: an allegedly liberal former constitutional law lecturer is being cautioned about blowback, the erosion of democracy, and national security by former heads of supersecret spy agencies!

Secrecy-driven violence in government breeds fear and surrender of conscience. When Mr. Obama was campaigning for president in 2007, he was reviled by Hillary Clinton, Joseph Biden Jr., and Mitt Romney—then presidential candidates—for declaring that even if Pakistani leaders objected, he would go after terrorist bases in Pakistan. Romney said he had "become Dr. Strangelove," according to the *Times*. Today all three of candidate Obama's critics have decided to go along with egregious violations of our Constitution.

The *Times* made the telling point that Obama's orders mean "the Defense Department can target suspects in Yemen whose names they do not know." Such is the drift to one-man rule, consuming so much of his time in this way at the expense of addressing hundreds of thousands of preventable fatalities yearly here in the US from occupational disease, environmental pollution, hospital infections, and other documented dangerous conditions.

Based on deep reporting, Becker and Shane allowed that "both Pakistan and Yemen are arguably less stable and more hostile to the United States than when Obama became president."

In a world of lawlessness, force will beget force, which is what the CIA means by "blowback." Our country has the most to lose when we abandon the rule of law and embrace lawless violence that is banking future revenge throughout the world.

The people in the countries we target know what we must remember. We are their occupiers, their invaders, the powerful supporters for decades of their own brutal tyrants. We're in their backyard, which more than any other impetus spawned al-Qaeda in the first place.

So, lawyers of America, apart from a few stalwarts among you, what is your breaking point? When will you uphold your oath of office and work to restore constitutional authorities and boundaries?

Someday, people will ask—where were the lawyers?

12.

ON CONGRESS AND CIVIC ENGAGEMENT

Americans: For Most Roads Ahead, It's All about Congress!

DECEMBER 4, 2020

We know their names! We've given immense power to 535 people to do good or bad. To 100 Senators and 435 Representatives. Unfortunately, some 1,500 corporations control most members of Congress. Think about all the dreams for a better world that could come to be realized if our elected officials worked for the big majority of Americans instead of for Big Business interests.

Let's go through a short list of Big Deals:

1. Do you want a living wage for all Americans? The superhighway is through Congress.

2. Do you want universal, more efficient, free-choice health care with an emphasis on the prevention of disease and injury? The superhighway goes through Congress.

3. Do you want a fair tax system that makes the big corporations and the wealthy pay their fair share for a change? Take it through Congress.

4. Do you want to stop your tax dollars from being spent on corporate welfare, corporate-powered wasteful budgets in Washington? Congress can do that.

5. Do you want to eliminate corporate defrauding of government programs like Medicare and Medicaid? Take it to Capitol Hill.

6. Do you want your tax dollars to be used to create good-paying, non-exportable jobs—workers to repair and upgrade the public facilities or infrastructure in every one of your communities?

7. Do you want to cut the presently un-audited, bloated military budget; stop the boomeranging empire overseas; and redirect your tax dollars back home to pay for the necessities of life? That means getting it through Congress.

8. Do you want to end all the financial rip-offs such as overcharges and penalties, sky-high credit card and payday loan interest rates and fees?

9. Do you want to end the near-zero interest rates on your savings, where you are lucky to get one-quarter of 1 percent interest while the government charges many times that for student loans?

10. Do you want to protect your families and your children's children from climate catastrophes—worsening by the year?

11. Do you want to quickly move away from fossil fuels to self-reliant, local, cleaner, renewable solar, wind, and hydropowered energy, plus huge energy conservation?

12. Do you want to stop big companies from directly exploiting and tempting your children with junk food and sugary junk drinks that lead to spiraling obesity and related diseases?

13. Do you want Congress to stop the digital-age child molesters (a.k.a corporations) that undermine parental authority and promote violent and addictive entertainment programs?

14. Do you want members of Congress to give you what they have given themselves in the way of retirement security that is part of workers' compensation?

15. Do you want a pathway to universal basic income long backed by leading conservative and liberal economists?

16. Do you want a modern, convenient mass-transit system (that will diminish traffic congestion) like what Japan and western Europe have had for years?

17. Do you want across-the-board paid vacations, paid family sick leave, daycare, and free or low-cost college tuition? (Many years ago, people like you in other countries got these social services through their parliaments.)

18. Do you want to take back control of what you already own from corporations—the public lands, public airwaves, massive public research and development? (Remember you already own these great public assets and pay for them in direct and indirect ways.)

19. Do you want clean and fair elections and electoral districts that stop the buying and renting of politicians? (This is the first step in breaking the big-money chains on Congress by the corporations).

There are so many more congressional actions that could brighten the horizon. Congress could lead the way on affordable, available housing; repeal anti-union laws; push the White House to wage peace (diplomacy) rather than repeatedly threaten or use military force; ratify arms control; advance consumer, labor, and environmental protection treaties; and push the executive branch to enforce civil rights laws and develop stronger corporate crime laws. The list of what should be done is long and overdue.

The road to a more just society runs through Congress and the members of Congress who are working for you, the people.

You may ask, what about obstruction of Congress by the executive branch and the judiciary? Congress controls the purse, confirms the judges, has the tax-paying and the war-making authorities—as designed by our Founding Fathers, who never envisioned Congress abdicating those powers.

In my little paperback book, *Breaking Through Power: It's Easier Than We Think*, I write about the past battles for justice writ large that have been waged in Congress. None of these efforts took more than 1 percent of the people—actively engaged, connected, and knowledgeable—reflecting majority opinion. How did they win? They had a laser focus on Congress and state legislatures—lawmaker by lawmaker.

Why don't tens of millions of Americans—who are hurting, deprived, underinsured, underpaid, disrespected, stressed out, and obstructed from a better life—form Congress watchdog lobbies? Imagine summoning your senators and representatives to *your* organized town meetings to receive *your* majority-supported instructions on how to use the power you've given them.

Americans care for seventy million pet dogs every day. Spend a fraction of that time taking care of your representative and two senators. Maybe people can start using their cell phones to call their members of Congress while safely walking their dogs. For ideas on how to form your own congressional watchdog group see: "Become a Congressional Ratwatcher," https://ratsreformcongress.org/become-a-congressional-ratwatcher/.

Speaker Pelosi and Majority Leader Schumer: Use the Lame-duck Session for the People

NOVEMBER 30, 2022

Dear Speaker Nancy Pelosi and Majority Leader Chuck Schumer,

On July 23, 2022, twenty-four prominent civic advocates and leaders, many of whom you know, made a Zoom presentation for congressional candidates and staff about how to readily defeat the worst GOP—by numerous measures—in history. These presenters were brought together by Mark Green and me. It was not easy to get through the screen of corporate-conflicted political and media consultants to reach candidates. This is a problem the Democratic Party has to confront as it looks back to see why winnable congressional contests were lost or just narrowly won.

Visit winningamerica.net and judge for yourselves how effective these policies, strategies, tactics, messaging, rebuttals, slogans, and techniques for GOTV would have been if they were applied before the election on November 8, 2022.

The DNC [Democratic National Committee], DCCC [Democratic Congressional Campaign Committee], and DSCC [Democratic Senatorial Campaign Committee.] were apprised of these suggestions. They seemed to approve, but whether they conveyed them with the requisite urgency to their candidates is doubtful. Our hunch is that the effort to spread the word was minimal, and when some of the suggestions were used, it was too little too late. It is not far-fetched to say: if we had adopted the principle that all of us are smarter than any one of us, we would in many instances have taken close losing and winning races over the finish line with comfortable margins and majorities.

Turning to the present opportunities until January 3, 2023, the following suggestions—some repeated, some new—are submitted to the current Democratic Congress to roll up its sleeves, hold concise hearings, pass overdue legislation, or at least conclude the session with a popular agenda to greet the incoming Trumpster Dumpster at the House of Representatives. The Democrats have one "last clear chance" to present an agenda that will benefit the American people where they live, work, and raise their families.

Hearings: Hold one or two days of precise hearings on necessities—for children, women, workers, consumers, local communities, and the climate crisis—to frame the electoral policy contest for 2024. Invite strong input from civic community groups known or knowable to you.

Legislation: Pass bills to (1) raise minimum wage to fifteen dollars, (2) enact Representative John Larson's Social Security protection bill (HR 5723), (3) ratify (statutorily) Biden's student debt forgiveness program, (4) require a corporate crime database (HR 9362 and S. 5141—just introduced by Representative Mary Gay Scanlon [D-PA], Representative Jamie Raskin [D-MD], Senator Richard Blumenthal [D-CT], and Senator Richard Durbin [D-IL]), (5) ratify the Environmental Protection Agency clean air regulation invalidated by the US Supreme Court, (6) require Senate confirmation of the national security adviser and White House counsel, (7) adopt a concurrent resolution finding that Donald J. Trump was implicated in the insurrection against the United States and is thus disqualified from holding any office of the United States or any state under Section 3 of the Fourteenth Amendment, (8) propose "Medicare for all," (9) require penalties if the Pentagon fails to comply with a 1992 federal statute requiring that auditable budgets be submitted to Congress, (10) pass a resolution calling on President Biden to begin cease-fire negotiations with Vladimir Putin on the war in Ukraine, (11) repeal the huge Trump tax cut of 2017 for the super-rich and large corporations; enact the long-overdue restoration of a stock transaction sales tax to raise revenues to support important social safety nets and diminish enlargement of the deficit, and (12) enact pending electoral reform legislation.

What can't pass through Senate "reconciliation," or with GOP support, remains on the table to inform the citizenry that the outgoing Congress strove toward the idea of being a Congress for the people and exercising more of its constitutional duties.

The above is doable under an accelerated rhythm of an outgoing Democratically controlled Congress. Recesses would need to be curtailed, but how does that compare to the enhancement of the lives and livelihoods of the American people, who all bleed the same color, who are about to be assaulted by the incoming cruel and corrupt gerrymandered House GOP?

You have about half a dozen legislative deadlines and priorities to enact. However, you have many committees and subcommittees with budgeted staff ready to move on the suggested legislation and other bills and resolutions. Make history, not excuses of being preoccupied with bills on your table. You can decentralize these initiatives and loosen the reigns of your highly concentrated management for the sake of the greater good both inside Congress and, most importantly, throughout the land.

Thank you.

Looking forward,

Ralph Nader

Moving Street Protests
from Futility to Utility

JUNE 6, 2020

The nationwide street protests following the gruesome murder of George Floyd, who was pinned to the ground and choked by a Minneapolis police officer and three accomplices, were spontaneous and diverse. No leaders, charismatic or otherwise, put out the call for people to turn out in the face of militarized police legions. *It was a wondrous display of civic self-respect.*

Showing up is half of democracy.

The *New York Times* asked some of the protesters who stood in solidarity why they turned out. Their responses boiled down to inner compulsions that required action. A municipal employee in Minneapolis, Don Hubbard, said, "I feel like if I don't come out here, and we don't all show up, then what are we doing?" And he added, "We're letting this man die in vain."

In Los Angeles, Beatriz Lopez replied, "I felt I had to go. I had been asking, 'What can I do?'"

Beth Muffett of Austin, Texas, declared "If you're not standing up for George Floyd, who's going to stand up for you? It's just a level of wrongness, that I couldn't say no to going out to try to do something."

Young Chad Bennett (age twenty-two) from St. Louis said the video of Mr. Floyd left him "numb." He added, "It's a silent rage, I guess."

The personal and conscience-driven feelings that arise from these people and many others are not uncommon.

These protesters are well aware of previous mass demonstrations that did not lead to reforms and did not even result in prosecutions of the felonious police officers.

"Not this time" is the sentiment of these seekers of justice against the broader criminal injustice system. The attorney general of Minnesota, Keith Ellison, promptly brought second-degree murder charges against the knee-choking police officer. The signs carried by protesters called for

618

defunding bloated municipal police budgets and using the proceeds for housing, education, and health care. "Abolish the police" speeches meant establishing community-shaped security for neighborhoods.

Even the presence of premeditated vandalism of stores and other properties could not overshadow the historic, continuing grievances of Black Americans.

They face racism daily. It is built into conditions of discriminatory poverty—no jobs or low-paid jobs, or unprotected work that is too often dangerous in nature. As tenants, many African Americans are defenseless against evictions and landlord safety code violations. They are ripped off as borrowers (payday loan rackets); defrauded as consumers (the poor pay more for less); and grossly underserved by a wide array of public services, such as health care, crumbling schools, and inadequate mass transit, where they experience ongoing discrimination. They are arrested and imprisoned more often than white people for similar offenses. Then there is the obstruction or suppression of their voting rights in Republican states. They face public harassment and targeted racism while walking, jogging, or driving. Add it all up and their suppressed pain, despair, dread, fury, and fear for their children can't be ignored anymore.

No matter how many books, articles, or documentaries expose this aggregate life under "the new Jim Crow," little changes. Even concerned politicians routinely break their promises to communities of color.

How then can this current moral force avoid dissipation once the media loses interest and the protesters become exhausted? How can such widely praised demonstrations produce real change?

Seize the movement. Immediately secure funding from enlightened or guilt-ridden wealthy residents of these cities to form full-time citizen watchdog groups leveraging the reforms demanded by the protesters. Some permanent presence must be established to thwart the status quo ante. That's what seizing the moment means.

The collective street experiences must become the engine for massive early voter registration and voter turnout by Black and Hispanic Americans. Such a turnout is essential to replacing many of the corporatist racists, like Senate ruler Mitch McConnell of Kentucky, with elected officials who will stand with and for the people.

The conscious raising of such massive vocal challenges to the dominant powers brings new *leaders* to the forefront to run for office, to forge new advocacy groups, to join existing groups, and to litigate and educate and motivate.

Innocent Americans died and were injured in these peaceful protests. Many others risked batons, harmful tear gas, pepper spray, and other weaponry. Awareness, authenticity, and resolve can be the products of such confrontations. These are seeds for a strengthened, enlarged democracy of justice, freedom, and equality.

Again, seize this moment! Big-time!

America's Streets and Squares Are Waiting: Massive Rallies Work!

NOVEMBER 7, 2019

Around the world people are marching, rallying, and demonstrating in huge numbers. Some of these countries are ruled by dictators or plutocratic regimes; others are considered democracies. Despite the peril of protest, people are seeking justice, freedom, and decent livelihoods.

Many boast about the United States being the oldest democracy in the world. While there are some street protests in the US, they are sadly too few and far between. Rallies calling attention to climate disruption have received less public support and media attention than they deserve. Likewise, the Parkland rally in Washington, DC, against gun violence could have received more follow-up publicity. And we all remember the massive Women's March the day after Trump was inaugurated in Washington, DC. The subsequent Women's Marches have attracted smaller crowds and therefore less media coverage.

It is not as if our country doesn't have a historic tradition of sustained demonstrations. Mass protests have carried the labor movement, the farmer movement, the civil rights movement, and the antiwar movement to breakthroughs. These mass protests alone were not the sole drivers of political action—books, articles, editorials, pamphlets, posters, and litigation were essential. But visible displays of aggregated people power had a profound effect on those politicians' actions. When politicians put their fingers to the wind, the repeated rumble from the masses is what fills the sails of change.

It is not as if mass injustices are absent in the "land of the free, home of the brave." Sadly, the informed populace is just not showing up in an organized, big-crowd fashion—the way they did to challenge the nuclear arms race and nuclear power in the 1970s and '80s. In the era of the iPhone and internet, activists have greater access to organizing tools than ever—no postage stamps or costly long-distance telephone calls are needed.

Consider these candidates for mass demonstrations proximate to where the decision-makers are located. Millions of young people are being gouged by student loan creditors and for-profit colleges. Whether it is the US Department of Education's high interest rates or the exploitation by for-profit universities, the abuses are outrageous, cruel, and, in the latter case, often criminal.

Total outstanding student loans amount to over $1.5 trillion. These burdened young Americans know how to contact each other for free; they also can raise money instantly using new crowdfunding technology. They know how to use the visual arts and the verbal arts. Congress can reverse the predatory practices in higher education. Where is the advocacy from millions of student loan debtors? They could have a huge impact if they surrounded the Capitol or held smaller rallies around congressional offices back home, especially in the coming election year.

Millions of workers are making, inflation-adjusted, less than workers made in 1968. The federal minimum wage, frozen at $7.25, is the culprit. The House of Representatives finally bestirred itself to pass a $15.00 minimum wage stretched over a number of years. But when the Walmart-indentured members of the Senate look out their windows, it would be nice to see masses of workers surrounding their Senate offices, prior to some insistent personal lobbying.

There are no mass labor rallies in front of Trump's antilabor White House either, even though the headquarters of the AFL-CIO are just yards away on Sixteenth Street NW. The face-off of AFL-CIO president Richard Trumka versus Donald Trump is overdue.

Millions of minorities are suffering voter suppression. Civil rights leaders are angry. They anticipate Republicans at the state and federal level to again erect all kinds of insidious roadblocks that disproportionately affect people of color the most. Abuses in the Florida and Georgia races were rampant in 2018. Presidential races in swing states are also plagued by voter suppression tactics. All signs point to a more intrusive stripping of eligible voters in the 2020 election.

Where are the marches before the offices and headquarters of the states' culpable legislators, secretaries of state, and governors?

A quarter of our country's families are poor. The Poor People's Campaign, led by the Reverend William Barber and local pastors, has been protesting in the streets in North Carolina and other states. Their protests deserve far greater attendance. The media has given them too little coverage. But massive demonstrations in major cities and before state legislatures and Congress, with coordinated demands and large photographs of key politicians fronting for the rich and powerful, will get mass media coverage.

Tens of millions of Americans have no health insurance or are severely underinsured. Thousands of lives are lost annually as a result. This is a problem in America but not in other developed nations that have systems in place that prioritize their citizens' health. Getting sick or injured without medical care is far too frequent in the US. Those who suffer from this deprivation can be motivated to take to the streets. The health care industry's soaring profits and megarich bosses should move additional Americans to rally for "Medicare for all"!

These rallies can be led by physicians and nurses tired of the paperwork, the bureaucracy, and the health insurance companies denying access to health care for their patients and arbitrarily rejecting doctor-recommended treatments.

In the 1940s, President Harry Truman proposed to Congress universal health insurance. Americans still do not have Medicare for all and are paying the highest prices, premiums, and out-of-pocket bills in the world—not to mention the human suffering caused by an inadequate health care system.

What a great street story for television, radio, and print newspapers! Think of the tragic human-interest stories, straight from the heart, by mothers and fathers with children who have limited or no access to health care.

Other marches can come from the homeless and the desperate tenants spending over half their income on rent in the many communities where there is a shortage of affordable housing.

All these mass turnouts can pass contribution buckets or tout websites and raise money from the crowds for the next round of even larger protests. At each event, a list of demands can be presented to decision-makers. At each event, protestors can go to the offices where the decision-makers are or insist that these lawmakers speak to the assembled protestors.

There are many innovations to make these action rallies more impactful, more motivating, and more mass-media-centric. There also have to be some enlightened billionaires, worried about their country and their descendants, who want to provide the modest amount of money necessary for event organizers and focused political action. Show up, America!

To Democrats: Make Labor Day a Workers' Action Day

AUGUST 17, 2022

Labor Day presents a great opportunity for the Democratic Party to tout their election-year story of being on the side of labor—as opposed to the GOP, which is invariably backing the wealthy and giant corporations.

Unfortunately, the Democrats have not been taking advantage of the one national holiday dedicated to working people. It is not too late. Labor Day has been turned into a sales day by the big-box chains, but the Democrats can revive the true purposes of this day. Imagine thousands of public events for the working classes to give voice to their rightful needs and protections.

Never mind the dwindling Labor Day parades. Instead, organize rallies and assemblies in neighborhoods around real reforms and redirections, and respect that all workers (regardless of their political labels) want for themselves and their families.

Invite workers and their children to these festive gatherings—with refreshments, nutritious snacks, and music (taking proper pandemic precautions). If necessary, do it virtually and distribute snacks via food trucks. Present a vibrant, coherent proworker mandate complete with what the Democrats have already enacted or proposed against the unanimous opposition of the Republicans in Congress.

The Democrats, against the filibustering opposition of the Wall Street Republicans, stand for a living wage (they passed a fifteen-dollar minimum in the House of Representatives, which was blocked in the Senate), expanding Medicaid and Medicare, providing child care and paid family leave—all blocked by the Republican Party of *dread*, *anxiety*, and *greed*.

The Democrats push for more worker health and safety protections while the GOP senators and representatives want to continue to weaken the Occupational Safety and Health Administration and cut its tiny budget for workplace inspections and enforcement of protective standards.

The child tax credit of some $300 per month to about sixty million children was set for an extension this past January. In spite of cutting child poverty by over 30 percent, the Republicans blocked its extension, just as they blocked the Democrats' effort to restore some of Trump's giveaway tax escapes for corporations and the super-rich to pay for this crucial assistance to America's children and critical infrastructure jobs in the midst of a pandemic.

Congressman John Larson (D-CT) has proposed a comprehensive update for Social Security (benefits have not been upgraded for fifty years), but the Republicans are signaling a filibuster in the Senate. Worse, the chairman of the National Republican Senatorial Committee, corporate felon Senator Rick Scott (R-FL), wants to sunset all federal legislation, including Social Security and Medicare, in five years. He actually put it in writing (see *An 11 Point Plan to Rescue America*: https://www.politico.com/f/?id=0000017f-1cf5-d281-a7ff-3ffd5f4a0000).

Then there is labor law reform to make it easier for workers to form unions. This is the seventy-fifth anniversary of the notorious Taft–Hartley Act—the worst antiworker law in the Western world. The Democrats passed a bill in the House that partially repeals this giant handcuffing of American workers, but again the Republicans are blocking it in the Senate.

The Pension Rights Center (see pensionrights.org) has a ready-made agenda to protect and expand worker retirement systems.

The Democrats should highlight the worker respect and dignity issue. Focus on companies like Amazon, which is perfecting "digital monitoring" of workers and tracking their every minute, including limited bathroom breaks. Millions of Americans working remotely now have "Big Brother" electronically monitoring them, as Aldous Huxley predicted in his 1932 novel *Brave New World*. The GOP is not protecting minimal worker privacy.

The list of immediately perceived proworker contrasts between the Democrats and the Republicans goes on. Publicizing these deep livelihood improvements, where workers live, work, and raise their children, is far superior to the failed billions of dollars spent on vacuous political television ads.

On Labor Day, Democrats should join with and showcase the working people whom the Democratic Party has been distancing itself from under the controlling dictates of their corporate-conflicted political and media consultants. The latter gets 15 percent of the amount spent on all TV ads. Do you think they want to give us these big bucks for a superior, realistic ground campaign? How about organizing a campaign that speaks honestly about ending the corporate-managed, job-destroying foreign trade that has left our country defenseless—without, for example, domestic protection of key medicines (such as antibiotics), protective equipment, and essential microchips?

Bring all these long-overdue advances in just treatment of workers (many of them long available in Western nations) to the voters in the form of a printed "voters guide" handed out widely on a large card, on which one side asks voters to check yes or no on the issues, such as full "Medicare for all" or a fifteen-dollar minimum wage. The flip side of the card can show that Democrats side with workers, and the Republicans back Wall Street over Main Street and big business domination of America.

There is still time to arrange for celebratory Labor Day events. Workers are eager to voice their claims to America's promise to their fellow workers and other Americans. It is also a good way to attract volunteers to get out the vote on Election Day this November.

Bear in mind that what works for Labor Day can also work in the two months leading up to Election Day. Activist voters, give your party a push in this direction. They should be landsliding the worst GOP in history instead of worrying about losing the House and Senate to the dictatorial Trumpsters bent on stealing elections through voter manipulation, suppression, and purges.

Excluding the Civic Community
Excludes Lifesavers

OCTOBER 23, 2019

The lawmakers are doing it. The candidates are doing it. The mass media are doing it. All are excluding from their arenas the leading citizen groups as never before, since the early 1960s. The nonprofit national advocacy and research organizations that led the way for social reforms are being shut out of the political process. These groups were pioneers in consumer rights, environmental protections, labor rights, and whistleblower protections. These groups fought for freedom of information laws and practices and access to justice in ways that have made our country better in so many ways.

Television anchors like Judy Woodruff (*The News Hour,* PBS) and Chuck Todd (*Meet the Press,* NBC) prefer to interview reporters, political consultants, or tired columnists instead of knowledgeable civic leaders who use facts and speak truth to power.

One result of this marginalization is that the public discussion of key services and safeguards for the people is often vapid and fact-starved. For starters, the talking heads who are invited on news shows rarely, if ever, speak of the corporate crime wave, the corporate welfare scandals, or many preventable mass casualties that flow from corporate negligence and cover-ups. The few news articles on such subjects are often thin and untimely because reporters are not in regular touch with citizen groups, instead choosing to rely on irregular official leaks and occasional insider information.

Take, for example, the current discussion on "Medicare for all" or single-payer health insurance. The Democratic presidential candidates and other progressive lawmakers who support catching up with dozens of other industrial nations are not making the strongest case for this basic human right. They say that all Americans should have access to health care, referring to the unaffordable price of care.

The corporatists and some of these Democratic presidential hopefuls attack Medicare for all, asserting that the program would be prohibitively expensive by citing wild projections from biased think tanks. Bernie

627

Sanders rebuts by proposing overdue restoration of higher taxes on the wealthy and big business. He asserts that whatever increases there are on the middle class would be more than made up by no longer having to pay health insurance premiums and out-of-pocket costs.

Moreover, most advocates of single-payer do not stress the millions of ailments and injuries that persist because people cannot afford health insurance to get diagnosed and treated in a timely manner. According to the *Wall Street Journal*, roughly thirty million Americans are uninsured and eighty-six million Americans are underinsured. And about forty thousand of them die from that same deprivation each year. Such casualties due to lack of insurance do not happen in countries with universal insurance.

Furthermore, little mention is made of Canada's far more efficient single-payer (public insurance, private delivery of care) that covers every Canadian at half the average per capita cost of that in the US. Canada also has free choice of doctor and hospital, in contrast to the cruel, narrow networks in the US. Canada has better outcomes, less billing fraud by far, and fewer casualties due to "medical error and negligence." This is because the US has a serious problem of overdiagnosis and overtreatment, due to profit motives built into our chaotic, wasteful, corrupt, and profiteering system.

Single-payer means one billing agent in Canada, not inscrutable bills from 1,500 insurance companies with manipulated codes and discriminatory fees (for example, many hospitals charge the uninsured more in the US).

In Canada, there is far less anxiety, dread, and fear about medical bills than in the US. Imagine what that is worth!

In the US people worry that if they change jobs, they'll lose their insurance. In Canada, physicians practice medicine, not complex bookkeeping. In the US, physicians plead for permission to treat their patients, while slow-paying insurance companies look out for their corporate bottom line.

The sheer administrative costs in the US are, as a percentage of overall costs, more than double the administrative costs in Canada. Health care in Canada is on average less than $5,000 per capita per year; in the US it has just soared over $10,000 per capita per year. Canada spends 10 percent of its gross domestic product on health care and covers everyone; the US is reaching 18 percent of GDP while leaving out tens of millions of people.

No one in Canada has to go bankrupt due to medical bills, as is the case half a million times a year in the US. Drug prices for the same drugs are lower in Canada than in the US due to the bargaining power of the Canadian single-payer system. Just in terms of correlating health care data, single-payer detects what works and what doesn't far better than the secret proprietary data of many US insurance companies (which excessively compensate their executives). For example, in 2017, Aetna paid its CEO, Mark Bertolini, nearly $59 million as compensation (see the *Hartford Courant* article published on April 7, 2018). These salaries and compensation packages come out of your pockets, as do the copays and deductibles. The maddeningly complex fine-print exclusions add insult to injury.

In the US, people resort to GoFundMe campaigns to collect money for major operations that cost far more than they would in Canada. After all, to get the same procedures, all Canadians have to do is show their Medicare card, which is given to them at birth.

At the extreme, people in the US commit minor crimes just to go to jail to get health insurance. Recently, a couple in their seventies in Washington State took their lives due to being so overwhelmed by their soaring medical bills.

These and other examples further illustrate the advantages of a single-payer system. These numerous points were conveyed in a printed pamphlet personally delivered to dozens of members of Congress (see page 108, "25 Ways the Canadian Health Care System is Better than Obamacare for the 2020 Elections" and singlepayeraction.org). Some of these deliveries were followed by my personal calls. To date, not one office, other than Congressman Jamie Raskin's, acknowledged receipt. Nor have any of these lawmakers or the presidential candidates used such obvious arguments in this pamphlet or other available materials to rebut or to explain. Rarely do any media outlets present the overwhelming advantages of a single-payer health care system.

Recently, liberal columnist Mark Shields appeared on the *PBS News Hour* and mindlessly characterized single-payer as being too expensive.

When Medicare was established in 1965, the elderly had no trouble giving up their private health insurance plans that could at any time have been weakened, dropped, or not renewed. Just as today, workers with private company plans can be forced to accept less coverage or be laid off without any coverage. Mr. Shields seemed to have forgotten the fear that workers have about the unilateral power of companies to change the rules and delay or limit the benefits.

The foregoing case for a single-payer health care system is just one example of how corporate power prevails when there is media and political exclusion of the informed and experienced civic community. Speak up, people!

Statehood for the District of Columbia

SEPTEMBER 19, 2019

It is important for Democrats and Republicans to give voice to people whose voice is not heard inside the corridors of power. More than six hundred thousand of those people live in the District of Columbia. As the capital of this nation, the District is the symbol of the freedoms for which this nation stands. The light of democracy shines from the District, but does not illuminate this city. The core is hollow. The values of equality and political participation that the city promises are denied right here in our nation's capital.

Most Americans do not know, and many would find it hard to believe, that under our current system, DC residents are second-class citizens. The District is denied local control—Congress must approve the District's budget and can override any action of the city government. At the same time, District residents do not have even one voting representative in Congress that controls them. DC is effectively a colony, with all local decisions directly subject to change by a Congress largely out of touch with local realities.

Here is an important issue, involving the democratic rights of over half a million people, and yet there has been no debate whatsoever, and most Americans are unaware of the issues involved. Statehood for DC is a perfect issue for the Democratic presidential primary debates. All the Democratic primary candidates for president should pledge to make District residents first-class citizens of the United States, or explain why they think District residents should continue to be denied rights that other Americans take for granted.

Most people who live outside of the District do not know that DC citizens pay more than $2 billion a year in federal income taxes—more than several states—yet cannot elect people to decide how their money is spent. DC residents have served and died in our armed services over the last half century in disproportionately high numbers, but have no representation in Congress that decides whether or not to go to war. The US is the only democracy in the world that deprives the residents of its capital city the basic rights granted to other citizens.

Even more damaging than the lack of congressional representation is the colonial-style control that Congress exerts over the District. Adding one—or three—DC representatives to the 535 members of Congress would, by itself, do little to solve this problem.

Unaccountable power is by its nature abusive. The places where unaccountable power is exercised are, and must be, dysfunctional. Unaccountable power is uninformed. Members of Congress don't know this city. They don't know what's right for its people. They approve the budget and all the legislation, but they do not themselves have to live with their decisions. They foist pet projects on citizens who are perfectly capable of deciding these issues locally. They prevent the District from taxing income where it is earned. They regularly overturn the judgment of local elected officials—on public health, tax, budget, school issues—all with impunity.

Unaccountable power is destructive. It chokes the ability and destroys the responsibility of people to govern themselves. There is no place in the world where second-class citizens live side by side with first-class citizens and fare as well. It just doesn't happen. What happens to a community where the people cannot exercise authority, where there is no democracy? People stop participating. They don't run for local offices. The civic culture of the community withers away.

President Clinton objected to Congress's arbitrary use of its colonial power over the District. In 1999 he wrote a veto message chiding Congress for attempting to block District decisions that he correctly argued were local matters in the areas of: advocating statehood; access to special education, abortion, and drug policy; among other issues. But he did not aggressively push for full local control and self-determination for DC.

The results of congressional interference and the inefficiency of colonial-style management are as distressing as they are predictable. I have often been criticized for saying that there are few major, real differences between the Democrats and the Republicans. On this issue, the difference between the Democrats and the Republicans is very clear: Republicans do not believe that District residents should have the right to full local control or self-determination, and they do not intend to do anything about the current situation; Democrats believed that District residents have the right to local control, but they also did not intend to do anything about the situation. Until now.

The District of Columbia has been taken for granted by the national Democratic Party for too long. This is the year to send a message. Unfortunately, District voters don't have very many ways to send a message to the leaders in Washington, despite living in the shadow of the Capitol. Their local representatives have been disempowered; they have no voting representatives in Congress. Their best chance to send a message and make their voices heard is through a vote in the presidential election.

I support full local control of the District of Columbia, outside of a small federal enclave. Furthermore, I support a referendum for the voters of the District to choose their future status. Statehood should be one of the options, as should a return to Maryland. I support statehood, but more than that, I support the right of DC voters to choose their own future.

To those who say that the District is too small to be a state, (two states have smaller populations) and propose other solutions, I say that Congress has lost the right to impose its will on DC: after two hundred years of being second-class citizens, District residents have the right to choose for themselves.

To those who say that DC needs to get its house in order before we can move to full local control, I say, "Voting is a right, not a privilege." As Eleanor Holmes Norton has said for years, local control is what will make it possible for the District to start fixing its problems. With legislative and appropriations delays, regular governing confusion, and congressional interference eliminated, the District would be more able to deal with its pressing problems. The solution for the problems of democracy is more democracy!

Chuck Todd, Labor Day,
and Getting Serious

SEPTEMBER 4, 2019

Labor Day has come and gone. To most people it's a day off and a splash of sales. The symbolism and meaning that inspired this national holiday back in 1894 has long since dissipated. Labor Day parades are affairs of the past, with very few exceptions, and those that still exist are facing dwindling participation—in the era of Donald the corporatist, no less.

Part of this neglect stems from major unions and their large locals. Labor leaders, year after year, miss the opportunity to speak through the local and national media about what's on their mind regarding the state of workers today. I have urged labor leaders to develop a media strategy for Labor Day, since it is their one big day to give interviews and submit op-eds. Having major events or demonstrations on the needs of working families would invite coverage.

Even the usual excuse that the corporate press is not that interested goes away on Labor Day. The major labor chiefs just don't take advantage of this yearly opportunity. That is one reason why, over the years, raising the minimum wage, adopting card checks for union-desiring workers. pressing for full "Medicare for all," and repealing the notorious anti-union Taft–Hartley Act of 1947 have remained at such low visibility.

On the other hand, the editors and reporters are not exactly reaching out for, say, interviews with Richard Trumka, the former coal miner who rose through the ranks and became the head of the AFL-CIO labor federation in Washington, DC. Trumka versus Trump has a nice ring to it, but someone has to hit the bell.

This Labor Day, the *Washington Post* and the *New York Times* had touching stories of workers in various jobs from a human-interest point of view. There was little space devoted to labor policies, labor reforms, worker safety, the persistent private pension crisis, and the huge power imbalance in labor/management relations.

NBC's *Meet the Press*, anchored by Chuck Todd, is symptomatic of the media's indifference to showcasing labor leaders on Labor Day.

Chuck Todd, the quick-witted former citizen organizer, has lost control of his show to his corporate masters in New York City. He cannot even stop them from replacing his show entirely on the few Sundays when the NBC profiteers think there are more profits showing a major tennis, golf, or soccer tournament. My repeated complaints about this blackout to NBC chief Andrew Lack, or to the corporatist chairman of the Federal Communications Commission, have received no reply.

Obviously Chuck is working in a tough environment for any self-respecting journalist. But this past Sunday, *Meet the Press* reached a new low from its beginnings under the news-savvy Lawrence Spivak over seventy years ago. *Meet the Press* has become a dittohead to the regular news shows' saturation coverage. Todd covered Hurricane Dorian and the shootout in Texas, along with whether Joe Biden is too old for the presidency. Repetitious and dull—he added nothing new for the audience.

The shrinking range of *Meet the Press* has been going on for some years. It focuses, with other network shows, on questioning politicians or their surrogates—sometimes the same guests on multiple shows—about inconsistencies, gaffes, thoughtless statements, or current political controversies. We don't need to see yet another round with Trump's Kellyanne Conway, who plays with Todd's sharp questions.

The NBC corporate masters tell or signal to Todd whom he can invite for his roundtable. He should never have corporatists from the American Enterprise Institute without having people from the Economic Policy Institute, Public Citizen, or Common Cause.

Brit Hume, before he went over to Fox, once told me that the real purpose of the Sunday shows was to let the Washington politicians have their say so they stay off the back of the networks. That was his way of explaining why the questions put to them were not as tough or deep as they could be.

Todd can be a tough questioner, but he is trapped in a cul-de-sac of predictability, trivia, and redundancy that demeans his talents.

Along with the other Sunday morning network news shows, Todd stays away from the all-important civic community—historically and presently the fountainhead for our democratic society. It is hard to name any blessing of America, great or small, that did not start with the work or demands of citizens. Improved civil rights and liberties, safer consumer products, workplace conditions and environments, nuclear arms treaties, and much more began this way. Citizen groups continue as watchdogs, documenting, litigating, lobbying, and pushing the powers that be on behalf of the American people.

In 1966, I was invited on *Meet the Press* by the legendary Lawrence Spivak to first highlight, on Sunday national TV, what needs to be done about unsafe cars. That helped auto safety action to move faster in Congress. The civic leaders of today are largely shut out from these forums. Civic startups cannot reach larger audiences and shape the politics of the day.

None of this is unknown to Chuck Todd. He has allowed his hands to be tied with golden handcuffs. One can almost sense his impatience with his roundtable guests spouting guarded opinions or conventional speculations suited to their current careers. But Chuck is very polite with them and his interviewees. As he has said, if you really go after these guests, they won't come back next time. But why such a small pool? There are plenty of other fresh, courageous, accurate voices he can invite "next time." It's that his corporate bosses won't let him.

Todd has much more potential than to continue his increasingly trivialized, though sometimes temporarily sensationalized, role as an anchor of a withering show "brought to you by Boeing." He should request reassignment or resign for more significant journalistic challenges. He really doesn't need the money anymore.

Make Congress Accountable

MAY 29, 2022

Congress's failings and subservience to corporatism are historic in scope.

This is the fiftieth anniversary of our Congress Project that profiled in detail members of Congress. No citizen group has ever done this before or since.

Our 1972 Congress Project provides a context for measuring the decline of Congress, both in its near abandonment of its constitutional powers vis-à-vis the executive branch and its collective subservience to the many forces of corporatism over the people's necessities.

Congress was relatively productive in the early 1970s but could have done much more to address people's needs. While enacting groundbreaking legislation on consumer, environmental, and worker safety protections, Congress dragged its feet on full "Medicare for all," strengthening the antiquated federal criminal laws, labor law reform to facilitate union organizing, housing and mass transit programs, and, of course, its oversight and constitutional duties regarding the Vietnam War quagmire.

Bills languished that sought to establish a strong federal regulatory presence for pensions, drinking water safety, and safer food products, from farms to families.

Strong amendments to the 1966 Freedom of Information Act, pioneered by Democratic California representative John Moss, were blocked by both federal bureaucrats and corporate lobbyists.

With expectations for that Congress rising, commensurate with its constitutional authority and its visibility to the populace, our Congress Project embarked on an unprecedented profiling of every member running for reelection in November 1972—the year of the Nixon versus McGovern presidential contest. It was a massive undertaking. We strove to produce magazine-size political biographies of each senator and representative. Teams of undergraduate, graduate, and law school summer interns were supervised by full-time stalwarts to assure that each intern produced several high-quality profiles.

Other teams also worked long hours to produce books on key congressional committees such as Judiciary, Commerce, and Rules. These efforts required digging, interviewing, and working with about a thousand volunteers in all fifty states.

We conducted personal interviews with the lawmakers, whether they liked it or not. Such was the presence of the "Nader Raiders" in those days, when the mainstream media covered far more progressive civic initiatives than is the case today.

Given the tight deadlines, preparing the profiles of thirty or more pages each was a Herculean task. An intern even traveled with me to Copenhagen, Denmark, where I was attending an event, so I could review dozens of draft profiles on the plane so he could immediately fly back to Washington with the edits.

The leadership in the House and Senate reserved large rooms so that final drafts of the profiles could be reviewed for factual accuracy by the legislators themselves. On the appointed days, the lawmakers came to these rooms one by one and read every page. Whether they wanted to or not, they deemed it the better part of political prudence to accept our entreaties for maximum accuracy.

Imagine anything remotely like this response and humble spectacle occurring today. On publication day in the fall of 1972, we held news conferences in Washington and throughout the country with piles of printed profiles for reporters. We also prepared what turned out to be the best-selling book ever on Congress, titled *Who Runs Congress?* Requests for copies of the profiles poured into our office from citizens keen to learn more about their congressional representatives.

There never was another Congress Project of this magnitude by anyone. Passing years witnessed an increase in official source coverage of Congress, including C-SPAN, and a stiffening resolve by some members of Congress to not again be, in their inflated words, "humiliated," "ordered around," or "subjected to biased reporting" in such a very personal, specific manner.

The solons of Congress just didn't want the people back home to know much beyond what members of Congress said in their choreographed newsletters, radio and TV reports, and occasional town meetings. Members of Congress didn't like their unedited voting records reported in detail. They intuitively knew that "information is the currency of democracy," and most of them, with few exceptions, wanted to determine what currency was released and printed.

Fast-forward to today. The failings of Congress are historic in scope and regularity, given its constitutionally specified authorities, such as dutiful executive branch oversight and the power to declare war. Congress no longer works a five-day week—it's in on Tuesday, out on Thursday afternoon or evening, not counting ample recesses. Members of Congress spend enormous time raising campaign money, even though they exclusively can change how elections are funded nationwide.

Congress must come closer to and be more of the people's common good. Communicating with Capitol Hill is far more difficult in this Internet Age. Serious citizens who try all forms of communication often only have the option to leave desperate, brief messages for an increasingly unresponsive Congress voicemail.

Two simple bills, if enacted, would go a long way toward making members of Congress identify with their sovereign voters—to be more part of "We the People" instead of "We the Congress."

Bill No. 1: Congress members will have no employment benefits that are not accorded to all American workers, including pensions, health insurance, and deductible expenses. As for wage ratios, members will be paid no more than ten times the federal minimum wage.

Bill No. 2: Anytime the US is engaged in armed warfare, declared or undeclared by Congress, all age-qualified, able-bodied children and grandchildren of senators and representatives shall be immediately conscripted into the armed forces for military or civilian rendition of services.

Sharing in the benefits and burdens of the people would nourish the desire by members of Congress to become part of the solutions.

Who will introduce these bills and start this vibrant public conversation?

Demand Critical Congressional Hearings—
Long Overdue, Avoided, or Blocked

JANUARY 30, 2019

Earlier this month I wrote a column listing twelve major redirections or reforms that most people want for our country (see page 662: "It's Your Congress, People! Make It Work for You!"). All of which require action by Congress—the gatekeeper. Now Congress must hold informative and investigative public hearings to inform the media and to alert and empower the people.

The US Government Publishing Office (GPO) explains a congressional hearing as follows:

> A hearing is a meeting or session of a Senate, House, joint, or special committee of Congress, usually open to the public, to obtain information and opinions on proposed legislation, conduct an investigation, or evaluate/oversee the activities of a government department or the implementation of a Federal law. In addition, hearings may also be purely exploratory in nature, providing testimony and data about topics of current interest.

Here are my suggestions for a dozen long-overdue hearings in the House of Representatives, now run by the Democrats:

1. Hearings on the corporate crime wave, which is often reported by the mass media. Yet Congress, marinated in corporate campaign cash, has ignored, if not aided and abetted, corporate criminals for many years. Hearings on corporate crime, fraud, and abuse must be a top priority (see more at corporatecrimereporter.com).

2. Hearings on the causes of poverty—e.g., the frozen minimum wage, tens of millions uninsured or underinsured for health care, unaffordable housing, lack of criminal justice reform, and low utilization of

tort law. These hearings will address public outrage about how our rich country treats the poor among us.

3. Hearings on the need to fund the small congressional Office of Technology Assessment to provide in-house advice to Congress about big technological and scientific decisions—such as the boondoggle ballistic missile defense, electromagnetic or cyberattacks, driverless car hype, runaway artificial intelligence, nanotech, biotech (see: Bill Joy's "Why The Future Doesn't Need Us" in *WIRED*) and many other unassessed innovations.

4. Hearings on the overwhelming tilt into *speculation,* rather than *investment,* by the financial markets (e.g., Wall Street). The focus on speculation can cause grossly unproductive investments in the form of stock buybacks and off-the-charts executive compensation, which weaken the economy and keep shareholders (whose overpaid managers often don't allow them to vote on such decisions) powerless. These matters need congressional review.

5. Hearings on consumer protection—the myriad of recent controls and manipulation of consumers and their spending, savings, and credit, along with the first real investigation of fine-print contract servitude or peonage—all topics neglected by congressional committees.

6. Hearings on fundamental reform of our tax laws. Aggressively examining our tax laws' perverse incentives, unjust escapes, privileges and immunities, and estimated (by the Internal Revenue Service) $400 billion a *year* of uncollected tax revenue will enlighten taxpayers and members of Congress. A hearing on this is long overdue.

7. Hearings reviewing and evaluating our failed military and foreign policies—their costs, their boomerangs, and their unlawful, violent impact on innocent peoples and communities abroad are vital.

8. Hearings on the planet's environmental disruptions—from the climate crisis to water usage, from soil erosion to deforestation to the oceans' pollution and deoxygenation. A hearing on this could increase grassroots action.

9. Hearings on electoral reforms—dealing with campaign finance corruption to gerrymandering, voter repression, ballot access obstruction, unequal treatments, and more. A hearing on this might really help to "drain the swamp."

10. Hearings on needed and unneeded government-funded and operated projects, including varieties of infrastructure or public works and how to make them more efficient and cleaner—all topics that will make the case for rebuilding our communities.

11. Hearings on shifts of power from the few to the many, so long denied and abused. A hearing on these matters will help empower the people to more easily band together as workers, consumers, small taxpayers, voters, litigants, and audiences of the public airwaves and cable channels.

12. Hearings on the benefits of opening up an increasingly closed Congress, with concentrated power in the four leaders of the House and Senate at the expense of committee and subcommittee chairs as well as individual members. Doing so will help make Congress more accountable for the people. When Congress cuts budgets for committees and advisory institutions, such as the Congressional Research Service and the Government Accountability Office, it becomes more reliant on corporate lobbyists. These lobbyists work as congressional staffers before they return to their corrupt influence-peddling (the so-called K Street crowd). (See: "Why is Congress so dumb?" by Congressman Bill Pascrell Jr. in the *Washington Post*.) It also needs to be emphasized that routine appropriations hearings in both House and Senate must step up mightily to exercise far bolder supervision of executive-branch departments and agencies. (The Senate's confirmation hearings on nominated judges and high officials must also be far more rigorous and open to more witnesses to testify.)

There you have it—people, citizens, voters, students, and teachers. We need these and other such congressional hearings to make up for the years of deliberate inaction and avoidance. Send your senators and representative your suggestions and the above list. Demand more production from their $5 billion-a-year congressional budget.

United States Capitol switchboard: 202-224-3121.

How About a Civic Group to Oppose a Cashless Society?

SEPTEMBER 1, 2022

The most perceptive ancient historians and philosophers could not have foreseen a time when a certain type of mass convenience and abundance would become a threat to democracy, justice, and dispersed power. Welcome to the incarcerations of the credit card payment system gulag and the corporate state's drive to stop consumers from paying with cash.

So long as you have a credit card and a credit score, you're in a world of easy credit (no down payments, etc.) and high interest rates, especially on unpaid monthly balances. All it takes is swiping your card and pushing buttons at retail establishments or online to make a purchase.

If you are in the lower 20 percent of the income scale, unbanked and outside the gulag, consumer protections are really weak. Rip-off practices such as payday loan rackets and check-cashing gouges proliferate.

For over a decade the screws have been tightening to coerce people into the credit-debt economy. Both the corporations and the government are to blame.

Try renting a car or getting home insurance without a credit card and credit history. Try using FedEx or UPS without a credit card. More retail outlets are experimenting with cashless transactions, even in places like the District of Columbia, where a law barring discrimination against cash purchases goes unenforced.

"Cash" is defined for this article as paper money, checks, and money orders. Many state laws define cash as only paper money.

The government, for example, is turning the screws by forcing Social Security recipients into receiving electronic monthly *direct deposits* or prepaid debit cards instead of receiving a check in the mail. This started in 2010. If you don't have an "E-ZPass" on the Massachusetts Turnpike, an electronic camera catches your license plate and bills you with an added fee, even though you were willing to pay cash, for which there is no toll gate.

Last month, the city of Newburgh, New York, converted its coin-only parking meters to cashless meters on the city's business corridor streets. According to Blaise Gomez of News12 Hudson Valley, florist Christine Bello said the city is out of touch with its largely low-income demographic. "They eliminated an entire portion of my customer base by making this strictly cards," she related. "So many of my customers do not have credit cards. They don't have bank accounts. They don't have smartphones. What were they thinking?"

Ms. Bello is speaking for tens of millions of poorer Americans who are being denied, excluded, penalized, and harassed simply because they want to use paper cash and coins, which is "legal tender." Isn't that what 31 USC 5103 stipulates—that "United States coins and currency (including Federal Reserve notes and circulating notes of Federal Reserve Banks and national banks) are legal tender for all debts, public charges, taxes, and dues"? Except for the loophole, which is that vendors can give you notice that they don't accept cash, unless you are in one of the few states with laws declaring cash must be accepted.

There are many inducements for vendors getting you into the credit card economy. First, you lose control over your money. The ever-tightening tentacles of their fine-print contracts dictate the terms of their grip over you and any remedies you may have to challenge abuses. While losing your bargaining power under this consumer servitude, you also are losing your privacy big-time compared to buying with cash. "Data mining" takes over and sends your purchase history and profiles to anyone in the world willing to pay or anyone able to hack. Corporate Big Brother—Equifax and Facebook—is profiting from your personal data.

With credit, you are more likely to make impulsive purchases and not be able to control your children's buying escapades. Debt, high-interest payments, and maybe harassment by bill collectors enter your life. Some who live beyond their means are seduced by the gambling industry's lure of riches.

A new Gallup poll reports that 64 percent of respondents said it is "likely the US will be cashless in their lifetime"! Other countries are moving to cashless faster—some for authoritarian motivations. Just try being a tourist in Europe without a credit card.

There is a class stratification in the poll. The lower a person's income, the more likely they use cash for most purchases. The higher their income and the younger they are, the more likely they use credit/debit cards or other digital payment systems. Interestingly, however, far more US adults say they would be "upset" if the US becomes a cashless society (46 percent) than the ones who say they would be "happy", with such an outcome (only 9 percent).

A majority (56 percent) of Americans, Gallup finds, say they "like to have cash with them at all times when they are outside their home."

The poll registers a sharp partisan difference: "Republicans are most resistant to a shift to a cashless economy, with 60 percent saying they would not like it." Independents register 45 percent and Democrats register 28 percent taking that rejectionist position.

While the COVID-19 pandemic contributed to the shift from cash, all the corporate pressures and extreme surveillance capitalism are going in that direction. Even the union-owned Amalgamated Bank recently announced that its Washington, DC, branch is now a "cashless bank." Imagine a "cashless bank" where you can no longer cash a check or get money for petty cash!

The ever-increasing loss of consumer freedom is a daily work in regress by the fine-print commercial planners of growing consumer peonage. They have corporate contract attorneys who brag about each step they originate, including blocking you from going to court for your grievances and relinquishing other rights.

There is no time to lose. Consumers need an all-American advocacy organization to protect and defend the use of paper cash, checks, and money orders for the consumers' control, freedom, and the privacy these payment systems enable. We invite people interested in helping to create such an organization to write to Protect Cash, P.O. Box 19367, Washington, DC 20036, or send an email to info@csrl.org.

It's Your Congress, People!
Make it Work for You!

JANUARY 3, 2019

Congress is the constitutionally delegated repository of the sovereign authority of the people (the Constitution starts with "We the People," not "We the Congress"!). Most of the changes, reforms, and improvements desired by a majority of people have to go through Congress. Incentives for change often start with congressional elections or grassroots organizing. But sooner or later, change has to go through the gates of our national legislature on Capitol Hill.

This point is so obvious that it is astonishing so many reformers fail to regularly hammer home that we must intensely focus on Congress.

Just 535 humans (senators and representatives) need your votes far more than they need fat-cat campaign contributions.

Guess what the following twelve redirections or changes have in common with one another.

1. Instituting a living wage, much higher than the long-frozen federal minimum wage of $7.25 per hour.

2. Covering everybody with full "Medicare for all," or what is called a single-payer system, with free choice of doctor and hospital, is much cheaper and has better outcomes than the present complex, bureaucratic, price-gouging, claim-denying, profits-first chaos in the US.

3. Moving swiftly to a more efficient renewable, solar-based, wind-powered energy system that diminishes climate disruption and toxic pollution.

4. Achieving cleaner air, water, soil, and food for a healthful environmental for today and for coming generations.

5. Enacting clean elections reform and strong, enforceable laws against public corruption.

6. Reforming the criminal justice system, especially regarding nonviolent offenses, sentencing, and prisons.

7. Stopping taxpayers from being required to pay for very costly corporate welfare, or what conservatives call "crony capitalism," in all its many forms.

8. Enforcing the criminal and civil laws against corporate rip-offs, thefts, and hazardous products, and hearing the voices of workers, consumers, and those from beleaguered communities (especially on the public's airwaves, unfairly controlled by the monetized gatekeepers called radio and television stations).

9. Protecting access to justice for wrongfully injured people to have their full day in court with trial by jury as demanded by the country's founders and our Constitution.

10. Protecting public lands—the national and state forests and the national parks and wilderness regions—from profit-driven corporate encroachment and despoliation.

11. Reevaluating the loss of lives from unconstitutional, boomeranging wars abroad that spread death and destruction, making more people our enemies. These wars have also taken trillions of taxpayer dollars that could have been used to rebuild our community infrastructure— schools, highways, bridges, public transit, libraries, health clinics, drinking water and sewage works, and environmental cleanups.

12. Making it easier for consumers, workers, and small taxpayers to band together for civic action and a powerful seat at the table with big businesses and their government toadies.

These twelve advances have the following in common:

1. They have majority public-opinion support—in some cases huge support—which means many liberal and conservative voters agree, which can produce an unstoppable political movement.

2. Most of them cost nothing or little to implement, bringing more efficiencies and less damage to our society. *Wisdom* is less expensive than constant folly or deep greed!

3. They are understandable. People relate to the experiences, agonies, and dreams for a better life and livelihood for themselves and for their families.

4. They provide people with a sense of empowerment and accomplishment—traits necessary for a worthy democracy to work. Cynicism and withdrawal begin to be reversed in favor of engagement and new civic institutions necessary to our posterity.

5. They all have to go through our Congress—a good majority of only 535 people whose names we know become much more responsive to citizen action, people-driven town meetings, civic agendas, and democratizing procedures inside Congress.

Start by inviting the old and new members of the House of Representatives and the Senate to your town meetings. Five hundred citizens clearly signing a petition will get a senator to attend; considerably fewer names a US representative.

When you have them face-to-face with no flak, you'll see what "We the People" can accomplish. It has happened before in American history; it must happen again. (For more advice, see ratsreformcongress.org.)

Are the New Congressional Progressives Real? Use These Yardsticks to Find Out

DECEMBER 12, 2018

In November, about twenty-five progressive Democrats were newly elected to the House of Representatives. How do the citizen groups know whether they are for real or for rhetoric? I suggest this civic yardstick to measure the determination and effectiveness of these members of the House both *inside* the sprawling, secretive, repressive Congress and *back home* in their districts. True progressives must:

1. Vigorously confront all the devious ways that congressional bosses have developed to obstruct the orderly, open, accessible avenues for duly elected progressive candidates to be heard and to participate in congressional deliberations, from the subcommittees to the committees to the floor of the House. Otherwise, the constricting congressional cocoon will quickly envelop and smother their collective energies and force them to get along by going along.

2. Organize themselves into an effective caucus (unlike the anemic Progressive Caucus). They will need to constantly be in touch with each other and work to democratize Congress and substantially increase the quality and quantity of its legislative/oversight output.

3. Connect with the national citizen organizations that have backers all around the country and knowledgeable staff who can help shape policy and mobilize citizen support. This is crucial to backstopping the major initiatives these newbies say they want to advance. Incumbent progressives operate largely on their own and too rarely sponsor civic meetings on Capitol Hill to solicit ideas from civic groups. Incumbent progressives in both the House and the Senate do not like to be pressed beyond their comfort zone to issue public statements, to introduce tough bills or new bills, or even to conduct or demand public hearings.

4. Develop an empowerment agenda that shifts power from the few to the many—from the plutocrats and corporatists to consumers, workers, patients, small taxpayers, voters, community groups, the wrongfully injured, shareholders, consumer cooperatives, and trade unions. Shift-of-power facilities and rights/remedies cost very little to enact because their implementation is in the direct hands of those empowered—to organize, to advocate, to litigate, to negotiate, and to become self-reliant for food, shelter, and services (Citizens Utility Board provides an example of what can come from empowering citizens).

5. Encourage citizens back home to have their own town meetings, some of which the new lawmakers would attend. Imagine the benefits of using town meetings to jump-start an empowerment agenda and to promote long-overdue advances such as a living wage, universal health care, corporate crime enforcement, accountable government writ large, renewable energy, and real tax reform.

6. Regularly publicize the horrendously cruel and wasteful Republican votes. This seems obvious but, amazingly, it isn't something Democratic leaders are inclined to do. Last June, I urged senior Democrats in the House to put out and publicize a list of the most antipeople, pro–Wall Street, and prowar legislation that the Republicans, often without any hearings, rammed through the House. The senior Democrats never did this, even though the cruel GOP votes (against children, women, health, safety, access to justice, etc.) would be opposed by more than three out of four voters.

7. Disclose attempts by procorporate, antidemocratic, anti-human rights, and other corrosive lobbies that try to use campaign money or political pressure to advance the interests of the few to the detriment to the many. Doing this publicly will deter lobbies from even trying to twist legislator's arms.

8. Refuse PAC donations and keep building a base of small donations as Bernie Sanders did in 2016. This will relieve new members of receiving undue demands for reciprocity and unseemly attendance at corrupt PAC parties in Washington, DC.

9. Seek, whenever possible, to build left-right coalitions in Congress and back home that can become politically unstoppable.

10. Demand wider access to members of Congress by the citizenry. *Too few* citizen leaders are being allowed to testify before congressional hearings—and there are *fewer* hearings in general. Holding hearings is a key way to inform and galvanize public opinion. Citizen-group participation in hearings led to saving millions of lives and preventing countless injuries. Authentic congressional hearings lead to media coverage and help to mobilize the citizenry.

Adopting these suggestions will liberate new members to challenge the taboos entrenched in Congress regarding the corporate crime wave, military budgets, foreign policy, massive corporate welfare giveaways, or crony capitalism.

The sovereign power of the people has been excessively delegated to 535 members of Congress. The citizens need to inform and mobilize themselves and hold on to the reins of such sovereign power for a better society. Demanding that Congress uphold its constitutional obligations and not surrender its power to the war-prone, lawless presidency will resonate with the people.

Measuring up to this civic yardstick is important for the new members of the House of Representatives and for our democracy. See how they score in the coming months. Urge them to forward these markers of a democratic legislature to the rest of the members of Congress, most of whom are in a rut of comfortable incumbency.

If It Takes the Rats to Wake Us and Congress Up, Bring Them On! This Book Shows How!

NOVEMBER 20, 2018

Let's get down to the all-important matter of congressional performance. No matter how pollsters ask the question—"Do you approve of Congress?" or "Do you have confidence in Congress?"—less than 20 percent of people respond positively. Four out of five Americans disapprove of what Congress has been doing and are presumably disappointed about what Congress is not doing. That's an overwhelming unhappy majority. There are many changes, reforms, and redirections for our country that conservatives and liberals both agree on (see my book, *Unstoppable: The Emerging Left-Right Alliance to Dismantle the Corporate State*, Nation Books, 2014). There would be more agreements were we more alert to the divide-and-rule tactics of our political/corporate rulers and rejected such manipulations outright.

For decades, I've argued that it is easier than we think to change what comes out of Congress—the smallest yet most powerful branch of government under our Constitution.

Our history demonstrates that if 1 percent or fewer citizens, *reflecting majority public opinion*, roll up their sleeves and focus together on their two senators and representatives, they can prevail. Other consumer and environmental advocates and I did just that years ago with far less than 1 percent of the people (which is about 2.5 million adults) actually engaged in moving our agenda. Together we championed laws that reined in the auto industry, the corporate polluters, and other industries to save lives and prevent injuries and illnesses. Because majority public opinion supported us.

Our approach then was to put out factual documentation of these corporate harms and perils and get our research covered by the news media and programs like the *Phil Donahue Show*. People would feed back their demands and concerns to the senators and representatives of Congress, where we were pushing member by member. Reforms followed. I've given numerous examples of these citizen endeavors in my book *Breaking Through Power: It's Easier Than We Think*.

It still can happen, even though the news media hardly covers conventional civic activity anymore, and great shows like Donahue's are no longer on the air. We shouldn't be discouraged, however—we just have to shift strategies and find new ways to get more Americans revved up to feel and focus their own sovereign power exclusively rooted in the Constitution. "Corporations" and "companies" aren't even mentioned in that storied document. As the Constitution says, "We the people . . . do ordain and establish this constitution for the United States of America."

So here comes my new fable, *How the Rats Re-formed the Congress*, replete with examples of how little it took to change Congress beyond our greatest expectations. Once the rats stormed up the toilet bowls of these smug solons and transformed the place from the bottom up, action followed. When the American people found out how the congressional biggies tried to cover up their embarrassment—their ineptitude at not even being able to control a rat infestation—massive public derision flooded the televised and radio airwaves and social media.

Suddenly, people all over our country—at home, in the bars and restaurants, at their clubs—snapped to attention and began believing that "there are only 535 of them on Capitol Hill, many misusing our sovereign power delegated to them, but we're millions."

In "civic" waves from the hinterlands, the people move to take control of Congress away from the giant corporations and their greedy lobbyists. You'll laugh yourselves serious as you turn page after page and start *feeling, believing, thinking* that "we can do this; let's go, America!"

Enough of not paying hardworking, impoverished workers a livable wage; enough of people being denied health insurance and ripped off by the credit sharks; enough of our children being directly assailed with junk food and violent advertising, bypassing parental authority; enough of trillions of our tax dollars not coming back to us for superior public services in our crumbling communities but instead going to corporate welfare (crony capitalism) and the infernal, very profitable corporate war machine in addition to more tax escapes for the wealthy.

Enough of the fossil fuel industry poisoning our soil and water and disrupting our climate. Enough of the corporate bosses and their indentured politicians; enough of the big-time crooks and their dirty elections. Enough, enough already!

A few early readers found *How the Rats Re-formed the Congress* to be "disgusting" or "revolting," to use their words. Reading the back cover presents indictments of the "disgusting" and "revolting" Congress whose majority lets American men, women, and children get sick and die in great numbers from preventable perils in hospitals, in toxic workplaces, and in toxic products and environments. Other readers have called the book "uplifting," "optimistic," and "empowering."

The rumble from the people grows, and the leaders they generate break out in rallies and support for progressive agendas nationwide. Huge numbers of people surround Congress night and day, week after week, until the people's pressure becomes unbearable for recalcitrant members of Congress.

This external pressure permeates Congress with specific calls for reforms backed by the dramatic demand that the politicians get it done in an election year *or else!* The faster these long-overdue changes come—many long installed in western European democracies—the more the corporate big boys reel on their heels, unable with their tired bullying and intimidating ways to block the will of the people.

Wall Street and its lobbyists warn about "economic collapse" and "mass layoffs" if the citizenry's agenda passes Congress. Corporate front groups are created to disrupt the peaceful crowds. These corporate tactics don't work anymore. The agitated media publishes story after story about the corporate crime wave, the rip-offs of consumers, and the tax monies that Congress wasted.

Backing up the book is a helpful website on organizing Congressional Ratwatcher Groups in every congressional district. The material is readable, accurate, and relieves your feeling that such an effort is too difficult and won't produce results.

You can get an autographed copy of *How the Rats Re-formed the Congress*, or discounted autographed books in bulk for your circle of friends, by going to ratsreformcongress.org. See how the rats led the *way* until the people, just like you, entered the *fray.*

Ten Million Americans Could Bring HR 676 into Reality Land—Relief for Anxiety, Dread, and Fear

MARCH 22, 2018

Polls show that over 125 million adults in our country already favor full "Medicare for all," with free choice of doctor and hospital outside of stifling networks. I say "already" because, as of yet, there is no major national campaign underway showing that an "everybody in, nobody out" system of health care costs less, has better outcomes, is simpler, and avoids maddeningly inscrutable or fraudulent bills, copays, deductibles, and additional trapdoors set by a bunch of greedy corporations. The campaigns that exist today are receiving too little on-the-ground assistance for such a widely supported issue.

A supermajority of only 535 members of Congress—senators and representatives—can make that decision. The bill—HR 676, the "Expanded and Improved Medicare for All Act"—is now supported by 121 House Democrats—two-thirds of all the Democrats in the House of Representatives. So that's a good start.

HR 676 has been referred to several regular committees of the House whose chairs are all Republican corporatists, so there have been no public hearings. The bill, not surprisingly, is not moving at all.

Millions of Americans have had the bitter experience of denials of health care, staggering bills, pay-or-die drug prices, and even loved ones dying because they couldn't afford health insurance (about thirty-five thousand a year based on Harvard Medical School experts). So, in the next month, imagine what would happen if just 10 million of the 125 million who support full Medicare for all wrote, telephoned, or emailed their two senators and their representative demanding action and a written response by their lawmakers (who don't pay postage).

Just ten million Americans making the smallest effort—perhaps ending with a demand for a town meeting back home to educate the negative solons—would strike the Congressional Dome like a thunderbolt. Are there a dozen leaders among you up for launching such an electrifying *internet mobilization*?

Not to be confused with other lesser health insurance bills, mostly in the Senate, HR 676 is the real thing. It covers "all individuals in the US with free health care that includes all medically necessary care, such as primary care and prevention, dietary and nutritional therapies, dental services, and vision care." No more premiums, copays, or gaping deductibles.

How does HR 676 pay for all these services? Five ways: (1) from existing sources of government revenues for health care, (2) by increasing personal income taxes on the top 5 percent of income earners, (3) by instituting a progressive excise tax on payroll and self-employment income, (4) by instituting a tax on unearned income (such as on capital gains), and (5) by instituting a tax on stock and bond transactions. Amounts that would have been appropriated for federal public health care programs, including Medicare, Medicaid, and the Children's Health Insurance Program (CHIP), are transferred and appropriated to carry out this bill.

Presently, all Canadians are covered at an average per-capita cost half of what Americans—insured and uninsured—are having to spend for health care. The system proposed in HR 676 is similar to Canadian Medicare. It includes public funding and free choice of private delivery of health care. It also has provisions for better recordkeeping, prevention, and quality control. There is even transition retraining for all those clerical and administrative jobs that would not be necessary after displacement of the present bloated, wasteful, redundant health care subeconomy.

What would happen to the giant health insurance companies such as Aetna and UnitedHealthcare? They would be prohibited from selling insurance that duplicates the benefits provided under HR 676. They could only sell benefits that are *not* deemed "medically necessary," such as certain cosmetic surgery operations.

Representative Keith Ellison (D-MN), the deputy chairman of the Democratic National Committee (DNC), is officially the lead House Democrat on the bill, which indicates that the DNC may be getting a little more interested in endorsing such legislation.

Meanwhile, Representative Ellison is talking it up everywhere he travels. He says: "One of the consistent applause lines we're all hearing is: 'We need Medicare for all.' There's a lot of folks who feel that it's time for us to organize around that. It's a better policy, at a better price. People in labor, people all over the country, they're going to be driving the public conversation, raising the dialogue about this. . . . What some people think is a really important progressive position is just what the rest of the industrialized world does."

Medicare for all is what the Pentagon does. It is what President Harry Truman wanted from Congress back in the 1940s! *It is time.*

So will the first ten million Americans step up and be counted by sending messages directly to their senators and representatives in the month of April? The amount of time required to send a letter, an email, or a telephone call is so brief that activated citizens could be called the modern "minutemen" for universal health insurance. Just think of all the tasks you do every day that take far more time, like trying to figure out bills, denials, and exclusions from this basic human right.

Go to singlepayeraction.org to get the details, the motivation, and the groups with which to connect. The congressional telephone switchboard is 202-224-3121. Make sure to give your legislators your name and contact information; they'll take the call or letter more seriously.

Senators Call for Al Franken's Resignation

DECEMBER 6, 2017

Many Democratic senators have demanded that Senator Al Franken resign immediately from the US Senate over accusations by six women that Senator Franken made unwanted advances and engaged in sexual harassment. Strange, isn't it, that these same demanding senators are not demanding now that Donald Trump resign as president?

Mr. Trump has boasted and bragged about his sexual aggressiveness toward resisting women and has been accused by more women regarding more serious charges so far than the case of Senator Franken. Mr. Trump has responded by slandering these women, while Senator Franken has shown deep contrition and self-criticism. Why the double standard, senators?

The same double standard holds true for Minority Leader Nancy Pelosi's demand for Congressman John Conyers's resignation, while avoiding demanding the same of tortious Donald J. Trump. Demanding the same result for gross behavior demonstrates a modicum of courage and even-handedness that's lacking here, because these senators know that unlike Franken, tweeting Trump will go after them with wild, continual denunciations—repeated by the mass media.

Moreover, why have a Senate Ethics Committee investigation process at all if righteous double-standard clamor is deemed to suffice? These senators should be mindful that having a due-process procedure and then ignoring it can someday come back to bite them.

Of course, there are many other double standards in Congress, such as backing aggressive illegal wars with mass civilian destruction without war declarations (Iraq) and authorizations and appropriations resulting in millions of innocent casualties abroad (Libya). Some of these senators run for the presidency without any objection by their senatorial colleagues.

The Super Bowl of Civic Action
for the People

SEPTEMBER 19, 2016

To have a democratic society that brings out the best in its citizens, people have to show up—to vote and to attend city council meetings, rallies, marches, and other serious gatherings that reflect the public interest. They also need to support progressive candidates and run for office.

Showing up is half of democracy. We invite you to attend, in person, our four-day Breaking Through Power conference in Washington, DC, featuring some of the most accomplished civic leaders and thinkers as well as opportunities for you to become energized and engaged wherever you live or work.

Whether you see yourself as a dissatisfied voter, a civically minded teacher, a curious student, a fed-up consumer, or a dismayed taxpayer—or if you are looking for ways to make your community better—you'll come away with knowledge, tools for action, and connections with others who want to make a difference.

Visit breakingthroughpower.org to see the conference speakers—people who long ago decided they were going to dedicate their time and talent to make our country responsive to the necessities and aspirations of its people.

The first day—September 26—is about building civic skills and breaking through apathy. You can see David Freeman talk from his experience of advising presidents and governors and running four big public utilities, including the vast Tennessee Valley Authority, and wisely lay out a practical path to economical renewable energy with environmental respect.

Have you been ripped off? Hear Oliver Hall of the Center for Competitive Democracy talk about using small claims court or the people's courts. They are located everywhere.

Thinking about a community-based business? Listen to the nation's expert, Neil Seldman, from the Institute for Local Self-Reliance, talk about how community business is revolutionary.

Want to engage with the safe, nutritious food movement? You'll be shown the way by the leading safe-food advocate—who has done it for forty-five years—Dr. Michael Jacobson.

Whether it is empowering consumers, getting corporate money out of politics, knowing the safeguards for whistleblowing, or building public opinion behind your proposals, advocates who are among the best in the country are ready to share their experience and enthusiasm with you at the Breaking Through Power conference.

Let's say you're a teacher and you want to convey civic skills to your students and motivate them to overcome their apathy and work for needed change. You couldn't have a better day's retreat. There is even a talk on the civic engagement of business leaders by Mitch Rofsky, who founded the delightfully proconsumer motor club called the Better World Club (betterworldclub.com).

The second day is a huge eye-opener and brain-filler. Did you know that "We the People" actually own the greatest wealth in our country? I'm referring to the vast public lands, onshore and offshore; the research and development, funded by taxpayers, that enabled today's new industries; the huge capital amassed in the form of pension and mutual funds and individual shareholdings. But corporations control their uses and reap the profits, abetted by their influence over Congress and government officials in Washington. Imagine if we took back reasonable control over those assets that we already own. A society beyond our optimistic dreams would emerge, assuming that we provided "eternal vigilance."

Well, that's what day two is all about—our savings, our natural resources, and our other "commons" being shaped to fit your needs and those of your descendants.

Day three will respond to interest about ways to start a citizen group by featuring the heads of some of these groups exhibiting different models. The afternoon is devoted to DC statehood—the New Columbia to replace the Washington, DC, colony and abolish the servitude that blocks the residents of our nation's capital from having voting representatives in Congress.

Day four, held at historic Constitution Hall, celebrates the two great liberation movements that provide us with self-actuating freedoms to have our day in court and make contracts fair. Naturally, the big corporations are irritated by challenges to their overreaching, so over the decades they have weakened the law of torts—the remedies for wrongful injuries—and perfected the anticonsumer, one-sided fine-print contracts that await you when you enter into the marketplace of goods and services. Our rights to fair contracts and to use tort law are under constant attack from the promoters of crony capitalism. Attend the Breaking Through Power Conference and learn what you can do to defend yourself.

You'll be engrossed by advocates who have successfully represented people like you and by scholars who can clearly demonstrate what is at stake when we decide to strengthen the fundamental freedoms to use tort law.

Consider these four days the Super Bowl of Civic Action that can equip you to seek justice and protect yourself from wrongful impacts on your living condition.

There's no substitute for attending the events and meeting with similarly motivated citizens like you.

BREAKING THROUGH POWER: MAY PROGRAM

MAY 23–26, 2016, at Constitution Hall in Washington, DC, with civic mobilization designed to break through the power of the corporate/political complex.

BREAKING THROUGH POWER means securing long-overdue democratic solutions made possible by a muscular new civic nexus connecting local communities and Washington, DC.

On these four days, speakers will present innovative ideas and strategies designed to take existing civic groups to higher levels of effectiveness.

DAY ONE—MAY 23, 2016—will feature an unprecedented series of presentations by seventeen successful citizen advocacy groups of long standing.

DAY TWO—MAY 24, 2016—brings together a large gathering of authors, documentary filmmakers, reporters, columnists, musicians, poets, and editorial cartoonists who will present important content that deserves more exposure via the mass media.

DAY THREE—MAY 25, 2016—will be dedicated to enhancing the waging of peace over the waging of war. We will assemble leading scholars with military and national security backgrounds such as retired colonel Lawrence Wilkerson, the former chief of staff to Secretary of State Colin Powell; veterans' groups such as Veterans For Peace; and longtime peace-advocacy associations to explain how peace is more powerful than war.

DAY FOUR—MAY 26, 2016—will unveil a new civic agenda (much of which has left-right support) that could be advanced by engaged and enraged citizens in each congressional district. The agenda includes recognized necessities ignored by Congress for decades and will be presented by a veritable brain trust of recognized advocates for the well-being of present and future generations. The idea on this day is that each speaker presents the substance of each demand for later pickup by citizens back home serving their senators and representatives with formal summons to their own town meetings to educate these politicians and instruct their duties on their return to Congress.

Revitalizing the people to assert their sovereignty under our Constitution is critical to the kind of government, economy, environment, and culture that will fulfill human potential and respect posterity.

The Rumble from the People Can Work

DECEMBER 31, 2015

If only the people who engage in "road rage" would engage in "corporate rage" when they are harmed by cover-ups or hazardous products and gouging services—then aloof CEOs would start getting serious about safety and fair play. With press report after press report documenting how big business stiffs millions of its consumers and workers, why is it that more of these victims do not externalize some of their inner agonies by channeling them into civic outrage?

It has happened on occasion and with good results. After Candy Lightner lost her daughter to a drunk driver, she founded Mothers Against Drunk Driving (MADD) in 1980 as the only way she could deal with her intense grief. Asked what her principal motivation was in building a national movement to put homicide-producing drunk drivers behind bars, she replied: "Revenge."

Medical malpractice victims or their next of kin have started special lobbying associations to stop the attempt by insurance companies and physician lobbies to weaken the rights of patients to have their full day in court against their negligent harm-doers. They also inform the public about the need to discipline bad doctors and careless hospitals so as to reduce some of the hundred thousand fatalities a year (according to the Harvard School of Public Health) from malpractice.

Jean Rexford started such a group—the Connecticut Center for Patient Safety—in 2005 to press for quality health care through the media and before the state legislature.

Joanne Doroshow, a public interest lawyer, has gathered people injured by defective products as well as negligent medical procedures to testify and lobby a callous Congress often on the verge of usurping the state courts and these vulnerable victims' access to justice.

For the most part, however, Americans swallow their grievances and try to muddle through their disrupted lives with subdued anger. A major reason for this external passivity is that the plutocrats and oligarchs have signaled that it is futile to even try to make a challenge or a ruckus. The "you can't fight the big boys" feeling starts in the schools, where youngsters are given no instruction and no experience (such as learning how to use small-claims courts) in pursuing their remedies when defrauded or wrongfully injured. They are scarcely educated about our courts of law and the duty and role of civil juries—rooted in the Seventh Amendment to our Constitution—in judging the facts about wrongs.

Let's refer to some recent examples. You may have read news stories about drug companies suddenly spiking the cost of specialized drugs a hundredfold or more, or "price gouging of old drugs," in the words of Dr. Martin A. Makary of Johns Hopkins. The era of the $1,000-per-day pill has arrived.

Picture the scene—companies that have monopoly patent ownership of drugs (many based on taxpayer-funded research and development) are essentially telling their customers with life-threatening diseases that they have to "pay or die" for unique drugs that are priced at more than $100,000 per patient per year, unless they have an insurance company to pay the tab. Already those insurance companies that do pay, along with Medicaid and Medicare, are staggering under the sharp surge in costs during the past two years. A casual Congress is just starting to notice its responsibilities here.

On December 22, 2015, the *New York Times* reported that Fred Kellerman, a retired car salesman from Los Angeles, was receiving a drug for free for his rare neuromuscular disease. The drug improved his life dramatically.

Then he learned that a pending FDA approval, with a seven-year patent monopoly, could raise the price to $100,000 per patient. There are thousands of terrified patients and families in the same situation as Mr. Kellerman. Fright needs to motivate organization. They would receive media and congressional attention with their heartfelt stories and expressed sense of injustice.

Gilead Sciences bought a company that had a drug to cure hepatitis C with a twelve-week regime. It started selling the drug for $1,000 per pill in 2013—or $84,000 for the full treatment. In one year, Gilead took in more than $10 billion from the drug, Sovaldi.

But in Egypt, a poor country where there are nine million people suffering from hepatitis C, Gilead agreed with the government to sell it for ten dollars a pill, which are then dispensed free by the Health Ministry to ailing Egyptians.

"Do you Americans love Egyptians more than yourselves?" asked Hany Tawfik, one of the first Egyptians to take sofosbuvir (Sovaldi), according to the *New York Times*, adding, "Why aren't you putting pressure on Gilead to sell to you at a reasonable price, too?"

Good question. And why aren't more students and recent college graduates organizing to rebel against their gouging student loans—an exploitation unheard of in other Western countries? Why aren't consumers who are being sued unlawfully by aggressive debt collectors or being crammed on their telephone bills charged for so-called services they never requested?

Short of organizing into a demanding group, why can't more people just shout out via telephone, letter, email, or text message to anyone who could do something or at least spread the word? Just a growing rumble from the people has gotten elected officials moving, including President Richard Nixon, who signed wonderful bills into law that he never wanted. But he feared the rising *rumble from the people*. Who can stop you from rumbling?

Happy New Year!

Sending Citizens Summons to Members of Congress

JULY 24, 2015

With the long congressional recess in August through Labor Day approaching, "We the People" have the opportunity to do more than complain about Congress and individual senators and representatives.

There are many issues affecting you and your communities that need to be addressed by members of Congress. Over the years, it has become increasingly difficult to reach the legislators in Washington, DC, and when they return to their districts and states, they often only attend public events and ceremonies where they do little more than shake hands and smile.

In-person town meetings by members of Congress—which are diminishing in number—are often stacked and controlled. The locations, attendees, and even sometimes prescreened questions fail to provide citizens an opportunity to make their case to their legislators. Politicians crave predictability; they are control freaks.

Our 535 senators and representatives need to be reminded that they were sent to Washington, DC, by voters back home who entrusted them with the well-being of their communities and country. Many of these lawmakers then become indentured to corporate campaign cash that they must constantly beg for, often compromising with what is in the best interest of their constituents. For all this corporate campaign cash, these corporations want something in return—government contracts, giveaways, tax loopholes, weak corporate law enforcement, and other privileges and immunities, especially for giant multinational corporations that have tightened their grips of crony capitalism on Washington.

So what happened to your votes and your trust in your elected representatives? They were nullified and replaced with ungrateful politicians who have forgotten that the authority lies with the people.

It is time, during this August recess, for "We the People" to shake up Congress and shake up the politics across the land. If anyone is skeptical of this possibility, they should recall August 2009, when the Tea Party noisily filled the seats of some town meetings called by senators and representatives in a Congress run by the Democrats. That is how the Tea Party movement came to public visibility, with the daily help of Fox News.

After that experience, many members of Congress were forced to reevaluate the power and influence of town meetings.

My proposal of a Citizens Summons can begin the process of showing your elected legislators who is truly in charge, as befits the preamble to the Constitution—"We the People." I am including below a draft Citizens Summons to your senators or representative. It covers the main derelictions of Congress, under which you can add more examples of necessary reforms.

Your task is to start collecting signatures of citizens—members of citizen groups, labor unions, and any other associations that want a more deliberative democracy. The ultimate objective is to reduce inequality of power.

Shifting power from the few to the many prevents the gross distortions of our Constitution, our laws, our public budgets, and our commonwealth that currently favor the burgeoning corporate state.

May you give your lawmakers a memorable August recess; they deserve to be shown the workings of what our founding fathers called "the sovereignty of the people."

THE CITIZENS SUMMONS TO A MEMBER OF CONGRESS

Whereas, the Congress has tolerated the expansion of an electoral process, corrupted by money, that nullifies our votes and commercializes both congressional elections and subsequent legislation, creating a Congress that is chronically for sale;

Whereas, the Congress has repeatedly supported or opposed legislation and diverted the taxpayer dollars to favor the crassest of corporate interests to the serious detriment of the American people, their necessities, and their public facilities—such as access to safer consumer products, health care, and other basic social safety services. It has opposed raising the inflation-ravaged minimum wage and fair taxation; allowed endemic waste, fraud, and abuse by contractors; and authorized massive corporate welfare subsidies and giveaways;

Whereas, the Congress has narrowed or blocked access to justice by millions of Americans, leaving them unprotected and defenseless in many serious ways while giving corporations preferential treatment and allowing them full access to influence the three branches of government;

Whereas, the Congress has imposed trade-treaty despotisms over our democratic institutions—the courts, legislatures, and executive departments and agencies—subordinating our domestic branches' abilities to preserve and enhance labor, consumer, and environmental standards to the domination of global commerce's "bottom line." It has endorsed the usurpation of our judicial process by secret tribunals under the World Trade Organization, and other similar invasions of US sovereignty;

Whereas, the access to members of Congress has increased for corporate lobbyists and decreased for ordinary citizens; therefore, the citizens of [INSERT state (for senators) or the congressional district (for representatives)] hereby *summon* you to a town meeting or meetings during the August recess (ending September 7, 2015) at [INSERT place of known public convenience]. Your constituents will establish an agenda of how Congress should shift long-overdue power from the few to the many, both in substantive policy and through the strengthening of government and civic institutions;

We deem this *summons* to be taken with the utmost seriousness as we gain grassroots support throughout your [INSERT congressional district, or state for senators]. We expect to hear from you expeditiously so that the necessary planning for our town meeting can take place. This People's Town Meeting reflects the preamble to the Constitution that starts with "We the People" and the supremacy of the sovereignty of the people over elected representatives and corporate entities;

Be advised that this *summons* calls for your attendance at a town meeting run by, of, and for the people. Please reserve a minimum of two hours for this serious exercise of deliberative democracy.

Sincerely yours,

[The names of citizens and citizen groups]

How Birth-Year Legacies Can
Better Our Country

JANUARY 5, 2015

It is a new year and I'd like to propose a new American tradition: making birth-year legacy gifts to lift our country's future. Many Americans born in the same year—say, from 1924 to 1944—could form a unique affinity group to conceive and fund endowed institutions that improve our country's "life, liberty, and the pursuit of happiness."

For example, there are over two million Americans who are seventy-six years old, born in 1939. They have many different interests, backgrounds, and income levels, from billionaires to those barely making it. It is not too far a stretch to believe that many would like to do something to benefit their descendants—Americans who will inherit our country.

These legacies can take the form of significant, self-renewing nonprofit civic institutions either at the national or regional level. No hidden agendas, no obscure profit motives, no self-aggrandizement—just extending the torch of wisdom and foresight and imagining brighter futures.

Benefactors could come up with their own ideas. Here are some of mine:

1. Organize afterschool clubs for youngsters that advance civic skills and civic experience in local communities;

2. Develop and share project ideas to make it easier to strengthen more self-reliant communities;

3. Start a movement to simplify our laws, red tape, overly complex forms, and the omnipresent fine-print contracts;

4. Establish an annual national "Showing Up for Citizen Engagement Day" to rediscover best practices for a better America;

5. Organize for affordable and open access to justice forums for all Americans;

6. Award moral courage prizes in all 3,007 counties in the US so as to recognize and support courageous people who stand tall;

7. Create facilities for participatory neighborhood sports—both organized and unorganized;

8. Build two thousand civic community centers, as Mr. Andrew Carnegie did when he funded the establishment of over two thousand free libraries a century ago;

9. Create arboretums in communities nationwide to increase understanding and enjoyment of nature;

10. Institute broad prison reform and rehabilitation for adults and juveniles—this is already receiving left-right support;

11. Enact public financing of public elections and other electoral reforms to give voters more voices and choices;

12. Promote faster conversion to solar energy and energy efficiency;

13. Endow departments of civic practice in universities and colleges so students can learn how to practice democracy, civil rights, and civil liberties;

14. Advance full "Medicare for all," with greater efficiency and free choice of doctors and hospitals;

15. Organize scientists and technologists to consider the consequences of their work in society;

16. Organize congressional accountability watchdog groups in all congressional districts for long-overdue reforms such as fair taxation,

corporate law enforcement, reduced corporate welfare, and judicious allocation of public budgets for the necessities of the people.

By now, you may be thinking of your own proposals and wondering how you can launch these birth-year legacy gifts. Well, out of each birth year can come those who have the means, the time, the imagination, and the skills to jump-start the process. Each birth year can have its own unique approach to establishing future betterments that can be operated in perpetuity.

There are many trillions of dollars of wealth possessed or controlled by people with birth years from 1924 to 1944. Most of this is dead money— money markets and other investments that do little to initiate needed changes. At the same time, many Americans think our country is moving in the wrong direction.

Mr. Carnegie could have left all his fortune to his descendants or to charities. Instead, besides endowing scientific institutions, his legacy is the millions of people who used and continue to use libraries that otherwise would not have been built in their communities to educate, enlighten, and inspire the citizenry. Shrewdly, this Scottish immigrant required towns and cities to provide the land before he paid to build the libraries as a way of signifying a public commitment to maintain them.

Perhaps the first step for the birth-year initiative is to hold gatherings around the country simply to discuss the idea of legacy gifts by birth year.

Developing the kind of elan or spirit within birth years that we see in some universities and college alumni classes could be transformational for our nation and its relation to the rest of the world. For it wouldn't just turn money into action for the common good; it would also arouse what now are too many discouraged people to engage in purposeful, exciting elderly living with new friends and stimulation.

Activating older generations of Americans to share their knowledge and experience with the young certainly expands the latent potential of the human journey.

For help getting started on your own birth-year project, please contact us at info@nader.org, or write to P.O. Box 19367, Washington, D.C. 20036, for preliminary advice.

The Democrats Can't Defend the Country from the Retrograde GOP

OCTOBER 18, 2013

Congress, which polls show the American people would like to replace in its entirety, has kicked the can down the road again, putting off the government shutdown until January 15 and another debt-ceiling showdown until February 7.

The polls also show, convincingly, that people blame the stubborn Republicans more than the Democrats for the adverse effects of the impasse on workers, public health, safety, consumer spending, recreational parks, and government corporate contracts.

There is another story about how all this gridlock came to be, fronted by the question: "Why didn't the Democrats landslide the cruelest, most ignorant big-business-indentured Republican Party in its history during the 2010 and 2012 congressional elections? (See "The Do Nothing Congress: A Record of Extremism and Partisanship" [https://nader.org/wp-content/uploads/2014/02/GOP-Outrageous-Votes-10-2012v3.pdf].)

There are a number of answers to this fundamental political question. First and most obvious is that the Democrats are dialing for the same commercial campaign dollars, which, beyond the baggage of *quid pro quo* money, detours the party away from concentrating on their constituents' needs, in a contrasting manner with the GOP.

Democrats like Representative Marcy Kaptur (D-OH) tell me that when the House Democrats get together in an election year, they go into the meetings talking about money and walk out talking about money, burdened with the quotas assigned by their so-called leadership.

Last year, House Democratic leader Nancy Pelosi (D-CA) was reported to have attended four hundred fundraisers in DC and around the country for her campaigning Democrats. Helping Democratic candidates with fundraising is a major way she asserts her control over them. Over 90 percent of the Democrats in the House defer to her and do not press her on such matters as upping the federal minimum wage, controlling corporate crime, reducing corporate welfare giveaways, reasserting full "Medicare for all," diminishing a militaristic foreign policy, and other policies reputed to be favored by the party's Progressive Caucus, numbering seventy-five representatives. Instead, the Progressive Caucus remains moribund, declining to press their policy demands on leader Pelosi, as the hardcore Tea Partiers do with their leaders.

So when election time comes around, voters do not know what the Democrats stand for other than to save Social Security and Medicare from the Republicans. Former senator and presidential candidate Gary Hart, now living in Denver, said last year that the local Democrats in Denver didn't know what the national Democrats stood for.

The 2010 election was crucial for the winners in the state government races who gained the upper hand in redistricting decisions for a decade. That meant more gerrymandered, one-party-dominated districts. The Republicans won a majority of those gubernatorial and state legislative races and took over the US House of Representatives with Speaker John Boehner (R-OH) and his curled-lip deputy, Eric Cantor (R-VA).

And there is also President Obama's political selfishness. Obama knew that he could not govern with a knee-jerk Republican House of Representatives intent on blocking any Democratic proposal. Yet he did not provide serious campaign support or progressive policy leadership for Democratic candidates. Consequently, he was overcome in 2011 by Republican demands for sharp cuts in federal budgets serving people (while exempting corporate entitlements from similar cuts). And, during his first term, he was beset by the specter of government shutdowns and Republicans in Congress refusing to raise the government's debt ceiling to pay current debts.

So you'd think that in 2012 President Obama would have run arm in arm with congressional Democrats. No way. He signaled his going-it-alone approach not only by turning down a Democrat's request for $30 million from his billion-dollar campaign hoard, but also by his lack of interest in campaigning with local congressional candidates as he traveled around the country. The House Democrats were dismayed but kept quiet.

So he got the Boehner/Cantor duo for another two years after the 2012 election. That meant another shut-the-government-down, don't-lift-the-debt-ceiling imbroglio—a clash that crowded out all the necessities and the matters of justice that our government is supposed to champion. The greed and power of the Walmarts, the Exxons, the Aetnas, the Lockheed Martins, and the rest of the global corporate power structure that has turned its back on taxpaying American workers and their families remain unchecked by our government.

Fast-forward to the elections of 2014. No House Democrat believed, until the recent congressional impasse, that the Democrats would win back the House in 2014. Given that many House-passed Republican votes since 2011 sided with big business—on the wrong side of fair treatment of children, student borrowers, workers, women, consumers, and small taxpayers; and of providing necessary public services—one would think the Democrats should win next year in a slam dunk. Not likely, unless the Republican echo chamber, with its mad-dog extremists, hand control of the House to the Democrats.

From the 1940s to the 1990s, the Republican Party did not behave as badly as today's snarling version of the GOP. Yet the Democrats were still able to beat Republicans in most congressional races. Imagine what presidents Franklin D. Roosevelt, Harry S. Truman, John F. Kennedy, and Lyndon Baines Johnson would have done with today's crop of Republican corporatists and rabid ideologues.

Today's Democrats with very few exceptions are dull, tired, and defeatist. They regularly judge themselves by how bad the Republican Party is, instead of how affirmatively good they could be for our country and its politically alienated people. They cannot even muster themselves to battle for a higher minimum wage on behalf of thirty million American workers, just to a level equal to 1968, inflation-adjusted, that is supported by over 70 percent of the people.

Neither Senate Majority Leader Harry Reid nor House Minority Leader Nancy Pelosi is really taking this minimum-wage fairness issue to the people and directly confronting the Republican Party. Yet they both profess to believe in "catching up with 1968." They just don't believe in themselves enough to generate the focused energy to make it happen.

Does Congress Need an Ombudsman to Look After Its Case Work?

APRIL 30, 2022

Want to see Republicans and Democrats come together?

Just revive legislation introduced in 1965 by prominent Wisconsin Democrat Henry S. Reuss—an administrative council of Congress (HR 4273), informally called an ombudsman or "tribune of the people." The administrative council, as an arm of Congress, would handle part of the "casework" to lighten the burden of Congress members and aides. Congressman Reuss saw "casework" as so burdensome on staff and limited office budgets "that it interferes with more important legislative and policy-making functions."

Fifty-seven years later, casework is more alive than ever. Walk into congressional offices and you will see staff jammed together, with their computers and phones, dealing with personal constituent complaints. Same for staff back in the district offices.

Reuss pointed out that it takes time from representatives and senators as well. He referred to cases such as requests for assistance in dealing with federal agencies, including the Veterans Administration, the Social Security Administration, Railroad Retirement Board, Selective Service System, and US Citizenship and Immigrations Services. For many of these citizens, their members of Congress were their last resort.

The population of each congressional district has grown from about 410,000 in 1963 to around 760,000 today. And the complexities of citizen interaction with the federal bureaucracy have created more demand on congressional offices.

For example, the number of staff working in senators' offices on Capitol Hill and in state offices has almost doubled since the 1970s, but Senate staff members still only number about 4,000—or an average of 40 per senator. This number does not include committee staff or leadership staff. Add those and you are up to a total of 5,717 Senate staff members. (See *Senate Staff Levels in Member, Committee, Leadership, and Other Offices;* Congressional Research Service, October 19, 2020.)

Total House staff stood at 6,329 in 2021—or an average of only 15 per member. Total House staff, including committee and leadership staff, stood at 9,034 in 2021 (*House of Representatives Staff Levels in Member, Committee, Leadership, and Other Offices*, Congressional Research Service, September 2, 2021).

As introduced, the administrative council would receive the cases from members, process them, and return them to the members for review and responses to their constituents.

In this way, members could avail themselves of the council's expertise and still take credit for case resolutions, while reducing burdens on staff.

An important added benefit would come from the pooling of complaints by the council to discern patterns demanding reform or cessation of such practices. The council would recommend changes to federal agencies and departments, and, if needed, recommend broader legislative corrections.

With his typically thorough explanation, Representative Reuss grounded his proposal in the Constitution's First Amendment: "Congress shall make no law . . . abridging . . . the right of the people . . . to petition the Government for a redress of grievances."

The response by his colleagues took the popular congressman aback. It was overwhelmingly negative and bipartisan. Members were not about to let go of their control of their response to private citizens asking for help the citizens would never forget. It was and is seen as a reelection given.

Never mind the more expert treatment they could take credit for in their response. Never mind the value of the council discovering patterns or trends calling for reform stemming from the aggregations of individual cases. And never mind freeing more staff for the primary purposes of their legislative job description. Members of Congress wished to call out the agencies directly and display their prowess on these personal matters mishandled by the federal bureaucracy.

HR 4273 and its companion bill, S. 984, introduced by Senator Claiborne Pell (D-RI), never went anywhere. With the Newt Gingrich (R-GA) era's staff and committee budget cuts in 1995 and 1996 still bedeviling congressional capacities, members remain mired in the same zero-sum game of attending to their legislative and big-time oversight duties and casework.

No such tensions occur, however, with what to do when constituents send substantive nonpersonal communications on policies and members' practices. Ignore them. Do not even acknowledge their receipt. It has become part of the "incommunicado" culture on Capitol Hill. Over and over again, people tell us of these discourtesies, these affronts from supposed public servants.

After a while, people stop trying to get through to their member of Congress altogether, even ones whose political leanings are congenial with that of the citizens. They see a voicemail Congress as hopelessly beyond reach.

In 2019, the House of Representatives established a small Select Committee on the Modernization of Congress. Its relatively low profile may indicate contemplation over matters long rejected, before recommendations are made. At least we can entertain that prospect.

Let the People Know—Put Full Texts of Government Contracts Online

JUNE 6, 2013

Openness in our government is essential for a healthy democracy. When citizens and voters have access to information about the inner workings of their government and representatives, they can cast informed votes. However, when this information remains in the shadows, citizens are left without access to the information necessary for them to properly exercise their civic powers and responsibilities.

Certainly the regular disclosure of how our government spends our tax dollars is extremely important.

In 2006 and 2009, legislation was passed that advanced open government initiatives. With the creation of USASpending.gov in 2006, the public was given access to a searchable online database that discloses federal financial awards and their recipients. In 2009, the Recovery Act included openness provisions that created a public website to track recovery spending and formed a board that would oversee the Recovery Act funds to prevent waste, fraud, and abuse. These were good first steps, but there is much that is left to be done.

Just last month, President Obama signed an executive order and a policy directive that would officially require data generated by the federal government to be made available to the public online. As with all open government initiatives, this is a welcome development. But again, President Obama and his colleagues in Congress can—and need to—do more.

Attempting to build on the foundation of the 2006 and 2009 transparency laws, Republican congressman Darrell Issa and Democratic senator Mark Warner have been working to advance the Digital Accountability and Transparency (DATA) Act in the House and Senate. The DATA Act passed the House in April 2012, but was not acted on in the Senate and died in committee in the 112th Congress. The Senate Committee on Homeland Security & Governmental Affairs did, however, hold a hearing to discuss the bill, titled "Show Me the Money: Improving the Transparency of Federal Spending."

During this hearing, despite bipartisan support in Congress, White House representatives from the Office of Management and Budget and the Treasury Department balked at the bill, giving insight to improvements that could be made. Comptroller General Gene Dodaro, however, made it clear that a law is needed to specifically enumerate what information must be reported.

The DATA Act was reintroduced in the 113th Congress (HR 2061 and S. 994) at the end of May 2013 and unanimously passed the House Committee on Oversight and Government Reform. It aims to improve the quality of publicly accessible government information, set uniform data standards, collect spending data, and examine the information to root out waste, fraud, or abuse.

Neither the president's executive order nor the DATA Act, however, has gone far enough. There remains one crucial provision that is notably absent from both proposals: making full contract texts available online. Unfortunately, when it comes to government spending and government contracts, the devil is in the details. Providing this degree of public access to reporters, scholars, taxpayer associations, and more competitive bidders would be an important step forward. It would help keep corruption in check, hold government accountable for its actions, propagate best practices in contracting, give rise to significant taxpayer savings, and encourage fiscal responsibility.

Each year hundreds of billions of dollars in federal government contracts, grants, leaseholds, and licenses are awarded to corporations. Taxpayers should be able to easily access clear and concise information on how their tax dollars are being spent by the government at all levels. This is especially needed in an era of massive outsourcing to large private corporations.

States across the country have been implementing their own open-government initiatives in the past several years. States leading the way by consistently moving toward making full contract texts of all direct government spending available online include Arizona, Arkansas, Connecticut, Delaware, Indiana, Kentucky, Massachusetts, Michigan, Mississippi, Nebraska, Ohio, Oklahoma, Pennsylvania, Rhode Island, South Carolina, South Dakota, Utah, and Texas. Requiring federal agencies and departments to post the full text of all federal contracts online would be the logical next step.

Concerns about confidentiality or cost of such an endeavor are vastly overblown. The computer age should make it possible to efficiently allow for certain redactions related to only legitimate concerns about genuine trade secrets and national security in contracts before they are posted online in a publicly available database.

To repeat: Let the people know now. No more secret contracts and other deals.

Putting the full text of these contracts online could give taxpayers both savings and better value; allow the media focus to more incisively on this vast area of government disbursements to inform the wider public; encourage constructive comments and alarms from the citizenry; and allow research by scholars specializing in the daily government procurement, transfers, subsidies, giveaways, and bailouts.

Capitol Hill's Rabid, Ravaging Republicans

OCTOBER 25, 2012

Has there ever been a more crazed, cruel, antipeople, corporate-indentured, militaristic, or monetized Republican Party in its 154-year history? An about-to-be-released list of some of the actual brutish votes by the House Republicans, led by Speaker John Boehner and Representative Eric Cantor, will soon be available to you from the House Democratic Caucus.

Lest you think this is just partisan propaganda, these are real, recorded votes in the House of Representatives.

The Republicans seem to have it in for women, and not just against health insurance covering reproductive health care, funding for Planned Parenthood's many services, or privacy for the medical records of victims of rape and incest. The Republicans voted *en masse* to repeal protections keeping health insurance companies from discriminating on the basis of gender.

On other consumer protections—forget it. The Republicans are indentured to the worst of their corporate paymasters. The Republicans either do nothing to help or actually push for rollbacks. No minimum wage to give thirty million Americans the same pay workers got back in 1968, adjusted for inflation. The Chamber of Commerce says no. So Boehner and Cantor curtsy.

In a frenzy, House Republicans have voted to repeal the Affordable Care Act thirty-three times. Be assured their hatred for Obamacare is not because they want full "Medicare for all." It is because they want to voucherize Medicare and hand patients over to the avaricious Aetnas and Pfizers who return the favor with campaign cash.

House Republicans rage against any attempts to stop the shipping or outsourcing of American jobs to communist and fascist regimes abroad that know how to keep their workers in powerless penury. Why? Because that is what the unpatriotic US global corporations want them to do. Anything Big Oil wants, it gets—retain big subsidies and tax breaks, weaken

pollution restrictions, lease everywhere, and even give relief to oil companies when they damage the Gulf Coast.

House Republicans have a conflict of interest between their families'
lungs and their corporatized minds. Resolution? Vote to weaken the
Clean Air Act and drinking-water safety standards; cut funding for these
cancer-preventing, health-protecting programs while pushing for more
military weapons and bloated Pentagon budgets. The Republicans went
so far as to vote for polluters over children, pregnant women, and people
who live in nursing homes and assisted living facilities. These Republicans
voted to block the Environmental Protection Agency (EPA) mercury and
air toxics standards that the agency estimated would save twelve thousand
lives every year and prevent more than one million asthma attacks.

With unseemly fervor, House Republicans want to generally weaken
the National Labor Relations Board and labor laws. But when it comes
to protecting the lowest tax rates and loopholes for the very wealthy, they
are Horatius at the bridge. When the top 2 percent engage in financial
fraud (credit cards, mortgages, student loans, abuse of seniors) or urge
privatizing social security, the Boehners and the Cantors are block-tack-
ling anyone in the House who begs to push law and order for the rich and
corporate or keep the "security" in Social Security.

For the poor, let them eat less. Hunger in America is real. But not real
enough for the Republicans to stop wanting to cut these food programs.
While Republicans campaign against Obama for not doing anything to
lower gasoline prices, they are voting against measures to regulate oil and
gas speculators who drive up gas prices, a fact recognized by the CEO of
Exxon a few years ago in a Senate hearing.

The above are just a sample of what the House Republicans passed or
blocked. Even worse are what many of them wanted to summarily abolish,
such as the EPA, the Occupational Safety and Health Administration, and
the Internal Revenue Service. The meat-axing Republicans have trouble
telling the public how the important *functions* performed by these agencies
would be handled. The Republicans dismiss the work of health and safety
agencies as junk science (e.g., regarding climate change). Fortunately, the
Senate has rejected most of their madness.

How do such people get elected? Is it just money and smooth slogans?
Is it a lack of competition in rigged districts? Is it a winner-take-all, two-
party duopoly where more than half the voters sit out the election? Is it

shocking disengagement by the cynical or hopeless public, shorn of any rigorous expectation levels?

For the time being, you can read the report. Ponder the fate of our republic. Ask why we have almost unconditionally given up our enormous sovereign power of "We the People" to those out-of-control, raging members of Congress.

Pompous Prevaricators of Power

MAY 15, 2012

A friend who works in Congress and actually reads the *Congressional Record* suggested that a collection of excerpted falsehoods by Republicans on the floor of the House of Representatives and Senate would make compelling evidence for the truth of economist Albert Hirschman's book *The Rhetoric of Reaction* (1991).

Professor Hirschman, a very original political economist, found throughout American history the following three propositions were commonly used to counter social justice efforts:

1. *The Perversity Thesis* states government action only serves to exacerbate the problem being addressed;

2. *The Futility Thesis* holds that attempts at social policy will simply fail to solve the problem;

3. *The Jeopardy Thesis* argues that the cost of the proposed change or reform is too high and will lead to disaster.

The only people who know more about this sequential rhetoric than Mr. Hirschman are corporate lawyers and their corporate clients' publicists. For over two hundred years they and their corporations have opposed virtually every advance for better and fairer lives for the American people using propaganda that fits into Hirschman's framework. Whether it was the abolition of slavery, child labor, the seventy-hour week, women's right to vote, trade union rights, the progressive income tax, unemployment compensation, social security, and, of course, the various regulatory standards protecting consumers, worker safety, and the environment, the arguments against them have been pretty much the same.

As the fascinating Cry Wolf Project (crywolfproject.org) staff observed:

"We've heard these all before. Perversity: if you raise the minimum wage, you'll increase unemployment. Futility: tobacco warning labels won't stop people from smoking. And Jeopardy: it's a 'job killer.'"

The Cry Wolf Project presents verbatim quotations from the corporate bosses from years past and then lets their words speak for themselves. Here is a sample:

Henry Ford II, in 1966, on long-overdue safety standards such as laminated windshields, dual-braking systems, collapsible steering wheels, and seat belts: "Many of the temporary standards are unreasonable, arbitrary and technically unfeasible. . . . If we can't meet them when they are published we'll have to close down." To his credit, ten years later on national television, Mr. Ford recognized that due to federal regulations, cars were safer, more efficient, and less polluting.

His fiery vice president, Lee Iacocca, said in 1970 that the Clean Air Act "could prevent continued production of automobiles . . . *and* is a threat to the entire American economy and to every person in America." Mr. Iacocca did recant his opposition to air bags as head of Chrysler in a full-page ad headlined "Who Says You Can't Teach an Old Dog New Tricks?"

Other corporate barons were more intransigent. Reacting to a law that established the federal minimum wage and ended child labor, a spokesman for the manufacturing industry in 1938 unleashed this volley: "The Fair Labor Standards Act constitutes a step in the direction of communism, Bolshevism, fascism, and Nazism."

Social Security received a broadside from the chairman of the board of Chase National Bank. In 1936, top-brass banker Winthrop W. Aldrich called it a "grave menace to the future security of the country as a whole and to the security of the very people it is designed to protect."

His down-the-line executive successor, the haughty James Dimon, has been spouting cataclysmic claims about the Dodd–Frank reforms that are modestly designed to avoid another multitrillion-dollar Wall Street bailout by Washington. Haughty, that is, until last week when Mr. Dimon, CEO of JPMorgan Chase, revealed at least a $2 billion gambling bet that his company lost in the high-flying business of complex-derivatives trading linked to corporate debt.

What a cruel irony. Mr. Dimon's bank and half a dozen other giant banks are now corporate welfare kings deemed "too big to fail" (as well as too big to be taxed fairly). Unfortunately, Social Security recipients and other taxpayers are still the ones who will pay for any future bailouts. This is what America has been reduced to by the multinational casino capitalists who long ago abandoned any allegiance or patriotism toward the country that bred them into present-day giants.

Outlandish assertions are not restricted to members of Congress or the corporate world. Ronald Reagan was a jovial genius at nutty declarations, as when he told reporters that submarine-launched nuclear missiles can be recalled or that approximately 80 percent of our air pollution stems from vegetation. So prolific was the former Hollywood actor that Mark Green collected Reagan's pronouncements in a classic 173-page paperback titled *Reagan's Reign of Error* (1987).

With the velocity of modern communications, media, and the internet, who can keep up with the separation of facts and truth from lies, propaganda, and what is now called "magical thinking"? Far more people have become rich and famous for telling lies and falsehoods than people who have a habit of telling the truth and reciting facts. The former get promoted, host radio shows, receive large advances on books, and are elected to office.

In 2002, the ultracorporatist senator Saxby Chambliss defeated incumbent Georgia senator Max Cleland, whose legs were amputated as a result of injuries he suffered in the Vietnam War, with ads showing a photo of Cleland along with photos of Saddam Hussein and Osama bin Laden, by way of questioning Cleland's patriotism. Fellow Republican senator John McCain called Saxby's ads in 2002 "worse than disgraceful—reprehensible." In 2008, Saxby was reelected.

The forces of accountability for what public personages exclaim have to come from a more demanding citizenry. People have to punish these charlatans who think they can distract, degrade, or fool the public. Don't buy their garbage or let the prevaricators garner your votes.

A handy question people can always ask is "What's your evidence?" That starts an entirely new dialogue, doesn't it?

Callers Say, "Can't Get Through"; Callees Say, "Don't Want to Let Them Through"

JULY 28, 2022

Most of us play the role of both Caller and Callee. Guess which role rules? The Callee. I've lost count of how many older adults tell me, week after week, how hard it is to get through to powerful Callees. Especially by telephone! The latter includes your local electric, gas, and telephone company; your bank and insurance company; your members of Congress (or their staff); your local, state, and federal government agencies. It never used to be that way.

Imagine the days when you'd pick up your phone, dial, and get through to a human being. You couldn't be waylaid by the evasive robotic operator who gives you the "press one, or two, or three, or four" drill. Unfortunately, when you select "one," you often get another automatic recording. At some point you get a *voicemail* opportunity, which is really *voicefail.*

Oh, say the younger people—what about trying email or text messaging? Clutter, filters, distractions, and sheer overloads can't adequately describe the ways Callees can keep you from getting through to a human. The more difficult it is, the more people repeat their attempts, and the more overload there is for the digital gatekeepers. Call this the Callees' power plays.

The Bureau of Labor Statistics measures white-collar labor productivity. If they measured the sheer billions of hours wasted by people trying to contact members of Congress, white-collar labor productivity would be far lower than its present level.

Here are some areas of abuse. Our Constitution's First Amendment protects more than freedom of speech, press, and religion. It adds the "right to petition the Government for a redress of grievances." "Grievances" include more than personal affronts or injustices, such as petitions to get the government to enact or repeal policies, practices, or other behaviors. I am confident in saying that members of Congress and their staff have never been more unresponsive to serious petitions (letters, calls, emails, and old-fashioned petitions) on important issues than today.

Their prompt responses are reserved for donors and ceremonial requests (graduations, birthdays, weddings, funerals, and friends). Civic groups supporting a member's already-chosen legislative priorities find their staff have a working relationship with a congressional office. But try to get through to a member of Congress to sponsor a congressional hearing or expand their portfolio to urgent new arenas—yes, keep trying.

It is near impossible to get through to even friendly members (or senior staffers) of Congress on grave matters of undeclared wars, the starving of the Internal Revenue Service (IRS) budget to aid and abet massive tax evasions by the super-rich and big companies; serial, lawless rejections of congressional authority under the Constitution by the White House; or even restoring the staff of congressional committees that Newt Gingrich cut in 1995 when he toppled the House Democrats. Nonresponses everywhere.

It is so bad that we wrote to every member of Congress and asked them what their office policy toward responding to serious communications was. Only one in 535 offices responded.

Of course, there is the absorbing activity known as "constituent service"—intervening for people back home not getting responses from federal agencies for their personal complaints. Some responsiveness to constituents' personal stories is widely believed to be good for reelection. (See my column on page 691: "Does Congress Need an Ombudsman to Look After Its Case Work?," published in the *Capitol Hill Citizen* newspaper—capitolhillcitizen.com).

If the Congress in the sixties and seventies was as unresponsive as Congress is today—ironically in the midst of the communications revolution—we couldn't have gotten the key consumer, environmental, worker safety, and health laws; the Freedom of Information Act; and other laws enacted. Clearly if you cannot communicate consistently with the 535 members of Congress and staff, who are given massive sovereign powers by "We the People" (right in the preamble to our Constitution), you cannot even start to get anything done on Capitol Hill.

There is one democracy-wrecking exception—corporate lobbyists who grease the system with campaign money and assorted inducements and temptations dangled in real time and in the future. The lobbyists for the oil, gas, and coal industries; the banking, insurance, and brokerage companies; the military weapons manufacturers; the drug, hospital, and nursing home chains; corporate law firms; the corporate media; and others of similar avarice do get access. They get the private cell phone numbers of our elected officials, because they invite members and staff to luxurious gatherings and travel junkets, as well as more formal fundraising or political action committee venues.

This phenomenon of elected officials being incommunicado toward civic communities is a process enacted by the powerful to control the less powerful. Make no mistake. This same tale of two systems of access is everywhere. Big banks (Bank of America is one of the worst) and utility companies have algorithms that tell them how they can hire fewer workers for customer service if they can make consumers wait on recorded lines or fail to answer emails and letters. The big companies want customers to just give up.

The courts are culpable as well. People have complained about not even being able to get through to small claims court for hours at a time. The Postal Service is not known for quick telephone pickups, as it's still under control of Trump's nominee, Louis DeJoy. Not to mention what the GOP did to the IRS's budget for responding to ordinary taxpayers.

But some companies are a bit more responsive, such as FedEx or your local small family-owned retail business.

The lack of access is a serious problem that degrades quality of life with heightened stress and anxiety. And in some cases, during an emergency or disaster, the lack of a response has dire consequences.

More than fifty billion robocalls a year have seriously disrupted people answering their telephones, even from neighbors down the street. The Federal Communications Commission and Federal Trade Commission are just not aggressively pressuring the communications companies to use the latest software to thwart these robocall outlaws. These agencies themselves are notoriously incommunicado.

What to do? Be more vociferous. Favor politicians and merchants who pledge to have humans answer phones and not make you wait, wait, and wait to give them your thoughts, your business, and your complaints.

Your suggestions, readers, will be most welcome.

SELECTED LETTERS

Speaker Pelosi to Revive the Office of Technology Assessment

AUGUST 3, 2020

House Speaker Nancy Pelosi
Office of the Speaker
H-252 US Capitol
United States Congress
Washington, DC 25015

Dear Speaker Pelosi,

A critical arm and intellectual infrastructure of Congress—the Office of Technology Assessment (OTA)—has been defunded since Speaker Newt Gingrich ordered such after he toppled the complacent Democrats in November 1994. This left Congress without sound independent advice by some 140 scientists and technologists on a long list of decisions by the Congress to oversee, stop, reduce, or start funding for scientific and technological programs.

Not until 2009–2010, when the Democrats regained control of both Houses, did a broad coalition of scientists, civic advocates, and members of Congress—led by Democratic representative Rush Holt (a former Princeton University scientist)—urge you as Speaker to revive the OTA. A distinguished number of Nobel laureates, former staff and officials of the OTA, and your Democratic colleagues sought hearings backed by an impressively documented case for refunding. To no avail. You then opposed public hearings and apparently told aides that you did not want to give the Republicans an opportunity to accuse Democrats of creating another bureaucracy on Capitol Hill. (The OTA's budget was a parsimonious $21 million in its last year. A bureaucratic OTA is a figment of fevered Republican imagination.) It is very alarming that the damage Gingrich did in lobotomizing Congress continues after him. The number of expert congressional overseers has been slashed beyond the bare bones, while the massive executive branch to be overseen has grown topsy-turvy and for the worst.

So, another decade was lost. Another vacuum of credible advice by Congress's own OTA (as has occurred to a lesser extent with the diminished Government Accountability Office [GAO] and Congressional Research Service) enveloped sectors and issues such as artificial intelligence, systemic invasions of privacy, boondoggle, huge ballistic missile defense and nuclear upgrade expenditures, climate disruption, Boeing 737 MAX, genetic engineering, citizen surveillance technology, autonomous vehicles, nanotechnology, COVID-19, fracking, computer procurement waste, atomic energy, renewable energy, health care, medical devices, pharmaceuticals, food additives, catastrophic environmental disasters (such as the BP oil spill), occupational safety, the controlling power of corporate algorithms, consumer product hazards, and more.

What filled this vacuum was corporate-driven pseudoscience (see former OSHA director David Michaels's new book, *The Triumph of Doubt: Dark Money and the Science of Deception*), which twisted and tortured legislation and appropriations. Business lobbyists thwarted oversight while the number and experience of congressional staff overseers shrank. This is a serious situation now under your watch.

There followed an open sesame for unscrupulous corporations that arrested prudent ways to avert trillions of dollars in waste, imperiled the American people and other peoples abroad, inverted perverse priorities, and resulted in bad, dangerous decisions that have ramifications to this day.

You can now move toward action-driven enlightenment despite Republican control of the Senate. Your House majority can create a unicameral OTA and fund it without the affirmation of the Senate majority wallowing in its Dark Ages. The House OTA can be reconstituted functionally as an arm of the House independent of the Senate. Acting on behalf of the House alone, you cannot be blocked by the Senate as you were in 2019 when the House included $6 million for the bicameral OTA in its House-passed version of the Legislative Branch Appropriations Act, 2020 (HR 2779). As a matter of law (31 USC 1105, 1107, and custom), neither the Senate nor the president can interfere with the budget proposed by the House for itself, including the funding of House committees or House offices.

You and your colleagues can make an overwhelming substantive case for funding a House OTA based on scores of audits, investigations, and reports that invite first-class advice, assessment, and testimony from your own public servants. The small technology unit in GAO, while useful for GAO's culture, is not sufficient. There is a massive backlog of congressionally neglected work to be done. Consider how pathetic the questioning has been by committee members, already deprived of adequate staff (the Gingrich model), of the Silicon Valley executives once Congress finally got these imperial bosses to agree to come and testify. Similarly, both Democrats and Republicans have been seriously fact-deprived in their hoopla of support for failed attempts at deregulating and boosting the prematurely hyped autonomous vehicles pushed by the industry, especially in 2017 and 2018. Worse has been the automatic annual funding by Congress of the megabillions of dollars for the ballistic missile defense boondoggle, criticized by leading technical experts, without oversight since its inception during the Reagan years.

Corporate lobbyists and installed corporate-indentured officials in the executive branch will no doubt oppose such a revived OTA. Its reports will be staples of public congressional hearings. Congressional ignorance has consequences. Your iron control of the House of Representatives can make Republican opposition flaccid and evidentially self-serving to their greed and corporatism. Please use your power to address the problems that stem from the absence of OTA and fund it this time.

The undersigned are sending this letter to other members of Congress, numerous scientific and engineering associations, individuals, distinguished academic and nonacademic scientists and technologists, and, of course, the media.

Please do not prejudge from the last decade. As recent events and civic energy demonstrate, this is a new era with new possibilities once deemed politically difficult in those past years of inertia and self-censorship. Seize the hour!

Two of the undersigned, in their exercise of civic duties, have written you several letters on important matters without ever receiving an acknowledgment, much less a serious response. Is this your established office practice, apart from constituent services for your San Francisco residents? The right of citizens to petition for redress of grievances is enshrined in the First Amendment in furtherance of self-government. Public officials should act accordingly.

Sincerely,

Ralph Nader, Esq.
Bruce Fein, Esq.
Claire Nader, Ph.D.
Joan B. Claybrook, Esq.
Louis Fisher, Esq.

Letter to Alexandria Ocasio-Cortez

JULY 31, 2020

Representative Alexandria Ocasio-Cortez
229 Cannon House Office Building
US House of Representatives
Washington, DC 20515-3214

Dear Representative Ocasio-Cortez,

Your going to the floor of the House of Representatives to take to task Representative Ted Yoho for his disgusting and sexist epithet following your exchange with him exposed to a national audience the range of such foul talk by more than a few male members of the House. Words matter, for they often clothe wrongful attitudes and the conditions behind them.

You are in the eye of the mass media—deservedly so. But such an asset for communicating your actions, policies, and observations may not last very long. At least that is often the history of authentic political figures who take on entrenched interests even from elected office. Ever-higher expectations for your work toward a more just society invite the following suggestions.

Consider three actions to address official inertia and wrongdoing that you could take.

First, the savage sexual predator in the White House, Donald J. Trump, has engaged in more than boastful misogynistic language. He has sexually abused and assaulted many women and repeatedly lied and publicly vilified his victims in the process. As you know, tort lawsuits filed by some of these women are pending in the courts. The Me Too constituency has the opportunity to make Trump's predatory behavior an issue in this year's presidential campaign. However, the media and civic groups have failed to continue to make Trump's deplorable behavior an issue. So has Congress, including both female and male Democratic legislators. In

697

early February, we hand-delivered personally the enclosed letter to nearly a hundred House Democratic members, including all eighty-nine Democratic women House representatives. The staff was more than courteous in receiving what amounted to a documented petition to have a House committee investigate this deeply rapacious behavior. Mr. Trump's "abuse of the public trust," in our Founders' language, should not be ignored.

I delivered the letter directly to your office. Not one of the nearly one hundred members, including Speaker Nancy Pelosi, even bothered to respond. The lack of response resulted, not surprisingly, in no media coverage by any of the twenty reporters, columnists, and editors in the mass media who had previously covered Trump's brutish assaults. Is he too terrible to hold accountable?

Don't you think it is worthy of a House committee's time to investigate a pattern of behavior that is a destructive role model for boys and young men—as Trump continues to get away with what a small fraction of such transgressions have cost Democratic senator Al Franken and Democratic congressman John Conyers?

Second, the *New York Times* reported a few days ago your demand for Governor Andrew Cuomo to adopt, with the legislature, a "billionaire tax" to help a deficit-ridden New York bolster the state's social safety net. Political observers don't expect action on this proposal. On the other hand, the New York Public Interest Group (NYPIRG), one of the leading student advocacy groups in American history, assembled a diverse coalition of fifty civic groups and held a press briefing led by NYPIRG director Blair Horner on May 28, 2020. Your office was sent their persuasive media release (see attached) demanding that Governor Cuomo stop rebating some $40 million a day from the tiny stock-transfer sales taxes that the state collects and electronically sends back to Wall Street brokers.

This rebated progressive sales tax is well-known to state and congressional legislators. There was no response from you or your staff or from any other members of the New York State Congressional Delegation. Given New York State's $16 billion budget deficit this year, the estimated $16 billion in rebated tax revenues could help provide assistance to struggling communities statewide. Isn't this worth your immediate attention?

Please take the lead here and help shine your media spotlight on something critically important to illuminate.

Third, you'll remember how President Trump violated the "speech and debate clause" in our Constitution when he pressed Israeli Prime Minister Netanyahu to bar the entry of two members of Congress traveling to Israel and the Palestinian West Bank in the exercise of their constitutionally protected oversight duties. At the time we urged the excluded Rashida Tlaib and Ilhan Omar to make more of this impeachable offense— unprecedented in American history, according to two constitutional law specialists. Our letter (attached) to Speaker Nancy Pelosi, as well as similar ones to you and other members of the House, went unanswered, except for a call from Representative Tlaib's office. You can still send Mr. Trump a stiffly written warning to never try this again, with many members of the House cosigning. Otherwise, Trump will just add this to his lengthy list of impeachable offenses that the Democrats let him get away with, absent even an official condemnation to deter such dictatorial behavior by succeeding presidents.

Were you and the class of 2018 in the Democratic camp more connected from the outset with national progressive citizen groups on a regular basis—meeting with them in your offices, listening to their recommendations—the above three actions might not have been neglected. Right after the 2018 election, I wrote the attached column putting forth several tests that would determine how serious the congressional newcomers were about getting fundamental neglected actions underway, not just saying the right words and issuing good public statements. History shows that legislators cannot get much done without the close engagement of the civic community (e.g., civil rights and environmental groups, unions), and the civic community can't get any laws or public hearings without the legislators. Social justice causes require regular close cooperation, consultation, and open acknowledgment of such to persuade the media that these civic groups have a power base in Congress and vice versa. Alas, this was not done, with few exceptions, not even by the heralded "Squad."

We welcome your considered response to each of the above suggestions, notwithstanding many months of unsuccessful striving to connect and having you and others respond to matters of contemporary importance. These include matters of war and peace, and of White House constitutional, statutory, and treaty violations (see attached list of twelve impeachable offenses we assembled that were placed in the *Congressional Record* by Congressman John Larson, December 18, 2019). Eleven offenses were completely set aside by your party's leadership, including some strongly recommended for action by the House Judiciary Committee.

Thank you.

For Peace and Justice,

Ralph Nader

Open Letter to the Women in Congress

FEBRUARY 24, 2020

Think of Elizabeth Cady Stanton, Sojourner Truth, Susan B. Anthony, Angelina Weld Grimké, Alice Paul, and Jeannette Rankin. Recall their courage and leadership in comparison with the courage needed to request an investigation of President Trump's treatment of women.

It does not take many conversations with women lawmakers and their staff on Capitol Hill to sense the deep indignation over the recidivist serial sexual predator now inhabiting the White House as president. Since his selection by the Electoral College, Donald Trump has been embroiled in numerous tort lawsuits alleging sexual assaults with sworn testimony by aggrieved plaintiffs. He has called the charges by aggrieved women lies and showered his accusers with degrading fulminations. The credible accusations by many women, under oath, of Trump's very brutish, violent, rapacious assaults are overwhelming. As has been his practice in a bankruptcy-ridden business career, Trump has thus far escaped being deposed under oath because of the well-honed dilatory tactics of his attorneys (unlike Bill Clinton, who was deposed under oath in a tort case asserting sexual aggressions and then impeached by the House of Representatives for lying about sex).

Through his last three years as president, Trump has persisted with non-stop slander of women, whether they are accusing him of sexual assault and battery—a felony in every state—or whether they displeased him by denouncing him for sexist behavior or other practices. On national television and before large rallies, Trump has called the chairwoman of the House Financial Services Committee "low-IQ Maxine Waters" repeatedly. Never any remorse nor apologies. He just doubles down with his unprecedented intimidating misogyny in action.

Last year, Trump singled out two female members of Congress by urging the prime minister of Israel to deny these two women visas to exercise their oversight responsibilities regarding US foreign policy in Israel and Palestine. In so doing, he violated the spirit if not the letter of the "speech or debate" clause of Article I, Section 6, Clause 1, of the Constitution. Trump has never selected any male members of Congress for such exclusions. He refuses to express regrets or promise never to repeat this violation of the critical separation of powers under our Constitution. He has denied the House Speaker appropriate military aircraft for hazardous foreign travel while exercising her official oversight responsibility. Trump has always had difficulties with strong women.

Democratic women lawmakers led by Senator Kirsten Gillibrand forced the departure of Senator Al Franken and Representative John Conyers for past inappropriate sexual advances. It did not matter enough that these two Democrats were champions of women's rights in Congress. There was an absence of due process, particularly regarding Senator Franken's request for an ethics proceeding that was pending before the Senate Ethics Committee, despite expressions of remorse. Both women and men in both chambers just said "get out now" to both Democratic legislators. Senator Franken and Representative Conyers complied.

What of Republican Donald Trump? His blatant sexual transgressions, boasted over national television shows, were far, far greater in number and levels of felonious violence than the above legislators. Moreover, his rise to public notoriety that in turn gave rise to his plan for the White House was partly based on his outrageous outbursts on television shows, such as those on the Howard Stern show, and what went on about his treatment of women behind the scenes of Trump's show *The Apprentice*.

As related by one of Trump's sexual victims, Natasha Stoynoff, in the *Washington Post* op-ed page on November 7, 2019: "Two weeks ago, 43 new allegations of sexual misconduct by Trump surfaced in a new book, 'All the President's Women: Donald Trump and the Making of a Predator,' by Barry Levine and Monique El-Faizy. My sisters and I were not surprised: we suspect there are even more out there."

This book was given major coverage in the *New York Times*. A reporter there told me she was surprised at the mild response to the feature by the Me Too movement engaged in the protection of women from sexual assaults and harassments. This same citizen constituency created public awareness that led to some two hundred powerful officials in the business, sports, entertainment, and academic worlds being ousted. The book's coauthor, Barry Levine, wrote that "Trump's actions helped catalyze the #MeToo movement."

Has Donald Trump—the bully and sexual predator—become too terrible to challenge, too much of a criminal sexual marauder gravely abusing his power and public trust, to justify impeachment and removal from office? Republican Trumpsters take note—Trump's offenses are rooted in state statutory crimes. In addition, he criminally paid hush money to a porn star late in the election year of 2016, which is itself rooted in the violation of federal campaign finance laws having criminal penalties. Senator Kirsten Gillibrand has denounced Trump, the kingpin of sexual predators in the White House. In December 2017, Gillibrand said to CNN's Christiane Amanpour in an exclusive interview:

"President Trump has committed assault, according to these women, and those are very credible allegations of misconduct and criminal activity, and he should be fully investigated and he should resign. These allegations are credible; they are numerous," said Gillibrand, a leading voice in Congress for combating sexual assault in the military. "I've heard these women's testimony, and many of them are heartbreaking."

If he does not "immediately resign," she said, Congress "should have appropriate investigations of his behavior and hold him accountable."

Other members of Congress made similar demands at that time. Why no action since that declaration? Why the surrender?

Public hearings by the House of Representatives and the Senate—where the women who've been assaulted testify *under oath,* followed by a demand that Donald J. Trump appear before congressional committees to respond under oath—are a critical component of the lawmakers' belief that *no one is above the law.* These are clearly inquiries with legitimate legislative purpose to discover the extent of violations of the laws pursuant to the available probative evidence on the record and what laws need to be strengthened.

The women in Congress have the facts, the morality, and the law squarely on their side. Moreover, a CNN national poll released on November 27, 2019, reported that 61 percent of women are ready to impeach *and* remove Donald Trump from his office.

On January 30, 2020, over two dozen women legislators in the House of Representatives, led by representatives Jackie Speier, Lois Frankel, and Brenda J. Lawrence, cochairs of the Democratic Women's Caucus, sent a letter to President Trump reprimanding him, with graphic detail, for his "continuing derogation of women in your rhetoric and policies." It ended with the plea: "Mr. President, instead of being the biggest bully on the playground, why don't you set a moral example for our children?" This unprecedented admonition received almost no media, much less a response. Letting Trump get away with a sharp verbal slap on the wrist does little to counter violent behavior against women for all too many men and boys to find acceptable.

Where is the call for congressional hearings? If these accusations by scores of women, some made under oath, turn out to be either felonious crimes or tortious wrongful injuries, such offenses are impeachable or grounds for resignation. The public has a right to know the facts and the violations of pertinent applicable laws to this boastful, unrepentant sexual sadist.

Our Founders cited serious abuses of power or violations of the public trust as a prime definition of the clause "high crimes and misdemeanors," including by no less an advocate of a strong executive than Alexander Hamilton.

Imagine the horrible precedent for future presidents and wannabe presidential candidates that is being established by not moving to hold Donald Trump accountable to the rule of law. Having gotten away with racist/bigoted policies and incitements to violence, this serial fabricator cannot be allowed to escape accountability for these egregious, chronic offenses. As collateral harm, he is shredding further the moral fiber of our society among impressionable youths, as detailed this week in the *Washington Post* (see: washingtonpost.com/graphics/2020/local/school-bullying-trump-words).

By comparison, note how the lawmakers in Albany, New York, reacted in March 2008 when the *New York Times* reported that Democratic governor Eliot Spitzer had paid a prostitute for her service at the Mayflower Hotel in Washington, DC. Legislators, especially Democrats, told him if he did not resign immediately, he would be impeached. He resigned two days later with remorse. After ending a promising political career, he subsequently said: "I resigned my position as governor because I recognized that conduct was unworthy of an elected official. I once again apologize for my actions."

It is true that Spitzer's conduct occurred while he was governor. Trump's conduct, as far as is known, preceded his taking office but is civilly *sub judice* and still vulnerable to criminal prosecution. Moreover, his conduct in office is deeply misogynistic and offensively sexist, with regular, crudely phrased ("She's not my type") denials, not under oath, of violent encounters described in great detail under oath (or ready to be described) by his accusers. At the least, a congressional investigation would discover more of the facts and move a long-overdue process of accountability forward.

I write this letter from decades of indignation over the cruel, discriminatory treatment of half the human race by the dominant male culture and its laws. As a law student I started writing about these blatant repressions, including some states prohibiting women from serving on juries as late as the 1950s. I challenged our law school dean as to why only fifteen women were admitted to our class of over five hundred. Later, I wrote articles and sponsored books on the corporate marketplace discrimination and exploitation of women as consumers, workers, patients, and debtors. I never would have envisioned, after years of successful advances of the rights of women by organized women, that such continued inaction toward President Donald Trump would presently prevail in the powerful seats of the US Congress.

This letter does not in any way exonerate male legislators and staff who mostly are willing to pass the responsibility for action to their female counterparts. I have been told and have seen women staffers with frustrated, reddened faces and moistened eyes when this issue of nothing being done is raised with them directly. Perhaps they think it is not for them to speak up before their principals do, but it may be necessary for them to take the first steps.

Speaking for the scores of Trump's victims, Natasha Stoynoff asks: "But for us, the question remains. Will this, finally, be the time when enough people care?"

The clock of history is ticking, Congress.

Sincerely,

Ralph Nader

Letter to President Trump

JUNE 26, 2020

Dear President Trump:

Do you think you have enough on your table these days? Wait until the Israeli government, fortified economically and militarily by US taxpayers, illegally annexes a large region of the Palestinian West Bank, including the Jordan Valley, next month. That is the declaration of the Israeli prime minister.

This flagrant violation of international law, once again confirmed by various countries and the United Nations, is expected to unleash crushing repression and violence, which will be broadcast and shown by photojournalists around the world. This annexation will lead to demonstrations condemning you and the prime minister. Inside Israel, there is strong opposition from retired high military and security officials, as well as members of the Knesset from which the prime minister is not seeking approval. Sound familiar?

The collateral damage from this unilateral seizure of 30 percent of what is left of Palestinian land (the West Bank is about 20 percent of the original Palestine) will include a rupture of warming relations between Israel and nearby Arab countries, especially Jordan; alienation of your friend Recep Tayyip Erdogan, president of Turkey; and unintended consequences that will be arriving at your door as the COVID-19 pandemic widens. Even with your limited attention to detail, your inability to recognize the consequences of international disputes, and your short attention span, you should be able to envision how much time and energy this war crime will take from you.

For the Palestinians, there will be more dread and devastation. Half of their food comes from the Jordan Valley. It would spell the end of the "two-state solution" and lead to the possible dissolution of the Palestinian Authority's security arrangements with the Israeli occupation. That would mean more Israeli patrols, more destruction of homes, more innocent Palestinian casualties, and more responsibility on you stemming from your reckless, mindless endorsement of annexation several months ago.

You can prevent these calamities. First, you need to stop your bigotry against the Palestinian Arabs and desperate Syrian Arab refugees that make you a leading anti-Semite against the Arab peoples. There is, in your regime (Michael Pompeo), the spreading of the "other anti-Semitism," a term James Zogby used to title an address he gave years ago at an Israeli university. Ever since the South Carolina primary in 2016, when you, out of the blue, assailed two poor newly arrived Syrian refugee families who had fled the horrors of their war-torn country, you have expanded your politically motivated hatred of powerless, impoverished Arabs. For example, at a recent rally in Minnesota, you bragged—even gloated—about cutting off $500 million a year in aid provided to desperate Palestinian families. You broke a humanitarian program supported by Democratic and Republican presidents since 1950 in recognition of the role that the US has played in that region. You have fully backed brutal Israeli actions against defenseless Palestinians and their children. What the Israeli regime does in the coming months will be ascribed to you, a multifaceted anti-Semite against Arabs. You could stop this atrocity, but you are actually inciting what are in essence territorial war crimes. Your political allies in Israel welcome such racist evocations from the White House. Politicians in the Israeli government's coalition have expressed over the years the vilest epithets against Palestinians, so racist that if you bothered to read them, it would shock even your limited sensibilities.

And what is the Palestinian grievance at its core? Israel's founder, David Ben-Gurion, put it concisely in a widely reported comment: "It was their land and we took it." Now you are depriving these Palestinian descendants from having their tiny independent state, endorsed by previous US presidents. Their poverty has worsened because of occupations, blockades, and regular attacks by the military. Add the deprivation of water, taken by Israel; plus, according to Israeli historian Ilan Pappé, Israel "has recently escalated its spraying of pesticides on Palestinian fields in Gaza and increased harassment of fisherman."

This is one fast-arriving crisis that you brought onto yourself. It is not too late to stop. Your advisers, including your son-in-law, know full well that the prime minister will not make the annexation move without your concurrence. Tell the prime minister NO and he will comply. You are known as a control freak. Exercise this trait and you'll prevent multiple eruptions in the Middle East that may be uncontrollable and create another foreign policy crisis in your administration.

Domestically, a majority of American Jews oppose this annexation and other Israeli policies that seriously harm Palestinians and also undermine democratic freedoms in Israel. J Street and Jewish Voices for Peace are gaining many more adherents. Even AIPAC has reportedly expressed disapproval of the prime minister's racist policies and the move toward annexation, privately signaling that they won't push back against lawmakers who criticize the plan. Where does that leave your political calculations?

On the eve of the 1956 elections, President Dwight D. Eisenhower handily won acclaim and reelection while stopping Israel's collaborative invasion of Suez with Britain and France.

Act now: say NO to annexation.

Sincerely,

Ralph Nader

An Open Letter to Chairwoman Yellen, from the Savers of America

OCTOBER 30, 2015

Dear Chairwoman Janet Yellen:

We are a group of humble savers in traditional bank savings and money market accounts who are frustrated because, like millions of other Americans over the past six years, we are getting near-zero interest. We want to know why the Federal Reserve, funded and heavily run by the banks, is keeping interest rates so low that we receive virtually no income for our hard-earned savings, while the Fed lets the big banks borrow money for virtually no interest. It doesn't seem fair to put the burden of your Federal Reserve's monetary policies on the backs of those Americans who are the least positioned to demand fair play.

We follow the reporting on your tediously overdramatic indecision as to when interest rates will be raised—and no one thinks that when you do, it will be any more than one-quarter of 1 percent. We hear the Federal Reserve's board of governors and the various regional board presidents regularly present their views of the proper inflation, unemployment rate, and stock market expectations that influence their calculations for keeping interest rates near zero. But we never hear any mention of us—the savers of trillions of dollars who have been forced to make do with having the banks and mutual funds essentially provide a lockbox for our money while they use it to make a profit for their firms and, in the case of the giant banks and large mutual funds, pay their executives exorbitant salaries.

We are tired of this melodrama that exploits so many people who used to rely on interest income to pay some of their essential bills. Think about the elderly among us who need to supplement their Social Security checks every month.

On October 27, the *Wall Street Journal* headlined the latest rumors of twists and turns inside the secretive Federal Reserve: "Fed Strives for Clear

709

Signal on Rate Move: As 2016 approaches, the central bank hopes to better manage market expectations."

What about the expectations of millions of American savers? It is unfortunately true that we are not organized; if we were, we would give you and Congress the proper signals! Please, don't lecture us about the Fed not being "political." When you are the captives of the financial industry, led by the too-big-to-fail banks, you are generically "political." So political in fact that you have brazenly interpreted your legal authority as to become the de facto regulator of our economy, the de facto printer of money on a huge scale ("quantitative easing" is the euphemism for artificially boosting the stock market), and the leader of Washington bailout-machine crony capitalism when big business, especially a shaky Wall Street firm, indulges in manipulative, avaricious, speculative binges with our money.

When it comes to the Fed, Congress is mired in hypocrisy. The anti-regulation/deregulation crowd on Capitol Hill shuts its mouth when it comes to the most powerful regulators of all—you and the Federal Reserve. Meanwhile, Congress goes along with the out-of-control private government of the Fed—unaccountable to the national legislature. Moreover, your massive monetary injections scarcely led to any jobs on the ground other than stock-and-bond processors.

So what do you advise us to do? Shop around? Forget it. The difference between banks, credit unions, and mutual funds may be one-twentieth or one-tenth of 1 percent! That is, unless you want to tie up money that you need regularly in a longer-term CD or treasury bill. Even then interest rates are far less than they were ten years ago.

Maybe you're saying that we should try the stock market to get higher returns. Some of us have been impelled to do that, but too many have lost their peace of mind and much money in the market.

The Fed's near-zero interest rate policy isn't helping younger people with student loans (now over $1.3 trillion), whose interest rate ranges from 6 to 9 percent. It doesn't help millions of payday loan borrowers or victims of installment-loan rackets—mostly the poor—whose interest rates, rolled over, can reach over 400 percent!

Chairwoman Yellen, I think you should sit down with your Nobel Prize–winning husband, economist George Akerlof, who is known to be consumer-sensitive. Together, figure out what to do for tens of millions of

Americans who, with more interest income, could stimulate the economy by spending toward the necessities of life.

For heaven's sake, you're a "liberal" from Berkeley! That is supposed to mean something other than to be indentured by the culture and jargon of the Federal Reserve. If you need further nudging on monetary and regulatory policies of the Fed, other than interest rate decisions, why not invite Berkeley professor Robert Reich, one of your longtime friends and admirers, to lunch on your next trip home?

Start imagining what we, the savers, have to endure because of plutocratic crony capitalism for which the Federal Reserve has long been a leading tribune.

Can we expect your response?

Sincerely yours,

Savers of America

Letters to a President:
Return to Sender

APRIL 8, 2015

President Barack Obama
The White House
1600 Pennsylvania Avenue, NW
Washington, DC 20500

Dear President Obama,

I am enclosing a copy of *Return to Sender: Unanswered Letters to the President, 2001–2015* (Seven Stories Press), which contains over a hundred letters that I sent to you and President George W. Bush. They were almost entirely unanswered and unacknowledged.

One of these letters asked you about the White House's policies regarding letters it receives. I raised this issue early in your first term with the director of the Office of Presidential Correspondence (OPC), Mike Kelleher, who said there was no specific policy regarding responses, but that he would get back to me after the OPC considered the matter. He did not.

Citizen correspondence is important both for you as president and for them. For the citizens, it is an opportunity to circumvent the barriers presented by the media and governmental institutions to directly access the White House. For presidents, letters help, as you have said, escape "the bubble" (e.g., the ten letters from citizens you read each evening). Letters from citizens also convey ideas and observations that alert you to conditions, issues, and urgencies at hand and occasionally provide you with an opportunity to publicly discuss the point raised by an ordinary citizen who penned such a letter.

Just the other day, when you were visiting Ohio, a chance question to you from a person in the audience elicited your view that mandatory voting would "be transformative" and exists in a number of other democracies, such as Australia. Those few words alone will stimulate a public discussion in an era of low voter turnout, including the pros and cons of having a none-of-the-above option for voters.

Letters can be very valuable by asking questions that offer you an opportunity to respond on matters or issues not ordinarily addressed by the press corps or officials or members of Congress. (Incidentally, the first annual review of the White House press corps and its interaction with the president appears in the current issue [March/April 2015] of the *Columbia Journalism Review*, funded by the Helen Thomas Fund. She would like that!)

There are many other potential benefits of sending letters to presidents. For example, during Secretary of Energy Steven Chu's entire four-year term, many of the major antinuclear power groups could not obtain a meeting with him. Although he had met numerous times with representatives from the nuclear industry, he would not respond to our several letters and calls so that he could hear and respond to the empirical positions and recommendations of experienced groups whose overall views he did not share. I wrote asking if you could intervene and urge him to meet with us. Also, you needed to know about this rejection by your secretary of energy. There was no response.

I understand that you and your staff send courtesy responses to invitations to events around the country and that you respond to letters about highly visible issues, such as the auto industry bailout, with form letters. Of course, you also respond to political allies and supporters in some fashion. But that leaves out many letters reflecting the knowledge and position of many engaged Americans who should neither be stonewalled nor overlooked.

Here is what I recommend:

1. Issue a policy on responding to letters with whatever classification you choose to make it so that people can know what to expect.

2. At the very least, these active citizens should receive an acknowledgement of receipt of their letters and emails. This is what the prime minister of Canada does, regardless of whether the letters are supportive or critical. Additionally, the prime minister refers letters to the appropriate ministry for further review. Without even an acknowledgement, citizens might become cynical and/or stop writing.

3. Have your staff select the letters with ideas, proposals, or suggestions that they think would make a good annual public report to the American people. Include critical letters that point out shortcomings. This has a salutary effect on "the bubble" and goes beyond the few letters that all presidents use as political props.

I'll conclude with an invitation, which you may wish to reconsider, that appears in my book *Return to Sender: Unanswered Letters to the President, 2001–2015*. On May 4, 2012, I sent a letter to you urging you to address a proposed gathering of a thousand leaders of the nonprofit civic community at a hotel ballroom near the White House, at your scheduled convenience. These leaders head diverse groups supporting justice for consumers, workers, small taxpayers, the poor, and other environmental, health, housing, transportation, and energy causes. These organizations represent many millions of Americans across the country who support them with donations and volunteer time. There was no reply. Then, I sent the letter to First Lady Michelle Obama's East Wing. Her staff at least responded, writing that you had no time. Well, what about any time this year?

Jimmy Carter addressed just such a group of civic leaders after his election in 1976. The event was very successful and helped give greater visibility to this very important civic sector in our society. I found your White House's response disingenuous, in as much as you have traveled across the country and the world directly promoting by name for-profit US companies and the jobs these companies create. (In India, it was for Boeing and Harley-Davidson motorcycles.) Well, the nonprofit sector employs millions of Americans, and its growth and services are good for the society, are they not?

I hope you and the family will enjoy perusing this book and possibly gaining some insights and ideas that will enhance your service to our country, its people, and its interaction with the rest of the world. This volume could have been called a "bubble-buster," except we could only wonder whether these letters were ever given access through that self-described encasement.

Sincerely yours,

Ralph Nader

Open Letter to Plaintiff Trial Lawyers

AUGUST 13, 2012

Dear Plaintiff Trial Lawyers of America:

The common law of torts, which came from England to the thirteen colonies, has been elaborated in tens of thousands of judicial decisions with one basic message—if a person suffers a wrongful injury or harm, he or she can seek redress in court with a trial by jury. This is the civil justice system working through the evolving law of torts. It is this body of law that especially focuses on protecting the physical integrity of human beings, their reputations, and their property.

The two initiators of the common law are the plaintiff and the attorney. Over the years these two movers have challenged and prodded the courts into building the greatest civil justice system in the world—one that, despite its insufficient usage, strives to keep up with community values and the risks of existing and new technologies.

The civil justice system, when not straitjacketed, works to compensate victims for various losses, punish the perpetrators in the more heinous cases, and deter future injudicious or reckless behavior. The courtroom door is more open to claimants due in substantial part to the contingent fee. The injured, poor or not, only pay their attorneys in cases where they prevail.

As a judicial system of public decision-making, the civil justice system has to conform to a range of refereeing far beyond what is in place for decisions by legislatures, executive agencies, and global corporations. Disputes are first refereed by the very nature of the adversary system and its rules of evidence and cross-examination. The judge referees the interpretation of the law, and the jury referees the facts. Then the judge referees the jury's decision, followed by the appeals courts. The entire process is open.

Trial counsel expanded the embrace of tort law with a refereed steadiness, expressed so concisely by the former dean of Harvard Law School, the celebrated Roscoe Pound, who wrote: "Law must be stable, and yet it cannot stand still."

Unfortunately, even before the massive assault on the tort system by the corporatists and their ideological allies, the civil justice courts did not serve enough of the millions of people suffering injury or illness caused by negligent or intentional behavior. The costs of specific litigation, such as medical malpractice or complex corporate torts, removed all but the cases with the most accessible evidence and greatest damages from the calculus of the trial attorney. By comparison with other countries, however, the American law of torts, with all its limitations—textually and operationally—remained far superior and continued to evolve, though haltingly, through the decisions of some of the finest judicial minds in our country. Until, that is, the 1980s, when the backlash by the wrongdoers' lobby and their ever-profitable insurance company bell ringers intensified their attacks.

Until that decade, the common law had expanded to include damages for pain and suffering, the infrequent but necessary punitive damages, loss of consortium, joint and several liability, comparative negligence, and other doctrines. Again and again, plaintiff attorneys could take credit for bringing cases, having little chance of success but nonetheless enlarging the core of more humane legal arguments presented in open court. Sometimes pioneering trial lawyers prevailed against powerful defendants with far greater resources, such as the asbestos and tobacco industries. This benefitted their clients and our society as well.

The law of torts cannot stand still, because evolving expectations by society toward greater care, caution, and anticipation atrophy or are repressed if they are not regularly transformed into prudent legal rights and responsibilities.

It cannot stand still because the evidence acquired in the course of litigation pierces the veil of corporate and professional secrecy and allows the use of newly discovered information in the preventative process of health and safety regulation. For example, evidence acquired in tire products liability cases led to the federal tire safety law of 1966.

Having initiated and materially gained from their overdue and proper expansion of the common law of torts, plaintiff lawyers should more vigorously embrace a presumed trusteeship to defend what they helped bring about. Such a trusteeship could be invaluable in confronting the tidal wave of what grotesquely became known as "tort reform." This corporate lobbying drive first focused on state legislatures. This assault was amply greased by falsehoods and campaign cash and ultimately shaped the elected judiciary in many states. Blatant insurance industry propaganda, along with occasional insurance or reinsurance company strikes, or tactical refusals to sell insurance coverage, got headlines.

The "tort deform" juggernaut gathered steam in the 1980s as a peculiar phenomenon began to emerge. At the same time that some trial lawyers achieved very considerable wealth from their breakthrough litigation successes, their resistance, once muscularly organized, began to flag before the gathering storms. This anomaly only worsened in the 1990s and in the first decade of the twenty-first century. Although riches were amassed by the creative litigators involved in asbestos, tobacco, and other mass tort victories for workers, patients, and public health policies, inadequate resources were directed toward countering the commercialist movement that infected elections, legislatures, and the judicial confirmation process to shred tort law.

The recent history in Texas illustrates this point only too well. Commencing in 1991, the wealthiest trial bar in the country lost legislative battle after legislative battle designed to destroy the wrongful injury remedies of injured Texans. It started with the weakening of the workers' compensation law by an increasingly antagonistic legislature. In drumbeat succession, lawyers for people harmed by negligent or chronically incompetent physicians and manufacturers of defective products were rendered less and less able to pursue the legitimate rights of their clients in the courts.

"Tort deform" laws tied the hands of judge and jury—the only people who see, hear, and evaluate the evidence before them in open court. Campaign money flooded both absentee state legislators and judicial candidates who showed their responsiveness to the legislating of judicial outcomes that were uniquely antiplaintiff in tort cases. From corporate interest, money talked loudly. Now the judiciary, especially the Texas Supreme Court and the indentured Texas Legislature and governor, have cruelly turned against these innocent victims and their attorneys, restricting their meaningful access to the courthouse.

The venerable Texas constitution of 1935 said, "The right of trial by jury shall remain inviolate." In 2003, the ravenous corporatists, including of course the insurance industry, decided to take on an important section of the Texas constitution and of Texas democracy. Their millions of dollars placed a provision on a statewide ballot initiative. The proposed constitutional amendment, "Prop 12," would, in the words of Craig McDonald, director of Texans for Public Justice, "take power away from communities, judges and juries and give the Texas Legislature the absolute unfettered power to grant special interest groups special protections from the harm they might cause in the future and dismantle the checks and balances system that's been the backbone of our government." Passing the amendment was considered an uphill struggle in the opinion of some observers who overestimated the resolve and smarts of the trial lawyers. Corporate cash—which could easily have been matched but wasn't—and deceptive television ads won the vote for Mammon, Greed, and Cruelty by a margin of 51 to 49 percent of those who chose to vote. The predictable further weakening of Texas tort law followed. The resolve of the trial bar in protecting the law of torts was inadequate or inept.

Why have the Texas trial lawyers—no shrinking violets to past contests of power—lost again and again? Needless to say, they had the arguments, the evidence, the heartrending cases of avoidable deaths, injuries, illnesses, and family anguish. They had the contrast of corporate bosses, with rubber-stamping boards of directors, paying executives huge compensation and bonuses even while these bosses were taking down their own companies, workers, and shareholders. Remember Enron. After all, these years of "tort deform" paralleled the greatest corporate crime wave in American history. Weren't there several dozen trial lawyers—each worth hundreds of millions of dollars, and even a billion or two—who could contribute the money and talent needed to get the truth to the people and mobilize ready and able citizen and labor groups to build the voting power needed to preserve tort law in Texas? It seemed that the very traits of individualism and self-regard that drove them to their courtroom victories—cases involving asbestos, tobacco, medical devices, and toxic release—hindered the kind of sustained, collective organization that so many advocates pleaded with them to support.

The sterling, publicized work of Texans for Public Justice led by Craig McDonald and Andrew Wheat (tpj.org), with its tiny budget, was an operating example of what an expanded public investment would have accomplished. By contrast, the "tort deform" lobby spawned many well-funded state-based astroturf groups against so-called "lawsuit abuse," and several national groups as well.

The loss of the constitutional referendum in Texas was the result of poor strategy, a low advocacy budget compared to corporations' expenditures, excessive delegation by leading trial lawyers to their unimaginative professional association in Austin, and especially the exclusion of ideas and participants by those lawyers' misguided consulting firms.

Loss after loss in state after state—severe limits on damages, abolition of joint and several liability and the collateral damage rule, restrictions on expert witnesses and jury autonomy—revealed another vulnerability of the trial lawyers that did not go unnoticed by their adversaries. The trial lawyers had no second-strike capability to roll back bad legislation once enacted. Moreover, they had no power, or chose not to exercise it, to improve tort law that had fallen behind the times. They signaled to the corporate insurance lobby that they could be steamrolled again and again, unlike groups who regroup and become stronger after suffering a defeat. They relied on campaign contributions instead of full-bodied grassroots campaigns. Their presumed trusteeship had little energy or capacity for self-renewal.

All the missteps of the trial lawyers did not keep their corporate opponents from constantly magnifying the power of the trial bar so as to raise more money and give the impression that they were fighting Goliath when in reality they were the giants, from the US Chamber of Commerce on down. The trial lawyers were like Davids with broken slingshots.

To be sure, the trial lawyers and their civic allies are not without their history of victories in New York, Florida, Ohio, Illinois, and other states during this period. But they have been smaller and less frequent in the past twenty years. The biggest victories are defensive—holding the shrinking fort—with truly offensive turnarounds going the way of the Mauritius Dodo bird. The "mighty" trial lawyers of California cannot even mount an inflation-adjusted campaign to bring the 1976 cap on pain and suffering—a stagnant $250,000 lifetime cap—up to 2012 dollars, or about $1 million. This is the case even though the then and current governor Jerry Brown in his 1992 statement expressed his regret for supporting such a draconian limit that has caused so much deprivation, cruel mimicry in other states, and a required reduction in adjudicated jury verdicts above that limit for horrendous injuries from medical malpractice.

To be sure, plaintiff lawyers have developed some sterling ways to teach the public about their legal rights—such as the People's Law School seminars. They collaborated in the late eighties with the Johns Hopkins School of Public Health to publicize consumer product defects and other harmful conditions based on their proven case files. But these good efforts are not diffused throughout the country and often fade away. Seventy thousand full-time plaintiff trial lawyers can do much, much better for the lives, health, and safety of the American people for whom they are the first responders.

Their potential is seen in the adoption of a proposal I made more than thirty years ago for them to start a public interest law firm that they called Trial Lawyers for Public Justice (now called Public Justice)—a nonprofit organization to take important cases that commercial law practices would not undertake. The success of Public Justice (publicjustice.net), led by the resourceful Arthur Bryant, is convincing evidence of how much more could have been done in state after state with modest draws on the trial bar's discretionary income.

As detailed in the work of Joanne Doroshow's Center for Justice and Democracy (centerjd.org), studies have shown that civil litigation by the injured is in decline by several measures. Far fewer than 10 percent of actionable tortious acts ever move to the stage of a legal complaint. It is harder and harder for these Americans to have their day in court. People slated for jury pools are constantly misled and lied to by the barrage of propaganda in print, TV, and radio about the civil justice system (again, see centerjd.org). Actual trials are declining in number, and court budgets are being radically cut in some states.

I was introduced to the law of torts at Harvard Law School in 1955 by the legendary Warren Seavey's casebook and in 1956–1957 by the writings of professor Thomas F. Lambert Jr., the director of the first trial association known as NACCA (the National Association of Claimants' Compensation Attorneys). The *Nader v. General Motors Corp.* case brought by leading trial attorney and author of the treatise *The American Law of Torts*, Stuart Speiser, helped advance the right of privacy and is often included in legal casebooks.

For decades I have testified, written, and fought for the legal rights and remedies of wrongfully injured children, women, and men in the workplace, marketplace, home, and environment. Illustratively, in 1986 I traveled to more than forty states to help stem the massive assault on the tort system fronted by the insurance lobbies, often with the formidable J. Robert Hunter, whose expert testimony as a leading property-casualty insurance actuary impressed many a state legislator in that critical year.

In almost every state, there were a few trial lawyers who stood very tall on the trial lawyer association ramparts against the tortfeasors' lobbies. The vast majority paid their modest annual dues and practiced law. Year after year the ramparts weakened. Our country's tort law can be considered mortally wounded in many states, with the congressional minions of the wrongdoers' battalions thirsting to federalize and codify downward the entire common law of the fifty states—for a "mess of pottage."

It is time to call for a grand, multifaceted mobilization of the American people who believe in their constitutional right of trial by jury and their full day in court based on the principle and affordable practice that every wrongful injury requires a righteous remedy and fair compensation paid by the perpetrators of those harms. This should be a movement for responsibility and accountability for those wrongdoers. Plaintiff trial lawyers should come out of their cloistered and defeatist corners to lead this community-based restoration and expansion of refereed civil justice and deterrence under law.

If you and other colleagues are interested in this call to action and what it will take to effectuate, please call or write to me ASAP for further elaboration and a mutual exchange of suggestions.

Sincerely yours,

Ralph Nader

Upholding and Defending the Constitution

JUNE 14, 2012

Honorable Patrick Leahy
Chairman, Senate Committee on the Judiciary
United States Senate
Committee on the Judiciary
224 Dirksen Senate Office Building
Washington, DC 20510

Honorable Lamar Smith
Chairman, House Committee on the Judiciary
United States House of Representatives
2138 Rayburn House Office Building
Washington, DC 20515

Dear Chairman Leahy and Chairman Smith:

The recent detailing by the *New York Times* of a secret White House self-styled "kill list" frightfully reminiscent of practices by totalitarian regimes is a lethal assault on the Constitution and the rule of law. We are convinced that you are legally and morally obligated by your constitutional oath to hold prompt and comprehensive hearings into the constitutionality of President Obama's secret unilateral death decrees against citizens and noncitizens alike. In perpetrating the appalling violations, the president simultaneously plays the role of secret prosecutor, judge, jury, and executioner in scornful defiance of the Constitution's separation of powers and checks and balances.

We believe that inaction despite constitutional authority to investigate a prima facie case of presidential "high crimes and misdemeanors" under Article II, Section 4, of the Constitution would make you complicit. As Edmund Burke observed, "All that is necessary for evil to triumph is for good men to do nothing."

An inexhaustive list of the constitutional violations disclosed in the *New York Times* story would include:

1. The president has ordered killings without time-honored procedural safeguards against error and injustice and beyond constitutional authority under Article II or otherwise—the very definition of tyranny, according to the Founding Fathers. The killings are not authorized by the 2001 Authorization for Use of Military Force or other congressional action. They are not exercises of inherent Article II war powers of the president according to Supreme Court precedents. Justice Robert Jackson warned in *Youngstown Sheet & Tube Co. v. Sawyer*, 343 US 579, 642 (1952) (concurring opinion):

   Nothing in our Constitution is plainer than that declaration of a war is entrusted only to Congress. Of course, a state of war may, in fact, exist without a formal declaration. But no doctrine that the Court could promulgate would seem to me more sinister and alarming than that a President whose conduct of foreign affairs is so largely uncontrolled, and often even is unknown, can vastly enlarge his mastery over the internal affairs of the country by his own commitment of the Nation's armed forces to some foreign venture.

2. Suspected terrorists are ordered killed by the president with no attempt to capture—a violation of the War Crimes Act of 1996, as amended, 18 USC 2441.

3. The killings are also war crimes because they serve no legitimate military objective. William A. Daley, White House chief of staff in 2011, is quoted as saying: "One guy gets knocked off, and the guy's driver, who's No. 21, becomes 20? At what point are you just filling the bucket with numbers?"

4. With no authority from Congress, the president secretly delivers terrorist suspects to foreign governments (with the potential of torture) in violation of due process.

5. The president recklessly orders killings justified by a totalitarian theory of guilt by association. The *New York Times* reports that all military-age males in a strike zone are deemed imminent dangers to the United States and killed (no matter how nonexistent or remote in time their conceivable future involvement in a terrorist act). The dead are counted as "militants" unless there is explicit posthumous intelligence proving them innocent! The logic is Orwellian. An official maintained: "Al-Qaeda is an insular, paranoid organization—innocent neighbors don't hitchhike rides in the back of trucks headed for the border with guns and bombs." A dissenting official commented: "It bothers me when they say there were seven guys, so they must all be militants. They count the corpses and they're not really sure who they are." The story also reported that "today, the Defense Department can target suspects in Yemen whose names they do not know." In these operations, known innocents have been regularly killed in Afghanistan, Pakistan, and Yemen, including sixteen-year-old United States citizen Abdulraham al-Awlaki and his seventeen-year-old Yemeni cousin while eating dinner.

6. The rule of law has succumbed to the rule of men. Thus, State Department legal adviser Harold Koh voiced confidence in the self-styled "kill list" because it is screened by White House adviser John O. Brennan, whom Koh praised as priestly and "a person of genuine moral rectitude."

7. Suppose you believe that President Obama is benignly motivated to achieve justifiable ends. It still seems undeniable that constitutionally enshrined procedural safeguards against tyrannical government are being trampled. The precedents ratifying absolute presidential power set by Obama will lie around like a loaded weapon ready for use and abuse by any future White House occupant. "The history of liberty has largely been the history of observance of procedural safeguards," the Supreme Court lectured in *McNabb v. United States*, 318 US 332 (1943).

8. The president recklessly ordered the killing of Baitullah Mehsud despite being told by his advisers that his wife would also be a casualty,

and that Mehsud himself was a risk to Pakistan, but not to the United States. The predator drone attack predictably killed his wife and perhaps other nearby family members.

9. The *New York Times* writes regarding Obama's first drone strike in Yemen on December 17, 2009: "It killed not only its intended target, but also two neighboring families, and left behind a trail of cluster bombs that killed more innocents. . . . Videos of children's bodies and angry tribesmen holding up American missile parts flooded YouTube, fueling a ferocious backlash that Yemeni officials said bolstered Al Qaeda."

10. The president regularly authorizes so-called "signature" strikes that purport to target military training camps or suspicious compounds allegedly controlled by militants based on shaky evidence shielded from outside review. The *New York Times* reports that officials at the State Department have joked that when the CIA discerns "three guys doing jumping jacks," the agency is convinced they are at a terrorist training camp.

11. Former director of the CIA and director of the National Security Agency Michael Hayden lamented: "This [killing] program rests on the personal legitimacy of the president, and that's not sustainable. I have lived the life of someone taking action on the basis of secret [Office of Legal Counsel] memos, and it ain't a good life. Democracies do not make war on the basis of legal memos locked in a Department of Justice safe."

Inside the executive branch, there are many silent dissenters to the White House's vandalizing of the Constitution that imperils national security. Some of these patriots need the protection of your committees to speak out. We urge you to display the moral and intellectual courage against tyrannical practices that gave birth to the United States. One should not become an accomplice in the incremental destruction of the American republic and violate one's constitutional oath to uphold our Constitution and the rule of law.

Be steeled by Tacitus's judgment on the fall of Rome: "The worst crimes were dared by a few, willed by more, and tolerated by all."

Sincerely,

Bruce Fein, Constitutional Attorney
Ralph Nader, Attorney, Public Advocate
Lt. Col. Tony Shaffer, Retired Intelligence Officer
William Quirk, Professor of Law – University of South Carolina School
of Law
Theresa Amato, Attorney, Public Advocate
Marcus Raskin, Social Advocate, Political Activist
Lynne Bernabei, Esq., Civil Rights Attorney
Greg Kafoury, Esq., Civil Rights Attorney
Carl Mayer, Attorney and Social Advocate
John Whitehead, Constitutional Attorney
Mike Ferner, Former President, Veterans for Peace

Cc: The Member of the Senate Committee on the Judiciary, the Members of
the House Committee on the Judiciary

An Open Letter to Yankees Brass: Nader Decries In-Game Ads on Radio Broadcasts

JUNE 8, 2012

Randy Levine, President
Brian Cashman, General Manager
New York Yankees

Gentlemen:

When I was growing up in Connecticut, I'd listen with pleasure to Mel Allen's radio broadcasts of the New York Yankee games.

The commercials were reserved for the commercial breaks—between half innings.

Now the commercials have become a significant part of the broadcast.

You are forcing your radio announcers—John Sterling and Suzyn Waldman—to read an untold number of ads during the game.

Pitching matchups, double plays, pitch counts, rallies, calls to the bullpen, the umpire alignment, a pitch that paints the corners, the game-time temperature, even the national anthem are sponsored by car dealers, insurance companies, junk-food outlets, among others.

I had an associate listen to the June 1, 2012, radio broadcast of the game between the Yankees and the Detroit Tigers, which the Yankees won 9–4.

He came up with twenty-two in-game ads that disrupt the flow and excitement of the game broadcast and undermine your responsibilities as a guardian of the national pastime.

Do you know how irritating these ads are to your listeners?

Have you no boundaries or sense of restraint?

Have you no mercy on your play-calling broadcasters?

The corporate commercial creep continues unabated, not only on radio broadcasts but also on the playing field. What's next, uniforms pasted with ads?

That's apparently being discussed too. (See "Are Oakland A's uniform ads a vision for the future?" *San Francisco Business Times*, March 26, 2012.)

I am asking that you stick to baseball in between the half-inning commercial breaks. Let the fans enjoy the "moment."

After absorbing the attached commercialized play calls from your June 1 game broadcast, please call us to discuss how to avoid having your sponsors placed in a highly visible Hall of Infamy by your irritated fans.

Sincerely

Ralph Nader, Founder, League of Fans